Sign Languages of Aboriginal Australia

Cultural, Semiotic and Communicative Perspectives

G. C.
LIBRARY

Sign Languages of Aboriginal Australia

Cultural, Semiotic and Communicative Perspectives

ADAM KENDON

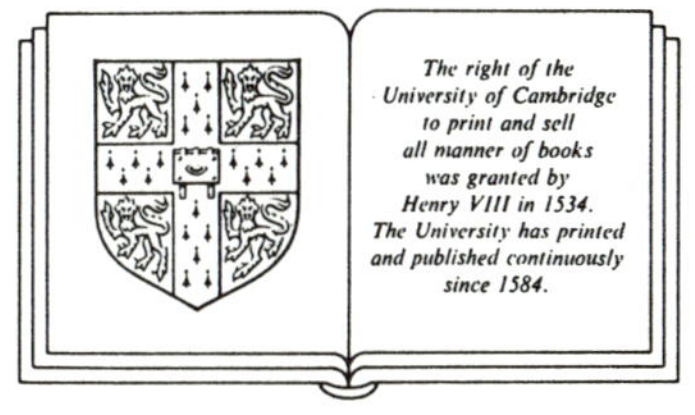

The right of the University of Cambridge to print and sell all manner of books was granted by Henry VIII in 1534. The University has printed and published continuously since 1584.

CAMBRIDGE UNIVERSITY PRESS

CAMBRIDGE

NEW YORK NEW ROCHELLE MELBOURNE SYDNEY

Published by the Press Syndicate of the University of Cambridge
The Pitt Building, Trumpington Street, Cambridge CB2 1RP
32 East 57th Street, New York, NY 10022, USA
10 Stamford Road, Oakleigh, Melbourne 3166, Australia

First published 1988

Printed in Great Britain at the
University Press, Cambridge

British Library cataloguing in publication data

Kendon, Adam
Sign languages of Aboriginal Australia:
cultural, semiotic and communicative
perspectives.
1. Australian Aboriginal sign languages
I. Title
001.56

Library of Congress cataloguing in publication data

Kendon, Adam.
Sign languages of Aboriginal Australia: cultural, semiotic, and communicative perspectives / Adam Kendon.
p. cm.
Includes bibliographies and index.
ISBN 0 521 36008 0
1. Australian Aborigines – Sign language. I. Title.
GN666.K44 1988
001.66—dc19 88-15003
CIP

ISBN 0 521 36008 0

Contents

List of illustrations

Maps

General illustrations

Illustrations of signs

Preface

Whenever a person engages in utterance, either speech or gesture may be used, but, commonly, both are employed at the same time. Yet, speech and the gestures, or, rather, gesticulations that may accompany it, express things in very different ways. Whereas in speech use is made of recombineable elements which must be organized into constructions governed by rules of syntax, in gesticulation meanings are presented in a seemingly direct, holisitc fashion, often as depictions of spatial relationships or patterns of movement. Furthermore, unlike the forms used in speech, forms used in gesticulation are, for the most part, improvised in context. They are not codified like the elements of spoken language.

The question of how such different modes of expression are related to one another and how these relationships may be explained has been of interest to me since 1968, when I became acquainted with R.L.Birdwhistell's work in kinesics. Since then I have published a number of papers on this topic (e.g., Kendon 1972, 1980b, 1983, 1985b, 1986b). This work, along with that of McNeill (1985, 1987), Schegloff (1984), and others, has established that there is an intimate relationship between speech and gesticulation and this, as McNeill has argued, appears to show that imagistic expression and verbal expression are both fundamental in the process of utterance.

A useful contrast to studies of gesticulation would be provided if one could examine cases where speakers had available a system of gesture that was codified and which could serve independently of speech. This could help to clarify the differences between various kinds of gestural expression and add to our understanding of the relationship between medium of expression and mode of encoding. In addition, the study of such a case might also provide a worthwhile contrast to the situation that obtains for the deaf, among whom codified gesture systems (i.e. sign languages) are developed quite separately from any spoken language. Such a study might throw additional light on the the extent to which the medium employed in a linguistic system may govern its structural characteristics.

Among Australian Aborigines we can find cases where codified gesture systems or sign languages have been developed by speakers. These systems are used as full substitutes for speech in some circumstances and they are also often used in association with it. In 1978, while a Senior Research Fellow in Anthropology at Australian National University, I decided to gather material on such a sign language from Warlpiri women at Yuendumu. I thought that a fairly restricted investigation would be enough for the questions I had in mind; however, I soon discovered that Australian Aboriginal sign languages had never been studied in any depth and, in particular, the whole question of how they relate to the spoken languages of their users had received virtually no attention. The existence of such a gap in knowledge was an attraction in itself, but I also realized that the comparisons in which I was interested could not be dealt with adequately in a short time. Once involved in the study of these sign languages, various additional issues demanded attention. The work developed its own momentum, and the result is this rather large book.

Despite its size, this book must be considered preliminary in many respects. In several places I have had to make do with insufficient data. This is particularly true for the comparative studies reported in Chapters 11 and 12. I hope, however, that what I have been able to say will be sufficient to show that further work would be worthwhile, if such is still possible. Further, when I began this work ten years ago, in addition to studying the structure of these sign languages and how they are related to their associated spoken languages, I had hoped to include observations on how the use of sign language among Aborigines structured daily interaction. I still regard this as important and interesting; however, although there is some discussion of this, detailed studies have yet to be done, and most of what I say about it is based only on casual observations. Systematic collection and analysis of relevant data has yet to be undertaken.

Throughout the book I have made use of a notation system in describing signs which has been adapted from the system originally developed by William Stokoe in his pioneering linguistic analysis of American Sign Language. Details of this system are given in Chapter 5 and the symbols employed are given in Appendix I. Although the use of this notation system is very advantageous in exposition and analysis I am aware that many readers may feel it to be a stumbling block. I have endeavored to give verbal descriptions of signs wherever possible and I have also provided numerous illustrations. Several readers of this book in draft have assured me that it is perfectly possible to grasp what is said without first mastering the notation. I hope, therefore, that people will not be deterred by the curious symbols that will often be encountered.

For institutional support during the period of research that led to this book, I am grateful to the Department of Anthropology, Research School of Pacific Studies at Australian National University in Canberra; the Australian Institute of Aboriginal Studies, Canberra; Connecticut College, New London, Connecticut; and Indiana University, Bloomington. I have received financial assistance from the National Science Foundation, Washington, D.C. (BNS-8024173, 1981-1982 and BNS-8503271, 1986-1988), the Australian Institute of Aboriginal Studies, Canberra (grants in 1981, 1982, 1984-1986 and 1987-1988), the Wenner-Gren Foundation for Anthropological Research, New York (1982), the American Council of Learned Societies, New York (1982) and the Department of Anthropology, Research School of Pacific Studies (1985). The John Simon Guggenheim Memorial Foundation of New York appointed me to a Fellowship in 1983-1984 and this provided me with an additional year in which to analyze material. Chapter 10 in the present book is one of the main outcomes of this period of support.

I would like to thank Roger Keesing for welcoming me to his Department as a Visiting Fellow on repeated occasions; Thomas Sebeok of Indiana University for permitting me to work at the Research Center for Language and Semiotic Studies; and Michael Herzfeld of Indiana University for helping with the institutional negotiations that were associated with the second of my two awards from the National Science Foundation and for his help as Project Director for this grant.

These institutions and individuals have helped to create the environment without which this work could not have been accomplished, but there are many others who have assisted generously in the work itself. First, my thanks go to Mary Laughren who showed an interest in my idea of studying Warlpiri sign language from the beginning. She has helped me by smoothing my visits to Yuendumu and by introducing me to some of the Warlpiri women with whom I have worked. In particular, however, she has placed her unrivalled linguist's knowledge of the Warlpiri language at my disposal. She has read most of the present book and has offered numerous suggestions and pointed out my many errors. I have tried to follow her advice wherever I could. David Nash and Jane Simpson have also taken an enthusiastic interest in my work. I am indebted to both of them for intellectual, nutritional and logistic support during my field trips to Elliott and Tennant Creek. Jane Simpson put me in touch with Warumungu people during my stay at Tennant Creek and she has assisted me in several Warumungu elicitation sessions, provided me with unpublished material on Warumungu language and has patiently answered my numerous queries. David Nash has been an unfailing source of information on all sorts of topics. He provided me with linguistic material and advice in regard to Warlmanpa and Mudbura, generously making his unpublished materials on these languages freely available. He has also advised me on many linguistic matters. He has read most of the chapters of this book and they have benefited much from his numerous corrections and suggestions. For other linguistic help, I am grateful to Harold Koch for material and advice on Kaytej and to Avery Andrews and

Jenny Green for help with Anmatyerre. It should be stressed, however, that any errors that remain are entirely my responsibility.

I am grateful to the Council at Yuendumu for permission to stay in that community and carry out my inquiries. Judy Nampijinpa Granites and Dolly Nampijinpa Granites were my first teachers of Warlpiri sign language. Subsequently, I worked a great deal with Winnie Nangala and Ruby Nangala Robertson. I am most grateful to them and thank them for their patience and good humor during our many sessions. At Elliott I worked with Pharlap Dixon and Hilda Kingston in studying Mudbura sign language. Powder Raymond helped with Djingili. At Tennant Creek I was shown Warumungu sign language by Bunny Narrurla and Annie Phillips Narrurla. Bunny Narrurla was also able to help me with Warlmanpa sign language, but here I am also indebted to a number of others, including Donald Graham Jupurrula, and a Nampijinpa who is now deceased. For Kaytej, I am grateful to Daisy Akemarre and several other women of the Kaytej community, Tara. For Anmatyerre sign language I am grateful to Lucky Long and June Napangardi, among others. During my stay at Neutral Junction for the Kaytej work, Greg and Janet Broad provided me with hospitality. Mick Arundel and Karen Collas of Ti Tree stored some of my equipment and later provided hospitality and space to work when I was gathering Anmatyerre material. In Canberra, thanks are due to Michael Leigh, film archivist at the Australian Institute of Aboriginal Studies for assistance in working on film material in the Institute's film archive; to Douglas Smith, technical officer at the Institute for technical assistance; and to the staff of the Institute's library who have been extremely helpful over the years.

The book has been read in draft in its entirety by William Washabaugh. I have altered both the form of argument and presentation in many places in the light of his comments and criticisms. Judy Kegl also read most of the book and has offered many useful suggestions. Bonnie Urciuoli read the first eight chapters and made valuable and detailed comments. Françoise Dussart has helped me in many ways with her knowledge of Warlpiri culture, especially from a woman's point of view. She has read Chapters 4, 11 and 14. Nicolas Peterson and Isobel White have read Chapters 2, 3, 4, and 14, Harold Koch has read Chapters 7 and 8, Jim Wafer has read Chapter 11, William Stokoe and Brenda Farnell have read Chapter 13, and Michael Jackson, John Morton and Ian Keen have read Chapter 14. I am most grateful, in each case, for the comments that these readers have provided and as far as possible I have tried to follow their advice. Nevertheless, I am wholly responsible for everything written.

The production of the text has been carried out exclusively on an Apple Macintosh™ computer. Mathew Ciolek assisted me in the early stages of my encounter with this marvellous machine and has been an important source of advice since. Camera ready copy was prepared on equipment in the Coombs Computer Unit and the Department of Anthropology, Research School of Pacific Studies in Canberra. Most of the photographs that appear in the book were taken by myself, however in 1981 Peter Bartlett, of Yuendumu, took a number of the photographs that show individual signs. I thank him for his help in this, but apologize to him for not being able to remember which particular photographs to credit him with. The line drawings in the book have all been prepared from photographs. Most of the drawings were made by Brett Hatherly but the handshape drawings that appear on pp. 121-125 were drawn by Kate Dorrough and Gregory Myers. I am grateful to Peter Herel of the Department of Graphic Investigation at the Canberra School of Art for putting me in touch with these artists. The reproduction of Plate II from W.E.Roth's monograph of 1897 that appears on p. 23 was prepared by the photographic department of the Australian Institute of Aboriginal Studies, but all other illustrations were prepared for publication by Photographic Services of Australian National University. I am grateful to G.L. Walsh for permitting me to copy from his comparative illustrations of stencilled hands and Queensland hand signs. Mervyn Meggitt has kindly allowed me to copy his data tables that appear on p. 382. I would like to thank Plenum Press, New York and A.R.Taylor of the University of Colorado for permitting me to reproduce the map that appears on p. 411; Oceania Publications of Sydney University for permission to use material in Chapter 9 that also appears in their journal; and Mouton de Gruyter of Berlin for permitting me to use material in Chapter 10 which they had previously published. Details of place of previous publication is given in a chapter note in each case.

The work on Aboriginal sign languages that has resulted in this book has taken much longer than I ever thought it would. It has caused me to shuttle back and forth between the United States and Australia several times, often at great inconvenience to my family. My wife has put up with several long absences. During the final stages of the writing of the book, most weekends have been fully occupied as well. Despite this, she has supported my efforts in every way. Such words of thanks as I might offer here, no matter how elaborated, cannot do justice to what is her due.

Canberra, June 1 1988

Orthographic conventions and descriptive terms

Warlpiri, Warlmanpa, Warumugnu, Mudbura

Vowels: a, i, u. Lengthened values are shown by doubling: aa, ii, uu

Consonants:

	bilabial	apico-alveolar	retroflex	lamino-alveolar	dorso-velar
stops	p	t	rt	j	k
nasals	m	n	rn	ny	ng
laterals		l	rl	ly	
flaps		rr	rd		
glides	w		r	y	

This orthography is the so-called Modern Practical Orthography or 'p t k' orthography, which is now employed in the bilingual education programs in Warlpiri at Yuendumu, Willowra and Lajamanu. It was originally developed by Lothar Jagst for Warlpiri and subsequently modified by Ken Hale. It may be used in writing Warlmanpa, Warumungu and Mudbura, although in these languages the retroflex flap, rd, does not occur. In Warumungu, and to some extent in Warlmanpa, certain consonants also show lengthening. This is indicated by doubling.

Anmatyerre and Kaytej

Vowels:

	front	central	back
high short		e	we
high long	i		
high long (Kaytej)	ey		
low long		a	ew
low (Kaytej)		a	
dipthong (Kaytej)	ay		

Consonants

	bilabial	alveolar	retroflex	inter-dental	lamino palatal	velar
stop	p	t	rt	th	ty	k
nasal						
pre-stopped nasals	pm	tn	rtn	tnh	tny	kng
lateral		l	rl	lh	ly	
flap		rr				
glide	w		r		y	h

This orthography is that developed for Arrernte (Aranda) and is used in Arrernte language programs at the Institute for Aboriginal Development in Alice Springs.

Abbreviations used in interlinear transcription are given in the introduction to Appendix II.

Signs

Signs are described in notation. This notation system is fully explained in Chapter 5 and the values of the symbols used are given in Appendix I. Signs are also often referred to by a label, based on a common gloss for the sign. This is written in upper case. The label is usually in the language with which the sign is associated, but occasionally an English label is used where no Aboriginal language correspondence exists. In Warlpiri, verb signs are always labelled with a corresponding spoken form in the non-past tense and division between root and tense inflexion is not shown. Where spoken forms are given, morpheme breaks are shown by hyphens. Gestures that are not signs are referred to by a name (e.g. Point) or a descriptive phrase (e.g. Points down). Underlining shows the temporal extent of the gesture in relation to the speech, where appropriate.

In the verbal descriptions of signs the following anatomical and kinesiological terms are employed:

Ipsilateral: belonging to or occurring on the same side of the body as something (e.g., active limb); *contralateral*: belonging to or occurring on the opposite side of body opposite (e.g. as active limb).

Forearm rotation: *supination*, clockwise rotation in right arm, anticlockwise rotation in left arm; *pronation*, anticlockwise rotation in right arm, clockwise rotation in left arm.

The shoulder joint may be *extended* , bringing the upper arm toward a forward horizontal position; it may be *retracted*, bringing the upper arm towards a position behind the medial plane of the body; it may be *elevated*, moving the upper arm toward a lateral horizontal position or, further, to a vertically upward position.

Digits of the hand are referred to as follows: thumb, thumb; index finger, 1; middle finger, 2; third finger, 3; fourth finger (little finger or pinky), 4. Joints of the digits are proximal (knuckle), A; medial, B; distal, C. Bending at these joints is *flexion*, straightening is *extension*. Digits may also be spread, or *abducted*, or brought together, or *adducted*. The thumb may be moved so that it is held in front of the palm of the hand, in which case it is said to be *opposed*.

1 Introduction

1.0 Scope

The use of complex gesture systems or sign languages by Australian Aborigines, especially in central Australia, has been reported since the late nineteenth century. Their use in connection with initiation and mourning rituals has been noted, as well as in hunting and other everyday situations, and a few sign vocabularies have been described. However, no work has provided any extended description and analysis and there has been only one discussion that has raised the question of the relationship between these sign languages and the spoken languages of the people who use them (Miller 1978). This book is thus the first work in which these sign languages are studied in detail. Findings are presented from a study of the sign languages in use in seven Australian Aboriginal groups, all from an area referred to in this book as the North Central Desert, with particular attention to the sign languages of the Warlpiri, Warumungu and Warlmanpa. Material collected by other observers is reviewed, but for the most part what is presented here is based on an analysis of original material collected in the field between 1978 and 1986. We provide a description of the structure of these sign languages and an account of how they are related to the spoken languages of their users. We compare sign languages from different locations within the North Central Desert, as well as from other places in Aboriginal Australia. This permits a comparison of dialect formation in signed and spoken languages. Aboriginal sign languages are also compared with sign languages of the deaf, on the one hand, and, on the other, with sign languages developed in other communities of hearing people, such as the Plains Indians of North America. These comparisons suggest how mode of use, presence or absence of a spoken language model and the morphological type of the associated spoken language, all contribute to sign language structure. Finally, in an effort to account for the widespread use of signs and the frequent development of sign languages in Aboriginal society, we examine Aboriginal face-to-face interaction and draw attention to certain special features that appear to favor sign use.

While this work should be regarded as a contribution to Australian Aboriginal communication ethnography, it is also a contribution to the comparative study of semiotic systems. Two issues of importance for this may be mentioned. First, since the sign languages to be dealt with here are sign languages developed by speakers for use as an alternative to speech, we may expect that they will show a direct relationship to spoken language. Yet what sort of a relationship can this be? The medium of sign language, that of visible bodily action, or *kinesis*, as it may be termed, has properties very different from the vocal medium of spoken language. If a sign language is developed that preserves some aspects of spoken language structure, what aspects does it preserve and how does it preserve them? On the other hand, to what extent does such a sign language make use of the expressive possibilities of kinesis and develop expressions that are not found in spoken language? Answers to such questions will throw light on the nature of language representation, and will further our understanding of how the medium of expression influences the structure of the code represented.

Second, the use of the of kinesis as a language medium may not only have consequences for the structure of the code. Because it is silent, and because it requires for its reception sight rather than hearing, it may be used in circumstances different from those of speech. Because it is produced by bodily movements which are also used for many other kinds of activities, it may be perceived by others to be a different kind of communicative activity, even though it may encode the same things as spoken language. To use a sign language, thus, may have consequences both for the kinds of communicative functions it serves and also for the social role of the user. Just as there is a relationship between the medium of a language and its structure so, we suppose, there is a relationship between the medium of a language and its functions.

1.1 Primary and alternate sign languages

The term *signing* will be used to cover any sort of use of gestures in communication where the gestures are *codified*, that is, where they have standardized forms and can commonly be used as alternatives to spoken expressions. Signing is, thus, distinct from other aspects of communicative kinesis, such as may be observed in the communicative functions of spacing, posture, orientation, movement style, facial expression, and the use of uncodified gesture, such as gesticulation (gesturing that co-occurs with speech). Where the number of codified gestures used is relatively small and where they are not used as an autonomous mode of discourse, we may speak of *sign use*. Where the codified gesture vocabulary is large, and where codified gestures can be employed as a mode of discourse on their own, then we may speak of *sign language*. The distinction between *sign use* and *sign language* cannot be sharply drawn and much of the time we shall not insist upon it. It is useful to bear it in mind, however. In many parts of Aboriginal Australia, - in Arnhem Land, for instance - sign use is widespread, but there has been no development of signing as a fully autonomous mode of discourse. There is, thus, strictly, no *sign language*. In the northern region of the central desert, on the other hand, most older women can use codified gestures as an autonomous mode of discourse and thus can be said to use *sign language*. The men and young people in these areas, on the other hand, although they engage in *sign use* to a fair degree, do not command *sign language* (even though many of the gestural items they use are the same as those used by the women within the sign language).

Most of the discussion in this book is concerned with *sign language* in the sense just indicated. However, in several Chapters we consider data from parts of Aboriginal Australia where there is sign use, although problably no full-fledged sign language has developed. Thus in Chapters 2 and 3 observations on sign use among Australian Aborigines are discussed, regardless of whether or not they were made within the context of a well developed sign language system. This is also done in Chapters 11 and 12, where we undertake sign vocabulary comparisons throughout Aboriginal Australia. The reason for this is that, in this book, the complex sign languages of the North Central Desert of Australia are regarded as but special elaborations of a widespread propensity among Aborigines to use signs as a mode of communication. This propensity becomes the topic of a special investigation in Chapter 14.

The sign languages studied in this book have developed as alternatives to speech for use during periods of mourning or in connection with male initiation rituals, when silence must be observed. They are also used extensively in ordinary circumstances, both as a substitute for speech, when speech is not convenient, and as an accompaniment to it, often appearing instead of ordinary gesturing. In terms of origin and use, thus, these sign languages are quite different from those that develop in deaf communities. As Stokoe (1980) has emphasized, sign languages developed in deaf communities are systems in which "not just the output signal but also the processes for forming words and sentences operate without any connection to speech or sound" (op. cit., p.365). "Other sign languages," he continues, "may more or less completely and unambiguously mediate general or special interaction, but these are generally learned and used by persons already competent in some spoken language, and hence they differ from sign languages acquired as their native languages by persons who cannot hear speech and by children of deaf parents" (ibid.). Stokoe suggests that the term 'sign language' be reserved for such language systems, but he does not put forward another term by which systems of the sort dealt with in this volume can be designated.

It might be as well to employ a term for these other systems that would not include the word 'language'. In regard to the Aboriginal systems dealt with here, as we shall see, we find that they are not fully autonomous systems and might be better thought of as systems that *represent* spoken language, rather than as languages in their own right. Some of the other gesture systems that have been developed by speaker-hearers, such as the systems in use by certain religious orders or the systems developed in work situations, where it is difficult to use speech, are relatively simple and for this reason might be thought not to qualify as true languages. Nevertheless, the use of the term 'sign language' to refer to these various systems is so well established that I have decided to retain it. I suggest that modifiers be introduced to draw the distinction that Stokoe so rightly insists on. I propose that sign languages proper, as Stokoe would have it, be termed *primary sign languages*, while sign languages developed by people already competent in some spoken language be termed *alternate sign languages*. The word 'alternate' is suggested, for these systems are typically developed for use as an alternative to speech in circumstances where, for whatever reason, speech is not used.

The systems in use by the Aborigines of central Australia are probably the most complex alternate sign languages ever to have been developed. Besides these, the most well known are the sign languages of the Plains Indians of North America and those developed in certain monasteries. The Plains Indians of North America used a complex sign language, apparently as a means of communication between groups who did not share the same language, but it was also used in narration both in religious contexts and for public entertainment (Mallery 1972 [1881], Clark 1982 [1885], West 1960, Taylor 1978). Sign languages also developed for use in the monasteries of the Cistercians, Cluniacs and Trappists, who follow a rule of silence laid down by St. Benedict in the sixth century. Although the rule of silence discouraged all forms of communication, a limited repertoire of signs was permitted, to meet essential needs. In addition to this, unofficial sign systems of varying complexity developed, each monastery apparently using a somewhat different system. One system, in use in a Cistercian monastery in the United States, has been studied in some detail by Barakat (1975). Many of the other accounts of these systems have been reprinted in Umiker-Sebeok and Sebeok (1987). An alternate sign language of some complexity was also at one time in use among the women of the Baraninskiy region of Armenia. In this region it was the custom for married women not to speak when in the presence of their affinal relatives and a sign language was used instead (Karbelashvili 1936).We will discuss some of these sign languages again in Chapter 13, where we compare the Australian Aboriginal systems with others. As we shall see, there are considerable differences between them in how they relate to the spoken languages of their users.

Alternate sign languages that are somewhat more limited in development have been reported in use in various occupational settings. The simple systems of gesture signals in use by auctioneers, skin divers, crane operators, broadcast engineers, and the like (Brun 1969, Crystal and Craig 1978) could be included here; however more complex systems have developed in work settings which permit communication about more than just the immediate task. The best known of such systems are those developed by workers in the sawmills of British Columbia and elsewhere in the northwest of North America. An example from British Columbia has been described in some detail by Meissner and Philpott (1975). An account of a similar system from Oregon has been provided by Johnson (1978).

An alternate sign language is to be distinguished from an invented *manually coded language*. Manually coded languages are those systems which have been developed by educators as a means of conveying spoken languages to the deaf by manual actions. These codes include fingerspelling systems and systems such as Signed English, in which manual actions have been devised to represent the words and morphemes of English (Wilbur 1979 provides a review). It would appear that all such systems presuppose a written form of spoken language and it is this form of language that is conveyed. Alternate sign languages, even those developed in literate societies, do not rely upon written forms of language in any systematic way.

Alternate sign languages are also to be distinguished from those forms of signing used by the deaf, and by hearing people in interaction with the deaf, that are strongly influenced by spoken language. In these forms of signing, signs from the primary sign language used by the deaf are used as equivalents of words in the spoken language. The morphological and syntactic processes characteristic of primary sign languages tend not to be used. Instead, utterances are constructed following the word order of the spoken language and some signs may be invented to mark spoken language grammatical inflections. Such spoken language influenced forms of signing, although they often incorporate elements from manually coded language systems, particularly fingerspelling, have not been specially invented.They have evolved through linguistic contact between the deaf and the hearing. In the United States, English influenced forms of signing of this sort are referred to as 'sign English', 'signed English' or 'pidgin sign English'. Some further discussion of these in relation to the sign languages studied in this book will be found in Chapter 13.

1.2 The medium of sign language and linguistic structure

Primary sign languages have attracted increasing attention from linguists, since the pioneering work of Stokoe (1960) on American Sign Language. An important reason for this interest has been that they raise the question of the relationship between linguistic structure and linguistic medium. It is becoming clear that they show structures very different from spoken languages and it is possible, therefore, that claims about the nature of the general language faculty, hitherto based exclusively on the study of spoken languages, may have to be modified.

Sign languages are organized in the kinesic medium, the medium of visible bodily movement, that is. This has properties very different from the medium of speech. Whereas, in speech, linguistically significant units can be organized in temporal sequence only, in the kinesic medium forms may be constructed which contrast in their spatial organization, as well. Furthermore, the instrument of sign language expression, the body, has a number of spatially separated parts which can be used as articulators, simultaneously. Linguistically significant expressions can be constructed that, all at once, involve the head, action in the face and bodily orientation, as well as the hands.

Research on the organization of primary sign languages has shown that these properties of the kinesic medium have been extensively exploited at every level of organization. At the level of sign structure (analogous to the phonological level of a spoken language), the features of location, handshape and movement pattern by which each sign is distinguished from another within a given lexicon, are not sequentially rearrangeable, as phonemes are, but must be thought of as simultaneously realized aspects of a unitary act. To be sure, it has been shown that in terms of how they are actually produced, signs have a temporal organization (Studdert-Kennedy and Lane 1980, Liddell 1984), but it seems clear that at the sub-lexical level we do not have units that can be separately uttered. Whereas it is possible to pronounce an instance of a single phoneme, one cannot produce a unit of a sign's structure in isolation. At the morphological level, it has been shown how differences between such categories as noun and verb may be realized through an inflection of movement (Supalla and Newport 1978). Special forms known as 'classifiers' have been found, which are used as pro forms for classes of objects, such as 'legged creature', 'vehicle', 'solid cylindrical object', and the like, depending upon the handshape employed. These then can be used in complex constructions in which they may be moved around or positioned in space, thereby becoming incorporated as part of a verb (Wilbur 1979, Stokoe 1980, Supalla 1986).

At the syntactic level, also, there are many ways in which sign language appears to be distinctive, because of how the properties of the kinesic medium are used. For example, it has been shown that, because multiple spatial locations may be established for person reference, multiple pronominal reference within a single sentence is possible. This also makes possible the spatial expression of relationships between verbal arguments by modifications in the spatial movements of a verb sign. Furthermore, spatial relationships may be displayed directly, for example, by using the two hands in relation to one another, so that separate prepositional forms are not needed (Liddell 1980).

The fact that the language is articulated by the body, an entity with several different parts which can be deployed in relationship to one another, is also made use of. For example, in American Sign Language distinctive patterns of facial action may be extended over a signed clause as a way of marking its grammatical status, as in subordination, relativization, interrogation, and the like (Liddell 1980, Baker and Cokely 1980). As a result of these and other features, signed sentences in primary sign languages can rarely be analyzed simply as linear strings of elements, as spoken sentences can. A different grammatical model seems to be required (cf. Stokoe 1972, DeMatteo 1977, Kyle 1983).

Alternate sign languages, we have said, are to be distinguished from primary sign languages because there is a radical difference in their origins and use. The extent to which they may differ structurally from primary sign languages, however, is a matter to be resolved by comparative investigation. In the study of Australian Aboriginal sign languages undertaken here, it will be important to explore the extent to which such alternate sign languages are also found to exploit the kinesic medium in the way primary sign languages do. If we were to find that the Aboriginal sign languages examined were structured according to their own principles, as if they were primary sign languages, this would provide strong grounds for the view that the structure of a linguistic code is highly dependent upon the properties of the medium in which it finds expression.

In this book we shall, from time to time, draw comparisons between the Aboriginal alternate sign languages studied here and primary sign languages, as exemplified by American Sign Language (ASL) and British Sign Language (BSL), among others. As we shall see, the principles that govern the formation of manual signs appear to be much the same in the two kinds of sign language. The processes by which concepts come to be represented in manual form also appear to be very similar except that, in the case of the alternate sign languages studied, the concepts expressed tend to be the same as those expressed in the associated spoken languages. Differences emerge when we consider grammatical organization and the construction of discourse. The structured use of space and movement for grammatical purposes that is so well developed in primary sign languages appears to be developed to a much lesser degree in Australian Aboriginal alternate sign languages. In the Australian Aboriginal systems, furthermore, very little use is made of the face or other parts of the body besides the forelimbs, as a linguistic resource. This is also very different from what has been found for primary sign languages. As will be discussed later, these differences appear to stem directly from the fact that the alternate sign languages dealt with here have developed to become something close to a form of spoken language representation and they do not ever function as the sole and only available linguistic system, as is the case for primary sign languages.

1.3 Some terminological considerations

In discussing sign language in this book I have followed the lead of William Stokoe (1960, 1978). He was the first investigator to undertake a systematic linguistic analysis of any sign language and his work remains the foundation of most that has been done in this field since. In his monograph *Sign Language Structure* (1960), a study of American Sign Language, he outlined the the linguistic units in terms of which the structure of any sign language can be understood. He also developed a notation system which was then used in his *Dictionary of American Sign Language* (Stokoe, Casterline and Croneberg 1965). It is this that serves as the basis for the notation system used in the present work.

Despite my attempt to build upon the work of Stokoe, I have deviated from him in some ways. This is most notable in regard to terminology. Here, not only have I not followed Stokoe. I have also not followed the practices of most other writers in this field. Let me explain my policy with regard to this.

Stokoe's approach to the analysis of sign language was modelled explicitly after the methodology of structural analysis developed in spoken language linguistics, especially by American structural linguists such as Bloomfield (1933) and Trager and Smith (1951), among others. Stokoe recognized, however, that in many ways sign language structure was very different from spoken language structure. He proposed, therefore, a new terminology for sign language linguistics that paralleled the terminology employed in spoken language linguistics but which, at the same time, introduced new concepts where needed. This would appear to be a very reasonable strategy. Unfortunately, his terms have not been widely used. Later writers have sought to introduce their own terminology, in place of Stokoe's, and there has also been an increasing tendency to speak of sign language in terms borrowed from spoken language linguistics without any modification.

Stokoe's approach to terminology in this field is a good one, but because his terms have never become widely current I have not used them here. Thus, for the three aspects in terms of which the structure of a sign may be described, roughly speaking the sign's location of enactment, the arm and hand posture employed and the pattern of movement involved, I have used the terms Sign Location, Sign Actor and Sign Action, rather than Stokoe's terms. He had proposed *tabula, designator* and *signation* for these aspects, and recommended the use of the abbreviations *tab, dez* and *sig*. These terms are somewhat obscure, however, and the plainer terms offered here (which are derived from Stokoe's later attempt to re-explain his original analysis - see Stokoe 1978) seem easier. Stokoe also suggested the term *chereme* for the features by which signs contrast with one another, on analogy with *phoneme*. This seems quite appropriate, but again, it has also been dropped from virtually all discussions of sign language and so it has not been used here.

Other writers on sign language have introduced other terms. Thus, Klima and Bellugi (1979) proposed *parameter* for what is here called the aspect of a sign, and *prime* for particular organizations within an aspect, such as a particular handshape, location or movement. I have avoided using these terms also. They are borrowings from mathematics, and do not seem to be appropriate.

I also have not followed the practice of using terminology from spoken language linguistics without modification, to discuss sign language. Thus I will not speak of sign language phonology and I do not refer to contrastive handshapes or other elements of sign structure as phonemes, as is becoming customary. I do not do so partly because I am not fully convinced that our understanding of sign languages will be enhanced if it is discussed with the terminology of spoken language linguistics. Despite obvious and considerable similarities in the organization of sign languages and spoken languages, there are also very considerable differences, such as those mentioned above, which may ultimately prove to be of great importance. To use spoken language terminology when discussing sign language, without reservation, could well lead to these differences being overlooked or unduly played down.

Finally, I have resisted using explicitly linguistic terminology to discuss sign language for reasons that are peculiar to the present work. In this book, sign languages *and* spoken languages and their interrelationships are discussed in some considerable detail. In order to avoid the need to qualify repeatedly any term that is used, to indicate whether it refers to spoken language or sign language, as far as possible I use a separate terminology for each system. The terminology of spoken language linguistics, especially in its more technical aspects, is used in this book *only* to discuss spoken languages.

To discuss sign languages, as far as possible I have used unspecialized terms and I have tried to avoid new coinages.

1.4 Plan of the book

The book falls roughly into three parts: two sections on Australian Aboriginal sign languages generally, with a special study of the sign languages I myself have recorded in between. I begin with a review of the history of the study of Aboriginal sign languages. Note is taken of certain curious early beliefs by Europeans about Aboriginal sign language, such as the belief that it represented freemasonry. I also discuss why these sign languages have received so little attention, notwithstanding the enormous amount of attention that has been paid to virtually all other aspects of Aboriginal life and culture. This is followed, in the next chapter, by a survey of all the accounts of Aboriginal sign languages that I have been able to find, early or recent, published or unpublished. This is undertaken with a view to arriving at some conclusions about the geographical distribution of these sign languages, the extent to which they appear to have varied in their degree of development, and the various functions they appear to have had.

Chapter 4 provides an outline of the ethnographic situation of the groups from whom I have gathered material, a sketch of the linguistic and cultural relationships between them, and an account of the specific methods used in this study. I then commence a detailed investigation of the sign languages recorded. Chapter 5 provides a description of sign structure, showing how signs in these sign languages are formed and what specific features distinguish them from one another. This discussion is followed by an examination of the relationship between sign form and sign meaning. Many signs can be seen to be derived from pantomime or descriptive gestures. Chapter 6 explores this issue and develops a framework in terms of which the process of sign formation may be analyzed.

Chapters 7 and 8 explore in some detail the relationships between these sign languages and their associated spoken languages. In Chapter 7 sign organization is compared with spoken language morphology and in Chapter 8 we look at how various aspects of spoken language grammar find representation in sign. It is concluded that these sign languages are a sort of compromise between a fully autonomous system, like a primary sign language, and a system that is nothing but a representation of the spoken language. There is some indication that the more sophisticated and knowledgeable a user of one of these sign languages is, the more closely is spoken language represented. This representation is almost wholly at the level of spoken language semantic units, however. The tendency for signs to be established that represent spoken units, such as syllables, is very limited indeed. We suggest that this is a consequence of the medium. Whereas a graphic medium, when used to represent a spoken language, can readily represent aspects of its spoken form, the kinesic medium is quite limited in its capacity to do this. The use of the kinesic medium also gives rise to the development of representations which, in respect to certain kinds of meanings, do not map on to the semantic units of the spoken language. This is true, especially, of certain meanings that have regard to spatial concepts and concepts that involve some notion of movement through space. Such concepts can be more economically rendered directly in gestural form, and this is what we find.

In Chapter 9 we examine discourse in sign language and compare it to spoken language discourse. Specifically, we offer an analysis of two Warlpiri stories which had been recorded on one occasion in sign only and on another occasion in speech. Comparison between the two versions shows that the signed version has much in common with the spoken version in terms of the sequential organization of semantic units. However, modes of expression peculiar to the kinesic medium are used from time to time. Once again we see how the sign language is neither fully autonomous in its organization, nor fully dependent on the spoken language for its structure.

In Chapter 10 we again look at the relationship between sign language and spoken language, but in a different way. Here we look at how signs and words are related when they are used simultaneously, within the same utterance, as is not uncommon. The purpose of our analyses in this Chapter is to see the extent to which signs used together with speech may convey meanings additional to what is conveyed in words. It is found that, on the whole, signs are not used in this way. They are found to parallel verbal meaning closely. Only when the speaker ceases to use sign, and engages in pointing, pantomime or other forms of uncoded gesture, do we find that the kinesic channel serves to convey additional meanings. Signs, thus, are clearly different from gestures. They appear to represent meaning in the same way that lexical forms in the spoken language do. Despite the apparent separateness of the vocal and kinesic channels, if both are being used for lexical encoding at the same time they can only provide parallel meanings.

The next two Chapters examine signs in the North Central Desert sign languages in relation to signs reported from other parts of Australia. In Chapter 11 we examine signs for kin terms. The special character of kin signs as signs in which some part of the body is pointed to is discussed. This is shown to relate to the Aboriginal conceptualization of kin relations in terms of different kinds of bodily mediated interaction. In Chapter 12 we compare larger vocabulary samples both among the North Central Desert groups and also among other vocabulary samples. It is shown that sign languages interrelate with one another differently from spoken languages. It is suggested that processes of sign language diffusion may be different from spoken language diffusion, and the reasons for this are discussed. We also show that the sign languages of the North Central Desert constitute a special and somewhat separate development, in comparison to sign languages elsewhere in Australia. It is suggested that this is a consequence of their intensive use as substitutes for speech during prolonged periods of speech taboo connected with mourning, a practice that is not followed elsewhere. On the basis of certain Australia-wide comparisons of some signs, it is tentatively concluded that the sign languages of the North Central Desert are a relatively more recent development, as well.

The book concludes with two chapters that seek to place the main findings within wider perspectives. Chapter 13 compares Aboriginal sign languages with other semiotic systems. They are compared both to primary sign languages, other alternate sign languages, and other language codes, including acoustic language codes and graphic systems such as writing. These comparisons illustrate how, for a given semiotic system, the medium in which it is fashioned, its function, and how it is related to other semiotic systems, all play a part in shaping its character. Chapter 14 examines the question as to why signing appears to be such a widespread practice among Aborigines. The main characteristics of Aboriginal sociality are reviewed, the special features of Aboriginal face-to-face interaction are described, and it is suggested that the communication requirements that these features engender mean that signing is particularly useful in Aboriginal society.

2 Aboriginal sign languages observed: a history

2.0 Aboriginal sign language as a focus of study

Sign language among the Australian Aborigines, though it has received passing notice quite often, has rarely commanded much serious attention from ethnographers or linguists, or indeed from other observers of Aborigines. Hitherto, almost all that is known on this topic has been derived from the work of four of the main pioneers of Australian ethnography: Alfred Howitt, Walter Roth, Baldwin Spencer and Francis Gillen. Since their work (Howitt 1890, 1891, 1904; Roth 1897,1908; Spencer and Gillen 1899, 1904, 1927), we find only the sign list for the Aranda published by Carl Strehlow (1978 [1915]) and the brief reports of Warner (1937), C.P. Mountford (1938, 1949) and Berndt (1940), before we come to the important but isolated paper of Meggitt(1954). Thereafter, apart from the aborted work of La Mont West (1963), no further work on the topic is reported until the publication of Wick Miller's (1978) brief but valuable discussion of Western Desert sign language, Wright's pictorial dictionary of Warlpiri sign language (Wright 1980) and my own work (Kendon1980a, 1984, 1985a, 1986a, 1987).

Given the tremendous amount of work that has been done on Australian Aborigines, [1] this is a remarkable record of lack of interest. It is clear from Roth and more especially from Spencer and Gillen (1904) that sign language has an important place among the communication practices of Aborigines, yet it has not been regarded as a topic of sufficient interest or importance to be studied in its own right by more than two or three investigators for all of this century.

This lack of interest in sign language among the Aborigines is due to a number of factors. Undoubtedly, many investigators who have been struck by it have not attempted to work on it for technical reasons. Whereas there are well established methods for writing down spoken languages, until recently there have been no easy means for notating signs. Further, since sign language plays no part in the daily life of most members of our own society, its use being wholly confined to the deaf community, most investigators, however interested they might be in it initially, are likely to find that it appears very difficult to study because they have no previous conception of it. In addition, the use of sign language in Aboriginal daily life, though widespread, is nevertheless specialized and limited. Its intensive use in the North Central Desert, for example, is confined to older women, for the most part in association with the observation of speech bans connected with mourning. Its use elsewhere is occasional, or confined to special periods, such as during male initiation ceremonies. To an outsider it thus may not appear to be central to people's lives. In consequence, whereas, for ethnographic work, it is virtually essential to study the spoken language it is clearly not essential to study sign language for this purpose.

It is notable, however, that both Roth and Howitt accord sign language a prominent place in their work. Roth's (1897) treatment is presented as the fourth chapter of his book, immediately following his discussion of spoken language and prior to any ethnographic descriptions. Howitt (1904) devotes an entire chapter to various communication systems, such as message sticks and smoke signals, and this includes an extended treatment of sign language. The subsequent lack of attention to sign language, thus, is not to be accounted for wholly in terms of the kinds of factors just listed above. If it had continued to be seen as something of as much interest as Howitt or Roth saw it to be, there is no doubt that we would today be much better informed on the topic than we are.

Howitt, Roth and Spencer and Gillen belong to a phase in the development of anthropological research in Australia during which direct observation was for the first time being made of Aborigines by people with scientific training and for whom the study of Aborigines was their primary business. These observers were interested in all aspects of Aboriginal life and set as much value on detailed description as they did upon accounts that were guided primarily by more general theoretical interests. Elkin (1963) has distinguished this period as the Phase of Fortuitous, Individual Field Projects. It extends roughly from about 1890 to the First World War and it resulted in a large amount of detailed descriptive ethnography. Subsequently, anthropological research became more systematic. It began to be undertaken by people who were trained as anthropologists in the first instance (none of the pioneer ethnographers started their careers as anthropologists: Howitt was a geologist, Roth was a surgeon, Baldwin Spencer was a zoologist) and this meant that they were trained to do work in terms of what was deemed most relevant from the point of view of general anthropological theory. Sheer ethnographic description was given less emphasis. As a result, only those aspects of Aboriginal culture deemed relevant to the prevailing theoretical preoccupations of the time received detailed attention. This certainly did not include sign language. The prevailing theoretical climate, profoundly influenced by the interests of Radcliffe-Brown (appointed the first Professor of Anthropology in Australia at Sydney University in 1926) meant that great emphasis was placed upon the study of social organization and ritual from a structural-functionalist point of view. As Meggitt (1954, p. 2) observed of this period "attention was being fixed more closely on problems of social organization rather than on cultural content".

Meggitt, in fact, appears to have been quite aware of the unorthodox nature of the paper he published on sign language, given the prevailing theoretical climate, for he writes as if he felt he was under some obligation to justify its publication. After noting the extreme lack of information on the subject, especially given the very large amount of fieldwork that had been done on Aborigines up to that time, he writes: "It may be objected that this [lack of information] is of no great consequence, the subject being one of dilettante rather than of scientific interest." He then goes on to reply to this possible objection by saying that sign language ought to be of interest because it is a practice of some importance in the daily lives of Aborigines, and therefore should not be ignored by ethnographers. However he adds that, in addition, its study may help to throw light "on the way in which Aborigines think about things, how they view their socio-geographical environments and why they single out some features for attention rather than others" (p.3).

Aboriginal sign languages have also not received any attention from linguists. Of the early observers who presented systematic data on one or more Australian language, only Roth also presented material on sign language, as we have already mentioned. Systematic linguistic work by people specializing in linguistics has only been undertaken in Australia since about 1950 and the interest has been primarily in the grammatical description and comparative study of Australian languages, with a view to arriving at a typological and genetic classification of them. Some linguists working in the field have noticed sign language and some have collected occasional notes on the topic, but it has generally been treated as a topic quite peripheral to what has been looked upon as the main task of linguistics. Nevertheless, it is perhaps surprising that there is no mention of sign language in the recent general treatises on Australian languages by Wurm (1972), Dixon (1980) or Yallop (1982), although there is a brief discussion of it in a more popular book by Blake (1981).

The lack of attention paid to Aboriginal sign languages for the last seventy years or so may also be seen as part of a lack of interest in gestural communication in general, that has prevailed for much of this period. A review of the history of the study of sign language and gestural communication shows that, whereas these topics commanded much interest among major investigators at the end of the nineteenth century, interest in them dwindled almost to nothing until a revival began round about 1970. In the latter half of the nineteenth century, under the influence of Darwin's evolutionary theory, there was much discussion of the question of language origins (Stam 1976), and several important figures of the time considered the study of gesture and sign language to be very relevant to this question. Thus Edward Tylor (1878) devotes much space to the topic in his *Researches into the Early History of Mankind* and Wilhelm Wundt, likewise, in his *Volkerpsychologie*, devotes a major section of his volume on language to a discussion of gesture and sign language, which he saw as a kind of intermediate stage in the process by which fully articulate language emerged (Wundt 1973[1921]). There was, thus, at this time, a theoretical climate within which the observations on Aboriginal sign language of Howitt and Roth would have had some relevance, beyond having an interest as part of a complete and detailed description of Aboriginal customs. However, after the first decade of the present century, there was a marked shift in the theoretical climate in anthropology, linguistics and psychology, which turned investigators away from historical studies towards a concern with synchronic studies of systemic structures. Thus a major reason why the study of gesture and sign language might be of more general theoretical interest was removed and this undoubtedly contributed to a decline of interest in them (Kendon 1982).

To this we may add that it is only quite recently that the whole phenomenon of face-to-face communication has become a major focus of attention. The study of ethnography of speech (Hymes 1974), conversation analysis (Schenkein 1978), discourse analysis (Stubbs 1983), and semiotics (Eco 1977), inevitably generate interest in the variety of communication practices employed in interaction. The effects of this in Aboriginal Studies have only lately begun to be felt (see Malcolm 1982 for a comprehensive review and also Sansom 1980 and Liberman 1982a, 1982b, 1985. This work receives further discussion in Chapter 14). Thus, since the whole question of interpersonal communication and interaction was not an issue for linguists and anthropologists for most of this century, it is perhaps not surprising that detailed studies of communication practices among Aborigines are very few in number and that sign language, in particular, should have received the scant attention that it has.

In the earliest period of observation of Aborigines, that which precedes the era of Howitt, Roth and Spencer and Gillen, such knowledge as was available derived from the accounts of explorers and settlers whose contact with Aborigines was incidental to their main activities. Some of these people, the explorers, especially, were very sympathetic to Aborigines and took much interest in them and accumulated much valuable information. Most others were either only mildly interested or indifferent, if not actually hostile, and their information is fragmentary at best.

Very little in the way of reports of sign language stem from this early period. Evidently, sign language was something that people observed only after prolonged and intimate contact with the people who used it. Howitt himself comments on this. He remarks that when he first saw the Dieri (of Cooper's Creek, South Australia) using gestures he took it to be an expression of defiance or command to depart, but afterwards, he writes "when I became better acquainted with these tribes, I came to see that these gestures were part only of a complete system of handsigns" (Howitt 1891, p. 94). Elsewhere (1904) he notes how early explorers observed the use of gestures by Aborigines but did not realize that these gestures "were not merely the natural aids to speech, but, in fact, formed part of a recognized and well-understood system of artificial language" (op. cit., p. 726). Indeed, it seems probable that most of these early observers would not have recognized a sign language for what it was, even if they had noticed it. As we shall see, there is evidence that sign language sometimes was noticed, even as early as the 1850's, but that in such cases it was mistaken for something else.

The history of the study of Australian Aboriginal sign language, then, is not a very rich one. Nevertheless, as we shall see in the review to follow, it is not without some curious aspects.

2.1 A history of observation of Australian Aboriginal sign languages

The earliest report of sign language recognized as such for any Australian Aboriginal group appears to be that of Gason (1874) for the Dieri of Cooper's Creek, South Australia. Samuel Gason was a police trooper in charge of two men at an isolated police post at Lake Hope. This had been established in about 1864, shortly after European settlers had begun to run cattle in the region and required protection from the Aborigines (Bonython 1971). Gason became very well acquainted with the Dieri, he learnt their language and participated in their initiation rituals (Howitt 1891, p. 83). He was persuaded to publish his observations of the Dieri, together with some account of their language in a small monograph in 1874. This monograph was subsequently reprinted in whole or in part in several different works of compilation (including Woods 1879 and Curr 1886). In this monograph Gason says: "Besides the spoken language, they have a copious one of signs - all animals, native man or woman, the heavens, earth, walking, riding, jumping, flying, swimming, eating, drinking, and hundreds of other objects or actions have each their particular sign, so that a conversation may be sustained without the utterance of a single word" (Gason 1874, p. 35). Unfortunately, Gason provides no description of this sign language. He adds: "This dumb language, of which I possess a thorough knowledge, cannot be described in words" (loc. cit.).

Only a very few signs of the Dieri are known to us. Howitt (1891), in his account of the Dieri, provides a description of some 65 signs, 44 based on descriptions supplied by his correspondent, the Rev. H. Vogelsang (a Lutheran missionary), 16 by Gason, the remaining five being his own. According to Howitt (1891), who also quotes Gason as his source, Dieri mourning ritual included the maintenance of prolonged speech taboos by the deceased's spouse - widow or widower. This speech taboo was sustained for longer periods by women than by men. In the case of widows it could last for many months, for they had to wait until all of the white clay with which they had bedaubed themselves had completely worn off. Howitt also notes that male novices were also placed under speech taboos during their periods of seclusion. Such speech taboos were applied in association with each of the four different initiation ceremonies that Howitt describes.

Prior to Gason's report, the only published reference to what might be sign language among Aborigines is the curious account by the explorer John McDouall Stuart of his observation of 'masonic signs'. The account is to be found in Stuart's journal of his fourth expedition into central Australia, which he undertook in 1860. Stuart describes an encounter with four Aborigines, including an older man and two younger men who, Stuart thought, must be a father and his two sons. The encounter took place at Keckwick Ponds, which is just south of what is now known as Attack Creek, where Stuart was turned back by a large and hostile group of Aborigines. The Aborigines he encountered on this occasion were almost certainly Warumungu. Stuart describes how the four men approached his camp about an hour before sundown on 23 June 1860:

> One was an old man, and seemed to be the father of these two fine young men. He was very talkative, but I could make nothing of him. I have endeavoured, by signs, to get information from him as to where the next water is, but we cannot understand each other. After some time, and having conferred with his two sons, he turned round, and surprised me by giving me one of the Masonic signs. I looked at him steadily; he repeated it, and so did his two sons. I then returned it, which seemed to please them much, the old man patting me on the shoulder and stroking down my beard. They then took their departure, making friendly signs until they were out of sight. (Hardman, ed. 1865, p. 213)

As several different authors were to comment later, it seems likely that the 'Masonic sign' Stuart saw was a sign belonging to the sign language that was later found to be in extensive use among the Warumungu.[2] However, this report by Stuart apparently contributed to widely circulated rumors that 'freemasonry' was practised by the Aborigines and several investigators appear to have taken this idea seriously enough to inquire further about it. Thus E.M. Curr included as Question 80 in the printed Questionnaire that he circulated in the 1870s, as he gathered data for his monumental *The Australian Race* : "Have your Blacks any Masonic signs?" (Curr 1886, Vol.2, p. 206). And again, in the questionnaire circulated in 1904 under the authority of Malcolm A.C. Fraser, the Registrar General of Western Australia, we find as Question 30: "Any use of Masonic signs observed among the natives in the district?"

According to Elizabeth Salter (1971, p.112), Malcolm A.C. Fraser was inspired to circulate this questionnaire by John Fraser, of Maitland, New South Wales. John Fraser had reminded him in 1900 that it was "a pity your colony [Western Australia] had done nothing toward a record of your Aborigines". Malcolm Fraser persuaded his Government to provide funds for an assistant to compile all information available on Western Australian natives and he appointed Daisy Bates to the post. It was she, in collaboration with Malcolm Fraser, who designed the questionnaire. This questionnaire contained a number of questions about Aboriginal customs, as well as extensive word lists. It was sent to every policeman, magistrate and settler throughout the colony. The question on masonic signs may have been suggested by Curr (his questionnaire had been circulated in Western Australia), but equally likely, it may have been directly suggested by John Fraser himself, for it appeared that he believed that the Aborigines used masonic signs.

John Fraser had written a short treatise on the Aborigines of New South Wales (Fraser 1882a) which had won him election to the Royal Society of New South Wales and which had also won him its Money Prize (of £25). He subsequently wrote on Australian and Polynesian languages and he edited a collection of L.Threlkeld's work on Awabakal, a New South Wales language (Fraser 1882b). He was appointed by the New South Wales Commissioners for the Columbian Exhibition in Chicago to write a short book on the Aborigines of New South Wales which was to be distributed at the Exhibition. It is in this book (Fraser 1892) that he expresses his belief that the Aborigines used masonic signs. Thus, he writes (op. cit., p. 24): "In several instances, blacks in their wild state, and in places far removed from contact with white civilization, have been known to make use of masonic signs when approached by white men." As proof of this he quotes at some length from a previously unpublished private letter from a Mr Bedford, a staff surveyor in Queensland. Mr Bedford writes of an incident in 1882 or 1883 in which he saved the life of an Aborigine he was about to shoot, because the Aborigine addressed him with what he took to be a masonic sign. This man was the last left alive of several with whom Mr Bedford and his "well armed party" of Kanakas had had a skirmish. The fight was "short, sharp and decisive". At the end of it "only one black was left - a very tall and powerful specimen, evidently a chief". Mr Bedford continues:

I had just covered him with my rifle and in another instant he would have dropped, when, to my utter astonishment, he gave me in rapid succession three or four times, the penal sign of the master mason, and thereupon stood to order. I instantly answered him, and, going nearer, I gave the signs of entered apprentice, fellow craftsman and master mason, which he appeared to understand. My next five or ten minutes were fully occupied in saving him from the wrath of my boys. But when I had succeeded in making them understand that he was not to be harmed, I turned round to our captive and found he was gone! He had dived head foremost into the very long grass, and wriggled through it like a snake, he got clean off, for not one of us could find him; I was much disappointed at this, for I wanted to question him, and through him I might have succeeded in forming friendly relations with the tribes round about.

John Fraser concludes his discussion of Mr Bedford's letter by quoting from Stuart's journal (he refers to him as "Sturt"[3] - a confusion W.E. Roth also falls into, as will be noted below), but adds that "in the region where this incident happened to Captain Sturt (sic), the blacks have an extensive system of gesture language" (op. cit., p. 25) and he suggests that "Captain Sturt's adventure was only an incident of this gesture language but I can scarcely explain the experience of Mr Bedford, in Queensland, in the same way. I leave it unexplained."

To revert to Mr Bedford's letter for a moment, it is worth adding the closing portion of it that Fraser quotes. Mr Bedford writes:

Our Right Worshipful D.G.M., the Hon. Charles Augustus Gregory, formerly Surveyor-General of Queensland, one of our earliest explorers, told me that he also found traces of free-masonry amongst the blacks of the north-west of Queensland, although not so unmistakable as those I have narrated.

A.C. Gregory, it may be added, was a prominent freemason (he joined the Craft in 1855), as well as being one of Australia's most important explorers (Birman 1979). He was thus a man of some influence. Gregory does not make any reference to masonic signs among Aborigines in his journals (Gregory and Gregory 1884); however Mr. Bedford was not the only man to whom he mentioned this observation. He also mentioned it to a J. Malbon Thompson who reported it in the February 1902 issue of *The Science of Man* (Thompson 1902, p.15). Daisy Bates had come across this, for she refers to it in the manuscript for her projected book on Western Australian natives (Bates ms. n.d.).

The rumor of "freemasonry among the blacks" is thus not due to Stuart alone.[4] Since, as we know from later observation, sign language was widely used in north-western Queensland, it is likely that Gregory's observation of 'masonic signs' in this part of the country, perhaps like that of Stuart's, really refers to an observation of sign language. Like John Fraser, however, I am inclined to leave Mr Bedford's experience unexplained!

W.E. Roth was also influenced by Stuart's observation of masonic signs, but in his case (as, with hindsight, we might expect), the result was a critical study of the idea and then, realizing that it was erroneous, some of the most detailed accounts of Aboriginal sign language available. In his *Ethnological Studies in North-West-Central Queensland* (Roth 1897), Roth includes a chapter entitled "The Expression of Ideas by Manual Signs: A Sign Language". This begins with some brief but very acute observations on the nature and use of the sign language and contains careful descriptions of 213 signs, with notes on their origin, use, and the group to which each sign was attributed. All his descriptions are accompanied with excellent drawings (Fig. 2.1). It remains to this day a most valuable source for information on sign language in this part of Australia. Indeed, it is the only detailed information on this area that we have.

In the Preface to the book Roth gives an account of how he came to recognize the existence of a sign language among the Aborigines in the district where he worked as a doctor. He encountered it quite accidentally for the first time at Roxburgh Downs, on the Upper Georgina River:

> I was out on horseback one day with some blacks when one of the "boys" riding by my side suddenly asked me to halt, as a mate of his in front was after some emus, consisting of a hen-bird and her young progeny. As there had been, apparently to me, no communication whatsoever between the boy in front and the one close to me, separated as they were by a distance of quite 150 yards, I naturally concluded that my informant was uttering a falsehood, and told him so in pretty plain terms, with the result that, after certain mutual recriminations, he explained on his hands how he had received the information, the statement to be shortly afterwards confirmed by the arrival of the lad himself with the dead bird and some of her young in question. The reported use of "masonic" signs attributed to the blacks by Captain Sturt [sic], who had been in close proximity to these districts some half a century ago, immediately flashed across my mind, and the possibility of such signs being ideagrams [sic], the actual expressions of ideas, led me on step by step to making a study of what I subsequently discovered to be an actual well-defined sign-language, extending throughout the entire North-West-Central districts of Queensland.

Roth took "Captain Sturt" seriously enough, at first, to trouble to investigate his claim. In his introduction to the chapter in which he presents descriptions of the signs he says "So far as my limited knowledge of the craft [of freemasonry] allows, I have tested these people over and over again, repeatedly submitting them even to strict cross-examination, but have never succeeded in corroborating the gallant explorer's statement. I can only conclude that what he conscientiously believed to be aboriginal masonic signs are really the ideagrams which I am about to describe" (Roth 1897, p.72).

We may now consider the contribution of E.M. Curr. In the 1840s he had managed a sheep run for his father near Shepparton in Victoria, where he came into contact with the Bangerang. Unlike many of his contemporaries, he was sympathetic to these Aborigines, treated them with much respect, and learnt something of their language. After a varied life which included travel on horseback through the Middle East and work as an importer of horses to New Zealand, Curr returned to Melbourne as Chief Inspector of Stock in the region. From 1873 onwards he became interested in the possibility that a study of the languages of the Aborigines might throw light upon their origins. In pursuit of this, he compiled a vocabulary list of 125 items and a series of questions which he sent to as many people as possible. Among these questions, as already mentioned, he had included as Question 80 a question about freemasonry. He also included as Question 65: "Do your Blacks use signs instead of words? To what extent, and what particulars can you state?" The returns were presented in his *The Australian Race* (Curr 1886). In this book, he summarizes the findings of his survey in a long introductory chapter, and then presents details of the vocabularies and the answers to his Questionnaire which he received from over 200 correspondents. Although there are many shortcomings to this work, it is nevertheless of great value, for it gives the only documentation available for many groups whose languages and customs have since disappeared.

Extracts from Roth's notes to illustrations shown in Fig. 2.1

Fig. 2.1 (opposite) shows Roth's drawings for signs for mammals (from Plate II in Roth 1897). Roth collected material from ten groups in an area centered on Boulia in northwest Queensland (see Fig. 12.2). These were.(in Roth's orthography) Pitta Pitta (PP), Boinji (Bo), Ulaolinya (Ula), Wonkajera (Wo), Walookera (Wal), Undekerebina (Und), Kalkadoon (Kal), Mitakoodi (Mit), Woonamurra (Woo) and Goa (Goa). For each of the signs illustrated, Roth added a description and an explanation of the sign's form. Thus for Fig. 1. Dog, he says "Finger-tips all touching top of thumb: flexion at wrist. Finger-tips represent the toe pads." For Fig. 7. Rat, he says "The one hand is the animal's head: it is in the act of being struck with a stick, etc." He also notes which groups have the sign and describes any variants. Here we give Roth's identifications, followed by his abbreviations of the groups where he recorded it : 1. *Dingo, Dog*. For all groups except Undekerebina. 2. *Horse*. PP, Bo, Ula, Won, Wal, Und. 3. *Horse*. Mit. 4. *Cattle*. PP, Bo, Und. 5. *Cattle*. Mit. 6. *Rat*. PP, Bo, Ula, Won, Wal, Und. 7. *Rat*. Woo, Goa. 8. *Porcupine* (Echidna hystrix). PP, Ula, Won, Wal, Und, Kal. 9. *Porcupine*. Mit. 10. *Porcupine*. Bo. 11. *Bandicoot*. Bo. 12. *Bandicoot*. Mit. 13. *Bandicoot*. PP, Won, Wal. 14. *Bandicoot*. Kal. 15. *Bandicoot*. Bo. 16. *Bandicoot*. Ula, Woo, Goa. 17. *Opossum*. Kal. 18. *Opossum*. Mit. 19. *Opossum*. Bo, Ula, Won, Wal. 20. *Opossum, Opossum string*. PP, Woo, Goa. 21. *Paddymelon: Small species of kangaroo*. PP, Ula, Won, Wal. 22.*Paddymelon*. Kal. 23.Mit. 24.*Kangaroo: Any large species of Macropus*. PP, Ula, Won, Wal, Und, Mit, Woo, Goa

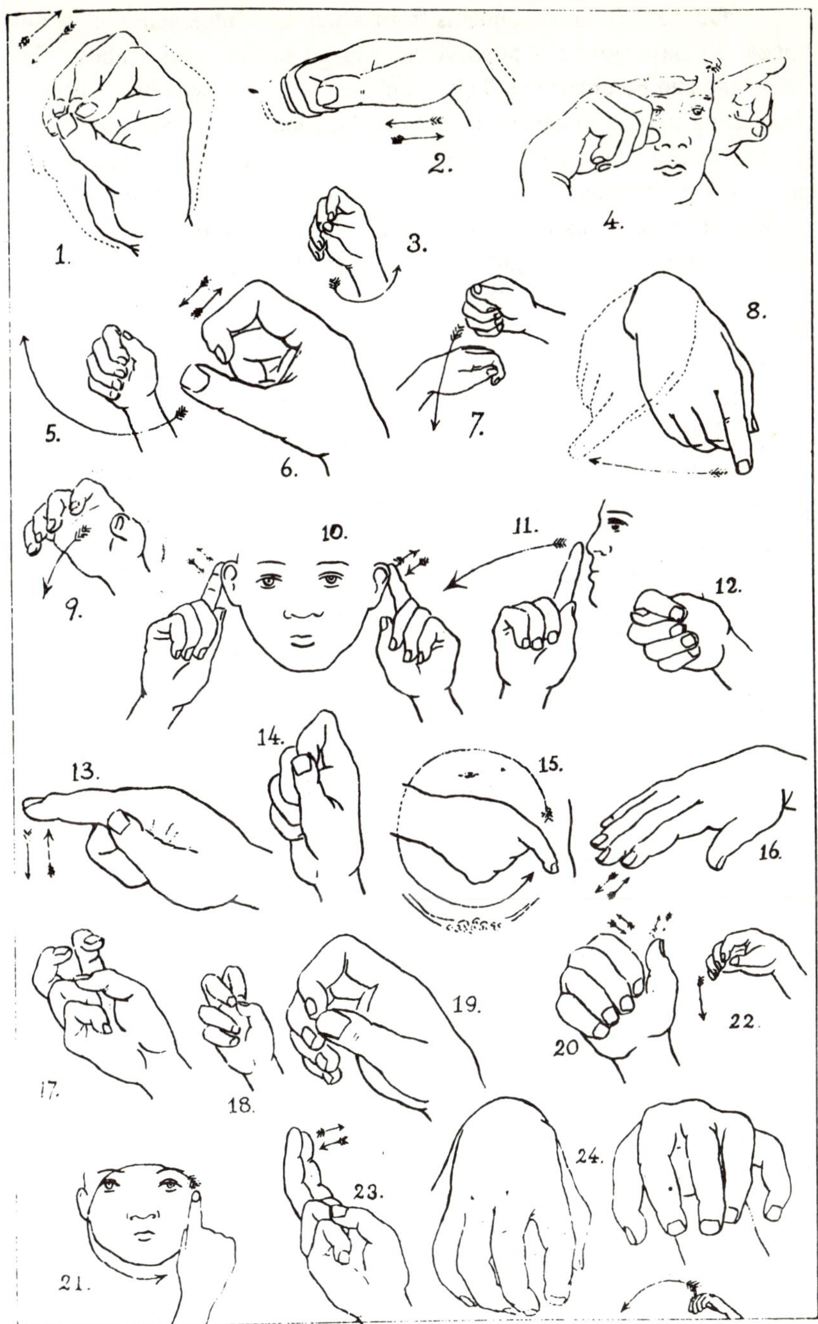

Fig. 2.1 Plate II from Roth (1897) illustrating signs for mammals.

Of the 200 correspondents from which Curr received replies, only 11 appear to have given a positive answer to his questions about Gesture Language and Freemasonry. This, combined with his own observations of the Bangerang people made some years earlier, led him to conclude: "Though communication by signs has been reported to prevail in a few tribes, the practice is exceptional, the Australian being noticeable for the little use he makes either of signs or of gesticulation" (Curr 1886, Vol. 1, p.26). This seems surprising, in the light of what soon was to become evident from the observations of Howitt, Stirling, Spencer and Gillen, Roth, and others. However Curr based his statement firmly upon the information he had gathered from his numerous correspondents and his conclusion was correct, given the information he had at his disposal at the time.

Such a conclusion, erroneous as it proved to be, is less a reflection on Curr than it is a reflection on the poor qualities of observation of so many of his correspondents. Curr appears not to have corresponded much with the people who sent in answers to his questions and in this he contrasts with A.W. Howitt, who also made extensive use of the questionnaire as a means of gathering information about Aborigines. Howitt was originally trained as a geologist and had the benefit of some scientific education (Curr's education included a British Public School and a period of study in France). Furthermore, Howitt, after he had entered into collaboration with Lorimer Fison (leading to their joint work *Kamilaroi and Kurnai*, Fison and Howitt 1880), came to have a definite theoretical position he wished to explore. Whenever a correspondent showed an intelligent interest in answering his questions he would enter into correspondence with him, following up many of the answers he received with further more detailed questioning (Mulvaney 1971).

Howitt's main interest was in social organization and marriage practices, for he was, as a result of Fison's influence, intent on developing a theory of the evolution of society as illustrated by the Aborigines. However, he was interested in all aspects of Aboriginal culture and in at least some of the questionnaires he circulated he included a question about sign language (but not about freemasonry, as far as I know) and, as we have seen, he accorded quite a prominent place to this topic in two different articles and also in a chapter in his major book (Howitt 1904).

The section on sign language in his *The Native Tribes of South East Australia* is in large part a re-presentation of a paper he had published earlier (Howitt 1890). Howitt does not accept the idea that the extensive use of gestural communication among some Aboriginal groups is due to any "paucity of language" (as some had suggested). He goes on to note that there is a good deal of variation in the extent to which gesture is used in different groups. He says "Some have a very extensive code of signs, which admit of being so used as to almost amount to a medium of general communication. Other tribes have no more than those gestures which may be considered as the general property of mankind" (pp.723-724). He states that his own observations and the information he had received from correspondents leads him to the conclusion that "the use of sign language is more common in Central and North-eastern Australia than in the South-eastern quarter of the Continent" (p.724). He remarks that this variation in use is difficult to explain, but he offers the following hypothesis as a possible way of accounting for it:

> The reason for this may perhaps be found in the vast extents of open country plains, sandhills, stony tracts which occur in the interior of Australia as, for instance, in the Lake Eyre basin.
>
> A stranger is seen there from afar off, and can be interrogated at a safe distance by gesture language as to who he is, where he comes from, and his intentions. In the coastal regions or in the forest-clad mountain ranges which lie alongside the Great Dividing Range, separating the coast lands from the interior, such would not be the case, and gesture language could not be made use of at a distance, except in rare cases. (p.724)

Howitt does not seem to be fully convinced by this hypothesis, offering it, perhaps, as the most plausible, for he adds: "I venture this supposition, but without laying much stress upon it" (loc. cit.). It does seem rather unlikely, for the main functions of these complex gesture languages, as we shall discuss in more detail later, have to do with communication in circumstances where speech is avoided for ritual reasons, and not for such limited functions as communication at a distance, although it certainly is useful for this purpose and may be observed being used in this way at times.

Howitt continues his review by citing examples of groups which, on the one hand, have complex gesture languages, such as the Dieri; groups which have virtually no use of gesture, such as the Kurnai of Gippsland on the Southeast coast (which Howitt knew well from first hand acquaintance); and groups which were intermediate between these two extremes. He concludes by remarking that the "systematic use of gestures by the Australian aborigines in lieu of words, or in connection with speech, seems to have been almost overlooked until lately by writers on the native tribes of Australia" (p.726). He remarks, however, that there are great difficulties in the way of investigating the use of gesture language, suggesting that "the ordinary inquirer needs to be almost specially trained to the work" (p.726). He admits to being able to treat of the subject in only a superficial way, and concludes with descriptions of some 63 signs attributed to ten different groups, mostly from South Australia and New South Wales, the descriptions all being derived from those supplied by his numerous correspondents. The descriptions, like those to be found in the earlier paper on the Dieri already mentioned, suggest that in many cases the gestures his correspondents had described were those made either in long distance contact, as often as not with Europeans, or gestures used when in closer contact with Europeans in the course of efforts to make themselves understood.

Despite Howitt's interest in this topic and the greater recognition that he gives to it in comparison to Curr, it is clear that he himself made few detailed observations. It is also clear that his correspondents also made few observations. The nature of the gestures they did describe suggests how little intimate contact they actually did have with the Aborigines they were writing about.

Following Howitt, the next observer to remark in detail on sign language among the Aborigines was W.E. Roth, whom we have already mentioned. Roth became interested in collecting information about Aborigines while he was Surgeon in the Boulia district of North-West-Central Queensland. The duties of this position were sufficiently light to allow him to learn to speak Pitta Pitta, to write its grammar, and to collect a large amount of detailed information about the Aborigines living in the area, all within the space of three years. As already remarked, his treatment of sign language is excellent, and it remains to this day among the best accounts we have. In 1898 Roth moved to Cooktown, to take up an appointment as Northern Protector of Aborigines for Queensland, an office he took very seriously, much to the annoyance of the local settlers who wished to exploit Aborigines as cheap labor (Pope and Moore 1967). During his time in this office (1898-1905) he collected a great deal of information about the Aborigines of the Cape York Peninsula, again paying attention to sign language where it could be observed. Some of these observations were published (Roth 1907, 1908), but others remain in manuscript form. It is to Roth that we owe much of what little is known about sign language in the Cape York Peninsula area.

Other early observers of Aborigines also remarked on the use of sign language. E.C. Stirling, as a member of the Horn Scientific Expedition which, in 1895, traversed much of northern South Australia and the southern part of what is now the Northern Territory, was quite struck by it. As the anthropologist on the expedition, he was responsible for Section IV of the report in which the anthropological observations were presented. He includes a section on sign language. In this section (Spencer 1896, Part IV, pp.111-126) he remarks that although he had been made aware, by the observations of various writers, that many groups of Aborigines made use of signs, it was "a great surprise to us to find that these signs constituted, in the districts visited, a very extensive system of gesture language, which is not only much used, but is capable of indicating a very large number of objects, as well as simple ideas concerning them" (op.cit., p.111). He states that among the Aranda and Luritcha signs were observed to be in constant use. He also cites the observation of Francis Gillen (at the time Post and Telegraph Station Master at Alice Springs, and Aboriginal Sub-Protector and Special Magistrate) that north of the MacDonnell Ranges "the sign language reaches a still higher development" (op.cit., p.111). He adds that he noticed that some Aborigines were much greater adepts at sign language than others and, he adds "I think, generally speaking the lubras [i.e. women] excelled the men in readiness of execution" (op.cit., p.112). He concludes with a description of forty-two signs, with several variant forms noted. The descriptions are careful and, on the whole, interpretable, and accompanied by clear drawings.

Baldwin Spencer (see Mulvaney and Calaby 1985) was also a member of the Horn Scientific Expedition and it was on this journey that he first met Francis Gillen and began his famous collaboration with him. Gillen had already learned to speak Aranda when Spencer met him, and had accumulated a large body of observations. An outline of these observations was included in Part IV of the Report of the Expedition. Gillen does not mention sign language in this Outline although, as Stirling's reference to Gillen's observations makes clear, he had certainly made observations about it.

Spencer and Gillen refer to sign language in several places in their publications; however they do not offer any descriptions of any detail, with the exception of 64 signs from the "very many" that were shown to them on one occasion by an old Aranda man. These descriptions are given as an Appendix to their book *The Arunta* (Spencer and Gillen 1927) and re-printed in Baldwin Spencer's *Wanderings in Wild Australia* (1928). They are further discussed in Chapter 11.

From the remarks Spencer and Gillen make about sign language in various places in their books, it appears that they were most impressed by the use of sign language among the Warumungu. Although they certainly observed it to be in use elsewhere in the central and north central desert regions, it seems clear that the Warumungu were, in their observation, the most prolific and extensive users of it:

> One of the things that struck us most when wandering around the Warramungu (sic) camps was the fact that so many of the women were under a ban of silence. Many times when we spoke to a woman she signified by putting a finger to her lips that she was not allowed to speak. If four men, each of them belonging to a different section of the tribe, happened to die within a short time of one another, there would not be a single woman in the whole camp who would be able to utter a word.
>
> They did not seem to mind in the least, and those who were under the ban of silence chattered gaily away on their fingers. Without making any sound, except that of laughing, they easily communicated with one another by means of their remarkable system of gesture language. Their conversation deals with matters of a concrete, rather than an abstract nature,

and it is simply wonderful to watch the way in which they can express themselves. (Spencer and Gillen 1912, pp.389-390).

Spencer and Gillen add that sometimes the women of the Warumungu preferred not to have the ban of silence lifted and they reported an encounter with one old woman who, they were told, had not spoken for twenty-five years (op.cit., p.394).

Aranda sign language was also observed by Carl Strehlow, who includes in his treatise on this group (Strehlow 1907-1922) a description of 290 signs for 454 meanings. Strehlow remarks that the sign language "has an astonishing importance for and is perfected to a remarkable degree by the Central Australian natives" (Strehlow 1978 [1915], p. 349). He offers little in the way of further observations on its use, however, and neither in the section on sign language, nor elsewhere in his treatise, does he mention extended speech taboos, either in connection with mourning ritual or with the rituals of male initiation. He does, in one place, mention that if a brother of someone who has died has been living elsewhere, he may be informed of the death by means of sign language. He makes no mention of the practice of widow's silence, however.

Strehlow's descriptions of the signs of the Aranda remains the most complete for this group to date. Unfortunately, he provides no details about how he acquired these descriptions (whether they were based on demonstrations from women or men, for instance) and many of his descriptions (at least in the Chewings translation that is now available in Umiker-Sebeok and Sebeok 1978) are very hard to follow.

After Strehlow's account, as we have already observed, we have to wait until 1954 for the next substantial contribution to this subject, when Meggitt published his paper on Warlpiri sign language. Thereafter, the next publication of significance is Miller (1978). Apart from Basedow's (1925) derivative account, the only other publications to be noticed in this period are those of Mountford (1938, 1949) on the Ngada and the Warlpiri, respectively; Berndt (1940) who published a note on some signs shown him by an old survivor of the Jaralde of Murray Bridge, South Australia; Lloyd Warner (1937) who describes signs he observed in North East Arnhem Land in an appendix to his book; and Love (1941) who describes the kinship signs of the Worora.

From the foregoing it will be seen, then, that until 1978, despite the initial interest expressed in the nineteenth century, Aboriginal sign language has been little investigated. This chapter may be aptly concluded with a further quotation from Meggitt (1954), which remains almost as true today as it did when he wrote it:

...we really know very little about their sign languages. Indeed, we still have to undertake the pedestrian tasks of classifying such sign languages, even if only in the most general terms, and of mapping their distributions before we can begin to tackle the problem of their significance" (p.2).

It is to be hoped that the remainder of this volume will serve to render this statement by Meggitt at least partially outmoded.

Notes

[1]Greenway's (1963) bibliography lists over 10,000 items up to 1959 (and this is a selection from over 22,000 that he had compiled).

[2]As to what the gestures were which Stuart mistook for a masonic sign, we can only guess, of course. However, it may be worth noting that according to one account of the rituals of freemasonry, the Sign of Fidelity of the Second Degree in a Craft Lodge is described as "Right hand on left breast with thumb squared upwards" (Hannah 1953, p. 81). It is conceivable that one of the Warumungu signs for 'water' could be mistaken for this masonic sign. Stuart had tried to get information about water, as he explains. Perhaps he had made himself understood, and the Warumungu were replying with the sign for 'water' in which the center of the chest is tapped with the fingertips, all fingers fully extended and adducted (held together - a 'flat' hand). Perhaps the Warumungu, seeing Stuart use so many gestures and grasping the topic of his gesturing, presumed he knew a kind of sign language and so used a relevant sign from their own. As we may guess from Stuart's account, this produced a rather surprising response in the strange white man!

[3]Charles Sturt (1795-1869) is mainly known for his exploration of the Murray river system around 1830. J. McDouall Stuart (1815-1866) accompanied Sturt on his last expedition into the Simpson Desert, 1844-1846, and then himself led three further expeditions into the center of Australia. His encounter with the 'masonic' Warumungu took place during his second expedition in which he was attempting to find a permanent route to the north from South Australia.

[4]The editor of Stuart's journals, W. Hardman, must bear some of the responsibility for this, also. He heads page 213 of his edition of Stuart's Journals "Native Freemasons!", thus drawing attention to the 'masonic' signs Stuart claims to have observed. As a more recent editor of the same journal has noted (Stuart 1983), Hardman showed considerable contempt for Stuart and doctored his journals in various ways in an attempt to improve their literary quality and their popular appeal.

3 Aboriginal sign languages observed: a geographical review

3.0 Introduction

In this Chapter primary references to sign language among Australian Aborigines will be discussed. Included here is a discussion not only of the well-known sources already referred to, but also all mentions, in both published and unpublished writings, that I have been able to find. Where appropriate, I have also included personal communications from people who have not published their observations, but with whom I have talked or corresponded. The aim of this discussion is to establish as complete a picture as possible of where in Australia Aboriginal sign language has been observed and to review the uses that have been reported for it. In undertaking this survey, particular attention has been paid to reports of the presence of speech taboos, whether in connection with mourning rituals or initiation rituals, or both. In general we expect that the more extensive are speech taboos, the more likely are we to find the development of complex sign languages.

The results of this survey are presented geographically in Figure 3.1 and in tabular form in Table 3.1. With one or two exceptions I have included in the Table only those instances where specific reference is made to sign language or to speech taboos, or both, either indicating the presence or the absence of these practices. Most writers on Aborigines make no mention of these topics, but we cannot assume that just because they are not mentioned, they are absent. Only specific mentions, positive or negative, can serve as sources of information for this survey.

The discussion is organized geographically and will generally follow the order of entries in Table 3.1. These entries have been grouped by region, for the most part following the Culture Areas of Australia proposed by Peterson (1976), based on the major drainage basins of the continent. Within Peterson's regions we have made some subdivisions (Fig. 3.1). Thus we have divided his South East Coast into a South Coast region, and a Southern and a Northern East Coast region. We discuss Aboriginal groups in Victoria and the southern hinterland of New South Wales separately from those found in the high country of northern New South Wales and southern Queensland, even though both of these areas are included in Peterson's Riverina culture area. In addition, we have considered a North Central Desert area separately from the rest of Peterson's Western Desert. The North Central Desert, as defined here, extends northwards from the MacDonnell Ranges to the boundaries of the Gulf and Fitzmaurice drainage basins and westwards to include all of what is usually taken to be traditional Warlpiri territory. As we shall see, in terms of sign language development and the application of speech taboos, this area seems somewhat distinct.

The Aboriginal groups mentioned within regions are entered in Table 3.1 in a south to north sequence as far as possible, with groups to the west being listed before those to the east, where two or more are on the same latitude. The regions are also listed in a south to north sequence in a succession of four passes across the continent. The names employed for the Aboriginal groups are usually those favored by Tindale (1974), except where those preferred by literate native speakers differ from Tindale, (thus I use 'Warlpiri' instead of Tindale's 'Walpiri'), or where his suggestion is different from a very well known name (thus I have retained 'Tiwi' rather than use Tindale's recommended 'Tunuvivi'). In such cases Tindale's version is given in square brackets. In other cases, common alternatives to Tindale, or an author's original spelling, is given in round brackets. I have also followed Tindale in arriving at the geographical placement of groups referred to in Fig. 3.1, locating the group in the center of what he proposes for its area of occupancy, without putting in his boundaries, however.[1]

Table 3.1 lists the name of each of the groups for which there is a mention of sign language or speech taboo. In the next column we enter information on the nature of the sign language mentioned. 'Present' means that the use of sign language is mentioned specifically by the author or authors listed in the Observer column, 'Absent' means that a definite statement has been made that it is not used. A question mark preceding an entry indicates either that we have inferred Present or Absent from statements made by the author or that we are uncertain as to the reliability of the statement of the author in question.

Where further information is available on the nature of the sign language we have summarized this in the Table by the words 'limited', 'developed' or 'highly developed'. 'Limited' indicates that, so far as we can tell, only a small vocabulary of signs was in use, and this was not employed as a general alternative to speech, but either as a supplement (as, for instance, with the use of kin signs among the Worora) or as an alternative in quite limited circumstances such as hunting. 'Developed' indicates that there is evidence for an extensive vocabulary of signs (more than a hundred items, at least), and that signs could be used as an alternative to speech in a variety of

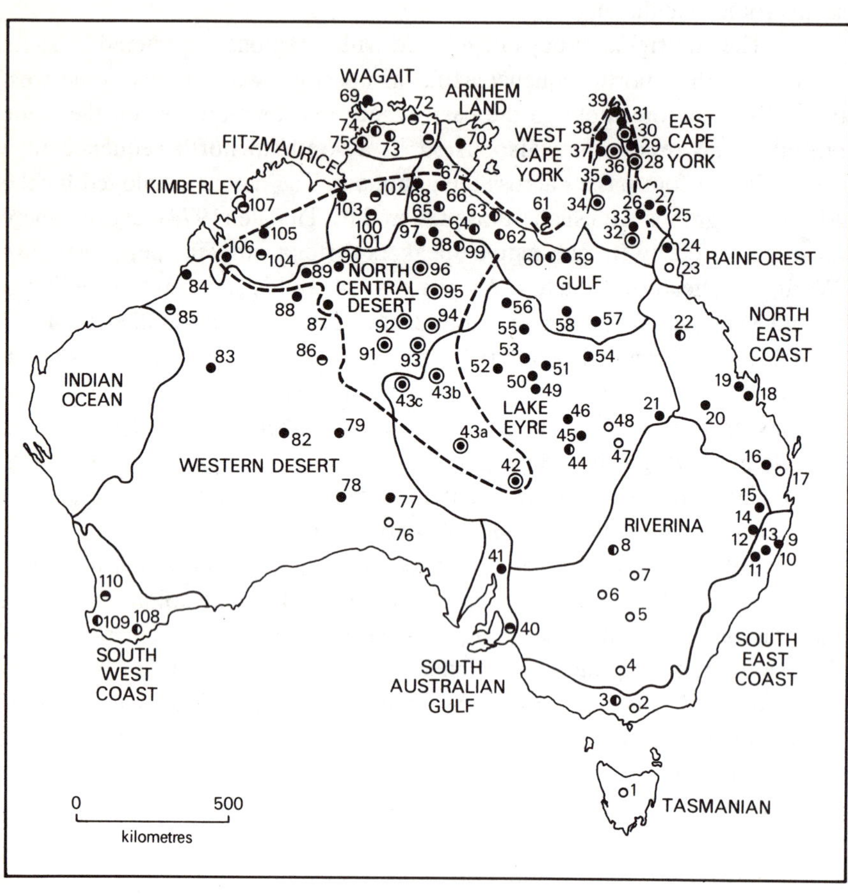

Fig. 3.1 Culture areas of Australia (modified after Peterson 1976) and distribution of sign language reports. Speech taboos associated with mourning observed within areas enclosed in broken line. These taboos are observed only by women in the North Central Desert, perhaps by men as well in Cape York. Empty circle: Signing absent; Left half full: Signing may be present, reports uncertain; Upper half full: Signing present but limited; Full circle: Signing present; Full circle with outer ring: Sign language highly developed. To identify groups see numbers in Table 3.1

situations. 'Highly developed' indicates that there is evidence that there is a full-fledged sign language with an extensive vocabulary (more than 500 items, and usually much larger than this) and that it could serve as an alternative to speech in all situations of daily interaction. It should be added that the information available on which these judgements are based is often slender. In general, more confidence may be placed on the 'highly developed' or 'developed' judgements than on the 'limited' judgements.

3.1 Geographical distribution of sign languages

A consideration of Table 3.1 and Fig. 3.1 will show that Howitt's (1904, p. 724) conclusion that sign language "is more common in Central and North-eastern Australia than in the South-eastern quarter of the continent" does not need to be altered, although we may add to it in several ways. Thus we may add that sign language appears to have been very well developed in Western Cape York, there is some evidence for its presence in Arnhem Land, but it appears to be absent or much attenuated in the northerly parts of the regions further to the west. It appears to have been in general use throughout the Western Desert, although not developed to so high a degree as it is in the central desert regions. Evidence for sign language use in the extreme west and southwest is scant. Detailed discussion of the information available for each of the several regions of Australia will now follow.

3.2 Tasmania, the South Coast, Southern East Coast and Southern Riverina

Sign language appears not to have been used in Tasmania. At least, I have not found a mention of it either in Robinson's journals (Plomley 1966) or in the book by H.L. Roth (1899), the two major sources of information on Tasmanian Aboriginals. For the South Coast we have Howitt's (1890) observation that the Kurnai of Gippsland "have no gesture language" although he adds: "they made use of certain signs in lieu of words, when they were for some reason or other prevented from using or were reluctant to use the words themselves" (p.638). Apparently, when a death was announced or some reference was to be made to a dead person, an indication of the relationship of the deceased was given, together with pointing gestures, rather than that the name of the deceased be mentioned. On the other hand he says that "the Woiwurung Kulin, (i.e. Waradjeri in Tindale's nomenclature) who inhabited the Yarra watershed, had a much more extensive code of signs which are recorded herein so far as I have been able to obtain them" (p.639).

Unfortunately, however, only one sign attributed to this group is listed in the short description of signs that is appended to his paper.

TABLE 3.1 References to sign language among Australian Aborigines

Region and tribe	Sign language reference	Speech taboos	Observers
TASMANIA			
1. Tasmanians	No mention		Robinson (1829-1834) (See Plomley 1966)
SOUTH COAST			
2. Kurnai [several groups]	Absent		Howitt (1890,1904)
3. Wurundjeri	Present		Howitt (1890)
SOUTHERN EAST COAST AND SOUTHERN RIVERINA			
4. Pangerang	Absent		Curr (1883)
5. Wiradjuri	?Absent		Cameron (1881)
6. Barindji	?Absent		
7. Wongaibon	?Absent		
8. Naualko	??Present		Teulon (Curr 1886)
NORTHERN EAST COAST (INCLUDING GREAT DIVIDING RANGE)			
9. Kumbaingirri?	Present	Male	Mathews (1898)
10. Dainggati	Present	initiates	
11. Anaiwan	Present		
12. Kitabal	Present		
13. Jukambal	Present		(Sommerlad 1966)
14. Kambuwal	Present		Purvis-Smith
15. Keinjan	Present	Women at corroborrees	Hall (c.1925)
NORTH EAST COAST			
16. Wakka-wakka	Present		Wurm 1957 (p.c. 1987)
17. Kabikabi	?Absent		Mathews (Curr 1886)
18. Darambal	Traces		Roth (1898)
19. Koinjmal	Traces		Roth (1898)
20. Kairi	?Present		Middleton (Curr 1886)
21. {Tambo 'mutilated hands' stencils}			Walsh (1979)
22. Ilba	?Present		Chatfield (Curr 1886)
RAINFOREST			
23. Gulngai	?Absent	No mention	Roth (1900b)
24. Tjapukai	Present		West 1961

Table 3.1, continued

Region and tribe	Sign language reference	Speech taboos	Observers
EAST CAPE YORK			
25. Guugu Yimidhirr [Kokoimudji]	Present	No speech taboos for male initiates	Roth (1908, 1909) West 1961 de Zwaan (1969)
26. Kokowara	Present		Roth 1898 (1908)
27. Kokojawa	?Developed		Roth 1898 (1908) West 1961
28. Ombila	Developed		West 1961
29. Pontunj	Present		West 1961
30. Pakadji (Koko Yao)	Developed	?Widows	West 1961
31. Otati	Present		Pim c. 1900 (Thomas 1906)
WEST CAPE YORK			
32. Kutjal	Developed	Widows	West 1961
33. Kokomini	Present		Roth 1899 (1908)
34. Yir Yoront [Jirjoront]	Developed	?Mourning	Sharp 1933-1936
	Developed	When shamed (Sharp 1934)	McBride 1970 at Edward River (probably Yir Yiront)
35. Wikmunkan	Present	Widows	McConnell (1937) Sutton (1978)
36. Kandju	Developed	Widows	West 1961
37. Winda[u]winda (Linngithig)	Present	Mourning Male initiates	Hale c. 1960
38. Jupangati	Present	Mourning, certain relatives	Roth 1900a (1907)
39. Ankamuti	?Present		McLaren (1946[1926])
SOUTH AUSTRALIAN GULF			
40. Jaralde [Jarildekald]	Limited		Berndt (1940)
41. Anjamatana [Wailpi]	Present		Mountford (MS n.d.)

Table 3.1, continued

Region and tribe	Sign language reference	Speech taboos	Observers
LAKE EYRE			
42. Dieri	Highly developed	Widows and widowers for several months Male initiates	Gason (1874) Howitt (1891) Stirling 1896)
43a.Aranda (S) (Arrernte)	Highly developed	Widows (for relatively	Belt (Curr 1886) (S.Aranda)
43b. Aranda (E)		short period	Stirling (1896)
43c. Aranda (W)		Male initiates	Strehlow (1978[1915]) Spencer and Gillen (1927)
44. Kungadutji	?Present		Hughes (c.1880)
45. Bidia	Present	Advanced	Duncan-Kemp (1933)
46. Marulta	Present	male initiates	Duncan-Kemp (1933)
47. Wadjalang	?Absent		Curr (1886)
48. Kuungkari	Absent		Heagney (Curr 1886)
49. Julaolinja	Developed	Advanced male	Roth (1897) for
50. Wongkadjera	Developed	initiates in	Julaolinja to
51. Pitta Pitta [Pitapita] (and Boinji)	Developed	Pitta Pitta and Kalkudunga	Kalkudunga inclusive
52. U[A]ndekerebina	Developed	at least	
53. Waluwara	Developed		
54. Koa	Developed		
55. Kalkadunga	Developed		Urquhart (Curr 1886)
56. Wakaja (Workia)	Present		Roth (1897)
GULF			
57. Wanamara	Present		Roth (1897)
58. Maithakari	Developed		Roth (1897)
59. Kukatja (Kurtja)	Present	?Male initiates	Black (1975)
60. Kalibamu	?Present		Armit (Curr 1886)
61. Lardiil	Present	Male initiates	Woolston and Trezise (1966) Keen (1969) Roughsey (1971) Levy (1974)
62 Karawa	?Present	Widows and	Spencer and Gillen
63. Janjula	?Present	other bereaved	(1904)
64. Binbinga	?Present	women	
65. Wilingura	?Present		
66. Alawa	Present	Widows	Spencer and Gillen (1904) Lockwood (men only) (1962)
67. Ngalakan	Present	Male	Spencer (1914)
68. Mangarai	Present	initiates	
69. Tiwi [Tunuvivi]	Present		Priest (1986)

Table 3.1, continued

Region and tribe	Sign language reference	Speech taboos	Observers
NORTH EAST ARNHEM LAND			
70. Duwal,etc.	Present		Warner (1937)
('Murngin' Yolngu,			
Gupupuyngu)			Williams (1981)
WAGAIT			
71. Rembarunga	Limited		McKay (1972)
(Rembarnga)			
72. Wurango	Limited		Robinson (c.1880)
73. Wulwulam (Woolwonga)	?Present		Bradshaw (1891)
74. Djerimanga (Wolna)	?Present		Bradshaw (1891)
75. Larakia	?Present		Bradshaw (1891)
			(not sighted)
			Foelsche (Curr 1886)
			Parkhouse (1895)
WESTERN DESERT			
76. 'Antakarinja'	No mention	No speech	Berndt and Johnston (1942)
(Wirangu,		taboo for	
Kukatja or Mirning)		widow	
77. Kukatja (Luritcha)	?Developed		Stirling (1896)
			Strehlow (1978 [1915])
78. Ngalea	Present		Basedow (1904)
79. Pitjantjatjara			
[Pitjandjara]	Present		Love (1941-1945)
80. Yakuntjatjara			Tindale and Fry (1933)
81. Nangatadjara (Alingara)	Present		Basedow (1904)
82. Ngadadjara	Developed	Male initiates	Mountford (1938)
(Ngada, Ngaada		Male initiates	de Graaf (1968) Gould (1969)
Ngadadara,etc)			Miller (1971)
83. Mardudjara	Present	Male initiates	Tonkinson (1978)
84. Karadje[a]ri	Present		Piddington (1932)
85. Nyangu[a]marta	Limited	Male initiates	O'Grady, p.c. 1986
86. Pintubi	?Limited		Daphne Nash, p.c. 1981
87. Ngardi	Present	Widows	Mathews (1900)
			Tsunoda (1981)
88. Kokatja	Present		Hadfield and Hadfield (1977)
(Wangkajunga)			Tsunoda (1981)
(?Wangkatja)			McGregor (p.c. 1984)
89. Djaru	Present	Widows	Mathews (1900)
			Tsunoda (1981)
90. Wandjira	Present		Tsunoda (1981)

Table 3.1, continued

Region and tribe	Sign language reference	Speech taboos	Observers
NORTH CENTRAL DESERT			
91. Ngalia (=S. Warlpiri)	Present		Strehlow (1978 [1915]) Harney (1952)
92. Warlpiri	Highly developed	Widows ?Male initiates Mothers, etc. in connection with male initiation	Strehlow (1978 [1915]) Mountford (1949) Meggitt (1954) Terry (1974) Wright (1980) Dail-Jones (1984)
93. Anmatyerre [Anmatjera]	Highly developed	As for Warlpiri	Kendon 1985
94. Kaytej [Kaitija]	Highly developed	As for Warlpiri	Chewings (1936) Bell (1983) Kendon 1985
95. Warumungu [Waramanga]	Highly	As for Warlpiri. developed	Stationmaster (1895) Crauford (1895) Spencer and Gillen (1904) Linklater (1940) Chakravarti (1967)
96. Warlmanpa	Highly developed	Widows, etc. Male initiates	Kendon 1985 D.Graham 1984, p.c.
97. Mudbura [Mutpura]	Developed	Widows Male initiates	Spencer (1914) McConvell (1976) Kendon 1985 P. Dixon, p.c. 1984
98. Djingili [Tjingili]	Developed	Widows Certain male bereaved (?) Male initiates	Spencer and Gillen (1904) Linklater (1940) Kendon 1985 P.Raymond, p.c., 1984
99. Kotandji	?Present	Widows	Spencer and Gillen (1904)
FITZMAURICE			
100. Ngarin(g)man	Present	Widows	Rose (1984, and p.c.)
101. Ngaliwurru		?limited for short period	
102. Wardaman	?Present	Widows	Spencer (1914)
103. Mariu	Present	Widows	Mathews (1900)

Table 3.1, continued

Region and tribe	Sign language reference	Speech taboos	Observers
KIMBERLEY			
104. Konejandi (Kuniyanti)	Limited		McGregor, p.c.1984
105. Kitja	Present	Widows	Mathews (1900)
106. Njikina	Present	Widows	Mathews (1900)
107. Worora	Limited		Love (1917, 1941) Wong (1974) Kendon and Silverstein (film, 1975)
INDIAN OCEAN			
No reports			
SOUTHWEST COAST			
108. Minang	?Limited		Bates (1904 MS)
109.Wardandi	?Limited		Bates (1904 MS)
110. Pindjarup	?Present		Roth (1902)

Inland, on the other side of the Great Dividing Range, in the southern Riverina, such reports as there are that can be taken as bearing on this subject indicate that sign language was generally absent. Curr (1883) makes no mention of sign language for the Pangerang, with whom he had considerable contact between 1841 and 1850, the years during which he was operating a sheep run which his father owned near Shepparton. He says of them (p. 295): "When speaking there is a remarkable absence of gesticulation." I have also found no reference to sign language or speech taboos in Dawson (1981 [1881]), nor in those sections of Brough Smyth (1878) which cover this part of Australia. Both of these books contain much detailed information on the Aborigines of Victoria, although not all of it is fully reliable.

For tribes further to the north, in south central New South Wales, we only have the observations of A.L.P. Cameron, one of Howitt's correspondents (Cameron 1881 MS). He writes from Balranald in regard to the Wiradjuri, the Barindji and the Wongaibon. In reply to Howitt's questions on gestures he says (p.4): "they have an imperfect gesture language; thus a shake of the head, as with us, means no, a shake of the hand at a distance, means no, waving the hand round the head and then pointing in a certain direction means that he is going that way." From this one gains the impression that these Aborigines had a limited repertoire of gestures that served in occasional communication, but that their system was no more elaborate than that of groups that have no sign language. We do not count Cameron's observations as evidence for even a 'limited' sign language.

For a group just to the north of the area from which Cameron reported, however, there is a faint suggestion of the presence of a sign language, at least of a limited sort. Thus Curr (1886, Vol. II, pp. 186ff) prints his list of questions and the responses to them provided by Greville N. Teulon, in reference to the Bakundji on the Darling River. This group was probably what Tindale identifies as the Naualko. Curr's questions 64, 65 and 66 asked, respectively, if "the blacks" had any "crests or totems", if they used signs instead of words, and whether they drew or painted. Curr quotes Teulon as saying "To these three questions the answers were invariably 'No ', but I feel inclined to believe that, excepting so far as painting is concerned, they were false." Evidently Teulon suspected the presence of a system of gestures among these people. However, to Curr's Question 80 ("Have your Blacks any Masonic Signs?") Teulon replied "I have never heard of any" (op. cit., p. 206).

Teulon's impression that there might be a gesture language is thus barely hinted at. It seems safest to conclude, and this in spite of Howitt's remark quoted above about the Waradjeri, that for the South Coast, inland Victoria and southwestern New South Wales, no elaborate system of gestures serving in any language-like fashion had been developed. I think we must conclude that the same is true for the East Coast, at least south of Coff's Harbour, for in the scanty literature available on the Aborigines of this region, I have found no mentions of either sign language use or speech taboos. The absence of sign language from this area has been noted by other writers. For example, John Fraser remarks in his booklet on the Aborigines of New South Wales: "the natives of the interior have a very full and elaborate system of gesture language, while our tribes on the eastern coast have nothing of the kind" (Fraser 1892, p. 68).

3.3 Northern East Coast, North East Coast and Rainforest

Further north, from Coff's Harbour and beyond, we encounter several reports that indicate that sign language was used in this area. Mathews (1898), writing of several groups located near Coff's Harbour, and somewhat inland (the Kumbaingirri) says of the male novices, during their period of seclusion which lasts for about ten days or two weeks, that "if they want anything they are not allowed to ask for it, but must make a sign to the guardian who has charge of them" (p. 62). Just to the north and west of the Kumbaingirri and straddling the Great Dividing Range we find the Kambuwal, the Jukambal and the Kitabal of the Tenterfield district, and just to the north of this, in the Warwick district we encounter the Keinjan. Reminiscences of settlers in these districts suggest sign language usage among these groups. Thus G. Purvis-Smith, of Boorook, in reminiscing about the Aborigines of the Tenterfield district from the 1890s remarked "They also spoke on their fingers similar to the deaf and dumb" (Sommerlad 1966, p. 3). For the Keinjan, who inhabited the Warwick district, we have the observations of Thomas Hall. According to a memoir he wrote on the Warwick district, Hall settled in the area as a boy in about 1853, being fourteen in 1858 (Hall, c. 1935). In a pamphlet entitled "A Short History of the Downs Blacks known as the Blucher Tribe" (Hall c. 1925), he reports on many aspects of their customs, including initiation ceremonial which he claims to have witnessed personally. In a section on sign language he says: "At corroborees [i.e. public ceremonial performances] the old gins and married women whose husbands were alive had the first position, then came the young unmarried women and girls. No talking or whispering was allowed among the women, but instead a system of deaf and dumb speaking was known to each female, by which they conversed at leisure. This was taught as one of the women's parts of their Bora ceremony, and no male was ever allowed to learn these on penalty of death." We take this as suggesting that sign language was in use among the women of the area, although I think we may remain skeptical on Hall's last claim, that it was not permitted of the men, on pain of death. Other accounts of the Keinjan and associated groups are very sketchy (e.g. MacPherson 1902, 1904; Mathews 1907; Kelly 1935). I have not found any as detailed as Hall's and I have thus been unable to corroborate his observations on this point.

Just north of this area, extending northwards and westwards from Brisbane, is the Waga or Wakka-Wakka. Wurm (personal communication 1987), in 1957, interviewed two elderly male speakers of Dungidjawu, a dialect within this area. They showed him a number of signs and confirmed that signs were extensively used in this area. Signs were also used to the north of this area, for Roth (1898), in a report on his visit to the Rockhampton district, says he found "traces of gesture language" among the older members of the Darambal and Koinjmal people that he encountered. Later (Roth 1908) he published descriptions of 18 signs that he had recorded there.

From the inland regions of the North East coast area we have brief references that suggest the presence of sign language among the Kairi who lived in the district of Springsure, Queensland. Curr's correspondent, Thomas Middleton (Curr 1886, vol. III p. 91), describes four signs which he had observed in use among these people. This is a very limited set, of course;

however the signs he describes are characteristic of forms that are found in other places in Queensland, and have the character of gestural units of a sign language, rather than being general gestures, such as those described by Cameron for tribes in southern New South Wales. Thus, he gives: "Puffing out the cheeks indicates absence of water; placing thc fist on the forehead indicates the presence of Walleroo; stroking the face with open fingers, a kangaroo; and the arm held up and hand bent down, an emu."

It is somewhat to the south and west of Springsure, in the region of Tambo, in the central Queensland Sandstone belt, that Walsh (1979) has described an extensive occurrence of hand stencils in association with other kinds of rock art. These include many stencils of hands which appear to have fingers missing or which are otherwise distorted. These have been referred to as 'mutilated hands'. Walsh suggests, however, that such shapes could be achieved by making a stencil with the hand held in various poses. He draws parallels between the hand poses that may be inferred from these stencils and some of the handshapes reported in the sign language data of Roth (1897) from North-West-Central Queensland (Fig. 3.2). Although this is some 600 kilometers west of the region in which the 'mutilated hand' stencils occur, Walsh suggests that, on other grounds, there is enough cultural continuity to make the comparison valid. He suggests that the 'mutilated hand' stencils may actually be stencils of hand signs, comparable to those described by Roth. If Walsh's interpretation is accepted, this can be taken as additional evidence for the presence of sign language in this area. [2]

Further north still, from the Cape River district, Curr includes reference to a report from a Mr Chatfield, referring to the Ilba. Curr says (1886, Vol. II p. 477) "Mr Chatfield expresses himself as having a fancy that there are some faint traces of freemasonry amongst the tribe." Such a 'fancy' may perhaps indicate that Mr Chatfield had observed a use of gesture that was more stylized and elaborate than ordinary gesticulation. This may, thus, count as a possible observation of sign language use. In another case, in reference to the Kalkadunga (Kalkadoon) of North-West-Central Queensland, where we know from Roth's account (Roth 1897) that a well developed sign language was in use, Curr reports that his correspondent F. Urquhart "says in reply to one of my printed questions that this tribe (i.e. the Kalkadunga) has Masonic signs" (Curr 1886, Vol. II, p. 327). Curr continues: "As only one other of my correspondents makes this assertion in connection with our Blacks, it seems certain that Mr. Urquhart has been mistaken, as such an institution would not be confined to a few tribes, nor would it have escaped the notice of the many Masons who have written to me on the subject." Of course, Urquhart was mistaken about the freemasonry of the Kalkadunga, but since we know from

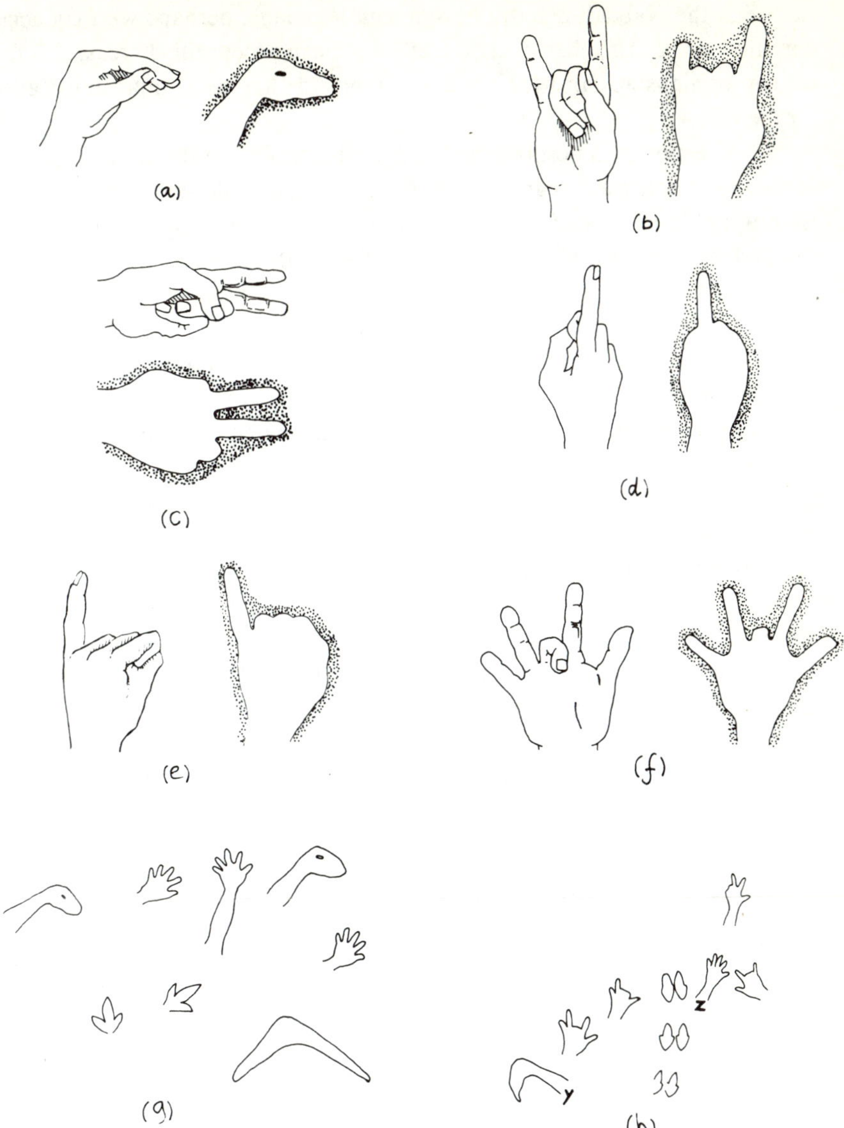

Fig. 3.2 A comparison of signs recorded by Roth in North-West-Central Queensland with stencils of 'mutilated hands' (after Walsh 1979). (a) Turkey bustard; (b) Bad; (c). Emu; (d) Woman, copulation; (e) Small caterpillar, grub, etc.; (f) Spear, woomera-spear; (g) Composite stencil panel, using a combination of stencil 'V' boomerang, emu feet and hands; (h) Composite stencil panel using a combination of stencils of a variety of small marsupial paws and various hand 'signal' stencils. The stencils marked Y and Z in this panel were executed in yelowish ochre, the remainder in red

Roth that the Kalkadunga did have a sign language, perhaps we may accept that this is what Urquhart had noticed. If we can accept this here, we suggest we can perhaps accept Mr Chatfield's 'fancy' as having similar implications for the Ilba.

The next area north of the North East Coast is the Rainforest, the home of the so-called Barrinean type of Aborigine (Tindale and Birdsell 1940). Ethnographic details of these groups are quite scanty; however there is a detailed report for the Gulngai by Roth (1900b MS). It is remarkable that Roth makes no mention of sign language or of speech taboos, despite mentioning many other things. Given his interest in the topic, it seems likely that a lack of mention may, in this case, be taken as evidence for its absence. West (1960-65), on the other hand, made film recordings of two Tjapukai women (the Tjapukai are a group who lived to the north of the Gulngai, extending to the fringes of the rainforest) who showed some facility with signing. However, in his recording we may note an extensive amount of pointing and little differentiation in handshape. This suggests that signing among these people may not have been very highly developed.

It seems clear, from these reports, that sign language was in use along the North East Coast, at least from Coff's Harbour northwards as far as Townsville, and that this area of use extended inland and westward, over the ranges. It seems likely, indeed, that sign language was in use all the way from south east Queensland westwards to northwest central Queensland, where, as we know from Roth's (1897) account, sign language was quite elaborate and used extensively.

3.4 Cape York Peninsula

The picture here is very different. Especially towards the northern end of Eastern Cape York, and throughout Western Cape York, there is good evidence of widespread sign language use by both women and men, and that the sign languages, at least in some cases, were developed or perhaps even highly developed.

Early reports, for Eastern Cape York, may be found in Roth (1898 MS) and Roth (1908). In these reports Roth describes a number of signs for a variety of different groups. He offers no comment on circumstances of use; however, in a description of initiation ceremonial for the Guugu (Koko) Yimidhirr he says there is no speech ban imposed on male initiates (Roth 1909, p. 170). More recent observations of sign language among the Guugu Yimidhirr and related people are by West (1961-1965) and de Zwaan (1969).

West made film recordings from two Guugu Yimidhirr women and de Zwaan made a film recording in which some sixty signs were demonstrated by an elderly Guugu Yimidhirr man. Several of the signs recorded by de Zwaan are the same as those described by Roth for this area, sixty years before. West's films are not accompanied by transcriptions. Furthermore, they appear to comprise narrations or snatches of conversation, rather than demonstrations of individual signs. It is impossible to derive any details of vocabulary from these films; however it is possible to examine them for certain features of sign formation characteristics. One can compare the rate at which signs are produced; the signing space used; the extent to which signing is done only with the hands; or whether it involves whole body action and the face; whether the signing is one handed or two handed; the extent to which it appears to require differentiated hand shapes. By such criteria one can make an estimate as to the extent to which the signing depicted represents a 'limited' or 'developed' sign language. A 'developed' system will show much hand shape differentiation, consistency in the space used for signing, a tendency for most signing to be done with but one hand, and restricted use of face and body. In such signing, meaning is conveyed through a large vocabulary of lexical signs. Pantomime and improvisation are at a minimum.

By these criteria, the sign language recorded by West from the Guugu Yimidhirr appears to be highly pantomimic and improvisational in character. Extensive space is used, there is much whole body action and face action, and there is little differentiation in the hand shapes used. This is in contrast to what may be observed in the sign language recordings West made from representatives of groups further to the north, especially the Ombila and Pakadji. The signing recorded from members of these groups is mostly one handed, uses restricted space, uses much hand differentiation and is rapid, and does not involve the use of the body or face. These are all marks of a highly developed sign language. In this area speech taboos were observed by widows and, as is clear from West's films, the best signers he recorded were women. West comments on this himself in the notes that accompany these films and he states that the women who were most proficient at signing all stated that they had learned sign language as a result of observing speech taboos during widowhood.

The most northerly group in East Cape York for which there is some indication of the presence of sign language is the Otati, located at Shelburne Bay. N.W. Thomas (1906, p. 32) states that he has in his possession a sign vocabulary for these people collected by Captain Pim for G.C. Seligman.[3] Pim also collected spoken vocabulary for the Otati (Ray 1907) and presumably this sign vocabulary was collected at the same time. Finally, we may add McLaren (1946[1926]) who remarks in reference to the people of Simpson Bay at the very tip of Cape York (probably the Ankamuti) that "they could also converse by gestures" (p. 113).

For Western Cape York there is good evidence that sign language was (until very recently, perhaps still is) in widespread use and that it was developed or highly developed. West (1961-1965) recorded sign language from the Kandju of the Archer River district. He notes that female signers reported that they had learned sign language when observing a ban on speech while in mourning as widows. McConnell, writing of the Wikmunkan and adjacent groups which included the Kandju (McConnell 1937) also reports that speech taboos are observed by widows, and although she makes no mention of sign language, in view of West's films and notes it is clear that it was in use. Sharp (1934), writing of the Yir Yiront, reports sign language use by persons who withdraw from society temporarily when shamed (p. 41). In his field notes (1933-1934) vocabularies of sixty or seventy signs are described. McBride (1970) made films of signing at the Edward River Mission. From his films it is clear, as it is from the films of West, that sign language in this region of Western Cape York was, or is, developed and in widespread use.[4] Only small vocabularies of signs have actually been described from this region, however. Roth (1900a MS) records some 24 signs from the Jupangati of the Pennefather River district (between Port Musgrave and Albatross Bay) which he later published (Roth 1908).

Sign language use has been reported by Hale (1960) for the Windawinda, a group immediately to the south of the Jupungati. Hale describes about sixty signs and he also includes a few notes on the occasions of sign language use. According to his informant, at the death of wife or husband the nearest relatives of the deceased are addressed in sign language by the deceased's spouse - the speech taboo thus applied to both widows and widowers. Further, in male initiation ritual during certain periods of seclusion the novices, though permitted to talk among themselves in lowered tones, must use only sign language to non-novices. He adds that signs were also used in long distance communication. Hale's informant stated that signs are learned by all from an early age.

Roth also reports on some of the circumstances of sign language use in this district. The sign language, he says, is used by men during hunting or fighting expeditions, but it is also used in connection with burial and mourning customs. The near relatives of certain deceased people "remain dumb for some few months after the death" (Roth 1900a MS, p. 47). Part of this ritual is described in more detail in Roth (1907). He describes how the son or sons of the deceased's sisters carries a 'pau-to'- the fibula bones of the deceased wrapped up in bark, bound round with twine. Two, three or more men together may be responsible for preserving these relics. Roth continues:

Furthermore, the portions of the deceased's flesh (thighs and feet) when originally cut from the corpse are baked in the ashes, and cut up into little bits to be eaten one or two at a time morning and evening by the same individual or individuals who are responsible for carrying the "pau-to". The eating process takes from two to three months, sometimes longer, to complete, and throughout all this period the person remains dumb, and is known as "te-itima": he is supposed to actually lose the power of speech, and though going about his business as usual expresses himself only by signs, claps his hands if he wants to attract other people's attention, maintains the signs of mourning and lets his hair grow. But during all this loss of speech, the "te-itima", when done with the eating of human flesh, has gradually discovered the murderer....

Also in West Cape York, but further south, in the district of the tributaries of the Mitchell River, we have Roth's account of signs for the Kokomini of the Middle Palmer River, and West's (c. 1961-1965) film recording of signing from women and men of the Kutjal, from an area between the Lynd and Walsh rivers.

3.5 South Australian Gulf

There are two reports of sign language from the South Australian Gulf. Berndt (1940) interviewed an old man of the Jaralde. This group originally occupied a region in the extreme south of this area, near Murray Bridge. Berndt's informant described a number of signs and also commented on their use. The signs described are few in number and are all performed with arms in full extension. They are well adapted to long distance communication, which is apparently the use to which they were put. There is no evidence for any sort of developed or highly developed sign language here. Mountford worked for a number of years among the Anjamatana (Wailpi in Tindale 1974) who lived on the Western slopes of the Flinders Ranges in the most northerly part of the South Australian Gulf region. He was preparing to write a book on these people and planned to include a section on their sign language (Mountford, n.d., listed in Stone 1958 and annotated in A.I.A.S. Library catalogue). No details of this sign language are available to me at time of writing.

3.6 Lake Eyre

This vast and largely arid drainage basin extends from the dry deserts of western New South Wales to just a little west of the route of the Port Augusta-Alice Springs highway, and northwards to include the Channel Country of Queensland, the district of Boulia and as far north as the Barkly Highway. It includes Alice Springs and the Simpson Desert that extends to the southeast.

There is evidence that sign language was in use throughout this region, except in the most north-easterly portion, east of Jundah and Eromanga. In this area are found the Wadjalang and Kungkari (Kunggari in Tindale), and for both groups we have remarks by Curr's correspondents that suggest an absence of sign language. Thus in reference to the Wadjalang, Curr (1886, Vol. III, p. 79) reports that his correspondents assert that "Freemasonry is unknown.". In reference to the Kungkari, Curr's correspondent, J. Heagney, is reported to say "no sign language exists among these tribes" (Curr 1886, Vol. II, p. 377). These mentions are, admittedly, scant evidence for drawing any firm conclusions. Unfortunately there are almost no other sources of information. It is nevertheless consistent with the observations of observers from further south and to the east that sign language, if present at all, was developed to only a rudimentary degree.

For the rest of the Lake Eyre region, sign language is reported fairly frequently. From the reports available, one gains the impression of two somewhat different regions of sign language use. On the one hand there are those peoples of the Channel Country and the Boulia District among whom sign language appears to be used during speech taboos imposed on advanced male initiates. This includes the sign language described in some detail by Roth (1897). On the other hand we have the sign languages of the Dieri and the Aranda which, from all that can be gathered, were highly developed and were employed by women who observed extended speech taboos when in mourning.

Roth (1897), writing of the Pitta Pitta (Pitapita in Tindale) and Boinji, states (p. 177): "During the progress of the muruk-kundi rite the novitiate for this degree (fourth) is allowed to converse orally only with the members of the same paedomatronym, though he may speak in the sign language with any others - a rule strictly enforced and continued for some few days subsequently." (Note that this appears to be a very similar rule to that reported by Hale 1960, above, for the Windawinda on Western Cape York). Likewise, Alice Duncan-Kemp (1933) refers (p. 192-193) to youths of what she calls a Cooper Creek tribe (probably Bidia or Marulta), going through "the yellow ochre or third degree" ritual. She says that during this time "tribal etiquette forbade them to speak except by signs". Thus the practice Roth describes clearly extended well into the Channel country at least as far south as Durham Downs on the northerly reaches of Cooper Creek. On the other hand, Roth makes no mention of any speech taboos in connection with death or mourning for this part of the country and he makes no mention of the use of sign language by women.

For the Dieri, on the other hand, at least if we are to accept Gason's statement (quoted in Chapter 2, p.17) sign language was highly developed. It was used in connection with speech taboos maintained at times of mourning. Of this group Howitt (1891) writes:

> ....the near relations [of the deceased] dress in mourning by smearing themselves over with white clay. Widows and widowers are prohibited by custom from uttering a word until the clay has worn off, however long it may remain on them. They do not, however, rub it off, as doing so would be considered a bad omen. It must absolutely wear off itself. During this period they communicate by means of gesture language. (p. 72)

Elsewhere, Howitt adds "the women mourn and are speechless much longer than the men" (op. cit., p. 89).[5] Unfortunately, as we noted in Chapter 2, we have almost no record of Dieri sign language.

For the various groups referred to as Aranda,[6] we have several different observers mentioning the use of complex sign language. E.F. Belt in Curr (1886, Vol. I, p. 422), for the Southern Aranda (Macumba River) says "there is a sort of sign language in use". For the Aranda in the region of Alice Springs we have the evidence of statements by Stirling (1896), Spencer and Gillen (1927) and Strehlow (1978 [1915]) that sign language was widely used and probably highly developed. Spencer and Gillen (1927) comment on the speech taboos followed by novices in male initiation ceremonies and by widows among the Aranda (p. 433, p. 600), this being a time when sign language was used extensively. Stirling (1896, p. 112) remarks that the women are much more adept at sign language than the men, and this also is compatible with sign language, in this region, being used mainly by women in connection with speech taboos connected to mourning. In this respect the situation in regard to sign language in this area is similar to that which prevails further north in the North Central Desert.

Some record of sign language among the Aranda has been made, at least for the region near Alice Springs. Strehlow (1978 [1915]) provides a description of 290 signs (covering 454 meanings) and Spencer and Gillen (1927) give descriptions of sixty-four signs. Detailed discussion of differences and similarities between sign languages in different parts of Australia will be found in Chapter 12. We may note here, however, that a comparison between signs gathered in the North Central Desert region with the Aranda signs described by Strehlow, on the one hand, and the North-West-Central Queensland signs described by Roth (1897) on the other, suggest that the Aranda sign language had more in common with North Central Desert sign languages whereas the Queensland sign language appears to be very different. We suggest, with all due caution, given the extreme limitations of available information, that the sign languages of the Aborigines of the Channel Country and the Boulia district constitute one dialect group, whereas the sign language (or sign languages) of the area occupied by the Aranda comprises another, which itself is perhaps related to the dialect group of the North Central Desert.

We suggest that this difference may be related to differences between these regions in how sign language was used. In the former area it was used by men as part of their initiation ritual. In the latter area its main development was by women, who practised more or less prolonged speech taboos in connection with mourning. As we shall see, this practice appears to have reached its most extreme development in the North Central Desert and it is there that we find Aboriginal sign languages to have reached their highest degrees of complexity.

3.7 Gulf

This area stretches from the Norman River in the east as far as the Roper River, just south of Arnhem Land in the west. It extends northwards to the Gulf of Carpentaria, from the uplands in northern central Queensland and the Barkly Tableland. Information on sign language in this region is scant. In the eastern part, and east of the Leichardt River, which is also the easternmost boundary of the circumcision rite, Roth (1897) reports sign language among the Wanamara and the Maithakari in the southernmost portion of this region. Black (1975) recorded a number of signs from a Kukutja man at Normanton and he indicates that sign language was used among these people in male initiation ceremonies. Armit, one of Curr's correspondents, indicates that he had observed some usage of gesture in communication among the Kalibamu, who immediately adjoined the Kukutja on the coast to the west (Curr 1886, Vol. II, pp. 300-305).

Among the Lardiil of Mornington Island, Roughsey (1971) reports on the use of sign language in male initiation ceremonies. He writes that prior to circumcision the boy would be taken with his mother's brother and a few other men visiting. "During this time he would be taught many things, including sign language, for he wouldn't be allowed to speak for six moons or more after the ceremony" (p. 58). A little later he says:

> After the ceremony [of circumcision] the boy is kept in seclusion; he uses only sign language to talk to people and can eat only certain foods, as others would make him unclean. For about six months the boy is in the charge of his uncle, who shows him all the secrets of hunting and teaches him the tribal laws. (p.60)

A small amount of this sign language has been recorded on film by Woolston and Trezise (1966), and the process of teaching how it should be used is briefly shown in a film by Levy (1976).

A further observation on Lardiil sign language has been provided by Sandra Keen (1970). She reports that it is used by the sub-incised men of the Eastern Lardiil as a component of a form of the special language, Damin, that all men must speak for a period between the ceremony of sub-incision and a ceremony of 'squaring up' with various relatives. (For an account of Damin see Roughsey 1971 and also Dixon 1980, pp.66-67, Hale 1982, Hale and Nash 1987.). It is said that the men of the Eastern Lardiil were unable to learn the proper Damin but spoke a 'no-good' form of it instead. According to Keen, in 'no-good' Damin use was made of a vocabulary of only eight meaningless words which, spoken in varying orders, were used to convey the emotional tone of the utterance, while the content was conveyed by means of the same sign language that was normally used by a man just after he had been circumcised. This is an interesting instance of speech serving in the role of gesticulation in relation to sign language.[7]

To the west of the Leichardt River the picture seems somewhat different. For the Karawa, Janjula (Anula), Binbinga and Wilingura (Willingara), who occupied the area between the Calvert River in the East to the Arnold River in the west, we have Spencer and Gillen's (1904, p.554) testimony to the practice of speech bans on widows, mothers and certain other female relatives of the deceased extending for a period until the second and final burial of the corpse. For these groups we may infer the presence of sign language; however Spencer and Gillen themselves do not mention it and I have found no other accounts of these peoples that do. For the Alawa (Allaua), on the Roper River, Spencer and Gillen (1904) likewise report the practice of speech taboos for female relatives in mourning but they again make no reference to sign language.

Philip Roberts, an Alawa man whose autobiography has been published by Lockwood (1962), refers to the use of sign language among men, but makes no mention of its use among women. He indicates that there is a speech ban in association with circumcision: "In my case it [i.e. the initiation ritual] involved circumcision with a razor blade ... a ban on speech with specified tribal relatives for two years" (p. 28). Elsewhere Roberts refers to how the "expressive finger-talk which is common to all tribes" (p.121) is used in conjunction with broken English as a means of communication between people who do not share the same language. He adds: "Finger-talk is also constant among men who speak the same tongue. It not only saves unnecessary speech but has the added advantage that evil spirits cannot hear it" (loc. cit.). However although he gives a fairly detailed description of what happens when a man dies, and describes how the widow should behave, he makes no mention of any taboos on speech for her.

The extent of development of sign language among the Alawa, as for the other groups of the Gulf region, is difficult to assess from these reports. It is also not entirely clear how extensive the speech bans followed by widows and other females were (or are), nor do we have any clear indication of the extent to which sign language may have been used by them, or indeed by the men of these groups. It seems likely that sign language was used among these peoples, but also, because it has not received much mention, it seems likely that it may not have been very highly developed.

3.8 North-East Arnhem Land and Wagait

For North-East Arnhem Land Lloyd Warner makes the following statement: "All the tribes of northeastern Arnhem Land have a very elaborate sign language which is used between people who do not understand each other's spoken languages, between the deaf and dumb, and by young men observing taboos of silence after certain initiations" (Warner 1937, p. 515). Warner describes sixty-seven signs. He does not discuss speech taboos or the use of sign language elsewhere in his book, however, although its use is referred to in a myth he quotes (p. 80). A number of signs from this part of the country have also been described by Williams (1981). The signs are described by means of photographs and they are demonstrated by women. Their use is not discussed.

Elwell (1982) working at Maningreda, which is located on the coast at the very western edge of the N.E. Arnhem Land area, reports the use of sign language in the settlement where people speaking many different languages are to be found. She indicates that the sign language is the same for all language groups. She says:

> Sign language appears to be a traditional but silent 'lingua franca', at least in the Maningreda area. Everyone understands it and uses it at various times, for example: between relatives who are not permitted to speak aloud because of a taboo placed on their oral communication; when communication is required over a distance, especially when silence is essential, as in hunting situations; as a way of introducing oneself to a stranger and finding out about that person; to communicate with deaf people (who are thus not socially isolated, as tends to be the case among European Australians); and, finally, when no common language exists between people. (pp. 89-90)

She indicates that there is a good deal of variation in sign language competence and expresses the view that it is likely that it is not a complete language but that "it is merely a pidgin, used only for limited communicative purposes in a restricted range of topics". She concludes her remarks by adding that much further research is needed before its role in such a multilingual community can be properly assessed.

Elwell's comments may provide some corroboration for Warner's observation that sign language in this region is used between people who do not share the same spoken language. It has been suggested quite often that this may be a function of sign languages in Australia. However, at least in the North Central Desert region to be discussed below, this function seems unlikely. Multilingualism is widespread, especially in regions such as Arnhem Land (Brandl and Walsh 1982), and, furthermore, sign language varies a good deal from one place to another. However, from what Warner and Elwell say, both discussing the same area, perhaps we should accept that inter-lingual communication may be a function of sign language in this part of Australia.

Information on sign language for the coastal region to the west of N.E. Arnhem Land, the area termed Wagait, is extremely limited. McKay (1972) describes about twenty signs for the Rembarunga (Rembarnga), whose traditional territory was just south of the N.E. Arnhem Land area, between the Cadell River and the edge of the escarpment country. To the north, in the Darwin area, Bradshaw (1891) has recorded a few notes on sign language among the Wulwulam on the Mary River, the Djerimanga on the coastal plains at the mouth of the Adelaide River and for the Larakia in the region of Darwin (at time of writing, I had not seen these notes). Of the Larakia, also, Foelsche (in Curr 1886, I, p.255) states that they "can communicate with their arms to some extent, as far as they can see each other distinctly". Parkhouse (1895), also writing about the Larakia and neighboring groups, states "There is a wide range, too, of handsignalling" (p.647).

For the Tiwi of Melville Island and Bathurst Island, Charles Priest mentions 'finger-talk' (1986) in the course of describing recollections of his life among these people in the late 1920s. He writes: "In addition to their spoken languages the Tiwi had a sign language, usually referred to as 'Finger talk', whereby they could convey messages by movements of their hands and fingers. Such a language was very useful when stalking game or transmitting messages which they might desire to keep secret from third parties. No doubt its vocabulary was limited, but it served a useful purpose." I have not come across a reference to the use of signs among the Tiwi elsewhere.

3.9 Western Desert

In Peterson's division of Australia into culture areas, the Western Desert extends all the way from the boundaries of the Lake Eyre region, westwards to the coast at Eighty Mile Beach in the north, and to include all of the Gibson Desert, the Great Victoria Desert and the Nullarbor Plain. It covers virtually half of the Australian continent. In the present work, however, we have excluded from the Western Desert an area here termed the North Central Desert. This includes the Lake Woods drainage basin, extends southwards to the MacDonnell Ranges and westwards to include the Tanami Desert and all of what is included in traditional Warlpiri territory. As we shall see, there appear to be some differences in sign language development and usage between the

North Central Desert and the rest of the Western Desert region. It may be noted that this westernmost boundary of the North Central Desert region distinguished here coincides with the boundary proposed by Wurm and Hattori (1981: Map 20) between the Ngarga group of Southwest Languages (which includes Warlpiri) and the Wati Group, which extends over all of the rest of the Western Desert.

So far as the Western Desert as here regarded is concerned, it appears that, throughout this region, sign language was and still is widely used, at least by men. Mountford (1938), de Graaf (1968), Gould (1969) and Miller (1978), for the Ngadadjara, refer to the use of sign language by men in initiation ceremonies as a means of preventing novices from hearing what is planned for them, as well as mentioning its use in hunting and revenge expeditions, when silence is essential. Tonkinson (1978, p. 74), for the Mardudjura, mentions that male novices may only use sign language when they are secluded and Piddington (1932, p. 68), for the Karadjeri, describes how the initiates on their 'walkabout' in the company of their guardians may only mumble to attract attention and use gestures to communicate their needs. Goddard (1983), writing of the Yankunytjatjara (Yakuntjatjara) of the eastern Western Desert, mentions (p. 325) that signs may be used instead of the auxiliary language (*anitji*) by those who are not fluent in it. *Anitji* is used between certain categories of relatives of a boy who is undergoing certain processes of initiation. Liberman (1982b, p. 319), writing of Pitjantjatjara speakers, mentions more everyday uses of sign. He states that "Aboriginal people continually employ a code of hand signs that is more than merely a series of gestures, in that it also has semantic and syntactic properties. Aboriginals may converse using hand signs alone, but usually hand signs are employed to carry the central aspect of a message, while the talk signifies around it."

These reports are in clear contrast with what we know of sign language use in the North Central Desert, where, at least in the more southerly parts of this region, men use little sign language, whereas women use it a great deal. The imposition of prolonged speech taboos on widows and other female relatives of the deceased appears not to be the practice in the Western Desert, except in its extreme northern periphery (at least, I do not find it reported). Thus Berndt and Johnston (1942), in their account of death, burial and mourning ritual at Ooldea in South Australia (Pitjantjatjara speaking peoples), explain the various restrictions that are imposed on the widow, but they make no mention of sign language or speech taboos. Indeed, they say that the "widow must speak respectfully of her late husband" - a statement which seems clearly to imply the absence of any speech taboo. The other writers on peoples of the Western Desert, mentioned above, also make no mention of speech taboos on women, nor do they mention the use of sign language by women.

For the northern periphery of the Western Desert region, however, along the edge of the Kimberley and among the peoples adjoining the North Central Desert region, we have come across reports of sign language in use by women. Mathews (1900) mentions widows' silence and the use of sign language by widows for the Ngardi and Djaru. Tsunoda (1981) reports that he has recorded some sign language from these groups and also from the Kokatja (for which no widows' silence has been reported, however) and the Wandjira.

Descriptions of some Western Desert signs are available and a few recordings have been made. Miller (1971) describes some 270 signs and offers a fairly detailed discussion (Miller 1978) of the characteristics of the sign language that he recorded at Warburton Ranges Mission (Ngadadjara speakers). Mountford (1938) describes a few signs for the same people. He also states (Mountford 1976) that he collected a large number of signs on film but adds (p.63): "It was a misfortune of no mean order that the whole film was spoiled by a faulty camera." A few signs have been recorded by Tindale and Fry (1933) from Ernabella, and Love (1941-1945 MS.) collected notes on about fifty signs from Ernabella. Hadfield (1977) recorded a video tape of some signs by a Wangkatja (Nangatadjara, Tindale) speaker in the course of recording materials for a language course.

From the few published reports and recordings available, it is difficult to arrive at any clear assessment of the extent to which sign language in this region can be considered developed. It appears to have had (or to have) quite a large vocabulary. However, since very prolonged speech taboos do not appear to have been observed, even by young male novices, we would not expect the sign languages of the Western Desert to show the very high degree of development that we encounter in the North Central Desert, which will be discussed next.

3.10 North Central Desert

As we have already indicated, it is in the North Central Desert region, from the MacDonnell Ranges northwards as far as the edge of the Arnhem Land escarpment and the rivers that drain the Fitzmaurice area - up to Newcastle Creek - and westwards to the edges of the area traditionally occupied by the Warlpiri, that we find Aboriginal sign languages to have reached their highest development in Australia.

To my knowledge, the earliest mentions of sign language in this area are by two respondents to a questionnaire drafted by J.G.Frazer and circulated by E.C. Stirling, published in 1895 in the *Journal of the Anthropological Institute of Great Britain*.[8] Both mentions (we may infer) are in reference to the Warumungu. Thus, the Stationmaster at Powell's Creek Telegraph Station reports, in response to Question No. 52 (What ceremonies take place at death?):

> After a death a general wailing ensues and may continue for two or three days, the women score their heads and thighs till blood flows freely. The older women may refuse to speak for two or three months, expressing their wishes by handsigns, a species of deaf and dumb language, in which both men and women are wonderfully proficient. The men score their thighs only. (Stationmaster 1895, p. 178)

Lindsay Crauford, a correspondent from Victoria River Downs Station, wrote in response to questions 47 and 48 (concerned with in-law and brother-sister taboos):

> The following came to my notice during my residence at Powell's Creek. The first man and woman I got to come in were two old people with three youngsters. I found the woman could not or would not talk, and that she communicated with her husband and children by signs. I imagined she was deaf and dumb, until I got other women, and found them the same. After some time, I found out from these natives that when a woman is married and has children she is not allowed to speak at all until she has done breeding. I found that all the unmarried girls and old women were allowed to talk. Also that the young boys (only certain ones) were not allowed to talk when certain chief men of the tribe were present. After a lot of persuasion I got the first old man to let his lubra speak, after that he could never stop her again. She is still at Powell Creek. Her name is Numigilly. This is the only tribe I know of that has this custom. (Crauford, 1895, pp. 181-182)

I have not been able to find another report that would confirm Mr. Crauford's observation that married women among the Warumungu, or any other group, use only sign language during their years of childbearing.[9]

Spencer and Gillen (1899, 1904) were the first widely read writers to report the use of sign language in this area. They were especially impressed with its extensive use and high degree of development among the Warumungu. As they also report, it is among the Warumungu that the longest periods of silence are observed by widows - sometimes widows would forgo speech altogether for as much as two years, and, as mentioned in Chapter 2, Spencer and Gillen report one case of an old woman who had not spoken for twenty-five years.

The practice of extended speech taboos for widows and certain other female relatives of the deceased extends south to the Kaytej (Bell 1983) and

Anmatyerre and westwards to the Warlpiri. It is among these groups that we encounter a clear difference in competence at sign language between men and women. I have been repeatedly told, by both men and women, that the men do not know or use sign language and in one systematic survey of sign language use at the Warlpiri community of Yuendumu (Kendon 1984) this was amply confirmed. However, it should be added that women at Yuendumu told me that although the men there do not know or use sign language, they are much more knowledgeable about it at Willowra. I have not had an opportunity to visit Willowra and I have, thus, not confirmed this with any observations of my own. However, as described in Chapter 4, Meggitt did observe sign language use among Warlpiri men at Hooker Creek (now Lajamanu) in the 1950s and, as mentioned below, among the Warlmanpa, the Mudbura and the Djingili, men do know and use sign language. It is possible, thus, that the restriction of sign language competence to women is a characteristic of the more southerly peoples of the North Central Desert and that this becomes much less, the further north one goes.

Among older Warlpiri women at Yuendumu sign language is in constant use, whether people are under a speech ban or not (Dail-Jones 1984). As will be seen in more detail in Chapter 4, sign language among Yuendumu women is used as an accompaniment to speech, and it is used as an alternate mode of communication when speaking is too great an effort or when, as where people are separated by some distance, talking loudly is either inappropriate or too much trouble. It is also used as a means of private communication and it is used whenever the speaker feels especial reverence or respect for what she is talking about.

In regard to the Warumungu, we have already referred to Spencer and Gillen's (1904) observation of extensive sign language use by women in this group. Men evidently also knew sign language too, for Spencer (1928) refers to the use of sign language by men in the context of a visit to a corpse that had been placed in a tree as the first stage in the burial procedure. The corpse was visited at dawn for the purpose of determining whether it had been disturbed by the spirit of the murderer. It was hoped that the spirit might be observed, or its clues might be noted, so that the identity of the murderer could be determined. Spencer describes how, as they approached, they kept hidden from view as much as possible and communicated in sign language "so as not to attract the attention of the spirit of the murderer should it happen to be hovering about" (p.487). As further evidence of knowledge of sign language by Warumungu men, we may mention Chakravarti's (1967) report in which he states that he collected some sign vocabulary from men. However, he notes that women, especially young women, were making extensive use of it.

Among the Warlmanpa, where sign language is used as extensively as it is among the other North Central Desert groups, men appear to have knowledge of it as well as women. At least I have recorded a good deal of sign language from a senior Warlmanpa man, who also told me that young men had to learn it for initiation ceremonies.

Somewhat to the north of the Warlmanpa are the Mudbura and Djingili. Sign language is known by both men and women among the Mudbura. It has been recorded from men by McConvell at Wati Creek (McConvell 1976), and by myself at Elliott in 1984. I have also recorded sign language from Mudbura women. Sign language is also known and used among the Djingili by both men and women. Spencer and Gillen (1904) refer to speech taboos imposed on younger men in connection with initiation and this is also mentioned by Linklater (1940). Evidently younger men who do not yet have gray hair observe a speech taboo in mourning deceased relatives, as do women.

Use of sign language in this area has also been mentioned by a nineteenth century observer, G.H.Lamond (Lamond 1986). In giving an account of a journey from Queensland to the Kimberleys undertaken in 1885, Lamond describes observing Aborigines using signs near Newcastle Waters. He says:

> I went up to see Mr. Goss, and we were talking out near the Station [Newcastle Waters] blacks' camp. There were about six strangers there. Mr. Goss [Newcastle Waters lessee] asked the boys if they had heard anything about the natives seeing us up at the thirty mile water-hole. They shook their heads. They were standing about twenty yards apart and I was watching them closely. Their arms were hanging down on either side of their bodies and I could see, first one lot moving their fingers, and then the others; like making signs. I asked Mr. Goss about this. He told me that out in that part [west of Newcastle Waters] they have a deaf and dumb language, so they were talking to one another by signs with their moving fingers. (Lamond 1986, pp. 34-35)

This observation is of some interest in that it suggests how signing is done in circumstances where communication is being conducted inconspicuously.[10]

3.11 Fitzmaurice and Kimberley

From my own material, my impression is that sign language among the Djingili and Mudbura may not be as fully developed as it is further south among the Warlmanpa and Warumungu. As one proceeds northwards out of the desert area and into the Fitzmaurice and Kimberley areas a further attenuation of the degree of sign language development appears to occur. In the Fitzmaurice region there is a report of sign language among the Ngaringman and Ngaliwurru (now centered around Victoria River Downs); however the sign language appears to be restricted in its vocabulary and although widows do observe silence on bereavement they do not do so for more than a few days (Rose, personal communication 1984, also Rose 1984). Spencer (1914, p.250) refers to the silence of widows among the Wardman of the Willeroo district, although he does not mention sign language. Mathews (1900) refers to widow's silence and to sign language for the Mariu in the Bulloo River district.

In the Kimberleys we find that widow's silence and the presence of sign language is reported for tribes along the Fitzroy River and south of the King Leopold Ranges. Thus McGregor (1984, personal communication) reports sign language for the Konejandi and Mathews (1900) mentions it for the Kitja and Njikina. These areas constitute the southerly parts of the Kimberleys which are adjacent to areas of high sign language development. In the more northerly parts of the region sign language appears either to be quite limited in its development or absent. In regard to the Worora, Love (1917) states that:

> Apart from the gestures denoting relationships, the Worora have not developed a system of these signs to the extent that occurs in some of the Central Australian tribes, in which use of gestures has attained the level of a sign language. The Worora, however, have signs for a great many animals and birds and, in many cases, a different gesture for the male and female of a species. (p.22)

Love (1941) describes ten kinship gestures which, he says, may be used to accompany spoken reference to kin. In 1975 Kendon and Silverstein made a film of an old Worora man demonstrating a number of animal signs.[11]

The only other Kimberley group for which I have information at present is the Wenambal of the Forrest River area. This group has been reported on by Kaberry (1935). From her account of death and deferred mourning ceremonies it is apparent that the widow is not enjoined from speaking. Kaberry says: "The widow and everyone else refrain from using the dead man's name, but I found that in taking genealogies it was always the wife who displayed the greatest reluctance in uttering it" (p.37). Such a remark seems to imply that the widow was not under a general ban on speaking.

3.12 Indian Ocean and Southwest Coast

These are the two regions of Australia for which the least information relevant to sign language is available. For the Indian Ocean region I am aware of no relevant reports which refer specifically either to the presence or to the absence of sign language. For the Southwest Coast some rather sketchy information is available, however. Roth (1902), summarizing notes on the Pindjarup of the Bunbury district made by F. Robert Austin, an assistant surveyor in Western

Australia, says (p.69): "They were not an emotional people, and were able to express themselves by signs independently of speech." Among the papers of Daisy Bates (held in the National Library, Canberra) one may find a number of copies of the printed questionnaire she and M.A.C. Fraser circulated in 1904. In this questionnaire, as mentioned in a previous chapter, there is a question asking for details of sign language and a question asking if any Masonic signs were to be observed. A few respondents gave answers to the first of these two questions. These responses are given in respect to the Minang of the Mount Barker district and the Wardandi of the Whicher Range. Bates (Ms 365, XI, 5) herself offers some general comments on the distribution of sign language in the Southwest, thus indicating that there was some development of it in the region at one time. She notes that it was more highly developed in plains and open country than it was in the hilly country. She favors the idea that this can be accounted for by saying the sign language would not be useful in hilly country because it could not be so easily used for long distance communication, and in this she appears to follow Howitt (1904).[12]

3.13 Sign language distribution and speech taboos

From the foregoing survey it appears that sign language, though widespread, has been developed to varying degrees in different parts of Australia. The most complex sign languages are found in the North Central Desert area, in particular among the Warumungu and the Warlpiri. This development is associated with the imposition of extended speech bans on female relatives of the deceased as part of mourning. Extensive use and a high degree of development of sign language also prevails in Western Cape York and here, too, it appears to be associated with extended speech bans imposed on the bereaved, although here these bans are not always confined to women. As we move northwards from the North Central Desert into the Gulf, and into the southern regions of the Fitzmaurice and Kimberley areas, sign language appears to become attenuated. Such reports as are available suggest that it is quite limited in development or even absent from the more northerly parts of these areas. However, there is evidence of some development of sign language in north east Arnhem Land.

Eastwards of the North Central Desert, in the western parts of Lake Eyre, from north-west central Queensland southwards to Lake Eyre itself, there are a number of reports that suggest that in the most southwesterly parts of this area sign language was well developed and used during speech bans imposed in mourning, much as in the North Central Desert. In the more northerly parts of the Lake Eyre area, in the Channel Country of western

Queensland and northwards into north-west central Queensland, sign language appears to have been developed and used in connection with speech taboos imposed on male initiates rather than on females in association with mourning. The occurrence of sign language in this area may have extended eastwards as far as the uplands of the Great Dividing Range.

East of this area there is little information on sign language use until we reach the coastal regions. There is some evidence to suggest that sign language was quite well developed in the northern part of East Cape York, but in the more southerly part it was much less developed. Sign language has not been reported from the Rainforest area. South of this, however, there are a few reports that suggest its presence both on the coast and inland as far south as Coff's Harbour. South of Coff's Harbour, including all of the rest of the East Coast and the South Coast and all of the Riverina, sign language appears not to have been developed at all. I also know of no evidence for the use of sign language in Tasmania.

West of Lake Eyre and the North Central Desert, throughout the Western Desert area, it appears that sign language was widely used, at least by men. Various authors have reported seeing signs in use in hunting and the use of sign language by male novices during periods of 'walkabout' in connection with initiation ceremonial have been reported. Speech taboos imposed on women have not been reported for the Western Desert and the one observer to have commented on the matter (Miller 1978) suggests that in the Western Desert men are more adept at sign language than women. As far as the extreme western areas are concerned - Indian Ocean and South West Coast - information seems too scant to draw any firm conclusions.

How is this distribution to be accounted for? One possibility that should not be overlooked is that it is a consequence of the history of European contact with Aborigines. It is to be noted that sign language appears to be absent or attenuated in just those areas of Australia where European settlement came first and where it was most intensive. Sympathetic and detailed observation of Aboriginal customs was rare until about 1880, and by this time Aboriginal society throughout the South and East Coast, as far north as Eastern Cape York and throughout the Riverina, had all but disintegrated. Furthermore, as Howitt (1891) has remarked, it seems that sign language is something that is easily overlooked unless the observer has more than a casual contact with the society which uses it. We may imagine this would especially be true of such a mode of communication, as it is associated with practices which involve seclusion and social withdrawal, such as male initiation or mourning.

Against this, there are two things that may be said. In the few detailed accounts that we do have from these regions that were written before

Aboriginal society had fallen apart, there is no mention of sign language. Second, there is Howitt's testimony to its absence in these southern regions. Howitt did engage in a good deal of first-hand observation and he was careful and critical in his evaluation of the responses of his correspondents. Although it cannot be ruled out that sign language was used throughout this part of Australia and was simply overlooked until it was too late to observe, it seems that we are on fairly firm ground in rejecting this hypothesis.

In Howitt's view, as described in the previous Chapter, the widespread occurrence of sign language use in the desert interior of Australia and its apparent absence from the well-watered and forested regions of the southeast was to be accounted for by the fact that in such regions communication at a distance by gesture would be of little use, whereas it could be used in open country. Howitt put this idea forward only in a most tentative fashion. There are several grounds on which it may be rejected. In the first place, the fact that sign language was well developed in Western Cape York, a region of low-lying rivers and swamps and certainly not of open country, is in itself a strong reason. Second, however, from what we know of sign language use among Aborigines, it is clear that it is far more than a simple signalling system. In many areas, as we have seen, it can serve as a full alternative to speech in all circumstances. It is not obvious why such an elaboration would have occurred if its main function was that of long-distance communication, as Howitt's hypothesis seems to imply.

Two general hypotheses to account for the elaboration of sign languages in Aboriginal societies have been put forward by Divale and Zipin (1977). They propose that hunting societies are likely to develop sign languages because gestural signalling, a silent mode of communication, will be highly useful to hunters since it enables them to coordinate their activities without scaring away the game. They also suggest that sign languages might develop in situations where there is frequent contact between people who speak different languages. They seek to demonstrate support for these hypotheses by means of a statistical evaluation of the association between hunting as the economic base for a society and the presence of sign language and of the association between small society size (which is suggested by them as an indication of frequency of contact with speakers of other languages) and the presence of sign language. They use as data material gathered from the Human Relations Area Files. They do find that all societies reported as having sign language are hunting societies, however there are also many hunting societies for which the presence of sign language has not been reported. Since all hunting societies tend to be small in size, they are unable to present any evidence in relation to their second hypothesis.

Divale and Zipin may well be right when they suggest that the practice of hunting is likely to promote the development of gestural signalling systems. In Chapter 14 we shall suggest that there are certain quite general characteristics of face-to-face interaction in Aboriginal society that appear to favor the use of gesture and sign language as autonomous modes of communication. However, it is not obvious why such gestural communication, which, in hunting, need only be quite simple, should ever evolve into the highly complex sign language systems that we find in many Australian Aboriginal societies. As to the idea that sign languages might develop where people speaking different languages come into contact, this seems most unlikely, and it is certainly not the reason for the development of sign languages in Australia. Although it has been reported quite often that Europeans coming into contact with natives for the first time attempted to use gestures to communicate with them (see Hewes 1974 for a review of many of these accounts), there is no case reported from anywhere in the world where, with prolonged contact, a sign language has developed.[13] Invariably, some form of spoken language is employed, such as a pidgin or trade jargon, or those coming into contact learn each other's languages.

In Australia, where there are many places where speakers of different languages are in frequent contact with one another, multilingualism is widespread (Brandl and Walsh 1982). No instances of the use of sign language instead of spoken language in these circumstances have been reported.[14] In those cases where a use of sign language between people who cannot understand each other's language has been claimed in Australia (Howitt 1890, Roth 1897; Warner 1937; Terry 1974; Roberts in Lockwood 1962), no detailed description has been given and the only instances mentioned are those in which very short term accidental contacts are involved. From what one can gather from these accounts, the incidents described are examples where gestures have been used in a way quite similar to the attempts by Europeans to use gestures in their first contacts with natives. As we shall see in Chapter 12, there is evidence that sign languages of adjacent groups who speak different languages are more similar to one another than the spoken languages. In such a case it is conceivable that sign language could be used between people who could not understand one another's speech. However, if this occurs, this almost certainly is a result of people already sharing a sign language. It is not the circumstance which leads them to create one.

The circumstance that does quite clearly favor the development of a complex sign language is the circumstance where people who otherwise would use speech are prevented from doing so in *all* of the circumstances in which they would normally use it. In Aboriginal society such a circumstance frequently prevails, as we have seen, because of the widespread practice of speech taboos. It is clearly this that promotes the development of sign language, at least in Australia. It is remarkable that Divale and Zipin make no mention of it.

As we have seen, there are two main circumstances in which speech taboos are found in Aboriginal society: in association with male initiation and in association with mourning. In male initiation ceremony the novices are often subject to a speech taboo. In some societies, such as the Lardiil, this may be for as long as six months. In mourning, in many places close relatives of the deceased, especially female relatives, are required to observe speech taboos of varying lengths which may, as in the case of the Warumungu, extend for widows for as long as two years.

The tabooing of speech for mourners and male novices can be understood in terms of the link both have with death. The initiation ceremony for males in Aboriginal society is seen as a process whereby the boy dies and the man is born. Thus the period of the novice's liminality is often treated as a kind of semi-death and restrictions are placed on communication and other aspects of behavior, since persons who are dead are not able to communicate, and are certainly not able to speak. Preventing speech may also have important functional consequences. It is a good way of emphasizing the withdrawal of the person from normal social intercourse, which is a necessary part of the process whereby instruction in the sacred secrets and laws of the group can be impressed upon the novice. In addition, because expression is much restricted in such circumstances, this may have the effect of dampening or quelling the novice's feelings. It helps to make him passive in the face of the ordeals to which he is subjected. In the case of mourners, observing a speech ban may have a similarly dampening effect upon the emotions.(Glowczewski 1983 makes this suggestion.) Refusing to speak, also for mourners, is a way of withdrawing from normal participation in society, which is a common feature of mourning everywhere. It may also, perhaps, be interpreted as part of a process whereby the mourner, for a time, takes on some of the characteristics of a dead person.[15] It is significant, in this connection, that Sharp (1934), writing of the Yir Yoront, notes that while suicide is unknown, persons who feel deeply shamed may act as if they are deaf and dumb ('shut ear'), and communicate only by signs. If this is the origin of speech taboos in mourning, they have nevertheless become institutionalized and now have their own explanations.Thus the imposition of speech bans on close relatives is explained as a way of making sure that the spirit of the dead person will not be attracted back to the places where those to whom it was close in life are living.

The development of extended speech bans undoubtedly provide the circumstances in which elaborate sign languages will develop. Once these have developed, as among the Warumungu and the Warlpiri, the sign language may then come to be used generally, at least by those who are often liable to observe speech taboos, as is the case with older women in these societies. We expect a direct correlation with the extent of speech taboo and the length and frequency with which it is imposed and the elaborateness of sign language. Thus to account for the distribution of sign language in Australia requires that we understand the distribution of speech taboos.

Bearing in mind the limited information which seems to be available on the topic, it would seem that the tabooing of speech by female relatives of the deceased, particularly the widow, is found among the Dieri, northwards and westwards among the Aranda, throughout the North Central Desert area and northwards into the southerly regions of the Kimberleys, Fitzmaurice and western end of the Gulf areas. It does not extend westwards into the Western Desert nor eastwards into the northwestern parts of Lake Eyre. However, in both of these areas we find the imposition of speech taboos on male novices. This is a curious distribution. It perhaps suggests that the imposition of speech taboos on female relatives of the deceased is a practice that developed in the North Central Desert, spreading a little northward, but extending southwards to a considerable degree. If we suppose that the practice is kept up the most in the place of its origin, this would suggest that it is a practice that began among the Warumungu and spread from there. We suggest that the practice of tabooing speech as part of the male initiation process is the older practice. Widows' silence is a newer development that has spread outwards from its center of origin in the country of the Warumungu. Evidence in support of this idea that North Central Desert sign languages constitute a distinct and possibly more recent development is presented in Chapter 12.

The snag in this idea is the presence of speech taboos as part of mourning ritual that is found in Western Cape York. Ethnographic information on the tribes in the eastern part of the Gulf area is extremely limited. Those few accounts that I have been able to find make no mention of speech taboos in connection with death. The question remains, then, as to whether mourning speech taboos arose twice, which is what the model proposed here would suggest. If a connection between Western Cape York and the Gulf can be established in this respect, however, then it might be equally plausible to suppose that the practice has spread southwards from Cape York, across the Gulf and southwards through the North Central Desert.

3.14 Sign language and 'special language'

We conclude this Chapter with a comment on sign language in relation to 'special language'. Both may be regarded as transpositions of spoken language into another form, but they are otherwise very different. The transposition of spoken language into the kinesic medium, which is what we encounter in Aboriginal sign languages, has radical consequences not just for the structure of the resulting code, but for the way the user is perceived as a social being. These consequences are far more profound than those that follow from the use of a vocal special language.

'Special languages' are systems of talk developed for use by interactants in special relationships or in certain ritual situations, in which special modes of pronunciation, special vocabularies, or peculiar semantic transformations are employed. Capell (1962) has surveyed these and suggests three types: secret languages used only by men at male initiation ceremonies; special 'avoidance' or 'respect' languages, used between people who stand in an in-law relationship; and, of apparently more restricted distribution, special languages used between people in a 'joking' relationship. Examples of secret language have been partially described for the Warlpiri (Hale 1971), the Lardiil (Dixon 1980, Hale 1982, Hale and Nash 1987) and the Nyagnumada in Western Australia (O'Grady 1956). Avoidance languages have been described for the Dyirbal by Dixon (1971, 1972) and for the Guugu (Koko) Yimidhirr by Haviland (1979a, 1979b). Other special forms of talk include 'play' languages, such as the so-called 'rabbit' talk of the Akarre (Eastern Aranda) of Harts Range in Central Australia (Turner and Breen 1984), and 'baby talk', which has been described for the Warlpiri (Laughren 1984a).

A consideration of these accounts of special languages suggests that they serve as a means of indexing the interaction as being between people who are in a particular kind of relationship. Sign languages, on the other hand, are devices whereby people who otherwise would not or could not communicate at all are enabled to do so. One might say that the employment of a sign language marks the user as having assumed a certain quite general condition, as having entered into a particular general state that affects all aspects of his life. Using a special language, on the other hand, indicates that the participants in the specific interaction in which it is used are in a particular relationship with one another, but they are not otherwise transformed as social beings.

Thus it is to be noted that, as far as we have been able to determine, sign language is not used routinely as a form of communication between people in an avoidance relationship.[16] Such people either do not communicate directly at all, or they do so by way of a special 'avoidance' or 'respect' language. Further, in those cases where a 'mystic' language is used in male initiation ceremonies, in so far as any information about their use is available, it appears it is reciprocal between the initiates and those who teach it. Learning the 'mystic' language is part of the process by which the initiate acquires the power and the knowledge of the initiated. Sign languages, on the other hand, appear to be taught to novices so that they may communicate their essential needs during a period when they are considered symbolically dead, and thus not really capable of communicating at all. Other uses of sign language are, as we have seen, by people who are in mourning - a state of partial withdrawal from all forms of normal social intercourse, or, as reported by Sharp among the Yir Yiront, by people who have imposed their own form of withdrawal on themselves. Its other, occasional, everyday uses are to serve as a way of communicating when speaking is either impossible or undesirable. Sign language thus does not count as a form of talk at all.

A user of sign language in Aboriginal society, thus, is regarded as communicating in an altogether *different* manner. To transpose one's mode of communication from the vocal medium to the kinesic medium does not only have consequences for the structure of linguistic system. It also has consequences for how one is perceived as a social being.

Notes

[1]Tindale's (1974) work is the most comprehensive treatment of Aborginal 'tribes' available. As many recognize, it contains a number of errors (perhaps inevitable in a work of this nature). I use it as a guide here, however, because, despite its errors, it is fully documented. By tracing Tindale's references it is usually possible to establish which Aboriginal group is being referred to even if, for whatever reason, it is preferred to refer to in a different way or to establish its associated geographical area differently.

[2]As will be noted in Fig. 3.2, some of the 'mutilated hand' stencils are combined in panels with other figures. If Walsh's interpretation of these as representations of hand signs is correct, this use of them raises the interesting possibility that they were serving as linguistic symbols in these panels. If so, this would represent a step in the direction of true writing among Aborigines.

[3]A search of the various places where the papers of N.W.Thomas are still to be found has failed to locate this manuscript.

[4]It should be noted that the two men in the film by McBride available at the Australian Institute of Aboriginal Studies are deaf. However, McBride did film many non-deaf signers at Edward River (McBride, p.c., 1985).

[5]See also Gason's responses to Frazer's questionaire (Gason 1895).

[6]Arremte is now the recommended spelling. I have retained 'Aranda' here, however, as being more familiar.

[7]This may, perhaps, be compared to the 'grunting' that may accompany signing by North Central Desert women when observing the speech taboo (see Chapter 10 for further discussion).

[8]It will be noted, however, that people were certainly aware that complex sign languages were used in this part of Australia before this date. This is clear from the passage from John Fraser, quoted above (p.40), which was published in 1892.

[9]I am indebted to David Nash for bringing these two mentions to my notice.

[10]I am grateful to David Nash for drawing my attention to this passage.

[11]A copy of this film is on deposit in the library of the Australian Institute of Aboriginal Studies.

[12]These comments on sign language by Bates are not included in the extracts from her manuscripts published under the editorship of Isobel White (Bates 1985), presumably because they are rather brief and derivative and not part of her body of firsthand observations.

[13]The sign languages that were used by the Plains Indians of North America may be an exception to this statement. However, the evidence seems to suggest that the use of sign language as a lingua franca by the Indians of the Plains was a late development and was an adaptation in the use of sign languages already employed by various tribes. See Chapter 13 for further discussion.

[14]Elwell's observations at Maningreda referred to above may possibly be an exception. Further research in this context would be most valuable.

[15]In addition to becoming silent, mourners in many parts of Australia bedaub themselves with white clay and this may also be a simulation of a death-like state. Aboriginal corpses are often treated in various ways, including having their skin removed, being singed or heated over a fire, and being exposed for desiccation. The corpse takes on a lighter colored appearance as a result so that being white is a characteristic of death. This perhaps accounts for why the pale skinned Europeans were so often mistaken for returned spirits, when first encountered by Aborigines (see Reynolds 1982).

[16]Roheim (1974, p. 29) says: "Strehlow (i.e. Carl Theodore Strehlow) writes that a man may not speak or go anywhere near his real mother-in-law in the camp, but if they meet in the bush he may use *ankatja kerintja* (taboo talk) or sign language and converse with her from a distance." This is the only reference to the use of sign language in an avoidance interaction that I have come across. At Yuendumu I was told quite definitely that sign language was never used in this way.

4 North Central Desert background

4.0 The environment

In the Chapters to follow we undertake a detailed study of several aspects of sign language in the North Central Desert. The basis for this is original material collected from seven Aboriginal groups between 1978 and 1986. Sign language material was gathered from Warlpiri at Yuendumu, Anmatyerre at Ti Tree, Kaytej at Tara Community near Neutral Junction, Warumungu and Warlmanpa at Tennant Creek, and Mudbura and Djingili at Elliott. In this Chapter we shall provide some ethnographic background for these groups and some further details on sign language use among them. In the final section we give an account of how the sign language material was gathered. Fig. 4.1 shows the North Central Desert region with an indication of the areas traditionally occupied by the seven groups here considered. The places where sign language data were actually gathered are also shown.

The region within which these seven groups reside coincides with a rather poorly defined inland drainage basin which extends northwards from the Macdonnell Ranges as far as the edge of the Gulf drainage area and the Arnhem Land escarpment. It is bounded to the east by a chain of hills that extends to the Davenport Range, but north of this the region extends eastward to the Queensland border to include the Barkly Tablelands. Its westward extent is less easily defined, merging with the Western Desert beyond the chain of (usually dry) lakes that extends from Lake Amadeus in the south to Gregory Lake in the north, near Balgo, which is fed by Sturt Creek. The main rivers include the northward flowing Lander and Hanson rivers to the south and the southward flowing Newcastle Creek to the north. These rivers are dry for the greater part of the year, although permanent waterholes and soaks may be found along them in places. The Lander and Hanson rivers both dissipate in floodouts but Newcastle Creek empties into a series of permanent waterholes known as Newcastle Waters and, when rain is heavy, into Lake Woods.

Rainfall throughout the region is highly unpredictable. It can vary from anywhere between only three or four centimeters in some years with upwards of more than seventy centimeters in others.[1] It can also show marked local variations. Most rain occurs during the period between October and March. In

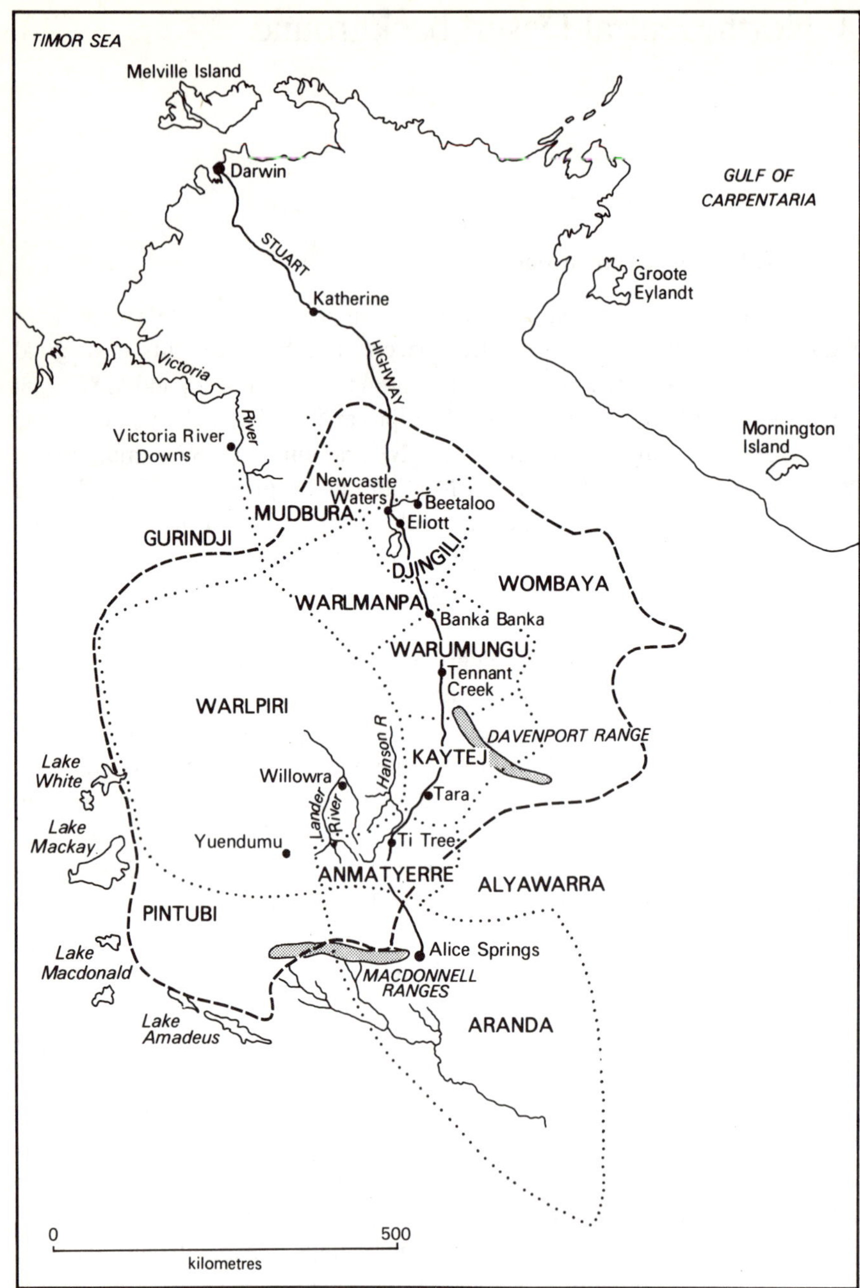

Fig. 4.1 The North Central Desert (area enclosed by a heavy broken line) showing the approximate areas occupied before European contact by the Aboriginal groups discussed and the places where sign language material was gathered in 1984-1985

the more northerly parts of this region, rainfall may average about 36 cm per year, with lower averages to the south. Daytime temperatures range from upwards of 35° C during the summer months to between 15° and 20° C during the winter. The region is thus hot and arid. Compared to the Simpson Desert to the southeast and the Western Desert to the west of the Tanami Desert, however, it is somewhat better watered and there are few areas completely without vegetation. In the more southerly parts there is extensive mulga scrub. Further north this gives way to grasslands with scattered acacias, grevilleas and hakeas. Along the creeks large Eucalypts may be found, including *Eucalyptus camaldulensis*, the red river gum, which grows in the sandy creek beds.

4.1 Traditional culture [2]

Prior to European contact the inhabitants of this region, as in the rest of Australia, were nomadic hunter-gatherers. During much of the year they lived in small groups, of variable size and composition, usually of two or three families, each including a man and his wife or wives and children, but often including other relatives as well. Commonly, the group might include two or more brothers-in-law, since a man, in the early part of his married life might spend time with his wife's group. Thus the group could include his wife's sisters, and their husbands, as well as his wife's mother. From a woman's viewpoint, it will be seen that her circle could include her mother and one or more mother's sisters, her own sisters (real and classificatory), as well as her own daughters (Peterson 1970, Hamilton 1980, Bell 1983). These small groups would remain camped near waterholes, the women spending part of each day foraging for vegetable food and pursuing small game, the men hunting for larger animals, although, on occasion, spouses foraged together. After a short spell camped in one place, the group would then move on to another waterhole. Typically these small bands roamed over an extended area, regularly visiting various locations within it, often interacting with other bands affiliated by kinship and ritual ties. During periods of localized abundance of food (which typically occurs three or four months after a major fall of rain), these small bands would coalesce into large gatherings, sometimes of hundreds of people. During such times important ceremonies would be carried out, most notably the elaborate cycle of ceremonial associated with male initiation. On these occasions there would often be gatherings that would include people from several different groups who had been specially invited to take part.

The size of the areas or subsistence domains through which such wanderings occurred and the extent to which there were local groups associated with particular tracts of land varied somewhat in association with environmental differences. Much of the area occupied by the Warlpiri and Warumungu, for instance, is open sandhill country with highly dispersed water resources. The composition of the local groups was fluid and open and the areas over which they moved were quite large. In comparison, the Anmatyerre and Kaytej lived in country that is better watered and segmented into small regions by small ranges of hills. The local groups were less open in their composition and were more closely connected to particular tracts of land.

Fig. 4.2 Sparse mulga scrubland south of Yuendumu, Northern Territory

Although food resources are not always abundant in this region and in times of drought can be very scarce, a wide variety of types of food is available. There are several kinds of underground tuber (*Ipomea* and *Vignea* spp.) fruit bearing herbs, such as the bush tomato (*Solanum* spp.), shrubs, such as conkerberry (*Carissa lanceolata*) and trees, such as wild orange (*Capparis* spp.). Numerous species of grass and tree yield edible seed which may be ground to flour and used for making dampers and this is a particularly important food source in some areas. There are also many animals that can serve for food. There are a number of species of kangaroo as well as smaller marsupials. With the entry of Europeans to Australia, rabbits and feral domestic cats spread into the region, and these are now are hunted, as well.

There are numerous species of lizard, some quite large, and many species of birds, including the emu and the turkey bustard. Insects that are exploited for food include the honey ant, found in the more southerly parts of the region, the wild bee and several species of Cossid larvae or witchetty grubs.

Culturally, the groups considered here have much in common. Although they speak different languages (see 4.5), they share the same

Fig. 4.3 Ridge of sandstone hills (Walbri Range) southwest of Yuendumu

material culture, the same economy, and the same principles of social organization. In all North Central Desert groups considered here, the system of kin relations, explained further in Chapter 11, is of the so-called Aranda type. In this, four lines of descent are recognized, terminologically, in the second ascending generation and preferred marriage is with Ego's classificatory Mother's Mother's Brother's Daughter's Daughter (MMBDD), in the case of a male, and with Mother's Father's Sister's Daughter's Son (MFZDS), in the case of a female. In all groups the system of grouping kin into eight named subsections is employed. Patrilineal, matrilineal and generational groupings (moieties) are also recognized and these divisions become important, especially, in connection with the organization of responsibility in preparing for and enacting rituals.

All of the groups considered share similar beliefs concerning the role of totemic heroes. These heroes travelled the country before humans lived there, in a period of 'time out of time' usually referred to in English as the Dreamtime or the Dreaming. As they travelled, they left evidence of their activities in the form of rock formations, waterholes and trees, and they established how ceremonies should be performed and how people should behave in daily life (so-called 'Law'), as well as the functioning of the natural

Fig. 4.4. Winnie Nangala with a catch of goannas (*Varanus*, sp.)

world and the place of all people, animals and plants within it. The power or 'life force' (Glowczewski 1983) of these totemic heroes resides at each of the places along the path the hero traversed where some activity was engaged in and, in particular, at those places where the hero is said to have emerged from the ground, or to have re-entered it at the end of its voyage. These locations of emergence and re-entry and of activities along the way are sacred sites at which ceremonies must be performed from time to time. There are numerous tracks of the heroes of the Dreamtime traversing the whole central desert region, often crossing from the area of one group into that of another, with the result that ceremonial responsibility for sacred sites is often shared between different groups.

Every individual is affiliated with several totemic heroes in a number of different ways. Each individual receives a totemic spirit from the place where his or her mother became aware of being pregnant, or where the father had it revealed to him that a child was to be born to his wife. This is the individual's so-called conception Dreaming. An individual may also receive a totemic affiliation as a result of a revelation dream (*kurruwalpa* in Warlpiri) by the father, and also sometimes by the mother. There are also totemic affiliations which are acquired in virtue of both the patriline and the matriline one is born into. It is these totemic affiliations, especially, that have implications for an individual's ritual responsibilities which he or she will gradually acquire once adulthood is attained.

Small patrilineal descent groups are recognized as totemic cult lodges. Each such group has ritual responsibility for one or more totems and has a spiritual affiliation with one or more sites where the totemic hero emerged, engaged in some exploit, or came to rest. These groups perform ceremonies in which aspects of the totemic hero's exploits are enacted. They also perform various ceremonies which ensure the continued abundance of the totemic species and of human fertility.[3] Ceremonies with many of the same functions are performed separately, by both men and women, at least in many parts of Australia (Elkin 1979, Glowczewski 1983, Bell 1983, Myers 1986). Each sex regards these ceremonies as the special domain of the other and, to varying degrees, aspects of them may be maintained as sacred and secret. In respect to many of the men's ceremonial, any breach of this secrecy can result in extreme sanctions. Women and uninitiated males may be killed if found to have witnessed a secret ceremony, even if only by accident. Men who violate the secrecy of women's ceremonial may become sick, even seriously ill. For men, only those who have passed through the initiation ceremonial of circumcision and subincision may be fully instructed in these ceremonies. For women, it is those who are older and who have borne at least two children who may be fully instructed in women's ritual, although girls and younger women may also receive partial instruction. Other rituals, also performed separately by men and women, include 'love magic' rituals (*yilpinji* in Warlpiri). Men may use these rituals to try to ensure their own attractiveness to women and to incline the affections of reluctant promised wives. Women may use these rituals to attract lovers, to ensure the steadiness of their husbands, and also as a means of more general 'emotional management' of relations between men and women (Bell 1983). In ceremonies associated with male initiation, mortuary ceremonies and a number of other religious ceremonies, both men and women participate, with reciprocal and complementary roles.

The separate and, to some degree, parallel sacred and ritual life of men and women is but a part of a separation of the sexes that is found in these societies in almost every sphere of life. This has been discussed by White (1974), Hamilton (1980), Bell (1983) and Myers (1986, p. 248 ff.). Although, of these authors, only Bell is concerned with North Central Desert Aborigines, the statements made by the others, who are concerned with Western Desert peoples, apply nevertheless. White (p.39) writes that a "notable feature of Aboriginal social, economic, and ritual organization is the high degree of segregation between the sexes". She observes that this role segregation is much more pronounced in the arid central desert regions of the continent than it is in the lusher north. Hamilton (1980), writing mainly of the Pitjantjatjara speaking peoples of northern South Australia (Eastern Western Desert), argues that the segregation of the sexes both economically and ceremonially is such that the society may be thought of as having a "dual social system" - a two track model with separate men's and women's societies which intersect only through the reciprocities of kin and affinal obligations. Thus she concludes (1980, p. 12) from a review of the extractive and subsistence activities of men and women "that the division of labour by sex in this area is so thoroughgoing and complete that it can better be understood as two separate systems". Bell (1983), in her work on the Kaytej at Ali Curung (formerly Warrabri), likewise suggests that, ceremonially and economically, men and women lead parallel and only occasionally intersecting lives. Myers (loc. cit.) writing of the Pintupi, a Western Desert group adjacent to the south western part of Warlpiri country, states that "men and women occupy rather autonomous domains". He adds that "Pintupi believe that there is 'men's business' and 'women's business,' and that it is inappropriate for either sex to intrude on the proper concerns of the other." This separateness and autonomy of women's lives, which is as characteristic of the central desert as it is of the Western Desert, may be one of the factors that sustains and encourages women to maintain sign language as a separate communication system. This point will be returned to in Chapter 14.

Ceremonies connected with the process of 'making men', that is, the process of transforming boys into fully initiated men with access to knowledge of the Dreaming, with an understanding of the obligations of adulthood and who are entitled to marry and have children, are of central importance in all these groups. These ceremonies involve the separation of youths in seclusion camps in which they undergo various kinds of instruction. They culminate in circumcision and the selection of the novice's future potential mother-in-law. Speech taboos are observed in connection with this ceremonial, both by the novices and by certain of their kinswomen, especially mothers and potential mothers-in-law. Sign language is used by these kinswomen at this time and, to a more limited extent it may be used by the novices, also.[4] In all of these groups, in a subsequent ritual, males also undergo subincision.

Death is attended by elaborate ceremonial in which both men and women inflict injury upon themselves. In all groups the kinswomen of the deceased observe more or less prolonged speech taboos (see below). Traditionally, in all groups considered here (in contrast to the Aranda to the south and to the groups living to the north of the desert) two stage burial was practised. Immediately after death the corpse was exposed in a tree. After an extended period, which could be at least a year, the bones were then removed and a final ceremony conducted in which the remains were disposed of. Nowadays, European practices of burial are followed.

4.2 The contemporary situation [5]

Today no Aborigines in this area live a traditional nomadic existence sustained only by the natural resources of the environment. Most Aborigines now live in settlements, in towns, or in settled camps near towns and obtain most of their provisions by buying from stores. A certain amount of hunting is still carried out and expeditions into the surrounding bush to gather traditional vegetable foods and small game are undertaken whenever possible, but such activities are for most no longer part of the daily routine except, perhaps, for those who live on outstations (see below), where traditional foodstuffs have come to occupy a larger place in everyday diet than has been the case in recent years.

Settlement life has inevitably led to many changes. Whereas in traditional times, large concentrations of people were occasional, settlement life has meant that people now live in large associations all the time. This has led to the development of problems in health which were previously not encountered. These problems are exacerbated by the fact that standards of accommodation with associated facilities such as the availability of water and plumbing are far below what is needed in such circumstances. Living continuously in large groups has also led to many increases in social tensions. In many settlements, groups that traditionally were not closely associated may find themselves living in close proximity, in many cases in territory with which they have no ritual attachment. For example, the settlement of Warrabri was established in 1956 to accommodate Warlpiri and Warumungu people who had been living at the settlement of Phillip Creek.[6] Warrabri, however, is not situated in the traditional area of either group, but in the area of the Kaytej. The Kaytej were not consulted over the establishment of Warrabri and the result has been an unhappy one, with many tensions arising between the Kaytej and the other groups who live there.

A further consequence of settlement life, however, has been an intensification of certain aspects of ritual life. Bell (1983) suggests, for instance, that the camp quarters traditionally set aside for widows, single women, and women temporarily without their husbands (the *jilimi* as it is termed in Warlpiri) in settlements is today much enlarged and this has led to an intensification and elaboration of women's ritual life. It is quite possible that this has also had the consequence, at some settlements, of leading to a greater elaboration of sign language, as well.

Some settlements, such as Yuendumu, were started as government ration stations. Other settlements, such as those at Willowra or Ti Tree, or further to the north, Banka Banka and Newcastle Waters, are derived from the communities of Aborigines that became established in association with cattle stations. Aborigines were originally attracted to stations because of the European food they could obtain. The station owners encouraged such gatherings to settle down, because these people could then more readily serve as a source of cheap labor. Many men took on work as stockmen while a few women worked as domestic staff. Furthermore, many cattle stations were centered near a permanent waterhole or other favored spot, places which were also important for the Aborigines.

There are two small towns in this region, Tennant Creek and Elliott. Tennant Creek was originally a relay station on the Alice Springs-Darwin telegraph line, but following the Tennant Creek goldrush in 1933 it developed rapidly as a small town. Tennant Creek, though small, offers many of the features of an urban center. There are several Aboriginal camps on the town's fringes and in recent years there are many Aboriginal families living in houses in the town.[7] Elliott was established during World War II as a supply depot for the work of upgrading the Stuart Highway between Darwin and Alice Springs. It now has two roadhouses, a campground for tourists, a police station, a school and a health facility. Approximately 500 Aborigines were living there in 1984, some in houses, but most in two different camps, one to the north of the town and one to the south.

4.3 History of European contact

European contact in this region began in 1860 with the explorations of J. McDouall Stuart. This contact intensified soon thereafter with the construction of the overland telegraph line which ran from Adelaide to Darwin and was completed in 1872. The telegraph line was operated by a series of relay stations - Alice Springs, Ti Tree, Barrow Creek, Powell Creek - and the officers in charge were among the first Europeans in the region with whom the Aborigines had prolonged contact. The route along the line was, of course, used for overland transport and somewhat later a highway known as the Stuart Highway was built close to it. The Stuart Highway was metalled during World

Fig. 4.5. Two views to show the open character of contemporary Aboriginal living arrangements in the North Central Desert. Above, outlying camp at Yuendumu. Below, Six-Mile, Anmatyerre settlement near Ti Tree. Drawn from photographs

War II and more recently it has been completely re-surfaced and re-aligned and is now a modern high speed road which carries much traffic. Aboriginal groups living in areas which lay in the path of the telegraph line and the highway suffered increasing disturbance from 1870 onwards. Where land was taken up for stock, they found themselves suddenly deprived of free access to land they had always used and in conflict with the pastoralists when they speared cattle. The influx of miners at the times of the various gold rushes (at Hall's Creek in 1885, at Tanami beginning in 1909, at Granites in 1932 and Tennant Creek in 1933) also had an important impact. While miners did not interfere with Aborigines' use of the land to the extent that the pastoralists did, their presence nevertheless gave rise to conflicts from time to time. The miners brought with them supplies of interest to Aborigines and, to a limited degree, offered Aborigines employment.

The Northern Territory was originally administered as part of New South Wales, but in 1862 the new state of South Australia took responsibility and this continued until 1914, when it was separated from South Australia and became a Territory administered by the Commonwealth government. In order to encourage settlement, and in the hope of developing the Territory as a source of revenue, the South Australian government, and later the Commonwealth government, gave pastoralists and prospectors a free hand. Pastoral leases were taken up, at first fairly close to Alice Springs, and also further north at Tennant Creek, Banka Banka and in areas bordering on the northern edge of Warlpiri country. From the first there was conflict between Aborigines and pastoralists and there were many incidents in which fighting occurred, usually ending with the Europeans gaining the upper hand. From 1890 the government sought to regulate relationships between settlers and Aborigines. In 1892 several Aboriginal reserves were declared and it eventually became policy to confine Aborigines to these areas. Subsequently, an assimilationist approach came into prominence and efforts were made to train Aborigines to live in a European manner. Since Aborigines were granted full citizenship (1967) and since the passage of the Aboriginal Land Rights Act (Northern Territory) in 1976, official government policy has been to encourage self-determination. Extensive areas of the Northern Territory have now been returned to Aboriginal communities as freehold and many settlements are now self-governing communities in charge of local Aboriginal Councils, although effectively still operated by European employees.

Few Aboriginal settlements have a secure economic base (Young 1981). While a settlement such as Willowra was originally established as a cattle station and is operated as such today, more typical are settlements such as Yuendumu or Lajamanu (formerly Hooker Creek) which had no original economic justification. The inhabitants are almost completely dependent upon government funds in the form of unemployment benefit and pensions, or government funded positions, as in education (as teacher aides) and health care (as health care workers).

Since the establishment of Aboriginal freehold land with the right of the owners to demand royalties from mining companies operating within the boundaries of Aboriginal land, there has been some influx of funds from this source. One result of this has been a great expansion in the availability of motor transport with the consequence that it has become much easier for many to move away from settlements and travel to or settle in places close to traditional sacred sites. This has greatly facilitated the 'outstation' movement, in which satellites of the larger settlements are established in favorable spots where people can live in closer association with their traditional country. To some extent this has led to a repopulation of areas of the North Central Desert that had been abandoned a generation before. The greater availability of motor transport has also made it possible for large ceremonial gatherings to be held more easily and, according to some, there has been a recrudescence of ceremonial life in recent years, with many ceremonies being revived (Kolig 1981).

Of the groups from which we have gathered sign language material, the Warlpiri are by far the largest and most vigorous and it is estimated that there are upwards of 2000 Warlpiri speakers. They have long had the reputation of being highly aggressive and expansionist and in recent years they have extended their 'country' considerably. Warlpiri 'country' today extends as far north as Lajamanu (Hooker Creek) and there are sizeable groups of Warlpiri living in Tennant Creek and even Katherine. It has also extended eastwards into areas formerly populated with Anmatyerre.

The territorial expansion and vigor of the Warlpiri is undoubtedly connected to the fact that their main centers were not close to the telegraph line or the Stuart Highway. Furthermore, apart from some short-lived mining activity in the Tanami Desert, the land they occupied had little to offer the European and in large measure they remained undisturbed until the end of the second decade of the twentieth century and most did not become established on settlements until after the second World War. In contrast, the other groups considered here occupied land that was crossed by the telegraph line and the highway and which also was somewhat richer and thus offered itself as somewhat more suitable for running cattle. In consequence, the Anmatyerre, Kaytej, Warumungu and Warlmanpa, and also the Mudbura and Djingili, have been much more disturbed and are now much reduced in numbers.

4.4 Interrelations between groups

As will be seen in Fig. 4.1 the area traditionally occupied by the Warlpiri adjoins to the east the areas of all of the groups considered here except for that of of the Djingili. Meggitt (1962) has provided some details of how these groups interrelated, although from the perspective of the Warlpiri. According to him, the Warlpiri engaged in extensive trade and ceremonial exchanges with the Mudbura and the Gurindji to the north, these groups serving as a sort of intermediary, in both material things and in certain ceremonies, between the Warlpiri and the groups living further to the north. However, the relationship with these groups was not an intimate one, and they did not intermarry. Meggitt states that the Mudbura tend to regard the Warlpiri as "uncouth trouble makers", a sentiment which one may still hear expressed today. The Warlpiri and the Warlmanpa had a much closer relationship. Their languages are extremely close, they intermarried freely, and they share many cultural practices in common. In some ways the Warlmanpa could be considered a northern extension of the Warlpiri, differing from them little more than the way the four divisions of the Warlpiri - the Lander, Ngalia, Walmalla and Waneiga[8] - differ among themselves. The Warlpiri had little contact with the Djingili; however the Djingili have long had an intimate relationship with the Mudbura and they have also had much contact with the Warumungu (Spencer and Gillen 1904). According to Meggitt, the Warlpiri were not on good terms with the Warumungu. In the area where the territories of these groups adjoined, there was much skirmishing, the Warlpiri often stealing Warumungu women. Most Warlpiri had little contact with the Kaytej, although the Lander Warlpiri did intermarry with Kaytej to some extent. According to Meggitt, the Warlpiri regarded the Kaytej as a "sullen, suspicious and hostile people who were best left alone", an opinion of them apparently shared by other neighboring Aboriginal groups as well (Meggitt, 1962, p. 39). The Kaytej apparently returned the compliment, deeming the Warlpiri to be "hungry buggers; hungry for land, for young men, for sex" (Bell 1983, p. 60). The Kaytej interacted with the Warumungu extensively and shared ceremonial responsibility for many sacred sites along their northern border. The Anmatyerre, in contrast, were held in high regard by the Warlpiri, the Ngalia Warlpiri, in particular, maintaining extremely close relations with them, sometimes claiming them as "half Warlpiri", much as the more northerly Warlpiri claimed this of the Warlmanpa.

These relationships probably remain much the same today, although there have been some changes in the places where the members of these groups are now mainly to be found. The Mudbura, for many years concentrated at Newcastle Waters, now mostly live in Elliott. Most of the

Djingili are now to be found in this town, also. The Warlmanpa have moved eastwards and are concentrated mainly at Banka Banka and Tennant Creek. Tennant Creek remains the traditional center for the Warumungu, although they have suffered much disturbance for many years (Nash 1984) and many additional groups of Aborigines are to be found there. In addition to Warlpiri and some Warlmanpa, Kaytej and Alyawara now also reside in the town. The Kaytej now mainly live at or near Tara, near Barrow Creek, which is more or less at the center of their traditional area. However, a significant number are also to be found at Ali Curung (formerly Warrabri), a settlement established south of Tennant Creek in the northern part of Kaytej country. This settlement was founded in 1956 as a relocation settlement for the Warumungu and Warlpiri of Phillip Creek, when this had to be closed. Phillip Creek, somewhat to the north of Tennant Creek, was founded in 1945, but failed for lack of water. In recent years the Warumungu and most Warlpiri at Ali Curung have moved away and the population is now mainly Kaytej (Bell 1983, p. 8). The Anmatyerre still live in their traditional area. Today they are found mainly in camps at Mount Allen, close to Warlpiri country, at Napperby, in camps in the creek near Ti Tree homestead and in a newly established camp a few miles south of the town of Ti Tree on the Stuart Highway.

4.5 Linguistic relationships[9]

The languages spoken by the groups considered here fall into four divisions: Arandic (Anmatyerre and Kaytej), Southwest Pama-Nyungan (Warlpiri, Warlmanpa and Mudbura), Waramungic (Warumungu) and Djingilic (Djingili). All but Djingili are members of the Pama-Nyungan language family, which extends from the Paman languages in Cape York to the Nyungan languages in the extreme southwest. Djingili has characteristics which suggest that it is quite distinct from other Australian languages and must be regarded as belonging to a group of its own. It is distinguished by the fact that it has a four-class gender system and that there are obligatory suffixes on the verb that cross reference gender class, person and number of the subject, object and indirect object of the sentence. The other languages considered here are all Pama-Nyungan. As is characteristic of the languages of this group, all bound morphemes are suffixes and grammatical relations are given by morphological markers on nominals. They do not have gender and the verb need not (although in some languages it may) bear any information about its arguments.

Grammatical differences between the six Pama-Nyungan languages considered here are found mainly in the structure of the verb and in the treatment of pronouns. In Warlpiri, and the closely related languages of Warlmanpa and Mudbura, there are several conjugations and a verbal auxiliary is employed which carries information about tense and to which may be attached clitic pronouns and their associated case suffixes. These languages also have a system of free pronouns. Number distinctions are singular, dual and plural, both with exclusive and inclusive forms. In Warumungu there is no verbal auxiliary and pronouns do not occur as bound forms. A special feature of this language is the occurrence of a large set of pronominal forms which are complexes of subject and object. These complexes, which often take forms which cannot be derived as compounds of the independent subject and object pronouns, function as free forms and can either precede or follow the verb.

In Kaytej and Anmatyerre there are no verb conjugations. However, there are a number of tenses that are not found in the other languages and there are suffixes that attach to the verb stem, preceding the tense suffix, that indicate number. There is no verbal auxiliary and pronouns occur as free forms only. For dual and plural pronouns there are different forms according to the nature of the kin relationship of the persons referred to (see Chapter 8 for an explanation of this for Kaytej).

Phonologically, Warlpiri, Warlmanpa and Mudbura are quite similar to one another as they are also to Warumungu. Warumungu is distinctive, however, in that it has two series of stops that contrast in length. Kaytej and Anmatyerre display the distinctive phonological characteristics of the Arandic languages. When compared to Warlpiri, for example, they show extensive initial dropping of consonants and often of the following vowel with the result that many words that appear to be very different on the surface are in fact closely related. For example, *purlka* 'old man' in Warlpiri becomes *erlkwe* in Kaytej. They also employ nasally released stops which do not occur in the other languages considered here.

There are, of course, substantial vocabulary differences between these languages (Table 12.3, p.380 presents some illustrative lexicostatistics); however there are also many borrowings and words which are shared by several of them. Especially to be noted is the frequent occurrence of the same word in two or more different languages, but with quite different meanings. This feature is thought to be related to the practice of borrowing a word from another language to replace one that is phonologically similar to the name of someone recently deceased. Several of these languages, notably Warlpiri, have a large number of synonyms which also may have arisen as replacement words for those which become taboo as a result of a death.

The relationship between these linguistic differences and differences in sign language will be discussed in Chapter 12. As we shall see, these differences do correlate to some extent. However, geographical proximity and degree of interaction between groups also play an important role so that, for instance, although the southern Warlpiri and the Anmatyerre speak very different languages, they yet share far more in common in regard to sign language than these Warlpiri do with the Warlmanpa, despite the closeness of the latter two languages. In Chapter 12 we shall put forward a number of reasons why neighboring groups should maintain different spoken languages, and yet come to have much in common in respect to their sign languages. Evidently sign languages diffuse and differentiate according to somewhat different principles from spoken languages.

4.6 Ritual contexts of sign language use

As mentioned in Chapter 3, in the North Central Desert speech taboos are observed in connection with male initiation, but the main circumstance in which they are observed is in connection with mourning, when kinswomen of the deceased may remain silent for prolonged periods and use only sign language for communication. Here the main features of these ceremonials will be outlined to indicate the place of speech taboos within them. Detailed accounts of both initiation and burial and mourning rites can be found in Spencer and Gillen (1904) for the Anmatyerre, Kaytej and Warumungu and in Meggitt (1962) for the Warlpiri. Bell (1983) provides important material on the role of women in these ceremonies, based mainly on fieldwork carried out between 1976 and 1978 among the Kaytej at Warrabri.

Male initiation. Male initiation ceremonial follows a broadly similar pattern in all groups. When a boy reaches about thirteen years of age, or begins to show signs of puberty, he is removed from the general camp and taken into seclusion by his sister's husband, who is his guardian throughout the ceremonies, and an elder brother. This event is attended by several ceremonies which serve to mark the boy's departure from the company of his family, especially from his mother, and his separation from women. A number of totemic ceremonies are also performed, the first of a long series in which the novice receives instruction. After these initial ceremonies, which may last a few days, the novice is then taken on a long journey by his guardian and an elder brother.[10] On this journey he learns the topography of the region, its flora and fauna and is instructed in the skills of hunting and finding water. He is introduced to his more remote relatives who are invited to attend the circumcision ceremony. This takes place soon after the novice's return from his wanderings, which may last two or three months. The operation itself is preceded and succeeded by an important series of ceremonies. These include ceremonies which serve to instruct the novice further in the totemic mysteries and in the Dreamtime Law and ceremonies in which again he bids farewell to the womenfolk and playmates of his childhood. There is also a ceremony in which the boy's 'mother-in-law' is nominated. Among the Kaytej, at least, as Bell (1983) describes it, in the course of this ceremony, the boy is brought to a place where his 'mother-in-law' is sitting and she, covered in red ochre, rubs her body against his. This action is regarded as comparable to rubbing against a sacred object to absorb its power. Thereafter, the 'mother-in-law' is considered to be in a highly dangerous state and must observe a speech taboo until the whole process of initiation is completed.

Circumcision is performed by three men, who may be the novice's future wife's father, wife's mother's brother or a mother's brother's son. This latter person is the equivalent of a future wife's father for the initiate. The actual operation is carried out by one man, preferably someone who can be a father-in-law to the boy (i.e. a maternal nephew). After he has been circumcised the novice again goes into seclusion for two or three months. He is not reintegrated into normal daily life until after he has been formally reintroduced to his circumciser who, following the operation, has regarded the boy as 'dead'. When he rejoins the normal life of the tribe the youth now spends most of his time with the single men and may now attend many totemic ceremonies or increase ceremonies from which he had previously been barred.

From the time the boy is seized and taken into seclusion until after circumcision is completed, he is enjoined to remain silent as far as possible. The extent to which he learns to use signs, however, appears to vary. As mentioned in Chapter 3, signs were used by novices for extended periods among the Mudbura and Djingili and probably also among the Warlmanpa. However, this appears to be much less true of the Warlpiri. Meggitt (1962 and personal communication 1985) suggests that the novice is expected to communicate as little as possible and thus any signing that he may do is of a quite rudimentary character.

The novice is released from all restrictions on communication in a special ceremony. Among the Warlpiri this takes place between the novice and his circumciser upon their first meeting after the operation. On this occasion gifts of food are exchanged and the circumciser touches the boy's mouth with some of the vegetable food the boy has brought. Thereafter he is allowed to speak. Among the Warumungu gifts of food are exchanged with the men of the novice's wife's matriline and these men hold out their hands so the novice may bite their fingers. Among the Anmatyerre and Kaytej the novice is released from silence after circumcision in a ceremony in which he exchanges gifts of food with his mothers and sisters. They touch his mouth with a yam and this releases him from silence and permits him to speak with his mothers and sisters.

The ceremony of circumcision is recognized more or less explicitly as a ceremony in which the boy is killed (Meggitt 1962, p. 294) and there are many aspects of the behavior of others that are reminiscent of mourning. Here, it is particularly relevant to note that women may not utter the names of the initiates at any time and at several different stages of the initiation process the boys' sisters and mothers and future mothers-in-law wail and engage in other activities that are also observed at a real death.This includes the observance of speech taboos and the use of sign language by the mothers and potential mothers-in-law of the boys (Dail-Jones 1984; Dussart, personal communication). In addition, during certain stages of the ceremonies the mothers of the initiates are also regarded as 'dead'. Their names may not be uttered and they may only be referred to by sign language.

At a somewhat later stage, and before a boy can marry, he must undergo the operation of subincision. Among the Warlpiri, subincision is carried out two or three years after circumcision. The operation is again associated with seclusion and the revelation of totemic mysteries, although to a much lesser extent. The novice undergoing subincision, however, is not required to be silent but may talk freely (Meggitt 1962, p. 311). Among the Warumungu it is carried out soon after the circumcision wound has healed, and the novice remains under communication restrictions until after it has been completed (Spencer and Gillen 1904, pp. 354-364).

Death and burial. Ceremonials connected with death and burial are also quite similar for all groups in this area and it is in association with these, of course, that speech taboos are most widely observed and that sign language finds its most extensive use. Upon the death of an adult man or woman, the immediate reaction is to wail. The men gash their thighs, the women cut off their hair and gouge their heads with burning firesticks to inflict deep wounds.In traditional practice the body was removed some miles from the main camp and was placed in a platform in a tree and covered with branches. Once this had been done, the period of silence began for those women who were to observe it. Nowadays, women cease to speak from the moment of death and become silent as soon as they have finished wailing. The body is disposed of by burial. Among the Warumungu, at least, a more or less extended ban of silence is observed by the deceased's actual or classificatory wife, mother-in-law, mother, father's sister or sister-in-law. Meggitt (1962, p.323) reports that while the Warlpiri at Hooker Creek and Powell Creek followed this custom, at Yuendumu only the widow must observe the speech taboo. Warlpiri women I spoke with at Yuendumu in 1982, however, stated that the classes of kinswomen of the deceased who must observe it include the deceased's mother, mother's sisters and deceased's mother-in-law and her sisters, as well as actual and classificatory widows.[11] Note that the speech taboo is not observed for a deceased parent, nor is it observed for a deceased sibling. The speech taboo is observed for varying lengths of time, according to the closeness of the relative to the deceased, the status of the deceased, and the extent to which the death was expected. In general, the speech taboo would be observed for only short periods after the death of a very old person or a baby, but for much longer periods after the death of someone in the prime of life, especially if a man, or someone very prominent in ritual. The widows maintain it for as long as it takes for the spirit of the deceased to be avenged, however. This is often about a year.

If the death is due to wounds inflicted by a known person, it may be avenged by having the killer punished by spearing or even by having him killed. Where the death is not caused in this way, and provided the person is neither very old nor a small baby, the death may be considered due to sorcery and an inquest is held to determine the culprit. This is carried out by the men of the deceased's matriline. The traditional procedure was as follows. The men conducting the inquiry visit the corpse in the hope of encountering the ghost, who may be hanging about and who may be questioned about the identity of the killer. When making such a visit the party attempts to remain as silent and as inconspicuous as possible. As mentioned in Chapter 3, Spencer and Gillen (1904, also in Spencer 1928) describe one such visit to a Warumungu tree burial and they report that members of the party, all males, communicated by signs. If the ghost is not met with, the tree and the ground beneath are carefully examined for clues. The direction of flow of any fluids that have dripped from the body may give a clue as to the direction of the killer's camp. The tracks of animals or insects in the sand may also provide clues. The body is also inspected for any unusual marks, fissures or discharges. The position of these on the body may indicate the kin relationship of the killer to the deceased. For instance, if the fissure is in the shoulder, the person may be a younger brother, if in the thigh an older brother, and so on. The body parts 'read' in this manner are the same as those that are touched in signing kin relations (see Chapter 11). Once the various clues have been noted and pondered, a decision is made as to who the killer might be. An attempt will then be made to punish him, either by magical means, or by means of a revenge expedition in which a party of men seek him out and spear the killer to death.

Eventually, when the corpse has fully dried out, the skeleton is taken out of the tree and its bones are smashed up and tipped into an ant's nest. The arm bones, however, are brought back bound up in a special wallet of hairstring. Among the Warlpiri these bones may then be circulated among the deceased's mother's brothers and used by them in sorcery. Among the

Warumungu, as described by Spencer and Gillen, the arm bone is brought back to the main camp and after a short period of time in which it is kept by a mother of the deceased a ceremony is then performed at which it is smashed and then buried in a small hole. Thereafter, the spirit of the deceased is thought to go back to the location from whence it came, there to reside with the other spirits of the same totem until it returns, reincarnated in someone else.

After these final ceremonies the women observing the speech taboo may be released from it in a special 'mouth opening' ceremony. The actual way in which this is enacted varies from one group to another. Among the Warlpiri, this ceremony is conducted by the woman's husband's mother's brother (in the case of a widow) or the woman's elder brother (in the case of a bereaved mother). In this ceremony the woman prepares food and paints herself with white stripes. She then squats near a low mound in the middle of the general camp. The men of the deceased's matriline and of the woman's matriline gather round and touch the woman on the head with a switch of leaves. They then rub some of the food the woman has prepared on her mouth so that it may be opened. Thereafter she is permitted to speak. Among the Warumungu the speech taboo is lifted by the woman's classificatory sons. The woman presents food to the men who are releasing her and she then bites a finger of each one of them.

The explanation for the observance of the mourning speech ban generally given is that those who observe it are "too sorry" to speak. Further, however, since the ghost of the deceased remains in the vicinity until its death has been avenged, it is important not to do anything to attract its attention or to anger it, lest it come back to cause trouble. The voices of the women closest to it may well attract it, hence it is important for them to remain silent, or at least to refrain from producing any articulate speech. Signing may sometimes be accompanied by a sort of grunting. However, a woman observing the speech taboo will keep her mouth clamped tight shut and on no account will she utter an articulated sound.

Although close male relatives of the deceased do not observe a ban of silence they, like everyone else, observe a ban on pronouncing the deceased's name or any word that bears some resemblance in sound to the deceased's name. This can last for a long time and requires that substitute words be found for the words that cannot be pronounced. New words may be invented, resulting in many synonyms in the language, or words from neighboring languages may be borrowed (Nash and Simpson 1981). The signs for the words that may not be pronounced are not replaced, however.[12]

4.7 Other contexts of sign language use

As we indicated in 3.11, among the North Central Desert groups studied here sign language use is not confined to the ritual contexts just described. Among older women, especially, it is in frequent use, whether a speech ban is being observed or not. It is used as an accompaniment to speech, and it is used as an alternate mode of communication when speaking is too great an effort or when, as where people are separated by some distance, talking loudly is either inappropriate or too much trouble. Thus, Dail-Jones (1984), working at the Warlpiri settlement of Willowra, writes (p. 176):

> It is during sorry business that sign language becomes an important and predominant form of communication for certain female relatives. Even if a woman is not under a speech ban, she must still be able to understand the signs of those who are. After the deaths of two old men in Willowra in June 1982, many closely related women were still under a speech ban six months later. Possibly due to the fact that often the only means for communication for women is sign language, older women tend to use sign language continuously, even when they are not under a speech ban. [I]n Willowra sign language is used throughout the year by the older women, to either accompany verbal communication, or to serve as a substitute for it.

Dail-Jones also notes some other occasions when sign language is prominently used. She observed that the mothers (both real and classificatory) of the boys who were undergoing initiation would, at certain stages in the ceremony, engage in sorrowing, including the observance of a speech ban and the use of sign language. She also observed the use of sign language during verbal fighting. Typically, women arguing will stand up and shout at one another, at the same time extending their arms fully forward and signing with great emphasis at the same time.

Françoise Dussart, while studying women's art and ritual at Yuendumu, has also made a number of observations on sign language use in daily life.[13] She notes that the very old women, who almost never leave the *jilimi* (single women's quarters), use sign language a great deal, both when making requests and when asking about people coming into the camps (especially if it is a stranger), and also in self-directed monologues. In response, the younger women who look after them often reply to them in sign language.

Another context of sign language use that Dussart noted is when someone is angry. Thus when a woman is very angry about something another has done, in discussing it she may switch into sign language. Sign language is likewise used when a woman is gossiping about another or saying things she intends for only a very limited audience. Another common context of sign language use is at the clinic. Women waiting for the attention of the

Fig. 4.6 Warlpiri women conversing in sign language near Yuendumu. From 16mm film, YSL XIII (1978)

Fig. 4.7 Warlpiri women conversing in sign langauge at Yuendumu. The woman in the center is observing a speech taboo. Note the spatial arrangement of the participants. From 16mm film YSL IV (1978)

nurse or doctor will exchange information about their symptoms in sign language (although if really sick, they do not talk at all, but merely groan).

When women are making preparations for ritual, sign language may also be used extensively. Sign language will be used, in particular, when discussing Dreaming sequences, especially those which are related to men's secret ceremonies or to men's ceremonies in joint ceremonial. Using sign language in this context is a way of showing one's respect for what one talks of. It is also a way of talking quietly about something which the speaker may not be entitled to know or to speak of. Sign language may also be used when referring to especially powerful or important parts of the ritual that is in preparation. This observation is corroborated by Bell (1983, p. 36), who writes: "During initiation time I was often alerted to women's precise knowledge of male rituals, but it was not for open discussion. The information was transmitted in signs or in the songs, dances and designs of rituals at which I was present."

Thus, apart from its convenience as a form of communication when speech is difficult, use of sign language in non-ritual contexts seems to be commonest for matters that are of a private nature or for matters which are regarded as deserving of respect. The use of sign language when one is angry perhaps serves both as a way of drawing attention to what one is saying, but also as a way of reducing the aggressive impact of one's utterances.

These observations are quite similar to those of Glowczewski (1983) who worked among the Warlpiri at Lajamanu (Hooker Creek). She notes the use of signing by women in mourning, but adds (p. 238, n. 2): "I was able to note that this [sign] language is used to 'speak' of sacred, secret things but also for gossip and to calm anger. Often women on the point of arguing would suddenly stop speaking and continue communicating through gestures. We could perhaps interpret the use of this language as a means of controlling different emotions."

As we stated in 3.11, at Yuendumu it is generally accepted that only women use sign language, although we suggested that there are some indications that further to the north sign language knowledge and use may be less exclusively confined to women than it is in the south. A systematic survey of sign language use at Yuendumu undertaken in 1982 (Kendon 1984) amply confirmed men's ignorance of sign language. Although men were asked to participate in this survey, very few did so, and those that did showed very little knowledge of sign language. From my experience in other communities, also, it seemed clear that it is the women who are regarded as the experts in sign language. Thus at the outset of my visits to the Anmatyerre at Ti Tree and the Kaytej at Tara it was made clear to me that only the women would be able to show me sign language. However, although men in these communities make no claim to use sign language, it seems likely that they have some competence in it and probably do make use of some elements from the sign language occasionally. From the survey carried out at Yuendumu it appears that almost everyone in the community knows and uses a small number of signs - including, for example, signs for 'no', 'wait', a general interrogative sign, signs for common activities such as 'playing cards' and 'hunting'. Signs for such common items as 'water', 'tea', 'chewing tobacco', 'money' and the like are also quite widely known, as are signs for some of the main kin terms such as 'spouse', 'father' and 'siblings'. However, knowledge of an extensive vocabulary of signs and ability to use this in daily conversation is confined to women over the age of thirty. There is a clear relationship between the frequency with which a woman has experienced bereavement and her ability to use sign language. However, it is also clear that the learning of sign language is an integral part of becoming a member of the circle of older women who are most deeply interested in women's ritual life. Knowledge of sign language, thus, is a mark of being 'in the know' in respect to 'women's business' as well as being something that is needed in order to be able to cope with periods of mourning.

Meggitt (1954, and personal communication 1985) observed men making some use of sign language during his period of fieldwork with the Warlpiri at Hooker Creek (now Lajamanu) beginning in 1953. He observed much sign language use in 'silent hunting' (i.e. hunting without a motor vehicle) and also by men during initiation ceremonies when they did not want the novices to know what was in store for them. The novices themselves were placed under communication restrictions and could use sign language. However, he adds that there was little incentive for them to learn an elaborate system since all communication was discouraged. At later stages in the initiation process novices learn a special language (*jirliwirri* - described by Hale 1971). An actual ban on speech, thus, is not maintained for very extended periods in Warlpiri initiation. Meggitt (1954 and personal communication 1985) observed, in the 1950's, that women used sign language to a greater extent than men, and that they commanded a much fuller knowledge of it. He agrees with me (see Kendon 1984, p. 557) that men may have made more use of sign language in earlier times than today. However, he thinks that they never used it in as wide a range of circumstances as women, and thus never commanded the extensive vocabularies that women commanded in the past and do still today.

4.8 Gathering sign language material

Work on gathering sign language material was begun in 1978 with Warlpiri women at Yuendumu. In that year, two visits were made, each of about two months. A third visit of three months was made to Yuendumu in 1981 and a fourth visit of two months was made in 1982. Work on gathering sign language materials from other groups in the North Central Desert was undertaken in 1984 and 1985 and in 1986 I made another visit to Yuendumu to make video-recordings of sign demonstrations for the purposes of creating a video dictionary of Warlpiri sign language.

In 1978, about 600 signs were elicited using a Warlpiri vocabulary and they were recorded in notation and verbal description. Photographs of handshapes were made and about 10,000 ft of 16 mm sound synchronized film was exposed, recording sign language in use in a number of different informal situations. I also recorded several narrations in sign language, and from three different women sign language translations of about seventy test sentences were recorded which were designed to explore ways in which various aspects of Warlpiri grammar are rendered in sign. These materials were shown to the individuals who appeared in them and were glossed by them into Warlpiri.

In 1981 I worked intensively for three months with two women, Winnie Nangala and Ruby Nangala Robertson. Most of this work was in the form of elicitation sessions, as far as possible carried out in Warlpiri. All elicitation sessions were video-taped and the signs recorded were subsequently transcribed to index cards. I began by using prepared lists of words for which sign equivalents were sought, organized by semantic domain. However, as the sessions progressed my informants often volunteered new examples. I often attempted to engage in sign conversation and Ruby and Winnie, as well as others often conversed informally in sign among themselves, much of which was recorded. In this way, many new signs were obtained, together with much material pertinent to their use. All signs recorded in 1978 were re-elicited and recorded on video-tape and an effort was made to record examples of all signs at least twice. For many signs there are often many more than two examples recorded, however, especially as at least two women were almost always present whenever sign language work was being done. Also, in 1981, the correctness of my rendering of many signs was checked by 'reading' signs back to informants from the notation that had been made for it and asking them for recognition. In this way, notations could be checked and amended where necessary. In addition, several more sign narrations were video-taped and spoken versions of the same narrations were also recorded, for the purposes of comparison (see Chapter 9 for some analysis of this). Still photographs of several hundred signs were also made.

In 1982 I undertook to survey the extent of knowledge of sign language at Yuendumu (Kendon 1984). In this work I interviewed upwards of sixty women, ranging in age from fifteen to over sixty years of age, using a standard elicitation list of 172 items. Not only did this yield information directly relevant to the question at hand, but, in the course of these sessions, many new signs were also recorded and, naturally, I also took the opportunity to work with women I had come to know well from previous visits to check examples brought up in the survey work and to continue to expand the general sign language vocabulary. In all, about 1500 Warlpiri signs have been recorded. In 1986, all these signs were re-recorded by my two main informants in a systematic fashion to provide a tape that will serve as a video component of a Warlpiri sign language dictionary.[14]

During all of these visits, in addition to the more or less formal elicitation sessions and narration recording sessions, I went on many 'hunting' and firewood gathering expeditions and a number of other excursions. On these occasions much information was provided about the signs for the plants, animals and topographical features encountered. Furthermore, since many women in addition to my regular informants joined these expeditions, I was often able to confirm signs from a wide range of different people.

The work in gathering sign language material from other language groups was carried out in a similar manner. During this phase of the work my visits in each case lasted only a few weeks and, except in the case of the work on Warumungu and Warlmanpa sign language at Tennant Creek, return visits were not made. On my second visit to Tennant Creek it was possible to check further on signs previously recorded, and also to extend the material in the light of what had been gathered before. A systematic video-tape recording of all Warumungu signs collected was made by Bunny Narrurla and Annie Philips Narrurla during this second visit and it is hoped that a dictionary of Warumungu signs, similar to the one for Warlpiri, will eventually be made available. The vocabularies collected include about 900 signs each for Warumungu and Warlmanpa, upwards of 500 for Anmatyerre and Kaytej, about 400 for Mudbura and 300 for Djingili. These vocabularies are not exhaustive, but they contain material that pertains to all of the semantic domains that are important in these cultures, except secret-sacred domains.

In all of this work, initially, as elicitation material, vocabularies drawn up in advance were used, but once the work got underway elicitation became a highly collaborative process with informants often taking the initiative in what aspects of vocabulary should be explored. All sessions were video-taped and I always set up a monitor so that the sign language experts, as well as myself, could see what was being recorded. In this way informants were often able to correct their own performances on the spot in cases where there were errors or an insufficiently clear recording had been made.

Notes

[1]Nash (1984) gives annual rainfall figures for Tennant Creek between 1874 and 1984. Meggitt (1962) provides rainfall figures for various parts of Warlpiri territory.

[2]This section owes much to Meggitt (1962), for Warlpiri, Spencer and Gillen (1904) for Anmatyerre, Kayte and Warumungu, and Bell (1983) for Kaytej and Anmatyerre. I am also indebted to Nicolas Peterson and Françoise Dussart for comments and additional pieces of information.

[3]When performed by men, such ceremonies have been termed 'increase' ceremonies and these are recognized among the Warlpiri, for instance, as being an activity of a highly specific sort. There is a special verb that refers to this type of activity which is used only by men and only in reference to these ceremonies.

[4] For a discussion of sign language use by male novices in the North Central Desert, see below.

[5]Meggitt (1962) and Bell (1983) contain useful discussions and summaries. For more detail see Hill (1951) and Rowley (1970, 1976), among others. See Young (1981) for an account of the present day economy of two north central desert settlements, Yuendumu and Willowra.

[6]Hence the name it was given: 'Warra' from the first two syllables of 'Warramunga' and 'bri' from the last syllable of 'Warlbri' (Bell 1983, p. 72).

[7]See Nash (1984) for a history of Aboriginal experience in Tennant Creek.

[8]As proposed by Meggitt (1962). Some authorities recognize fewer divisions than this.

[9]See Wurm (1972), Dixon (1980), Wurm and Hattori (1981), Yallop (1984) and Blake (1987). For specific languages see Hale (1974, 1983), Swartz (1982) and Nash (1985) for Warlpiri; Green (1984) and Purle, Green and Heffernan (n.d.) for Anmatyerre; Koch (n.d.) for Kaytej; Evans (1982) for Warumungu; Nash (1979) for Warlmanpa and Chadwick (1975) for Djingili. Information on Mudbura taken from Nash (Unpublished manuscripts).

[10]This journey is much curtailed or omitted in present day initiations. Indeed, the whole procedure is much shortened, usually so that it fits within the school holiday period.

[11]Françoise Dussart, of Australian National University, who studied women's art and ritual at Yuendumu between 1983 and 1985, confirms this statement. Does this difference with Meggitt's report reflect poor information on the part of his informants (who were not living at Yuendumu) or does this suggest that the southern Warlpiri, since Meggitt wrote, have adopted Warumungu and northern Warlpiri practices?

[12]At least, not as far as I have been able to observe.

[13]I am very grateful to Mlle Dussart for making her unpublished notes on sign language use at Yuendumu available to me.

[14]This is to be made available from the Australian Institute of Aboriginal Studies, Canberra.

5 Sign structure

5.0 Introduction

We begin our study of the sign languages of the North Central Desert (the NCD sign languages, as we shall refer to them) with an examination of the parts of the body that are employed in the production of signs, and how they are organized and moved to produce the contrastive configurations of action that function as lexical units in these languages.

Signs, in any sign language, are produced by distinctive patterns of movement and postures of the body. In all sign languages, to any observer, the most salient parts of the body employed in signing are the arms and hands. Other parts of the body are often involved, however. First of all, movements of the hands and arms may often be done in relation to a particular part of the body, such as the forehead, the nose, chin, the chest, and so on. For example, in Warlpiri, to sign *ngurra* 'camp' (Fig. 5.1), with all the fingers curled together, one places the hand in contact with the cheek. Second, some signs may involve movements of the face, eyes or head. Thus, in Warlpiri, the sign for *wita* 'small' (Fig. 5.2) includes a wrinkling of the nose, as well as a hand action. The use of the face as part of signing is uncommon in the NCD sign languages, however, although in primary sign languages it is of particular importance.

A manual sign can be analyzed as a phrase of movement in which the hand or hands are moved away from a rest position towards some region in space or towards some part of the body, and then away again. As the hand approaches this location, the hand itself comes to assume a distinctive organization, or *handshape*. That is to say, the fingers of the hand come to be disposed in a particular fashion - curled together into a fist, held straight out, splayed wide apart, or any one of the five digits alone, or in combination with one or more others, may be extended. A very large number of different handshapes are possible, of course, but a given sign language is found to make use of just a few - typically about forty. Sign languages differ in terms of which handshapes they make use of.

In performing a sign, the hand not only comes to assume a particular shape as it approaches the apex of its excursion. It may also engage in a characteristic movement, which is distinct from the preparatory movement by

Fig. 5.1 NGURRA 'camp'

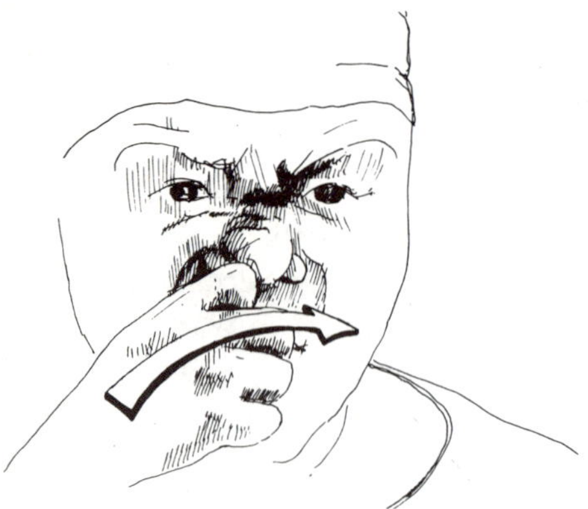

Fig. 5.2 WITA 'small'

which the hand is transported to the sign's location of articulation. For example, in Warlpiri, to sign *lawa* 'no', the hand is held with all five fingers extended and spread so that the palm of the hand is facing to the signer's left.[1] The forearm is then rapidly pronated, 'flipping' the hand with a rotary movement to the right (Fig. 5.3). It will be seen that, before this movement is performed, the hand must be moved forward into a suitable space in front of the signer. Such a preparatory phase of the movement phrase by which the sign is enacted is not part of what is distinctive for this sign and it is ignored in the systematic notation system that will be described later. The 'flipping' movement is distinctive, however. If the hand, again with the same shape and orientation, is moved into the same initial position and then is rotated back and forth on the forearm, rather than being 'flipped' to the right, this would be a way of doing a sign for *jarrampayi* 'large lizard, sp.'.

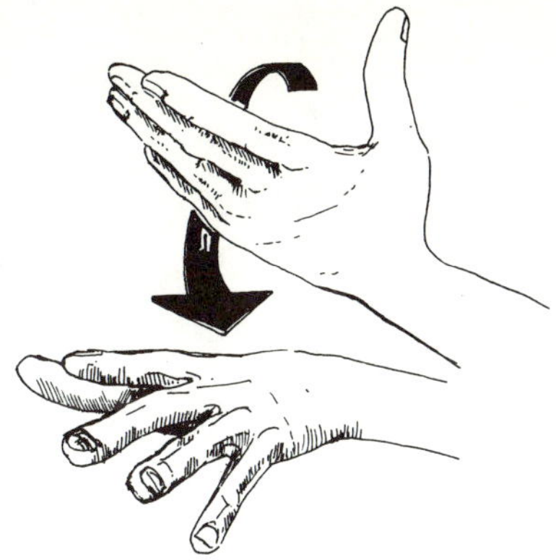

Fig. 5.3 LAWA 'no'. This sign serves for a wide range of negating expressions

Although, as we shall see, the majority of signs in NCD sign languages are adequately performed with one hand, a significant proportion in each require two hands. In some of these two handed signs, both hands assume the same handshape and perform the same pattern of movement simultaneously. However, there are many signs in which one hand acts in relation to the other. Typically, the left hand is held out to serve as something the right hand can touch, or move in relation to. The sign for 'short, cut off (as a piece of wood)'in both Warlpiri (*rdankarlpa)* and Warumunugu (*parlkarr*)the left hand is held as a fist, while the right hand, with fingers spread and with the palm facing downwards, is lowered sharply to contact the left hand (Fig. 5.4). In one Warlpiri sign for *maniyi* 'money', common at Yuendumu, the left hand is held flat, fingers extended with the palm up while the right hand, with only the index finger extended, makes a circular movement on the palm of the left hand (Fig. 5.5).

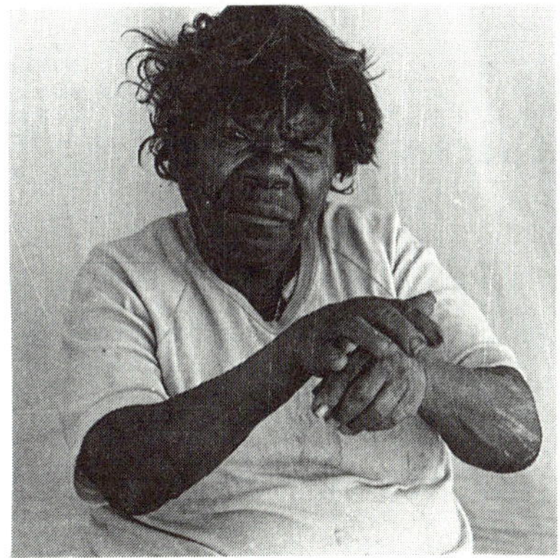

Fig. 5.4 RDANKARLPA (Warlpiri), PARLKARR (Warumungu) 'short, cut off'

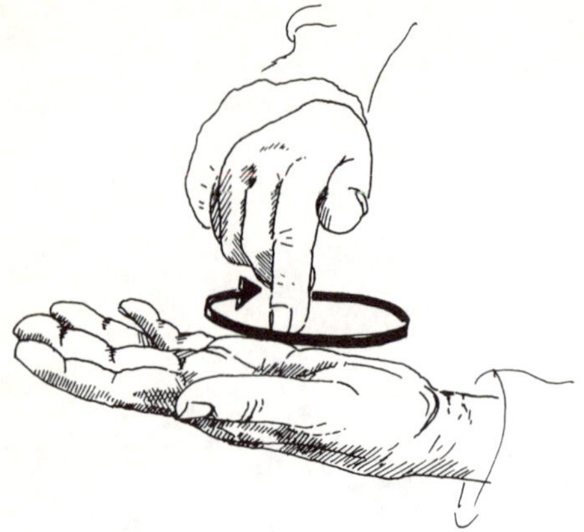

Fig. 5.5 MANIYI 'money' (Yuendumu)

As we shall see, it is possible to describe signs systematically in terms of the locations used, the handshapes assumed, the patterns of movement employed and, in the case of two handed signs, in terms of how the hands are related to one another as the sign is performed. In these terms we shall see that sign structure is fundamentally the same in all the sign languages here considered. That is, the NCD sign languages are very similar to one another in the extent to which the signs are produced by one or two hands, the extent to which non-manual body parts are involved, in the range of non-manual body parts involved, the range of distinct handshapes used and the patterns of movement employed in their enactment. In comparison with primary sign languages such as American Sign Language (ASL) or British Sign Language (BSL), however, there are some important differences. In contrast to these sign languages, NCD sign languages make almost no use of facial action in sign formation, the great majority of signs are adequately performed with only one hand, and the range of handshapes employed and the range of body-locations used is significantly different.

5.1 Some principles for analysis

In presenting an account of the structure of signs in these Australian Aboriginal sign languages we have followed the approach originally developed by Stokoe (1960, 1978) for the description of signs in American Sign Language. Following his most recent formulation (Stokoe 1978), we regard signs as actions which can be viewed in terms of three aspects. These aspects are *what* acts, the *action* taken and *where* the action is done. These we shall here term *Sign Actor, Sign Action*, and *Sign Location*, respectively. *Sign Actor* refers to the body parts employed in the production of the sign and how they are organized as they do so. *Sign Action* refers to the pattern of action that is undertaken to produce the sign. *Sign Location* refers to where the Sign Actor is placed as it carries out the Action that is characteristic of the sign. Signs may be compared with one another in terms of Sign Actor configurations, Sign Action patterns and Sign Locations. A sign language can be shown to have repertoires of distinctive Sign Actor organizations, movement patterns and locations. Comparisons between sign languages may be made in terms of the items within each of these aspects that they make use of.

It will be noted that I have followed Stokoe in maintaining that there are only three aspects in terms of which a sign should be viewed. A number of sign linguists have suggested that a fourth aspect be distinguished, that of the orientation of the hand in respect to the signer's body (e.g. Friedman 1977). It has been suggested that, because there are a number of signs which differ only in how the hand is oriented, orientation should be established as a fourth aspect. Certainly, there are examples of NCD signs that would support this. For instance, 'elder sibling' in all NCD sign languages studied is signed by patting the thigh with the back of the hand. To sign 'cousin' (more precisely, Mother's Brother's Child or Father's Sister's Child) one also pats the thigh, but with the palm of the hand. How the hand is held, however, whether with the forearm in pronation so the palm faces downwards or with the forearm in supination so the palm faces upwards, or whether it is held in some position in between, is part of the way in which the entire articulator of a sign is organized, along with the finger arrangement, so that the sign may be carried out. Orientation is thus really but part of the aspect what acts, or Sign Actor, as we have termed it. It does not emerge as a further aspect on the same level as Sign Location or Sign Action.

To distinguish orientation as if it were a fourth aspect adds difficulties to the description, as soon as we deal with signs in which the orientation of the hand changes as part of the action, and there are very many of these. In the case of the sign for *lawa* 'no' mentioned above, for instance, are we to specify the orientation at the beginning of the sign's action, or at the end, or are we to introduce a symbol to indicate how it changes? To do this is to introduce an approach to the analysis of signs that requires us to describe how the sign develops over time which is quite different from the aspectual approach adopted here (but see Chapters 9 and 10 where how signs are produced as phrases of movement becomes important).[2]

The basic features of the approach to the analysis of signs we have followed here will now be illustrated by a few examples. The sign used in Warlpiri for *wati* 'fully initiated man' is performed by moving a hand rapidly across the upper chest with the fingers held in a certain arrangement

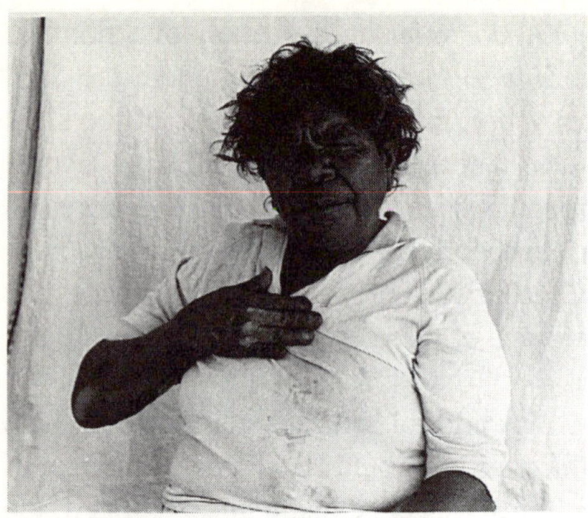

Fig. 5.6 WATI 'man, fully initiated'. Hand drawn across upper chest

Fig. 5.7 YAWULYU 'Women's ceremonies, etc.' Hand drawn across upper chest

Fig. 5.8 NGAPA 'water' Hand taps center of upper chest twice

(Fig. 5.6). The Sign Actor here is the right forelimb, with the hand held so that all of the fingers are fully extended and adducted (held together - the hand is a 'flat' hand). The Sign Action consists in moving the hand rapidly from left to right (together, also, with some flexion of the fingers) and the Sign Location is the upper chest in association with which this movement is performed.

The sign WATI may be compared with the Warlpiri sign for *yawulyu* 'women's ceremonies' in which Sign Action and Sign Location remain the same; however the Sign Actor is now different. The fingers of the hand are now arranged so that only the index and second fingers are extended and held in abduction, the fingers thus forming the shape of a V (Fig. 5.7). It will be seen, thus, that the use of the 'flat' hand in WATI and the use of the V hand in YAWULYU is what serves to contrast these two signs.

On the other hand WATI contrasts with a sign for *ngapa* 'water' because the Sign Action is different. Sign Location is still the upper chest and the Sign Actor is still the right forelimb with the hand held in a 'flat' arrangement as in WATI. However in the Sign Action the center of the upper chest is touched twice in rapid succession by the fingertips of the hand, and in this the sign is distinct from the sign WATI (Fig. 5.8).

By systematically comparing signs in regard to these aspects, then, it is possible to establish the range of Sign Actor organizations that a given sign language makes use of, the range of different distinctive movement patterns or Sign Actions and the range of different Sign Locations. Symbols representing the distinctive Sign Actors, Actions and Locations can be established and thus a means by which the sign language may be economically and systematically written down can be devised. A notation system developed according to these principles was devised by Stokoe in his studies of American Sign Language and it is a version of this system that we have employed in the present work.

5.2 Features of the notation system

The symbols employed in this notation are based on those originally proposed by Stokoe, although we have found it necessary to add a number of new ones and some of the conventions adopted by Stokoe have been altered.[3] A complete list , with definitions, will be found in Appendix I.

For noting Sign Location symbols based on pictographs for parts of the body are used. For Sign Actor arbitrary labels for the hand postures encountered are used, together with a limited number of symbols to represent arm position, where needed, and directional symbols to indicate hand orientation. The labels employed for hand postures are derived originally from the letters used to label the hand forms used for the letters of the English alphabet in American finger spelling. For Sign Action there are symbols to indicate direction and manner of movement, nature and point of contact between active hand and passive hand or other body part, if this is présent, and certain other devices. There are also some additional symbols used to indicate relative position of the hands in two handed signs and a small set of operator symbols which serve to instruct the reader in how to read the symbol strings.

5.2.1 The basic formula

In writing down a sign the symbols are arranged in a special order, according to the following formula:

$$\mathsf{L}\ \ \mathsf{ap}\mathsf{HS}_{\mathsf{OR}}\ \mathsf{AC}$$

where L is Sign Location; **ap**, **HS** and OR are the three components of the Sign Actor - arm position, hand shape and orientation; AC is the Sign Action.

For example, the sign for *purlka* 'old man', in Warlpiri, is written in the following way:

$$\mathsf{O}{<}5_{\mathsf{T}\wedge}{}^{\mathsf{I}}$$

where O , the Location, refers to the face; <5 is the hand shape - in this case a shape in which the fingers are all extended and spread apart but at the same time are slightly flexed, so the hand is shaped somewhat like a basket,[4] the two subscripted symbols indicate the orientation of the hand in respect to the face - here they show that the hand is held so that the palm is toward the signer's face but the metacarpals point vertically; the superscripted symbol ^{I} is the Sign Action symbol and it indicates that the hand, held in the shape indicated, and before the face of the signer, is moved forward and back in a movement of short amplitude. The sign is illustrated in Fig. 5.9.

In many signs there are features of the Sign Actor (especially hand shape) that alter as a result of the Sign Action, or that alter in the course of it. In writing down a sign where this is to be shown, the organization of the Sign Actor is always noted at the point of commencement of Sign Action. The organization to which it changes is written in square brackets after the Sign Action symbols. Thus,

$$.{<}5_{\wedge\perp}{}^{\vee}[\,\mathsf{to}\,]\,'$$

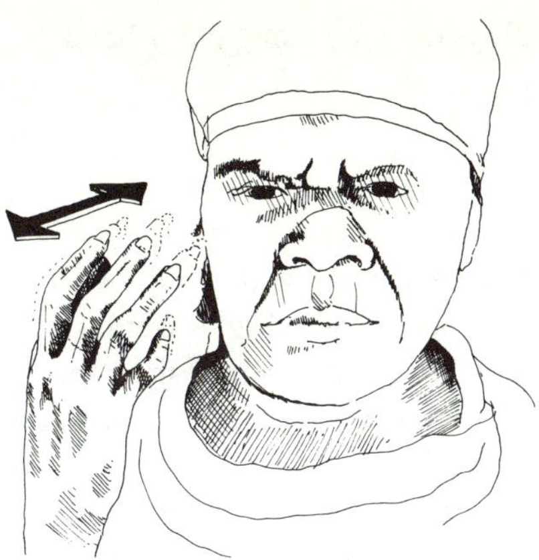

Fig. 5.9 PURLKA 'old man'

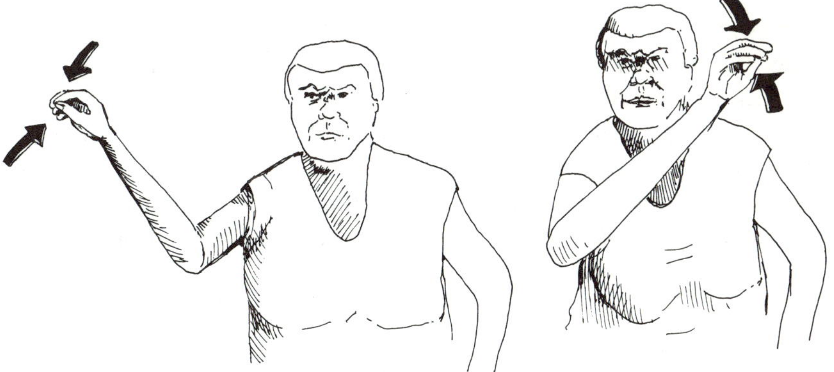

Fig. 5.10 MARNIKIJI 'conkerberry'

represents the Warlpiri sign for *marnikiji* 'conkerberry'. The . preceding the Hand Configuration symbol indicates that the Sign Location is in 'neutral space' (i.e., the sign is not enacted in any special relationship to another part of the signer's body); ᶜ5 is once again the 'basket' handshape, this time held so that the palm faces upwards with the metacarpals pointing away from the signer; the movement symbol ˇ indicates that the hand is moved downwards but, as the square brackets indicate, as the hand is moved downwards it is changed to a new shape, to, in which the fingers are all drawn together to be in contact with their tips. The superscripted ' that follows the square brackets indicates that the movement is repeated. The sign is illustrated in Fig. 5.10.

Where, as in most cases, the Sign Action does not result in a change in hand shape, it may result in a change in the orientation of the hand. It is sometimes a good idea to indicate this. This is done by using curly brackets instead of square ones, thus:

$$.B_{\top\wedge}{}^{\vee}\{_{\wedge\perp}\}$$

Here a 'B' hand (all fingers extended and held together) is held initially so that the palm is facing the signer and the metacarpals are pointing upwards. It is then lowered, but in such a way that at the end of the movement the hand is now oriented so that the palm faces upwards and the metacarpals point away from the signer. This is the sign for the Warlpiri expression *wiyarrpa* 'poor thing'. Note that we place in curly brackets only the orientation symbols. The hand shape symbol does not have to be given because it does not change.

5.2.2 Signs involving two hands

In the sign languages described here most signs are adequately and appropriately performed with one hand only, although it is not uncommon for many such one handed signs to be performed with both hands. This is done as a matter of style, perhaps as an emphasis device. However, approximately one fifth of the signs recorded in any of these sign languages require both hands for proper performance. Such obligatorily two handed signs may be either *symmetrical* or *asymmetrical*. In symmetrical signs both hands assume the same hand shape and they parallel or complement one another in action. In asymmetrical signs one hand plays a subordinate role in relation to the other. It may or may not assume the same shape as the active hand. The active hand may either make contact with the subordinate hand or it may perform its action in relation to it - in which case the subordinate hand serves as the Sign Location of the sign.

In the case of symmetrical two handed signs, the appropriate Hand Configuration symbols are written in sequence, the left hand being written first, with the relationship between the hands in space being given by a symbol placed between the two Hand Configuration symbols to indicate whether they are in parallel, crossed over, or one hand is in front of the other. Thereafter the Sign Action symbol is written in the usual place, and this indicates that both hands act together in the same way. For example:

$$\ulcorner A_{\top >}{}'A_{\top <}{}^{\div}$$

is a sign given at Yuendumu for 'coat' (Fig. 5.11). Here the signer holds her two fisted hands before her chest, palms of the hands facing herself, and she then moves the hands apart. ⊓ refers to the chest, A is the hand shape 'fist'. ' is placed between the two HC symbols to indicate that they act in parallel. ÷ indicates that the two hands are drawn apart. Similarly,

.JA>⊥'JA<⊥˜~

represents one of the signs for *turaki* 'motor car, truck' at Yuendumu. Both hands in 'fist' shape are held up on vertically raised forearms (as indicated by the symbol J in the ap (arm position) position in the formula). Action is again parallel, but we see from the Sign Action symbols that the hands are moved up and down (˜) and in alternation (~) with one another (see Fig. 5.12.).

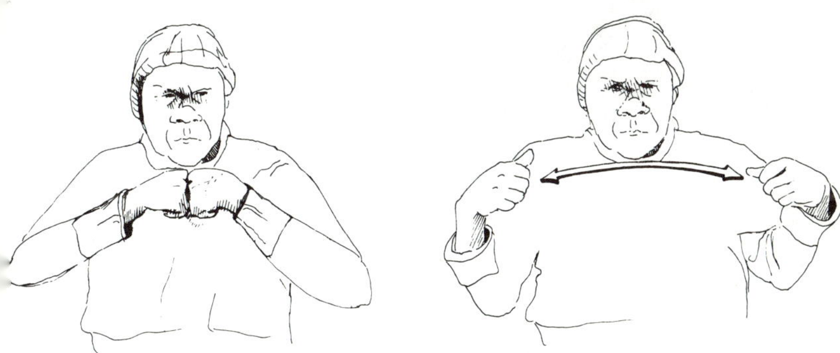

Fig. 5.11 COAT

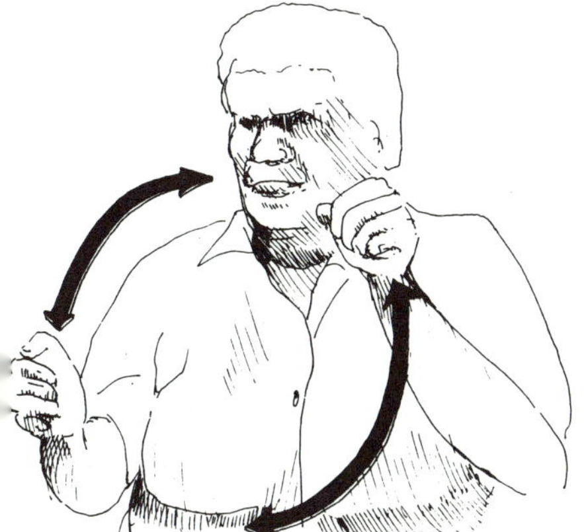

Fig. 5.12 TURAKI (two handed) 'truck, car'

On the other hand in the following (a common sign for 'policeman' at Yuendumu and elsewhere - see Fig. 5.13.):

.JA>⊥ ‡JA<⊥

the two arms are held crossed over. Since, in this case, the two hands do not act in parallel but in *interaction* with one another, the Sign Action symbol is placed between the handshape symbols, rather than after them, as indicated by the ‡ placed between the two HC symbols.

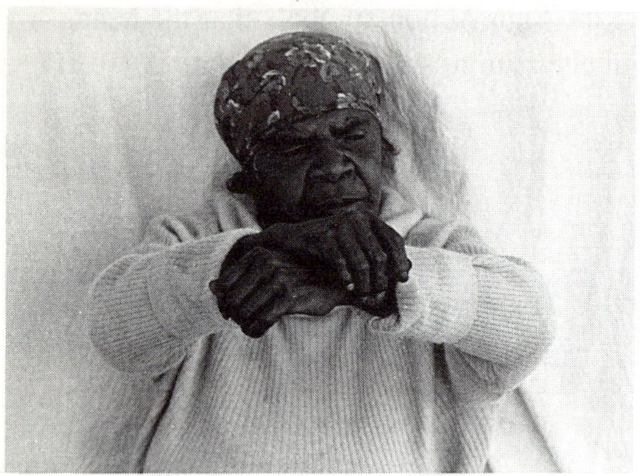

Fig. 5.13 POLICEMAN (Yuendumu)

In asymmetrical signs, in which one hand (almost invariably the left hand) acts in a subordinate manner to the other, again the left hand is indicated first and its subordinate relation to the other hand is shown by the use of a slash being placed after it. For example

.B^⊥\B<⊥ ˇ ʔ ˈ

represents the sign for 'hunting' in several different north central Australian sign languages (see Fig. 5.14.). The sign is enacted in 'neutral' space immediately in front of the signer. Both hands assume the 'B' or 'flat' handshape. The left hand is held with palm up, metacarpals facing away from the signer, while the right hand, held so that the palm faces to the left, is lowered to make contact with the palm of the left hand. The action is done twice (as indicated by the repetition marker) and the contact is made by the tips of the fingers of the right hand (as indicated by the contact symbol ʔ).[5]
Similarly,

.G⊤>\G⊤<@

Fig. 5.14 WIRLINYI 'hunting'. Side of active hand taps palm of subordinate hand twice

represents a Warlpiri sign for *pirdijirri* 'seedcake'. Here both hands assume the 'G' or pointing index finger shape. The left hand is held still while the right hand circles around it.

In a very few instances the subordinate hand is held above the active hand. This is indicated by using a rightward leaning slash rather than a leftward leaning one. Thus the Warlpiri sign for *watiya* 'tree, stick' is written as follows:

$$,G_{\vee\perp}/G_{\wedge<}{}^{\varphi\ \wedge}$$

Here both hands assume the pointing index finger shape. The left hand is held, palm facing downwards, metacarpals pointing away from the signer. The tip of the right index finger, palm held facing upwards, makes contact with the *underside* of the left index finger. It is then moved upwards, the finger sliding out from underneath the left finger it has been in contact with (Fig. 5.15).

Fig. 5.15 WATIYA 'tree, stick'

5.2.3 Compound and complex signs

In all of the sign languages examined here there are many semantically unitary expressions that require the performance of two (and occasionally more) distinct signs. This is well exemplified in Warlpiri or Warlmanpa sign language, for instance, where in the spoken language there are many verbal compounds in which a root verb is combined with a preverb to form a new verbal expression. Such verbal compounds in the spoken language are typically expressed as compounds in the sign language also (see Chapter 7). Signs that occur together in compounds are indicated by a compound juncture marker: ⁞, as in *kurnta jarri-mi* 'to be ashamed'(Fig. 5.16):

$$\mathrm{U}_{\top >} \backslash \Psi_{\top <}^{\ast \top \perp} \,\vdots\vdots\, \mathrm{tG}_{\top \wedge}^{\perp \blacksquare}$$

This is a compound of the sign for *kurnta* 'shame' and the sign for the inchoative verb *jarri-mi* 'to become'.

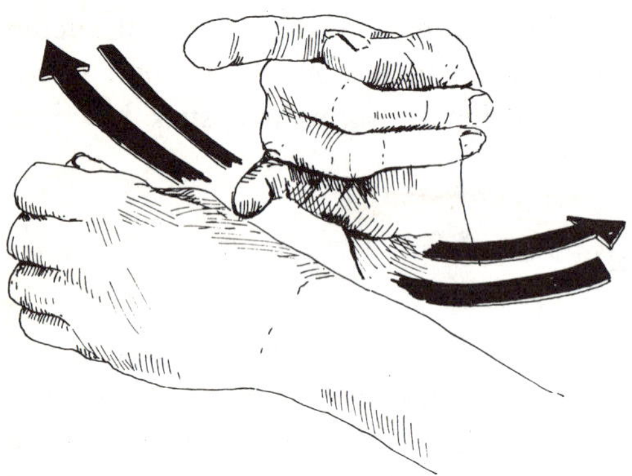

Fig. 5.16 KURNTA 'shame'

In other cases a sign may have two parts to its enactment, but such parts are not separate signs in the sense that there is no juncture between the parts. For example in the sign for the Warlpiri expression *kutukari* 'night' a 'B' hand is first placed, with palm down, so that its side is touching the middle of the upper chest, and then the hand is moved in a large arc away from the signer (see Fig. 5.17). This is written as follows, with the two parts of what will here be termed a *complex* sign separated by the juncture marker ;. Thus:

$$\sqcap \mathrm{B}_{\vee <}^{+} \,;\, \mathrm{B}_{\vee <}^{\perp \wedge \} \vee a}$$

Fig. 5.17 KUTUKARI 'night'

5.2.4 Sign action in the head and face

As mentioned above, the sign languages discussed here to differ from primary sign languages in that the head, and especially the face, is rarely used in actions that are integral to the language system. There are only a few signs where, at least in demonstration or emphatic signing, some facial action is involved. Where this is to be notated it is always placed first, before any Sign Location symbol. Thus the Warlpiri sign for *wita* 'small' involves a movement of the hand in relation to the nose, the nose being 'wrinkled' as this action is performed (see Fig 5.2.). It is written thus:

Z△X$_{T<}^{6\perp)}$

5.3 Sign structure analysis: the sample

With the help of the detailed explanations of the symbols provided in Appendix I it is hoped that the foregoing will enable the reader to grasp the main principles which guide the notating of signs in this work. Any further details that are needed will be described at appropriate places in the exposition to follow.

We will now present the results of analyses of the formational features of signs in the vocabularies collected.The topics covered include body part involvement in sign production (5.4) and Sign Actor organization (5.5), where we shall examine arm position, handshape and orientation from the point of view of how they establish contrasts between signs. Included here will be a consideration of handshapes in two handed signs where we shall show that certain principles of organization that have been established in primary sign languages also apply here. We shall then consider Sign Location (5.6). Here we shall discuss the repertoire of distinct body-locations that are employed in the NCD sign languages and we shall show that there is a relationship between the semantic domain of a sign and the body-location it uses. Finally we shall consider Sign Action, or movement (5.7), and conclude with an overall summary of the findings (5.8).

In the analyses to be presented, we confine our attention to the *simple* signs in the corpus. As mentioned above, in all of the sign languages examined a proportion of the vocabulary is made up of compound expressions, usually two-part forms. In most cases (although not in all) the forms of which the compounds are composed may also be used independently. To the extent that this is so, in discussing the frequencies with which the various sign forms occur in these sign languages, we have left the compound signs aside. The vocabulary samples which we have used in the analyses to follow, and the proportion of unitary and compound signs within each, may be seen in Table 5.1.

Table 5.1
Vocabulary samples and proportion of compound and unitary signs by group

GROUP	P	P%	N	N%	K	K%	R	R%
SAMPLE	1370	100	453	100	504	100	822	100
SIGN TYPES IN TOTAL SAMPLE BY GROUP								
Compound	433	31	61	13	32	6	217	26
Unitary	937	69	392	87	472	93	605	74

GROUP	L	L%	M	M%	J	J%
SAMPLE	663	100	374	100	300	100
SIGN TYPES IN TOTAL SAMPLE BY GROUP						
Compound	179	27	21	6	13	4
Unitary	484	73	353	93	287	96

P, Warlpiri; N, Anmatyerre; K, Kaytej; R, Warumungu; L, Warlmanpa; M, Mudbura; J, Djingili

5.4 Body part involvement in sign production

In all of the seven NCD sign languages discussed here, sign production is carried out almost exclusively by the hands and arms. As already stated, there are very few signs indeed that involve some action of the face as well and only one or two that may require a particular posture or movement of the head. The non-forelimb components of these signs are always done in conjunction with forelimb action. There are no purely non-forelimb signs. Furthermore, for the few signs that do involve face or head action, these components are most likely to be left out in rapid signing. In general, Sign Action in these sign languages is confined to the forelimbs. In signed discourse gaze-shift, posture-shift and facial expression do play a part (this is discussed in Ch. 9) but, as we shall see, these aspects of performance appear not to have any formalized role in the sign language system. They serve in ways that appear to be indistinguishable from the way in which they serve in spoken discourse. In this respect these sign languages differ from what has been reported for primary (deaf) sign languages, where facial action has been shown to have a crucial role to play, both lexically and grammatically (Liddell 1980, Baker and Cokely 1980, Vogt-Svendsen 1983).

The majority of signs in the NCD sign languages are performed with one forelimb only or they may be adequately performed in this way. As will be seen in Table 5.2, we find that upwards of 80% of all signs are one handed. This is very similar to what we have found in other samples of Australian Aboriginal sign languages. In Roth's (1897) description of signs from sign languages in North-West-Central Queensland, 74% are one handed, as far as may be judged from his drawings. Inspection of West's sign language film material taken from several different groups in Cape York (West 1961-1965) likewise shows that signing in this region of the continent is predominantly one handed. This strongly unimanual character of these sign languages is in contrast with what has been described for a primary sign language such as American Sign Language. Thus over half of the 2000 signs recorded in Stokoe, Casterline and Croneberg's *Dictionary of American Sign Language* (1965) require two hands for their performance.

Two handed signs are divisible into two sorts: those in which the two hands act in parallel to one another - two handed symmetrical signs, as we shall call them; and those in which one hand acts in a subordinate fashion in relation to the other - termed here two handed asymmetrical signs. As will be seen from Table 5.2, of the two handed signs, asymmetrical forms are twice as frequent as symmetrical forms, except in Mudbura and Djingili, where we find more symmetrical than asymmetrical forms.

It should be noted that, in Warlpiri sign language, at least, there appears to be a very strong tendency for signs to become unimanual. Signs which, in citation form, are given as two handed symmetrical forms are commonly observed in a one handed version. Two handed asymmetric forms may also be reduced to a one handed form in which only the active hand performs any action. Thus the sign MANIYI 'money'(Fig. 5.5), in the form in which it is usually cited, is done with the index finger of the active hand making a circular motion while pointing toward the palm of the subordinate hand ($.\,B_{>\perp}\backslash G_{\top<}^{\circlearrowleft}$). Yet it may often be signed with circular movements made with the index finger alone ($.\,G_{<\perp}^{\circlearrowleft}$). Likewise, WIRLINYI 'hunting' (Fig. 5.14), which in citation form requires the the palm of the subordinate hand to be contacted twice by the tips of the fingers of the active hand, which is held in a 'flat' (B) configuration (all fingers extended and adducted) with the palm facing to signer's left ($.\,B_{\wedge\perp}\backslash B_{<\perp}^{\,\scriptstyle ?\,'}$). This sign can also often be observed being made by tapping any convenient body part (such as a thigh) with the active hand, or even by making downward movements of the hand in free space. Other examples in which asymmetric signs have been observed to be performed with only one hand include the sign for 'rifle, gun',[6] PALKA 'body, present, actual' (Fig. 8.2)[7] and YAPUNTA 'abandoned'

It should also be noted that many signs that are cited in one handed form may often be performed by both hands acting in unison (it is occasionally hard to decide whether a sign should be classed as unimanual or bimanual symmetric because of this tendency). Such bimanual performances appear in emphatic signing, and sometimes in narrational signing, perhaps for stylistic effect. It might be added that bimanual asymmetric signs that have been observed in a unimanual form, as described above, are never performed as if they are unimanual signs performed with both hands at once. For bimanual asymmetric signs, in emphatic or animated signing, both hands are used in the form given when the sign is cited. The unimanual performance of bimanual asymmetric signs is typically observed only in quick signing or in signing when the signer is tired. There are a few instances, however (YURLTU 'rifle', for example, or JUKUJUKU 'chicken' - also Warlpiri), where the one handed form is so often used that it may be replacing the two handed form.

Bimanual signs, whether symmetric or not, are performed in front of the signer in the space into which the hands may easily reach, without the upper arms undergoing any marked extension or elevation. This space is referred to as 'neutral space' (marked by a dot in the place for the sign location symbol) and it is in this space in which the majority of one handed signs are performed also. As will be seen from Table 5.2, however, somewhere between just under a quarter to just over a third of all signs in the NCD sign languages examined are *body-articulated signs*, that is, they are performed in a definite relationship with some other part of the signer's body such as the forehead, the nose, the chest or the lower limbs. Once again we may notice that the sign languages here examined are all quite similar to one another in

TABLE 5.2

GROUP	P	P%	N	N%	K	K%	R	R%
PROPORTIONS OF UNITARY SIGNS BY GROUP THAT ARE								
1 ha. B	279	29	112	28	108	23	159	26
2 ha.Sym N	50	5	5	1	18	4	10	2
1 ha. N	475	51	240	61	301	63	371	61
TOTALS								
1 ha.	754	80	352	89	409	86	530	87
2 ha Sym B	11	1	0	0	1	0	0	0
2 ha Asym.	122	13	35	9	43	9	65	10
B	290	31	112	29	109	23	159	26
N	647	69	280	71	363	77	446	74
2 ha Asym.B	0	0	0	0	0	0	0	0
2 ha Sym.	61	6	4	1	19	4	10	2
2 ha Asym. N	122	13	35	9	43	9	65	10

GROUP	L	L%	M	M%	J	J%
PROPORTIONS OF UNITARY SIGNS BY GROUP THAT ARE						
1 ha. B	93	19	95	27	103	36
2 ha.Sym N	15	3	27	8	30	10
1 ha. N	333	68	208	59	133	46
TOTALS						
1 ha.	426	88	303	86	236	82
2 ha Sym B	1	0	0	0	8	3
2 ha Asym.	42	9	18	5	14	5
B	94	19	95	27	111	39
N	390	81	258	73	176	61
2 ha Asym.B	0	0	0	0	0	0
2 ha Sym.	16	3	27	8	38	13
2 ha Asym. N	42	9	18	5	14	5

1 ha: one handed; 2 ha: two handed; Sym: symmetrical; Asym: Asymmetrical; B: body located; N: neutral space.

respect to the proportion of body-articulated signs found in them. It is also to be noted that this proportion is not significantly different from the proportion found for body-articulated signs in primary sign languages.

Broadly speaking, then, as Table 5.2 reveals, in terms of overall trends for body part involvement in the production of signs, the seven sign languages here considered are very similar to one another. The only difference to be noted is that, for Mudbura and Djingili sign languages, we report a higher proportion of two handed symmetrical signs than two handed asymmetrical signs. Since our samples of these sign languages are the smallest we cannot be sure of how reliable this difference really is. At present we are not inclined to attach very much significance to it.

In one respect, however, there is a significant difference between these sign languages. This is in regard to the number of compound expressions found in them. This may be seen from Table 5.1. It will be noted there that in the sign languages of Warlpiri, Warlmanpa and Warumungu somewhat over one quarter of all signs are compounds, whereas many fewer compounds are encountered in the four other sign languages examined. This difference is associated with the fact that Warlpiri, Warlmanpa and Warumungu have a large number of compound spoken forms. For example, many verbs, especially in Warlpiri and Warlmanpa, are compounds of a root verb and a preverb. This compound morphology is reflected in the sign languages (see Chapter 7 and 8 for further discussion). Such compounding is not as widespread in Anmatyerre and Kaytej and, accordingly, we find a much lower proportion of compounds in their sign languages.

5.5 Sign Actor organization

Sign Actor, as defined above, refers to the organization of body parts that engage in the production of the sign. As we have seen, in the sign languages discussed here, with the few exceptions mentioned, signs are produced by the forelimbs. In considering how these are organized for sign production, three components must be considered: Arm Position, Handshape and Orientation. For two handed signs it will also be necessary to describe the arrangement of the hands in respect to one another, that is, Hand Arrangement. In this section we comment briefly on Arm Position and Orientation but devote most of the discussion to handshape.

5.5.1 Handedness

Prior to discussing each of these components a comment on handedness is appropriate. Throughout the account to follow, we assume that a signer's dominant hand is her right hand and, accordingly, when discussing one handed signs it is the right hand that is referred to. In two handed signs the dominant or active hand is assumed to be the right hand. In practice, at least in our observation, many signers appear able to enact signs with right or left hand with equal facility and may be observed switching from right hand to left hand and back quite freely. For most signs we have recorded, the handedness of the sign is of no consequence for its meaning. Some exceptions to this have been noted for some kin signs, however. As we shall see (Chapter 11) signs

Fig. 5.18 Signing while walking, Yuendumu. From 16mm film YSL II (1978)

Fig. 5.19 Signing using extended arm to address a distant recipient, Yuendumu. From 16mm film, YSL II (1978)

for kin relations generally do not distinguish sex. However, one Warlpiri informant and several Mudbura informants have indicated that handedness may be significant as an indicator of sex for at least some kin signs. Despite this, it is our impression that for most users of these sign languages, handedness is not usually relied upon as a form of linguistic contrast, even for the kin terms for which it was indicated by some informants.

5.5.2 Arm position

For most signs the position of the arm is 'unmarked'. That is, its position is simply that in which it is necessary to place the hand to achieve whatever Location may be distinctive for the sign. In notating signs, thus, reference to the Arm Position may usually be left out. However, there are a few signs which are distinguished from one another merely because the arm is held in a different position in their enactment. In other cases it is sometimes useful to note the arm position, either to make the description of the sign more explicit or as a way of noting a stylistic variation in its performance. For example, when a woman is signing to someone some distance off, or when she is signing emphatically, as in signing in argument, the arms may be fully extended and in certain kinds of directional inflections of signs the signer may vary the position of her arms (Fig. 5.19).

Arm position may be varied according to whether the upper arm is held elevated or not (upper arm elevation is written as ɿ), whether the forearm is held in a vertical position or not (vertical forearm is written as ɺ) and whether the arm is fully extended forward (⌃), laterally (⌃) or extended vertically (ɿɺ).

Signs in Warlpiri which contrast in terms of arm position only or for which arm position is marked include the following:

> The sign for *wiinywiinypa* 'gray falcon' is distinguished from the sign for *ngulajuku* 'enough, finished' only because, in WIINYWIINYPA the upper arm is held in elevation whereas in NGULAJUKU it is not (see Fig. 5.20). Thus we write . ɿG$_{\vee\perp\vee}$^{6} ' for WIINYWIINYPA but . G$_{\vee\perp\vee}$^{6} ' for NGULAJUKU.
>
> The sign for 'rifle' contrasts with that for 'Friday' because the former is done with an upraised forearm while the latter is not. Thus . ɺX$_{\top\wedge}$$^{\upsilon}$ for RIFLE and . X$_{\top\wedge}$$^{\upsilon}$ for FRIDAY.

We find full lateral extension of the arms in WARNTAMARRI 'single women's camp' This is written as . ⌐‹B˅ '⌐›Bˀ ∼ ˏ indicating that the signer stretches her arms outwards laterally and alternately flexes her wrists (see Fig. 5.21). The sign is depictive of the extended linear arrangement of a large single women's camp.[8]

Finally, in the sign for *jirdi ma-ni* 'to load spear thrower', we have an example in which the arm is upraised above the head. It is written as . ʅᒍO˄› ᵀ .

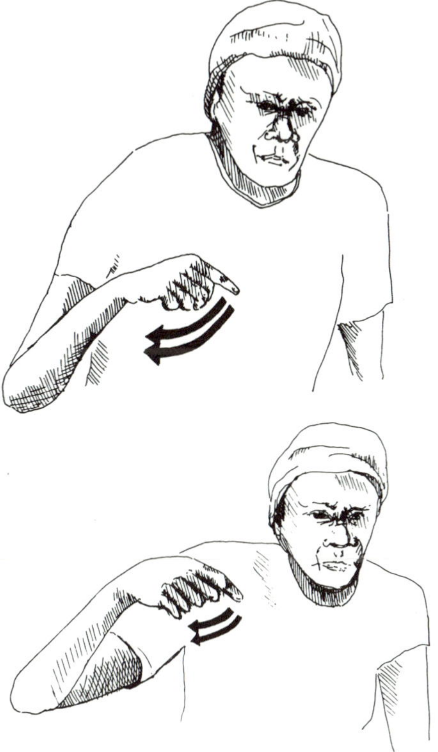

Fig. 5.20 A comparison between NGULAJUKU 'enough' (above) and WIINYWIINYPA 'gray falcon'(below) to show contrast in upper arm position

5.5.3 Handshape

An important way in which signs are distinguished from one another is in terms of how the digits of the hand or hands are arranged as the sign is performed. There are a very large number of possibilities - Klima (1975)

estimated it to be of the order of at least 1700 - and sign languages differ from one another in how they draw from this range.

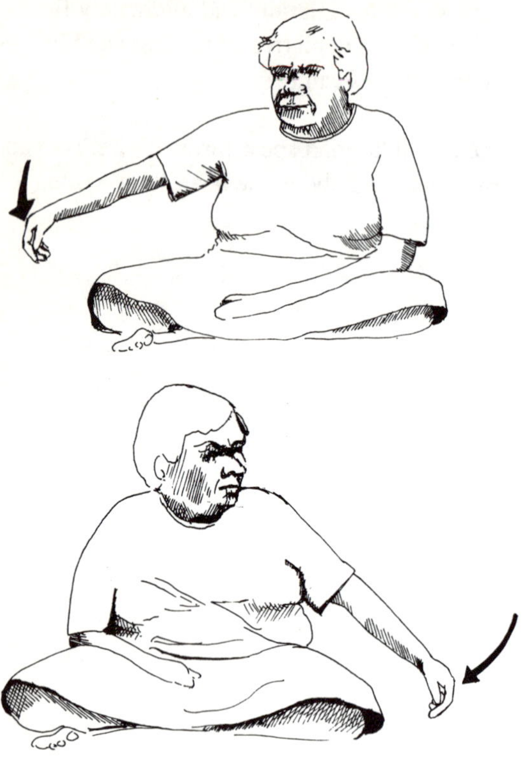

Fig. 5.21 Successive actions in WARNTAMARRI 'large single women's camp'

In the analyses we have undertaken here we have distinguished fifty-two handshapes. Several of these have proved to be variants of one another, however. Although, in the notation, we find it useful to be able to distinguish B, B̂, B̂, B5 and Bt, for example, it seems that these can in most cases be considered variant forms of the 'flat' hand (all fingers fully extended and held together) and can all be included under the symbol B+. O+ includes the forms O and ×o, both forms in which the fingers curl over to make a circle, mϚ+ includes several handshapes in which the middle finger is extended, L+ includes a 'bent' form of this handshape, as does Ɏ+. There is, thus, a set of 41 *emic handshapes*, and it is in terms of these that the analyses discussed here have been conducted.

All 52 handshapes are described in detail in Appendix I. It will be seen there that we have divided them into three major groups: Closed, in which the digits are all flexed, most to the palm of the hand; Open, in which all the digits are extended and sometimes spread; and Digit-extended, in which one or two (in one case three) digits are extended, the rest flexed to the palm of the hand.

Fig. 5.22 shows the 41 emic handshapes. Table 5.3 lists these and here we show the sign languages in which each occurs and the proportion of signs sampled in each language that each handshape accounts for. Table 5.4 shows how many of these handshapes are the same as or highly similar to the handshapes needed for a description of American Sign Language. In this table we show, for each coincident handshape in ASL, its rank order in frequency of use in that language (as given by Klima and Bellugi 1979) and we also indicate whether it is regarded as fully emic, a variant form, or whether it is a 'loan' form from fingerspelling. This information is taken largely from Friedman (1977).

Fig. 5.22 Emic handshapes for NCD sign languages

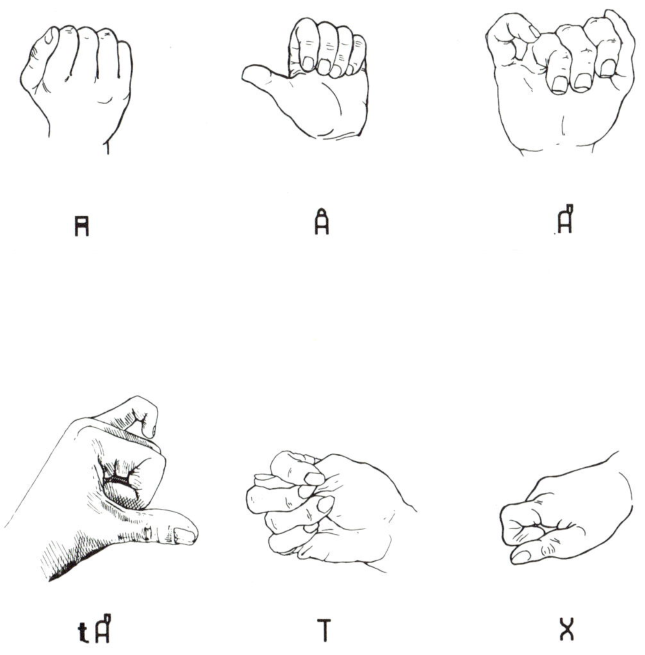

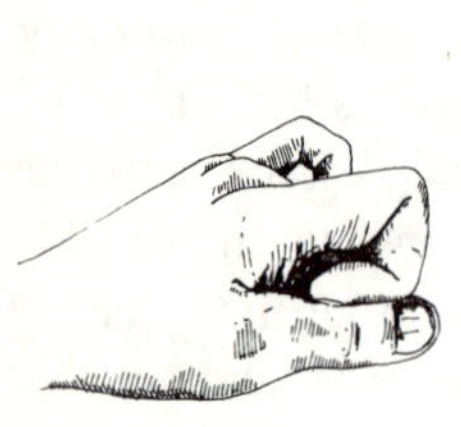

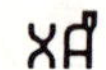

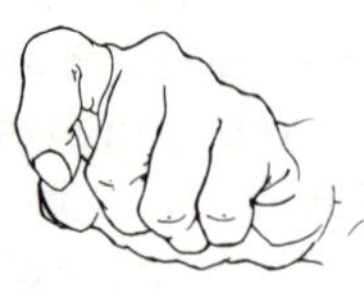

bO

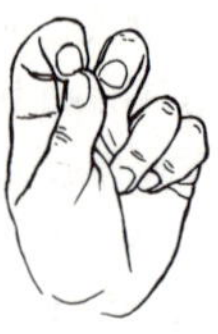

bO2

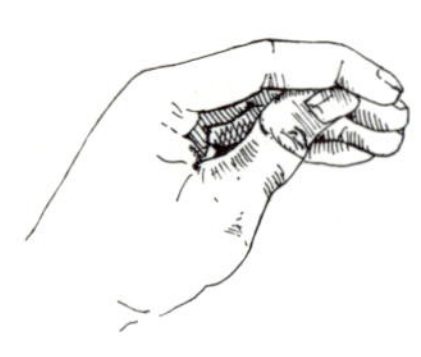

tO

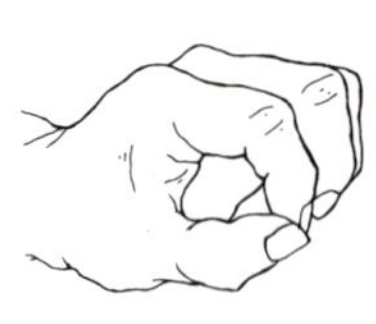

O

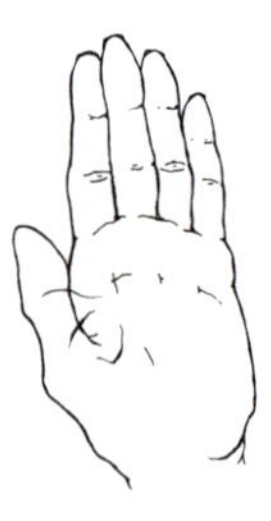

B

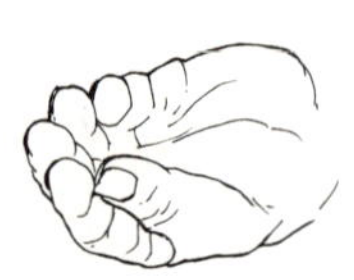

cB

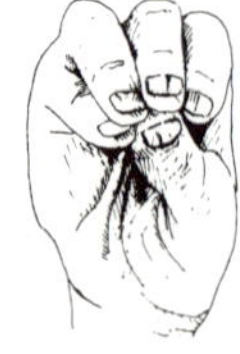

bB

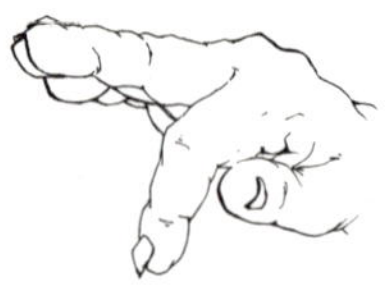

xB

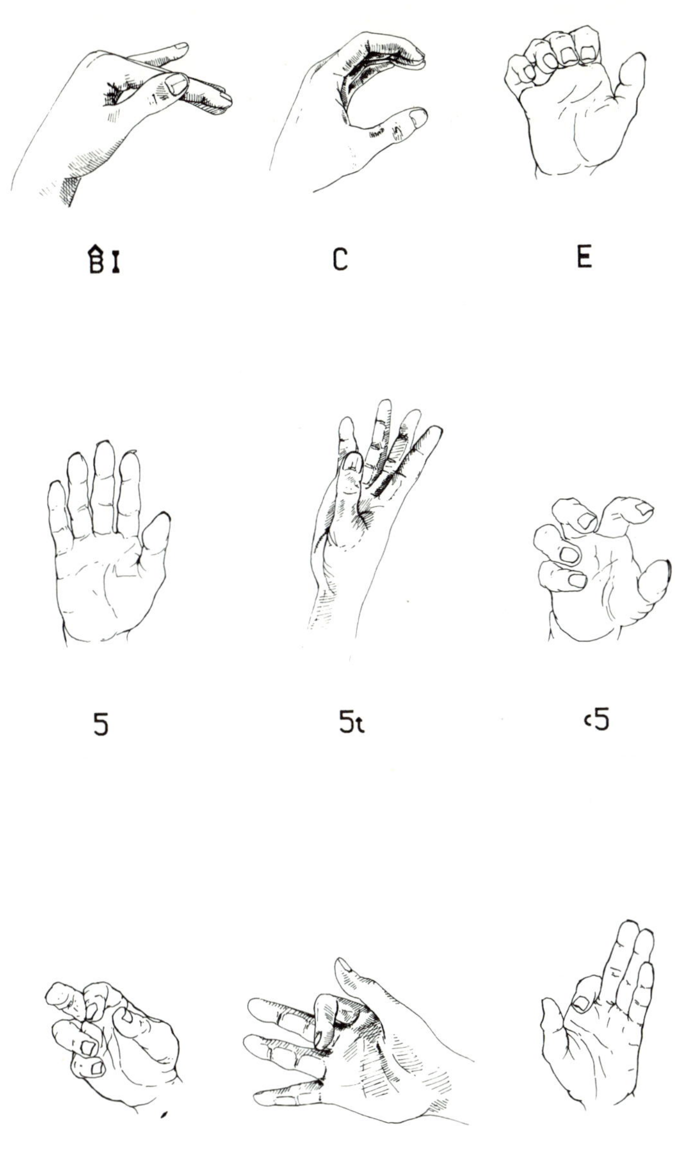
B̂I
C
E
5
5t
<5
<5m
X5
F

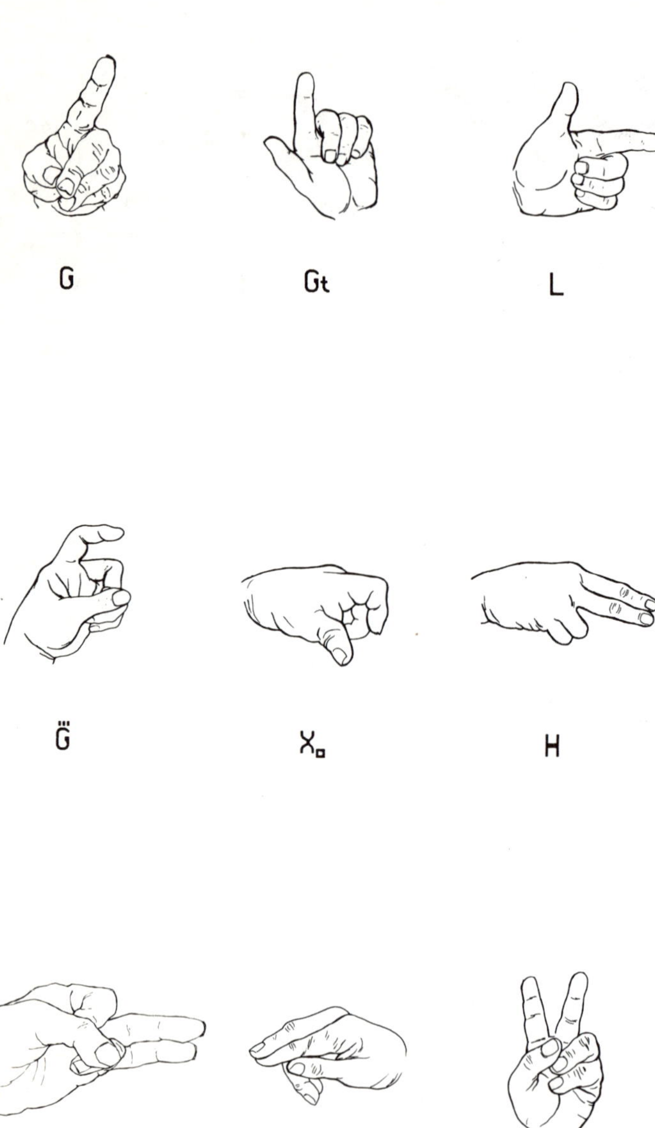
G
Gt
L
G⃛
X□
H
mH
R
V

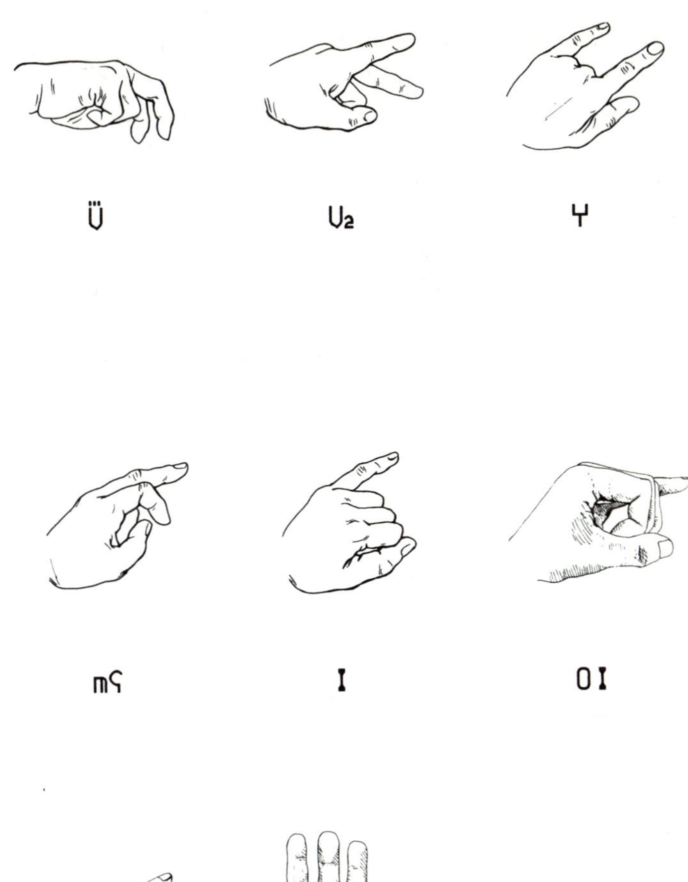

It W

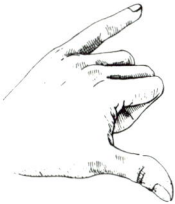

The signs considered in Table 5.3 include all the one handed and two handed symmetrical signs recorded in which there is no change in handshape during the course of the sign. Two handed asymmetric signs and signs involving handshape change will be considered separately. Inspection of Table 5.3 permits the following observations:

1. It will be apparent that the number of distinct handshapes in the emic set varies somewhat from one NCD language to another. Thus there are 35 handshapes for Warlpiri, 33 for Warumungu, 30 for Mudbura, 29 for Warlmanpa, 28 for Kaytej, 26 for Anmatyerre and 22 for Djingili. These differences are probably not very significant, for the sizes of the samples available vary and there is clearly some correlation between the number of signs sampled and the number of different handshapes described. Nevertheless these differences may reflect differences in the degree to which these sign languages have been elaborated. Among the Warumungu and Warlpiri, for example, sign language is very highly developed because its use is widespread in daily life. Among the Djingili, on the other hand, its use is today, at least, not nearly as extensive. The more restricted set of handshapes encountered in Djingili, as compared to Warumungu or Warlpiri, may be a reflection of this.

2. It will be seen that there is a high degree of overlap between these sign languages in the handshapes employed for the great majority of the signs in the sample. That is, it is as if these seven sign languages all draw from the same 'pool' of handshapes for the great majority of the signs in their lexicons. Thus there are 18 handshapes that are found in all seven languages. These 18 handshapes together account for between 85% and 97% of all signs in the samples examined.

3. Where the sign languages differ among themselves in the handshapes made use of, for the most part these differences are due to the fact that one or other of these sign languages has an additional set of handshapes which are extremely limited in their distribution. Thus Warumungu may be seen to have four handshapes which do not occur in the other sign languages, but these four handshapes have been recorded in only one sign each in the lexicon collected. Likewise, Warlpiri has three handshapes that it does not share with the other languages, but these, again, are found in only one sign each.

4. It will be seen that in each sign language there are a large number of handshapes that are highly specialized in their use. Thus, although each NCD sign language requires between at least 22 and 35 handshapes to describe the signs recorded in them, in each one of these sign languages only half of this repertoire is needed to account for ninety percent or more of the signs recorded. In each sign language we find that between one third and one half of all the handshapes distinguished account for one percent or less of the signs in the sample apiece. That is, in each sign language we find that about one third of the handshapes distinguished occur in three signs or fewer each.

Such a large number of highly specialized handshapes perhaps indicates a degree of unsystematicity in the processes by which signs are formed. It suggests that many handshapes may have been created *ad hoc* , so to speak. A consideration of the signs in which these rare handshapes occur, however, does not suggest that they are found only in signs that are very rarely used. Thus in Warlpiri we find that ơ (in which the first three fingers are curled over to rest on the thumb, but the fourth finger is extended at the A joint so that it forms a little 'hoop') occurs in but one sign, the sign for *turaki* 'truck, motorcar' (Fig. 6.17); ×B occurs but twice, in the sign for *parraja* 'coolimon', a common object of daily use, and in the sign for *pirrarni* 'yesterday'; and F occurs but once in *wardapi* 'goanna', a very commonly hunted lizard. In Anmatyerre we have C (a very rarely used handshape generally, as we have seen) being used for a sign that refers to a hole or burrow and in Djingili this same handshape is used in a sign that refers to the sun. In Kaytej F occurs but once, but in a sign for *artnwenge* 'child'. In Warumungu, which has ten handshapes that occur in but one sign each, we find, for instance, ьO2 in 'cigarette', U2 in *parrakurl* 'billy can', and XB̂ in *kana* 'digging stick'. In Warlmanpa ьB occurs in *maliki* 'dog' (this same handshape is also used in Warumungu for the same meaning) and R occurs in the sign for 'Tuesday'. In Mudbura the uniquely occurring handshapes include W in *murrkurna* 'three, few' and O I in *tarnkura* 'yellow'. Although there are also uniquely occurring handshapes in all of these languages that occur in signs that perhaps would not be used very often, as in signs for the names of certain trees and animals, as the foregoing examples make clear, there are many signs in common use that require a handshape unique to them.

5. A comparison between NCD emic handshapes and handshapes that occur in ASL is given in Table 5.4. ASL and NCD sign languages, of course, have nothing to do with one another. However, the comparison does serve to illustrate three points: first, that unrelated sign languages tend to use a similar number of different handshapes; second, that there are some handshapes that probably occur in all sign languages; third, that there are many differences in the handshapes made use of.

Table 5.3. The emic handshapes of seven NCD sign languages

The table lists all the handshapes found to be linguistically contrastive in seven NCD sign languages. The handshapes are listed by symbol, in order of frequency of use.For explanation of handshape symbols see Appendix I. SLs gives the number of NCD sign languages which uses the handshape. Remaining columns give the number of signs in the sample for each sign language in which each handshape occurs followed by the proportion of signs in each sample. Figures in % column rounded up, + indicates less than 1%. P, Warlpiri; N, Anmatyerre; K, Kaytej; R, Warumungu; L, Warlmanpa; M, Mudbura; J, Djingili.

Handshape		SLs	P	P%	N.	N%	K	K%	R	R%	L	L%	M	M%	J	J%
1	B+	7	143	20	95	30	62	17	67	15	66	19	80	28	81	34
2	G+	7	132	19	50	16	71	19	86	19	51	15	42	15	41	17
3	Y+	7	51	7	24	8	31	8	31	7	18	5	16	6	6	3
4	꜀5+	7	32	5	4	1	20	5	22	5	15	4	13	5	13	6
5	0+	7	30	4	15	5	19	5	27	6	21	6	14	5	8	3
6	H	7	30	4	11	4	14	4	20	4	15	4	9	3	5	2
7	꜀B	7	26	4	8	3	14	4	9	2	21	6	10	3	9	4
8	ƅO	7	26	4	4	1	2	+	11	2	9	3	2	+	8	3
9	X	7	24	3	13	4	15	4	13	3	7	2	6	2	5	2
10	G̈	7	23	3	9	3	14	4	15	3	13	4	3	1	10	4
11	U	7	20	3	6	2	13	4	14	3	12	4	6	2	2	1
12	R	7	18	3	13	4	8	2	11	2	4	1	13	5	8	3
13	5	7	17	2	11	4	15	4	28	6	19	6	21	7	14	6

Table 5.3, continued

Handshape		SLs	P	P%	N.	N%	K	K%	R	R%	L	L%	M	M%	J	J%
14	E+	7	12	2	3	1	8	2	15	3	11	3	6	2	4	2
15	Ü	7	10	1	6	2	3	1	6	1	6	2	5	2	4	2
16	to	7	8	1	1	+	1	+	6	1	3	1	7	2	8	3
17	Â	7	4	+	3	1	4	1	2	+	2	+	6	2	2	1
18	xB	7	2	+	3	1	5	1	7	1	4	1	2	+	1	+
19	mʕ+	6	28	4	7	2	9	3	12	3	10	3	3	1	0	0
20	X▫	6	19	3	8	3	11	3	15	3	13	4	5	2	0	0
21	L+	6	16	2	7	2	2	+	13	3	5	2	5	2	0	0
22	U2	5	8	1	3	1	1	+	1	+	1	+	0	0	0	0
23	5t	5	7	1	4	1	13	4	9	2	7	2		0		0
24	I+	5	4	+	2	+	0	0	0	0	2	+	2	+	0	0
25	ьB	5	1	+	0	0	4	1	2	+	1	+	0	0	1	+
26	F	5	1	+	0	0	1	+	0	0	1	+	4	1	2	1
27	ьO2	4	3	+	2	+	0	0	1	+	2	+	0	0	0	0
28	Gt	4	2	+	0	0	2	+	0	0	0	0	1	+	1	+
29	R	4	2	+	0	0	0	0	1	+	1	+	1	+	0	0
30	C	4		0	1	+		0	2	+		0	1	+	1	+

Table 5.3, continued

	Handshape	SLs	P	P%	N.	N%	K	K%	R	R%	L	L%	M	M%	J	J%
31	Ả	3	2	+	0	0	0	0	1	+	2	+	0	0	0	0
32	↑I	3	1	+	0	0	1	+	0	0	0	0	1	+	0	0
33	W	3	1	+	0	0	1	+	0	0	0	0	1	+	0	0
34	T	2	4	+	0	0	0	0	0	0	0	0	1	+	0	0
35	mH	2	0	0	0	0	0	0	3	+	0	0	1	+	0	0
36	tẢ	2	+		0		0		0		0		0		0	0
37	‹5mς	1	+	0	0	0	0	0	0	0	0	0	0	0	0	0
38	X5		0		0		0	1	+		0		0		0	0
39	B̂I		0		0		0	1	+		0		0		0	0
40	XẢ		0		0		0	1	+		0		0		0	0
41	It		+		0		0	1	+		0		0		0	0

Looking at Table 5.4, we find that there are twenty-two ASL handshapes that are similar to or the same as handshapes used in the NCD sign languages, and there are nineteen NCD handshapes that are not found in ASL. On the other hand, comparison with Friedman's (1977) inventory shows that there are ten ASL handshapes that do not occur in the NCD. Of the nineteen handshapes that occur in the NCD sign languages, but are not found in ASL, it should be noted, three are found in the set of 18 that are common to all seven NCD sign languages and, overall, eight occur in four or more of the seven sign languages studied.

Nevertheless, we may also note that the first and third most frequently occurring ASL handshapes ('flat' or B hand and 'pointing' or G hand) are among the three most commonly occurring NCD handshapes. On the other hand, the C hand is extremely rare in the NCD sign languages. This handshape is the fourth most commonly occurring in ASL and it is considered to be one of the so-called 'unmarked' handshapes. That is, it is a member of a set of some seven handshapes which, as Battison (1978) has pointed out, are the simplest to produce, show maximum degree of contrast in their shapes, and are used very frequently in a wide variety of contexts. At the same time, one of the most commonly occurring of all NCD handshapes - the 'horns' or Y hand - is quite infrequent in ASL, while a handshape in which the middle finger is extended - the mς hand - does not occur at all in ASL (it is reported in Chinese Sign Language, however), but is again a fairly common handshape in five of the seven NCD sign languages.

Thus although these NCD sign languages make frequent use of several of the same handshapes that are frequently used in ASL, it does not make use of one of these (C), and it makes very frequent use of another handshape (Y) that, in ASL, is considered to be complex. Perhaps the more frequent use of seemingly more complex handshapes that we observe in the NCD sign languages is related to the fact that these sign languages are not used much by people until they are upwards of thirty years of age.

5.5.4 Handshapes in two handed signs

As we have seen, two handed signs in these NCD sign languages constitute only a relatively small proportion of the sign lexicons. They are of two sorts: two handed symmetrical signs, in which both hands engage in the same action, and two handed asymmetrical signs, in which one hand serves as a locus for the action of the other. For both kinds of two handed signs we find, first, that the range of handshapes that are used in them is smaller than the range encountered in one handed signs; second we find that there are

Table 5.4 NCD Handshapes in order of frequency of use compared with occurrence of handshapes in American Sign Language

NCD handshape		ASL occurrence	NCD handshape		ASL occurrence
1	B+	1st	25	bB	o
2	G+	3rd	26	F	8th
3	Y+	+variant of Y	27	bO2	o
4	c5+	+	28	Gt	?+ loan
5	O+	7th	29	R	16th loan
6	H	10th	30	C	4th
7	cB	o	31	A'	o
8	bO	variant of O	32	O I	o
9	X	o	33	W	+
10	G̈	9th	34	T	+loan
11	U	6th	35	mH	o
12	A	2nd	36	tA'	o
13	5	5th	37	c5mϚ	o
14	E+	19th loan	38	X5	o
15	Ü	+	39	B̂ I	o
16	tO	variant of O	40	XA'	o
17	A	variant of A	41	It	o
18	xB	o			
19	mϚ+	o			
20	X₀	o			
21	L+	11th			
22	U2	o			
23	5t	o			
24	I+	+			

Loan: from fingerspelling; +: infrequent in ASL; o: not in ASL. [ASL data from Friedman 1977 and Klima and Bellugi 1979]

several handshapes that are much more common in two handed signs than they are in one handed signs, while handshapes common in one handed signs are rare in two handed signs; third, in regard to two handed asymmetric signs, the range of handshapes in the subordinate hand is much more restricted than the range of shapes used in the dominant hand. The relevant data are presented in Table 5.5.

5.5.5 Two handed symmetrical signs

In the case of two handed symmetrical signs, taking all seven sign language samples together, we find that of the 41 emic handshapes distinguished, only 19 occur in these signs and these, on the whole, are the most commonly occurring handshapes. Thus, of the 19 handshapes found in two handed symmetrical signs, 14 belong to the set of eighteen that occur in all seven sign language samples and 3 are handshapes that occur in six of the seven sign languages.

However, when compared to the frequency with which these handshapes occur when one handed signs are counted, it appears that a number of these common handshapes are much more common in two handed signs. Thus within the sample of two handed symmetrical signs, the five most commonly occurring handshapes are B, G, 5, O and A, whereas when one handed signs are considered, the five most commonly occurring handshapes are B, G, Y, c5 and H. Particularly notable is the increased frequency with which A is used in two handed symmetrical signs (and in asymmetrical ones, as we shall see) as compared to its occurrence generally, and the rarity with which both H and mG are used, when, in the large sample, these handshapes are among the most common.

5.5.6 Two handed asymmetrical signs

Here a distinction must be drawn between the *subordinate* hand, on which, or in relation to which the *dominant* or active hand engages in action characteristic of the sign. In a study of handshapes in two handed signs in ASL, Battison (1978) showed that handshapes in the subordinate hand were restricted to a set of seven 'unmarked' handshapes: two versions of the 'fist' handshape (A and S - a handshape difference that, for these NCD sign languages, is not noted as significant), and handshapes equivalent to O, C, G, B and 5. Handshapes in the dominant hand were not restricted in this way.

For the NCD sign languages examined here, we can report similar findings. We find, that is, that the range of handshapes found in the subordinate hand is much more restricted than the range found in the dominant hand and that the handshapes that most commonly occur in the subordinate hand include handshapes that belong to the restricted set found in ASL.

TABLE 5.5 Handshapes in two handed signs [all NCD sign languages taken together].

SY	Total	Cum. %	SUB	Total	Cum. %	DOM	Total	Cum.%	EQH	Total	Cum. %
B+	45	25.71	B+	148	43.66	B+	135	39.82	B+	110	53.66
G+	29	42.28	A	82	67.85	G+	49	54.27	G	29	67.80
5	22	54.85	G	29	76.40	A	38	65.48	cB	25	80.00
O+	16	63.99	cB	26	84.07	cB	28	73.74	A	17	88.29
A	11	70.28	U	23	90.85	5	19	79.34	O+	9	92.68
‹5+	7	74.28	O+	12	94.39	H	9	81.99	H	6	95.61
ьo	6	77.71	H	6	96.16	X	9	84.64	X	3	97.07
Ψ+	6	81.14	X	4	97.34	O+	9	87.29	U	3	98.53
H	5	84.00	Ψ+	3	98.22	ьo	8	89.65	tG	1	99.02
ƒn	5	86.86	5	3	99.10	mς+	7	91.71	Es	1	99.51
G̈	4	89.15	ьo	1	99.39	Ψ+	7	93.77	ьo	1	100
cB	4	91.44	to	1	99.68	5t	6	95.54			
X	3	93.15	E+	1	99.97	U	4	96.72			
to	3	94.86				E+	3	97.60			
X▫	3	96.57				Gt	2	98.19			
L+	2	97.71				L+	1	98.48			
E+	1	98.28				Ü	1	98.77			
mς+	1	98.85				I+	1	99.06			
C	1	99.42				X▫	1	99.35			
Â	1	99.99				Â	1	99.64			
						‹5	1	99.93			

Thus we find only 13 handshapes occurring in the subordinate hand in asymmetrical signs. Of these B, A, G and U (which indicates that the hand assumes no particular shape at all) account for 85% of all handshapes found in the subordinate hand in these signs. However, we also find a number of other handshapes occurring in the subordinate hand, which are never found in the subordinate hand in ASL. Thus cB and ×O occur with a fair degree of frequency, and there are also occurrences of H, Y, 5, E and ьO.

With regard to the dominant hand, we find that the range of handshapes used is greater: 21 different handshapes are used in the dominant hand of asymmetric signs. However, we find that of these handshapes, 15 belong to the set of 18 common handshapes and that the handshapes B, G and A account for over 65% of all the signs in the sample.

Once again we may note that the relative frequency of occurrence of handshapes that occur in the dominant hand in these asymmetric signs differs from the relative frequency of handshapes found to occur in one handed signs. Thus A and cB are much more common as dominant handshapes than they are in the one handed sample, whereas the handshapes Y, mC and c5 that are commonly employed in one handed signs are rarely encountered in asymmetric signs. Also we may note that U, the 'unspecified' handshape which occurs quite often in the subordinate hand of asymmetric signs (and virtually never occurs in one handed or two handed symmetrical signs) is very rare as a dominant handshape.

Finally, with regard to two handed asymmetric signs in which the handshapes in both hands are the same, as in . cB ^⊥ \ cB v< ×, the sign for *muurlpa* 'care, in company with' or .G >⊥ \ G <⊥ *⊥, the sign for *yarda* 'again' (both Warlpiri), we find that only 10 handshapes occur in these signs and that B, G and A account for nearly 80% of them.

5.5.7 Orientation

Orientation refers to the way the hand (or hands) is held in respect to the signer's body. As explained above (p.101), in the approach taken here we consider hand orientation, along with arm position and handshape, to be components of Sign Actor organization. It is not treated as a fourth Aspect, as some have proposed. Unlike arm position, which usually does not have to be specified, we find that it is useful to describe hand orientation in most cases, however, whether or not it makes a critical difference between one sign and another. This is because, in many signs, various hand orientations could be adopted, so, if it is not specified, mistakes could be made in interpreting the notation. For example, in a sign such as Warlmanpa MAJU 'bad', in which the hand, held with index and third fingers only extended, is flexed twice at the wrist (. H$_{\vee\perp}^{?}$ '), orientation must be specified as 'palm down, metacarpals facing away from signer'. If not, the reader might perform the sign with some other orientation, palm facing upward or to the signer's left, for instance, and in these cases it would not be intelligible.

As mentioned earlier, there are cases where hand orientation is critical, although there are not very many of these. We gave 'elder sibling' and 'cousin' as an example of two signs that contrast only in whether the palm was oriented upwards or downwards. Another example, in this case from Warlpiri, is the contrast between one of the two signs for *ngapa* 'water' and a sign for *kuntulpa* 'cold, cough'. In the sign for 'water' the center of the upper chest is tapped twice with the palm of the hand facing inwards (⊓B$_{\top<}^{\times}$ ' : see Fig. 5.8). The sign for 'cold, cough' is the same, except that the palm now faces upwards so that contact with the chest is made with the side of the hand (⊓B$_{\wedge<}^{\times}$ '). There are some signs where hand orientation may be omitted, as in signs in which all that is necessary is for a body part to pointed to or touched. For example, in Warlpiri, to sign *lirra* 'mouth' or *kakarda* 'back of neck', it is only necessary to touch these parts of the body with an extended index finger, and hand orientation need not be specified.

In the descriptions of orientation provided in the notation, we indicate by means of symbols subscripted to the Hand Configuration symbol, first the orientation of the palm of the hand and second, if necessary, the orientation of the metacarpals of the hand. In a few signs where the fingers are flexed at the A-joints (knuckles) so that the digits are pointing in a direction different from the metacarpals we have found it convenient to insert a third orientation symbol. These symbols are directional symbols. They indicate the directions of up ($_\wedge$), down ($_\vee$), toward signer ($_\top$), away from signer ($_\perp$), left ($_<$) and right ($_>$). These directions are all given from the point of view of the signer.

5.6 Sign Location

5.6.1 Neutral space

Somewhat more than two-thirds of all signs in each of the seven NCD sign languages are performed in 'neutral space', that is in the space immediately in front of the body into which the signer can easily reach, without extending the upper arm. A few signs, as we have seen, require a distinct arm position for their enactment and, as in the case of the examples given (both from Warlpiri:

WARNTAMARRI 'single women's camp', for instance, or JIRDI MA-NI 'load spear thrower'), as a result, employ space far to the sides of the signer or above her head. In addition, there are a few signs which, although enacted in space in front of the body, are nevertheless consistently enacted high up or low down in this space and in which high or low level of enactment appears to be a distinctive feature of the sign. Accordingly, in the notation, the neutral space marker is followed by an indicator as to whether 'upper neutral space' or 'lower neutral space' is being employed (⌒ and ᴗ, respectively). Thus, in Warlpiri, it appears that level of neutral space is the only way in which the signs for *yantarli* 'campbound' and *kukujuku* 'wait, not ready' are to be distinguished (Fig. 5.23 and 5.24). These are written as follows:

.ᴗcB^⊥ ⑨ YANTARLI

.⌒cB^⊥ ⑨ KUKUJUKU

Other signs in Warlpiri in which level of space is a distinguishing feature include *rdangkarlpa* 'short' as compared to *waralywaraly jarri-mi* 'to hang down' in at least one of its forms; and *kipirli nga-rni* 'graze, as kangaroo' as compared to *wantawanta* 'red ant'.

5.6.2 Body-located signs

Body-located signs, that is, signs that are performed in contact with or in a definite association with a part of the body (other than the second hand), comprise between 20% and 30% of the signs sampled in each of the NCD languages. To describe these, 36 different body locations must be distinguished. These are listed in Table 5.6 (locations marked * are combined, e.g. shoulder includes left shoulder, right shoulder and both together) in which is also given the number of languages in which each body location distinguished has been observed and the number of signs, overall, which it accounts for.

From Table 5.6 it will be seen that of the 36 body locations required, 14 are found in all seven languages. These account for between 74% (in Warumungu) and 88% (in Mudbura) of all the body-located signs in each sample - virtually 80%, for all languages taken together. As with handshape, so here, we find that each sign language has a proportionately high number of body locations that occur in a very few signs.

Of the 36 body locations distinguished, 11 are in the head and facial region, 9 in the upper body - neck, upper chest and shoulders - 9 in the thoracic (including abdominal) region, 4 arm locations and 3 lower limb locations. Taking all sign languages together, we find that, on average, 60% of all body-located signs are articulated in the facial region, 30% in the upper body and thoracic regions, the remainder in relation to the limbs. This is quite similar to what is found in primary sign languages. In ASL, for instance, as here, there are more locations of articulation in the facial region than there are in the lower regions of the body, and a higher proportion of body-articulated signs are articulated in the facial region than in other regions. However, we

Fig. 5.23 YANTARLI 'camp-bound, staying at home'

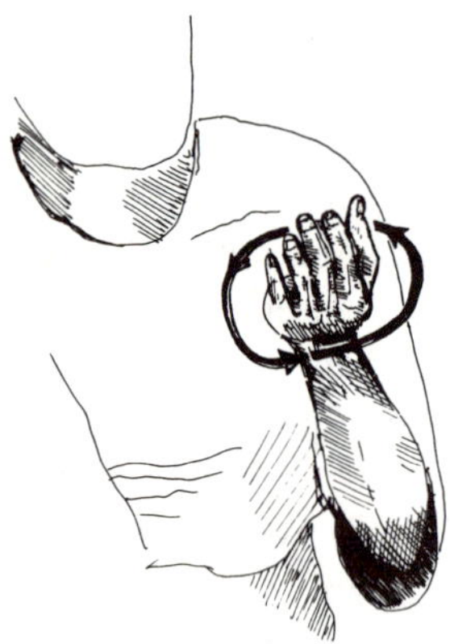

Fig. 5.24 KUKUJUKU 'wait, not ready'

may also note that these NCD sign languages make use of articulation locations that do not commonly occur in ASL. Thus, in the NCD sign languages we find that in the thoracic region there are distinctions between shoulder and front of shoulder, between upper chest and thorax, and between thorax and specific locations in relation to the breasts. We also find that there are a number of signs that employ the lower limbs as loci of articulation. The thigh is used in all seven NCD languages, the knee is used in five of them and the lower leg in three. All of these are locations that do not occur, or occur extremely rarely, in sign languages such as ASL or BSL.

The use of lower limbs as a location for signs in these sign languages may in part reflect the fact that the users of these sign languages do not live in furnitured environments and spend much time sitting on the ground. Lower limbs are thus more readily accessible as sign locations and are also much more visible for such purposes than they are among people who spend much time among tables and chairs. The use of such locations, as well as the use of locations such as the female breast as a locus of articulation for signs, may also reflect a different sort of attitude to the human body from that found in Western industrialized societies, the context in which BSL and ASL have evolved.

5.6.3 Body-articulation locations and handshape

An analysis of the relationship between handshape and location of articulation for body-located signs (see Table 5.7) shows that the greatest variety of handshapes are found in the signs articulated in the facial region. Thus, taking all the sign languages together, signs articulated in the face, side of face, mouth and chin regions employ on average nearly fifteen handshapes per location. In contrast, signs articulated in relation to other parts of the body employ only about four to six handshapes per location.

These findings, and those mentioned earlier concerning the relative proportion of signs in the vocabulary using locations within different bodily regions, are in line with those reported by Siple (1978) for ASL. She pointed out that recipients in sign language interactions direct their gaze to the facial area of the signer the greatest proportion of the time. They rarely track the movements of the hands when signs are made out of the facial area. Since it is in the central areas of the visual field that the greatest amount of detail is discriminated, it might be expected that signs performed where they are most likely to be seen with central vision will show the greatest degree of differentiation in terms of location. We might also expect that the range and nature of the handshapes employed in this area will be more highly differentiated. Siple found, for ASL, not only that there were more articulation locations differentiated in the facial region, but that signs performed in this region showed a greater variety of handshapes and included a higher proportion of the more complex handshapes than did signs performed in the thoracic regions.

Table 5.6 Body locations in seven NCD sign languages

Body Part		Presence	SLs	Total	Cum. %
Cheek	3	PNKRLMJ	7	116	12.42
Chin	ᵕ	PNKRLMJ	7	98	22.91
Face	○	PNKRLMJ	7	97	33.29
Thorax	[]	PNKRLMJ	7	90	42.93
Mouth	ᗜ	PNKRLMJ	7	89	52.46
Forehead	⌒	PNKRLMJ	7	52	58.03
Eyes	⏏	PNKRLMJ	7	40	62.31
Shoulders*	┌┐	PNKRLMJ	7	34	70.13
Abdomen	└┘	PNKRLMJ	7	32	73.55
Thigh	╲	PNKRLMJ	7	31	76.87
Upper chest	⊓	PNKRLMJ	7	29	79.98
Ear	?	PNKRLMJ	7	25	82.66
Sides*	[ ]	PNKRLMJ	7	23	87.68
Neck	π	PNKRLMJ	7	21	89.94
Nose	△	PNKRL J	6	39	66.48
Breasts*	[▪▪]+	PNKRLM	6	24	85.22
Shoulders,frnt*	┏┓	PNKRLM	6	18	91.86
Knee	┐	PNKRLM	6	13	93.25
Below eyes	⏏	PNKRL	5	11	94.43
Armpit	˥	PNKRL	5	8	97.32
Upper arm	ɿ	PN RL	4	9	96.47
Forearm	ɺ	P R M	3	10	95.5
Crown	^	P MJ	3	8	98.18
Calf	›	RL J	3	6	98.82
Neck back	π	PN R	3	5	99.36
Elbow	V	P R	2	2	99.89
Hip	ι	P	1	3	99.68
Upper lip	△	P	1	1	100.00

Presence: groups in which location occurs, SLs: number of sign languages, Total: total signs per sample per location. Sample: 934 signs.

Table 5.7
Handshape types by body area in NCD sign languages

Area	#Area	HC by Area	CH %	OH %	DEH %	Σ Signs	Signs by Area
Head & Face	11	14.9	18	35.6	46.3	583	60.8
Upper Body	10	5.9	10.7	52.3	36.9	195	29
Limbs	7	3.8	0	80.6	19	88	9.18
Thoracic	8	4	28.3	55.4	16.3	92	9.6

Upper Body: :neck, shoulders, upper chest; Thoracic : sides, breasts, abdomen; #Area: number of distinct locations; HC by Area: average no. handshapes per location; CH: % closed handshapes; OH: % open hands; DEH: % digit-extended hands

Findings from analyses of the relationship between bodily region of articulation and handshape undertaken here are similar. Thus not only do we find that signs articulated in locations in the head and face region use a greater variety of handshapes, we also find that, if we compare the handshapes that are employed in signs articulated in these different regions, the further away from the facial region one moves, the higher the proportion of simple Closed (A and O) and Open (B and 5) handshapes and the lower the proportion of the more complex Digit-extension handshapes. Thus, as may be seen from Table 5.7, the proportion of the more complex handshapes declines from 46% in the facial region and 37% in the upper body region, to only 16% in the thoracic region and 19% in relation to the limbs.

From these findings, and from others so far reported, it may be seen that the sign languages investigated here show, in the manner in which they make use of body parts as locations for articulation, similarities to other unrelated primary sign languages. This suggests that there are certain quite general principles which derive from general perceptual, anatomical and kinesiological considerations, which govern the way in which signs in any sign language are constructed.

5.6.4 Selection of body locations

So far we have written as if the body serves simply as a well differentiated spatial territory with many distinct features that can serve as a field in which spatial contrasts between manually enacted signs can be anchored. The various parts of the body have, of course, a functional significance in their own right and it would not be surprising if it were found that such functional significance were to play a part in determining which feature is selected for which sign.

That is, in general, we may expect that signs whose meanings are in some way connected with the functions of the different bodily parts will be formed in relation to those parts, if they are formed as body-articulated signs. To a very large degree we find that this is so. The body parts selected as locations in body articulated signs tend to be associated in some way with some aspect of the sign's meaning.

The semantic motivation for location selection in body-articulated signs is evident in general terms if we compare the frequency with which body-articulated signs occur in different semantic domains.[9] We find that in the domains of Body Parts, Human Classification, Kinship and Human Attributes, fifty percent or more of the signs are body-articulated. In contrast, in the domains of Animals (Mammals, Birds, Reptiles and Amphibians, and Invertebrates), Plants, General Attributes (includes Size, Shape, Weight, Color, Spatial Relations), and Verbs, 20% or fewer of the signs are body articulated.

Signs that refer to body parts include a high proportion of body-articulated signs because many of them (although not all) involve an action which indicates the body part referred to. Signs for kinship relationships have a high proportion of body-articulated signs because (as we shall discuss at greater length in Chapter 11) among the North Central Desert Aborigines (as among Aborigines elsewhere in Australia), different parts of the body are symbolic of different kin relationships. Signs for types of human beings (Human Classification) have a high proportion of body-articulated signs because many of them are derived from an indication of a bodily feature as a way of referring to a type of person. For instance, the sign for 'fully initiated man' in all seven sign languages (although not in other sign languages in Australia) is articulated in relation to the upper chest, doubtless because of the practice, followed in all these groups, whereby a man, when fully initiated, has conspicuous scars cut in his chest as a badge of status. Likewise, the sign for 'adolescent girl' in all seven sign languages makes reference to the breasts and the sign for 'European man' in all sign languages makes reference to the face, presumably because of the distinctive color that the face of such a person has. In the domain Human Attributes we also find a high proportion of body-articulated signs because signs for such attributes as blindness or deafness make reference to the eye or the ear, and many of the signs for physiological or emotional states refer to parts of the body that are involved in them - as in the eyes or face in 'sadness', the stomach area in 'hunger', 'satiation', 'worry' and 'happiness'.

On the other hand, in the domains of Animals, Plants, General Attributes, or Verbs (with the exception of those that are verbs of bodily function) far fewer body-articulated signs are encountered. Here we find that to the extent that signs are 'iconic', that is, to the extent that they may be seen as being derived from an action that is a representation of some Base (see Chapter 6), they are derived from pantomimic or spatial descriptive depictions which do not involve any reference to bodily parts or functions.

5.7 Sign Action

When considered as phrases of movement, manual signs comprise excursions of the forelimb or forelimbs from a position of rest to a spatial region that serves as the locus of articulation of the sign. The movement that transports the Sign Actor to the locus of articulation will be referred to as the *preparation*. The movement by which the Sign Actor is either moved back to rest position, or moved in the direction of the rest position is referred to as the *recovery*. In signed discourse, signs may succeed one another without any recovery movement or there may be a brief period of partial recovery before the next preparatory movement begins.[10] When the Sign Actor has been moved to the Locus of Articulation it may then engage in a pattern of movement distinctive for the sign. It is this that is referred to as Sign Action. It is the equivalent of what we have elsewhere referred to as the *stroke* of the gestural excursion (e.g. Kendon 1980b).

5.7.1 Pause

In some signs Sign Action comprises nothing more than a brief pause in movement. In such cases all that is required for the performance of the sign is that the hand, arranged in an appropriate shape, be moved to a location. Examples of such signs include, in Warlpiri, TIRINJI 'begging', in which a T hand is simply held forward on an upraised forearm: .J $T_{\wedge\perp}$ (Fig. 5.25); and JANGANPA 'possum', in which a hand in the $X_{\square}$ configuration is simply held forward in neutral space: .$X_{\square\vee\perp}$ (Fig. 5.26). In such instances there is no need to add a Sign Action notation. Signs performed in neutral space rather rarely have Sign Action of this sort. As we shall see later, it is more common among body-articulated signs where, in many instances, all that is required is that the hand be moved so that it approaches or makes contact with the appropriate body part.

Sign Action in one handed neutral space signs (other than Pause just mentioned) will be discussed in terms of five kinds, according to how the limb acts to produce the movement: movement of the Sign Actor in which the Sign Actor is displaced from one location in neutral space to another; forearm rotational movements; wrist movements; movements of the fingers within a handshape; movements of the fingers that change the handshape. The last four kinds of movement may or may not be combined with movement of the first kind.

5.7.2 Displacement movements

Here we refer to movements in which the hand is moved from one part of neutral space to another. For many signs such movements may be simple linear movements: upwards, downwards, forwards (away from the signer) or backwards (towards the signer), or to the left or to the right (in describing signs, movement is always described from the signer's point of view). Thus we have a simple upward movement in Warumungu JINKARLI 'proud': .tG$_{\vee\perp}^{\wedge}$; a simple downward movement in Kaytej ARLTERE 'white': .X$_{\vee\perp}^{\vee}$; movement to the right in Anmatyerre ALHAMPE 'orphan': .A$_{\wedge\perp}^{>}$; movement to the left in Anmatyerre INGWENTHE 'tomorrow': .B$_{<\wedge}^{<}$; movement forward, as in Mudbura NYUNGU- 'give': .B$_{\angle\perp}^{\perp}$; movement toward signer, as in Warumungu WIRRPINY 'all': .H$_{\wedge<}^{\top}$.

Displacement movements are often more complex than this, however. In many signs the path of movement may change direction, resulting in arc-like movements. Thus in Warlpiri KUTUKARI 'night' (Fig. 5.17), after initial contact with the upper chest, a 'flat' (B) hand is moved forward from

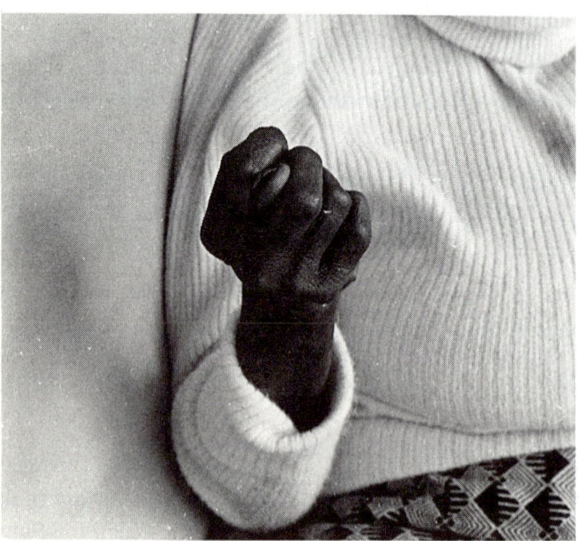

Fig. 5.25 TIRINJI 'begging'

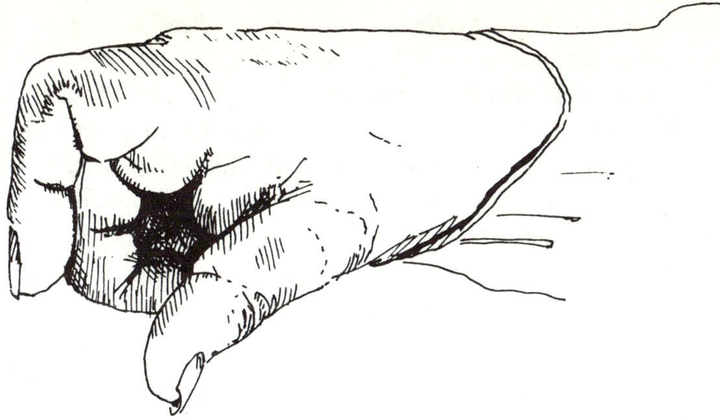

Fig. 5.26 JANGANPA 'possum'

the signer, but upwards and then downwards: $\ulcorner B_{\vee<}{}^{+}$; $B_{\vee<}{}^{\perp\wedge\vee\}}$ (the $\}$ at the end of the string of movement symbols means that the movements are to be read as occurring concurrently). A lateral arc-like movement is exemplified in PARARRI 'rainbow': $.\,\lrcorner X_{\vee\perp}{}^{\wedge>\vee\}}$.

Another sort of complication arises with repetition. Many signs are 'bisyllabic': there is a double pulse to the movement (e.g. in Warlpiri KANA 'digging stick' a 'flat' hand, held palm down, is thrust forward twice: $.\,B_{\vee\perp}{}^{\perp\,'}$). However, in many such instances the hand is displaced laterally before the second repetition occurs. Thus in Warlpiri YUWARLI 'house', for instance, a 'flat' hand held so the palm faces away from the signer is lowered twice, once in front of the signer and once displaced to the right: $.\,B_{\perp\wedge}{}^{\vee\rightarrow\vee}$. The spatial displacement is indicated by the arrow. If the displacement is to the left a left arrow is used. In some signs the overlaid spatial displacement is from side to side. This is indicated by a double headed arrow ($\leftrightarrow$). Where there is spatial displacement with repetition but no particular directions are to be specified, the sign action symbol is simply repeated after a space, as in Warlpiri JINTIRRJINTIRRPA 'Willie Wagtail, bird sp.': $.\,G_{\vee\perp}{}^{\perp\blacksquare\;\;\perp\blacksquare}$ ($^{\blacksquare}$ is a 'manner' marker, indicating that the forward movement is of short amplitude).

Another form of complication arises when one movement pattern is overlaid by another one. In Warlpiri PARNKAMI 'run', for instance, the hand is moved rapidly away from the signer, but as this movement is performed the hand is also moved rapidly up and down: $.\,X_{\vee\perp}{}^{\perp\sim\}}$. In other signs the movement may be modified only as the main movement is brought to an end. Thus in Warlpiri WIRI 'big', in which the main movement is a lowering of a 'bent V' hand in front of the face, as the movement is brought to an end the hand is shaken up and down slightly: $\bigcirc\dddot{U}_{\top\wedge}{}^{\vee\sim}$.

In addition to these linear movements and their modifications, we also find movements which are best described as side-to-side, up-and-down or forward-back. These are different from repeated left or right, up or down, forward or back movements. Whereas, let us say, when a simple forward movement is repeated only the forward movements are performed with definite 'efforts',[11] in a forward-back movement the movement in each direction is performed with definite and equal effort. Examples of Warlpiri signs involving such bi-directional movements include MALIKI 'dog': . G$_{\perp\wedge}$$^{\wr}$ (side-to-side), LAPAJI 'Port Lincoln parrot': U2$_{\wedge\perp}$$^{\sim}$ (up-and-down), and YULJULJU 'praying mantis': ▽O$_{\top\wedge}$$^{\perp I \wr}$ (forward-back).

A final kind of displacement movement to be mentioned is circular movement, in which the hand is moved round and round in consequence of whole arm action. Such circular movement may be either in the horizontal plane (the more common case) or in the vertical plane. In the notation system used here, this difference has not been indicated. While it is possible that further work will show that such a distinction should be made, our experience so far suggests that it is not consistently maintained and does not anywhere constitute a difference of contrastive significance. Signs which use circular motion in Sign Action include Warlpiri MULA 'egg': . G$_{\vee\perp}$$^{@}$, 'blood', in all seven sign languages: . 5$_{\vee\perp}$$^{@}$ (the exact form of the hand may vary in the extent to which the fingers are separated) and Warumungu PUNJJAN 'bite': . G̈$_{\vee\perp}$$^{@}$.

5.7.3 Forearm rotation

The forearm may rotate in a clockwise direction (so that the palm of the hand comes to face upwards - supination) or in an anti-clockwise direction (so that the palm of the hand comes to face downwards or even outwards, laterally - pronation). Both patterns of motion are common as a form of Sign Action and may also be combined with displacement movements in many signs. Signs such as Warlpiri LAWA 'no' employ pronation: . 5$^{\sigma}$ and Warlpiri 'interrogative' employ supination: . J L$_{<\perp}$$^{a\wedge}$. Some signs employ a combination of pronation and supination resulting in a twisting motion of the forearm. This may be seen in Warlpiri WARRIRNI 'to look about for something': . U$_{\vee\perp}$$^{\sigma a \leftrightarrow \wr}$.

A special movement that involves the forearm must also be mentioned, here termed 'tremble' and notated as ^{tr}. In this, the hand is trembled very very rapidly in movements of very small amplitude. It occurs in Warlpiri *warna* 'snake': . U$_{<\perp}$^{tr}; or in Warlpiri *karli* 'boomerang': . G̈$_{<\perp}$^{tr}, among others. It is a remarkable movement pattern, very difficult to execute properly by a European novice. It may be noted that rapid trembling is a movement pattern that is used elsewhere by Aborigines of the North Central Desert, most notably in dancing (cf. Dail-Jones 1984, p.300).

5.7.4 Wrist action

There are a number of signs in which the action is carried out from the wrist (again, often combined with displacement actions). The wrist can extend or flex, or combine these to produce a 'flapping' motion. The wrist can also engage in 'deviation' - that is, it can be moved laterally, either with the thumb leading the motion (radial deviation) or with the little finger leading the motion (ulnar deviation). All of these forms of motion are encountered in Sign Action in the sign languages studied here.

For example, wrist *extension* (hand bends back at the wrist) occurs in Warlpiri YUKAMI 'enter': . B$_{\vee\perp}$$^{\perp\Diamond}$; or in Warlpiri PARDIMI 'arise, sprout': . Ɏ$_{\vee\perp}$$^{\Diamond\wedge}$. Wrist *flexion* (hand bends forward at the wrist) occurs in Warlpiri YARUJU 'quickly': . H$_{\vee\perp}$$^{\Diamond\leftrightarrow\Diamond}$, in Kaytej ANGANKE 'crow': . Ɏ$_{\vee\perp}$$^{\Diamond}$ or in Warumungu MARAPUN 'possum': . X$_{\square\vee\perp}$$^{\Diamond}$. Wrist *flexion-extension* ('wrist flap') is found in certain bird signs where the bird is referred to by the flapping of the hand. Wrist *deviation* occurs in all signs for 'axe': . J B$_{\wedge\perp}$$^{w\text{ɑ}\,\prime}$. Here a twice repeated ulnar wrist deviation produces a chopping movement of the hand.

5.7.5 Finger movements: within-handshape movements

In a number of signs we find the Sign Action involves movements of the digits. Such movement, 'finger wiggle' as it has been termed, occurs within the framework of a given handshape and it does not result in any change of handshape. Finger movements that lead to change of handshape will be treated in the next section.

Within-handshape finger movement is indicated in the notation by ♎ in the Sign Action line. If it is necessary to indicate which digit or digits are involved in the action, these are indicated immediately after the finger movement symbol.

Within-handshape finger movement is observed only in nine handshapes: B 5 G H U tO ьO2 ьO and mϚ. In B and 5 hands, finger movement generally involves all digits. In G, H, mϚ and U hands movement is confined to the extended digit or digits. In ьO, ьO2 and tO hands, movement is confined to the thumb which is moved back and forth in continuous contact with the tips of the other digits.

To exemplify: in the case of B hand signs, we note examples in which the fingers are all flexed as the hand is moved, as in Warlpiri *wati* 'fully initiated man', in which the hand is drawn from left to right across the upper chest and the fingers are flexed as it does so: ⊓$B_{T<}^{>\Omega}$.

In signs involving finger movement within a 5 hand, two varieties may be mentioned, one where all fingers move simultaneously and in the same way, another where there is some differentiation of movement. A sign illustrating the first variety is Warlpiri PANU 'many'. Here a 5 hand is held up and the fingers moved back and forth in unison: . $5_{T\wedge}^{\Omega}$. The second variety is illustrated in a sign for 'single woman' or 'single man' common to several NCD languages. Here a 5 hand is lowered twice, displaced to the right as it does so, but as it is lowered digits 4, 3 and 2 flex slightly at the A-joints: . $5_{<\perp}^{\vee w\triangleleft \Omega}$ 432$^{\rightarrow\vee w\triangleleft \Omega}$ 432.

Signs in which finger movement occurs with handshapes where only one or two digits are extended include Warlpiri JARLA 'honey ant' in which the index finger engages in a kind of beckoning movement: . $G_{\wedge\perp}^{\Omega}$ '; or Warlmanpa WARTILYKA 'bustard' in which the middle finger is extended a couple of times: . $m\varsigma_{T\wedge}^{\Omega}$ '.

Finally, signs in which finger movement occurs within closed handshapes are, as we have said, all instances where the thumb is moved back and forth across the tips of the fingers. For instance, as in Mudbura PILYINGPILYINGA 'red': . $to_{\wedge\perp}^{*\Omega}$ t " or in Warlmanpa KINYUWURRU 'onion grass' : . $bo_{\wedge\perp}^{*\Omega}$ t ".

There is one special finger action that should be mentioned separately. For the sake of notational economy we have given it its own symbol, even though it would be possible to write it out in terms of the symbols already devised. This is the action we call 'fingersnap' in which, initially, the thumb tip is pressed against the tip of the second finger. It is then rapidly abducted and the second finger is allowed to 'snap' down onto the ball of the thumb. There is usually an audible click as a result of this action. To indicate this action we simply write ʄn. The orientation of the hand as the finger snap is performed is written using the orientation symbols as subscripts to ʄn . If, as is often the case, the hand is moved as the fingersnap is being performed, this movement is indicated by placing the movement symbols as superscripts, just as if ʄn was a Hand Shape symbol. Thus, for example, Warlpiri NYURRUWIYI 'long time ago' is written in the following way:

$$. fn_{<\perp}{}^{\vee < a \}}$$

As the fingersnap is performed the hand is moved downwards and leftwards and the forearm supinates.

The fingersnap occurs in several signs in each of the seven NCD sign languages.These signs all have in common either the meanings of extremes of time or space (as in 'long time ago', 'long way away'); or the meaning of sudden onset or completion of something (as in 'burnt', 'cooked', 'flare up', and the like).

5.7.6 Finger movement: handshape change

A second type of finger movement in Sign Action is movement that leads to a change in handshape. This is quite widespread in all of the NCD languages (occurring in roughly one tenth of all the signs recorded in each). In describing signs in which this occurs we first indicate the initial handshape and then, following the Orientation and any other Sign Action symbols that are needed, the terminal handshape is then given, in square brackets. Thus in Warlpiri, for the sign for *marlu* 'kangaroo' an 'O' hand (all fingers curved so their tips contact the tip of the thumb) is opened twice to a 'cupped 5' configuration (all digits abducted but partially flexed so hand is like a basket). The sign is written as follows (see Fig. 5.27):

$$. 0_{\vee\perp}[{<}5]'$$

In this case, where the orientation of the hand remains unchanged, the orientation signs for the second handshape are not written. In some cases there may be forearm movement or displacement movement as well and in such cases it is sometimes necessary to show the new orientation.We find that the number of different handshapes that are found as initial handshapes in shape-change signs is quite restricted. Twenty-nine handshapes are recorded as functioning as initial handshapes; however, of these, twelve are found in only one or two signs in the entire corpus examined, while nine handshapes account for 80% of all the cases found. These are listed in Table 5.8.

As will be seen, the handshapes that serve in shape-changing signs are, for the most part, simple Open or Closed handshapes. Digit-extension handshapes are much less common (with the exception of L). Two handshapes are found which occur mainly as initial forms. That is, in the signs in which they occur they are almost always transformed, and they virtually never occur in signs where no handshape change takes place. These are $\check{\text{t}}$o,

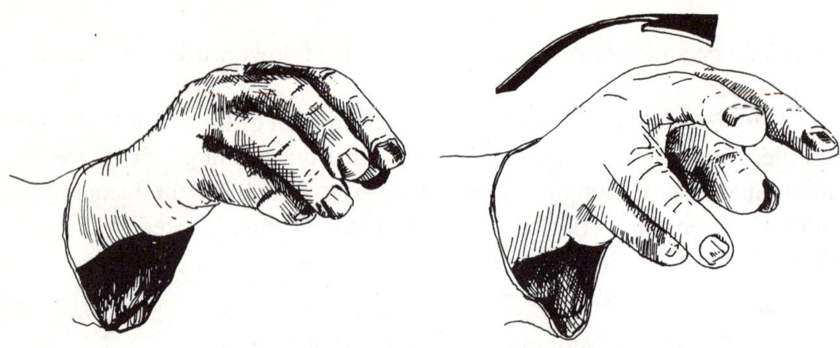

Fig. 5.27 MARLU 'plains kangaroo'

which occurs only in signs in which the Sign Action results in the hand closing to to (as in Warlpiri JANYUNGU 'tobacco': . to^⊥ [to]") and ᶜ5mϚ which occurs only in Warlpiri MANI 'get, cause' . ᶜ5mϚ<⊥ ᵅ[A^⊥] (Fig.5.28) and Warlpiri KURUWARRIKURUWARRI 'variegated'). The handshapes that never occur in shape-changing signs appear to be the more complex handshapes. They include: A T σ of the Closed shapes, ᶜB ьB ×B E, of the Open handshapes, and F G̈ mH mϚ U2 Ⴤ mϚ I of the Digit-extended handshapes.

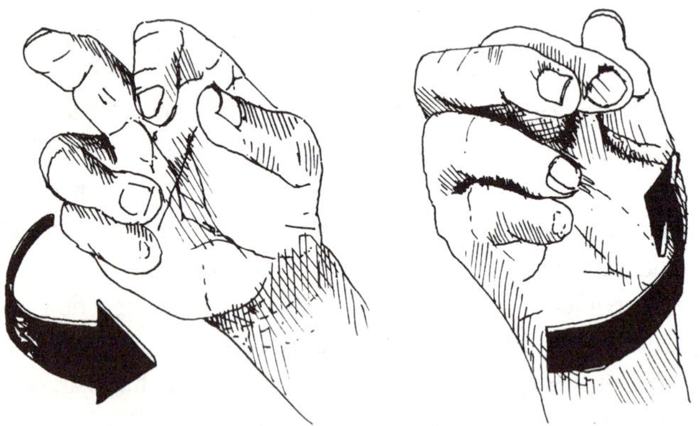

Fig. 5.28 MANI 'get, cause'

An examination of the handshapes into which these initial handshapes are transformed shows that a number of generalizations are possible. First, we find that Open handshapes always change to a Closed handshape, never to a different Open handshape. That is, for instance, B may change to G to or

Table 5.8 Handshapes that change in Sign Action

[Data from Djingili not included as very few examples]

Handshape	Total	P	N	K	R	L	M
5	30	11	6	3	3	3	4
O	19	5	4	1	2	2	5
‹5	19	12	1	1	3	2	
X	14	10		1	1	1	1
B	10	4	1		3	1	1
L	10	3	2		3	1	1
ьO	10		4		1	1	4
U	9	5	1		2		1
Gt	8	3		2	2	1	
5t	6	1		2	2	1	
Â	5	4			1		
to	5	4			1		
×O	4	4					
R	4	1		1	1	1	
A	4	2	1			1	
ťo	3	1	1			1	
C	3		1				2
H	2	1				1	
ьO2	2		2				
U⃛	2				1	1	
X▫	2			1	1		
G	2				1	1	
E	1						1
‹5mϚ	1	1					
G⃛	1					1	
U	1	1					
×B	1				1		
Bt	1					1	
B⃛	1	1					

A, but it does not change to 5, ‹5, or 5t. Likewise, Closed handshapes, such as A or X, are never observed to change to other Closed handshapes such as ьO or O. Third, Digit-extended handshapes such as G, H or U are very rare among the handshapes that do change, and they never change to a Closed handshape, only ever to another Digit-extended handshape.

In addition we find that for some initial handshapes there is a greater range of terminal handshapes than for others. Thus 5 has been observed to transform into to A E and Y; B has been observed to transform into G to Y and A. On the other hand a handshape such as X only ever transforms into G, H only ever transforms into U, U into H and L only ever transforms into bO.

Taking these generalizations together, it would appear that the occurrence of handshape-change is governed by two principles. First, the change that occurs is that which will give rise to the greatest contrast (thus, always Open to Closed and Closed to Open, never Open to Open or Closed to Closed). Second, the change that occurs is the result of action occurring only in those fingers that are active in the initial handshape. For example, in the X handshape, the index finger is fully flexed at all joints so that the nail is in contact with the tip of the thumb. The index finger is, thus, in this handshape, the digit that is active, all the others being held in relaxation. The only single action the index finger can engage in, given its posture in the X hand, is that of extension. That is why X only ever changes to G and not to some other handshape. In 5, on the other hand, where all five digits are fully extended and abducted, all five digits are active. A single phrase of finger action can lead to several different handshapes in this case because there are several different ways in which they can, in a single act, be rearranged into a new position.

5.7.7 Movement in two handed signs

Two handed signs, as we have seen, are divided into symmetric signs in which both hands act in the same way and assume the same handshape, and asymmetric signs, in which one hand serves as the locus in relation to which the other hand performs some action. In such cases the handshapes in the two hands may either be the same or different.

In respect to two handed asymmetric signs there is nothing additional that need be said about Sign Action, except in regard to contact, which will be treated in the next section. In respect to two handed symmetric signs, however, a few remarks should be added in regard to how the two hands may interact.

Where the two hands both perform in parallel, the Action engaged in is given after the second of the two handshape symbols, which are separated by a vertical bar to indicate that they act in parallel. Thus in the Warlpiri sign for *yarrara pi-nyi* 'winnow' both hands, palms facing one another, are lowered, trembling as they do so: . ɹ5>⊥ ' ɹ5<⊥ ˇtr . On the other hand, where the two hands move in relation to one another the Sign Action symbol is written between the two handshape symbols. Thus 'swag' (Australian English for bed-roll) in several languages is two hands moved round and round one another: . B⊤> ⑨B⊤<.

Interaction movements include Circle (⑨), as just mentioned, Approach (ˣ), Separate (÷), and Cross over (⁺). The Enter and Hold interaction movements that have been described in ASL I have not observed in the NCD languages.

5.7.8 Contact

In two handed asymmetric signs and in body-articulated signs the Sign Action quite often involves the hand making contact with the subordinate hand or other body part that serves as the articulation location. In the descriptions followed here we have distinguished Simple Contact and Durational Contact. In Simple Contact the hand just touches the articulation location, either initially or terminally. In Durational Contact the hand makes sustained contact during the enactment of the sign. In most cases this amounts to a brushing or rubbing of the articulation location.

In addition to distinguishing manner of contact in this way it is also often necessary to specify what part of the hand makes the contact. In some signs this is not needed, since the part of the hand that makes the contact may be predicted from the hand orientation, but in many instances, within a given orientation, the hand could make contact in a number of different ways. Thus we have distinguished a number of Contact Points.

Simple contact is illustrated in Warlpiri NGURRA 'camp' (Fig. 5.1). Here an O hand is simply placed in contact with the cheek: 3O<^ ˣ. More complex is the case of JUNGARRAYIJUNGARRAYI 'native tobacco, sp.' (Fig. 5.29). Here an O hand is placed in contact with the forehead, and then it is moved away in an arc-like motion. This is done twice: ⌒O⊤⊥ ˣ⊥ˇ}' . Note that the contact sign precedes the movement signs, indicating that it occurs first.

Durational contact is illustrated in Warlpiri MARNA 'grass', where a fist hand is moved toward the signer twice, rubbing against the other hand as it does so, which is also held as a fist: . A⊤> \A⊤< ⁎⊤ ' (Fig. 5.30). In Warlpiri, YARDAMANYAMANYA 'Bindi eye, plant, sp.', we note a rubbing

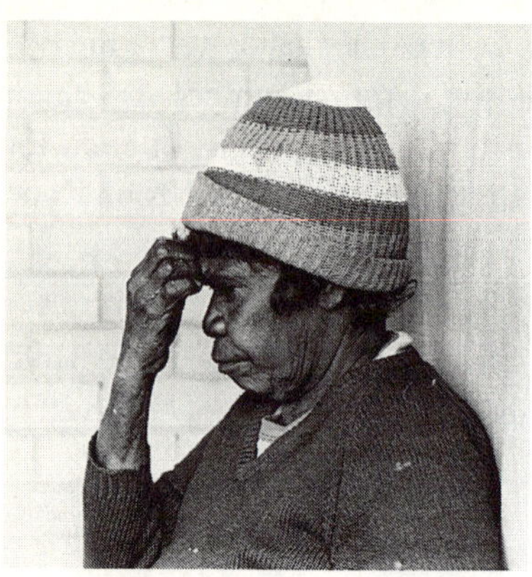

Fig. 5.29 JUNGARRAYIJUNGARRAYI 'native tobacco, sp.' The hand begins in contact with forehead and is moved away twice in a forward and downward direction

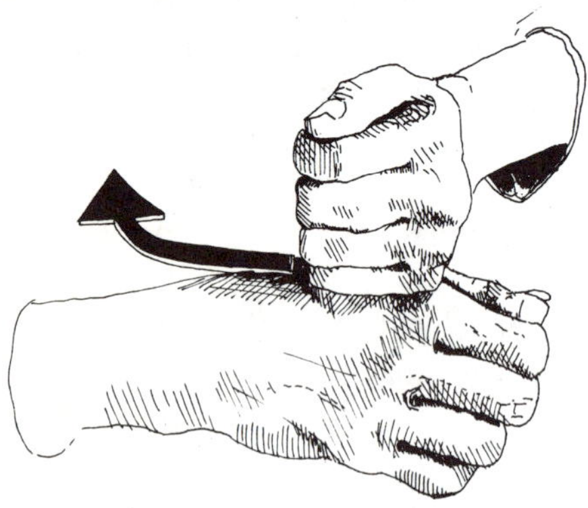

Fig. 5.30 MARNA 'spinifex grass'

action: . $U_{\top}$ › \ $5_{\vee\perp}$ $^{\ast h\}}$. The ^{h} following the contact sign indicates that contact is made, in this case, with the heel of the hand, rather than with the palm or the finger tips.

Contact points distinguished include heel of hand, just mentioned; palm of hand (noted as p); side of hand ($^{+}$); segment of digit ($^{▯}$); tip of digit (^{ᵃ}); and B joint of digit (^{bn}). In the case of digit contact points, where it is necessary to specify the digit making the contact this is done by inserting **t** for thumb or a number for digits 1 to 4, immediately after the contact point sign.

5.8 Conclusions

The foregoing introduction to the way in which the body parts are organized for the production of signs and to the range of different Sign Actor configurations, loci of articulation and patterns of movement found in the NCD sign languages here investigated suggests a number of general points.

As we stated at the outset, at the level of sign structure, it appears that these NCD sign languages do not differ from one another in any significant way. Thus, in the summary to follow, the statements to be made can be taken to apply to all of the NCD sign languages investigated.

1. The NCD sign languages are overwhelmingly systems of *manual* expression. Virtually no use is made of the face in sign formation. An examination of signed discourse (in this case only in Warlpiri signers) also shows that facial action does not appear to be formalized as a grammatical device. To be sure, as we shall see later (Chapter 9), when signing sentences or narrative, a signer may make use of gaze and posture shifts and of facial expression, but it does not appear that these usages are patterned in ways that are peculiar to sign language expression. They are little, if at all, different from the kinesic usages found when speech is being used.

In this respect, it would seem, these NCD sign languages differ rather markedly from such primary sign languages as we have knowledge of. In these sign languages, as has been shown by Liddell (1980) and Baker and Cokely (1980) for American Sign Language, by Vogt-Svendsen (1983) for Norwegian Sign Language, and by Kendon (1980c) for a primary sign language from the Lagaip Valley in Papua New Guinea, facial and other extra-manual action is of crucial importance both at the lexical level and at the grammatical level. That they do not play a part in these NCD sign languages is doubtless attributable to the fact that, in the first place, these sign languages are not primary, but are alternate sign languages and have, in consequence, a close association with the spoken languages of their users. Second, they are learned late in life. Evidence from the study of primary sign language acquisition suggests that extra-manual aspects of the sign language are not easily learned by hearing users of such sign languages or by those who have lost their hearing late in life and learned sign language as a result. The formal integration of facial action into a sign language appears to be something that occurs only when the sign language is truly primary: when it is the first language to be acquired, that is to say.

In regard to the NCD sign languages studied here, however, a further factor that would inhibit the use of the face in signing must be mentioned. We noted in Chapter 4 that when a woman is observing the mourning speech taboo she avoids any production of articulate vocalization. To ensure this, she tends to hold her mouth tightly closed, in a sort of clamp posture. This would certainly make it much harder to use the face expressively.

2. The sign languages of the NCD are predominantly *uni-manual*, and there is evidence that one of the processes of sign change in these sign languages is in the direction of one handedness. In this they appear to be similar to other Australian sign languages recorded from different areas (e.g. Roth's 1897 material from North-West-Central Queensland or West's 1961-1965 material from Cape York Peninsula) but, again, appear to be different from such other sign languages of which we have much knowledge.

3. We have discussed the formational characteristics of these sign languages in terms of the three aspects, here termed Sign Location, Sign Actor and Sign Action. The findings in respect to each of these aspects may now be summarized.

Sign Location. Approximately two-thirds of the signs recorded are enacted in space immediately in front of the signer's body in what has commonly been termed 'neutral space'. This is the space into which a signer may move her hand without extending her upper arm. There are a few signs that are distinguished from one another only in terms of whether they are enacted high up or low down in this space, but for the most part no differentiation within this space needs to be made. A few signs have also been encountered in each NCD sign language in which an extended upper arm or an upraised forearm, or both, is part of the Sign Actor organization distinctive for the sign. In such cases the sign may be enacted far in front of the signer, far to the side or above the head. Such instances are exceptional, however and, for the most part, in ordinary interaction, neutral space signing is done just in front of the body. However, such signing space may vary according to the circumstances of use. Thus in long distance signing the arms may be upraised; in emphatic signing (seen when signing is used in quarrelling) the arms may be fully extended forward; in signed conversations that occur between people when walking single file, signing may be done behind the back or above the head so that the person behind may see.

Roughly one third of the signs recorded are *body-articulated*. That is, the sign is performed in contact with, or close to, a non-manual part of the body. It was found that some 35 different body locations were used. We showed that most locational differentiation occurred in the facial region and that, in all NCD sign languages, of the body-articulated signs recorded, two-thirds were articulated in the facial region. We also found that there was some correlation between handshape and location of articulation, the more complex Digit-extended handshapes occurring more often in signs articulated in the facial region than elsewhere. These findings are similar to those reported from analyses made of other sign languages and may be interpreted in terms of the way features of the visual perceptual system influence the formation of signs.

We noted that the NCD sign languages made common use of a number of lower limb locations, which are very rare in sign languages such as ASL, and they also showed much more differentiation of locations in the thoracic region, including the use of the breast as a sign location.

Sign Actor. As already mentioned, in a few signs arm position appeared to be distinctive. In general, however, the discussion of Sign Actor could concentrate on the features of handshape and orientation. Orientation has here been treated as a component of the Sign Actor. We find it necessary to notate hand orientation, but it does not seem to merit extended separate discussion.

Hand shape requires extended analysis. We have distinguished fifty-two handshapes in all, but find that the emic set of handshapes (the hand-shapes that appear to be contrastive) varies from between twenty and thirty-five across the seven sign languages. However, between 80% and 97% of the signs in these languages are accounted for by a set of eighteen handshapes that are common to all seven sign languages. The range of handshapes employed, thus, is highly similar among them, although two of them - Warlpiri and Warumungu - were notable in that they used a number of highly specialized handshapes not found in the other languages.

A comparison between the handshapes found in the NCD sign languages and those described in ASL showed that while there was a fair degree of overlap, there were also some differences. Thus there are several NCD handshapes that do not occur in ASL and, likewise, a number of ASL handshapes that are not found in the NCD sign languages. However, it is notable that the number of different handshapes distinguished within each language is very similar to the number of handshapes distinguished in other sign languages - suggesting that the size of the emic handshape set is similar, regardless of the sign language under consideration.

It was found further, however, that some handshapes that are very frequently used in NCD sign languages are considered complex, or 'marked', in sign languages such as ASL where they occur with much less frequency. At the same time, a so-called 'unmarked' handshape - C - which is widely used in ASL was found to be very rare in use in the NCD sign languages. The frequent use of more complex handshapes in the NCD sign languages may reflect the fact that, unlike primary sign languages, they are learned by adults, relatively late in life.

It was found in respect to signs using two hands that the handshapes in common use in both the symmetric and asymmetric two handed signs were drawn from a restricted set of mostly the simple Open and Closed handshapes.

It was further found that in the asymmetric signs, the number of different handshapes found in the subordinate hand were far fewer than those found in the dominant or active hand. Furthermore, although they included some complex handshapes, on the whole they were confined to simple Open and Closed hands. These findings are quite similar to those that have been reported by investigators of primary sign languages, suggesting, once again, that there are entirely general principles of organization to be discovered.

Sign Action. Finally, in respect to Sign Action, we observed two special kinds of action: fingersnap and tremble. Otherwise, a wide range of action patterns are found to be employed and, in this regard, the NCD sign languages do not seem to differ in any marked way from other sign languages.

Overall, it may be said that although there are several ways in which, in formational terms, the NCD sign languages differ from a primary sign language such as ASL, there are enough important similarities to allow us to maintain the (perhaps rather unsurprising) view that the principles governing sign formation in the NCD sign languages are the same as those found operating in any other sign language. Because of the mode of production of signs, and given the characteristics of both the anatomical structure and the visual perceptual systems of the producers, we may expect all sign languages to display certain features in common. The results of the analyses of the formational characteristics of the NCD sign languages seem to be consistent with this position.

Notes

[1]I shall assume the right hand is being used, as it generally is. Handedness in signing is discussed below.

[2]Liddell (1984), drawing on earlier work of Don Newkirk, and others, has drawn attention to the way in which different parts of of a sign's performance occur in time and he has proposed a new approach to sign notation to take account of this. There are certainly many advantages to his approach for there are a number of features of sign structure that are more readily accommodated as a result. However, in this work we have made no attempt to follow Liddell. His approach requires a more fine grained analysis of sign structure than we have attempted. In our judgement, the aspectual approach that we have followed remains appropriate for the rather coarse analysis undertaken here. Liddell's approach provides a framework for the next step in any analysis of sign structure. It demands much greater refinement and depth.

There are also quite practical reasons for not following Liddell's approach in this work. First of all, an economical and practical system of notation has yet to be developed to accommodate it. Second, even if this was available I could not have used it, for at the time his article had appeared, most of the work for the present study had been completed. The task of revising my descriptions and the associated notation system in the light of his suggestions would have required an entirely new period of research. It was not thought feasible to undertake this.

[3]The alterations introduced are, for most part, those which proved necessary when adapting the notation to a font that could be installed in a Macintosh computer.

[4]In this case only Hand Configuration is noted since the arm position is 'unmarked' - i.e. the arm is simply held in the position needed to hold the hand in the location characteristic for the sign. For examples of signs in which arm position does have to be marked, see below.

[5]Contact symbols are explained below.

[6]Termed *yurltu* in Warlpiri, literally 'hollow', as in 'hollow log'.

[7]*Palka* also can occur as a preverb, as in *palka jarri-mi* 'to appear' or *palka ma-ni* 'to find'. It can also occur as a suffix. It is signed in the same way in all occurrences.

[8]*Jilimi* is the common expression for 'single women's quarters.*Warntamarri* refers to an especially large *jilimi* where sleeping places are laid out in an extended linear arrangement.

[9]Semantic domains used here are based partly on those suggested in Sutton and Walsh (1979).

[10]The question of sign juncture will be taken up in detail in Chapter 9.

[11]'Effort' meant here in the technical sense of Laban and Lawrence (1947). See also Dell (1970) for an account of this aspect of movement.

6 Sign form and sign meaning

6.0 Introduction

We turn now from a description of sign structure to an inquiry into sign form. Our question shall be, why do particular signs have the forms they do? In Warlpiri, why is *warungka* 'crazy, senseless' signed by pointing to each ear with a flat hand, or in Warumungu, why is *parlkarrparlkarr* 'gear, stuff' signed by twice slapping the left hand, held as a fist, with the palm of the right hand? As we shall see, signs come to have the forms they do as a result of several different factors. To a significant extent, they are shaped by certain system requirements, such as the need to keep signs distinct from one another, and that they conform to certain general patterns of organization, such as those that apply to two handed signs, or to signs in the facial region, as discussed in the last Chapter.

The operation of such system requirements does not provide a sufficient answer to our question, however. Although we may suppose that the differences between the Warlpiri signs for *ngurra* 'camp', *malirdi* 'son-in-law' and *warlalja* 'one's own kin', all of which are enacted in contact with the cheek (Fig. 6.1), can be accounted for in part in terms of the requirement that they contrast in handshape because they all use the same locus of articulation, we may still ask why the cheek is used for these signs and not some other body part; and we may still ask why the O hand is used for NGURRA, the 'curved B' for MALIRDI and the extended index finger hand for WARLALJA. Other handshapes, equally contrastive, it would seem, could just as well have been selected. Can any explanation be brought forward to account for the handshapes that are used?

It is widely assumed that signs in sign languages take the forms they do because they are derived from depictions of some feature of their meaning. There is a certain amount of truth in this idea and it does have value in giving an account of the origin of many signs in NCD sign languages, just as it does for many signs in other sign languages. If we are told that the Warumungu sign for *karnarnti* 'mother' is to tap the center of the chest with the finger tips of the right hand (⊓c5$_{\top <}$ $^{\vee}$ '), we are immediately tempted to suggest that the sign somehow makes reference to the mother's breast and thus expresses the

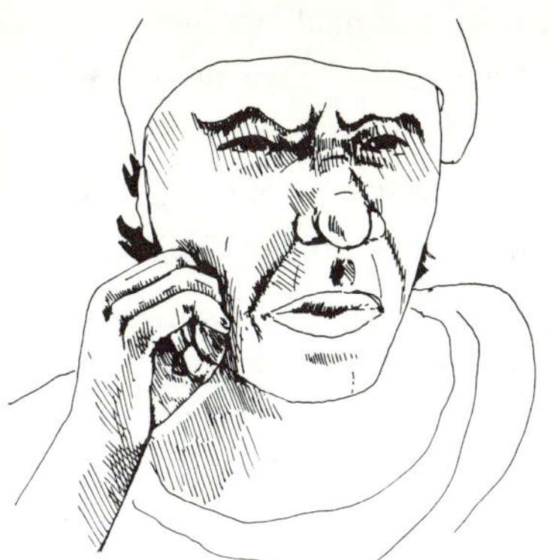

Fig. 6.1 NGURRA 'camp'

Fig. 6.2 WARLALJA 'one's own kin'

Fig. 6.3 MALIRDI 'son-inlaw, mother-in-law, etc.'

notion of 'mother' by referring to a part of the body that mediates the mother's most characteristic mode of relationship with her child. Likewise, if we are told that the Warlpiri sign for *puluku* 'bullock' is to point an extended index finger toward the side of the head and move it in a partial circle (3G$_{\vee <}$$^{\circlearrowleft}$), we immediately suppose that the sign expresses the notion of 'bullock' by depicting its horns.

A moment's consideration will show, however, that although we can, in cases like this, infer with some confidence that a visual image is being represented in the sign, at the same time, we must see that the enactment of the sign is only to be understood as being a possible *derivation* from such a representation. Touching the center of the chest twice with the finger tips of a spread hand is not in any sense an adequate depiction of a mother's breast or of the act of holding a baby to it. A circular movement of an index finger directed toward the side of the head does not constitute an accurate sketch of the shape of a bullock's horn. In short, it will be seen that a consideration of such examples shows that although the forms signs have can often be seen to originate in some kind of visual representation of an object or an action, in functioning as signs in the sign language they do not necessarily retain many of the features of such depictive gestures and they do not convey their meanings because they are depictive.

Nevertheless, it appears that the forms of a great many signs are to be understood in terms of the idea that, in creating a sign for something, bodily action is employed to create a concrete image of something connected to the meaning that is to be conveyed. In other words, signs are not created by combining features from an arbitrary repertoire within each of the three aspects. They are created as dynamic expressive forms which serve to present a concrete image of some pattern of action, form of movement, or physical shape. The activity required to create such a concrete image then becomes simplified and reorganized, so that it retains just those features which are required to maintain it as a distinctive form within the system of signs that the sign language makes use of, regardless of whether it also retains features that can be interpreted as representational.

The forms of a great many signs can be accounted for, thus, as a product of two processes which we shall term *image representation* and *sign formation*. By image representation is meant the creation of a gestural representation of some concrete image that has been selected as symbolic of the concept to be referred to. *Sign formation* refers to the process by which such gestural representations become transformed into expressions which are stable, shared by others, and which are structured in terms of both general formational constraints and the repertoire of contrastive locations, handshapes and movement patterns specific to the particular sign language.

We suggest that these processes are quite general, and will be found to be in operation in any sign language. We hasten to add, however, that there are other processes of sign formation in operation as well, which are also important. In American Sign Language, for instance, as discussed by Battison (1978), many signs show influences from English fingerspelling. Thus there are a number of ASL signs which can be shown to be derived from renditions in fingerspelling of English words. In other cases, ASL signs may be 'initialized', that is, they may be altered so that a handshape is used that is reminiscent of a letter in the fingerspelling alphabet. that is the initial letter of the English word commonly used to translate the sign. For instance, an ASL sign commonly translated as 'way' in English may sometimes be made with the W handshape from the fingerspelling alphabet, instead of the 'flat' hand that is otherwise used. Again, also in American Sign Language, many signs can be shown to be derived from a combination of two independent signs. The sign for 'home', for instance, has developed from a combination of the signs SLEEP and EAT. The sign for 'strawberry' is derived from a combination of the signs RED and SECRET. Such combinations are widespread, in fact, and are an important source of lexical innovation. In most cases, the signs that are combined in this way lose their separate identity, with the result that a wholly new sign is formed (Klima and Bellugi, 1979, Ch. 9).

In the NCD sign languages we find nothing comparable to initialization, and we rarely find compounding processes that are like those described for ASL. Compounding occurs most frequently in signs for expressions in the spoken language that are compounds.and in such compounds the two signs only occasionally fuse to form a new sign. They usually retain their separate identities and thus continue to match the agglutinative form of the compound in the spoken language. For instance, the sign for *parlkarrparlkarr*, mentioned above, has a reduplicate organization in part because it is related to a word in the spoken language that has a reduplicate structure. *Parlkarrparlkarr* is a reduplication of *parlkarr* 'short, cut off'. *Parlkarr* is signed by lowering the palm of the right hand sharply on to the ulnar side of the left hand, held as a fist (Fig. 5.4). The sign for *parlkarrparlkarr* 'gear, stuff' is signed, as we mentioned above, by hitting the fisted left hand twice with the palm of the right hand. The form of this sign, thus, in this case is to be explained as a kind of calque of the spoken form by which it is glossed.

Signs in sign languages may thus derive from importations from other semiotic systems (as with initialized forms in ASL), from the fusion of signs in combinations, or, as in the NCD sign languages, from a representation of the morphological structure of spoken language forms. Notwithstanding this, the process of image representation remains quite central in importance as a source of origin for signs. It is this process, and how sign formation processes operate in relation to it, that forms the subject of this chapter.

6.1 The form-meaning relationship: base and referent

When the form of a sign is governed by its meaning the sign is said to be 'iconic' or 'motivated'. To say a sign is 'iconic' is to suggest that it is a 'picture' of its meaning. To say that a sign is 'motivated' is to suggest that its form is somehow 'caused' by its meaning, although such an expression does not specify the nature of this causation.

A moment's reflection will show that where there is a 'motivated' or 'iconic' relationship between a sign's form and its meaning this relationship is far from straightforward. For instance, take the sign for 'fully initiated man' that occurs in all of the seven NCD sign languages considered here. In this sign a 'flat' or B hand, palm facing the signer, is moved rapidly from left to right across the signer's upper chest, often with the finger tips in contact, and usually with the fingers flexing as the action is performed ($\sqcap B_{\top <}{}^{> \divideontimes\, \Omega\, \rangle}$: see Fig. 5.6). Throughout this region of Australia it has been the custom for fully initiated men to have horizontal raised scars cut in their chests. These cicatrices are created largely for reasons of decoration (Meggitt 1962, p. 315) but they do serve as a highly obvious badge of the man's status. It seems likely that the sign that is so widely used to mean 'fully initiated male' is to be understood as deriving from a movement which serves to sketch the presence of these scars. However, it is to be seen that although the sign may be understood as originating as a representation of these scars, this is not what the sign means. The sign stands for the concept 'fully initiated male', just as does, say, the word *wati* in the spoken language of the Warlpiri or *kartti* in Warumungu. Thus it is necessary to distinguish between what is represented in the sign and the sign's meaning. Following Cohen, Namir and Schlesinger (1977) and Mandel (1977), the object or feature of an object, the action pattern or pattern of movement that the bodily action of the sign may be seen to be representing may be called the *base* of the sign. The meaning that the sign has when it is used in the sign language may be referred to as the sign's *referent*.

A few additional examples may help to make this distinction clear. In the sign used in Warlpiri to refer to an edible solanum fruit, *wanakiji* , the hand is held with all fingers flexed to the palm, except for the fourth finger, which is fully extended. The hand is then pronated several times to produce a succession of outward movements of the extended finger. The *base* of this is the employment of a little wooden tool, the *kajalarra* , to clean the solanum of its poisonous black seeds. However, the *referent* of the sign is the fruit itself. In the sign for *yawulyu* 'women's ceremonies' the tips of the extended index and second fingers (held in a V arrangement) are drawn from left to right across the upper chest (Fig. 5.7), the *base* of this sign being the lines that are painted across the upper chest as part of the ceremony (Fig. 6.4). Or again, in the sign for the verb *yi-nyi* 'give' a flat hand, palm upwards, is moved forward from the signer. The *base* of this sign is the action of presenting something on an open hand for someone else to take. The *referent* of the sign is the more general notion of giving, which is much broader than the concrete act of handing something to someone.

Fig. 6.4 *Yawulyu* designs worn during dancing at a public ceremony at Yuendumu

In the light of this distinction between base and referent, it will be seen that in considering how the form of a sign may be related to its meaning, there are three separate issues to be discussed. First, there is the question of the kind of relationship the action of the sign bears to its base. The action of the sign may sketch a feature of its base, as in the sign for *yawulyu*; the handshape assumed in the sign may model some feature of its base, like the handshape used in the sign for *kajalarra;* or the handshape and action of the sign may mimic some feature of a concrete pattern of action. There are, that is to say, different *techniques* by which a base may be represented in sign. Secondly, however, one may consider how the base itself was selected. For instance, to represent the notion of *wanakiji,* why is the tool used to prepare it for consumption selected as base, rather than some feature of the fruit itself? In Warlpiri sign language an extended index finger, wagged back and forth, is a common sign for *maliki* 'dog'. Evidently, a dog's wagging tail has been taken as base here. Dogs have many other characteristics, however, and any of these could equally well have been selected. Indeed, differences between signs in different sign languages can arise because a different base has been selected for a sign with the same referent. In Warumungu 'dog'(*kunapa*) is signed by holding the hand so that the fingers are all bunched together and sharply flexing the wrist. The dog's paw, and perhaps some characteristic movement pattern, appears to be the base here. Finally, there is the question of how the base selected is related to its referent. Does it stand as part for whole (as wagging tail stands for whole dog), is it linked by some form of association, is it related because it is something done to or by the referent, is it some symptom of it? The possibilities here are very many of course.

6.2 Techniques of base representation

From the point of view of how signs may be said to represent their base, we may distinguish *presenting* signs, *pointing* signs and *characterizing* signs. Characterizing signs may be further subdivided into *enactment* signs in which a pattern of action is presented and *depictive* signs in which some static feature of the base is presented. Depictive signs may be further divided into those that achieve representation of base features by modelling and those that achieve it by a process of sketching.

In the following paragraphs we shall illustrate the application of these various techniques for base representation ('iconic devices' as they have been termed by Mandel 1977), for the most part with signs drawn from Warlpiri and Warumungu sign languages. It should be stressed that the modes of base representation proposed here cannot be sharply distinguished. Furthermore, signs rarely exemplify only one mode of representation.. Usually we can observe at least two modes in operation at once, as when, for instance, in a widespread sign for 'emu' the handshape is derived from a *model* of the emu's head, but the sign action provides an *analogic enactment* of the mode of movement of the emu's head as it walks (Fig. 6.5). It should also be clear that a more refined treatment of this topic would certainly be possible. There are a

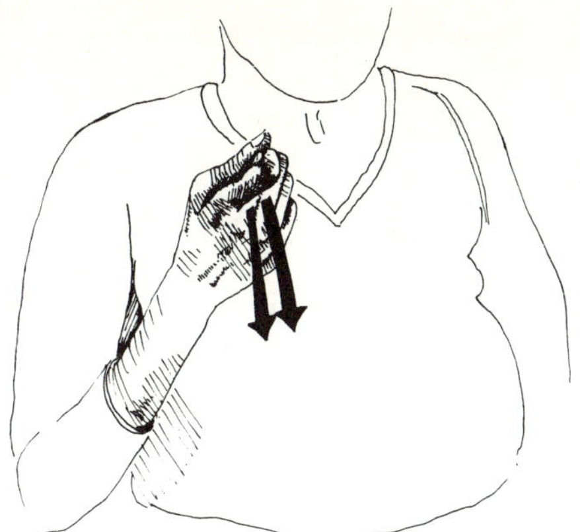

Fi.g 6.5 YANKIRRI 'emu' (Warlpiri)

number of signs which, though they clearly seem to derive from a base representation, cannot easily be described in terms of any of the above categories. What is said here, thus, is but a first approximation only to a treatment of this sort. As will be evident, however, it does appear to raise some interesting issues about the processes involved in the creation of signs in a sign language.

6.2.1 Presenting

In presenting, the base is a concrete object which is presented by the signer to the recipient either as the referent, or as a token of it. In the material we have gathered there are no examples of this in which actual objects are presented as bases in this way. Even if there were, it is unlikely that they could be considered part of the sign language, as such. Presenting, in the sense meant here, may be looked upon as a strategy that is open to users of sign, as indeed it is open to anyone engaged in referential discourse. It is probably employed mainly as a method of disambiguation.

Notwithstanding this, there are some signs which may perhaps be interpreted as involving presenting as a base representation strategy. Thus some signs for body parts involve a 'presentation' of the body part referred to, as in the sign for 'hand' in all of the NCD sign languages. In this sign (Fig. 6.6) the two hands are held in a special 'O' configuration, palms facing the signer, and the right hand is moved twice toward the signer, making contact with the other hand as it does so (. ×O$_{T}$ > \×O$_{T}$ <^{*T} '). Here we may note a combination of the presenting of the hand, which is held in a special configuration so that it is clear that the hand is not doing anything else, and, in the movement of the

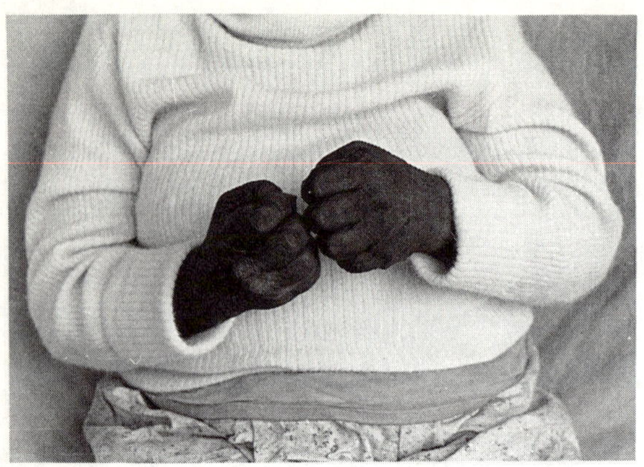

Fig. 6.6 RDAKA 'hand'. One hand moves toward signer while in contact with other hand. If done twice it may serve as a sign for *rdakardaka* 'sign language' (Warlpiri)

right hand, an indexing of it. In other cases we have instances where a body part is presented as a stand-in for something else. The signs for numerals in all NCD sign languages illustrate this, for they involve the holding up of one or more fingers, usually combined with a movement. Thus, for Warlpiri we have:

.tG⊥^ᵕ	JINTA 'one' (upraised index finger, palm outwards, wrist flexed)
.V<⊥›	JIRRAMA 'two' (index and second finger extended and spread, moved to the right)
.W⊤^	MARNKURRPA 'several' (three fingers held up)
.5⊤^ᴊᴄ '	PANU 'many' (all five digits held spread, wiggled back and forth)

Of these we may say that the fingers are being presented as instantiations of the number concepts.

6.2.2 Pointing

In pointing, a hand or some other body part (the head, the chin, the nose, the eyes) is directed toward something, which is then taken as the referent of the point. It is a widely used technique of reference, as much by speakers as by signers. Pointing, like presenting, is an open reference strategy and, like presenting, though it may be used by signers - for example to indicate direction or location or to indicate an object that is being referred to - in these sorts of uses it is no different from the way it is used by speakers and it is thus not a mode of expression that is peculiar to sign language. In Chapter 9, where we discuss the construction of discourse in Warlpiri sign language, we shall have occasion to show how general pointing is made use of in signing. Here we shall discuss the ways in which pointing serves as part of the way in which lexical signs are formed.

Most pointing signs consist simply in the directing of the hand to some part of the body that is to serve as the sign's base. There are also spatially directed pointing signs which serve as demonstratives, pronouns and directional and distance indicators. These will be discussed in a later section (8.3). We will consider body-part articulated pointing signs here.

Body parts that can easily be pointed to are commonly referred to in sign in this way. Thus, in Warlpiri (as in the other sign languages) the nose or the ear is touched by the tip of an extended index finger as a way of referring to 'nose' or 'ear' (as in *mulyu* 'nose': △G$_{\top \wedge}$ $^{\text{?}}$ or *langa* 'ear': ?G$_{< \wedge}$ $^{\text{?}}$). However, an examination of a number of such apparently simple body-part pointing signs shows that there are many different ways in which the pointing is done. Thus a number of different handshapes are employed (besides G we find Y O B etc.), the pointings may or may not involve contact with the body part pointed to, and a distinctive pattern of movement may be involved, as well.

These variations are consistent and are related to three factors: whether the base indexed by the point is directly visible or not, whether it is a specific location or an extended area of the body, and the nature of the relationship between the base of the sign and its referent.

Visibility. The difference between the way in which a visible body part is referred to in sign, as compared to an internal or invisible body part may be seen by a consideration of the following examples, from Warumungu sign:

⌒G$_{< \wedge}$ PURLUJU 'head' (Extended index finger touches forehead)

⌒G$_{\vee <}$ $^{\circledcirc}$ KUMPUMPU 'brains' (Extended index finger makes circular movements to the side of the forehead)

$\sqcap B_{T<}^{*\S}$ LAPPI 'chest' (Flat hand contacts chest palmside and is rubbed back and forth)

$\sqcap O_{T<}^{@}$ MANTURLKA 'heart' (Hand held with fingers curled and tips touching thumb makes circular movement in front of upper chest)

$[\,]Y_{\wedge<}^{\vee\ \vee}$ KALYUWARI 'lungs' (Hand held with only first and fourth fingers extended, lowered in front of each side of thorax)

$[\,]O_{T<}^{><}$ MALIMPARI 'liver' (Hand held with fingers curled to touch thumb is moved toward thorax)

These are all 'pointing' signs, in that the hand is directed toward the body part where the referent is located, but how the pointing is done varies according to whether the referent is visible or not. In general, it would seem, if visible body parts are signed by pointing to them the hand makes contact with the body part that is indexed. If the body part is internal and so not visible, the hand does not make contact. In such cases the hand may assume a shape other than G, and instead of making a simple excursion to its Location of Articulation, some pattern of movement may be engaged in instead. We can see how, in such instances, the pointing sign begins to acquire some of the features of a Characterizing sign.

Extent of area indicated. Likewise, we can compare signs in which two different parts of the body are referred to by pointing, but where the body parts in question overlap in area. Here we find that the G hand or a simple excursion movement is likely to be used for the body part that occupies a small area, whereas sweeping movements, often combined with a B hand or a 5 hand, is used for parts that have a more extensive area. Thus compare, from Warlpiri:

$\frown G_{T\wedge}^{\text{♀}}$ JURRU 'head' (Touch upper forehead with tip of extended index finger)

$\bigcirc\!<\!5_{T\wedge}^{\vee}$ MIPARRPA 'face' (Move 'basket' hand downwards in front of face)

In the first case only the index finger is extended. In the second case, all fingers are extended and spread, and held in a 'basket' shape. Note, too, that no body contact is made in the second sign.

Base-referent relationship. Finally, manner of pointing is varied in relation to how the item pointed to (the base) is related to the referent. This may be illustrated by comparing a number of Warlpiri signs which involve pointing to the ear or ears. For one of these, the referent is 'ear' and here an extended index finger simply touches the ear. The other ear signs are concerned with cognitive functioning, either effective or ineffective. Here the ear is used as the base, but it relates to the referent indirectly, for the ear now stands for 'channel of understanding'. This, it should be added, is a conception held throughout the North Central Desert and it is reflected in the spoken languages. Thus an expression for 'to understand' in Warlpiri is *langa-kurra ma-ni*, literally 'ear-ALLATIVE cause' or 'cause to go to the ear' and in Warumungu it is *pina ja-nta* literally 'ear stand'. Likewise, in Warumungu, an expression for 'senseless, crazy' is *kuwarta-kapurta* , literally 'ear-less'.

The signs for these various expressions all involve a hand movement toward the ear. However, if the meaning is positive - that is, such meanings as 'wise', 'knowing', 'understanding' - the hand assumes a handshape that is also found in signs concerned with movement through space; on the other hand, if the meaning is negative - such meanings as 'senseless, crazy', 'forget', and the like - the hand is a flat hand (B) which here, perhaps, suggests that the ear is blocked or covered. Thus we have, in Warlpiri:

?G‹^ ᵠ LANGA 'ear' (Touch ear with tip of extended index finger)

?Ч‹ ˣ ⁞ ‹5mϚ‹⊥ ᵅ[A]
LANGAKURRA MANI 'understand'
(Approach ear with 'horns' hand - index and fourth finger only extended; follow with sign MANI 'get, cause')

?Ч‹ ˣ PINA 'wise, knowing' (Approach ear with 'horns' hand)

?Y$_{\top <}^{)(}$ ⁞U$_{\vee \perp}^{\perp \blacksquare}$

MANNGI NYANYI 'ponder it, solve it, think it out' (Approach ear with 'horns' hand; follow with sign NYANYI 'see')

?B$_{<\wedge}^{)(}$ WAPARLKU 'not to know something' (Approach ear with 'flat' hand, palm facing ear)

??B$_{<\wedge}^{)(\ \ )(}$ WARUNGKA 'crazy, senseless, insane' (Approach both ears in succession with 'flat' hand)

?B$_{<\wedge}^{\int}$ ⁞ ‹5mϚ$_{<\perp}^{a}$[A]

WAJAWAJA MANI 'to forget' (Move 'flat' hand back and forth beside ear; follow with sign MANI 'cause, get')

It will be seen how only in the sign in which the ear as a physical object is meant (where base and referent are the same) do we have a G hand and physical contact with the ear. In the others the handshape varies according to the meaning of the sign. Furthermore here, where the base and referent are not identical, the base, though pointed to, is not touched.

The same phenomenon may also be illustrated by considering signs that involve the abdominal region as a location of articulation. In the following set (again from Warlpiri) the abdominal region is pointed to, first as a way of referring to the stomach, then in a sign for 'child of woman', presumably indicating the place where the child grows;[1] then, in a sign for 'hunger' it is pointed to as the region where feelings of hunger are experienced; finally, in signs for 'sated' or 'full up after eating', the abdomen is again pointed to. But, as will be seen, in each case the handshape is different. Once again, where the base and referent are identical we see the G hand is used and the Sign Action involves simple touching. Where the base and referent are not the same, other handshapes are used and the movement patterns are more complex:

⊔G$^{\varphi}$ MIYALU 'stomach' (Touch abdominal area with tip of index finger)

⊔B$^{\varphi}$ KURDUNA 'child of woman - sister's child,etc.' (Touch abdominal area with fingertips of 'flat' hand)

⊔B∧‹ ✻ʃ

YARNUNJUKU 'hunger' (Rub abdominal area back and forth with radial side of 'flat' hand)

⊔A∧‹ × ×

PIRDAKU 'sated, full' (Touch right then left side of abdominal area with fisted hand, palm upwards)

6.2.3 Characterizing

In Characterizing signs the base is represented by modelling or sketching its appearance or, where the base is an action or a movement pattern, the base is represented through the form of the sign's Action.

Modelling. Here the Sign Actor is arranged in a pose that suggests a feature of the shape of an object which serves as the sign's base. In Warlpiri, the sign for *ngirnti* 'tail, penis' exemplifies this: . mϚ∨⊥ 6 ' . Here an extended middle finger is presented, obviously depicting a thin appendage (Fig. 6.7). In one sign for *ngaya* 'cat' we have . ЬB⊥∧ ʃ, in which the extended digits are converged into contact with one another to create a fingertip arrangement that is suggestive of the arrangement of pads on a cat's paw (Fig. 6.8). In JILKARLKA 'prickle' we have . ‹5⊥∧ ʃ . Here it appears that the curved fingers suggest the prickles that stick out from the small burr of the 'bindi-eye' plant (Fig. 6.9).[2] In YAMA 'shade' we have . B⊥∧ ⊥▪ in which the flat hand appears to model a flat object that would obstruct sunlight and so create shade. It will be noted that in all of these examples there is a pattern of movement performed as part of the sign. This movement pattern appears to serve as a kind of marking device, 'bracketing' the handshape as the thing that is to be attended to, as if the mere movement of the handshape into signing space would be insufficient.

Signs may combine modelling with pointing. In the previous section some examples were included that illustrated this - as, for instance, ⌐×O⊤‹ ⑤ KURTURDURRU 'heart' or, perhaps, ⊔A∧‹ × × PIRDAKU 'sated, full-up'. Here the O handshape in the first instance suggests the shape of the thing being referred to; in the second example, the fisted hand perhaps suggests the lump or mass of food that is to be found inside the stomach.

Another way in which pointing and modelling may be combined is when one hand serves as the model, the other hand pointing to it. This is a

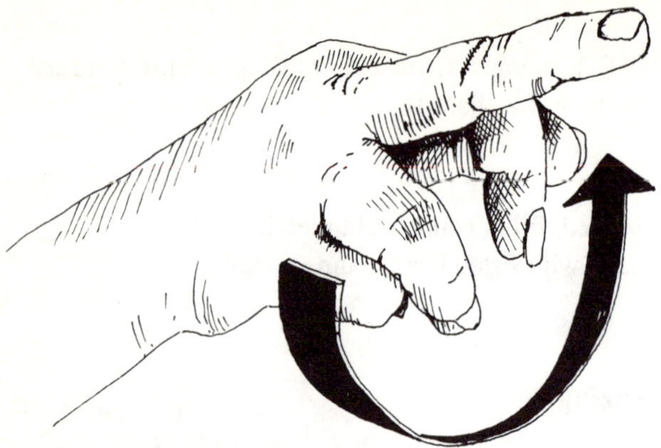

Fig. 6.7 NGIRNTI 'tail'

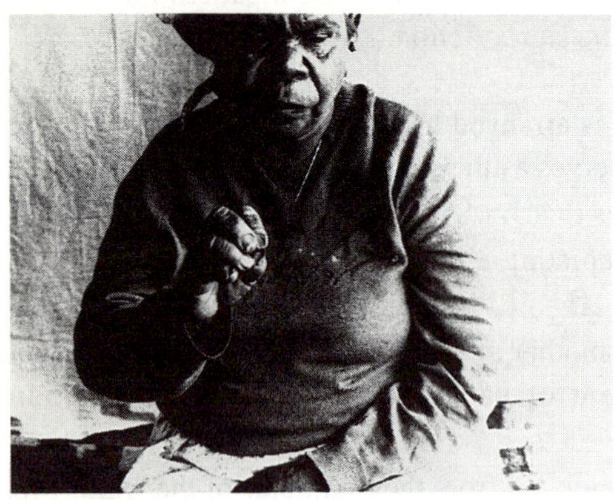

Fig. 6.8 NGAYA 'cat'

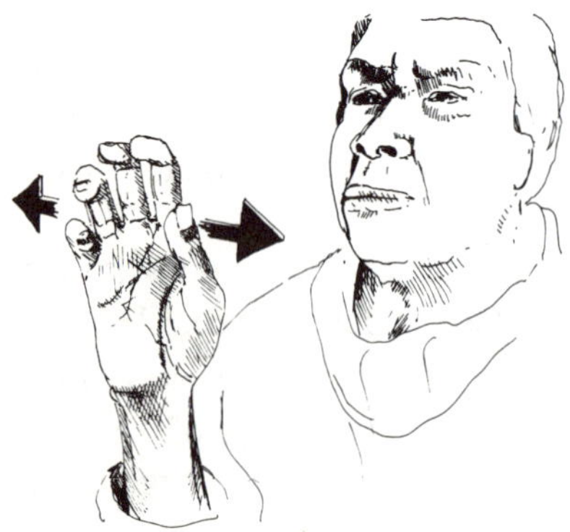

6.9 JILKARLA 'prickle'

possible interpretation of the sign . G∨⊥/G∧<⁑▮^ WATIYA 'tree, stick' (Fig. 5.15). Here the extended index finger of the inactive hand presents a model of a stick, while the movement of the active hand serves to point to it. A similar interpretation can be applied to the Mudbura sign for the same meaning - *kanti* 'tree, stick'. Here the forearm is held in front of the signer, thus presented as the exemplar of a long thin thing, while the extended index finger of the right hand is swept up and down against it as a way of pointing it out: J G∨⊥ I⁑. Somewhat similarly, in the Warlpiri sign for *kakalyalya* 'white cockatoo' we have ▽G̈⊤∧ ˀ ⁞G̈∨⊥ ʔ where the mouth is first pointed to and then a curved index finger is presented as a model of the shape of the mouth - that is, the curved beak of the cockatoo.[3]

Modelling may also be combined with enactment. This is common in signs for implements, where the hand assumes a shape suggestive of some feature of the implement and it then performs an action which is characteristic of the pattern of action engaged in when the implement is used. Examples from Warlpiri include:

. U<⊥[H]" NIPINIPI 'scissors' (Index and second fingers extended to form a V, repeatedly closed and opened)

. 5∨⊥ ⊤[E] YILJIRLI 'rake' (Fingers of hand fully spread. As hand is drawn toward signer, fingers flex slightly)

. G⊤>\G<⊥ ∨▮ "

TURURRU 'song sticks' (Right index finger fully extended taps left index finger repeatedly)

. G̈<⊥ tr< KARLI 'boomerang' (Index finger is held curved. The hand is trembled, then moved left)

Sketching. In sketching the hand is moved through space in such a way as to suggest the outline of something. Here movement describes an aspect of the appearance of the base, it is not a pattern of action. Rather few signs can be found which use what might be called 'pure' sketching. More commonly, it seems, the handshape used in the sketching sign assumes some of the character of what is being sketched, as when a flat hand is used, rather than an index finger, when something flat or with areal extension forms the sign's base.

Examples of 'pure' sketching signs in Warlpiri include MINGKIRRI 'termite mound', in which two extended index fingers move together to describe the outline of something tall and pyramidal, much as a termite mound is (. J G$_{\vee\perp}$ 'J G$_{\vee\perp}$$^{\div\vee}$); PULUKU 'bullock', in which an extended index finger describes a curving forward line, thereby representing the shape of the bullock's horn (3G$_{\vee<}$$^{\circlearrowleft}$); or MANIYI 'money', in which an extended index finger describes a circle, either in neutral space or against the open palm of the left hand, thereby representing the shape of a coin (. B$_{>\perp}$\G$_{\top<}$$^{\circlearrowleft}$).

Sketching signs using other handshapes where some aspect of the character of the object being sketched is thereby incorporated include YUWARLI 'European style house' in which a flat hand, in two forward strokes, appears to depict a sloping roof or, perhaps, a wall (. B$_{\perp\wedge}$$^{\perp\rightarrow\perp}$); MILPIRRI 'legs of rain', appearing as wide dark bands descending from the clouds to the horizon' - signed by moving upwards on a fully extended arm a horizontally held B hand (. ≏B$_{\top<}$$^{\perp\wedge I}$)); or WAKURLU 'head hair' in which a hand with fingers fully spread is lowered down the side of the face (35$_{\vee<}$$^{\vee}$).

Enactment. Enactment signs are those signs in which a pattern of action is characterized. Two main kinds of enactment signs may be distinguished: *mimetic* and *analogic*. In mimetic enactment signs, patterns of manual action that an individual might actually engage in serve as the base, such as chopping with an axe, throwing a boomerang, or moving the steering wheel when driving a car. We may also include here those signs that appear to use an interpersonal gesture or expressive action as a base. In analogic enactment signs, the Sign Action serves to present a movement that has features that are analogous to a movement pattern that is in some way related to the referent. For instance, signs which refer to 'progressing through space' (by walking, running, etc.), commonly involve the movement of the hand through space (often inflected for direction). Such movement is analogous to the actual movement of something through space, but it is not based upon any movement pattern that someone would actually engage in. To sign 'walk' in Warlpiri, for instance, one moves an upright fully extended index finger away from oneself in a series of jerky up-down movements (KARRKAMI 'walk': .G$_{\perp\wedge}$$^{\perp\sim\}}$).[4] The movement of the sign here does not derive from any movement pattern a walker actually engages in. Rather, it provides a movement analogue of a walker's movements, namely, that he moves through space in a definite line and bounces up and down slightly as he does so. In general, we find that mimetic enactment signs employ as bases patterns of action that are carried out with the hands. Analogous enactment signs characterize whole body actions (such as sitting or walking), features of movement patterns typical of animals, or dynamic images that represent more abstract concepts.

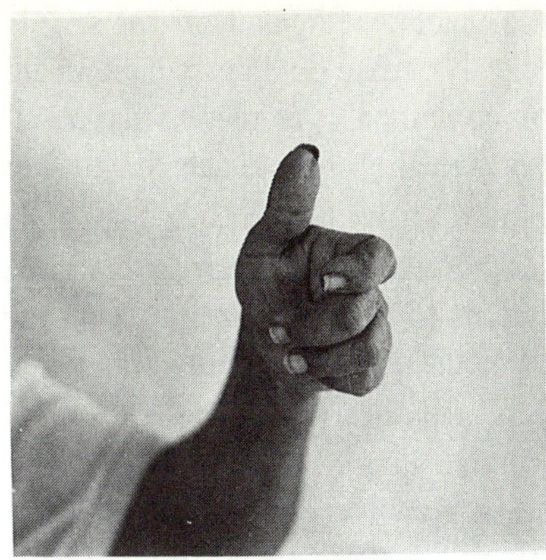

Fig. 6.10 KURLADA 'spear'. The hand is 'trembled'

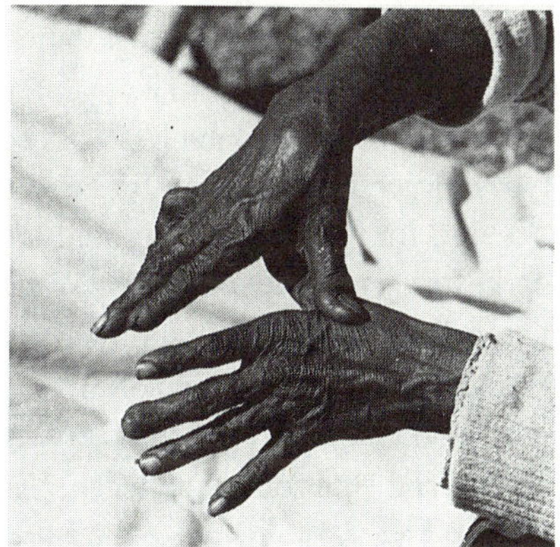

Fig. 6.11 PENSIONER (Yuendumu)

Mimetic enactment signs. Mimetic enactment signs are widely employed as signs for verbs that refer to activities that can be carried out with the hands. Thus we have, for *ma-ni* 'get, take', a sign in which a 'claw' shaped hand is rotated and, at the same time, the fingers are closed (. ᶜ5mϚ$_{\vee\perp}$ᵅ[A]), reminiscent of a grabbing action (Fig. 5.28). For 'hit with hand or held implement', throughout the group of sign languages considered here, we have a sign in which a 'flat' hand is rotated sharply back and forth (as, in Warlpiri, the sign for the verb *paka-rni* 'hit, kill': . B$_{<\perp}$ᵟᵅ) or, to take a more specialized example, the Warlpiri verb *mapa-rni* 'anoint, rub something on someone' is signed with a 'flat' hand making repeated downward movements of short amplitude, which are reminiscent of the action of smearing grease on some vertical surface, such as a person's back.

Many objects are signed by mimetic enactment signs. Here the base is a pattern of manipulative action characteristically carried out in association with the object. Thus, one widely used sign for 'coolamon' is to place a flat hand, with palm oriented upwards, near to or against the hip. This enacts the posture of the hand used when carrying a coolamon at the hip (ʯ B$_{\wedge <}$$^{)(\,\prime}$), as is common when using it to carry a baby. Another widespread sign for the same object, more common among older signers, is to flap a '5' or 'flat' hand (or such a hand with the index finger flexed at the first joint) outwards twice (. ×B$_{<\perp}$$^{\sigma\,\prime}$) in a pattern of action that is probably derived from the repeated tossing of the coolamon, which is done when it is used to winnow seeds by tossing them up and down. In Warlpiri a sign for *pangurnu* 'digging coolamon' is to make scooping movements with the right hand against an upturned left hand (. B$_{\wedge\perp}$\B$_{\vee\perp}$$^{* \top \,\prime}$), in an obvious imitation of scraping sand away, as one does with a *pangurnu* when digging out a soakage. In the Warlpiri sign for *kurlarda* 'spear' (Fig. 6.10) the hand is held with the thumb up, the index finger held in a hook, and the hand is trembled (. X$_{\square <\perp}$^{tr}), a form probably derived from holding a spear in readiness to launch it.

There are a number of signs for types of person, and even for certain animals, that are mimetic enactive. Thus a sign for 'Christian' is to hold the hands forward, palm to palm, in a praying gesture, and wave them back and forth (. ɹ B$_{>\wedge}$$^{\times}$ɹ B$_{<\wedge}$$^{\perp\leftrightarrow\perp}$). A Warlpiri sign for 'pensioner' (Fig. 6.11) is to press the thumb against the side of the left hand, imitating the action of making a thumb print, an early practice used in place of a signature when receiving pension checks (. A$_{\top >}$\5$_{\vee\perp}$$^{\times}$ t $^{\circ}$). A widespread sign for 'schoolteacher' is to perform a rapid lateral movement, overlaid with rapid 'wrist-flapping' movements with the hand held as if something is being held between the thumb and forefinger - clearly derived from the activity of writing (. ≙ ɓO$^{\omega \top}$). As for animals, a widely occurring sign for 'horse' appears to be derived from the action of pulling on reins (. E$_{\vee\perp}$$^{\circ \top \} \,\prime}$); a Warlpiri sign for *jukujuku* 'chicken' (Fig. 6.12) is to tap the left hand with the flexed second joint of the index finger of the right, evidently (as it was explained to me) representing the action of tapping an egg to break it (. U\X$_{\wedge\perp}$$^{b\cap}$); and a sign for *yimangi* 'fly' is to move an index finger rapidly in relation to one or both sides of the face, here representing the action of brushing flies away from the face.

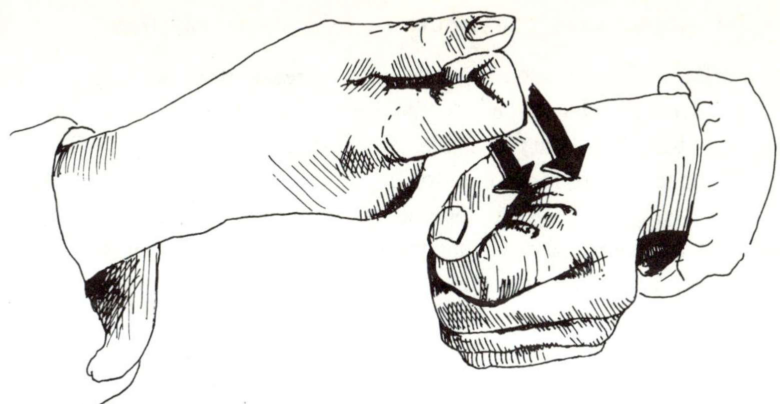

Fig. 6.12 JUKUJUKU 'chicken'

Analogic enactment signs. Analogic enactment is used in signs for activities that are not confined to the hands, but involve other parts of the body that are not employed in signing, such as the feet or the face. We already mentioned the sign for 'walk', above. Examples of the same sort include the signs for 'run', 'sit down', 'stand', 'kneel'.

Analogic enactment is also used in a number of signs for animals, where the Sign Action presents a movement pattern that is an analogue of a characteristic feature of the animal's movement. Thus, the Warlpiri sign for *maliki* 'dog' illustrates this, for here an erect index finger is wagged back and forth in a manner reminiscent of a dog's wagging tail. Likewise, in the sign for *yankirri* 'emu' the hand is held vertically on the forearm, bunched in such a way that the second joint of the flexed index finger slightly protrudes, and the Sign Action consists in a series of wrist extensions, producing a pattern of movement reminiscent of the emu's head movements as it walks: $.\,J\,X_{T\wedge}^{\circlearrowleft\,\prime}$ (see Fig. 6.5).

Analogic enactment also appears to be the device followed in certain signs for more abstract concepts, for example in certain signs relating to time or movement in space relative to the fixed environment. Thus we have a continual back and forth movement in the Warlpiri sign for *tarnnga* 'always, for a long time, eternal': $.\,J\,Y_{<\wedge}^{\,\S}$ (Fig. 6.14). In the sign for *jingijingi* 'pass through or across without stopping' we have the right hand, held as a fist, moving forward across the top of the stationary left hand, also held as a fist, brushing it as it does so: $.\,A_{T>}\backslash A_{T<}^{\ast\perp\,\prime}$.

6.2.4 Handshape and modes of base representation

There is a relationship between mode of base representation employed in a sign and the kind of handshape selected for it. This may be seen from a consideration of Table 6.1. In this Table 657 Warlpiri signs were classified in terms of the mode of base representation employed. For each such group the number of different handshapes recorded is given and the proportion of signs within each group that use B or G handshapes is also shown. Also given is the proportion of signs within each group in which handshape change occurs.

Table 6.1 Handshape (HC) and base realization mode in a sample of Warlpiri signs

MODE	No. of HCs	%G	%B	% with HC change
Pointing	16	38	38	2
Modelling	28	12	16	2
Sketching	12	34	35	7
Mimetic enactment	20	6	20	12
Analogic enactment	17	15	29	18

It will be seen from this Table that Sketching and Pointing employ the least number of different handshapes whereas Modelling employs the largest number. Sketching and Pointing also show the highest proportion of G and B handshapes, Modelling the lowest. Change in handshape occurs least often in Pointing, Modelling and Sketching, with greater frequency in the two Enactment categories.

These findings are fitting. Where base representation is accomplished by indexing or sketching, there we find the highest proportion of the simplest handshapes being employed - for what is important here is the direction in which the hand is moved, not the shape it assumes. In Modelling, in contrast, where the Sign Actor presents a shape, there we find the widest range of different handshapes. In the Enactive signs we also find a somewhat wider range of handshapes being employed. This reflects the fact that many of these signs have as their base a pattern of action which derives from object manipulation. In such cases, the hand often assumes a shape based upon the configuration it would show if the object being manipulated was being held. Consonant with this is the observation that the Enactive signs more often involve change of handshape than do the other kinds of signs.

6.3 Base selection

We must now consider the question of the principles that govern the selection of bases in the creation of signs. The first principle, an obvious one, is that the base must be something that is available for common observation. For example, if we consider how one might choose a base for a sign for 'sleep', one has available only the outward behavior of a sleeper. Aspects of inner experience, such as the dimming of consciousness, cannot serve as the base for a sign. Second, however, there are several different aspects to the outward behavior of a sleeper that could be chosen as a base for a sign for it. Thus one might choose some aspect of the physical posture of a sleeper, one might choose elements from the facial expression of the sleeper, for example closed eyes, or one might choose characteristic breathing patterns, or a noise, such as snoring. In general, we find that bases selected are those that have features that can easily be represented by actions of the hands. Accordingly, we find that heavy breathing or snoring have not been selected for representation in the sign for 'sleep'.

In the sign languages considered here, we find three different signs for 'sleep'. In these, the bases selected are: an aspect of a common posture of the head and hands in sleep, the posture of the whole body, and closed eyes. Thus in Mudbura, Djingili and Anmatyerre sign languages the sign consists in placing a hand against the side of the head: $3B_{<\wedge}^{\times}$. In Kaytej sign language we find that the whole prone body is selected for representation, for the sign comprises a highly abbreviated sketch of something horizontal on the ground: $.\mathring{A}_{\wedge\perp}^{<\sigma}$. In Warlpiri, Warlmanpa and Warumungu, the sign consists in lowering an index finger rapidly in front of each eye: ⌓$G_{\top\wedge}\Omega^{\vee}\ \Omega^{\vee}$, thereby indicating lowered eyelids. Note that in this last case, although facial action could be used to represent eye-closing, it is not. Eye closing is indicated by finger action. This follows a principle, noted in the previous chapter, that facial action is almost never employed in sign formation in these sign languages. In short, we see that the bases that are selected for 'sleep' are those aspects of the sleeper's overt behavior that can readily be represented by actions of the hands.

A third principle governing base selection appears to be the relative ease with which a representation device may be used to form a sign. It appears that of the four main modes of base representation illustrated above - Pointing, Modelling, Sketching and Enactment - some are much more commonly employed than others are. This is probably because some are much easier to use to create signs than are others. Thus, in an analysis of a sample of Warumungu signs we find that the two kinds of Enactment together account for about one half of the signs examined, and Pointing accounts for at least one quarter. Sketching, on the other hand, is least commonly employed, accounting for only 11% of the signs sampled (see Table 6.1). Pointing is commonly used because it is probably the simplest way to refer to something in gesture. Enactment, likewise, is straightforward, in that here we have a pattern of movement that can be mapped directly on to the pattern of movement it is used to represent, so this again may account for its widespread use. Sketching, on the other hand, the least often used, is perhaps the most difficult device to employ to represent something in gesture.[5] Sketching requires that a movement in space be interpreted as representing a static shape, rather than a movement. Further, to sketch something may require a succession of actions and this requires, in consequence, that the recipient be able to hold these actions in memory until they combine to form a pattern. Thus, to create a representation of something by sketching is much more difficult than to create a representation by pointing, or by enacting a movement pattern, and it is thus likely to be employed only when other modes of representation cannot be used.

It will be seen that if there are differences in the ease with which a mode of base representation may be used, then we may expect that this will influence what gets selected as a base. For example, Enactment, as we noted, appears to be the most frequent base representation device. This suggests that, more often than not, if there is a pattern of action that can serve to represent something, this is what will be chosen in the selection of a base for its sign. A comparison of the frequency with which different representation devices are employed in different semantic domains illustrates this point.

Table 6.2 presents such a comparison for a sample of Warumungu signs. From this it will be seen that there are considerable differences from one semantic domain to the next in what representation devices are employed. Thus, Pointing is the commonest representation device in the domain Body Parts and Enactment is the commonest representation device employed in signing Verbs. Mimetic Enactment is very commonly selected for Artifacts and Consumables, and quite often also for Plants. On the other hand, Analogic Enactment is commonly used in Topography and Animals. Sketching, used little in most domains, nevertheless appears quite often in Camp and Dwellings. It is not hard to account for these findings, as a review of some of the domains will show.

Many body parts can simply be pointed to, and since this is the most straightforward way to refer to them, it is not surprising that Pointing is the commonest mode of base representation in this domain. Many verbs refer to processes or activities that either are accomplished through actual bodily action, or may be represented by some pattern of movement. Hence we need not be surprised to find that most Verb signs are Enactment signs.

Table 6.2 Base realization mode and semantic domain in a sample of Warumungu signs

SEMANTIC DOMAIN:	A	B	D	E&F	G
Mimetic enactment (%)	8	25	14	36	58
Analogic enactment (%)	3	10	14	10	23
Modelling (%)	5	21	21	25	0
Sketching (%)	2	14	43	10	4
Pointing (%)	80	29	7	15	15
No.classified	57	28	14	55	26

SEMANTIC DOMAIN:	H	J - M	N	O - R	S	Totals
Mimetic enactment (%)	8	5	28	15	26	21
Analogic enactment (%)	25	20	5	25	57	26
Modelling (%)	22	34	48	6	4	15
Sketching (%)	28	13	5	19	4	11
Pointing (%)	19	28	14	35	8	25
No. of signs classified	36	82	21	68	140	528

Total number of signs in sample is 492; however totals in each Domain add to more than this because many signs can be classified as exemplifying more than one mode of base realization. A: Body Parts; B: Human Classification; D: Camp and Dwellings; E&F: Traditional and Modern Artifacts; G: Fire, Cooking and Consumables; H: Celestial Bodies, Weather, Topography; J-M: Mammals, Birds, Invertebrates; N: Plants and Plant Products; O-R: Time, General Attributes, Human Attributes; S: Verbs.[6]

In regard to Artifacts, here are included many implements of daily use and in many cases there is a pattern of action characteristically involved when they are used. It is this pattern of action that frequently forms the base for the sign which refers to them. In Artifacts we find, accordingly, that Mimetic Enactment is the commonest base representation device. For example, in Warumungu, we have as a sign for *kaarti* 'playing cards' a pattern of action that clearly is reminiscent of shuffling a pack of cards: the right hand, held flat with the palm facing left, is lowered sharply twice to make contact with the palm of the left hand: $.\,Bt_{>\perp} \backslash B_{<\perp}^{\vee + \prime}$ The second most often used mode is Modelling, in which the hand assumes a shape that is related to the shape of the implement in question. A simple example of this, combining both modes, is the Warumungu sign for *kayin* 'boomerang'. Here the index finger is extended, but curved, and the hand is moved upwards, the forearm pronated at the same time, in a movement which is reminiscent of a throwing action:

$$.\,\dddot{G}_{<\perp}{}^{a\wedge}.$$

We likewise find a high proportion of mimetic enactment signs in Consumables, based either on movement patterns involved in eating or drinking, or on movement patterns associated with the preparation for consumption. For example, various kinds of edible seed (for instance *jilpiriji*) are signed by drawing the index finger laterally to the right, either in front of or in contact with either the mouth or the chin, in a pattern derived from the practice of licking flour paste from the finger, a common way of eating edible seed in traditional times: ᵕG⌄‹ *›.[7] Signs for *tampa* 'damper' include forms which appear to derive from pressing or kneading actions, and in a sign for *janyungu* 'tobacco', manipulative actions are represented that are associated with rolling a wad of tobacco in ashes prior to chewing it.

Signs in the domain Animals, in contrast, employ virtually no mimetic enactment signs (we record two instances only: 'horse', in which the sign is derived from pulling on the reins in riding, and 'flies' in which the act of brushing flies from the face is represented), although there are a number that employ Analogic Enactment. With animals, it will be seen, there are few that have characteristic manipulative actions associated with them. Where Enactment is used as a representation device it is some aspect of the animal's characteristic movement pattern that is represented, as in the example of 'emu' given above. Pointing and Modelling are the most frequent representation devices in the Animal Domain. Pointing is common because in many cases a body part is pointed to as a way of referring to some analogous characteristic feature of the animal (as in WANGARLA 'crow' where the eye is pointed to as part of a compound sign indicating that the eye is white).[8] A common use for Modelling is to employ a handshape that imitates some aspect of the animal's foot. For example, in the Warumungu sign for *janapurlalkki* 'wedge tailed eagle', where the hand forms a 'claw' shape: . ᶜ5⌄⊥ ⌄▪ ; or, in Warlpiri, *ngaya* 'cat' where the digits are held in a bunched posture, imitating the arrangement of a cat's paw pads: . ЬB⊥^⊥ ⊥▪ .

In the domain of plants, in contrast, we have almost no instances of Analogic Enactment - again not surprisingly, for plants do not have characteristic movement patterns. On the other hand, Mimetic Enactment is more frequent because signs which take as their base the movement pattern associated with preparing the plant for use are quite common, as in the Warumungu sign for *muna* 'spinifex grass', where in the sign one fisted hand pounds upon another, a pattern of action that represents the activity of pounding the grass as part of the process of extracting wax from it: . A⊤› \A⊤‹ *⊤ ' (compare Fig. 5.32).

Finally, we may consider Camp and Dwellings. This is the domain where Sketching is more commonly used than any other representation device.

Here we are dealing with 'house', 'humpy', 'windbreak', 'road', and the like. These objects appear to have no characteristic movement pattern associated with them and it is hard to see how they could be modelled easily. Many signs in this Domain, accordingly, use rather extensive movements, sketching out the shapes of the objects referred to.

Base selection is thus governed by three main considerations: the base selected must be an observable, it must be something that hand action can represent, and there will be a tendency for those aspects that can be represented by Pointing, or some form of Enactment, to be favored over those aspects that would require Modelling or Sketching. This tendency will be tempered by the availability of features that can be represented by any of the representation devices suggested. However, other things being equal, we may expect Pointing or Enactment to be favored over Modelling and Sketching.

6.4 From representational gesture to sign

We have argued that many signs are created as dynamic gestural renderings of a concrete visual image, either of the visible appearance of something or of some pattern of action. However, it will be obvious that all of the signs we have cited as exemplifying various aspects of such representations are not in fact sketches, models or enactments. In their performance they only can be said to retain features which can be understood as deriving from such representational gesturing. As writers on primary sign languages have observed, concepts which have no lexical expression in a sign language may first be expressed by a complex pantomime. If there is need to repeat the expression, however, quite quickly the pantomime becomes reduced in various ways until it retains from the original only an element or two. Such elements as are retained are just those which serve to maintain the sign as a distinctive form, when taken in relation to the other signs in the system. They may not necessarily have much to do with elements that might help another interpret the sign as if it were still a depiction of something or a pantomime. Excellent examples of this process have been provided by Tervoort (1961) in a study of the creation of new signs in a group of young Dutch schoolchildren. More recent accounts include those by Klima and Bellugi (1979).

It has been pointed out by Frishberg (1975) and by Kyle and Woll (1985) that the process by which a pantomimic or depictive gesture becomes transformed into a lexical sign follows certain principles, which ensures that the form of the sign conforms to the 'phonological' system of the sign language. These principles include the following:

Symmetry. If the original representation involved the use of two hands, as the gesture becomes transformed into a sign, the two hands come to be symmetrical: they have the same handshapes and they perform, simultaneously or alternately, the same action.

Dominance. If the original representation involved the action of one hand in relation to the other, where this is retained in the sign, then one hand becomes passive and the location of action for the other. The passive hand assumes a handshape that is drawn from a quite restricted set, while the active hand can draw from a much wider range of handshapes.

Simplification. If the original representation involved multiple phrases of movement, as it is transformed into a sign it will reduce to two or one phrase of movement. There is also a tendency for two handed forms to become one handed and for two locations to be reduced to one.

Location changes. As they become signs, gestures performed in front of the mouth or face are likely to be articulated at the chin or side of the face; gestures made by one hand in relation to the left arm, are likely to be made in relation to the left wrist or hand; in general there is a tendency for signs to be performed in the center of neutral space, rather than at its edges.

To the extent that expressions can be shown to be symmetrical, to conform to the Dominance principle, to be simplified to two phrases or to one phrase of movement, to be one handed, to involve but one location of articulation, and to be articulated within a rather narrow spatial area, to this extent can they be regarded as 'sign-like'. Frishberg (1975) compared older American Sign Language signs with more recent versions and showed that the more recent versions were more 'sign-like' than the older versions. Where new expressions have been invented by signers, as reported by Tervoort and Klima and Bellugi, for instance, as these expressions are used repeatedly and come to be shared by others, a clear progression to 'sign-likeness' has been described.

In regard to the sign languages considered here, although we have no historical data and we have not directly recorded any instances in which a new expression has been introduced and stabilized, there are several ways in which we can show that comparable processes are in operation.

First, as we saw from the analyses presented in the previous chapter, in their structure, signs in the NCD sign languages conform to the principles of Symmetry and Dominance mentioned above (see 5.4.4). From this we may infer that new forms entering the sign language will be modified to conform to these principles. Second, as we also noted in Chapter 5, there is a strong tendency for signs in these NCD sign languages to become one handed. We cited (in 5.3) the Warlpiri examples of MANIYI 'money', WIRLINYI 'hunting', RIFLE and PALKA 'body, etc.' as examples where both two handed and one handed examples exist, but where there is evidence, at least in some cases, that suggests that the one handed versions are replacing the two handed forms. We also noted that extra-manual components of signs are very rare in NCD sign languages and where they do occur (as in Warlpiri WITA 'small' or WARLU 'fire, firewood') they are typically left out in most occurrences. Third, if we consider signs for non-traditional artifacts of very recent introduction, we find that a range of forms are in use. In several cases the forms in use by younger and less experienced signers are far less 'sign-like' than those used by older signers. The forms used by older signers, however, can be shown to be direct developments of the less 'sign-like' forms used by younger signers.

A good example of this last phenomenon is provided by the signs in use for 'playing cards' (both the objects and the activity) at the Warlpiri community of Yuendumu. The widely accepted sign for this among older women (the signing community at Yuendumu - see Ch. 4) is simply to hold up a fisted hand with the thumb extended and rapidly pronate the forearm a couple of times (.Å$_{<\perp}$ ª' - Fig. 6.13). Young people, and less experienced signers, however, do not use this sign. They commonly use a two handed enactment of the activity of dealing cards. This is quite variable in form but it is usually done so that the tip of the thumb of the right hand slides rapidly and repeatedly off the palm of the left hand, which is held flat, with the palm up but the fingers pointing slightly downwards toward the ground (Fig. 6.14).

Fig. 6.13 PARLPIRRPA 'playing cards' (noun and verb), one handed version

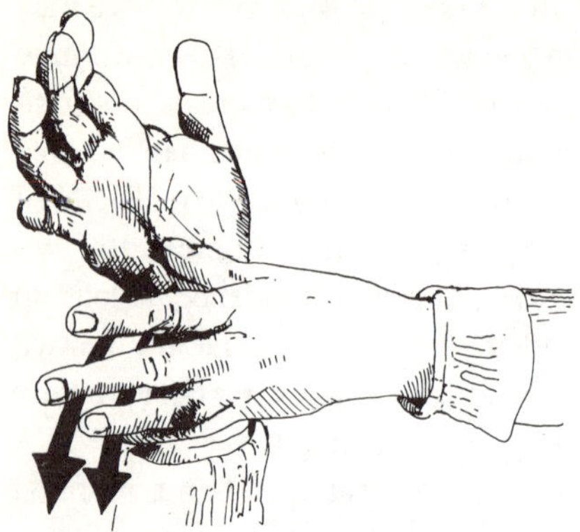

Fig. 6.14 PARLAPIRRPA, two handed version

The form used by older women may be seen as a development from the form often given by younger people and it will be seen that in several respects this development illustrates the operation of the sign formation processes outlined above. Thus, it will be seen that the repeated action of the right hand has been retained, although it has been simplified to a double pulse. There has been a reduction in the complexity of the Sign Action, that is. The use of the left hand has been dropped, once again illustrating the principle of simplification, and the right hand has moved upwards to perform the Sign Action in the space just in front of the signer's chest, which is the usual signing space for most other signs in the system. Thus there has been a location change which also conforms to expectations. The orientation of the hand has changed, too. It will be noted that if the palm-down orientation of the two handed enactment had been retained, the resulting sign would have been quite similar to the sign for 'washing' (. Å$_{T<}$$^{>}$ '). Also, note that by retaining the extended thumb, the sign maintains its difference from the signs for *ngapa* 'water' (. A$_{<\perp}$^{a} ') and *murnma* 'wait, not yet, not ready' (. A$_{<\perp}$$^{\sim\cdot}$), which are otherwise very similar.

As a second example from Yuendumu, the sign for *turaki* 'truck, car' may be mentioned. Among older signers the sign given is . O$_{<\wedge}$^{6} '. Here the hand is held in a specialized O form: the first three fingers held together and curved, with the tip of the index finger touching the tip of the thumb, and with the fourth digit held so that it is 'crooked' outwards in a small loop (see Fig.6.15). The Sign Action consists in a double pulsed forearm supination movement. Young people, when asked to give a sign for 'car', hold up both forearms with the hands held as if they are holding something, and the arms are then moved up and down in an alternating fashion, a form rather obviously derived from a pantomime of operating the steering wheel of a car (Fig. 5.12).

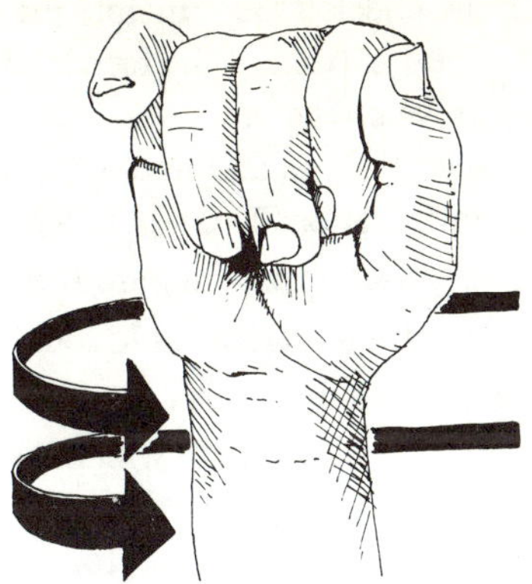

Fig. 6.15 TURAKI 'truck, car', one handed version (Yuendumu)

The one handed version given by older signers would appear to be derived from this, but once again, in its derivation, it shows the operation of the sign formation principles outlined above. It shows a reduction from two hands to one, and the Sign Action is reduced from whole arm actions which vary in the number of times they are repeated, to forearm action only, which is a single double-pulse movement phrase. We note, however, a specialization of the handshape. As a form of closed hand, it is clearly related to the handshape of the less 'sign-like' sign of the younger people. However, the 'crooked' little finger is an added complexity, which seems to go against the principle of simplification; but, as we saw with the change of orientation noted in the case of the previous example, so here, we see the introduction of a feature which serves to keep the sign distinct from other signs in the system. In this case, without the complication of the crooked little finger, the sign would be highly similar to the sign for *kurdu* 'child': $. 0_{<\perp}^{6}$, and would be indistinguishable from the plural form of KURDU, where the pronating action is repeated.

Finally, we may illustrate one of the principles governing Sign Location by considering the sign for *malirdi* 'son-in-law, etc.'. As we noted at the beginning of this chapter, in this sign a curved B hand is placed against the cheek: $3\dddot{B}_{T\wedge}^{\times}$. This sign can be understood as deriving from a gesture of covering the face with the hand and turning the face away at the same time. Among the Warlpiri (as indeed throughout Aboriginal Australia), a woman and her son-in-law are in an avoidance relationship. This means that they cannot be in one another's presence and may not speak to one another. Should by chance they encounter one another, they must each look the other way. A gesture to demonstrate this is to place the hand over the face and turn the head away. It seems most likely that the sign for *malirdi* has evolved from such a gesture. Notice here, however, how the curved B hand - a suitable handshape for covering the face - has been displaced to touch the cheek. One principle that governs sign location is that signs that are performed in front of the face tend to be displaced to the side. This appears to be what we see here.

It seems reasonable to apply similar considerations in accounting for a number of other signs that use the cheek as a Sign Location. Thus PAJARNI 'taste'(Warlpiri) is signed by moving an X hand (a closed form) forward from initial contact with the cheek: $3X_{\top\wedge}^{\times\perp}$. One sign for 'cigarette' is to touch the cheek with the middle finger and to twist the hand slightly: $3m\varsigma_{\top<}^{\,\,\ast\sigma}$. This would appear to be a displaced form of a modelling gesture in which the middle finger touches the mouth to suggest something long and thin extending from it. Likewise, the Mudbura sign for *walanypiri* 'pelican' is to perform a circular movement of the hand around the cheek, with index and middle finger extended. The sign presumably derives from a sketch of the pelican's large bag-like lower bill, but here again we see it has been displaced to the side of the face: $3H_{\top<}^{@}$.

6.5 Summary and conclusions

In this Chapter we have explored some of the ways in which the forms of signs may be accounted for. We have proposed that units of meaning find representation as a combined product of two main processes which we have here termed *image representation* and *sign formation.*

With regard to image representation, we suggest that in creating a representation for a meaning, some mode of action will be employed which bears a dynamic relationship to an image that has been taken as symbolic of the meaning intended. This image we have termed the *base* of the sign and we suggested five main ways in which, in gestural expression, such bases may be represented. We saw that the gestural modality permits some modes of representation to be more readily accomplished than others. We showed that there is a correlation between the kinds of things that are represented in sign and the modes of base representation that are adopted, and we interpreted this to mean that what images get selected as symbolic will be largely governed by the relative ease by which gestural representation may be accomplished. That is, there is an interaction between base (symbolic image) selection and the means available for representation. Thus we suggested that Pointing would be used wherever there was available a base that could be directly pointed to; and wherever a pattern of action could be used as a base, this would be selected in preference to something that would have to be represented by Modelling or Sketching.

The representations so produced, however, cannot serve as lexical items in a vocabulary system until they have become expressions that are shared by members of a communication community. That is, they must have standardized, repeatable forms and they must be incorporated into a shared system of referential usages. In becoming standardized, gestures or gesture sequences that are first created as image representations undergo certain processes of simplification. They tend to be organized so that they are units of action that are systematically contrastive with other units of action in the system. In consequence they come to be amenable to a phonologic-like analysis, as we demonstrated in the previous chapter.

It will be seen that one of the consequences of the process of sign formation is that whatever connection someone might perceive between the form of a sign and its meaning is very often lost. Thus the relationship between the form of the Warlpiri sign PARLPIRRPA 'playing cards' discussed above and the act of dealing cards would not be apparent, unless one already knew the developmental history of the sign we outlined. Likewise, the iconic origin of the one handed version of MANIYI would not be apparent, unless one also knew about the two handed version from which it is derived. In examining signs in these sign languages from the point of view of what mode of base representation might be involved in their derivation, there are very many for which it is not possible to offer any suggestions. They seem to be completely arbitrary. Many may appear to be arbitrary, however, simply because we have no access to the history of their development as signs.

We propose the foregoing as a general account of one of the most important set of processes by which signs come to have the forms they do. By illustrating their operation in the case of the NCD sign languages, we provide further insight into the nature of these sign languages - our primary aim in this book. At the same time, this also exemplifies the operation of quite general and fundamental processes that appear to be at work in the creation of all sign-linguistic systems.

Notes

[1]In Warlpiri a man may refer to his sister's child as *miyalu-warnu* 'stomach-originating'. See Chapter 11 for further discussion of kin terms and body parts.

[2]A ubiquitous weed at Yuendumu, yielding numerous small hard burrs which have extremely sharp prickles. Probably *Callotis hispidula*.

[3]Note the 'back assimilation' here. The curved index finger is used to point to the mouth, as well as to present a model for its shape.

[4]*Karrka-mi* may be glossed as 'walk' only in some contexts. It may also be used in contexts where *ya-ni* 'go' would also be appropriate. It does not always imply the bodily activity of walking as the English verb 'walk' does (Laughren, personal communication 1987). Nevertheless, although there is an overlap in usage, *karrka-mi* and *ya-ni* have quite different signs.

[5]If we were dealing with a graphic medium, in contrast, we would expect signs using Sketching would far outweigh any other sort.

[6]Semantic domains modified from Hale (1959) and Sutton and Walsh (1979).

[7]This explanation is suggested by Roth (1897) for very similar signs he recorded in Northwest Central Queensland.

[8]The crow referred to here is either *Corvus orro* or *Corvus benneti*. In the mature adult of these species the eye appears completely white, giving the impression that there is something wrong with its eye or that it is blind. This feature of the crow is referred to in signs in several of the sign languages considered here. In Warumungu the bird is also known as *miyil purnuru*, literally 'eye white'.

7 Sign organization and word structure

7.0 Introduction

In this and the succeeding three chapters, we shall investigate some of the ways in which the sign languages here under consideration are related to the spoken languages of the communities in which they are used. In this chapter we shall examine the relationship between sign organization and word structure. That is, we shall explore the extent to which unitary, reduplicated or compound signs are related to the phonology or morphology of the words that correspond to them. In Chapter 8 we investigate how sign renders the spoken language functions provided by grammatical endings, semantic case endings, derivational suffixes and enclitics, and also how person, space and time are expressed. In Chapter 9 we shall look at signed discourse in comparison to spoken discourse. Chapter 10 will report a study of how speech and sign are related when they are employed simultaneously, as they sometimes are by older women (see 4.6). This study throws additional light on the question of the level of meaning encoded by signs in these sign languages, and it also has implications for the more general question of the difference between gesture and sign .

As we have suggested previously, the Aboriginal sign languages considered here are best termed *alternate* sign languages. They have been developed by speakers as an alternative means of communication in circumstances where, for ritual reasons, the use of speech is prohibited. This is why we may expect these sign languages to show some influence from spoken language. The question remains as to what sort of an influence this may be. One possibility is that the units of the sign language might be set up as direct representations of sound units in the spoken language. Such a system would then be comparable to the speech surrogate systems exemplified in the so-called 'whistle languages' reported from Central America and the Canary Islands, or the 'drum languages' of Africa (Stern 1957).[1] As we shall see, in a limited way, phonetic characteristics of the associated spoken languages do exert an influence on the sign language. However, there appears to be a much more conspicuous influence from spoken language morphology. In several of the sign languages considered here, many signs reflect in their organization or their sign action aspects of the morphology of the spoken expressions with which they are glossed. Thus words that are related through a formational process such as reduplication often have corresponding signs that are related in the same way, even where the meanings of the unitary and reduplicated forms are unrelated. Words that can be analyzed as being compounded of more than one free form often have compound signs corresponding to them. Forms composed of a free morph and a bound morph likewise often have a corresponding sign that is a compound, the sign for the free form being followed by another that stands for the bound form.

It might be said of these sign languages, accordingly, that they are systems that represent the morphs of their associated spoken languages. However, this cannot be accepted without qualification. Signs are not always the direct correlates of spoken language formal units. Thus there are some morphs that are represented by several different signs, according to the meanings they have in particular contexts. In these cases, it would appear, the signs represent meaning in a more differentiated way than the spoken language forms. In other cases, as we shall see especially in Chapter 8, in regard to certain suffixes, and in Chapter 11, in regard to many kin terms, several different morphs are represented by but one sign. In these cases, signs may represent a more general category of meaning than the spoken language forms. In yet other cases, to be described in this Chapter, signs do not match word structure. A single sign may serve to convey a meaning that, in the spoken language, requires several morphemes for its expression, or we may find compound signs being used to convey a meaning that requires but a unitary form in the spoken language. In all cases, however, we find that signs can nevertheless be matched to spoken language meaning units at some level - whether this be morphological or lexical, as is most common, or, as in some cases, at the level of the idiom or collocation. That is to say, signs in these sign languages stand for the units of meaning that are provided for by forms in their associated spoken languages. They have not developed as representations of units of meaning separately from those that are provided by the spoken languages.

7.1 Sign representation of phonetic characteristics

As just noted, it is possible to imagine how the gestural medium could be used to represent a spoken language by means of contrastive gestures standing for the sounds of the language. Fingerspelling systems approach this, although in these the gestures are representations of letters in an alphabet and thus closer to a representation of the language in written form, rather than of the sound units of the spoken language. As will be clear from what has already been said in previous chapters, there is nothing about the NCD sign languages that invites a comparison with fingerspelling. In some cases, however, phonetic characteristics of the spoken language do appear to have an influence. This is shown by examples in which the same sign is used for more than one meaning, not because the corresponding spoken language expressions are semantically related (examples of this will be discussed later) but because they share something in common in how they sound.

For example, in Warlpiri *jija* 'shoulder' is signed by tapping the ipsilateral shoulder with the middle finger (Fig. 7.1, Γ mς ᵠ '), and the same sign is used for *jija* 'medical sister'. This is a homophone with *jija* 'shoulder' that results from an assimilation of the English word 'sister' to a Warlpiri pronunciation. Tapping the ipsilateral shoulder is also used to sign the first part of *ijanu wapa-mi* 'to visit one another', a complex verb formed of *jijanu,* a preverb (see 7.3.3), and the root verb *wapa-mi* 'move'. Similarly, also in Warlpiri, *winpiri* 'spearwood, tree sp.' is signed by a lateral sweep of the index finger (. G ⌄⊥ ˃). This same sign is also used for *wina* 'winner', *wiki* 'week', *wiki* 'whiskey', *Winjiyi* 'Wednesday', and *Winiyi* 'Winnie', a personal name. Here it looks very much as if the initial sound of all of these words, something very close to [wi:] in all cases, has been selected as a common element to which the lateral index finger sweep has been attached.

In further examples from Warlpiri, we have the same sign for *kirlilpi* 'bandicoot', *kirlilkirlilpa* 'roseate cockatoo, galah' and *kirlinpirlipirli* 'grass, sp.'(Fig. 7.2); the same sign for *mirdingi* 'European style meeting' and *mirdi* 'knee'; *jinti* 'female genitals' and *jintilyka* 'grasshopper, sp.' (Fig. 7.3) are signed in the same way; the sign for the first part of *luyurr nguna-mi* 'to be sad' is the same as the sign for the first part of *luyukurr yula-mi* 'to drone, buzz, as bees'; the sign for the English name 'Dolly' is the same as the sign for 'telegram' - again, because the Warlpiri pronunciations of the first two syllables, in each case, sound very similar.[2]

In Warumungu we find that the sign for *murtika* 'motor car' has the same handshape as the sign for *muṭinka* 'dilly bag' and that the sign for *juppa* 'just - sentence particle' is also used for *jupujupu* 'soup, stew' and *jupujupu* 'soap'. Also in Warumungu, in the sign for *tawun* 'town' an extended middle finger is lowered rapidly (. mς ⊤⌄ ˇ), evidently because 'town' is homophonous with the English word 'down'. It is of interest to note, incidentally, that the sign for the Warumungu expression for 'down', *kantu,* is different: the hand engages in a 'fingersnap' as it is lowered.

It will be seen that in the above examples the near-homophonous pairs in each case are homophonous only in respect to the first part of the words. Such treatment of near-homophones of this sort as if they are full homophones is also reflected in other aspects of language use. Nash (personal

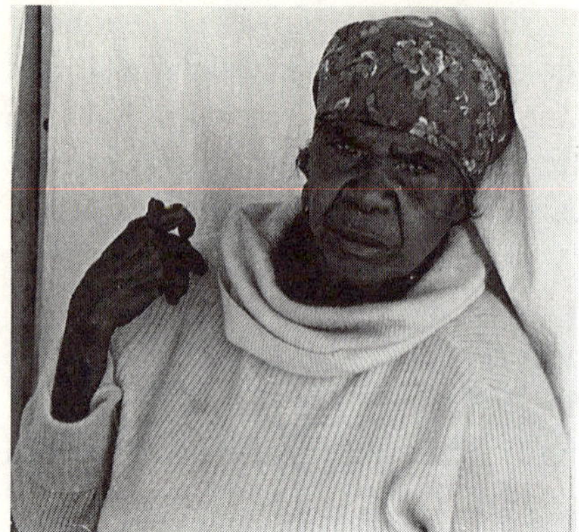

Fig. 7.1 JIJA 'shoulder'

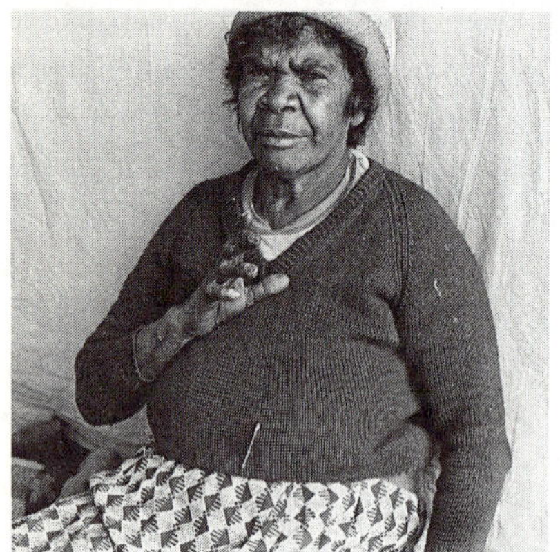

Fig. 7.2 KIRLILPI 'bandicoot'

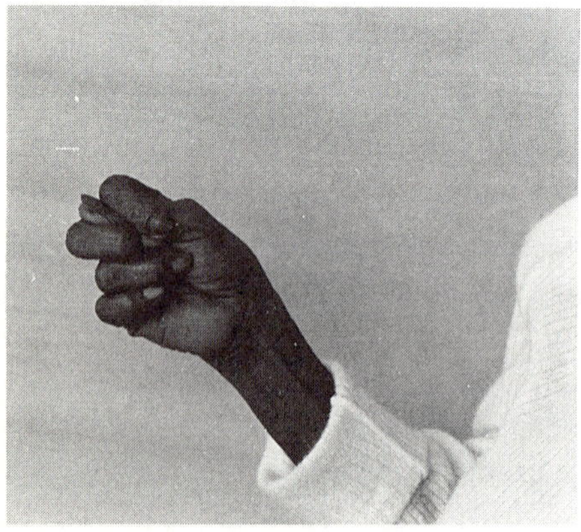

Fig. 7.3 JINTILYKA 'grasshopper, sp.'

communication 1986) points out that, in these central Australian languages, the taboo that extends to words that sound like the name of a deceased person, which is also taboo, also extends to words that are near-homophones in respect to the first part of the word only.

It should also be noted that several of the examples given above involve either English personal names or other English words. In Warlpiri I collected about seventy name signs and it is notable that a number of these served for more than one English name, in most cases for names that were highly similar in sound, especially when pronounced by Warlpiri speakers. Thus the sign used for 'Winnie', given above, could also serve for 'Willie'. 'Biddy', 'Betty' and 'Liddy' all took the same sign, as did 'Kitty' and Kevin'; 'Polly' and 'Nelly'; 'Jeanie', 'Jenny' and 'Jilly'; 'Ruth' (pronounced 'Ruju' in Warlpiri) and 'Ruby'; 'Jorna' and 'June'; 'Lornie', 'Lorna' and 'Morna'; and 'Peggy' and 'Belle' (pronounced *pila* in Warlpiri).

The phonetic representation suggested by the above examples is reminiscent of the phonographic principle found in the early development of writing, in which graphs were extended in their use to stand for words that are homophones or near homophones of the word for which the graph was originally established (see Chapter 13 for further discussion of this). It is of interest to note that a major incentive for the development of such phonographic representation apparently arose from the need to represent names and foreign words. As we have just seen, a rather high proportion of the examples of phonetic representation in the NCD sign languages includes names and English words.

It should be emphasized that, in the sign languages dealt with here, phonetic representation is of quite limited occurrence. This does not seem surprising. First of all, the development of systems representing the sound units of spoken languages took several millenniums. Furthermore, it seems likely that, for this to happen, the use of a graphic medium for language representation was essential. The enduring character of code elements in this medium makes it possible for people to compare them and classify them in various ways (Goody 1977) and an ability to do this was probably necessary if a set of code elements representing sound units in speech was to develop. In the third place, gestural units require more time to produce than spoken forms do (see Chapter 10). If gestural units were developed that were sub-lexical in function so that a recipient would have to synthesize a succession of units before being able to interpret them at the lexical level, this would greatly slow up the speed with which discourse could be accomplished.[3] The development of a gestural system in which each distinct gesture also serves as a unit of meaning seems much more likely, and this is indeed what we find.

7.2 Sign organization, Sign Action and word structure

Sign organization here refers to whether the sign, as a lexical item in the sign language, is unitary (accomplished in a single phrase of action), complex (two different phrases of action), or compound (composed of two signs, separated by a juncture). Signs can also be classified in terms of features of their sign action. They may be simple (accomplished in a single phrase of action), doubled (the action of the sign is repeated as a separate phrase, usually with spatial displacement) or reduplicated (same phrase of action repeated).

Some examples from Warlpiri may illustrate these distinctions.The sign for *ngapa* 'water' is a unitary sign. Here the hand is held up as a fist and trembled (. J $A_{<\wedge}^{tr}$). The sign for *kutukari* 'night' is a complex sign, because here the side of the hand is first placed against the chest, palm facing downwards, and then it is moved forward, away from the signer in an arc ([]$B_{\vee<}^{+}$; $^{\perp a}${$B_{\wedge\perp}$}). The sign for *payi-wiki* 'pay week' is compound because it consists of two separate signs: the sign for *payi* 'pay', in which the right hand, held flat, slaps the palm of the left hand as it moves downwards past it; and the sign for *wiki* 'week', in which the extended index finger is moved in a horizontal fashion to the left (. $B_{\top\perp}$\\$B_{\vee\perp}^{\top *}$! ⁞ $G_{<\perp}^{<}$).

In terms of the classification of Sign Action features used here, the sign for *ngapa* 'water', given above, is also an example of a simple sign. The sign for *marlu* 'kangaroo', however, is reduplicated. Here, the hand is held with the finger tips curled together in contact. The Action of the sign consists in *twice* expanding the fingers (. $O_{\vee\perp}$ [5t] '). A doubled sign is exemplified by the sign for *japirnpa* 'boil, sore'. In this sign the tip of the index finger touches each cheek in succession (33G ˀ ˀ). Another example of a doubled sign would be the sign for *yuwarli* 'house'. Here a flat hand, held so the palm faces away from the signer with the fingers pointing upward, but at a sloping angle, is moved downwards twice, the second time after the hand has been displaced somewhat to the right (. $B_{\ddagger\wedge}^{\vee\rightarrow\vee}$).

The overall extent of the relationship between sign organization, Sign Action and word structure within our material may be gauged from Table 7.1 for non-verbs and from Table 7.2 for verbs. In Table 7.1 we show the frequency with which unitary and compound signs are found in association with unitary (monomorphemic) words, compound words (words composed of two or more free morphemes) and suffixed words (words composed of a stem form and a bound morpheme of some sort). We also show how simple, doubled and reduplicated signs are distributed in relation to unitary words and words showing reduplication. Words that show reduplication are either words such as the Warlpiri *jukujuku* 'chicken', in which syllables are repeated, or words such as the Warlpiri *walyawalya* 'brown', which is composed of a repetition of the morpheme *walya* 'ground'. In Table 7.2 we show the frequency with which single and compound signs are found in association with root verbs or verbs which are compounds, usually of a preverb and a root verb.

For Warlpiri (P), Warumungu (R) and Warlmanpa (L) - the languages for which we have the most extensive data - the following may be seen from Table 7.1. There is a strong tendency for unitary signs to be associated with unitary verbal expressions, while compound signs are associated with compound verbal expressions. Thus, for these three languages, respectively, 93%, 96% and 96% of all unitary words are signed with unitary signs,

Table 7.1 Word structure and sign organization: nominals

	P	N	K	R	L	M
MONOMORPHEMIC WORDS						
Sign organization						
Unitary %[Σ]	93[730]	95[253]	98[324]	96[515]	96[391]	97[259]
Compound	7 [54]	5 [12]	2 [7]	4 [23]	3 [13]	3 [8]
Sign Action						
Single	69[542]	68[181]	59[198]	55[292]	62[252]	69[188]
Double	8[61]	8[22]	10 [32]	6 [34]	7 [28]	1 [4]
Reduplicated	23[181]	23[62]	30[101]	36[194]	30[124]	29 [79]
REDUPLICATED WORDS						
Sign Action						
Single	30[32]	33[5]	22[4]	19[11]	4[2]	78[15]
Double	21[22]	40 [6]	27[5]	25[15]	31[14]	5[5]
Reduplicated	49[51]	27 [4]	50[9]	55[33]	49[22]	15[3]
COMPOUND WORDS						
Sign organization						
Unitary	12[3]	38[11]	[4]	14[4]	16[2]	[0]
Compound	88[22]	62[18]	[2]	86[25]	84[11]	100[3]
SUFFIXED WORDS						
Sign organization						
Unitary	49[23]	83[5]	[6]	28[15]	38[11]	100[3]
Compound	51[24]	17[1]	[5]	72[39]	62[18]	[0]

whereas 88%, 86% and 84% of all compound words are signed with compound signs. Likewise, suffixed words also tend to be signed with compound signs, although it will be noticed that this tendency is not quite as strong. Thus, 51%, 72% and 62% of suffixed words in the three languages are signed by compound signs. Finally, reduplicated words are much more frequently signed with signs that either show double or reduplicated sign action than are unitary words. Whereas for the three languages 31%, 42% and 37% of unitary words, are signed with reduplicated or double action signs, such signs are associated with 70%, 80% and 80% of the reduplicated words.

A similar high degree of paralleling between the morphological structure of words and sign organization may be seen in respect to the data on verbs presented in Table 7.2. Again, for Warlpiri, Warumungu and Warlmanpa we find that whereas 95%, 83% and 96% of root verbs are signed

Table 7.2
Word structure and sign organization: verbs

SIMPLE VERBS	P	N	K	R	L	M
Sign Organization						
Unitary %[Σ]	95[115]	93[95]	94[83]	83[57]	96[45]	100[23]
Compound	5[7]	7[7]	6[5]	17[12]	4[2]	[0]
COMPOUND VERBS						
Sign Organization						
Unitary	17[63]	23[3]	53[9]	12[16]	16[25]	81[47]
Compound	83[307]	77[10]	47[8]	88[112]	84[133]	19[11]

with unitary signs, 83%, 88% and 84% of compound verbs are signed with compound signs.

For Anmatyerre (N) and Kaytej (K), the two Arandic languages in the sample, the pattern appears to be less strong. This is probably because the samples are smaller, with very few instances only in some of the categories. For the non-verb data we may see that for Anmatyerre there are probably enough unitary/compound instances to make comparison worthwhile, and there it will be seen that, as in the languages so far discussed, there are more compound signs for compound words, and unitary signs for unitary words than the reverse. For Kaytej, the data only permit us to compare the association of signs with unitary words and signs with reduplicated words. There we see 40% of unitary words are signed with reduplicated or double action signs, whereas 77% of reduplicated words are signed in this way. So far as the verb data is concerned, it will be seen that for both Kaytej and

Anmatyerre there is a higher proportion of compound signs associated with compound verbs than there are compound signs associated with root verbs, although the numbers available for comparison are perhaps insufficient for this to be considered significant. Overall, however, it will be seen that the number of compound signs in the sign vocabularies collected for these languages is much smaller than it is for Warlpiri, Warumungu and Warlmanpa. This reflects the fact that in these languages compounding and reduplication are less widespread.

Finally we may consider the Mudbura (M) data in these Tables (Djingili is omitted since there were too few compound expressions or compound signs in our sample to make comparisons worthwhile). Both for the non-verb data and for the verb data, it will be seen that the figures do not suggest much in the way of a correlation between word structure and sign organization. The sample is small, to be sure, but it is possible that this lack of correlation is a reflection of the somewhat different nature of Mudbura sign language, or at least of the way in which we sampled it, as compared to that of the other groups considered here.

Sign language material for the other five groups was gathered from older women who were active practitioners of it in their daily lives. Much of the Mudbura material was gathered from a man who, though highly knowledgeable, like all Mudbura men, used sign language rarely, except for fairly short periods when involved in certain ceremonies. The Mudbura sign language shown to us, thus, is probably less developed than the sign languages shown us by people from the other groups. Less frequent users of these sign languages show much less of a tendency to conform sign organization to the morphological structure of the corresponding words. We found this to be true among younger and less experienced users of sign among the Warlpiri. We suspect it is true in the case of the Mudbura data. The apparent lack of correlation between sign organization and word morphology in the case of the Mudbura data may thus reflect this less developed status.

In the sections to follow, we shall discuss in more detail some of the ways in which there is a relationship between sign organization and sign action and the structure of words in associated spoken languages. Examples will be drawn mainly from Warlpiri, Warumungu and Warlmanpa the languages for which we have the most extensive data.

7.3 Reduplication

Many words in the languages considered here, especially in Warlpiri, Warumungu and Warlmanpa, show *reduplication*. That is, there is a repetition of some segment or segments within the word. This has been studied for

Warlpiri by Nash (1985). He shows that in this language it can take several forms and serve several functions. It can function as a regular morphological process in pluralization, especially for nominals with human reference. In regard to verbs, it may serve to express repetition of action, distribution of action or to express plurality of agents or patients of action. However, there are also many instances of reduplicated words which have unreduplicated counterparts where, although there is often a semantic relationship between the unitary and reduplicated forms, because no general derivational process can be stated, the forms must be considered separate lexical items. Thus we have *yalyu* 'blood' but *yalyuyalyu* 'red' or *walya* 'ground' but *walyawalya* 'brown', where reduplication appears to serve to refer to a general quality of the concrete referent of the unreduplicated form. However, it may also serve as a kind of intensifier, as in *mungalyurru* 'sunrise' but *mungalyurrumungalyurru* 'before sunrise', or it may produce pairs of words that appear to have no semantic relationship, as with *pirli* 'rock, hill' but *pirlipirli* 'actual mother's mother's brother's daughter'.[4] Finally, there are also many words in Warlpiri which show reduplication but for which no unreduplicated counterpart has been recorded. In some cases of this sort, the unreduplicated form may have been lost, as perhaps with *kuntukuntu* 'fat, well fed' or *kurlpukurlpu* 'stingy, not generous'. In other cases, as in the names of many birds and other animals, reduplication appears to be used for onomatopoetic reasons, as with *kirlilkirlilpa* 'roseate cockatoo', *kuurrkuurrpa* 'boobook owl' or *jintirrjintirrpa* 'willie wagtail'. Although no one has undertaken a similar systematic study of reduplication in Warlmanpa and Warumungu, a review of available examples suggests that the above statements apply to these languages as well.

As we noted in the overall analysis presented in the previous section, signs glossed by spoken forms that show reduplication, are themselves likely to have a reduplicated character, as if the morphological feature of reduplication has been transferred to sign formation. A comparison of signs for those words where reduplication serves as a pluralization device and of signs for those reduplicated words which have unreduplicated counterparts shows that this does indeed occur in many cases.

As has been mentioned, reduplication in Warlpiri serves in the formation of plurals for certain nominals, especially those with human reference. Thus we have *wirriya* 'boy' but *wirriyawirriya* 'boys'; *karnta* 'woman', but *karntakarnta* 'women'; *kurdu* 'child' but *kurdukurdu* 'children'. Other nominals are pluralized by the addition of the suffix *-panu* or *-patu*, as in *marlu-panu* 'many kangaroos' or *maliki-patu* 'several dogs'. This suffix is also used for the pluralization of *wati* or *ngarrka* 'fully initiated man' which, exceptionally for the domain of human nominals, is not pluralized by reduplication.[5]

If we look at how pluralization in Warlpiri sign is achieved, we find it parallels the spoken language. Thus, we have recorded reduplication as a pluralization device for KARNTA 'woman', KURDU 'child', KAMINA 'adolescent girl', PURLKA 'old man'. However, the sign for *wati* or *ngarrka* 'initiated man' ($\sqcap B_{\top <}^{\Omega >}$), is not pluralized by reduplication but by the addition of a 'quantity' sign, generally glossed as *-panu* or *-patu*. This is performed by holding up a spread hand, palm toward signer, and moving the fingers back and forth ($.5_{\top \wedge}^{\Omega\ \prime}$). For those nominals in other domains which are not pluralized by reduplication, we likewise find that they are not pluralized in sign by this method, but follow the pattern just described.

Now consider the case of reduplicated words which have unreduplicated counterparts, where the two forms are treated as separate lexical items. If we compare the sign expressions that correspond to such word pairs, we find that, in many cases, the sign for the reduplicated expression is a reduplication of the sign for the unreduplicated expression. For example, in Warlpiri, for pairs with related meanings we have:

Mungalyurru
'early morning' : $\underline{\Omega}H_{\top \wedge}^{\circ}\ ;H_{\vee \perp}^{6}$

Mungalyurrumungalyurru
'pre-dawn' : $\underline{\Omega}H_{\top \wedge}^{\circ}\ ;H_{\vee \perp}^{6\ \prime}$

Palya 'spinifex wax' (Fig. 7.4): $.X_{\square < \perp}^{>6\}}$
Palyanjipalyanji 'sticky' : $.X_{\square < \perp}^{>6\}\ \prime}$

Walya 'ground' (Fig. 7.5): $.B_{\wedge \perp} \backslash A_{\wedge <}^{\vee \times}$
Walyawalya 'brown' : $.B_{\wedge \perp} \backslash A_{\wedge <}^{\vee \times\ \prime}$

For pairs with apparently unrelated meanings we have:

Japangardi
'subsection name'(Cf. Fig. 5.4) $.A_{\top >} \backslash 5_{\vee \perp}^{\vee \times}$

Japangardijapangardi
'cricket, sp.' $.A_{\top >} \backslash 5_{\vee \perp}^{\vee \times\ \prime}$

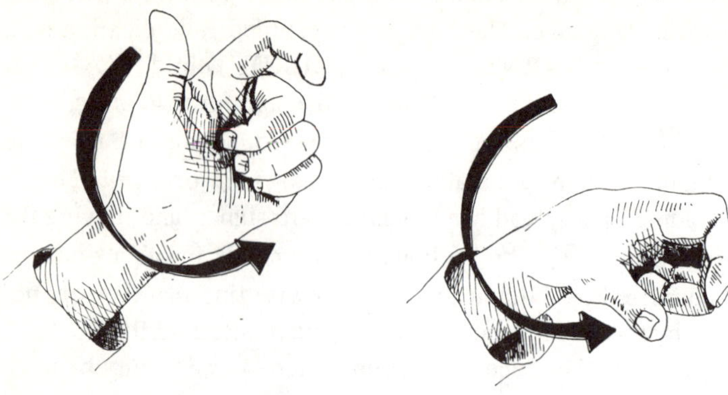

Fig. 7.4 PALYA 'spinifex wax'

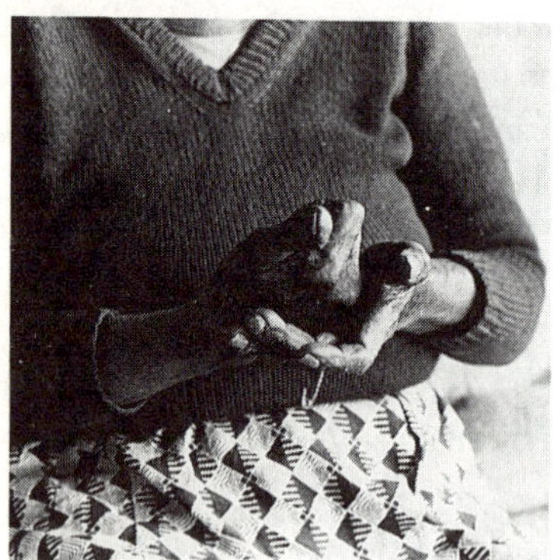

Fig. 7.5 WALYA 'ground'. Upper hand lowered to contact lower hand

Jarnpa 'kurdaitcha man'	$.\mathrm{G}_{\perp\wedge}{}^{\perp\blacksquare}$	(Index finger upwards, hand moves sharply out)
Jarnpajarnpa 'edible grub, sp.'	$.\mathrm{G}_{\perp\wedge}{}^{\perp\blacksquare\,\prime}$	
Wanta 'sun'	$.\mathrm{U}_{\wedge\perp}{}^{\vee}$	('V' hand, palm up, lowered slightly)
Wantawanta 'red ant, sp.'	$.\mathrm{U}_{\wedge\perp}{}^{\vee\,\prime}$	

From Warumungu, for pairs with related meanings we have:

Narra 'ground, dirt, earth'	$.\mathrm{E}_{\wedge\perp}{}^{\vee\blacksquare}$
Narranarra 'brown, earth-colored'	$.\mathrm{E}_{\wedge\perp}{}^{\vee\;\vee}$

Kilyirr 'sun' . U$_{\wedge\perp}^{\vee}$

Kilyirrkilyirr 'sunrise' . U$_{\wedge\perp}^{\vee\,\prime}$ or . U$_{\wedge\perp}^{@}$

Ngamuna 'breast, milk'] to$^{\times}$ or [ ] to$^{\times}$ $^{\times}$
(touch breast[s])

Ngamunangamuna 'tree with milky sap' [to$_{\top <}^{\wedge\,\prime}$

but with an apparently unrelated meaning we have:

Parlkarr 'short' (Fig. 5.4) . A$_{\top}$ > \B5$_{\vee\perp}^{\vee h}$

Parlkarrparlkarr 'things, goods' . A$_{\top}$ > \B5$_{\vee\perp}^{\vee h\,\prime}$

Here it may be noted that in some of these cases the reduplicated version is not an exact repetition of the action in the unitary form. For *narranarra* the repeated action also shows some spatial displacement, for *kilyirrkilyirr,* in some performances, the repetition of the lowering movement may become transformed into a circular action, and for *ngamunangamuna*, instead of touching the breast twice, the hand is moved upward past it twice - and this is done on only one side of the body.

In Warlmanpa, with related meaning, we have:

Larrpa 'already' . fn$^{a<}$ (fingersnap, pronate, move left)

Larrpalarrpa 'long time ago' . fn$^{a<\,\prime}$

but with possibly unrelated meaning we have:

Pulyurru
'soft, as of yam when ripe' . A> $_{\perp}$\L$_{\vee\perp}^{*\perp\,\prime}$ (L hand slides forward off fist)

Pulyurrulyurru 'red' fn$_{\vee\perp}^{\prime}$ (fingersnap twice)

There are also cases where the signs for each member of the pair are different, but these cases include examples where the meanings are obviously related, as well as cases where the meanings are probably unrelated. Examples from Warlpiri where the signs are different, although the meanings are related include

Kuruwarri 'ceremonial design on body, (Fig. 5.7) $\urcorner U_{\top <}^{\ast\ \text{ꝗ}\ >}$
Kuruwarrikuruwarri 'variegated' $.\,{}^{\varsigma}5\text{m}\text{Ϛ}_{\wedge\perp}^{\sigma\ '}$

Yukiri 'green growth, alive' $.\,\text{m}\text{Ϛ}\times_{1}{}_{<\perp}^{a\leftrightarrow\sigma}$
Yukiriyukiri 'green (color)' $.\,\text{Ч}_{\vee\perp}^{\varsigma}$

From Warumungu, likewise, we have

Pikka 'adolescent boy'(cf. Fig. 6.7) $.\text{m}\text{Ϛ}_{\vee\perp}^{\sigma\ '}$
Pikapikka 'children' $.\,0_{\vee\perp}^{\sigma\leftarrow\sigma}$

An example, again from Warlpiri, where both the signs and the meanings are different is

Pirli 'hill, rock, stone' $.\,\hat{E}_{<\perp}^{\underline{a}\ '}$
Pirlipirli 'Actual MMBD' $\text{F}\ t\text{G}_{\vee <}^{+}$ (side of G hand touches shoulder front)

Whether the signs within a pair are different or are reduplications of one another, thus, does not depend upon whether the words in the pair are related in their meaning. Indeed, in Warlpiri, for the unitary-reduplicate word pairs where there is no apparent relationship in meaning, there are more pairs where the signs are related by reduplication (or where they have the same sign), than there are pairs where the signs are different. We may conclude that so far as reduplication is concerned, the forms of the signs are influenced directly by the formal morphological organization of the corresponding spoken expressions. Sign reduplication is a direct borrowing from the morphological process of reduplication in the spoken language and it does not function here, at least, as an independent process of sign formation.

7.4 Compounds

In the languages considered here there are many expressions which are compounds of elements which can occur as separate words in other contexts. For example we have, in Warlpiri, *mulyupakarnu* 'thick scrub' which is composed of *mulyu* 'nose' and *paka-rnu* 'hit-AGENTIVE' (i.e. doer of action or 'hitter') thus, literally, 'nose hitter'; in Warumungu we have *jalangartata* 'scorpion' which is a compound of *jala* 'mouth' and *ngartata* 'crab'; in Anmatyerre we have *kwatyepwerre* 'lightning', which is compounded of *kwatye* 'water' and *pwerre* 'tail'.

As we saw in 7.2 almost all such compound words are rendered as compound signs in the sign language. An examination of these signs shows that they are comprised of a compounding of signs that match in meaning the components of the spoken form, when considered separately.[6] Thus, although *jalangartata* is a separate lexical item in Warumungu, we do not find that the sign for 'scorpion' is some separate depictive or enactive form (as one could easily imagine it would be). The sign is composed of two parts: a curved index finger touches the mouth in Part I and a 'claw' hand is lowered with a jerky movement in Part II: $\triangledown\dddot{G}_{\top\wedge}{}^{\text{ꝗ}}$ ⁞ $‹5_{\vee\perp}{}^{\vee\sim\}}$. Pointing to the mouth is done elsewhere as a way of signing *jala* 'mouth'. The 'claw' hand sign in Part II is the independent sign for *ngartata* 'crab'. Likewise, in Anmatyerre, *kwatyepwerre* 'lightning' is signed as a compound in which Part I is the sign for 'water' and Part II is the sign for 'tail': $.\,\text{J}\,\text{A}_{<\wedge}{}^{\text{tr}}$ ⁞ $\text{mç}_{<\perp}{}^{\sigma}$. In short, we find that in almost all cases where a given meaning is expressed by a compound word, it is this compound structure that is represented in the sign for that meaning.

In the spoken lexical compounds cited above, the separate components are the same whether they are used in the compound or separately. However, there are examples where the separate components have undergone some degree of phonological change, producing a 'fused' form. In some of these instances the signed versions of such 'fused' forms have retained their compound character, thus making clear the compound origin of the 'fused' spoken form. For instance, in Warumungu we have *Junkkarakur* , the name of a waterhole in Tennant Creek near the site of town (now used by Warumungu people as their name for the town). This is rendered in sign as a two-part sign: In the first part, an extended index finger is moved rapidly away from the back of the neck; in the second part, a spread C hand is moved rapidly toward the mouth: $\overset{\text{b}}{\pi}\text{G}_{\vee<}{}^{\vee\perp\}}$ ⁞ $\text{O}‹5_{<\perp}{}^{\top}$. In such a case we apparently have, first, a pointing to the back of the neck and second, a version of the sign for *warakur* 'waterhole'. This would appear to support the analysis of *Junkkarakur* as having been formed from a compound of *junkku* 'back of neck' and *warakur* 'waterhole'.

Similarly, the Warumungu sign for *Alikarrangi* 'Ali Curung', the name for the Aboriginal settlement formerly known as Warrabri, is a two part form in which Part I is a fusion of the Warumungu sign for *kunapa* 'dog' with a 'moving point', indicating movement through space; Part II is a sign which elsewhere serves as a way of rendering possessive and associative suffixes (see 7.5 and 8.1.2 for accounts of these): . B̂⊥^ ʔ [G]<::B⁶ . This sign could be glossed as 'dog+go past :: associated with'. The name *Alikarrangi* is actually derived from Kaytej *Alekerenge*, which is *aleke* 'dog' combined with *-arenge* 'possessive'. The site which has this name is a dreaming site where two dogs passed by. It will be seen that the Warumungu sign preserves these details, even though the name used is not a Warumungu form and has been so transformed from its original that its origin is not immediately obvious.

While almost all compound words are associated with compound signs, not all compound signs are associated with compound words. As may be seen from Table 7.1, there are, in each of the languages considered here, a number of instances where compound signs are glossed by unitary words. Some of these, as we shall see, turn out to be periphrastic constructions and thus do not have any relationship with spoken language morphology. However, in many other of these cases, we find that the words in question are complex in structure and though not true compounds, can be analyzed as partial compounds. In such cases the compound structure of the sign does seem to fit the word's structure.

In such partial compounds, although one part of the word might also occur as a free morpheme, the rest of the word does not occur elsewhere either as a free or as a bound form. For example, in Warlpiri, there are instances such as *kunapujupuju* 'backwards motion (of something that has a front and a back)' which is composed of *kuna* 'intestines, rear end' and *-pujupuju*. This, however, is a kind of onomatopoetic addition which has no true morphemic status. The sign would seem to reflect this, for it is composed of KUNA, followed by a segment in which an X handshape, continued from the X handshape used to sign KUNA, is moved rapidly forwards twice, sliding over the left hand, held as a fist. The double movement in this part of the sign reflects the reduplicative structure of *-pujupuju*, itself expressive of continuous or extended movement. Again, in Warumungu we have *ngamukurtu* 'bush banana' which is signed as NGAMUNA 'breast': KUMARNA 'coolamon'. Here, the first part of the word does seem related to *ngamuna* 'breast' but *-kurtu* is not a morpheme in Warumungu.[7]

The foregoing examples illustrate the extent to which sign structure can be influenced by the morphological structure of the words having the same meaning as the sign. As already mentioned, however, there are examples where this does not appear to be the case. Thus *kamulu* 'camel' is signed in Warumungu by first pointing over the shoulder to the back, and then holding the hand forward with a curved index finger. This sign is a sort of descriptive phrase, indicating the camel's hump. Likewise, in Warlpiri, to sign *kalwa* 'heron', in Part I the neck is pointed to; in Part II the index finger is moved upwards to indicate 'tall'. Here we also have a descriptive phrase, which may be glossed as "neck long". Again, to give a Warlmanpa example, the notion of *kujja* 'orphan' is signed by first giving the sign for 'mother' and following this with the negation sign, 5^{σ}, which may be glossed as 'mother without'. In Warlpiri *mangkurdu* 'rain-bearing cloud' is signed as NGAPA followed by a second part in which a B hand is waved back and forth in the direction of the sky.

It should be noted that, in all of these cases, the order of constituents in these descriptive phrases is the same as the order that would be followed if these phrases were spoken. That is, in all of the cases given above, the first sign of the phrase is a noun, the second modifies the noun, and this is just the order that is typically followed in the spoken language. Thus, where a descriptive phrase must be used in place of a single sign for something, either because the sign is not known to the signer or because no sign for the item in question has been established, the sign phrase that is employed nevertheless follows a spoken language organization.

The examples of descriptive sign phrases just given were provided by the most knowledgeable of our informants. However, when we undertook to compare signs from a large sample of women of different ages at Yuendumu (Kendon 1984) we recorded examples where the less knowledgeable signers gave descriptive sign phrases for expressions for which older signers knew a distinctive sign. It is also notable that several of the instances where a descriptive sign phrase is used for something for which there is a single word in the spoken language are instances of things that are of quite recent introduction. Thus for *yalyikapita* 'helicopter', *winmili* 'windmill', *piya* 'beer', and *pulijimani* 'policeman' (all from Warlpiri), among others, are all recorded as being signed with descriptive sign phrases. These observations suggest that where the signed expression does not pattern closely with the morphological structure of the corresponding word in the way exemplified above, we may be dealing with parts of the sign vocabulary that are less fully developed. In other words, it is suggested that as these sign languages develop, and as the skills of individual users of these sign languages develop, signing is approximated progressively ever more closely to the morphological structure of the spoken language of the sign users.

7.5 Suffixed forms

In the languages considered here many nominals can be analyzed as a combination of a free morpheme followed by a suffix. Thus we have, in Warlpiri, *kanaparnta* 'scorpion' which is literally *kana* 'digging stick' and the 'possessive' suffix *-parnta* . In Warumungu a policeman is commonly referred as *kilipartta* 'dangerous', which is literally *kili* 'danger, anger' followed by the 'possessive' *-partta* . In Warlmanpa we have *yurukanyanu* 'sad' which is composed of *yuru* 'face' and *-kanyanu* , a suffix meaning 'other, different'. The suffixes illustrated in these examples are derivational suffixes and, as in the examples given, serve to create new words. The signing of suffixes classed as cases - including the core grammatical cases of ergative and dative, and more peripheral cases of ablative, locative, and the prepositional and directional suffixes - will be discussed when we undertake a comparative review of the rendering of nominal suffixes in sign for Warlpiri, Warumungu and Warlmanpa in the next chapter.

As we saw from Table 7.1, words of this construction in Warlpiri, Warumungu and Warlmanpa are more often than not signed with a compound sign. An examination of the signs that are associated with suffixed words shows that where we have compound sign forms, these compound forms reflect in their structure the morphological structure of the spoken word. That is, we find that Part I of the sign is a sign for the free morpheme, when this is used elsewhere, and Part II is one of a number of special forms that function as signs for suffixes in the spoken language.

For example, in Warlpiri *kanaparnta* 'scorpion' is signed as . B$_{\wedge\perp}$^{I} :: B$^{\sigma}$ where Part I is also the sign KANA 'digging stick' and B$^{\sigma}$ is a hand motion that, among other things, serves as a way of rendering the possessive suffix *-parnta*. Likewise, also from Warlpiri, we have *jintakari* 'another one, different one', which is comprised of *jinta* 'one' and the suffix -*kari* 'other'. This is signed as . tG$_{\perp\wedge}$^{ʔ} :: ЬO$_{<\perp}$^{ʋ}, where Part I is the sign JINTA 'one' and Part II is a form that is used for the suffix *-kari* 'other'. In Warumungu *kilipartta* 'dangerous, policeman' is signed as a compound of the sign KILI 'anger' and a sign used only for the possessive suffix *-partta:* [ ]L$_{\wedge<}$$^{\vee\sigma}$ :: 5$_{\vee\perp}$$^{\vee}$[to].In Warlmanpa, *ngappapuru* 'rainy time', is composed of *ngappa* 'water, rain' and *-puru*, a suffix meaning 'during'. This expression is signed as [ ]B$_{T<}$^{ᵠ} ' :: A$_{T>}$ \G$_{<\perp}$$^{*\perp}$, where Part I is NGAPPA 'water' and Part II is a sign used only for rendering the durational suffix *-puru*.

However, as we noted in the discussion of Table 7.1, a higher proportion of suffixed forms are signed with a unitary sign than was found for compound words. A review of available examples suggests three reasons for this. First, there are a number of examples where a suffixed word is synonymous with other expressions which are single morphemes. In such cases we find that a unitary sign is usually the form given. For example, in Warumungu the wedge tailed eagle may be known as *warluwurru*, but it may also be called *janapurlalkki*. This word is composed of *janapurl* 'high side, i.e high up' and the associative suffix *-alkki*. However, the only sign we have recorded for it is a unitary form in which the hand is held like a claw and lowered sharply downwards: . ‹5$_{\vee\perp}$$^{\vee\blacksquare}$. Likewise, in Warlpiri, the dingo may be referred to as *warnapari*, a monomorphemic form. It may also be called *wirnkiwarnu* which is composed of *wirnki* 'wild' and *-warnu* 'belonging'. However, all forms we have recorded of the sign for dingo are unitary.

Second, there are examples where suffixed forms are signed with unitary signs, but where the sign can be understood as being derived from a fusion of the sign for the free expression and the suffix sign. The sign for the Warlpiri expression *witawangu* 'excessive, too much' illustrates this well. *Witawangu* (which itself is used as a suffix) consists of *wita* 'little, small' (a free form) and *-wangu* the privative suffix. A literal English rendering would be 'not little'. In the sign glossed as *witawangu* an O hand is moved with a supinating action and then immediately with a pronating action at the same time as it is opened into a 'spread' or 5 hand: . O$_{\vee\perp}$$^{a\sigma}$[5]. In this sign the initial hand shape is a 'closed' handshape, and thus related to the hand shape used for WITA 'small'; the supinating action with which the Sign Action begins is derived from the preparatory phase of the Sign Action of WITA, for in that sign the hand must first be moved up towards the face (WITA is articulated in relation to the nose). The pronating action, combined with the opening of the hand to the 5 form, is derived from the sign 5$^{\sigma}$ which, as we shall see, is widely used for negations, including the 'privative' suffix *-wangu*, as here. In short, in WITAWANGU, the sign begins as if it is to be WITA but is transformed without juncture into WANGU.

Other examples where a sign and a suffix sign have become fused to form a unitary sign include, in Warlpiri, PURRURDUWARNU 'ignorant', in which the hand in an H configuration is moved away from the head with the motion pattern used in 'privative' signs; WATARNPA 'always' in Warumungu, in which an initial upward movement of the extended index finger is terminated with a 'shaking' action, which is part of the way the suffix *-arnpa,* 'yet', is signed; and YURUKANYANU 'sad' in Warlmanpa, in which the handshape used in the sign for the suffix *-kanyanu* 'other' is assimilated to the location of articulation and the sign action that is used for the sign YURU 'face'.

Finally, there are a number of examples of signs for suffixed forms in which the sign for the free morpheme appears as an inflected form when the suffixed expression is meant. In these cases the Sign Action becomes modified. These instances are almost the only examples of sign inflection which is close to the kind of sign inflection observed in primary sign languages. They are all found in the domain of kinship. Many kinship expressions can have added to them what has been termed a ' 'gether' or 'dyadic' suffix. For example, in Warlpiri *jukuna* is used to refer to someone in relation to speaker as 'cousin' (i.e. Mother's Brother's Son or Daughter). To refer to two people in a cousin relationship - 'two cousins together' - the suffix *-rlangu* is added to form *jukurlangu.* JUKUNA is signed by patting the thigh (near the knee) twice with a flat hand, palm facing downwards: ⸜B$_{\vee\perp}{}^{\vee\times}$! '. To sign *jukurlangu* the hand, in the same configuration and orientation, is slid forward and back over the thigh: ⸜B$_{\vee\perp}{}^{*\perp\top}$. A similar modification of Sign Action is to be observed for the other kin expressions with the 'gether' suffix, not only in Warlpiri, but in Warumungu and Warlmanpa as well.

7.6 Signed verbs and verb morphology

Further illustration of the influence of spoken language morphology on sign organization comes from a study of the way in which expressions using complex verbs are rendered in sign. In Warlpiri and Warlmanpa, especially, but also in Warumungu, verbs may be formed from a compound of a root verb and a form known as a preverb. As we observed in 7.3, Table 7.2 indicates that in Warlpiri, Warumungu and Warlmanpa, the large majority of spoken verbs that are unitary are signed with unitary signs, while the large majority of spoken verbs that are complex, formed from a combination of preverb and verb, are signed with compound signs. As we shall see, this association between compound signs and compound verbs is correctly understood as reflecting a close relationship between the forms of the signs and the morphologies of the spoken language forms. It must be noted, however, that this relationship extends only to the verb root, together with the (uninflectable) preverb, if any. Other morphological features, such as inflections of the verb for tense and mood, are not rendered in these sign languages.[8]

Preverbs in Warlpiri have been discussed in some detail by Nash (1982, 1985). As a rule, a preverb occurs immediately prior to an inflected verb. It often has a kind of 'adverbial' function, but in many cases the combination of preverb and verb results in a complex verb stem which must be treated as a separate lexical entry. In such cases the preverb cannot be regarded as adverbially modifying the meaning of the root verb. A preverb differs from a nominal in that it cannot host any of the case suffixes, although it can host the directional enclitics, as can verb roots.

Forms that function as preverbs may derive from forms that have other functions in the language. For example, many nominals can function as preverbs, in particular when combined with the verb *jarri-mi* ,[9] which is referred to as a 'verb formative' and has no independent occurrence. Nominals may also function as preverbs when combined with *ma-ni*, both in its meaning 'get' and in its meaning 'cause'. Thus, *kurnta* 'shame' becomes the verb 'to be ashamed', when in the compound *kurnta jarri-mi*. Likewise, *ngurrju* on its own is glossed as 'good', but *ngurrju ma-ni* is the verb 'make, mend'; *yiri* on its own is 'sharp point' but *yiri ma-ni* is the verb 'to sharpen'.

However, there are also a large number of forms that function only as preverbs - Nash terms these the 'pure preverbs'. These include some forty or fifty forms that can combine with a wide range of verb roots - the so-called 'productive preverbs' - and a much larger number of forms that are highly restricted in their occurrence - the so-called 'unproductive preverbs'. The productive preverbs include forms that serve to specify various types of action, motion or position, forms that function as quantifiers of action, and forms that indicate a relationship between the action of the verb and something else (Nash, following Hale, terms them 'dative adjunct' preverbs). For example, one may combine the action type preverb *jaala* , with *wapa-mi* 'move', *ya-ni* 'go', or *nya-nyi* 'see' , to produce complex verbs all with the sense of 'back and forth' - as in *jaala wapa-mi* 'to move back and forth', *jaala ya-ni* 'to go back and forth' or *jaala nya-nyi* 'to look back and forth'. *Kutukutu* may be combined with a wide range of verbs with the sense of 'verb in any manner', as *kutukutu wapa-mi* 'move about in a random fashion, move about anywhere'. *Yarda*, an action quantifier preverb, can be combined to convey the sense of verbing 'again' or 'more', as in *yarda yi-nyi* 'give repeatedly'. *Jurnta,* a dative adjunct preverb, can be combined with a verb to convey the sense of verbing away from something or someone, or verbing to the disadvantage of something or someone, as in *jurnta ka-nyi* 'to carry away' or *jurnta nyina-mi* 'to sit away, to sit separately from the others'.

The non-productive preverbs are those forms that conform to the preverb pattern but in which the preverb component is found in combination with only one or two root verbs and cannot combine widely, as the productive forms can. In such cases it is sometimes found that the meaning of the root verb has become considerably altered. For example, *warla paji-rni* 'to restrain, to staunch' is a compound of *warla*, which does not otherwise occur, and *paji-rni* 'bite, cut'. It will be seen that the sense of 'biting' or 'cutting' does not appear to be preserved in the compound form. Likewise, *karri-mi* when used on its own means 'to stand'; however *palyupalyu karri-mi* is 'to flicker, as of flame, dart in and out, as tongue of snake'. Here again, the sense of 'stand' appears to have been much transformed, if not lost altogether.

Most complex verb forms in Warlpiri, as in Warumungu and Warlmanpa, as we have noted, are signed with compound signs. As we saw in the discussion of Table 7.2, in all three languages in which the preverb-verb construction is a common pattern, the signed equivalent of these forms is also a two part form. An examination of these shows that, to a large extent, the two part form matches the preverb-verb structure. That is to say, Part II of the sign is a form that would be used for the meaning of the root verb, when it occurs on its own; Part I of the sign is a form which serves to render the preverb.

For example, *jaala ya-ni* 'go back and forth' is rendered in a two part sign in which, first, a B hand is moved back and forth and, second, the sign glossed as *yani* 'go' is performed: . ꞁB‹› ⁞ Ψ⊥6. If the meaning expressed by *jaala nya-nyi* 'look back and forth' is to be signed, then we again have . ꞁB‹›, but followed with NYANYI as Part II. Likewise, *kutukutu wapa-mi* 'move about in any fashion' is signed as WAPAMI 'move, move about' preceded by a sign in which an O hand touches the back of the left hand, held as a fist, once on the left side and again once on the right: . A∨⊥\O∨⊥× × ⁞ G⊥∧∞. If the meaning is *kutukutu ma-ni* 'get in any fashion' (as in talking about 'getting firewood anywhere'), then we have . A∨⊥\O∨⊥× × ⁞ ‹5mϚa[A], that is KUTUKUTU followed by MANI 'get'. Again, where *nyina-mi* 'sit, be' is rendered in sign by rapidly closing a B hand to G handshape: . B‹⊥[G]; *jurnta nyina-mi* 'sit apart, away from' is signed as a two part sign. In Part I, corresponding to *jurnta*, the right hand, is lowered to make contact with the left hand, both hnads formed as a fist. Part II is NYINAMI, as just described and we have . A›⊥\A⊤‹∨× ⁞ B‹⊥[G]. When *jurnta ka-nyi* 'carry away' is signed we have . A›⊥\A⊤‹∨× followed by KANYI - signed as a 5 hand with the thumb held in opposition, waved back and forth: . 5t‹∧ʃ . When *jurnta ya-ni* 'go away from' is signed, we again have . A›⊥\A⊤‹∨× followed by the sign YANI 'go': . Ψ‹⊥⊥6. Thus, as in these examples, so in most others, no matter what root verb the preverb is combined with, it is signed in the same way.

Similarly, again most usually, the root verb is signed in the same way, regardless of the preverb it is combined with. This is so even when, in combination with a non-productive preverb, its meaning may have been completely altered. *Warla paji-rni* 'restrain, staunch' is signed with a circular motion of curved G hands for Part I, followed by the sign PAJIRNI 'cut, bite' in part II: . G̈⊤›'G̈⊤‹ᘓ ⁞ X□‹⊥a. *Karri-mi* 'stand' is signed by moving a vertically held index finger away from the signer: . G⊥∧⊥•. It is signed in the same way when combined with *palyupalyu* to form *palyupalyu karri-mi* 'dart in and out, as of snake's tongue'.

7.6.1 Preverbs and Verbs with more than one sign

The foregoing examples are all taken from Warlpiri, but similar examples can be adduced from Warlmanpa and Warumungu. They indicate that spoken language morphology is indeed a strong influence upon the associated sign language. However, as we have indicated, there are exceptions. There are examples where the same preverb is signed differently, according to the root verb with which it is combined. There are also examples where the root verb is signed differently according to the complex verb of which it is part.

Different signs for the same preverb may be illustrated from Warlpiri with the signing of the preverbs *tiirl* and *wuruly(pa)*. Thus, Part I of *tiirl paka-rni* 'split by hitting' (as split wood with an axe) is signed differently from Part I of *tiirl pardi-mi* 'open eyes'. In signing *tiirl paka-rni,* for Part I a closed hand is moved horizontally to the right (. X$_{\wedge\perp}^{>}$), whereas in signing *tiirl pardi-mi,* for Part I an open hand is moved to the right in front of the eyes, closing as it does so (ᗣ‹5$_{<}^{>}$[to]). Here the way Part I is signed, although in each case matching a morpheme in the spoken language as sign unit to spoken unit, the sign does not 'stand for' the morpheme. Rather, in each case it displays something of the meaning of the whole expression. Similarly, the preverb *wuruly(pa)* 'concealingly, secretly', when combined with verbs of motion such as *parnka-mi* 'run' or with verbs of transfer such as *yirra-rni*, is signed by sliding the right hand forward over the left, where both are held in a G configuration (. G$_{>\perp}$ \ G$_{<\perp}^{*\perp}$). In signing *wuruly wangka-mi* 'speak quietly, whisper' or *wuruly jarri-mi* 'to become quiet', on the other hand, Part I is quite different. In the first case it consists in a lowering movement of a B hand in front of the mouth (⊽B$_{\vee<}^{\vee}$ ⁞ B$_{<\perp}^{tr}$). In the second case an open hand is moved to the right in front of the face, closing to a G handshape as it does so (Ɔ‹5$_{<}^{>}$[tG] ⁞ tG$_{\top\wedge}^{\perp\bullet}$). It seems that, where the behavior referred to involves spatial displacement of some sort, the sign that matches the preverb unit has a space-displacement feature. Where spatial displacement is not involved, the sign unit that matches the preverb may have other characteristics, such as making reference to closing the mouth, as in the examples just given.

Root verbs, as we have seen, are generally signed in the same way in compounds, regardless of the preverb they are combined with and regardless of whether or not the meaning of the root verb is modified or completely transformed. In Warlpiri there is one exception to this, which involves the root verb *pi-nyi*. This may be glossed as 'hit' in some contexts but is better thought of as having the very general function of marking any action or process as 'punctate'. No sign for this root exists. Instead, expressions using this root are always signed with a form that serves to make the meaning of *pi-nyi* much more specific.

Pi-nyi, when used on its own, has the general meaning of someone or something acting on something in some way, usually with the implication of sudden or forceful action. It often has the meaning of hitting, striking or killing. Sentences which include expressions using this verb are signed differently, according to the kind of impact that is meant.Thus *wati-ngki karli-ngki marlu pu-ngu* [man-ERG boomerang-ERG kangaroo-ABS hit, etc.-PAST] would mean 'The man hit or killed the kangaroo with a boomerang.' The implication of this would be that he did this by throwing the boomerang at the kangaroo.If this sentence were signed the signer would use a sign for *luwa-rni* 'hit with missile' in which a curved index finger hand - the same as the one that is used in the sign KARLI 'boomerang' - is moved rapidly leftward, combined with a wrist flexion (. $\dddot{G}_{<\perp}{}^{<\wedge}$). Had a spear been used to kill the kangaroo, the spoken sentence could be the same (substituting *kurlada -ngku* 'spear-ERG' for *pirli-ngki*), but in signing it the sign for *panti-rni* 'pierce' would have been used instead ('crossed' fingers spring open to a V-like hand, as the hand is thrust forward: . $R_{\vee\perp}{}^{\perp}[U_2]$). A different sign again would be used to render the sentence *Karnta-ngu warna rralyku-ngu pu-ngu* [woman-ERG snake-ABS stick-ERG hit, etc.-PAST]. This would mean 'The woman hit or killed the snake with a stick' and to sign this the signer would use the sign glossed as *paka-rni* 'hit or kill by direct impact, usually with a club, etc.' in which a 'flat' hand is rotated back and forth by forearm rotation (. $B^{a\acute{o}}$)

Where *pi-nyi* occurs in combination with preverbs it has a more general meaning. In signed versions of these expressions we find that a wide range of forms are used in Part II. However, these forms are always forms that, elsewhere, would be glossed as root verbs. For example, *milya pi-nyi* 'recognize, know by sight' is signed with a special form in Part I (. $G_{>\perp}\backslash G_{\wedge\perp}{}^{*\top}$), followed by a form identical to NYANYI 'see' (V-hand, palm down: . $U_{\vee\perp}$). Evidently, in the signed form we see a specific reference to the use of the sense of sight that is implied in the verbal expression. Likewise, in the signed form of *laja pi-nyi* 'carry a large object', in Part I the signer touches her ipsilateral shoulder ($\ulcorner B^{\text{?}}$), in Part II a form identical to MANI 'get' (. $^{c}5m\varsigma_{<\perp}{}^{a}[A]$) is used. Here the sense of getting or picking something up that is implied in *laja pi-nyi* is given explicit expression in sign. A third example is the signing of *jakuru pi-nyi* 'to take leave of someone, to say words of departure'. Here speaking is implied in this expression, and in the signed version Part I is a special form, but Part II is identical to WANGKAMI 'speak, talk, make characteristic noise' ('flat' hand is trembled, held with palm facing left : . $B_{<\perp}{}^{tr}$).

These examples suggest that signs may, in some cases, actually provide a more differentiated representation of meaning than the spoken language. Morphemes such as *tiirl* or *pi-* must be regarded as forms that have several different meanings. This could indicate that we are dealing with different morphemes which are homophonous. Alternatively, which seems more likely, we are dealing with the same morpheme but one which must be regarded as having several different sub-meanings. It is these more specific sub-meanings that are represented in the sign language. Further examples, in respect to the sign representation of certain nominal suffixes in Warlpiri and Warumungu, are discussed in 8.1.2 under the heading of 'split representation'.

7.6.2 Unitary signs for compound verbs

Although most compound verbs are matched with compound sign expressions which, as we have seen, are in most cases appropriately regarded as gestural representations of morphological units in the spoken language, in each of our samples, there are a number of compound verbs which, when rendered in sign, are rendered as unitary forms. In the Warlpiri sample, for instance, there are over sixty examples of this sort.

Inspection of these examples shows that, in a few cases, signs which appear as unitary can be understood as resulting from a fusion of the two Parts. In these cases, the Sign Action or the handshape of Part I of the sign, the preverb section, is sufficiently similar to the Sign Action or handshape of Part II that the two parts can merge and there is no juncture between them. For example, *rdaku yirra-rni* 'put something into a large hollow container (e.g. firewood into a truck)' is signed as .O$_{\vee\perp}{}^{\vee}$[‹5];$^{\circlearrowleft}$. Here an O hand is lowered and spread, and this is followed by a wrist extension. YIRRARNI uses a spread hand with wrist extension (.5t$_{\vee\perp}{}^{\circlearrowleft}$). It will be seen that, in this case, the terminal handshape of Part I in RDAKU YIRRARNI is very close to this; thus there need be no juncture between this and Part II, here accomplished simply with a wrist extension movement. Likewise, *yanjaki ya-ni* 'go walkabout' is signed with a movement of a closed hand away from the signer, with contact with the cheek as its point of origin: 3X$_{\top\wedge}{}^{\times\perp\vee\circlearrowleft}$\{$_{\wedge\perp}$\}. Here the extension of the hand away from the signer - a feature of the Sign Action of YANI 'go' - is simply added to the movement from the cheek.

Most unitary signs for compound forms cannot be interpreted in this way, however. In most cases the compound verbs that are rendered by unitary forms are expressions whose meanings lend themselves very readily to representation by a single enactive action. Thus, in Warlpiri we find verbs such as *kurruru wapa-mi* 'spin, as of a top', *warru ya-ni* 'go around something', *wararrku parnka-mi* 'meander, as snake; as creek', *karipurdanji jarri-mi* 'turn around', *wira nga-rni* 'take off in flight' are signed with a unitary action. All of these, it will be seen, can be quite readily represented by a single action of the hand: spinning the hand round and round for *kurruru wapa-mi*, for instance, or simply raising a spread hand rapidly for *wira nga-rni*. Similarly, *muru pi-nyi* 'insert, shove into something', *wural pi-nyi* 'throw something far', *milmil pi-nyi* 'set spear in spear thrower' or *wuturr ma-ni* 'stretch tight', all are expressions that can be represented easily in a single pantomime-derived action, and this is what we find.

7.7 Sign expressions for non-traditional concepts

We will conclude this chapter with an examination of signs for non-traditional artifacts and ideas. It appears that there is a link between the way in which modes of referring to new things in the spoken language have been developed and how those things are expressed in sign. This provides a further illustration of the way in which signs established in the sign language are representations of units of expression in the spoken language.

The development of spoken language expressions for non-traditional things and concepts in Australian languages has been discussed by O'Grady (1960) for Nyangumarda and by Simpson (1985) for Warumungu. In the following discussion we have made extensive use of Simpson's paper. Several different processes have been distinguished. These include the adaptation of English expressions, the incorporation of words from other Aboriginal languages, the development of new words by combining existing roots with derivational suffixes of various kinds, and the extension of the use of existing words to cover new meanings.

Looking at the signs for new things, we find that where an English word has been adapted or where a word from another Aboriginal language is used, the sign that has been developed is distinct. However, in very many cases where the spoken language expression is a word derived from words already existing in the language, or where an existing word has had its meaning extended to refer to the new thing, the sign used for it is a parallel adaptation of an existing sign.

Where an English word is used, most commonly the corresponding sign is derived from an enactment of an activity pattern associated with the referent or from a depiction of one of its concrete features (cf. Chapter 6). Thus, to take examples from Warumungu, we have *pilankiti* 'blanket' signed by a movement of a 'flat' hand: $.B_{\vee\perp}{}^{\circlearrowleft}\,'$. For *nipi-nipi* 'scissors' (from the

English word 'snip'), the index and second fingers are extended and moved in imitation of the movement of the blades of scissors when cutting: $.U_{<\perp}[H]^{''}$. For *kaartti* ' playing cards' the sign is derived from an enactment of shuffling a pack of cards, in which the right hand, held 'flat', is lowered repeatedly to contact the side of the left hand, also held 'flat': $.Bt_{>\perp}\backslash B_{<\perp}{}^{\vee + '}$. *Puliki* 'bullock' is signed by a circular movement of the index finger directed towards the side of the head - clearly derived from a sketch of the bullock's horns. However, there are some examples where the corresponding sign appears to be derived from a homonymous meaning, either for a word in the Aboriginal language or, in a few cases, for another English word. We noted some of these examples in 7.2, when discussing phonetic representation in sign. We noted there that the sign for 'knee' is the same as the sign for 'European-style meeting' because of similarities in the sounds of the Warlpiri words used (*mirti* and *mirtingi,* respectively); or the sign for 'medical sister' is the same as the sign for 'shoulder' because the English word 'sister' becomes *jija* in Warlpiri, which is homophonous with *jija* 'shoulder'. To these examples we might add the example of *jiki-maniyi* 'check money' which is signed as a compound of a point to the cheek, followed by the sign MANIYI. Here 'check', when pronounced in Warlpiri, sounds like the English word 'cheek', and this apparently accounts for Part I of the sign. Likewise, in Warumungu, we encounter a downward movement of the extended middle finger for *tawun* 'town', evidently because this word sounds the same as the English word 'down'.

Where a word from another Aboriginal language is used, we also have a distinct sign. Sometimes this sign is peculiar to the particular group. At other times it may be shared with the group from which the word may have been borrowed. *Wawarta* 'clothes', in Warumungu, according to Simpson, is probably derived from a word in Wakaya. It is signed by a rightward sweep of a 5 hand (all fingers extended and spread): $.5_{\perp\wedge}{}^{>}$. *Wawarta* is also the word for 'clothes' in Warlmanpa and it is signed in the same way. *Wapawapa*, probably related to the Warumungu and Warlmanpa forms, is used in Mudbura. The sign for it also uses a spread hand, although the Sign Action is different. *Murrkarti* 'hat' is a word that, Simpson suggests, may have spread all the way from Kaurna, a language spoken in South Australia. 'Hat' is signed by a movement of the hand near the top of the head that probably derives from a sketching movement indicating a head covering.The word for 'hat' throughout central Australia is closely related to the Warumungu word cited and 'hat' is signed in the same way for all of the languages we have examined. *Timana* 'horse' in Warumungu, and in several neighboring languages, is also most likely derived from a word in an Aboriginal language (probably from an area to the east of the north central desert area). It is signed in Warumungu by a form that may be derived from a pantomime of holding and pulling on the reins when riding: . E$_{\vee\perp}$$^{\vee T}$)'. 'Horse', however, is also signed in the same way throughout the region we have studied, although in this case the word varies. In Warlpiri it is *nantuwu* (or *nantewe* in Kaytej and Anmatyerre).[10] Despite this last example, as we shall show in detail in Chapter 12, there is some evidence from our data that where words are shared between languages, the signs are more often the same than where words are different, suggesting that, to some extent, signs and words may spread together.

Signs for new concepts that are expressed in the spoken language by words formed from existing words by adding a derivational suffix are commonly signed as a compound of a sign for the root word followed by a suffix sign. Examples illustrating this will also be taken from Warumungu. In this language a common way of making new words is to add a suffix to an existing word to indicate that the new thing being referred to can be thought of in terms of its relationship to the other concept. A suffix widely used for this purpose is *-kari* 'belonging to'. Thus we have *jina-kari* 'foot-belong' for 'shoe', *warli-kari* 'thigh-belong' for 'trousers' or *nyinjji-kari* 'sitting-belong' for 'bicycle seat'. For each of these we have collected signed expressions. In each case the sign is a compound consisting of a root sign followed by . B$^{\sigma}$, the form used for 'associative' suffixes in Warumungu (see 8.1.2). Thus we have ×O$_{>\perp}$$^{\prime}$×O$_{<\perp}$$^{\times\prime}$ ⁞ B$^{\sigma}$, which is comprised of JINA 'foot' +ASSOCIATIVE for 'shoe', ⍀U$_{T\vee}$^{T} ⁞ B$^{\sigma}$ or WARLI 'thigh'+ ASSOCIATIVE for 'trousers', and so on. We have, in addition, collected signs of this type for *miyil-kari* 'eye-belong' for 'glasses', *murrka-kari* 'hair-belong' for 'hair clip' and even a three part sign (generally unusual) for 'hair oil' which, in Warumungu, is known as *wanguangu murrka-kari* 'alcohol hair-belong'. This is signed as . H$_{\perp\wedge}$$^{\$}$ ⁞ ^5t$_{T\wedge}$$^{\vee}$[to] ⁞ B$^{\sigma}$, that is WANGU 'bad', MURRKA 'hair' +ASSOCIATIVE.

These word forms and the signs that are patterned on them are also found for traditional items, we should add. One expression for 'widow' is *kupijja-kari* 'spinifex wax-belong', and this is signed accordingly.[11] The Warumungu name for a place where there are some spectacular boulders known as Devil's Marbles is *Wurtukari* or 'wind-belong' (so named because it is associated with Wind Dreaming) from *wurttu* 'wind' and the sign for it is a compound of WURTTU+ASSOCIATIVE

Another associative suffix used in Warumungu is *-partta* which is signed by closing a spread hand to a form in which only the index finger and thumb are extended. We encounter this in the expression *kili-partta* 'danger-having'. In Warumungu this is the expression commonly used for 'policeman' and the sign for 'policeman' that is used is a rendition of this: [ ]L^<ᵃ:: . 5v⊥ ˇ[ɓo], where Part I is KILI 'danger' and Part II is the suffix sign. Another suffix used in forming new words is *-warinyi* 'denizen of'. New things can be referred to in terms of where they are habitually found. Thus we have *skool-warinyi papulanyi* 'schoolteacher' (literally 'school-denizen-of European') which may signed as . tGv⊥ ˢ::Bᵟ::cBт^ ᵀ ᵀ.[12] The first sign in this compound derives from a pantomime of the activity of writing and is commonly used to refer to 'school' and also to the offices of Europeans. The second sign is the form used for 'denizen of' (the same as ASSOCIATIVE) and the third sign is the sign PAPULANYI 'European'.

Now consider signs for things which, in the spoken language, are referred to by existing words extended to cover new meanings. We again take examples from Warumungu. Money is referred to as *wangari* 'stone, rock, hill' - presumably because hard coins are like stones. A rifle or gun is called *jurlupu* 'hollow log'; a recorded image on video-tape or film is called *pawumpawu* 'ghost, deceased person'; alcoholic drink, drugs, petrol and oil are referred to as *wanguangu* 'dangerous, potent'; and the activity of writing, sewing and washing may be referred to using the verb *paka-* 'poke, spear'. In each of the cases mentioned, the signed expression for the modern object, substance or activity is the same as that used for the older meaning. Thus the sign used for 'rock, hill, etc.' (. E<⊥ ᵃ ') is also used as a sign for 'money'; the sign for 'hollow log' (3H⊥^ *⊥ ') also serves as a sign for 'rifle'; the sign for *wangu* 'bad', repeated, is used for *wanguangu*, whether this means 'potent, dangerous', or 'alcoholic drink'; and the sign for the verb *paka-* 'poke, spear' is used for both this meaning and for the meanings of 'write' and 'wash'.

Instances of the same kind of coordinate extension of word-use and sign-use may be observed in the other languages examined. Thus in Mudbura and Warlmanpa , as in Warumungu, the word for 'money' and 'rock' is the same, as is the sign (although the Mudbura sign for 'rock' differs from the sign used in Warlmanpa and Warumungu). In Warlpiri, *rampaku* means 'light in weight, not solid, weak, without force'. However, it can also be used to mean 'lightheaded, dizzy' and it is also now used to refer to European baked goods such as biscuits or leavened bread. The sign for all of these meanings is the same. *Pintapinta* means 'butterfly' in Warlpiri, but it is also used for 'aeroplane' and again the signs for 'butterfly' and 'aeroplane' are the same. Again, in Warlpiri, *pinti* is 'skin, bark' and it is signed with a spread hand closing to a 'tapered' hand, as the forearm is rotated to place the hand in a palm-up position: . c5v⊥ ᵃ[to^]. The fruit 'orange' is termed *pintikirli* 'bark-having' in Warlpiri and it is also signed in the same way as *pinti*.

In some cases we find that the sign for a traditional concept has been extended to cover new meanings, much as words have been in the examples given above, but that adaptations of English words are used to refer to these concepts in the spoken language. Thus, in Warlmanpa, *ngurrmarna* 'spider, spider's web' may be signed by rubbing together the extended index and second fingers: $.\mathrm{H}_{\vee\perp}{}^{\ast\Omega}$. This sign is also used to refer to *panjala* 'string', and it has been extended to refer to telegraph wires and, by further extension, to telegraph messages and telephones, and even to 'tape' (cassette or reel tape) and 'tape-recorder'. We find the same extension of sign-meaning occurring in Warumungu. In Warlpiri, on the other hand, the word *yinarrki* 'spider, spider-web' has not been extended to the meanings of string, wire, and the like. Instead the English derivative *waya* is used. This word is used for 'wire', 'fence' and 'wire' in the sense of a telegram, and by extension it is used for 'telephone'. It is not used for tape-recorder, however. The sign for this group of meanings is to move an extended middle finger horizontally to the left: $.\mathrm{m}\varsigma_{\top<}{}^{<}$.

From this last example, we may note that differences may arise between groups in regard to how non-traditional items may be expressed in sign, because of differences in how the spoken languages have been adapted. Thus we observed how the Warumungu use *kili-partta* 'danger-having' for 'policeman' and that the sign for this was KILI+PARTTA. In Warlpiri, on the other hand, the English-derived word *pulijimani* is used. To sign 'policeman' at Yuendumu, one wrist is crossed upon the other (representing the hands handcuffed or tied together). Similarly, whereas in Warumungu (and in Warlmanpa and Mudbura) the word for 'rock' is extended to mean 'money', and the corresponding sign is likewise extended, again in Warlpiri (at least at Yuendumu) an English-derived word *maniyi* is also used. The sign that corresponds to this is to describe a circle with the index finger of the right hand, often in relation to the palm of the left hand: $.\mathrm{B}_{>\perp}\setminus\mathrm{G}_{\top<}{}^{@}$.

7.8 Summary

This chapter began with a study of the extent to which the sounds of the associated spoken language influence signs. This was found to be very limited. It is confined to a few examples where words that share similar sounding first syllables are signed in the same way. It was suggested that this 'phonographic' process would have very limited application in a sign language because gesture, partly because it is relatively slow to produce, makes it difficult for recipients to synthesize elements presented in temporal sequence into meaning bearing units. For this reason we would not expect an alternate sign language to develop in the direction of a *speech* substitute. Fingerspelling systems that might be considered to approach these are based on already existing alphabetic systems and they thus do not represent speech units directly.

A comparison of sign organization with the morphological structure of the lexical items with which they are glossed showed that a close relationship is common. Unitary signs are often glossed with monomorphemic words, reduplicated signs are often glossed with words which have a reduplicated structure, and compound signs are often glossed with compound words or with words which have a root-suffix structure. This suggests that it is the morphological structure of the spoken language that has the greatest influence on the organization of signs. In regard to reduplication, this influence appears to be the most direct. Where a comparison could be made between signs for pairs of words in which one member is a reduplicated version of the other, sign organization was often found to parallel word formation, regardless of whether there was a semantic relationship between the words in the pair. Here, it seems, sign formation parallels the formal structure of spoken language closely and reduplication in sign organization is not operating as a sign-formation process separately.

In regard to the paralleling of sign organization with the structure of compound and suffixed words, although this was found to be widespread, certain exceptions were found in which more than one sign form was used to represent the same spoken form. Thus we cited examples where the same preverb was signed differently, according to the root verb it was combined with. We also described how, in Warlpiri, compound expressions containing the root verb *pi-nyi* are signed with different root verb signs, according to whether the *pi-nyi* compound verb made reference to cognition, speaking or carrying. There is thus not always a direct link between a spoken language form and a sign form. Where a spoken language form is used for more than one meaning, the signs corresponding to it may show differentiation accordingly.

We also discussed examples where compound words are signed with unitary signs rather than compounds. In several such cases it appeared that this arose because the concept being expressed could be expressed by gesture directly, with great ease. This was especially true of certain complex verb stems which refer to different modes of movement. Evidently, for certain meanings, in particular those that involve space directly, sign organization will diverge from the spoken structure. Further examples of this will be encountered in the next Chapter where we shall see that verbal inflections that make reference to spatial orientation and direction may not be represented in sign segmentally, but by way of modifications to the movements involved in the performance of the verbal sign.

The chapter concluded with a brief study of signs for non-traditional items. This once again demonstrated a close link between spoken language expression and sign. We described a number of examples in which the spoken expression for the non-traditional item was a compound form. The corresponding sign for the item was also a compound, structured in parallel with the spoken expression. Signs for non-traditional items, it thus appears, are not formed separately. The spoken language expression is established first and the sign expression is formed as a representation of it.

Notes

[1] See Chapter 13 for a more detailed consideration of these systems in relation to alternate sign languages.

[2] I am indebted to Françoise Dussart for drawing my attention to this example.

[3] Skilled fingerspellers can reach a speed of about 6 units per second, but words thus produced still lag behind their spoken equivalents. Where fingerspelled sequences are used repeatedly by signers, however, they typically become abbreviated in various ways and reorganized so that they conform to the formational principles of signs (Battison 1978).

[4] Such a woman would stand to a male ego as a mother-in-law. However, someone who is actually in this relationship would never be the mother of ego's wife. He would always marry someone who is the daughter of a woman who is classificatorily in this relationship, only. For further discussion see Chapter 11 and also Meggitt (1962, pp.147 and 151).

[5] According to Nash (1985, p. 130) *wati* can be reduplicated to form a plural; however Laughren (personal communication 1987) regards this as an example of the use of another, and more recently developed, pluralizing suffix *-wati* and not an example of pluralization by reduplication. In my own (much more limited) experience with Warlpiri I have only observed *wati* pluralized in the same way as *ngarrka,* that is, by the addition of the suffix *-panu* or *-patu.* Note that in spoken Warlpiri *panu* can be used with any noun with human reference, whether or not it reduplicates.

[6] We have encountered but one exception to this. This is the Warumungu expression *kartti purlungu* 'adolescent boy', literally *kartti* 'man' and *purlungu* 'child'. Although this is signed as a compound with Part I being KARTTI (⌐B$_{T<}$$^{*>\Omega\rangle}$), Part II is not the sign PURLUNGU (. O$_{<\perp}$$^{\sigma}$) but a form that does not occur elsewhere: . A\B$_{T<}$$^{*+a\sigma}$.

[7] This suggests that *ngamukurtu* may be analyzed as 'breast-like' - and certainly the fruit of the bush banana could be regarded as being shaped somewhat like a woman's breast. Support for this interpretation is perhaps provided by the fact that in Kaytej *altyeye* 'bush banana' is signed by a repeated touching of the breast: ▪] tO$_{T<}$$^{*\wedge''}$.

[8]For a discussion of temporal reference in NCD sign languages, see Chapter 8.

[9]Verbs in Warlpiri will be given with a suffix indicating the non-past tense. Signs for verbs are written in upper case, again with the non-past suffix, but without the hyphen.

[10]*Nantuwu* is also derived from a Kaurna word. *Nantu* is 'kangaroo'. In Kaurna horses were referred to as *pindi-kaurna* where *pindi* means 'European' (and also 'ghost' - Europeans were at first widely thought to be ghosts by Aborigines because of their pale appearance), hence 'horse' was refered to as 'European kangaroo'. See Teichelmann and Schürmann (1840). I am indebted to Harold Koch for this reference.

[11]In Warlpiri we have*palya-warnu.* 'bereaved mother'. *-warnu* is a Warlpiri associative suffix.(similar to the Warumungu *-kari*). *palya* means 'spinifex wax' but it also means 'dirt, soil'. The expression, thus, is literally 'dirt-having' - which may be an allusion to the fact that breaved people cover themselves with ashes. It seems likely that the Warumungu expression is parallel to the Warlpiri.

[12]It is quite unusual for a sign to have three parts. 'Schoolteacher' is more commonly signed simply by the first two signs in this compound, occasionally simply by the first one.

8 Signing spoken language grammar

8.0 Introduction

In this Chapter we look at how certain aspects of spoken language grammar receive representation in sign. We shall discuss how, in these sign languages, the functions of grammatical and semantic case suffixes, derivational suffixes and enclitics are rendered. We shall also consider determiners, space and time reference and the signing of personal pronouns. We shall see that although the sign languages here also follow closely spoken language morphology in many respects, they do not always do so. The ways in which they do not provide a further understanding of the nature of the units these sign languages represent. It also suggests some of the ways in which the users of these languages themselves analyze them. Which units are represented in sign, and which are not, provides a guide to which units speakers assign a status of 'separability' to. This may have implications for the status of units offered in grammatical analyses of these languages. For much of this discussion we shall rely upon data from Warlpiri and Warumungu; however in the discussion of personal pronouns we shall consider data from Kaytej, as well.

8.1 Nominal suffixes

As we saw in Chapter 7, lexical forms that can be analyzed as a combination of a nominal root with a derivational suffix are often rendered in sign language with a compound sign which consists of the sign for the root, followed by a special form, which serves to represent the bound morph. In this section the forms used to represent nominal suffixes are described. As we shall see, in several cases, the same sign form is used to represent two or more different suffixes. On the whole, where this is so, the suffixes that share signs are related to one another in meaning. There are also instances where the same spoken language suffix is rendered by a different sign, according to the type of nominal it is attached to. Here, it appears, a semantic difference that is implicit in the spoken language is made explicit in sign. Both kinds of examples support the more general point that it is the meanings of these morphemes that signs represent rather than their forms.

The rendering of bound morphs in sign language is something that only the most sophisticated and knowledgeable of signers have been found to do to any extent.[1] The most extensive material we have for this comes from the data provided by Winnie Nangala and Ruby Nangala for Warlpiri, and Bunny Narrurlu, Annie Phillips Narrurlu and Mary Napaljarri for Warumungu. In many instances we were led to recognize the existence of these signs when working with these informants in glossing texts they had previously recorded. Where such discoveries were made, their form and usage was confirmed in subsequent sessions by obtaining signed renditions of specially constructed sentences in which these bound morphemes were used.

8.1.1 Nominal affixes in Warlpiri and Warumungu

A detailed account of Warlpiri nominal affixes may be found in Nash (1985). For Warumungu the reader may be referred to Evans (1982). We have also relied upon an unpublished manuscript by Jane Simpson and Jeffrey Heath (1984) and have benefited from conversations and correspondence with Jane Simpson. A general discussion of affixes in Australian languages may be found in Dixon (1980), Yallop (1982) and Blake (1987).

Both Warlpiri and Warumungu are *suffixing* languages (some Australian languages use prefixes as well as suffixes). All of the morphemes to be considered here are added after the root. When rendered in sign they invariably have this position also. Nominal suffixes may be classed into four broad categories, according to their functions: grammatical case markers, semantic case markers, derivational affixes and enclitics. Examples of most of them, for both Warumungu and Warlpiri, will be found in Table 8.1 (see Appendix to this Chapter).

1. Grammatical case markers. These serve to mark the syntactic functions of nominals in sentences as subject or object. These mark what Dixon (1980) has termed the core cases and Nash (1985) the argument formatives. The absolutive, which is unmarked, is the case for the subject of intransitive sentences and for the direct object (often the patient) of transitive sentences. The ergative marks the subject of a transitive sentence (often the agent of an action). The dative has a variety of functions, but this includes that of marking the indirect object.

2. Semantic case markers. These have many functions, including those which, in English, are accomplished by prepositions. There are several such case markers and Warumungu has a slightly different set from Warlpiri. For both languages these include those which indicate spatial relationships (locative, 'on, in'; allative 'towards'; ablative, 'from') and relationships of origin and cause (elative); they indicate purpose or goal ('purposive dative'); and they indicate relationships of 'withness' (comitative) or 'having' (proprietive), of 'not having' (privative), of possession (genitive), and a relationship of causation (evitative or aversive), in which something is referred to as the cause of some action, or as a source of danger, as in the Warlpiri *maliki-kujaku* 'because of the dog' or 'for fear of the dog'.

3. Derivational affixes. These affixes attach to nominals to form new nominal stems. Most of them serve to modify the semantic content of the root to which they are attached but included here is the 'noun formative' affix which forms a nominal from a verb. Derivational affixes serve many functions. Thus there are diminutives, comparatives, 'alternatives' (which indicate that something is 'different' from something else), 'distributives', 'gentilics' (which indicate the locality of origin of someone, or the normal habitat of something), an affix marking something as the possession of someone, and so on.

4. Enclitics. This term refers to bound morphemes which can attach to any kind of word but which are never followed by a further affix and which may have semantic scope beyond the word to which it is attached, sometimes extending to a whole clause. They may sometimes function like sentence particles. To convey some sense of their functions, a few examples from Warlpiri may be mentioned. Thus we may give *-jala* 'after all, obviously'; *-juku* 'still, yet'; *-nya* 'emphatic, focus marker, interrogative'; *-wiyi* 'first'; and *-yijala* 'also'. Nash (1985) also counts the verbal auxiliary (not used in Warumungu) and the directionals (which indicate direction of something or some activity in relation to the speaker) as enclitics. However, these will be discussed in relation to sign language in section 8.3.

8.1.2 Sign language representations

Table 8.1 (see Appendix to this Chapter) lists all the nominal suffixes for Warlpiri and Warumungu for which we have definite information as to whether they are or are not rendered in sign language. This includes, for Warumungu, 13 semantic case endings and 18 derivational endings and, for Warlpiri, 15 semantic case endings and 21 derivational endings. Inspection will show that for both Warumungu and Warlpiri there are six signs that are used to represent two or more suffixes and that Warlpiri has 15 and Warumungu eight specialized forms, each rendering a single suffix each. In what follows we shall (1) comment on those endings which are not marked in sign, (2) discuss the signs that are used to mark two or more endings, (3) describe examples where the same suffix is represented in two different ways in sign and (4) conclude with a discussion of the specialized forms which also are used as free forms in the sign language.

1. Unsigned cases. There appears to be no special way by which the roles of subject, agent, object or indirect object of a sentence are indicated in sign. No suffixed forms of the sort to be described below have ever been observed to mark these cases and no other modifications of the signs according to grammatical role have been noted. We also have not recorded any instance where the locative case is signed.

Since the grammatical roles are marked morphologically in the spoken language, word order does not have any grammatical function. The absence of such marking in the sign language might lead one to expect that sign order could become important for this in signed discourse. In Chapter 9 we shall present the results of a study in which signed discourses are compared with equivalent spoken discourses. As will be reported there, we find the same consistencies in constituent ordering in both signed and spoken discourse. In both there is a tendency for sentences to have an SOV order, and there are close parallels between speech and sign in how this order is changed in the service of such rhetorical devices as emphasis, repetition, and the like. The evidence available at the moment provides no reason to suppose that, in signing, any special use is being made of sign-order to indicate grammatical role. We must conclude that in the interpretation of grammatical role in signed discourse the recipient is left entirely to rely on what may be inferred from the interactional context of utterance and prior knowledge of what is being talked about.

2. Generalized suffix markers. The two most widely used generalized forms found in both Warumungu and Warlpiri are 'flat hand pronation' and 'spread hand pronation'. In 'flat hand pronation' the hand is held with all fingers extended and together and is rapidly 'flipped' away from the signer with a forearm pronation. In notation: .B$^{\sigma}$. In 'spread hand pronation' the action is very similar, but here the hand is held with all the digits fully abducted (spread apart). In notation: .5$^{\sigma}$. This is very similar to the sign for negation (*lawa* in Warlpiri: see Fig. 5.3).

(i) B$^{\sigma}$ ('flat' hand pronation) is used in Warumungu to render:
-*kari* 'Genitive', as in *warli-kari* 'thigh-belong' (an expression for trousers)

-*warinyi*'Gentilic', as in *palamparr-warinyi* 'sky-dweller' (an expression for aeroplane)

-*alkki* 'Associative', as in *wurrmul-alkki* 'old-associated with' (of olden times)

-*wari* 'Adjective formative', as in *kilykily-wari* 'spotted' (*kilykily* 'spot'), *pilirr-wari* 'shiny' (*pilirr* 'shine, gleam').

It is also added to the personal pronominal sign when the possessive form is signed.

B^{σ} is used in Warlpiri to render

-*kurlangu* 'Possessive', as in *murkardi wati-kurlangu* 'hat man-POSS' (the man's hat)

-*kurlu* 'Associative', as in *wati maliki-kurlu* 'the man with the dog'

-*parnta* 'Pertaining to', as in *nyampu warna kulu-parnta* 'this snake is dangerous' (*kulu* 'fight, sting', etc.) (version 1)

-*jangka* 'Elative of origin or cause', as in *palya marna-jangka* 'wax is from spinifex grass'

-*warnu* 'Elative of origin or cause', similar to -*jangka*.

It may also be used to render -*nyanu* and -*puraji* 'possessives on kin terms', (e.g. *ngati-nyanu* 'his/her mother', *ngamirni-puraji* 'your uncle') although we also encounter $.\mathrm{G}^{\sigma}$ for these forms, which is the same except that only the index finger is extended instead of all digits.

It will be obvious that there is a good deal of overlap between Warumungu and Warlpiri in the use of these forms. In both, $.\mathrm{B}^{\sigma}$ is used for all of the suffixes that have a meaning of 'associated with'. However in Warlpiri this is extended to cover the notion of 'associated with because of origin'. Thus $.\mathrm{B}^{\sigma}$ is used for -*jangka* in signing an expression such as *ngurlu-jangka* 'edible seed-from'. This expression is used as a way of referring to a product of edible seed, for instance when prepared as a paste to be eaten. It would be as if one were to call flour 'ground seed product'.

A further point of difference with Warumungu is that in Warlpiri the two 'gentilic' forms, -*ngawurrpa* 'denizen of' and -*wardingki* 'native of' are rendered with a special form $.\mathrm{G}_{\perp\wedge}^{?}$. We should add that $.\mathrm{B}^{\sigma}$ is also used in Warlpiri by some signers to render the verb formative -*jarri-mi* , although this can also be done with $.\mathrm{G}^{\sigma}$.

(ii) . 5^{6} is used in both Warumungu and Warlpiri for all suffixes with a negative, privative or evitative meaning. Thus, in Warumungu it is used to render:

-mana 'Prohibitive', affixed to the verb infinitive, as in *jalupunju-mana* 'don't drink it'

-kupurtu 'Privative', as in *kuyu-kupurtu* 'without meat'

-kajji 'Lest, beware', as in *ngappa-kajji* 'beware of water' (i.e.'beware of rain')

and, in Warlpiri, likewise, it is used for:

-wangu ' Negative', when suffixed to the infinitive, as in *Nyina-ja wangka-nja-wangu* 'He/she sat without speaking'

-wangu 'Privative', as in *maniyi-wangu* 'without money'

-kujaku 'Lest, beware', as in *warna-kujaku!* 'beware of the snake!'

In both sign languages (as in all the other North Central Desert sign languages) 5^{6} is used to render 'no': *warraku* in Warumungu and *lawa* or *walku* in Warlpiri.

The foregoing are the only two forms that are of widespread use in both sign languages. The following forms have generalized uses either in Warumungu or in Warlpiri, but not both.

(iii) . $tG_{\top\wedge}^{\perp\blacksquare}$. The hand is held with palm facing the signer with the index finger and thumb extended and in contact. The hand is moved forward for a short distance. This form is used in a generalized way only in Warlpiri. It has been recorded as marking the following:

-kurra 'Allative - towards', as in *ngurra-kurra* 'towards the camp'

-wana 'Perlative - around, along edges of', as in *karru-wana* 'along the edge of the creek'

-nyayirni 'Excessive, of dimensions - very', as in *wiri-nyayirni* 'excessively big, strong'

and also, from one signer, as a device marking the dative ending *-ku* in contexts where this is functioning as a 'purposive dative', as in the sentence:

Nalija-rna-ngku	ka-ngu-rnu	nga-rninja-ku
Tea -1P subj.-2P obj.	carry -PAST-hither	eat-INF- PUR.DAT

'I brought tea to you for you to drink'

This has been recorded as being signed as:

NALIJA	KANYI	NGARNI	$tG_{\top\wedge}^{\perp\blacksquare}$
Tea	carry	drink	DAT

. $tG_{\top\wedge}^{\perp\blacksquare}$ has also been recorded in Warumungu as a marker for *-kuna/-kina* 'Allative', but it otherwise does not occur as a marker for bound forms, except for the verb formative *-ja-nta*. This, it should be noted, is also used in

Warumungu as the verb 'to stand'. $.\,tG_{\top\wedge}^{\perp\blacksquare}$ is used for it, as for the verb formative. This sign is also used in Warlpiri for *karri-mi* 'to stand'.

(iv) $.\,\lrcorner\,tG_{\top\wedge}^{\top\vee\}}$. Here the forearm is held up, palm of the hand facing signer, with the index finger extended, with extended thumb held in contact with it. The hand is drawn downwards and towards the signer. This form is found only in Warlpiri. It is used to sign the derivational suffix *-piya* 'like, similar to' and also the semantic case *-ngurlu* 'ablative - from'. Note, however, that *-ngurlu* in Warlpiri has two uses. It can be used to indicate spatial origin, as in *ngurra-ngurlu* 'from the camp' or *karru-ngurlu* 'from the creek'. It can also be used in a causal-origin sense. When it is used in this way it is signed differently, as will be described next. This is an example of what is here termed 'split representation', in which the same spoken language form receives a different sign language representation, according to its context of use.

3. 'Split representation'. This refers to instances where a morph with more than one meaning is represented in sign in more than one way. The examples to be described here may be compared to those described in 7.6.1. Like these, they show how signs may sometimes show a greater degree of form-meaning correspondence than is found in the corresponding spoken language expressions. In some cases this may provide evidence that a given morph should be properly regarded as two different morphemes, something that might not have been apparent if sign representation had not been considered.

In both Warumungu and Warlpiri, as in many other Australian languages, the ending that marks something as being the spatial origin of something is the same as the ending that marks something as being a causal origin. Both endings are called ablative, although some authors, such as Dixon (1980), suggest that there are really two case relations, ablative and causative. Dixon argues that these forms were distinct in Proto-Australian, but have converged in historical development. As we have just mentioned, *-ngurlu*, the ablative in Warlpiri, is signed differently according to whether it is being used in a spatial sense or in a causal sense. This difference in use of the ablative also appears to be marked in Warumungu signing.

The form used for the causal ablative in both Warlpiri and Warumungu is $.\,B_{\wedge\perp}\backslash A_{\top\vee}^{*\,?}$. Here the right hand forms a fist which is held in contact with the palm of the left hand. It is moved toward the signer by wrist flexion (see Fig. 8.1). For Warlpiri, this was first observed in the following sequence, in the signed version of the story *Yarnirnpa-Kurlu* ('The Reluctant Bride' - see Chapter 9 for an account). The story-teller signs:

WURNA	KARNTA	.B$_{\wedge\perp}$\A$_{\top\vee}$*ʔ	RDINYIRLPA
Travel	woman	*-ngurlu*	dissatisfied
JINTA	PARNKAMIRRA		
the one	runs thither [to a distant creek]		

('He travelled thither [to the creek] dissatisfied because of the woman' [the woman, his promised wife, had refused him])

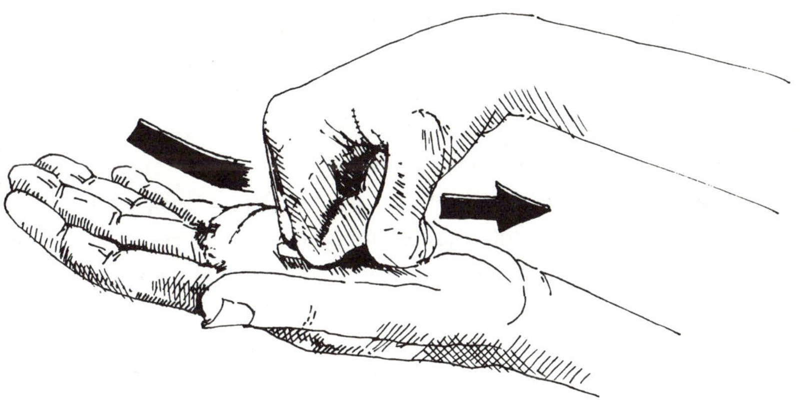

Fig. 8.1 Sign for causal ablative, *-ngurlu* (Warlpiri), *-ngara* (Warumungu)

In Warumungu, we have not recorded a sign for *-ngara* 'ablative' when this is used in the spatial origin sense, but when *-ngara* has a causal sense it is signed as in Warlpiri, as in *nyayi-ngara?* 'what-from?' - i.e. 'why?' - which we have recorded as being signed thus: .G$_{<\perp}$^{a} ¦¦ B$_{\wedge\perp}$\A$_{\top\vee}$*ʔ. Part I is a form of the general interrogative (used for several different interrogatives in Warumungu). Part II is *-ngara* 'causal ablative'.

In Warlpiri a separate causative is also used. This is *-jangka* and this, as we have seen, is signed with the 'flat hand pronation', .B$^{\sigma}$. This causative appears to have a somewhat different sense from *-ngurlu* as a causative, however.[2] Whereas *-ngurlu* is used to mean that something is the direct cause of some event (as the woman, in the example above, was the direct cause of the man running to the creek), *-jangka* is often used to mean that something is a causal product of something, as flour may be called *ngurlu-jangka* because it is 'from' edible seed.

A second example of 'split representation' is found in Warumungu in respect to the ending *-yilppi* 'very'. In certain contexts it is signed as follows: the index finger is extended but flexed into a sharp 'hook' and the thumb is at the same time fully extended so that it sticks up (see Fig. 5. 26). The hand is held so the palm faces the signer. The Action is a supinatory rotation of the forearm ($.\,X_{\square\top<}{}^{a}$). This form occurs (as a suffix marker) only in Warumungu, where it is also used to mark the endings *-kuwarta* 'Desiderative purposive' and *-ara* or *-arra* 'agentive excessive'. *-kuwarta* is used to indicate something as being the purpose of some action or activitiy, as in *Lippirriji-kuwarta apa-n* 'I am going for goanna, i.e. going out with the purpose of getting goannas' or as in *nyayi-kuwarta* 'what for?'. *-ara* or *-arra* indicates someone that does something to excess, as in *marnu wangka-j-arra* 'excessive talker, someone who talks too much'.

It is to be noted that $.\,X_{\square\top<}{}^{a}$ is used for *-yilppi* only when the nominal to which it is attached refers to some kind of human activity. *Nginngin-yilppi* 'thief' is a case in point. Here *-yilppi* has been attached to *nginngin* 'thieving', so literally it means 'thieving very'. When this is signed it is signed as a compound sign as follows: $.\,B^{a\sigma}{::}\;.\,X_{\square\top<}{}^{a}$. When *-yilppi* is used on nominals that do not refer to human activity, however, as in *wupparn-yilppi* 'too small' or *kumppu-yilppi* 'too big', it is, then signed in a different way. In such cases a spread hand is turned to a palm up position, all digits but the thumb and index finger being flexed to a closed position as it does so: $.\,5_{<\perp}{}^{a}[\,tG\,]$. This form is also used to render the definite plural *-yirtti* and the third person plural pronoun *ajjul* 'they'.

It will thus be seen that, in Warumungu, the form $.\,X_{\square\top<}{}^{a}$ is used to mark suffixes which refer to desire, or excessiveness of human activity, while $.\,5_{<\perp}{}^{a}[\,tG\,]$ is used to mark suffixes which refer to plurality or markedness of size or number in general. In both cases, what is being marked is something that is 'more than normal', but a distinction is drawn between what is 'more than normal' in human desire or activity and what is 'more than normal' in terms of objects in the non-human world. This distinction appears to be drawn in sign, where it is not apparent from the surface forms in the spoken language, as the case of the signing of *-yilppi* shows.

We encounter a third example of 'split representation' in respect to the Warumungu suffix *-partta.* This suffix occurs on a very few nominals with the meaning of 'having, characterized by', as in *kili-partta* 'danger having' (a form nowadays commonly used as a name for 'policeman', as we have seen). In such cases the suffix is signed by closing a spread hand so that only the thumb and index finger remain extended: $.\,5_{\perp}[\,tG\,]$. Note that this form differs from the 'more than' sign just described, in that there is no forearm supination. *-partta* also occurs as a suffix on a number of place names, however, as in *Aparrpartta*, a compound with *aparr* 'language', or *Kirtangarapartta,* a compound with *kirtangara* 'centipede'. These names are signed as compounds and Part II, which corresponds to *-partta* in these cases, is signed in quite a different way. A spread hand is lowered to make contact by its heel with the left hand, held as a fist: $.\mathrm{A}_{>\perp}\backslash 5_{\vee\perp}{}^{\vee\times h}$. This difference in the signs used seems to suggest that the *-partta* used in association with *kili* 'anger', where it has the force of 'having', is different from the *-partta* used on place names - or at least that it is nowadays perceived to be different.

The form used for *-partta,* where it occurs in place names, is the same as the sign that is used to render the nominal *partta* , which means both 'heel' and 'hard ground'. One is tempted to speculate, in consequence, that where *partta* occurs in place names it is not the same as the suffix *-partta*, but is actually the word for 'hard ground'. In such a case the places are being referred to not as *Aparrpartta* 'language-having' or *Kirtangarapartta* 'centipede-having', but as 'language-ground' and 'centipede-ground'. 'Ground' and 'place' may be semantically connected. Places are commonly named after the exploits of Dreaming heroes who enter and re-emerge from the ground at various locations along the paths they travelled. In effect, thus, these names would indicate the 'place of centipede' or the 'place of language'. If this interpretation is correct, once again we would have an example where differences in meaning of homonymous forms are recognized by different forms in the sign language.[3]

These observations on 'split representation' show how differences in meaning, though not reflected overtly in spoken language morphology, are yet retained in sign language. They are reminiscent of those examples described in Chapter 7 in which the Warlpiri root verb *pi-nyi* is rendered in sign differently according to the meaning of the complex verb stem in which it participates. These examples provide further support for our general thesis that these sign languages are representations of the semantic units of spoken language morphs, and only indirectly are they representations of their surface forms as such.

4. Suffix markers as free forms. The suffix marker signs that represent more than one suffix, with one exception, do not occur elsewhere as free forms in the sign language. Several of the specialized suffix markers - forms that render only one nominal suffix - also occur as signs for free morphs, however. In such cases there sometimes appears to be a relationship in meaning. In other cases the similarity may arise because of homophony.

(i) $.\,c\mathrm{B}_{\wedge\perp}\backslash c\mathrm{B}_{\vee<}{}^{\vee\times}$. In this sign the hands are held in a 'cupped' shape, the digits drawn together. The right hand, palm downwards, is lowered to contact the left hand, held with palm up. In both Warumungu and Warlpiri it serves to render the 'Proprietive' suffix, *-jangu* and *-parnta*, respectively, as in *kartti wijjartu-jangu* 'the man has a spear' (Warumungu) or in *karnta pangurnu-parnta* 'the woman has a scoop'. In Warlpiri this sign is also used for *muurlpa* 'together, in company'.

(ii) . U∖$\dddot{U}_{\vee\perp}{}^{\intercal}$. Here the right hand, held in a 'V' shape, but with fingers bent, is lowered to contact the left hand (handshape unspecified) or even any available body part if the other hand is being used for something else (Fig. 8.2). This form is used for the Warlpiri suffix *-palka* 'one able to, characterized by mode of action', as in *wiji-palka* 'thief' (although in the case where we have recorded this, PALKA was signed with one hand only and it was performed with assimilation to the previous part of the action, thus: . $B_{\wedge\perp}{}^{\sigma\langle\rangle a\rangle}$ ${}^{\sigma}[\dddot{U}_{\vee\perp}]$). It is also used for the free form *palka* 'body' and another use of *palka* to mean 'presence' or 'actual possession' and in combination with certain verbs, as in *palka ma-ni* 'to find', *palka jarri-mi* 'to give birth'. This may be a case of 'phonographic extension', where the suffix is given the same sign as the free form because they sound the same. On the other hand, some relationship in meaning at a very abstract level may be indicated. In Warumungu this sign is used for *ngattu* 'body'.[4]

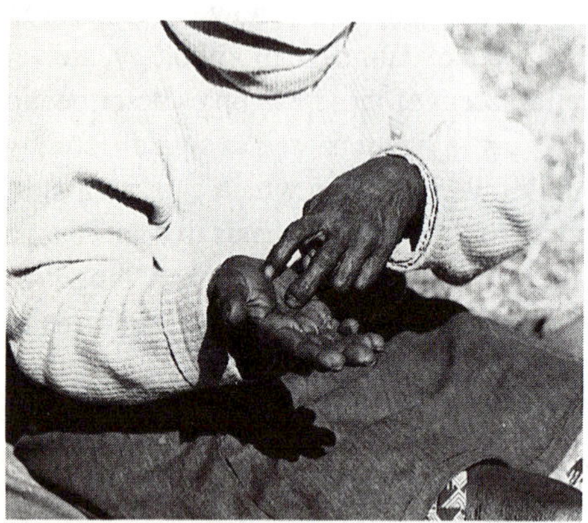

Fig. 8.2 PALKA 'body, etc.' (Warlpiri), NGATTU 'body' (Warumungu)

(iii) Other signs used in Warlpiri for derivational suffixes that are also used as signs for free forms with related meanings include the sign for the Warlpiri diminutive *-pardu*, which is the same as the sign used for *wita* 'small', and the sign for the dual *-jarra,* which is the same as the sign for *jirrima* 'two'. The special suffix *-palangu* which marks someone as belonging to any generation above one's own is signed by a form that is remarkably similar to the sign for *ngati* 'mother'. Whether there is any connection here is not certain. The suffix *-puka* 'bereaved kinsman' - as in *ngati-puka* 'bereaved mother' - is signed in the same way as *kuna* 'intestines, faeces' and *puka* 'rotten, stinking'.

-puka, it may be added, also occurs as an enclitic to mean 'even' or 'only'. There is some question as to whether the *-puka* in *ngati-puka* is related to this, or to the form used to mean 'stinking', etc. The sign evidence perhaps suggests the latter. Undoubtedly, someone who is dead is also likely to be rotten and stinking. *Ngati-puka*, in this case, could be interpreted literally as 'mother to stinking (i.e. dead) one'. This is plausible, on the analogy of such expressions as *ngati-puraji* 'mother to you' or *ngati-nyanu* 'mother to him/her/them'.[5]

8.1.3 Nominal suffixes: discussion

Of the endings discussed, as we noted, there is no sign language representation for the grammatical cases. As far as our evidence goes, it appears that, in signing, grammatical relationships are left to be resolved by the recipients. We suggest that in the context of everyday interaction this is not difficult and grammatical ambiguity rarely arises. In the context of normal interaction situations, when anyone produces signs, they will be taken to be 'saying something'. Recipients will attribute communicative intent to the signer and will thus give signs status as utterances. In doing so, grammatical case relationships will be attributed to the units of the utterance, since all utterances must imply such relationships. This can usually be done on the basis of semantic content alone. Animate items, especially human beings, dogs, and the like, are usually either subjects, agents or objects. Ambiguity is only likely to arise as to whether an animate item is agent or object, but which it is will usually be obvious from the content of the sentence. In normal circumstances, people do not say things like 'The man bit the dog' or 'The dog bit the man' unless they are describing an actual event (either real or imagined). Utterances of this sort, produced in normal situations, are always embedded in both situational and discourse contexts which make it quite evident who is doing what to whom. Signers, we suggest, can count on recipients to assume that they are producing an utterance that intends to 'say something'. In consequence, they can count on the recipient to resolve the grammatical relationships correctly. For this reason, there is no need for grammatical role to be marked in sign.

The endings that are signed include all those that make differences that a recipient could not be left to settle on the basis of context. Thus many of the endings that indicate change in spatial relationship or spatial orientation are signed, for these provide information that must be specified if ambiguity is to be avoided. If one were to utter 'meat creek man carry', for instance, the recipient would have no difficulty in deciding that it was the man who did the carrying and that it was the meat, and not the creek, that was being carried. But he would have to be told whether the man carried meat from the creek or towards it. Thus it is not surprising that the endings that express 'toward', 'from', and 'alongside of' are represented in sign. By the same token, we find that many of the derivational suffixes are also signed. Since these suffixes alter the semantic content of the stem to which they are attached, it is obviously crucial that this information be represented.

A number of different suffixes were found to have the same signs. Thus, 'associative' meanings of various kinds are all represented similarly, as are the various 'negative' meanings. An examination of the signs for these suffixes thus may suggest semantic relationships underlying different surface forms. However, we also encountered several examples of what we termed 'split representation' in which suffixes that have the same forms are signed differently, according to the kind of nominal to which they are attached. In the case of the ablative suffix, we saw that, in sign language, differences in meaning were marked that were, perhaps at one time, represented by distinct forms in the spoken language. In other cases, differences in sign may give a clue to the different status of otherwise homonymous forms. In either case, the phenomenon of 'split representation' shows that signs often represent meaning units in the spoken language rather than its surface forms.

As a final observation, we suggest that the suffixes that receive representation in sign provide evidence for the status that the speakers themselves assign to these spoken language elements. As we have seen, a number of suffixes have free counterparts, often with a semantic relationship between them. These are signed in the same way, whether they are bound or free. This suggests that such forms are perceived by the language users as having a status as separate lexical forms. Thus, we suggest, for users of Warlpiri, *puka* or *palka* are regarded as separate words, regardless of whether they occur phonologically as free or bound forms. On the other hand, the various 'associative' suffixes which are all signed in the same way, with a sign form that is of a quite simple nature, are perceived by these language users as less separable from the nominals to which they are attached. Finally, the forms that do not receive any sign representation are regarded as undetachable. Such endings are regarded as integral components of the word and are true inflections, therefore.

8.2 Time

In the spoken languages verbs are always inflected for tense and this, of course, conveys information about the temporal frame of the utterance - whether what is being referred to is occurring now, occurred in the past, will occur in the future, and so on. This information can also be conveyed, in addition, by the use of temporal adverbs - 'now', 'soon', 'yesterday', and the like. In the associated sign languages verb signs are not inflected for tense. Furthermore, we have not observed any use of spatial displacement of signing to indicate tense, such as has been reported in primary sign languages (Friedman 1975, Brennan 1983). In American Sign Language, for example, a so-called 'time-line' has been noted, by which the temporal frame of an utterance may be indicated by a spatial displacement of 'time signs', backwards if it is the past, forwards if it is the future. In Warlpiri and Warumungu signing, if the temporal frame of an utterance is given at all this is done by using a sign that is glossed by one of the temporal adverbs. Unlike comparable signs in American Sign Language these are not modulated in terms of a 'time line'. Typically, this temporal adverbial sign is placed at the beginning of the sentence. In addition, there are signs in both languages for the various times of the day - sunrise, midday, afternoon, sunset, night, and the like. There are also signs for the days of the week.

In Warlpiri, but not in Warumungu, the verb is always accompanied by an auxiliary. This is also inflected for tense and it also may have attached to it various pronominal clitics. The auxiliary, depending on its form, may occur, phonologically, as a clitic or as a word. If its form is monosyllabic, it is pronounced as a clitic, if it is polysyllabic it may be pronounced as if it is a word. Thus, in the present tense it takes the form *ka*, and is cliticized to the preceding word:

Wati ka wangka-mi
Man PRES speak-NONPAST
'The man is speaking'

Likewise, in the past imperfect it is a clitic *-lpa* attached to the nominal preceding the verb, as in

Wati-lpa wangka-ja
Man-IMPF speak-PAST
'The man was speaking'

In the future it takes the form *kapi* and in such a case may be pronounced as if it is a separate word. Thus:

Wati kapi wangka-mi
Man FUT speak-NONPAST
'The man will speak'

This is also true of the forms it takes in the conditional (*kaji*) and possibility (*kala*). In the definite past it is omitted (zero) as in

Wati wangka-ja
Man speak-PAST
'The man spoke'

No matter what form the auxiliary may take it is never rendered in sign. Here is another way in which the sign language deviates from a strict rendering of spoken language morphology. The fact that the auxiliary is not signed suggests that speakers regard it as an integral part of the semantic unit conveyed by the verb. In this it contrasts with the semantic cases and derivational suffixes which, though bound, as we saw in the previous section, are given separate rendition in sign. This suggests that speakers do treat these two kinds of endings as if they are separable semantic units, no matter that, phonologically, they do not occur as separate forms.

Although the temporal inflections of the verb are not reflected in sign, there are some kinds of verb inflections that are. For example, Warumungu verbs have a 'negative imperative' inflection and a 'fear' inflection. In the negative imperative the suffix *-mana* is added to the infinitive form of the verb, as in *nya-nji-mana*! 'Don't look!' This may be signed as $.\mathrm{U}_{\vee\perp}$ ⁞́5^{σ}, that is, the negational sign 5^{σ} is added after the verb sign. The 'fear' tense is formed in different ways according to the conjugation class of the verb. It is used to express such meanings as 'for fear of', or 'lest something'. Thus one might say:

Nya-ya, ama jaja-kurn
See-IMP he eat-lest
'Watch out, he might eat it'

To sign this one would again follow the verb sign with 5^{σ}. In Warlpiri the same notion is expressed with a special suffix *-kujaku* which is added to the infinitive form of the verb and this is likewise signed by following the verb sign with 5^{σ}.

8.3 Space

Signers can, and do, make extensive use of unformalized pointing as a means of spatial reference. However, there are also formalized modes of spatial reference which are correlates of spatial reference devices in the spoken language.

8.3.1 Locational cases and demonstratives

Both Warlpiri and Warumungu, as we have seen, have semantic cases that function as prepositions do in English to indicate the spatial relationship of things, and movement towards or away from them. As we saw, the case endings that refer to displacement in space relative to objects - 'towards' and 'from' - can be rendered in sign language with special signs. Both Warlpiri and Warumungu also have demonstratives with a spatial reference. Those for which we have sign equivalents in Warlpiri and Warumungu are listed below. It should be added that these signs are typically directionalized. That is, the signer directs her arm toward the point in space referred to. In this way, of course, information is provided by the sign that is additional to that provided by the spoken determiner alone, which does not by itself indicate a compass direction.

Inspection of this set of signs shows, first, that points in space that are far off are referred to with the upper arm upraised or with full arm extension. Second, it will be seen that the handshape adopted, at least in the series recorded from Warumungu, changes according to the precision with which the point in space is referred to. For the equivalents of 'this' and 'that' an index finger is used. For expressions that are vaguer in their spatial reference, *ngunju* 'somewhere' and *arttirta* 'anywhere', a 'B' hand and a 'spread' hand are used, respectively. In these signs, thus, there is an analogic relationship between the form of the sign and the distance and nature of the spatial extent of the location referred to.

Signs for demonstratives in Warlpiri and Warumungu

ENGLISH	WARLPIRI		WARUMUNGU	
This	nyampu	$.G_{\vee\perp}^{\vee}$	ngalinya	$.G_{\vee\perp}^{\vee}$
That	yalumpu	$.\imath G_{\vee\perp}$	alinya	$.\imath G_{\vee\perp}$
That yonder	yali	$.\imath\, \dot{\frown} G_{\vee\perp}$		
That beyond	yinya	$\imath\, \dot{\frown} G_{\vee\perp}$		
Somewhere			ngunju	$.B_{\angle\perp}^{\perp\blacksquare}$
Anywhere (over there)			arttirta	$.5t_{<\perp}^{\varsigma}$

8.3.2 Directionalization in the verb

In both Warumungu and Warlpiri there are morphemes by which the orientation and spatial relationships of agents and patients in relation to the speaker are marked. In Warumungu there are different suffixes attached to the verb stem that indicate whether the action is oriented toward the speaker, or involves movement toward him (the 'centripetal' or 'hither' suffix), or whether it is oriented away from the speaker or involves movement away from him (the 'centrifugal' or 'thither' suffix). These suffixes are inflected according to the tense of the verb, but in an irregular way.

In Warlpiri there are three directional clitics that can attach to the verb or preverb which indicate whether the activity referred to is being done 'thither', over there, away from the speaker, 'hither', in the direction of the speaker, or whether the activity is 'going past' the speaker or crossing his line of vision. Thus:

Wati-ngki ka	kuyu	ka-nyi-rni	ngurra-kurra
Man-ERG PRES	meat	carry-NONPAST-'hither'	camp-ALL.

'The man is carrying meat hither to the camp' (camp being where the speaker is).

or

Wati-ngki ka	kuyu	ka-nyi-rra	ngurra-kurra
Man-ERG PRES	meat	carry-NONPAST-'thither'	camp-ALL

'The man is carrying meat thither to the camp' (camp being away from the speaker).

or

Wati-ngki ka	kuyu	ka-nyi-mpa	ngurra-kurra
Man-ERG PRES	meat	carry-NONPAST-'past'	camp-ALL

'The man is carrying meat past [me] to the camp [over there]'

Data on how this directionalization of the verb is rendered in sign is available for Warlpiri for the 'hither' and 'thither' directionals. There are two ways in which this is done, depending upon the nature of the way the verb is signed. There are some sign language verbs which can be varied in the path through which they are moved in space or in how the hand is oriented as they are performed, and these variations are used systematically to express directionalization. There are other verbs which cannot be varied in this way. In sentences involving these, directionalization is accomplished by the use of an additional pointing sign.

Ka-nyi 'carry' is a verb which, when signed, can 'incorporate' the direction of carrying in respect to the speaker, by how the hand is moved through space. There are, in fact, three forms of this verb in the sign language:

(i) . 5t$_{\wedge\perp}^{\top d}$ *ka-nyi-rni* 'carry hither'. Here the hand, with fingers spread and thumb opposed, is held with palm up. The Sign Action consists in moving the hand toward the signer from an initial position of forward arm extension. The particular direction of this extension may vary, depending upon the relationship between the carrier and the origin of carrying.

(ii) $.5t_{\vee\perp}{}^{\perp\smile\}d}$ *ka-nyi-rra* 'carry thither'. Here the hand, with the same handshape, is held with palm facing downwards. The Sign Action consists in moving the hand away from the signer, the particular direction of this movement depending upon the relationship of signer to goal of the act of carrying. An example of how directionalization of movement of KANYI is used as a means of referring in sign to the Agent and Dative object of carrying is given in Chapter 9 in the discussion of signed discourse.

(iii) $.5t_{<\wedge}{}^{\varsigma}$ or, as a two handed form, $.5t_{>\perp}{}'5t_{<\perp}{}^{\ddagger\div'}$ *ka-nyi* 'carry'. This is the 'undirectionalized' form. Here the hand, again with fingers spread and thumb opposed, is waved back and forth. When done with two hands the hands repeatedly cross over and separate. These forms are used when the act of carrying is referred to without any reference being made to the direction of carrying, as in describing a dog running along carrying something or describing travelling and carrying one's gear. This form also is used when KANYI occurs in compounds, as in *japarlka ka-nyi* 'carry on hip - as of baby in coolamon', signed as $\urcorner B_{\wedge\top}{}'B_{\wedge\top}{}^{\circ}$ ⁞ $5t_{>\perp}{}'5t_{<\perp}{}^{\ddagger\div'}$ or *wingki ka-nyi* 'irritate eyes, as of smoke' signed as $.\Psi_{\vee\perp}{}^{a\wedge\}}$ ⁞ $5t_{<\wedge}{}^{\varsigma}$ *Ka-nyi* 'carry'.

Other verb signs which can be directionalized in a similar way include those which refer to movement through space, including PARNKAMI 'run', KARRKAMI 'walk', WAPAMI 'move', YANI 'go', PURAMI 'follow'. Many verbs of transfer can be directionalized, such as YIRRARNI 'put, place', YINYI 'give', KIJIRNI 'throw' MURUPINYI 'insert, push into', WURALPINYI 'throw something far'. There are also verbs of activities that do not incorporate spatial movement into their meanings but which, when signed, can be directionalized and, thereby, the location of the activity referred to relative to the speaker can be indicated. These include NGARNI 'ingest (eat or drink)' and WANGKAMI 'talk'. NGARNI is commonly signed by holding a 'basket' or 'claw' hand toward the mouth and 'trembling' it: $\triangledown c5_{\top\wedge}{}^{tr}$. However, the direction of orientation of the hand can be varied and the sign can be performed with the arm fully extended away from the signer in a specific direction, as a way of 'incorporating' a deictic movement into the sign to indicate who is engaging in eating. Likewise, WANGKAMI is signed by 'trembling' a 'flat' hand, $.B_{<\perp}{}^{tr}$, but the direction in which the hand is pointed as it performs the sign can be varied and the person engaged in talking (if other than signer herself) can thus be indicated.

Many other verb signs cannot be directionalized, however. In addition, as we noted with KANYI, when the verbs occur as part of a compound, directionalization tends to drop out. When direction is to be indicated with verbs that cannot be directionalized, a special 'direction marker' is added as a separate sign. An example of such a verb sign is MANI 'get' (and in compounds, 'cause'). In this sign the hand is held initially in the form of a 'claw', but with the middle finger extended somewhat more than the others. The forearm is then rapidly supinated and the hand is closed into a fist form at the same time: . ᶜ5mʕ<⊥ ᵅ[A^⊥] (Fig. 5.31). If direction is to be added to this, the orientation of the hand is not varied and the movement is not inflected. The verb is followed by a directionalized index finger point, moved distally if 'thither' is meant, proximally if 'hither' is meant. A textual example of this will be given in the next chapter.

8.4 Personal pronouns

In this section we shall discuss the way personal pronouns are signed in Warlpiri, Warumungu and Kaytej. As we shall see, there are a number of differences in how pronouns are signed in these languages, several of which can be directly attributed to differences between the spoken languages.

8.4.1 The personal pronoun systems.

In each of these three languages, as in most other Australian languages, there are independent pronouns for first and second person and in Warumungu and Kaytej there are independent pronouns for third person as well. In each language there are singular, dual and plural forms and for the first person dual and plural there are, in addition, inclusive and exclusive forms.

In Warlpiri there is also a set of clitic pronouns which attach to the auxiliary base and which serve to cross reference the arguments of the verb. Sentences can be constructed using only these cliticized forms, or they may use both independent and cliticized forms. As we saw in 8.3, even when the auxiliary occurs as a phonological word, whether or not it has pronominal clitics attached to it, it is not rendered in sign. Hence we need not be concerned further with these clitic pronominals here.

The independent pronouns take the same form whether they are in the subject or agent role. In Warlpiri and Kaytej they take an inflection for the object role but in Warumungu the object pronouns comprise a separate set. Warumungu also has a large set of 'fused' subject/object pronouns which are used whenever subject and object have pronominal reference in the same sentence. In many cases these fused pronouns can be understood as having arisen from a compounding of the subject/agent and object pronouns, but many others cannot, and they have a distinct form. Warumungu also has a distinct set of possessive pronouns, whereas in Warlpiri and Kaytej the possessive is formed by adding a special possessive suffix to the independent form.

In Kaytej, there is a further complication. The non-singular pronouns (duals and plurals) occur in three different forms. Which of the three is used depends upon the nature of the kin relationship between the persons referred to (Koch 1982). Form I is used when the persons are both members of the same (or alternate) generations and the same patri-moiety; Form II is used when the persons are members of the same patri-moiety but of opposite generations (i.e., where, relative to one another, one person is of the parental generation, the other of the child generation - see 11.1 for further explanation); Form III is used when the persons referred to are members of opposite patri-moieties, regardless of the generations to which they belong.

8.4.2 How the personal pronouns are signed

In signing personal pronouns we find that in all three sign languages three persons are distinguished and there are separate forms for singular, dual and plural. However, there is no formal way in which the inclusive-exclusive distinction is rendered in sign. Perhaps this is because such a distinction can so readily be indicated by a directional variation in the sign. All of the signs, except the first person singular, can be varied in how they are directed in space, so who is to be included or excluded can easily be shown by such variations. Accordingly, there is no need for this distinction to be expressed by separate fixed forms. This is another illustration of how the special expressive potential of the gestural medium will be used in the sign language, where this appears as a simpler solution. As a result, it will deviate from a close mapping of spoken language morphology.

Most of the personal pronoun signs are pointing signs. However, as we shall see, there are variations in both handshape and sign action by which distinctions in meanings are marked. The pronoun signs thus provide a further illustration of how pointing signs may, at one and the same time, *indicate* the referent and convey information about it. We discussed this phenomenon earlier in Chapter 6, in connection with signs for body parts.

The independent subject/agent pronouns for Warlpiri and Warumungu are listed in Table 8.2 and the sign equivalents are given in notation. Table 8.3 gives the subject-object forms for Warumungu. Table 8.4 lists the forms for Kaytej. These Tables are to be found in the Appendix to this Chapter. The discussion to follow summarizes the conclusions that may be drawn from an inspection of these Tables.

Singular forms. First, second and third person singular are signed in the same way in the three languages. For the first person, an index finger is lowered in front of the face and usually the finger is bent as this is done. For the second person, the hand, palm up, with index finger only extended, is moved in an upward arc-like path toward the addressee. For the third person, the hand with palm down and index finger pointing away from the signer is moved diagonally to the right, or it may be moved in any direction appropriate, if the current or habitual location of the person referred to can be pointed at.

First person dual. In each language this is signed in a different way, and the differences can be attributed directly to differences in the spoken languages. In Warlpiri the dual exclusive form is *ngajarra*, which can be analyzed as bearing the dual suffix *-jarra* which can occur on other nominals. *Ngali,* dual inclusive, can also occur as *ngalijarra*, thus also bearing the dual suffix. The way these are signed would seem to confirm this. They are both signed in the same way as compound forms. In Part I, an extended index finger moves away from the signer and back to contact the center of the chest. In Part II, a V hand, palm facing left, is moved to the right. This sign is the same as the Warlpiri sign JIRRIMA 'two' and it is also used for the dual suffix. In Warumungu the first person dual is a separate form, *ajjil* , and the sign, accordingly, is not a compound. It is signed in the same way as Part I of the Warlpiri sign just described.

In Kaytej, as we have mentioned, there are three different forms of this pronoun, as there are for all the other non-singular pronouns. The form used depends upon the nature of the kin relationship of the persons referred to. In sign, for the first person dual only, there are two forms. When the two parties are of the same patri-moiety and generation, the G handshape is used and the hand, palm up, is first moved forward, away from the signer, and it is then brought back so that the tip of the index finger touches the top of the signer's ipsilateral shoulder. When the two parties referred to are not of the same patri-moiety and generation, the hand is moved from a distal position to touch the center of the signer's chest, but the handshape is quite different. The index finger is extended, but sharply bent into a 'hook', and the thumb is extended and abducted (the $X_{\square}$ hand: see Fig. 5.29). It is notable that the Form I sign, which terminates in touching the shoulder, is similar in this respect to the sign used in Kaytej for *atyerre* 'younger brother or sister'. Since persons in the same patri-moiety and generation include persons who are classificatory siblings, it is appropriate that reference should be made to this relationship in this pronominal sign. The sign used as the equivalent of the Form II and Form III pronouns is similar in Sign Action to first person dual signs in the other languages, because contact is made with the center of the chest. The handshape, $X_{\square}$, however, is probably used here simply as a means of keeping the sign distinct from the Form I sign. It is not used in any related Kaytej kin signs.

First person plural. The signs for the first person plural are highly similar in all three sign languages. In all three a B hand is moved from a distal position to make contact with the center of the signer's chest. Note that whereas in the first person dual forms, the extended index finger is used, here a handshape in which all digits are extended is used. This difference appears to encode rather nicely the difference between a singular other and several others included in the meaning of these signs.

Second person dual. In Warlpiri a V hand, also used for JIRRIMA 'two' and the dual suffix *-jarra,* as we have seen, is here moved, palm up, in an arc-like movement toward the addressees. It is the same as the second person singular sign, but with a 'dual' handshape, that is to say. In Warumungu and Kaytej second person dual is signed by holding the index finger hand forward with the finger pointing upwards and alternately supinating and pronating the forearm.

Second person plural. In all three languages this is signed by moving a spread hand (5) horizontally from right to left. However, Warlpiri signers bring the fingers together into a 'tapered' handshape (to) as this movement is made, Warumungu signers leave the fingers spread, while the Kaytej signers close the hand into a G form (index finger only extended) as they move it.

Third person dual. In Warlpiri there are no fixed third person forms established in the sign language and this is no doubt related to the fact that spoken Warlpiri has no independent third person pronouns.[6] The third person can be indicated in sign in Warlpiri by pointing, as already mentioned. Where two or several third persons are to be mentioned, this is done either by sweeping the pointing hand back and forth, or by using a pointing hand with several fingers extended.

In Warumungu and Kaytej separate forms for the third person do occur in the spoken language and there are fixed forms for these in sign. For the third person dual, in both languages, the hand is opened into a handshape with extended fingers, but it is done differently in each one. In Warumungu the initial hand position is a variant of the ×B handshape, in which all fingers are extended, but the index finger is flexed at the second joint. Here, however, the thumb is adducted, pressed against the side of the index finger. In the Sign Action the index finger is suddenly extended and, at the same time, all digits are abducted, resulting in a 'spread' hand. In Kaytej, the initial hand position is one in which both index finger and thumb are extended. The index finger is then fully flexed and the thumb is brought into contact with it and then, immediately, the index finger and thumb are extended again. In Anmatyerre, we may add, the sign for second person plural also has this opening of the hand action. Here the hand is first held as a fist and then the index and second fingers are extended to form a U hand: .A$_{\vee\perp}$[U].

Third person plural. This is signed in the same way in both Warumungu and Kaytej. A spread hand, with palm down, is closed to a G hand. At the same time, the forearm is rotated to bring the hand into palm-up position.

Warumungu subject-object pronouns. For the fused forms which combine first person singular with second person singular and first person singular with second person dual, regardless of which is subject or object, special signs are used. For *arnanku* and *anajju*, first person subject with second person object, and vice versa, respectively, a 'spread' hand, held up with palm facing the signer, is lowered and closed to a G hand. For *arnampukku*, first person singular subject with second person dual object, a G hand, palm facing left, is supinated and then, as it is pronated, the handshape is changed to the ʟO form (tips of thumb and index finger in contact, all other digits flexed to palm).

All the other fused forms are signed using one of the signs for the simple pronouns. Which one of the simple pronoun signs is used for which fused form is not altogether straightforward, however. We do not find, as perhaps might have been expected, that the form matching either the subject or the object pronoun is always the one chosen. Which form is used depends upon whether there is a plural component to the fused form or not, and whether or not a first person form is involved.

The first person dual is used for any form in which this is combined with any other person in the singular, regardless of whether it is as subject or object. The first person plural form is used for any fused form where this is combined with second person plural or third person singular, whether subject or object, or where first person dual occurs as object with third person singular as subject. The second person singular form is used where it combines with third person singular, whether subject or object, and the second person dual form is used for any fused form in which it combines with second or third person singular. The third person plural form is used for any fused pronoun in which third person plural, second person plural or first person plural exclusive occurs, for any form that combines two duals and any form where third person dual is combined with second or third person singular.

Possessive pronouns. In Warumungu, as we noted, possessive pronouns differ in form from simple pronouns. Thus where *arni* is 'I', *ajjinyi* is 'mine'. In the other languages, on the other hand, the possessive is formed by adding a special possessive suffix to the simple form. In Warlpiri, for instance, we have *ngaju* 'I', but *ngaju-nyangu* for 'mine'. In all three languages, however, the possessive pronoun is signed in the same way. It is signed as the simple form followed by the form B^{σ} which, as we saw in 8.1, is widely used as a suffix marker for endings with the meaning of 'associated with'.

8.4.3 Signing pronouns: conclusions

The pronoun signs are pointing signs, but in the handshapes and movement patterns employed they illustrate well how, in pointing, the referent can both be indicated and some aspects of its nature can be encoded as well. Singularity is encoded by handshapes with a single digit extended, duality is encoded either by double digit extension or by duality of movement and plurality is encoded by multiple digit extension. Reference to self is encoded by self-oriented movement and where reference is to self and other as a unit, this is encoded by a distal-to-self movement which gives a direct visual expression to a 'link' between self and other.

In each sign language, we find a partial mapping of spoken language morphology in the signing of personal pronouns. Where independent personal pronouns are present, fixed signs have developed to match them. Where they are absent (or not always used), fixed signs are not to be found. Thus in Warlpiri, where an independent third person pronoun is often omitted, there are no fixed signs for them in the sign language. In Warumungu, in contrast, where independent third person pronouns are always used, they are rendered by fixed signs. The sign languages preserve the singular, dual and plural distinctions, but they do not preserve the inclusive/exclusive distinction. We suggested that this might be because who is to be included and who excluded can be easily indicated by pointing. No need arises for fixed forms to express this distinction, therefore.

The most conspicuous differences between the three languages in how the personal pronouns are signed occur in respect to the first person dual pronouns. The differences described are attributable to differences in the morphological structure of the spoken language forms of these pronouns. In Warlpiri, these pronouns bear the dual suffix, and they are signed, correspondingly, with compound signs. In Warumungu and Kaytej they are monomorphemic and the corresponding signs are unitary. However, in Kaytej there are three forms for this pronoun by which differences in the kin relations of the referent persons are marked. In Kaytej signing two signs for the first person dual pronoun occur, one corresponding to the spoken pronominal that indicates that the referent persons are of same generation and moiety (hence likely to be siblings), the other being used for the other pronouns which indicate that the referent persons are of different generations and moieties. Kaytej has three forms for all the other non-singular pronouns as well, but these differences are not reflected in the corresponding signs.

The evidence from how the personal pronouns are signed in these languages seems to hint at the greater salience of the first person in its singular and dual modes and of the second person in the singular mode. As we have noted, it is in respect to the first person dual forms that we find the greatest differentiation between languages, and in Kaytej the sign language only reflects some of the kinship relationship distinctions marked in the spoken language pronouns of this language in respect to this pronoun. We also saw, in the discussion of the fused subject-object pronouns in Warumungu, that it is only those forms that involve the first and second persons in singular and dual modes that are signed in a specific way. Presumably, at least those distinctions that are indispensable to orderly interaction are preserved in the sign language. The fact that first and second person pronouns are treated with more differentiation than third person pronouns suggests that it is the the participants who are immediately involved with one another.in the current interaction that require the clearest representation. Where several persons are co-present, if personal references must be made to them, it is especially important to be clear about who is to be included or excluded as 'present' to the immediately current address.

8.5 Summary and conclusions

From what we have seen in this and the preceding chapter, it is evident that, to a considerable extent, the signs in the sign languages discussed here are representations of equivalent items in their associated spoken languages. There is some influence from the phonological structure of these items, but it is morphological structure that is represented most extensively. However, it would appear that, often, it is not the surface forms of the spoken language that signs stand for, but the meanings represented by these forms.

Two kinds of phenomena show this. First, there are examples where several different spoken language forms are represented by but one sign. We saw this in the present Chapter in connection with the signing of several of the derivational suffixes in both Warlpiri and Warumungu. We shall encounter further examples in Chapter 11, when we discuss signs for kin relations. In these cases, signs may represent a more general category of meaning than the spoken language forms. Second, there are examples where a given morph, which has different meanings in different contexts, is signed differently, accordingly. For instance, we saw, in the previous Chapter, how, in Warlpiri, for certain compound verbs, the preverb may be signed differently, according to the root verb to which it is attached. In other examples, the same root verb was found to be signed differently, according to the compound it occurred in. In this Chapter, in what we termed the 'split representation' of certain nominal suffixes, we again observed how the same surface form in the spoken language may sometimes be signed in more than one way, thus representing directly its different meanings.

In the present Chapter we saw, however, that it is only the lexical items of the spoken language that are represented. We find no representation in sign of inflections of the verb for tense (and, in Warlpiri, of the verbal auxiliary and its inflections) nor is there any representation of the core grammatical case markings (argument formatives). We suggested that these may be omitted from representation in sign because, most of the time, the meanings they provide can be supplied by the recipient as part of the process by which an utterance is understood. The time frame of an utterance, like the core grammatical relations of its constituents, is inherent in its meaning. No sense can be made of any utterance unless grammatical relations and tense are provided. In the ordinary circumstances of daily interaction, recipients will construe utterances as if these features are provided, hence specification of tense and grammatical relations can be omitted without much loss.

There are other ways in which, in certain respects, signs deviate from a complete representation of spoken language morphology. Thus there are certain meanings, mostly to do with manner of movement and movement in space, that are given a direct representation in gesture, regardless of the morphological structure of the equivalent spoken language expressions. As we saw in Chapter 7, a number of compound verbs for kinds of movement ('taking off in flight', 'moving about in a circular fashion', and the like) were found to be represented in sign by gestural forms, and not by pairs of signs, each member of which represented a different part of the spoken language compound. We also saw, in this Chapter, how the separate morphemes in the spoken language by which directionality in the verb is given ('hither' and 'thither' clitics in Warlpiri, for instance) often do not find separate representation in sign because the sign corresponding to the verb in question can itself be inflected for direction in the course of its performance. Directionality is, thus, 'incorporated' into the verb sign directly. Likewise, again in this Chapter, in our discussion of signs for personal pronouns we saw that the main distinction not marked in sign was the inclusive/exclusive distinction. We suggested that different fixed signs marking this distinction had not been established because inclusion and exclusion can so easily be expressed by a directional variation in how a personal pronoun sign is performed. This is, thus, another instance where the properties of gesture as an expressive medium may be exploited so as to offer a simpler way of representing a given meaning than would be provided by following the spoken language structure.

Notwithstanding these various ways in which these sign languages are not complete representations of their associated spoken languages, the formal correspondence between the organization of signs and the morphological structure of the spoken language units to which they are equivalent is striking. They are clearly not like autonomous (whether primary or alternate) sign languages and they use expressive devices characteristic of such sign languages to a much lesser extent. As we have noted previously, it appears that the women who make the most use of sign language show representation of spoken language structures to the greatest degree. This is no doubt in part a consequence of the fact that these sign languages are learned relatively late in life, when spoken language structures are so firmly established that they constitute the most salient model for any alternative communicative system that might be developed. However, it may also be that we find such a high degree of representation of spoken language forms in these sign languages because of the kind of spoken languages that they are. These languages are highly agglutinative in character. That is, there is a close correspondence between the sequencing of morphemes in any construction and the linear arrangement of morphs in the corresponding utterance. To represent utterances in such a language in another medium by establishing forms that represent morphemes is a relatively simple matter. Were we dealing with fusional languages, on the other hand, we might expect that signs would match spoken language morphology much less closely.

Notes

[1]It is interesting to note, in this connection that Miller (1978), in his study of Western Desert sign language, did not find much correlation between sign organization and spoken language morphology. It will be recalled from Chapter 3 that in the Western Desert sign language, although widespread, does not show the same degree of elaboration as it shows in the North Central Desert. This is undoubtedly correlated with the fact that, in Western Desert society at no time is any group of individuals enjoined from speaking for along periods of time and in all circumstances.

[2]*-jangka* can also be used with the sense of spatial and causal origin of something.

[3]The semantic connections we are suggesting here receive some support from a comparison with Warlpiri. The sign for *-partta* that is used in these Warumungu place names is the same as the Warlpiri sign for *yirdi* 'name, base of something, origin of something'. In addition, note that the Warlpiri sign for *walya* 'ground' is very similar to the Warlpiri sign for *jurrku* 'place', and for *jukurrpa* 'Dreaming'. All of which seems to suggest that concepts of origin, source, for which things are named, locations and the ground itself are closely connected.

[4]*Ngattu* has some of the same range of meanings in Warumungu as *palka* does in Warlpiri. However it does not occur as a suffix.

[5]I am indebted to Mary Laughren for the interpretation of *ngati-puka* given here.

[6]*Nyanangu* is a determiner that refers to some antecedent (it may be glossed as 'that aforementioned') and in some contexts it may be used as if it is a third person pronoun. However, it is not always present and in this Warlpiri differs from Warumungu, where the third person pronoun is always used. Like the other independent pronouns, it takes *-nyangu* and not *-kurlangu* as the possessive suffix, unlike the other determiners.

Appendix: Tables for Chapter 8

Table 8.1: Warlpiri and Warumungu grammatical and semantic cases
[NS: no sign; NR: no sign recorded]

	WARLPIRI		**WARUMUNGU**	
GRAMMATICAL CASES				
Absolutive				
	Unmarked	NS	Unmarked	NS
Ergative				
	-rlu/-ngki	NS	Various forms	NS
Dative	-ku	NS	-ku	NS
SEMANTIC CASES				
Locative	-rla/-ngka	NS	As ergative	NS
Allative as locative, in Warumungu marks location of objects				
			-kuna/-kina:	$.\,G_{\perp\wedge}^{\perp\blacksquare}$
Allative	-kurra	$.\,tG_{\top\wedge}^{\perp\blacksquare}$	-kuna/-kina	$.\,G_{\vee\perp}^{\circlearrowleft}$
Perlative	-wana	$.\,tG_{\top\wedge}^{\perp\blacksquare}$		
Pergressive	-purda	?	-purtta	$.\,G_{\vee<}^{>}$
Ablative, spatial origin				
	-ngurlu	$J\,tG_{\top\wedge}^{\top\vee\}}$	-ngara	NS
Dative-purposive				
	-ku	$.\,tG_{\top\wedge}^{\perp\blacksquare}$	-ku	NS
Desiderative-purposive				
	-ku-purda	?	-kuwarta	$.\,X_{\square\top<}^{a}$
Ablative, as causal origin				
	-ngurlu	$.\,B_{\wedge\perp}\backslash A_{\top\vee}^{\ast\,\circlearrowright}$	-ngara	$.\,B_{\wedge\perp}\backslash A_{\top\vee}^{\ast\,\circlearrowright}$
Source, from; because, injured from				
	-jangka	$.\,B^{\sigma}$		

Table 8.1 continued

	WARLPIRI		WARUMUNGU	
SEMANTIC CASES, cont.				
Evitative: negative-purposive, 'lest'				
	-kujaku	. 5^6	-kajji	. 5^6
Privative:	-wangu	. 5^6	-kupurtu	. 5^6
Prohibitive	-wangu	. 5^6	-mana	. 5^6
Possessive	-kurlangu	. B^6	-kari	. B^6
(on pronouns)	-nyangu	. G^6		
Associative, proprietive	-kurlu	. B^6	-alkki	. B^6
Pertaining to	-parnta	. cB ʌ⊥ \ cB v< vx		
DERIVATIONAL SUFFIXES				
Proprietive, pertaining to	-parnta	. B^6		
Proprietive, pertaining to	-parnta	. cB ʌ⊥ \ cB v< vx	-jangu	. cB ʌ⊥ \ cB v< vx
Comparative: 'like'	-piya	⅃ tG Tʌ vT}	-antajji	. G v⊥ ᵒ
Other, another	-kari	ḃO <⊥ ᵒ		
Gentilic: 'denizen of'	-ngawurrpa	. tG ⊥ʌ Ɂ		
Gentilic: 'native of'	-wardingki	. G ⊥ʌ vɁ}	-warinyi	. B^6
Genitive excessive			-arra	. B^a [A]
One able to, etc.	-palka	. U\Ü v⊥ ᵠ	-ara/-arra	. X □T< ^a
Excessive, of behavior			-yilppi	. X □T< ^a
Excessive, very	-witawangu	. O^a6 [5 v⊥]		
Excessive, of dimensions	-nyayirni	. tG Tʌ ⊥▪	-yilppi	. c5^a [tG]
Diminutive	-pardu	△ḃO T< ^6		

Table 8.1 continued

	WARLPIRI		WARUMUNGU	
DERIVATIONAL SUFFIXES, cont.				
Dual	-jarra	. U‹⊥ ›	-kujjurr	. U‹⊥ ›
Definite plural	-patu	. ‹5⊥ ᵅ[tG]	-yirti	. ‹5⊥ ᵅ[tG]
Durative: still, yet	-juku	. tG⊥^ ᶦ	-arnpa	. tG⊥^ ᶦ
While, during	-puru	. A›⊥ \X⌄⊥ *⊥		
			-akurru	. ×Bᵟᵅ, 5ᵟᵅ
Pair in a kin relation			-nyini	\G*⊥
Pair in a kin relation	-rlangu	\G*⊥	-kurangi	\G*⊥
2P possessive, on kin terms	-puraji	. Gᵟ		
Anaphoric possessor, on kin terms	-nyanu	. Gᵟ		
Same generation	-purdangka	. B⊥^ ›		
Ascending generation	-palangu	. Yᵅᵟ		
Bereaved kinsman	-puka	. X⌄⊥ ˢ		
Capable of			-pulkarti	. B‹⊥[G]
'Side' (relative place)	-nginti	NR	-purl	NR
Defective, of body part	-kari		-murumuru	. bO‹⊥ ᵅ←ᵅ
Adjective formative	-pari/-nji		-wari	. Bᵟ
Associative, characterized by	-parnta	. Bᵟ	-partta	. 5t⊥[tG]
Place name suffix			-partta	. U›⊥ \5⌄⊥ ⌄×h
Resultative	-warnu	. Bᵟ		
ENCLITICS				
Directional, thither (CF)	-rra	See text		
Directional, hither (CP)	-rni	See text		
I say, obviously	-waja	. 5⌄⊥ ⌄		
Of course, obviously	-jala	. 5⌄⊥ ⌄		
First	-wiyi	. A‹⊥ ‹		
Only	-mipa	. tG⊥^ ᵓ		
Assertive	-ja	NR		

Table 8.2: Warlpiri and Warumungu personal pronouns

Warlpiri Independent Personal Pronouns

1ST PERSON		
Singular	ngaju(lu)	ƆG$_{T\wedge}$ ˇΩ
Dual Exclusive	ngajarra	[ ]G$_{\wedge\perp}$ ⊥T ⚲ ⁞U$_{<\perp}$ >
Dual Inclusive	ngali(jarra)	[ ]G$_{\wedge\perp}$ ⊥T ⚲ ⁞U$_{<\perp}$ >
Plural Exclusive	nganimpa	[ ]≏B$_{\wedge\perp}$ T ⚲
Plural Inclusive	ngalipa	[ ]≏B$_{\wedge\perp}$ T ⚲
2ND PERSON		
Singular	nyuntu(lu)	.G$_{T\wedge}$ ⊥{$_{\wedge\perp}$}
Dual	nyumpala	.U$_{\wedge\perp}$ ⊥
Plural	nyurrula	.‹5$_{<\perp}$ ‹[to]
3RD PERSON		
Singular	nyanungu	No fixed signs recorded
Plural	nyanugu-rra/-patu	

Warumungu Simple Personal Pronouns

1ST PERSON		
Singular	arni	ƆG$_{T\wedge}$ ˇΩ
Dual Exclusive	ajjil	[ ]G$_{\wedge\perp}$ ⊥T ⚲
Dual Inclusive	ayil	[ ]G$_{\wedge\perp}$ ⊥T ⚲
Plural Exclusive	ankkul	.B$_{<\perp}$ T ϑ ⟩
Plural Inclusive	anyul	[ ]≏B$_{<\perp}$ T ϑ ⚲
2ND PERSON		
Singular	angi	.G$_{T\wedge}$ ⊥{$_{\wedge\perp}$}
Dual	amppul	.G$_{\perp\wedge}$ ɑσ
Plural	a(rr)kkul	.5$_{<\perp}$ ϑ
3RD PERSON		
Singular	ama	.G$_{T<}$ σ›⟩
Dual	awul	.G$_{\perp\wedge}$ ɑσ
		×B ˣt$_{\vee\perp}$ [5$_{\vee\perp}$]
Plural	ajjul	.B$_{\vee\perp}$ ɑ[G$_{\wedge\perp}$]

Table 8.3: Warumungu Subject-Object Pronouns and Signs

First Person S ('I')		
+2nd P O ('you')	arnangku	$.5_{\top\wedge}{}^{\vee}[tG]$
+2nd P Dual O ('you two')	arnampukku	$.G_{<\perp}{}^{a\sigma}[\text{ʟo}_{\vee\perp}]$
+2nd P Plural O	arnturrkku	$.5_{\vee\perp}{}^{a}[G_{\wedge\perp}]$
('you several')		$.U_{<\perp}{}^{<}[G_{<\perp}]$
First Person Dual Exclusive S ('I and him/her')		
+2nd P O	ajilirnkki	$.G_{<\perp}{}^{\perp\top\perp}$
+2nd P Dual O	alkurntukku	$.5^{a}[tG]$
First Person Plural Exclusive S ('I and them')		
+2nd P O	ankulurnkku	$.5_{\perp}{}^{\vee a\}}[tG_{\top\wedge}]$
First Person Dual Inclusive S ('I and you')		
+3rd P O ('him/her')	ayil	$.G_{\vee\perp}{}^{\vartheta\top\}\vartheta}$
+3rd P Dual O ('they two')	anyuljarni	$.B^{\vartheta\top\}}⁞5^{a}[G]$
First Person Plural Inclusive S ('I and you several')		
+3rd P O ('him/her')	anyul	$.U_{\vee\perp}{}^{a}[G_{\wedge\perp}]$
First Person Dual Exclusive S ('I and him/her')		
+3rd P O ('him/her')	ajil, ajjil	$[\,]G_{\vee\perp}{}^{\vartheta\top\}\varphi}$
First Person Plural Exclusive S ('I and them')		
+3rd P O ('him/her')	ankkul	$.5^{a}[tG]$
First Person Dual Exclusive S ('I and him/her')		
+3rd P Dual ('them two')	ankuljarni	$[\,]B_{\vee\perp}{}^{\vartheta\top\}\varphi}⁞5^{a}[tG]$
Second Person S ('you')		
+First P O ('me')	angajju	$.L_{\top\wedge}{}^{\vee}[to]$ $.5_{\top\wedge}[G]$
+First P Dual O ('us two')	angajikki	$[\,]G_{\wedge\perp}{}^{\vartheta\top\}\varphi}$
+First P Plural O ('us several')	angankku	$[\,]B_{<\perp}{}^{\vartheta\top\}\varphi}$

Table 8.3 continued

Second Person Dual S ('you two')		
+First P O ('me')	ampulajji	.G∨⊥ ɑσ
Second Person Plural S ('you several')		
+First P O ('me')	akulajji	.5∨⊥ ɑ[G⊤∧]
+First P Dual O ('us two')	akularnkki	[ ]B<⊥ ɔ ⊤ ♀
Second Person S ('you')		
+Third P O ('him/her')	angi	.G∧⊥ ∨
+Third P Dual O ('them two')	angapulu	.G ɑσ
+Third P Plural O ('them several')	angajurnu	.5∨⊥ ɑ[G∧⊥]
Second Person Dual S ('you two')		
+Third P O	amppul	.G ɑσ
+Third P Dual O ('them two')	akuljarni	.5∨⊥ ɑ[G∧⊥]
Second Person Plural S ('you several')		
+Third P O	a(rr)kkul	.5∨⊥ ɑ[G∧⊥]
Third Person S ('he/she')		
+First P O ('me')	ajju	B∨⊥ ɔ ɑ}[G]
+First P Dual Incl. ('Me and you')	ayingkki	[ ]G<⊥ ∨ɔ ⊤} ♀
+First P Plural O ('me and you several')	anyungkku	[ ]bB∨⊥ ɔ ⊤} ♀
+First P Dual Excl. O ('me and him')	ajikki	[ ]B∨⊥ ɔ ⊤} ♀
+First P Plural Excl. O ('me and them')	ankku	.G∧⊥ ⊥▪
Third Person Dual S ('they two')		
+First P O	awulajji	.G ɑσ

Table 8.3 continued

Third Person Plural S ('they several')		
+First P O	ajulajji	.5[tG˯˃]⁞G˯˄ˇΩ
+First P Dual Incl.	anyuljarningkki	[ ]ьB˂⊥ ‹˯ ϑ ›ᑭ
	(Lateral movement of hand extended)	
+First P Plural Inc.	ankkuljarningkki	.5ˇ⊥ ᵃ[G]⁞[ ]B ϑ ˯ › ᑭ
Third Person S		
+Second P O	angku	.G˄⊥ˇ
+Second P Dual O	ampukku	.Gᵃ‹›σ››
+Second P Plural O	arrku	.5ᵃ[G]
Third Person Dual S		
+Second P O	awulurnkku	.5ᵃ[G]
+Second P Dual O	ajurntulkku	.5ᵃ[G]
Third Person Plural S		
+Second P O	ajulurnkku	.5ᵃ[G]
Third Person S		
+Third P O		?
+Third P Dual O	apulu	.5ᵃ[G]
+Third P Plural O	ajurnu	.5ᵃ[G]
Third Person Dual S		
+Third P O	awul	.Gᵃσ
+Third P Dual O	ajuljarni	.5ᵃ[G]
Third Person Plural S		
+Third P O	ajjul	.5ᵃ[G]

Table 8.4: Kaytej personal pronouns and signs

Pronoun	**Kaytej**	**Sign**
1P	ayenge	○G⊤∧ ˇΩ⟩
2P	nge	.G⊤∧ ⊥ˇ{∧⊥}
3P	re	.G⊤< d
1 Dual inc. (Form I)	ayleme	˥G⊤∧ ⊥ ⊤ ♀
1 Dual exc. (Form 1)	aylerne	
1 Dual inc. (Form II)	aylake	⊓X□⊤ ⊤ ♀
1 Dual exc. (Form II)	aylernake	
1 Dual inc. (Form III)	aylanthe	
1 Dual exc. (Form III)	aylernanthe	
1 pl. incl. (Form I)	aynangkerre	⊓ЬB⊤∧ ʔ ⊤ ♀
1 pl. exc. (Form I)	aynernangkerre	
1 pl. inc. (Form II)	ayneakerre	
1 pl. exc.(Form II)	aynernakerre	
1 pl. inc. (Form III)	aynantherre	
1 pl. exc. (Form III)	aynernantherre	
2 Dual (Form I)	mpwele	.G<⊥ ɑ6⊥}
2 Dual (Form II)	mpwelake	
2 Dual (Form III)	mpwelanthe	
3 Dual (Form I)	erlweme	.Gt∨⊥[A][Gt]
3 Dual (Form II)	erlwake	
3 Dual (Form III)	erlwanthe	
2 pl. (Form I)	errwangkerre	.5t<∧ <[tG]
2 pl. (Form II)	errwakerre	
2 pl. (Form III)	errwantherre	
3 pl. (Form I)	atangkerre	.5t∨⊥ ˇɑ[tG⊤∧]
3 pl. (Form II)	atakerre	
3 pl. (Form III)	atantherre	

9 Discourse in sign and speech[1]

9.0 Introduction

In this Chapter we undertake a comparative study of signed discourse and spoken discourse. We shall compare examples from two narratives that were recorded in sign language on one occasion, and in speech on another. The signed and spoken versions of these narratives were recorded by Winnie Nangala, an exceptionally knowledgeable Warlpiri signer who is also a gifted story teller. The analyses to be presented will throw further light on the question of how the Aboriginal sign languages considered in this book are related to the spoken languages of their users.

We shall begin with a discussion of the phrasal organization of signed discourse and establish criteria for distinguishing different kinds of juncture in signing. We shall then present a series of examples from the narratives we have studied which exhibit specific ways in which signed utterances and spoken utterances are both similar and different. We shall also examine the question of whether there are consistent differences in the ordering of constituents in signed and spoken constructions. The Chapter will conclude with some observations on the role of bodily posture and gaze direction in the construction of these signed discourses.

The reader should bear in mind that the analyses presented here are preliminary. They should be taken as providing suggestions for general conclusions about the nature of Aboriginal sign language discourse, and not as definitive findings. Other narratives have been recorded by Winnie Nangala and similar material has been recorded by Ruby Nangala, also of Yuendumu. In addition, signed and spoken narratives have been recorded from Warumungu speakers in Tennant Creek. Although this material has been examined, it has yet to be studied in any detail. It is hoped to present a more detailed treatment of this material in a separate monograph.

9.1 The narratives and their analysis

The two stories to be discussed here will be referred to as the Parraja Story and the Yarnirnpa Story.[2] The Parraja story is a story of the Dreaming, and explains the origin of a certain constellation of stars (the Pleiades). The Yarnirnpa story is a typical domestic story, referring to marriage practices.

In the Parraja story, there is an old man who is fed by his womenfolk. They bring him edible seed (*ngurlu*) and this he eats, but he eats not only the seed but the dishes on which it is brought, as well. Eventually, the women become furious, because they are losing all their dishes. In the end they have none left. They chase the old man with fire-sticks which they shove down inside him to make him vomit. He vomits forth all the dishes he has eaten. Thereupon, he chases them, finds their grinding stones and puts a curse upon them, but the women escape by going up into the sky to become a certain constellation of stars.

The Yarnirnpa story concerns a promised wife who refuses to go to her husband. As a result, the husband removes himself to a distant creek. There he catches game, while the bride's family trick her into going with them to find him. The husband presents meat to the bride's family. Finally she accepts him and they all return, presumably to live happily ever after.

Both of these stories have been told by Winnie many times. Probably the versions we have recorded are fuller than her normal tellings. They were done on special request, in front of a camera for the signed versions and, for the spoken versions, into a tape-recorder. Certainly, these were not typical story-telling circumstances. Nevertheless, it seems quite unlikely that this means that we have for analysis something completely different from what is typical of Warlpiri story-telling or Warlpiri sign language discourse.

The signed version of the Parraja story (referred to as Parraja 1) was recorded in July 1981 on half-inch VHS cassette video-tape and the spoken version (Parraja 2) was recorded approximately six weeks later. The signed version of the Yarnirnpa story (Yarnirnpa 1) was recorded on 16 mm film in 1978. The spoken version of this story (Yarnirnpa 2) was recorded both by tape recorder and video-tape in September 1981. The spoken versions of the narratives were transcribed from the tape recordings by a literate Warlpiri native speaker.[3] The signed versions were transcribed by the writer in close consultation with Winnie Nangala, who provided Warlpiri glosses for the signs.[4] Transcripts of the Parraja story in both versions, are provided in Appendix II.

9.2 Segmentation

In order to make a systematic comparison between the spoken and signed versions, it is necessary to establish units of discourse that are comparable. In both spoken and signed discourses it is to be observed that units of expression are organized into phrases or packages, each one constituting a 'next' in the development of whatever is being said. In speech, phrases may be distinguished in terms of intonational contours which mark off successive units of information. Such phrases tend to correspond to the grammatical clause, and, in discourse, they serve as units in terms of which it is built. In sign, as we shall describe below, a similar phrasal organization can be shown, structured in terms of whether or not the hands articulating the signs are moved out of the space used for signing towards a position of rest.

9.2.1 Segmentation of spoken discourse

For the spoken version of the Yarnirnpa story, the sound recording was segmented into phonological phrases, using intonation tunes and pauses as criteria. Units of discourse termed *P-units* were established. These are single intonation units or tone units (Crystal and Davy 1969) or two or more such units combined into a single grouping, where succeeding tone units are clearly subordinate to the first in the grouping. Usually not more than two tone units are combined into a P-unit, but where the speaker repeats the same expression over and over, as she does in some places, a P-unit may contain several tone units. The tone units or tone unit groupings established as P-units constitute minimal units of 'sense' from the point of view of their role in the discourse. They may, perhaps, be compared to Halliday's (1985a) 'information units' established for English speech. The sequences of speech which had been bounded by periods in the transcription of this story that had been provided were found to accord well with the units established as P-units on intonational grounds. For the spoken version of the Parraja story, only a transcription from the sound recording was available. In the analyses to follow we have assumed that, in this transcript, speech segments bounded by periods are, as in the Yarnirnpa story, the equivalent of what we are here calling P-units.

A more detailed account of P-units will be given in the next chapter, where their relationship to simultaneously accompanying signs and other gesture phrases will be discussed. These minimal discourse units may themselves be grouped into higher order units of various sorts. That is, in the telling of the story, a succession of events is narrated, there may be scene-setting comments and explanations, or there may be comments directed to the recipient of the story. These higher order units, or episodes, are listed for the Parraja story in Appendix II.

9.2.2 The sign as a phrase of movement

In order to analyze the signed discourse, criteria must be established by which successive signs may be distinguished and by which the organization of signed sequences into units of signed discourse may be understood. So far, very little work of this nature has been done with any sign language. For this reason, we describe the criteria developed in the present analysis in some detail.

In Chapter 5 we showed that for the purposes of a systematic description which permits signs to be compared with one another so that their distinguishing features may be characterized, it is appropriate to regard a sign as if it may be analyzed into three simultaneously realized aspects: Sign Location, Sign Actor and Sign Action. This approach does not concern itself with the actual process of sign production, however. It does not consider the way in which the articulation of a sign unfolds in time. For the purposes of transcribing signed discourse and of understanding how signs may succeed one another within an utterance and how sign phrases are constructed, the temporal organization of sign production must be considered. Accordingly, we here analyze signs as phrases of movement, following principles developed earlier for the analysis of gesticulation or gesturing that accompanies speech (Kendon 1980b).

The principles to be outlined have been developed for the transcription of signs or gestures from film or video-tape recordings to time-based charts. Accurate analysis requires the use of suitable analysis equipment that permits the repeated viewing of very short segments at a time, so that boundaries between phrases of movement can be established, and which also permit slow-motion and frame-by-frame viewing.[5]

Manual activity, whether it be signing or gesticulation, can be analyzed as a succession of movement phrases. In each of these phrases the forelimb (or forelimbs, in two handed gestures or signs) performs an excursion. That is, it is moved into a region of space or to a location in relation to the body, and then away again. As the limb approaches the apex of the excursion (which is the equivalent of Sign Location), its components may assume a distinctive posture (forming a handshape, for instance) and there may either be a brief halt in movement, or it may perform a pattern of movement that is distinct from the movements by which the articulator is moved toward or away from the apex of the excursion. After the performance at the apex, whatever it may be, the limb then is moved away, either all the way to some position of rest or, where another sign is to follow, simply somewhat away from the apex of the excursion just performed, before embarking on the next one.

The phase of movement in which the limb is being moved toward the apex of the excursion will be referred to as the *preparation*. The phase during which the limb is maintained at the apex of the excursion, whether it is being moved while there or whether it is held still there, will be referred to as the *stroke*. It is within the stroke that the distinctive characteristics of the sign being performed are fully realized. If the limb is returned to a rest position, this phase of movement is called the *recovery*. The term *partial recovery* may be used to refer to withdrawals from the excursion apex that do not result in a full return to the rest position.

For many signs, these distinctions within the complete movement phrase by which a sign is performed can be made quite readily. For instance, for the Warlpiri sign WARLU 'fire, firewood', the hand is held in an O configuration (fingers curled together, tips resting on the tip of the thumb) and moved away from a position, roughly in front of the mouth, with a particular motion involving forearm pronation (▽O$_{T<}$$^{\sigma}$). It will be seen that the hand must be positioned in front of the mouth before it can perform the stroke and the movement by which this is accomplished is clearly distinguishable as the preparation. On the other hand, with a sign such as WANTA 'sun', in which a V hand (index and second fingers only extended and held apart), held forward with palm upwards, is lowered slightly (. U$_{\wedge\perp}$ ˇ), it is often difficult to establish a point at which one can, with confidence, distinguish preparation from stroke. In some signs, also, one finds that the movement phase of recovery (or partial recovery) may completely overlap with the movement phase of stroke. For example, KUYU 'meat' is signed by making a downward movement with the hand in front of (or sometimes in contact with) the ipsilateral side of the thorax (ᗢB̂$_{T}$ ˇ). Sometimes this is performed in such a way that the hand simply 'flops' down to the lap and the recovery phase, thus, cannot be clearly distinguished.

9.2.3 Juncture in sign discourse

An examination of the signed discourses shows that the forelimb excursions of which signs are composed do not succeed one another in an even flow. Sometimes the signer lowers her hands all the way to a rest position and ceases all movement, before embarking on the next sign; sometimes she moves them toward the rest position, but continues to the next sign without pause; sometimes her signs succeed one another without any such relaxations between them. Such differences in the way in which signs succeed one another provide criteria for the division of the flow of signs into sign sequences. Here we shall propose four kinds of sign transition or *juncture*. These junctures serve as boundaries for two types of sign sequences.

If the signer lowers her hands all the way to the rest position and ceases movement altogether, this will be termed an R-juncture (Rest Juncture). This is marked in the transcript as |R|. The sequences of signs bounded by such R-junctures will be termed *R-units*. If the signer lowers her hands to the rest position but immediately thereafter embarks upon the preparation for the next sign, or if she lowers her hands part-way towards the rest position before embarking on the next sign, we recognize a C-juncture (Comma Juncture). This is marked in the transcript as |,| (or |R,| if it is desired to show that the hands moved all the way to the rest position). Sign sequences bounded by such junctures are referred to as *C-units*. Junctures between signs are Unmarked if the movement away from the Sign Location of a given sign serves as the Preparation for the next sign (that is, no Recovery phase can be identified). If a sign in the sequence succeeds its predecessor without any intervening phase of Preparation, a juncture of Affixation may be recognized. This is marked in the transcript as |+|.

R-units often comprise several signs that may be construed in relation to one another to form a unit of meaning that is the equivalent of an 'information unit' in speech. They usually constitute the meaning units out of which the discourse is constructed. In the analyses to be described later, in which we examine the sequential organization of sign sequences for evidence of syntactic ordering, it is the R-units that will be taken as our units of analysis. As we shall see, they may often be compared directly with P-units in the spoken versions of these discourses.

C-units, which by definition always occur within R-units, sometimes may be construed as units that have informational completeness, but they always comprise a unit of meaning that is either a subordinate or a coordinate component of the larger unit of meaning that may be construed from an R-unit. Signs preceded by a juncture of affixation are usually signs which, if given a verbal gloss, are the equivalent of bound morphemes in the spoken language, such as noun formatives, semantic case markers and certain derivational suffixes (see Chapter 8).

9.2.4 R-junctures

As we have stated, R-junctures are said to occur whenever the signer moves her hands to a rest position and ceases to move them. R-junctures are, thus, pauses in the sign flow. They are to be distinguished from those occasions when signing activity ceases while the articulators are still away from any rest position. That is, they are to be distinguished from *hesitations* which occur when an articulator ceases to move at any point during the preparation, initial stroke phase or recovery phase of a sign-phrase; and from *holds,* which occur if the articulator is sustained in the position it reaches upon the completion of a stroke. In *hesitations* a sign in progress is held up. In *holds* a completed sign is maintained for a period (this can have important functions: a hold is used at the end of R-units that serve as questions, for example). In R-junctures there is a cessation of sign activity of any sort.

R-junctures can be extremely short (in both Yarnirnpa 1 and Parraja 1 there are R-junctures that last for as little as a few tenths of a second), but in the two discourses here examined, R-junctures were found to be rarely above two seconds in length. Thus in Yarnirnpa 1 72% of all R-junctures were between one half a second in length and two seconds, with only 9% more than two seconds in length. In Parraja 1 67% of all R-junctures were between one third of a second in length and two seconds, with 18% over two seconds long. In Yarnirnpa 1 the mean length of R-junctures was 1.18 seconds, in Parraja 1 it was 1.4 seconds (excluding exceptionally long periods of non-signing, due to coughing, picking a prickle from clothing or the interruption of someone else).

It appears that there is some relationship between the length of an R-juncture and the status in the discourse of the R-unit that precedes it. Evidently, pause length, at least in these performances, was being used as a device for discourse organization. In both Yarnirnpa 1 and Parraja 1 R-junctures tend to be longer at episode boundaries within the discourse than they are between R-units within an episode. Thus, again excluding R-junctures with interruptions, the mean between-episode R-juncture length is 2.96 seconds in Yarnirnpa 1 and 2.74 seconds in Parraja 1, whereas for within-episode R-junctures the figures are, respectively, 0.96 seconds and 1.16 seconds. In Yarnirnpa 1 we find that 8 out of 9 topic boundaries have R-junctures longer than any that occur within the preceding episode segment; in Parraja 1 this is true for 12 of the 18 topic boundaries. If the R-juncture at the episode boundary is compared with the R-juncture that follows the first phrase of the next episode segment, it is in every case longer in Yarnirnpa 1 and it is longer in fifteen cases out of seventeen in Parraja 1.[6]

Another characteristic of R-junctures is that they are often associated with a distinctive orientation by the signer. This will be described in greater detail in a later section. However, in both Parraja 1 and Yarnirnpa 1 it is common for Winnie to direct her gaze at her addressee as she commences an R-juncture and to assume a new orientation as she ends it and begins a new R-unit. This is a pattern that is well established in speakers (Kendon 1967, Goodwin 1981) and it provides further justification for our decision to the R-unit as a unit of analysis that is equivalent to the P-unit in spoken discourse.

9.2.5 C-junctures

A C-juncture occurs when, between two signs, the signer lowers her hands all of the way or part of the way to the rest position but does not cease in her movement but embarks at once on the preparation for the next sign. Such junctures appear to occur at boundaries between repeated sequences, coordinated sequences, insertions, and sequences that are subordinate to or relative to a main construction. Thus in P1-45 we have ('Point' indicates a simple index finger point):

WIRI Point |,| YANURRPU WIRI Point MURUPINYI
Big that, coolamon big that shove inside
(That big one, that big coolamon he shoved inside himself)

Here the expanded repetition of YANURRPU WIRI DCT is separated from the first by a C-juncture.

Likewise, in Y1-20 we have (DIR indicates a directionalized movement of the hand, usually held with just the index finger extended):

WIYARRPA YANI WIYARRPA |R,| WIYARRPA YANI |R,|
Poor thing go poor thing, poor thing go,

WIRLIYA DIR YANI
footprints thither go
(the poor fellow went thither, the poor thing went thither, thither go his footprints)

A C-juncture serves to establish coordination between two separate constructions in P1-1:

NGURLU YURRPARNI PARRAJA KANYI |,| MURUPINYI
edible seed grind coolamon carry, shove inside
([they] ground the seed and [put it on] a coolamon and carried [it to him], he shoved it inside himself)

A somewhat similar use of the C-juncture may be seen in P1-19:

WAPALWAPAL WANGKAMI |,| JAPUKUKARI PAYIRNI
Guess about it, next time ask
([they] wondered what had happened [to the coolamons] and next time they asked [him for them])

In P1-4 we see how a C-juncture may be used to set off an inserted segment of a sequence:

KANYI MURUPINYI |pR,| KIRDA NYANU |,|
Carry shove inside , father REFLX POSS,
MURUPINYI
shove inside
(They carried to him [the food] he shoved it inside [himself], their father, he shoved it inside [himself])

Here Winnie inserts a specification of the agent of the action referred to by MURUPINYI, in effect creating a new sentence in doing so. It may be noted that the juncture that follows the first sentence is 'deeper' (i.e. the hands are lowered closer to the rest position) than the one that follows KIRDA NYANU. The effect, here, appears to be that of an insertion of KIRDA NYANU into a construction that was already complete.

Finally, an example may be given which illustrates how a C-juncture may be used to set off a relative clause. Thus in P1-30 we have:

PARRAJA PALKA MANI |,| KIJIRNI NYAMPU |,|
Coolamon really get thrown this

YURRPARNI KANYI
grind carry
([they] got hold of a coolamon, one that had been thrown away, they ground [seed] and carried it to him)

9.2.6 Unmarked junctures and affixation junctures

Signs that have no juncture marked between them succeed one another in such a way that, typically, the movement phase that follows upon the completion of the stroke phase of a given sign-phrase is the preparation phase of the next sign-phrase. Signs succeeding one another in this manner are members of the same constructional unit. It sometimes happens, however, that the movement phase succeeding a stroke is not a preparation for the next sign but the stroke of the next sign. In such cases the two signs appear to succeed one another in a fashion which suggests that they are closely conjoined, as if they are, so to speak, two syllables of a compound form. We have marked such transitions with |+| in the transcripts and refer to them as Junctures of Affixation. Junctures of this type can only occur where the succeeding sign is one that can be performed without any major change in handshape or location of action. Occasionally one may observe how a current sign is modified in anticipation of the sign that is to follow, if the following sign is to have an Affixation Juncture.

A few examples will be given to clarify this type of juncture. In P1-11 we have:

YINYI |+| DIR
Give thither [to him]

In Parraja 1, every time Winnie refers to the carrying of food to the old man, or to the giving of food to him, she always directionalizes the signs KANYI and YINYI by extending her arms fully to the right (Fig. 9.5). In this way she establishes the location of the recipient of what is given. This aspect of expression will be described later. In the instance under consideration here what we see is an index finger point following immediately upon the completion of the sign YINYI. In making the sign YINYI a 'flat' (B) hand is used, held with palm uppermost. In this case, Winnie extends her hand in this configuration to her extreme right and then immediately flexes all digits except the index finger to her palm. The index finger point thus follows YINYI immediately, with no preparation, almost as if it is part of the same phrase of action.

As another instance we may consider Y1-25:

FINGERSNAP	|H|	PURRAKU	|+|	PARNKAMIRRA
Cook		potable water		run thither

(He cooked [the meat], drank water and ran off)

In this sequence, the action of the sign PURRAKU serves at the same time as the preparation for the sign PARNKAMIRRA. To sign PURRAKU the hand is held with all digits flexed to the palm except index finger and thumb, which are held fully extended and adducted (the L hand). The palm is oriented toward the chin. The hand is drawn rapidly ipsilaterally (to the right, if the right hand is being used) and as it does so the index finger is flexed somewhat ($\smile \mathrm{L}_{\top <}{}^{>}\underline{\Omega}$). In the instance considered here, as Winnie performs the rightward movement of this sign she flexes her index finger until it is bent at all joints and so that the tip of the finger is resting on the tip of the thumb. The hand is now in the X configuration (fist, but index extended at A joint, so the nail lies against the tip of the thumb, also extended), which is the handshape used for the sign PARNKAMIRRA, which is here immediately enacted as Winnie moves her hand back across the front of her face and towards her left shoulder. There is thus no separately distinguishable phase of movement that can be identified as the preparation for PARNKAMIRRA. Were this sign not affixed, for instance, we would observe a brief segment in which the hand was moved to a new starting position during which, also, the hand configuration for the sign would have been formed. Here, as we saw, the hand configuration for PARNKAMIRRA was formed as the action of PURRAKU was completed. The action of PARNKAMIRRA could thus be embarked upon immediately, simply by reversing the movement that had been made for PURRAKU. In this example, it seems that Winnie is perhaps expressing the idea that the three activities followed one another in quick succession.

9.3 Comparisons between signed and spoken discourse

In the case of both stories, the signed versions are shorter than the spoken versions. Thus in Yarnirnpa 1 there are 55 R-units, compared to 360 P-units in Yarnirnpa 2. Likewise, in Parraja 1 there are 61 R-units, but 139 P-units in Parraja 2. There are several reasons for the greater length of the spoken versions. First, as regards the Yarnirnpa story, the spoken version is longer than the signed version because Winnie inserted several more episodes. This appears to be a matter of what she remembered to put in at the time of the telling, however. It does not seem to have anything to do with the nature of the medium in which it was told. On the other hand, both the Parraja story and the Yarnirnpa story are also longer when presented in spoken form because, in telling a story orally, Winnie uses a great deal of rhythmic, almost song-like repetition. There are many repetitions in the signed versions, also, but none of these are as extended. It is possible that, in signing, if rhythmical repetition is undertaken it has a different character from that which is to be observed in speech.

The signed versions may also be shorter than the spoken versions because, in respect to some expressions, signing can be more condensed than speaking. There are examples where the same unit of meaning may require numerous morphemes for its spoken expression, but may be expressed in a single sign in the signed version. It is notable, however, that there are rather few of these. As we shall see, on the whole the signed versions and the spoken versions are much more like one another than different.

If we compare R-units and P-units in terms of the number of signs or words they contain, on average, we find that that they are quite comparable. R-units vary in length from between one and fifteen signs in the texts here considered. The average number of signs per R-unit is 4.96 in Yarnirnpa and

4.7 in Parraja. In the spoken versions of these stories we find 2.54 words per P-unit in Yarnirnpa and 3.76 words per P-unit in Parraja.

In considering these figures it should be borne in mind that a 'word' is here regarded as a root noun or verb together with all of its attached clitics. A sign, on the other hand, is counted for each excursion of the sign-articulator. Signs are for the most part glossed as root nouns or verbs, but there are some which may be glossed as clitics, including noun-formatives, verb-formatives, certain of the case markers and the directionals. A simple comparison between words per P-unit and signs per R-unit would inevitably show a higher number of signs per R-unit, given the definitions adopted. However, if we count as one unit in the signed texts those sign sequences which may be glossed as a root noun or verb and clitic combination, we find that there are 3.88 such units per R-unit in Parraja and 3.7 such units in Yarnirnpa. In terms of units of expression that are functionally equivalent in the two media, thus, there appears to be a close comparability in length between P-units and R-units.

9.4 R-units and P-units compared

In this section some examples will be presented in which R-units from the signed versions of both the Parraja and Yarnirnpa stories are compared with comparable P-units in the spoken versions. This will allow us to see how signed and spoken expression are in some respects highly parallel, in other respects divergent. In general, it appears that both R-units and P-units are organized in the same way, in terms of the units of meaning that are expressed, and how these are combined.

9.4.1 Subject, object, the verb and directionality

In Example 1, from the Parraja story, Winnie describes how the women grind edible seed and carry it to the old man. Here the activity of grinding and carrying are expressed in both versions by separate lexical forms. In both, the lexical form for the activity of grinding (which perhaps can be taken to refer to the whole process of preparing the seed for consumption) is repeated several times. Such repetition is a characteristic device in spoken Warlpiri by which the extension of an action over a period of time may be expressed and, in this case, we see that the device is used in the signed version, as well.

Second, it will be noted that in neither the spoken nor the signed version is the subject or the object of grinding specified - that it is edible seed that is being ground and that it is the women who are grinding it, is understood. The absence of any reference to the arguments of the verb, even by way of a pro-form, is quite characteristic of spoken Warlpiri, however (Hale 1983 refers to 'zero anaphora' as a feature of Warlpiri). The absence of

Example I
(Parraja Story)

Signed version

P1-42	YURRPARNI	YURRPARNI	YURRPARNI
	Grind	grind	grind
	YURRPARNI	YURRPARNI	KANYI (DIR)
	grind	grind	carry (direction incorporated)

([They] ground and ground and ground and ground [edible seed] and carried [it] to him)

Spoken version

P2-34	Yurrpa-rnu	yurrpa-rnu	ka -ngu-lpa-lu -rla	
	Grind-PAST	grind-PAST	carry-PAST-IMPF-333P-DAT. Subj.	
	Ground	ground	carried	they to him

(They ground and ground and carried [seed] to him)

verbal arguments in the signed version, thus, cannot be regarded as a peculiarity of the sign language. So far, then, the two versions are in very close conformity to one another. Now we may note some differences.

In the spoken version, for the verb *ka-* 'carry', subject and object of the action are given by means of pronominal clitics, which follow the cliticized auxiliary, *-lpa*. In the signed version there is no reference to the subject or agent of the action of carrying and we find no separate sign by which reference is made to the object or beneficiary of the action. However, when we observe how Winnie performs the sign KANYI, we see that she extends her arms fully to her extreme right (Fig.9.5). In doing this, she indicates the meaning 'carry' but, at the same time, indicates the place to which that carrying was done. In this way she may be said to 'incorporate' into the sign performance a reference to the notion that something was carried from one place to another (as opposed to the idea of someone just carrying something which, in sign, is expressed by a nondirectionalized form of KANYI - see Chapter 8 for further discussion). Further, by directing the movement of KANYI in this way she is able to establish a location for the old man, who is the recipient of what is being carried. This location is then used in various ways throughout the rest of the telling of the story as a way of making reference to the old man. Details of how this is done will be described later.

'Incorporation' of the object of a verb by means of a directionalization of the action, as we have already noted (see Chapter 8), is possible for a number of signs in Warlpiri sign language - including, for example, all of the verbs of motion. It will be obvious that such 'incorporation' by directionalization or spatial inflection of movement of the verb sign is an efficient exploitation of the spatial properties of the medium of gestural expression. Not surprisingly, it is widely employed in primary sign languages. Fischer and Gough 1978 have provided a detailed description for American Sign Language.

A second point of difference between the signed and spoken versions, to be noted from Example I, is the absence of any marking for tense in the signed version. In the spoken version the verbs are inflected for tense, and information about tense is also carried by the auxiliary clitic (in this case *-lpa*). Again as noted in Chapter 8, in signed Warlpiri the auxiliary is never referenced, no matter whether it occurs as a phonologically word-like form or whether it occurs as a clitic. As we also saw in Chapter 8, verb signs themselves are never inflected for tense. Tense is left to be inferred from context, although a signed utterance can have, in initial position, a temporal adverbial sign such as PIRRARNI 'yesterday', JALANGU 'now', NGAKA 'soon', or JUKURRA 'tomorrow'. In this way an utterance may be given a temporal frame. However this device appears to be used only in circumstances where ambiguity about tense might arise. For the most part, the signer constructs utterances as if tense will be 'understood' from the discourse context.

From Example I, then, we see how spoken and signed versions are closely similar in the lexical items employed and that, at least in this example, the idea of repetition or continuation of an action is expressed in the same way in the two media. On the other hand we see how in sign, space may be used to establish a verbal argument, and in this the signed version diverges from the spoken, for in the latter a segmental expression for this must be employed.

Example II, taken from the Yarnirnpa story, again shows very close parallels between the signed and spoken versions. The example comes from the place in the story where the refused husband travels to a distant creek. There he spears a kangaroo, removes its intestines, and carries the animal round his neck to the place where it is to be cooked. As with Example 1,a close parallel will be seen to obtain between the signed version and the spoken version, especially in respect to Y1-23 and Y1-24, on the one hand, and Y2-35.4 and Y2-35.6, on the other. Once again, however, there are certain differences.

Example II
(Yarnirnpa Story)

Signed version

Y1-23 KUNA MANI
Intestines get
(He gutted [the kangaroo])

Y1-24 KUYU NYURDI MANI |+| Point (DIR)
Meat carry on neck direction
(He carried the meat round his neck thither)

Spoken version

Y2-35.4
Kuna-rra-lpa-rla ma-nu
Intestines-thither-IMPF.-3P DAT get-PAST
(He gutted [the kangaroo] for her over there)

Y2-35.6
Nyurdi-rra-lpa ma-nu
PREVERB-thither-IMPF. cause-PAST
(He carried it thither around his neck)

Consider the way in which directionality is handled in this Example. We saw, in the previous instance, how, with KANYI, the signer is able to directionalize the action and 'incorporate' in the very performance of the sign a reference to the transport of something to some specific location. In the present example, reference is also made to carrying something somewhere, but in this case the expression involves the use of the sign MANI. This is performed by closing to a loose fist a kind of 'claw' handshape, at the same time as the forearm is supinated (ᶜ5mϚ$_{<\perp}$ ᵃ[A]). This sign is always performed in the same way and it is never directionalized. Accordingly, we find here that Winnie indicates direction by means of a separate segment of action. She immediately follows MANI with a directionalized index finger point and in this way she refers to the direction of the activity she is discussing. This terminal Point serves just the same function as the directional clitic *-rra* which, as will be seen, occurs on the preverb *nyurdi* in Y2-35.5. It will be seen, however, that the signed version of the clitic occurs after the verb, at the end of the R-unit. In the spoken version it occurs on the preverb. In spoken Warlpiri this clitic has the freedom to occur on either the preverb or the verb. In signing, however, where this directional clitic is used, as far as present observations go, it always occurs at the end of a sequence, never in association with a pre-terminal element.

As will be noted in the next Chapter, this is also true when speaking and signing are used simultaneously. When Winnie told the Yarnirnpa story in words (version Y2) she signed at the same time. As she uttered Y2-35.4 and Y2-35.5, in both cases she signed the directional clitic at the end, even though, in both cases, in speech the directional clitic occurred in an earlier position, as may be seen. This seems to indicate that the directional, though cliticized in speech, is treated as a separate semantic unit, functionally equivalent to a separate word.

9.4.2 Parallels between sign organization and morphology

It may be noted in Example II how, in Y1-24, Winnie performs two signs, glossed NYURDI and MANI. This is a signed rendition of the compound verb *nyurdi ma-ni* 'carry meat round the neck', used in Y2-35.6. This is an example of how a compound sign is used to sign something that, in the spoken language, is expressed with a compound form. In Chapter 7 we showed that this correspondence between sign organization and spoken language morphology is widespread. What is of interest in the present context is to consider that we find this is done here, even though one of the signs employed is quite graphic in character and might be thought sufficient to express the notion of 'meat hanging round the neck'. The sign that is glossed as NYURDI is a double stroke sign in which the hand is drawn rapidly down from either side of the neck. The action apparently derives from a depiction of meat hanging round the neck. Despite the character of this sign, it is followed by the sign MANI - the sign for the verb *ma-ni* which is generally glossed as 'get' or as an abstract causative. Here it has no meaning apart from its occurrence in combination with *nyurdi*. Yet Winnie performs signs for the two parts of the verb. She does not employ a sign expression which, in a single unit, expresses the notion of carrying meat on the neck. She conforms her signed expression closely to the spoken language structure.

A similar instance of this may be noted in Example III, from the section of the Parraja story where the old man seeks his revenge on the women. While the women have gone off hunting he finds their grinding stones and 'sings' them. In preparing to do this he takes the grinding stones and places them in a long row. Although the signed and spoken versions of this episode are not as close as we have found for other examples, in both there is a passage in which the placing of the stones in a long row is described. Thus in Example III P2-117 and P2-118 are matched by the last four signs of P1-61. In the spoken version it will be seen that Winnie uses the phrase *kanardi yirra-rni* 'place in a row' (literally 'row of objects+put, place'), and the extended nature of this row is expressed by the repetition of this phrase, by the extension of the final vowel of the directional clitic *-rra*, and by the repetition of the verb *yirra-rnu-rra*. In the signed version Winnie does not use a lexical sign to match *kanardi*. Rather, she uses an extended graphic gesture in which the arm, fully extended to her right, is moved back in one long movement, at the same time being moved up and down (Fig.9.1). During the course of this movement the hand, with all fingers slightly spread, is held with fingers pointing to the ground. The result is a graphic depiction of placing a series of things in a row and, further, the extended nature of the gesture conveys the extended nature of the row of stones. However, after this graphic depiction is complete, Winnie performs the sign YIRRARNI 'to place or put', thus conforming her sign sequence to the structure of the spoken phrase *kanardi yirra-rni* 'to place in a row'. If she were relying on the graphic force of gesture alone, and not matching sign units to spoken constructions, this would not have been necessary.

Example III
(Parraja Story)

Signed version

P1-61 NGAMA |+| RLANGU KARI NGAMA |+| RLANGU KARI
Mother-and-daughter other mother-and-daughter[7] other

⌐BS$_{\vee\perp\vee}$ $^{\vee}$" →⟩ YIRRARNI PAMARRPA |+| tG$_{\top\wedge}$$^{\perp}$■
Depiction of many objects placed in a row | put | stone | ?Topicalizer

(He placed the several grinding stones in a row)

Spoken version

P2-117

Kanardi yirra-rnu,	kanardi yirra-rnu-rraaaa
In a row put-PAST	in a row put-PAST-thither
	(final vowel extended)

P2-118

Yirra-rnu-rra, yirra-rnu-rra, yirra-rnu pirli-ji
put-PAST, put-PAST, put-PAST stone-TOP.
(In a row thither he placed the stones)

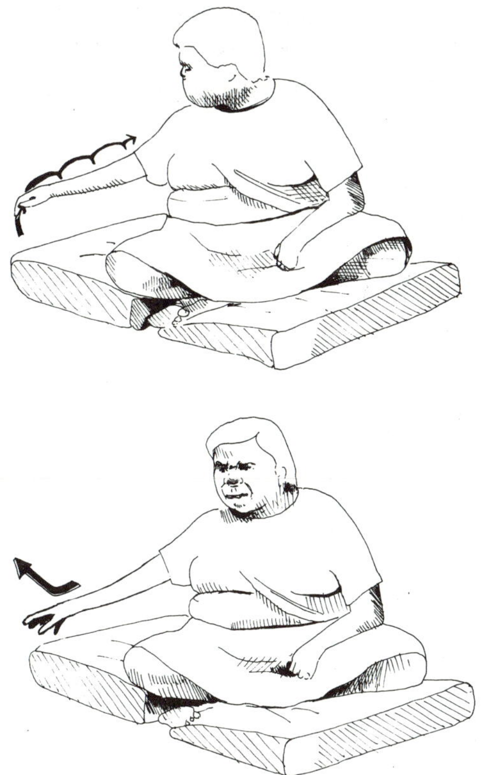

Fig. 9.1 Winnie signs KANARDI (above)YIRRARNI (below)'in a row put'. Drawn from the video recording YSL 1981 XII, Parraja 1

There is another way in which the signed and spoken version in this example are paralleled. In both versions she refers to the objects that are being placed in a row only at the very end of the discourse unit. In the spoken version a topicalizing clitic *-ji* is added. In the signed version an upraised index finger is affixed after the sign PAMARRPA. Perhaps this is a signed rendition of the topicalization clitic.

9.4.3 'Additional meaning' in sign

As we observed in Chapter 7, although the organization of the signed rendition of compound verbs usually parallels spoken language morphology, it does not always do so. There are a number of cases where a single gestural expression for a compound verbal form is used in preference. This is especially true for a number of compounds involving the root *pi-nyi*. An instance of this is given in Example IV, which may serve to illustrate a number of other points, as well. This example is taken from the Parraja story from the episode in which the women, exasperated at the loss of their coolamons, chase and catch the old man and force burning sticks inside him, thereby causing him to vomit up all of the containers he had swallowed.

Example IV
(Parraja Story)

Signed version

P1-53	WARLU Fire	MURUPINYI shoved inside (2 hands alternate action)	YURLKULYU vomit
	YIRRARNI put		
	NGAKA soon	WARLU |+| JANGKA fire CAUSATIVE	

(Burning sticks they shoved inside him, he vomited soon because of the burning sticks)

Note: WARLU 'fire, firewood' is here used to refer to the fiery sticks.

Spoken version

P2-100

Warlu-ju-lpa-lu-rla muru-muru pu-ngu.
Fire-TOP.-IMPF.-333P SUBJ.-3P DAT. shove inside-PAST
(Burning sticks they shoved inside him)

P2-101

Wuu! Wurruluku yirra-rnu-lpa wurruluku yirra-rnu-lpa
Wow! vomit -PAST-IMPF. vomit, etc.

wurrluku yirra-rnu-lpa warlu-jangka -rlu -lku.
vomit, etc. fire-CAUS.-ERG.-SEQ.
(Wow! He vomited and vomited because of those burning sticks!)

Once again, it will be seen that in terms of lexical elements the parallel between the two versions is very close. The spoken version is somewhat longer, but only because there is some repetition. We note also that, as before, there are no segmental signs by which verbal arguments are represented. In the spoken version these are conveyed by clitics on the cliticized auxiliary *-lpa*.

The point of interest here, however, arises from a comparison between the spoken version and the signed version in respect to the expression of the meaning 'shove in' - in the spoken version Winnie uses the compound verb *muru pi-nyi* for the action of shoving the fire sticks into the old man. In the signed version we have a unitary action, here labelled MURUPINYI. In performing this sign Winnie moves a hand rapidly downwards, from mouth level to stomach (Fig. 9.2). This action is a vivid gestural rendition of the idea of something being shoved into someone. In most places in its use in the Parraja story - and it is used many times - it refers to the action of the old man as he shoves into himself the food and the coolamons that are brought to him. Here it refers to the shoving inside him of the fire sticks, by the women.

It is to be noted first, that the sign in question is unitary, although it was glossed by the compound verb *muru pi-nyi* 'insert, shove something into something.' Second, however, it is to be observed that the form of this unitary sign varies according to the nature of the shoving or insertion that is being referred to. The form this sign takes here, as elsewhere in the signed version of the Parraja story, is a form that appears to express, quite specifically, the shoving of something inside someone. If the place into which something is to be shoved is a hole in the ground, or a bag, however, then the form of the sign is quite different. This is one of the few examples of signs in Warlpiri sign language in which the direct object of the verb is obligatorily 'incorporated', for, apparently, this sign cannot be performed without indicating the object of shoving. This is also an example of how a sign-unit in the sign language can, in its very form, provide information beyond that which is given by the verbal form with which it may be glossed. Although, by glossing the sign-unit with a spoken lexical equivalent, a parallel between the spoken discourse unit and the signed discourse unit can be drawn, the unit of meaning the sign-unit refers to is more specific and less abstract than that referred to by the spoken form, *muru pi-nyi*. In the spoken form, to specify what sort of insertion process is being referred to, additional words will be needed. Perhaps this is why, in the spoken version of the Parraja story, Winnie does not use the expression *muru pi-nyi* very often. She more commonly uses other forms, such as *ngurlkurr kiji-rni* which can be glossed as 'gulp down'. This has a more specific meaning than *muru pi-nyi*.

Finally, we may note here how, in Example IV, MURUPINYI is performed in a way that is quite different from its performance elsewhere in the signed version of Parraja. Whereas in all of the other instances it is performed as a single downward action of the hand, either by one hand or, sometimes, for emphasis, by both hands simultaneously, here the downward movements are performed three times, by two hands in alternation. In this way Winnie is able to convey the idea not only of the repetitive nature of the shoving down, but also, in the alternating hands, she conveys the idea of the multiplicity of agents responsible for it. Thus the meaning conveyed by the clitic *-lu* (third person plural subject) is also found in the signed version, but realized in a completely different way, through an inflection in the performance of the verbal sign.

Example IV provides a clear illustration, thus, of how, in terms of the sign-units employed in a given R-unit, a close parallel with the spoken version can be preserved and yet how, at the same time, additional meanings are brought in by the way in which the signs are performed.

9.4.4 Repetition in speech and sign

In the discussion of Example I it was noted how prolongation or repetition of an action was expressed in the spoken language by a repetition of the verb and that, in the example considered, the same device was used in the signed discourse. In Example I the verb in question was *yurrpa-rni* , in which, when signed, the hand is moved forward in a horizontal motion and as this is done the thumb is moved forward over the tips of the first and second digits. Such an action is a discrete action which may be repeated over and over again, as it is here. However, it is not the sort of action that can be extended in time. Other

9.2 MURUPINYI 'shove inside, swallow', from YSL 1981 XII, Parraja 1

verb signs, however, have a form of action that lends itself to temporal extension much more readily. Extended or repeated action, when such verbs are being used, is expressed by prolonging the action of the sign, rather than by repetition.

The sign for the verb *parnka-mi* 'run' illustrates this. It is performed by the hand being held so that the index finger is fully flexed, with its tip in contact with the tip of the thumb, the other digits flexed to the palm. The hand is then moved away from the signer, at the same time being moved up and down repeatedly. The sign may be inflected for direction. It may also be inflected for speed. In the Yarnirnpa story there is an episode in which the promised wife is taken by her family to where her promised husband is, in a distant creek in which prolonged running is described.This is given below as Example V. In the spoken version Winnie repeats the phrase *parnka-mi-rra-lu* 'they ran thither' numerous times. In the signed version, the single action of the sign PARNKAMI is greatly extended in time. In performing it, Winnie moves her hand very slowly upwards and leftwards, at the same time moving it back and forth rapidly in cyclic movements of very small amplitude. A single extended action, in this case, expresses the extension in time of the action of running and it corresponds in the spoken version to the repetition of the verb.

Where the action in question is expressed with a compound verb in the spoken language we find that extension or persistence of action is expressed by repetition of the complete form. In sign, however, either the preverb is repeated or the root verb is repeated. Repetition of the complete compound is rare. Thus, in Example III, we noted that in the spoken version Winnie repeated the compound verb *kanardi yirra-rnu* many times to convey the idea that the activity of placing the stones in a row was a prolonged one. In the signed version, in contrast, the graphic gesture that corresponded to the

Example V
(Yarnirnpa Story)

Signed version

Y1-16 PARNKAMI-------(DIR) WIRLIYA PURAMI------(DIR)
Run (action extended) tracks follow (action extended)
(They ran and ran following and following his tracks)

Spoken version

Y2-43.1
Parnka-mi-rra-lu parnka-mi-rra-lu parnka-mi-rra-lu
Run-NONPAST-thither-they, etc.

parnka-mi-rra-lu parnka-mi-rra-lu parnka-mi-rra-
(Thither they run and run and run and run and run and run and run)

preverb *kanardi* was spatially extended with numerous repeated component actions, but the root verb YIRRARNI was signed only once.

When compound verbs are signed repeatedly, which part of the compound is chosen for repetition depends in part upon the nature of the meaning to be conveyed by the repetition, but it also depends upon the nature of the action of the preverbal and verbal signs. This may be illustrated by two examples from an extended sign discourse recorded by Ruby Nangala (YSL 81 XIII 142-307).[8] In this discourse she is describing the processes of food gathering, transport to camp and preparation for storage. As we will see, in the first example, it is the sign for the preverb that is repeated. In the second example, it is the root verb sign that is repeated.

Ruby tells how many women go out to collect food and how they dig and dig and gather and gather and how they make many piles of food and how they cover these piles of food with loose earth (to prevent the sun from drying it out before they are ready to carry it back to camp). In several places in this discourse, she signs that this process of covering piles with loose earth is being done repeatedly in many different locations. For example in R-unit 50 in this discourse she signs as follows:

YURRUJURLA MILYI MILYI MILYI MILYI MILYI YIRRARNI
Pile loose earth, etc. put
---------------------extended arm-----------------------------
arm directed to a new
location for each enactment

Here she uses the signed equivalent of the spoken expression *milyi-ngka yirra-rni* 'loose earth-LOCATIVE put'. *Milyi-ngka* here behaves as a preverb. This is signed with a compound MILYI 'loose earth' YIRRARNI 'put'. In signing MILYI a bent V hand, held palm downwards, is flexed at the wrist: $\dddot{\text{U}}_{\vee\perp}{}^{\wp}$.

The action of the sign MILYI, it will be seen, is a discrete action that lends itself to repetition. The direction of the arm can be varied, thus suggesting the different locations of the piles that are to be covered. By repeating the preverb sign here in this fashion, Ruby is able to convey the sense of many piles in many different places, at the same time as she is able to convey the idea of the repetition of the action of covering these piles.

In another passage in the same discourse, Ruby refers to the fact that many piles were placed in many different places. She signs YURRUJURLA YIRRARNI 'pile put'. Here, however, the sign YIRRARNI is repeated several times, with the direction of the arm altered for each repetition, not the sign YURRUJURLA. YIRRARNI, like MILYI, is a single action sign which may readily be repeated. It is performed by lowering a spread hand and simultaneously extending the wrist: $5_{\vee\perp}{}^{\perp\vee\cup\}}$. The sign YURRUJURLA, on the other hand, is not like this. In this sign, both hands are lifted up, the hands being held with all fingers adducted and bent slightly, to produce a 'cupped' handshape. With the palms facing one another, the two hands are lowered, and moved rapidly in and out with cycles of very small amplitude at the same time: $\text{cB}_{>\perp}{}^{\text{I}}\text{cB}_{<\perp}{}^{\vee)(\text{"}\}}$. It will be seen that such a sign might well be suited to extended action (by extending it one might express the idea of a very large pile, for instance), but it is not well suited to repetition, and it is perhaps even less well suited to repetition with spatial displacement. Hence, in this case, even though it was the multiplicity of piles that Ruby wished to describe, she repeated YIRRARNI rather than YURRUJURLU because the action of YIRRARNI is easy to repeat many times while the action of YURRUJURLU is not.

9.4.5 Signs that do not match units in the spoken language

In the examples we have considered we have seen that there is a close paralleling between the sequencing of signs in R-units and the sequencing of words in P-units. We have seen that the semantic units to which morphemes in the spoken language are related are the same as the semantic units to which the sign units in the sign language are related. This is so even where the sign unit, because of its depictive or pantomimic character refers, in addition, to more specific and concrete meanings. There is no *a priori* reason why this should be so. Sign forms could be developed that would express, in a single phrase of action, something that would, in spoken form, take several lexical units to express. Indeed, as we saw in the case of the sign unit equivalent of the preverb *nyurdi* and of the preverb *kanardi* in Examples II and III above, sign units are found which could be used in this way. Winnie nevertheless usually treats forms such as these as if they were preverbs, for she follows them with the sign equivalent of the root verb, thus preserving the format of the spoken utterance. However, there are some instances where she employs sign forms which cannot be matched to semantic units in the spoken language. This is illustrated by the following examples.

The first example concerns the use of pointing. Winnie sometimes uses an index finger point instead of a lexical sign. This happens when the referent is immediately available to be pointed at. Thus, in the Parraja story, Winnie comments repeatedly on the big load the old man's stomach comes to contain as a result of all the food and other things he has swallowed. P1-8, from Parraja 1, which is but one instance of several sequences of this type, illustrates the way she expresses this in sign:

Point (to stomach)	PIRDA	MARDARNI
Stomach	full	possess

(His stomach was full).

In directing her index finger to her stomach here, as in other instances, the finger is simply moved directly toward its referent in a simple point. It is possible, however, to do more than merely point at something. The action of pointing can be varied in several different ways and, by such variation, something additional may be conveyed about the referent (compare discussion in Chapter 7). In these cases the action of pointing comes to be more than a means of referring to something. In one instance (P1-16 from Parraja 1) Winnie exploits this possibility of embellishing the act of pointing to good effect:

PARRAJA YANURRPU |R,| Moving-Point (to stomach) RDANJARR
Parraja *yanurrpu* point to stomach load
with a downward
motion

MARDARNI
possess

(The *parraja*, the *yanurrpu*; these were all shoved down in here [i.e. the stomach] which became fully loaded)

In this example, Winnie lists two different kinds of containers and then, by a 'shaped' point to her stomach, in which the index finger is first lifted up and then moved downwards as it is directed toward the stomach, she conveys the idea that the things she has listed have been put into the stomach which, as a result, is fully loaded. No spoken parallel to this R-unit can be established. In this case we have an instance of a sign-unit being inflected to convey information within a single unit of action that, in a spoken rendition, would have demanded several lexical items.

Example VI
(Parraja Story)

Signed version

P1-56 $B_{>\perp}{}^{'}$ $B_{<\perp}{}^{\perp}$ ${}^{\perp}\sim{}^{'}$ NGUNAMI

Depictive gesture lie down

(All the things he had swallowed lay scattered all over the place)

Spoken version

P2-107

Wurruluku yirra-rnu-lpa, wurruluku yirra-rnu-lpa,
Vomit-PAST-IMPF., etc.

parraja, yanurrpu, pangurnu, kilinjirri.
the *parrajas*, the *yanurrpus*, the *pangurnus*, the *kilinjirris*.
(He vomited up all the different dishes he had swallowed)

Another example in which Winnie uses a form of sign-unit that cannot be matched to any verbal equivalent is given in Example VI. This is taken from the section of the Parraja story in which the old man, having had the fire sticks shoved down inside him, vomits up all that he has swallowed. In the passage where this is described in the signed version (P1-56), Winnie is suggesting that all the things that he has swallowed are now lying all over the place. She does this by the use of a graphic action for which there is no direct verbal gloss in Warlpiri. Accordingly, it has no Warlpiri label and in the Example it is given in notation instead. The action consists of a succession of arm extensions, with the hands held with all fingers adducted and extended. The arms are extended in alternation, the fingers pointing towards the ground. In the first pair of arm movements the arms are extended somewhat laterally, in the second pair of alternating movements they are extended directly forward. In this way Winnie conveys the idea of many things lying on the ground in a widely spread array. She follows this sequence with the sign NGUNAMI 'lie down'. In doing this she once again preserves a spoken language format in her R-unit. However, the form that precedes it, as we have described, does not have any equivalent in spoken Warlpiri. In the passage in the spoken version of the story that is the closest to this expression that we can find, it will be seen that Winnie lists the objects that are vomited up. In this example we see what is perhaps one of the greatest differences between the sign language version and spoken version. Winnie does not transpose into manual form a spoken language expression. She uses here a primary gestural form, a form for which there is no spoken morpheme to which it can be directly matched.

Examples such as this are relatively few. For the most part, Winnie organizes her R-units very much as if the units of meaning to which each of her sign phrases refer are the same units of meaning to which spoken morphemes refer. The use of sign units which cannot be mapped on to semantic units which are the same as those which match words in the spoken language is quite uncommon. Even where Winnie uses sign forms that are highly depictive or pantomimic, she commonly employs them very much as if they are spoken forms, as we saw in the cases of the signing of *nyurdi ma-ni* and *kanardi yirra-rni*.

9.4.6 R-units and P-units compared: conclusions

We have seen, in the above examples, how in many ways the signed versions are organized very much in the same way as the spoken versions. At the same time, we have noted several differences. Where the action of the sign may be extended in time, this is the modification it will undergo to express extended action, where in the spoken language the verb is repeated over and over.

Likewise, where a sign can be directionally varied it will be, thereby expressing what, in the spoken language, is accomplished by a directional clitic. Where the sign cannot be directionally varied, however, a separate segmental sign is employed - although, as we saw, such a sign can only be placed at the end of a sequence. Apparently it does not have the same positional freedom that directional clitics have in the spoken language. Finally, we noted some instances of signs that vary in form according to the nature of the direct object of the action. Thus MURUPINYI varies according to the kind of thing into which the action of shoving was being done. In such a case, the sign does not express the same abstract unit of meaning that its verbal gloss expresses. It can be used to give concrete and specific meaning to the more abstract meaning to which the verbal equivalent refers.

9.5 Sign order and word order compared

In Chapter 8 we saw that in several of the NCD sign languages, at least, most of the clitics, including some of the case endings, can be rendered in sign, but that the endings which signal grammatical relationships within a clause (ergative and grammatical dative) are never marked in sign. This might lead one to suppose that, in these sign languages, sign order within a given construction would be more constrained than is word order. A comparison of constituent ordering in R-units and P-units suggests, however, that signed sequences and spoken sequences are quite similar in this respect. While word order is largely unconstrained by grammar in Warlpiri, and Warlpiri speakers are notorious for using very different word orders from one moment to the next, even when they are repeating something, there do seem to be certain preferences and conventions which serve functions such as topicalization and emphasis (Swartz 1984, Laughren 1984b). If we compare R-units and P-units in the two narratives considered here, it seems that the same kinds of preferences and conventions are operative in the sign language as they are in speech.

Thus, in the signed versions of both the Parraja story and the Yarnirnpa story, it was found that in approximately two thirds of all the R-units in which there is a verbal sign, the verbal sign is placed last. In most cases, in these R-units, only the object is given separate expression, but where the subject is given separate expression as well, it tends to be placed at the beginning of the sequence. In other words, in the signed versions we have what looks like a tendency for an SOV ordering. However, an examination of the constituent ordering of the P-units in the spoken versions of these stories suggests the same thing. Thus in the Yarnirnpa story, in the spoken version, of the 136 P-units in the discourse in which one or both of the arguments of the verb are referred to explicitly in separate lexical forms, 73% were verb final. The figure for the Parraja story, based on 74 P-units, is 76%. This may, of course, just reflect Winnie's preference. Nevertheless it is notable that she employs the same preferences in constituent ordering, no matter whether she is signing or speaking.

An indication that this preference may not be peculiar to Winnie, however, comes from an analysis of the constituent orderings given by Winnie and two other signers in sign translations of fifty one spoken sentences. The purpose of presenting these sentences was to see how various aspects of Warlpiri grammar would be handled in sign. The sentences included pairs in which Subject and Object were reversed (e.g., *Wati-ngki ka paka-rni karnta* 'the man hit the woman' vs. *Wati ka karnta-ngku paka-rni* 'the woman hit the man', and the like), the various pronouns were used, tenses were compared, and the use of negation and the interrogative was explored. The sentences were read to each signer separately and she was asked to provide a rendition in sign language. The sessions were recorded on 16mm film with synchronous sound.[9]

In presenting these sentences, many different constituent orderings were followed. This is quite consistent with the practice of Warlpiri speakers. Consistent with this, also, was the fact that, in giving signed versions of these sentences, the signers often did not repeat the constituent order that they had been presented with. If we compare the response versions of those sentences which had been presented with the verb at the end, with those in which the verb was not placed at the end, however, it is found that the signers rearrange the non-verb final sentences so that they have a verb final form, but they alter the ordering of the verb final sentences much less frequently. Thus of the 27 non-verb final sentences presented to two of the signers, the repeated versions were rearranged to have the verb at the end in 19 instances. The third signer was given 28 non-verb final sentences and she altered 17 of them. On the other hand, of the 23 sentences presented with the verb at the end, only 3, 6 and 9 sentences were altered on repetition, by each signer, respectively.

It would appear, then, that there are constituent order preferences, but that these preferences are the same, whether we are considering spoken utterances or signed utterances. This suggests that sign order is not employed as a means to establish grammatical relations any more than, in the spoken language, word order is so employed,

9.6 Extra-manual components in signed discourse

As we noted in Chapter 5, a notable feature of the North Central Desert Aboriginal sign languages examined in this work is that there is virtually no involvement of the facial muscles, either in the formation of individual signs or in the organization of discourse. However, in Winnie's performance of the signed versions of these narratives, we find that there is considerable patterning in her use of gaze direction and bodily orientation. Her use of these aspects of behavior appears to serve as a way by which she can label R-units in terms of their status in the discourse. It also serves as a way in which she can keep the various agents and beneficiaries of action distinct.

The role of gaze direction and bodily orientation has been analyzed in Parraja 1. It is found that R-units differ in the bodily and facial orientations associated with them in such a way as to suggest that they serve to frame each sequence differently according to who the agent or object of an activity is, or who is being addressed. In the Parraja story, as we have seen, there are the women who grind the seed, put it on containers and carry it; there is the old man to whom they give the food; there is also the old man himself, who shoves the food and containers in himself and who talks to the women. Later in the story there are the paths of movement followed by the women and the old man as they chase one another.

For utterances concerning the activity of the women, Winnie always uses an orientation in which she is turned slightly to her right, looking down (Fig.9.4). When the food is being given to the old man, as was noted earlier, in doing the signs for KANYI 'carry' or YINYI 'give', Winnie extends her arms to her extreme right, and turns in that direction also. This serves to establish a location for the old man (Fig. 9.3). When the women then go to the old man to ask him where the coolamons are or to demand that he give them back, for this segment of the story in which Winnie is quoting the speech of the women, she again uses an orientation in which she faces to her right, facing, thus, the location she has established for the old man (Fig. 9.4). By orienting in this direction she is able to define the signed sentence as being the speech of the women to the old man. For the old man's reply she uses a different orientation: she orients somewhat to the *left* which is, of course, appropriate as the reciprocal of the orientation used by the women as they talk to him (Fig. 9.5). Finally, Winnie from time to time repeats some utterance, or she makes a comment on what is happening. These utterances do not advance the story. They are, rather, made for my benefit. In these cases she uses an orientation in which she faces me directly (Fig. 9.6).

By noting the orientation that is associated with each R-unit, it is possible to establish the status of each one in respect to the discourse. Orientation and gaze direction are being used as utterance *frames*. They serve as a means whereby the signer is able to make clearer who is doing what, who is speaking, who is responding and which utterances are to be taken as extra-narrational and which as part of the story itself.

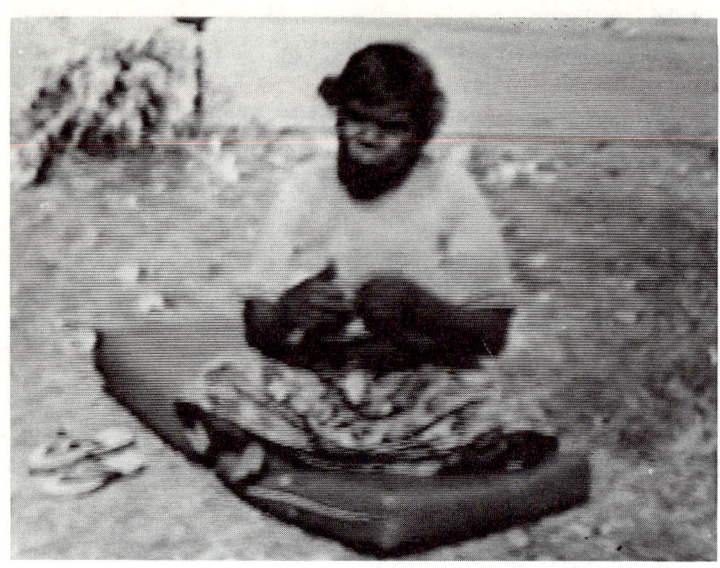

Fig. 9.3 Winnie signing YANURRPU in the orientation used when describing the activities of the women, from YSL 1981 XII, Parraja 1

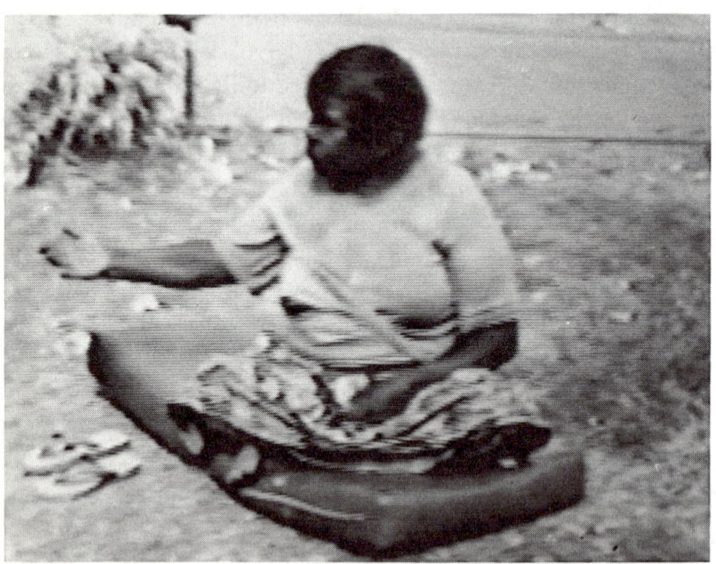

Fig. 9.4 Winnie signs YINYI 'give' and shows, by her orientation and arm extension, the location of the old man, from YSL 1981 XII, Parraja 1

Fig. 9.5 Winnie signs NYAPARRA 'where', quoting the women as they ask the old man where their dishes are, from YSL 1981 XII, Parraja 1

Fig. 9.6 Winnie signs WAJAWAJA, part of 'forget', quoting the old man's reply to the women. Note how her orientation is the reciprocal of her orientation in Fig. 9.5. From YSL 1981 XII, Parraja 1

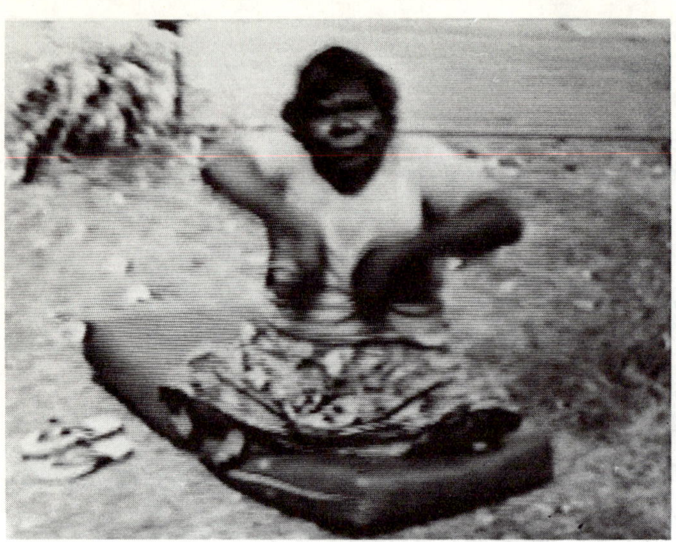

Fig. 9.7 A two handed version of MURUPINYI. Note Winnie's orientation to the camera, typical for repetitions and extra-narrational comments, from YSL 1981 XII, Parraja 1

Orientation during R-junctures may now be considered. Examination of the sign transcript of Parraja in Appendix II will show that the common pattern is for Winnie to orient her gaze toward the recipient of the story during R-junctures and to embark on a different orientation as she commences each new R-unit. For both narrations, it is found that there is a clear tendency for Winnie to establish recipient-directed face orientation during R-junctures. We find further that she is much more likely to orient away from her addressee as she begins the first sign of the next R-unit, and she is also likely to be orienting toward her addressee during the final sign of a given sequence just before an R-juncture. That is to say, Winnie is likely to look at her addressee as she comes to the end of a unit of discourse and then, as she commences signing again, she is likely to look away again. Such a pattern of orientation change is well known among speakers (Kendon 1967, Argyle and Cook 1976, Goodwin 1981, Webbink 1986). It seems clear that Winnie is here using orientation in association with R-junctures as a means of marking the major divisions of her discourse.

She does not look at her addressee in association with every R-juncture, however. An examination of the cases where she does not look suggests a further use of orientation as a device for exhibiting how successive R-units or discourse units are to be linked together by the recipient. What we find is that where Winnie sustains an orientation away from her addressee during R-junctures, the R-units concerned are closely linked to one another by topic. For example, in Parraja 1 R-units 19, 20, 21, and 22 all have R-junctures in which Winnie is looking to her extreme right, and not at the addressee. These R-units are connected because they constitute the successive components of an episode in which the women who have carried food to the old man on various coolamons, which he has swallowed, now resolve to ask him for them (19 and 20), ask for them (20 and 21) and receive a reply (22). Likewise, in Yarnirnpa 1, R-units 40 to 43 are all connected as units of a list of the several parts of the body of a kangaroo that is being divided up for distribution. Finally, we may note how, in Parraja 1, in R-units 16 and 17, 34 and 35, 36 and 37, 45 and 46, Winnie sustains an addressee orientation throughout both R-unit and R-juncture and in all of these cases she is repeating comments to the recipient of the story about the old man. In other words, R-units that are closely linked in topic may show a continuity of orientation during R-junctures, either away from the addressee or, as in the instances just mentioned, toward the addressee. We suggest, in short, that sustainment of the same orientation through R-junctures is another way in which a linkage between R-units in a discourse may be exhibited.

The use of orientation described here does not seem to be formalized. There appears to be considerable individual variation in the extent and consistency with which such framing behavior is employed. Furthermore, it seems quite similar to the way in which speakers often use posture and gaze direction as frames for spoken utterances. It seems likely that its use is part of what makes a story-telling a good performance, whether it is signed or spoken. However, we may expect that it plays a more important role in signed narration and that if signed narration were more common than it is in Warlpiri life, the use of gaze and orientation in utterance framing might become more systematically established.

9.7 Conclusions

There are several different ways in which the signed narratives may be compared to their spoken counterparts. First of all, we have shown that in sign, as in speech, distinct packages of discourse may be distinguished, here termed R-units and P-units, respectively. These units, it seems, have the same status in relation to the discourse in the two media. P-units are the packages of information out of which the spoken narrative is built. R-units serve in the same way and they are very comparable in size and content.

P-units and R-units may be compared in terms of their constituents: 'words' in the case of P-units, 'signs' in the case of R-units. Considering these as if they represent units of lexical meaning in each case, we find a close correspondence. Constructions, whether spoken or signed, have a similar structure. We described examples in which there was a virtual sign-for-word match. We showed, too, that the order in which the constituents of the discourse units occur is similar in the two media. To be sure, as Example VI showed, in the signed versions instances could be found where a single (usually) complex gesture was used to render the meaning of something that, in speech, would require a construction involving several lexical items. However, for the most part there is a close correspondence between the internal structure of P-units and R-units. This suggests that, in signing, the narrator takes the organization she would have followed were she speaking, and transposes this into a sequence of sign units which are ordered in the same way within a discourse unit as they would have been, had they been spoken.

However, we saw here that, as already noted in Chapter 8, only lexical morphemes find representation in sign. Markers of case relations, morphemes that mark tense, and pronouns, if they are cliticized, are not signed. Second, while we saw that complex lexical items, such as preverb-verb formations in the spoken language, are rendered by compound signs that match the morphological structure of the spoken form, we saw that this was not always the case. In some cases a unitary sign was found to be used instead. Further exploration is needed here. It may be that there are certain kinds of meaning that are more readily given direct representation in gesture than others and that it is in respect to these meanings that we will find a divergence between the formal organization of speech and the corresponding signed expression. These meanings may include spatial movement and actions that can be directly pantomimed.

These qualifications aside, this comparative study of signed and spoken narration suggests that the signed versions are very much like the spoken versions. As we have indicated previously, at least for the more sophisticated signers, these alternate sign languages are not fully autonomous systems but are built up as gestural representations of the semantic units provided by the spoken language. The findings presented in this Chapter only serve to reinforce this general conclusion.

Notes

[1]This Chapter is an expanded and altered version of a paper that has been published in *Oceania*, Vol. 59, June 1988

[2]*Parraja* 'flat wooden dish used for winnowing seed, carrying food, carrying a baby - coolamon'. *Yarnirnpa* 'shy, reluctant to participate socially'. In reference to a woman it generally refers to reluctance to accept men sexually.

[3]June Napanagnka Granites of Yuendumu.

[4]Dr. Mary Laughren assisted with this work on the Yarnirnpa story and I have consulted her extensively over the English translations.

[5]The method of analysis has been termed 'movement phrase boundary analysis'. See Kendon (1977, Appendix) for a detailed description. The equipment we have employed, for the film recordings, was a 16mm Bell and Howell Filmosound projector, specially adapted with a manual film-analysis handcrank; for video-tape we used a JVC cassette player with stop-frame and slow motion facilities.

[6]These observations are consistent with the findings reported by Gee and Kegl (1983) who show that pause length is related to episode structure in a story narrated by an experienced native signer of American Sign Language. Although the distribution of pause lengths in the two discourses here analyzed does not serve to parse the stories into well organized tree structures in a way that may be compared to Gee and Kegl, it seems clear that Winnie varies her R-juncture (pause) length consistently with major divisions in the story.

[7]Grinding stones comprise a large 'mother' stone and a small 'daughter' stone which is rubbed on the larger. The use of NGAMA |+| RLANGU here probably refers to this.

[8]From the 1981 series of video recordings made at Yuendumu. Copies are deposited at the Australian Institute of Aboriginal Studies in Canberra and at the Archives for Traditional Music, Indiana University.

[9]The sentences were prepared and presented by Dr Mary Laughren and the recordings were made at Yuendumu in August 1978. The films are deposited in the Library of the Australian Institute of Aboriginal Studies in Canberra from whom video-tape copies may be obtained by interested persons.

10 Signing and speaking simultaneously[1]

10.0 Introduction

In this Chapter we investigate the nature of the relationship between signs and elements of spoken language, when signing and speaking co-occur within the same utterance. This happens quite commonly, for older women often use signs while they are talking. We shall report that, for the most part, when signing occurs at the same time as speaking, sign meanings *parallel* verbal meanings. Occasionally, signs may be used as substitutes for words, as when they are used to complete an unspoken part of a sentence. Much less often, and only in special circumstances, are they used to provide additional meanings, or meanings that complement what is being said in words. On the other hand, if we consider passages in which, instead of signs, use is made of such gestures as pointing, pantomimic gestures, or gestures of interpersonal regulation, such as beckoning, we find that meanings additional to what are being spoken are being provided.

These observations are interpreted as supporting the view, advanced in previous chapters, that the signs in the sign languages treated in this book encode the same units of meaning as words in the associated spoken languages. However, we shall also argue that when used concurrently with speech, signs can only parallel spoken verbal output. This is because, when expressing meaning in lexical units, one cannot select for overt expression more than one such unit at a time. This is the case, regardless of whether one has at one's disposal more than one channel in which such units may be expressed. If the kinesic channel is to be used to express meaning that is supplementary to, or complementary to. what is being expressed lexically, it may only do so if it is being used to encode that information in a non-lexical fashion.

When expressing meaning in lexical units, whether signed or spoken, use is made of items which belong to a repertoire of standard forms, shared by others, which are organized into combinations or constructions, according to rules of syntax of some sort. Meanings expressed in this way may be referred to as *constructed meanings*. Meanings may also be encoded in another way. Use may be made of a configuration of action that encodes a specific meaning 'all at once'. Such an action, which may be either vocal or kinesic, though it develops in time, serves as a holistic representation, like a picture or an enactment. It is not built from recombinable elements and it is thus quite different from a linguistic construction. Meanings expressed in this way may be termed *presented meanings*. What we show in this chapter is that, when the vocal channel and the kinesic channel are being used simultaneously, when the kinesic channel is being used to produce *signs*, - elements of constructed meanings which are the equivalent of spoken words, that is to say - then meaning in this channel parallels the meanings expressed in the vocal channel. If the kinesic channel is being used to produce phrases of action that serve as presented meanings, on the other hand, then meanings in this channel may be *different* from the meanings expressed in the vocal channel.

The findings to be presented in this Chapter thus underline the difference between signs, whether they co-occur with speech or not, and gesturing that co-occurs with speech. Such gesturing, or gesticulation, has been the object of a number of investigations in recent years (Freedman 1977, Freedman, Van Meel, Barroso and Bucci 1986, Kendon 1972, 1980b, 1985b; Schegloff 1984; McNeill 1985, 1987). McNeill, in particular, has argued that gesticulations make manifest aspects of the intrinsic content of the utterance. They show, in imagistic form, the speaker's thought that motivates its linguistic structure. The study of co-speech signing presented in this chapter, shows, in contrast, that signs reveal only those aspects of the utterance that are encoded lexically. It confirms that signs encode content, in the same way as words. When used simultaneously with speech, they occur as word parallels and reveal no more of the content of the utterance than the spoken words do.

10.1 Circumstances of signing and speaking simultaneously

The practice of signing and speaking at the same time is widespread among the older women of the Warlpiri, and other North Central Desert groups (Liberman 1982b also mentions this for Western Desert men). I have observed it many times, but others, whose interest is not especially focused on sign language, have also noted it. Thus, Mary Laughren (personal communication, 1984) writes that Warlpiri women at Yuendumu: "...constantly mix sign and speech, either using them simultaneously or interchanging the two media". We have earlier (Chapter 3) quoted the observation of Dail-Jones, writing of the Warlpiri at Willowra, that "sign language is used throughout the year by the older women, to either accompany verbal communication, or to serve as a substitute for it". [2]

As yet, no systematic study of the occasions when women sign and speak at the same time has been carried out, although such a study could be very useful. A few observations may be cited, however, which suggest that signs are used with speech as a kind of emphasis device, when a speaker becomes animated, or when something sustained is being said.

One common circumstance in which sign is used with speech is during loud or forceful talk, as in argument, or when a woman is shouting instructions to others who are some distance off. For example, on one occasion at Yuendumu, on an outing to gather firewood, a woman was calling out instructions to her children as they were roaming about picking up sticks. She was trying to direct them to collect certain convenient pieces of wood that she could see. Her instructions were accompanied by signing which, as is common in such circumstances, was done with the arms held at full length, forward from the speaker, towards those she was addressing.[3]

A woman is also likely to sign as she is speaking, when animated or excited. Thus, when several women from Tennant Creek arrived by truck at Karlampurlpa, a small Aboriginal community to the northwest of this town, they immediately began excited 'greeting talk' with a number of women who were sitting in the shade of a tree. Some of these women crowded up to the truck and then, together with the new arrivals, they all sat together under the tree talking with great animation, catching up on one another's news. During all of this period, from the initial excited greeting talk and throughout the time when people were bringing each other up to date, the women signed continuously as they spoke. As the conversation became less continuous and people began to drift away, first news exchanges now finished, the talk became less loud and signing no longer accompanied it.[4]

Signing may also accompany speech in narration, as may be seen in the recordings to be discussed below. Munn (1973) has also noted this. Thus, she writes of how, in the telling of 'sand stories' by Warlpiri women "the process of narration consists of the rhythmic interplay of a continuous running graphic notation with gesture signs and a sing-song verbal patter. The vocal accompaniment may sometimes drop to a minimum; the basic meaning is then carried by the combination of gestural and graphic signs". (pp. 59-60).

In this Chapter, we shall examine some examples of simultaneous speaking and signing recorded on video-tape or film in which speakers were engaged in sustained utterance, either telling a story or engaging in extended commentary when gossiping. The examples examined here are thus examples of speech-concurrent signing during sustained discourse. It is possible that signs relate to speech differently, in emphatic, argumentative or other types of animated utterance. Whether this is so or not, however, must await the analysis of other kinds of examples.

The examples studied involve only speakers of Warlpiri. Narration in which speech and sign are used simultaneously has also been recorded for two

Warumungu speakers and for a Warlmanpa speaker. Simultaneous use of sign and speech has been observed in daily situations among Anmatyerre, Kaytej, Warumungu and Warlmanpa speakers. It seems unlikely that the conclusions reached in this chapter would not also apply in these other cases.

10.2 The material for analysis

For the analyses reported here, we have used three recordings of simultaneous speech and sign, recorded at Yuendumu by two different women. One is a video-tape recording of a narration by Winnie Nangala. The other two are sound-synchronous films of informal conversations. The narration is Yarnirnpa 2, already referred to in the previous Chapter. As already mentioned, the purpose of making this particular recording was to acquire a verbal version of a story which had already been recorded by Winnie in sign only. She had also been told that this story was to be recorded so that it could be transcribed and used, along with others, as a reading text for children in the Warlpiri bilingual education program that is in operation at the school at Yuendumu. Winnie was not asked to provide signs and indeed, at the beginning of the session in which this story was recorded, the video-equipment was not set in operation. Nevertheless, for all the stories she recorded on this occasion, Winnie signed as she spoke, as if this was her habit. As soon as this was noticed, video recording was commenced, but we had not intended to undertake it when the session started.

The two 16 mm films were made at Yuendumu on two different occasions in 1978 for the purpose of filming conversations in which sign language might be used. The first, YSL IV, was the last of four four-hundred foot rolls exposed during a lunch hour on the porch of a house. Several women were present, as well as numerous children and dogs. Among the women present was one who, at the time, was observing the speech taboo and used sign language exclusively. Talk ranged over a number of topics, including complaints about the behavior of various relatives and children, discussion of a misplaced bag of flour and a forthcoming excursion organized by the Baptist Church at Yuendumu. In the second film, YSL X, several women were filmed as they sat together awaiting the arrival of two others, prior to going on a hunting trip. The talk ranged from arrangements for a forthcoming Sports Weekend, to gossip about various relatives, a discussion of pensions and several other matters. The women present included two of those recorded in YSL IV, including the woman who was using sign language exclusively. In the analyses of this material to be reported here, we have concentrated on the utterances of one woman, Nelly, who, in both films, talked for extended periods.[5]

The recorded speech in both Yarnirnpa 2 and YSL IV and YSL X was transcribed in standard orthography for Warlpiri. The transcription of Yarnirnpa 2 was done from a high fidelity tape recording made at the same time as the video-recording. The transcription of YSL IV and YSL X was done from the original tape recordings made for the soundtracks of the films.[6] Complete transcriptions of all manual actions in these materials have been made. For Yarnirnpa 2, using a video-field numbered tape,[7] detailed transcriptions have been made for ten segments in which speech and manual action have been plotted on a common time base, the transcriptions being made to the nearest 1/30 of a second (range of accuracy from 1/6 to 1/30 of a second). All of the manual action for the entire 18 minutes has also been transcribed, however, with the action being coordinated to speech syllables and pauses.

Manual actions in both YSL X and YSL IV have been transcribed in detail. Copies of the films were made in which each frame was overprinted with a visible number. By the use of a Bell and Howell Filmosound 385 projector to which a Bell and Howell time and motion analysis handcrank had been added, transcriptions have been made of speech and manual action in which they have been plotted to a common time base to the nearest 1/24 of a second (range of accuracy from 1/12 to 1/24 of a second).

10.3 Units of analysis

In the discussion to follow we shall speak of the *vocal channel* and the *manual channel*. The units in the vocal channel are syllables, morphemes, words, P-units (phonological phrases at the level of the tone-unit or certain combinations of tone-units) and topic units. The units in the manual channel are G-units and G-phrases. A G-phrase may constitute a phrase of manual action identifiable as a *sign* in Warlpiri sign language, or it may constitute a *gesture,* that is a phrase of action that is communicative (pointing, beckoning, miming, and the like), but which is not identifiable as an element in the sign language.

As explained in the previous Chapter, the manual activity of producing a sign or a gesture can be analyzed as a phrase of movement within which the forelimb performs an excursion toward an apex. At the apex, the distinctive characteristics of the phrase become most evident, whether it is a sign or a gesture. Each such excursion will be termed a *G-phrase*. In transcribing the flow of signs a G-phrase is regarded as commencing from the earliest moment the limb can be detected as moving towards what will become the excursion's apex, to the last moment that the limb remains in the space of this apex. If the transcription is being done from film, for instance, the first frame of the film in which movement toward the excursion's apex can be detected counts as the first frame of the G-phrase, while the G-phrase is taken to end at the last frame before movement away from the excursion's apex can be detected. G-phrases are regarded as being contained within a unit of action here termed a *G-unit.* A G-unit is regarded as extending from the earliest moment at which the forelimb involved begins to move from a position of rest until the moment it returns to a position of rest again.[8] If a single gesture or sign is performed, then the G-unit contains but one G-phrase. Where, as in the discourses to be analyzed here, a succession of signs is performed without the hands returning to rest position between each one, then the G-unit may contain several G-phrases. Fig. 10.1 may be referred to for a graphic presentation of these units.

The flow of speech has been segmented into phonological phrases, using intonation tunes and pauses as criteria. The speech phrases established in the present investigation - P-units, as they will be called - are single intonation units or tone units that may be bounded by pauses, or two or more tone units in a single grouping where succeeding tone units are clearly subordinate to the first in the grouping.[9] At the outset of a P-unit there is always raised pitch and loudness, with more gradual pitch change and reduced loudness through the rest of the phrase. Subordinated tone units succeed one another without pause and initial raising of pitch and loudness in the subordinated tone units is slight compared to the first tone unit in the sequence. Usually not more than two tone units have been combined into a P-unit but some P-units may contain several tone units. This happens, in particular, in the case of repetitions, which are common in Yarnirnpa 2 and a characteristic feature of Warlpiri speech. For an illustration of this, the reader may be referred to Y2-7.4, quoted in 10.5, below. In the sequence in this example, the phrase "yakiri yakiri manu" is repeated four times. Each repetition constitutes a separate tone unit, but they have here been taken together to constitute a single P-unit in the present analysis.

The tone units and tone unit groupings treated as P-units here constitute the minimal units of 'sense' in the discourse. As mentioned in the previous Chapter, they correspond to the units Halliday (1985a) has distinguished in English speech as 'information units'. They tend to correspond to complete grammatical constructions. For Yarnirnpa 2, P-units agree well with the units of text separated by periods by the transcriber. They could be said to correspond to sentences, therefore. P-units have been grouped into higher level groupings or Topic Units, according to topic. As we shall note later, G-units may often extend over several P-units and in so doing serve to mark off Topic Units.

In order to show how signs and morphological units are related within the same utterance, P-units have been analyzed in terms of the words and morphemes they contain. I have followed Nash (1985) in deciding what to treat as a word and what to treat as components of a word. A *word*, so far as nominals are concerned, is a morphological unit which contains a stem and all of its suffixes. In the case of verbs, a word includes the root, its inflection and, in finite clauses, a verbal auxiliary. As described in Chapter 8, the auxiliary sometimes occurs suffixed to the preceding word and it sometimes occurs as an independent form, freely as the first or second constituent of a clause. Despite this, for present purposes the auxiliary has not been counted as a separate word. With regard to compound verbs, the preverb has been counted as a separate word in the present analysis.

The morpheme has also been used as a unit of analysis. In Nash's treatment, all morphemes in Warlpiri occur as distinguishable segments of speech. We are not faced with the problem of 'zero' morphemes or morphemes such as the past in irregular verbs in English, which do not have a separate segmental identification at the surface. For this reason, in Warlpiri, we may consider the morpheme as matching a unit of speech and it may therefore be compared to units of production in the manual channel.

10.4 Sizes of the samples analyzed

Winnie's narration in Yarnirnpa 2 is 18 minutes in length. It has been segmented into 364 P-units, of which 360 have been used in analysis. Four phrases were excluded because they were not sufficiently audible. 347 of these phrases are accompanied by manual activity, either signs or gestures, or both. 44 phrases are accompanied by gestures only and there are 30 phrases accompanied by a combination of gesture and sign. 273 phrases (76% of all P-units analyzed) are accompanied by signs. The recordings in YSL IV and YSL X are both 11 minutes in length. Nelly speaks intermittently throughout. She produces 91 P-units in all in YSL IV, and 99 P-units in YSL X. Of these, 60 and 59, respectively, were associated with signs, and 11 and 17, respectively, were associated with gestures.

10.5 An example

To illustrate how phrases in the manual channel are coordinated with phrases in the vocal channel, we shall take a close look at a small passage from Yarnirnpa 2 that has been transcribed in detail. This passage is presented in Fig. 10.1. In this passage, the prospective husband is being addressed by the girl's father's sister. She is urging him to be bold and claim his bride. The four P-units are thus united in a single Topic Unit. In Fig. 10.1, the single G-unit that extends over the four phrases 4.2, 4.3, 4.4 and 4.5 is diagrammed. The components of the constituent G-phrases - preparation, recovery[10] - are indicated by different line segments. The actual character of the action in the stroke in each case is not notated, however, but glossed in capitals. The transcription was done to the nearest one thirtieth of a second. There are several points to be noted:

1. The four P-units belong together in a single Topic Unit, as just noted. The manual activity associated with them is organized as a single G-phrase. This is characteristic. Although there are plenty of examples where successive P-units within a Topic Unit are separated by substantial pauses and where each separate P-unit has its own associated G-phrase (see Fig. 10.2, for example), speech that belongs to separate Topic Units rarely shares the same G-unit. Of the 93 Topic Units distinguished in Yarnirnpa 2, 79 (85%) are associated with the beginning of a new G-unit. There are six occasions when a new Topic Unit begins without any juncture in the concurrent G-unit. There are eight instances where the junctures are those of hold or partial recovery, rather than full recovery.

2. It will be seen that each new speech phrase commences simultaneously with the beginning of the *stroke* of a G-phrase. This means that Winnie must begin the preparation for a G-phrase in advance of beginning her speech. The G-phrases in this example are all signs, as is indicated by the glosses given in capital letters (the names of the signs are all in Warlpiri). The signs match the words that are being uttered. It will be seen, for instance, that in 4.3 the speaker performs the sign NGANGKIRI[11] and, at the very moment that she embarks upon its stroke, she also embarks upon her utterance of the word "ngangkiri". It will be seen that this coincidence between the onset of the first word of a phrase and its corresponding sign is achieved by the speaker beginning the preparation of the sign in question in advance of the speech with which the sign is to be associated. Thus eight thirtieths of a second before she begins the word "rdarri" of phrase 4.2, the speaker begins to move her hand up into the signing space appropriate for the performance of the sign RDARRI. There is a pause of seventeen thirtieths between 4.2 and 4.3 and during this pause the speaker re-positions her hands for the performance of NGANGKIRI. Here she appears to delay her speech slightly so that the word "ngangkiri" may begin the moment of the stroke of the sign NGANGKIRI

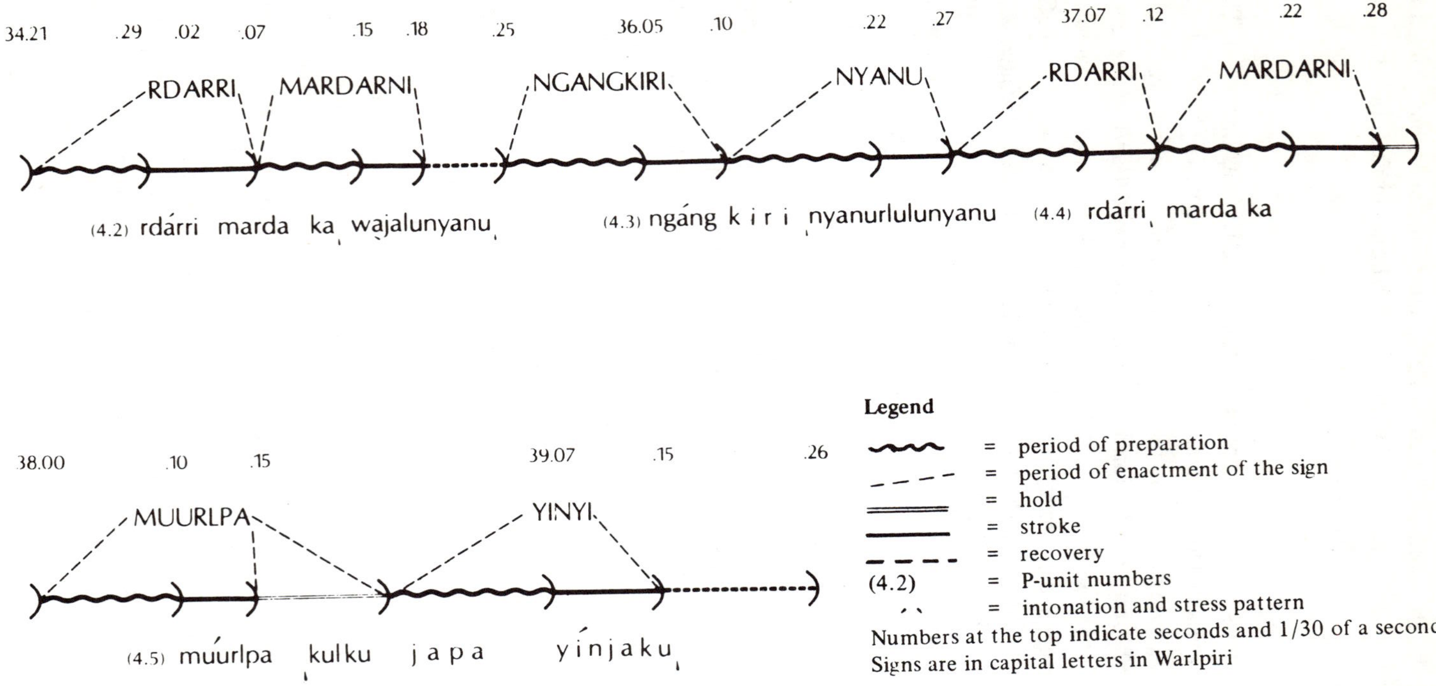
34.21 .29 .02 .07 .15 .18 .25 36.05 .10 .22 .27 37.07 .12 .22 .28
RDARRI
MARDARNI
NGANGKIRI
NYANU
RDARRI
MARDARNI
(4.2) rdárri marda ka wajalunyanu
(4.3) ngáng k i r i nyanurlulunyanu
(4.4) rdárri marda ka
38.00 .10 .15 39.07 .15 .26
MUURLPA
YINYI
(4.5) múurlpa kulku j a p a y í n j a k u
Legend
= period of preparation
= period of enactment of the sign
= hold
= stroke
= recovery
(4.2) = P-unit numbers
= intonation and stress pattern
Numbers at the top indicate seconds and 1/30 of a second
Signs are in capital letters in Warlpiri

Explanation of Fig. 10.1

Numbers in top row indicate seconds and thirtieths of seconds. Signs are labelled in capital letters in Warlpiri. Dotted lines extending from each label to the line below indicate the period of enactment of the sign. Periods of Preparation indicated by wavy line; Stroke indicated by straight line; Hold indicated by double line; Recovery indicated by dotted line (see text for explanation of these terms). Orthographic transcription of speech given on lowest line. Bracketed numbers are P-unit numbers. Intonation and stress patterns indicated by tone marks.

Translation of speech in this figure is as follows:

Rdarri marda-ka waja-lu-nyanu!
Grab hold-IMP indeed-333p SUBJ-REFLEXIVE
Grab hold [of her] yourself!

Ngangkiri-nyanu-rlu-lu-nyanu. Rdarri marda-ka
FZDH-REFLEXIVE-ERG-333P SUBJ-REFLEXIVE grab hold-IMP
Husband of my niece! Grab hold!

Muurlpa-ku-lku-japa yi-nja-ku
Together-DAT-SEQ-INTERROG give-INF-DAT
Is she not given for you to be together?

---

begins. Similar considerations apply at the commencement of "muurlpa" at the beginning of P-unit 4.5. For 4.4, preparation for the sign RDARRI is begun over the destressed final syllable of "-nyanu" of the preceding phrase. This "-nyanu" has no corresponding sign (the previous one does), but this enables the speaker to begin the first word and the first sign of the next phrase coincidentally.

The coordination of the stroke of a G-phrase with the utterance of the word corresponding to it that is illustrated here is found throughout. This is clear evidence that the planning processes for speech and sign are carried out in a completely integrated fashion. That is to say, spoken forms and signed equivalents are co-selected and their production is coordinated. The production of signs and speech together, thus, is a case of true 'simultaneous translation.'

3. It will be seen, however, that this kind of close coordination of the stroke of a sign with the spoken word with which it is associated only applies to the first word in each phrase. Subsequent words in the phrase may well be spoken before the sign sharing the gloss of the word is produced. Thus, in both instances of the occurrence of the compound verb *rdarri marda-*, though both the preverb *rdarri* and the root *marda-* receive a rendition in sign, it is only the first part that is precisely coordinated with the onset of the word. Subsequent signs do not necessarily fit over the words whose glosses they share, even though the boundaries of their G-Phrase components are coordinate with syllabic boundaries in the speech flow. Indeed, as will be seen at the end of phrase 4.4 the sign MARDARNI is executed *after* all speech belonging to 4.4 is over. While this is being done there is no speech. Speech does not begin again until the sign MARDARNI is completed and the hands have been moved into position to commence the stroke of MUURLPA.

This also is a phenomenon of general occurrence. If, in rendering a phrase in sign while speaking there is still signing to do, even though the speech of the phrase has been completed, the next spoken phrase will *not* begin until all signs belonging to the current phrase have been completed. This is further evidence that phrases of speech and phrases of sign are organized concurrently. The lag between speech and sign, discussed further below, is a consequence of differences in execution in these channels rather than in how they are organized.

4. The final observation to be made in respect to the example in Fig. 10.1 is that not all of the morphemes uttered have equivalents in sign. As we have seen in Chapter 8, there are a number of morphemes that do not have signed renditions, even when signing is being done without speech. However, we find that several of the morphemes in this passage that do not receive rendition in sign nevertheless can be rendered in sign. Presumably, some morphemes are left out in the signed accompaniment because to attempt to include them would lead to the development of too great a lag between speech and sign.

The lag between speech and sign that tends to develop comes about because it takes longer to perform a sign than to utter a word. Winnie's rate of production of signs, as measured over a five minute segment of her narrative, is 1.37 signs per second. She speaks at a rate of 1.55 words per second or at the rate of 3.82 morphemes per second. That is, her word production is about one and a quarter times faster than her sign production and her morpheme production is nearly three times as fast. A similar relationship between signing rate and speaking rate has been obtained from an analysis of Nelly's performance in YSL IV. Her rate of signing was there found to be 1.55 signs per second. She was found to speak at a rate of 2.06 words per second, one and one third times as fast as her rate of signing.

As the above example illustrates, the lag that develops between speech and sign is compensated for in three ways: signs are prepared for in advance of the beginning of speech, some morphemes are not rendered in sign, and any signing left over in a phrase is completed before any new speech is begun. Another possible way in which compensation for this lag could be accomplished might be mentioned. It might be possible for Winnie to complete a sign *before* speech begins and in this way avoid the necessity of completing a sign afterwards. This is never done. If it were, it would mean that Winnie might end up performing a sign of a given gloss but uttering a word of a different gloss. This, as we shall see, very rarely happens. To begin signing in advance would mean that signs and words would have to be planned for separately. All the indications are that this is not so. Production in the manual channel and production in the vocal channel are organized simultaneously as a single unit of action.

It may be noted that the lag of signs in relation to speech that we have described here is one of the ways in which speech concurrent signing differs from speech concurrent gesturing. In speech concurrent gesturing, or gesticulation, the G-phrases do not relate to words so much as to the unit of meaning that governs the combination of words that make up a speech phrase. The stroke of a phrase of gesticulation tends to co-occur with, or to precede somewhat, the point of greatest stress in a tone unit, and the whole phrase is often over before the tone unit is completed (Kendon 1972, 1980b; Schegloff 1984, McNeill 1985). Performing the stroke of a G-phrase after its associated speech phrase has finished is almost never observed. The observation that signs lag behind the words to which they correspond is specific evidence for their lexical status. Signs, it appears, represent the same meaning units as words, and are selected and arranged within the utterance in just the same way as are words.[12] Since, as we have seen, on average, signs take longer to perform than words, if they are being produced concurrently with them, it is not surprising that the final sign of a phrase will be left to be completed after the completion of speech, as we observe here.

10.6 Spoken meaning in the manual channel

From the foregoing we see that when signs and speech are produced in the same utterance, they are organized together. Yet, at the same time, not every component in the vocal channel is represented in the manual channel. A quantitative comparison suggests, indeed, that only about half of the elements spoken are represented in sign. Thus, if we compare the number of words in a P-unit that are matched by a sign with the total number of words per phrase, we find, in Yarnirnpa 2, that, overall, only 61% are matched. If we make the same comparison in terms of morphemes we find only 30% are matched by signs. A consideration of what kinds of spoken elements are represented in the manual channel, and what kinds are not, shows, however, that despite this quantitative disparity, most of the sense of what is being said is retained.

To begin with, we find that just about all nominals and any attached noun formative suffixes are represented, as are all the verbs. However, the sign organization employed does not always fully match the morphological structure of what is spoken and we also find that everything that contributes to the grammatical interpretation of what is said is left out. These points will now be exemplified.

First, in her signed accompaniment, Winnie quite often uses unitary signs for compound spoken expressions, instead of compounds. For example, in Y2-56.4 and Y2-57.1 she uses the compound *tarda ya-ni* 'sit down, alight'. Instead of signing it as TARDA YANI, however (as would be possible, for a sign for the preverb TARDA has been recorded), she uses a unitary sign PIRRIMANI 'sit down'. She preserves in sign the sense of what she is saying, thus, but represents it in a different way.

Second, where expressions are repeated several times, as is quite common, the signs do not always repeat all of the elements that are spoken. Where what is repeated is a compound verb, for instance, in sign, characteristically, only part of the compound is repeated, as may be seen in the following examples. In Y2-7.4 Winnie says:

YAKIRI YAKIRI YAKIRI
Yakiri yakiri ma-nu yakiri yakiri ma-nu yakiri yakiri ma-nu
(Demand promised wife-PAST)

YAKIRI MANI
yakiri yakiri ma-nu

In Y2-74.5 she says:

NYUYU NYUYU NYUYU NYUYU JARRI
Nyuyu jarri-ja nyuyu jarri-ja nyuyu jarri-ja nyuyu jarri-ja

(Gather together-PAST)

It will be seen that in the signed accompaniment, only the preverb is repeated. The root verb is signed only once, at the end of the sequence. This, as will be recalled from Chapter 9, is very similar to the way in which repetitions of compound forms are done when only signs are being used. Nevertheless, the signed accompaniment preserves the full sense of what is said, even though it does not represent all of the morphemes that are spoken.

In repetitions of this sort it is also to be noted that the strokes of the G-phrases do not necessarily coincide with the word to which they are matched in meaning, although they occur in an evenly spaced rhythm as do the words. Thus in Y2-74.5 it will be seen how the stroke of the sign NYUYU co-occurs with "jarri" in the verbal channel, the final signed JARRI occurring after all speech has ceased. This comes about because, in this case, the arms are lifted in preparation at the beginning of the first "nyuyu", thus displacing the stroke in respect to the words in the phrase. This can also lead to a reduction in the number of words in a repetition sequence that get signed.

Third, as we have mentioned more than once, tense inflections, the verbal auxiliary and any clitic attached thereto, and the grammatical cases, are never rendered in sign. This in itself accounts for a significant amount of the disparity between the number of elements spoken and the number that are signed. As we suggested in Chapter 8, however, the omission of these items may not subtract very much from the sense of the utterance.

Finally, use is made of directional variation in sign performance in such a way as to preserve information about spatial relationships given in speech, without at the same time matching the morphological structure of what is spoken. Thus where, in speech, a separate directional enclitic is used to convey information about the spatial orientation of some activity, in the signed accompaniment this may be conveyed by how the sign for the activity is actually oriented or moved in space.

For example, consider Y2-50.1 and Y2-50.2, presented below:

Y2-49.1

Points over right shoulder		NYANYI	MARDUKUJA	YANGKA
Miyitiyitiyi	ma-nu-lku-lpa	nya-ngu-lku-lpa	mardukuja	yangka-ngku-ju
Look from-side-to-side	PAST-SEQ-IMPF	see-PAST-SEQ-IMPF	woman	DET-ERG--TOP

(Looked from side-to-side then,[she] saw then [where she was] the aforementioned woman [i.e. his promised bride])

Y2-50.1

Rubs knee	NGURRJU	NYANYI (oriented to self)	POINT (to self)
Ngurrju-ngku-lkuuu	marda ka-ju	nya-nyi-rni	wajaaa
Good-ERG-SEQ	perhaps PRES -1P DAT	see-PRES-hither	indeed

(Perhaps she looks to me favorably now indeed)

Y2-50.2

NGURRJU		NYANYI (oriented to self)	NGURRJU
Ngurrju-ngku-lku	marda ka--ju	nya-nyi-rni	waja-ni
Good-ERG-SEQ	perhaps PRES-1P DAT	see-PRES-hither	indeed--TOP

(Perhaps she looks to me favorably now indeed)

Here Winnie is quoting the hero's thoughts about his promised wife as she is being brought to the creek where he is waiting. He believes that she will now look favorably towards him. In Winnie's use of NYANYI here, she orients the hand so it points toward herself. In the immediately preceding phrase, Y2-49.1, where she refers to the bride looking from side to side as she is brought to the creek, Winnie does not use a directional clitic and she does not modify the orientation of her hand in performing the sign. It will be seen that by using such directional modifications, Winnie can economize on the number of G-phrases needed to represent in sign what she is saying. Once again, thus, we may see how she may preserve in sign the sense of what she is speaking, while using a different structure to do so.

It should be added that in some instances within the signed accompaniment in Yarnirnpa 2, the directional clitic is represented as a separate segment of action. In such cases a separate pointing action with the index finger is performed, the finger being moved in an appropriate direction. The separate rendition of direction in this fashion occurs when the signed version of the verb in question is one that does not include motion through space in its meaning and for which the sign cannot be varied in its orientation.

Examples of this have been given in Chapters 8 and 9, and as we mentioned in Chapter 9, what is of particular interest is that the G-phrase representing the directional clitic may be placed in a different sequential position in the sign sequence from that which it occupies in the speech. It may be placed as the last G-phrase in the G-unit, often after the spoken phrase has been completed. In such cases we have an instance where the sequential organization of signing departs from the sequencing of the concurrent spoken forms.

An example is provided in Yarnirnpa 2 by Topic Unit 35, diagrammed in Fig. 10.2. It will be seen that the G-units associated with the P-units Y2-35.3 to Y2-35.7 all terminate in directional G-phrases which are added at the end of the sequence of signs, in several cases after the speech has ceased. In Y2-35.3 and Y2-35.6 the directional G-phrase is in the same sequential position as the directional clitic in the phrase. However, in Y2-35.4 and Y2-35.7 this is not so. Here Winnie signs the substantive components of these phrases first and then adds the directional, even though the directional in the spoken version occurs much earlier in the sequence, attached to the preverb.

This example would seem to support the view that in providing a signed rendition of her spoken utterance Winnie is not rendering the spoken forms by a simple process of word-to-sign transfer. She is rendering in manual form items which stand for the same semantic units as the spoken forms, rather than the spoken forms themselves. This point has been made in

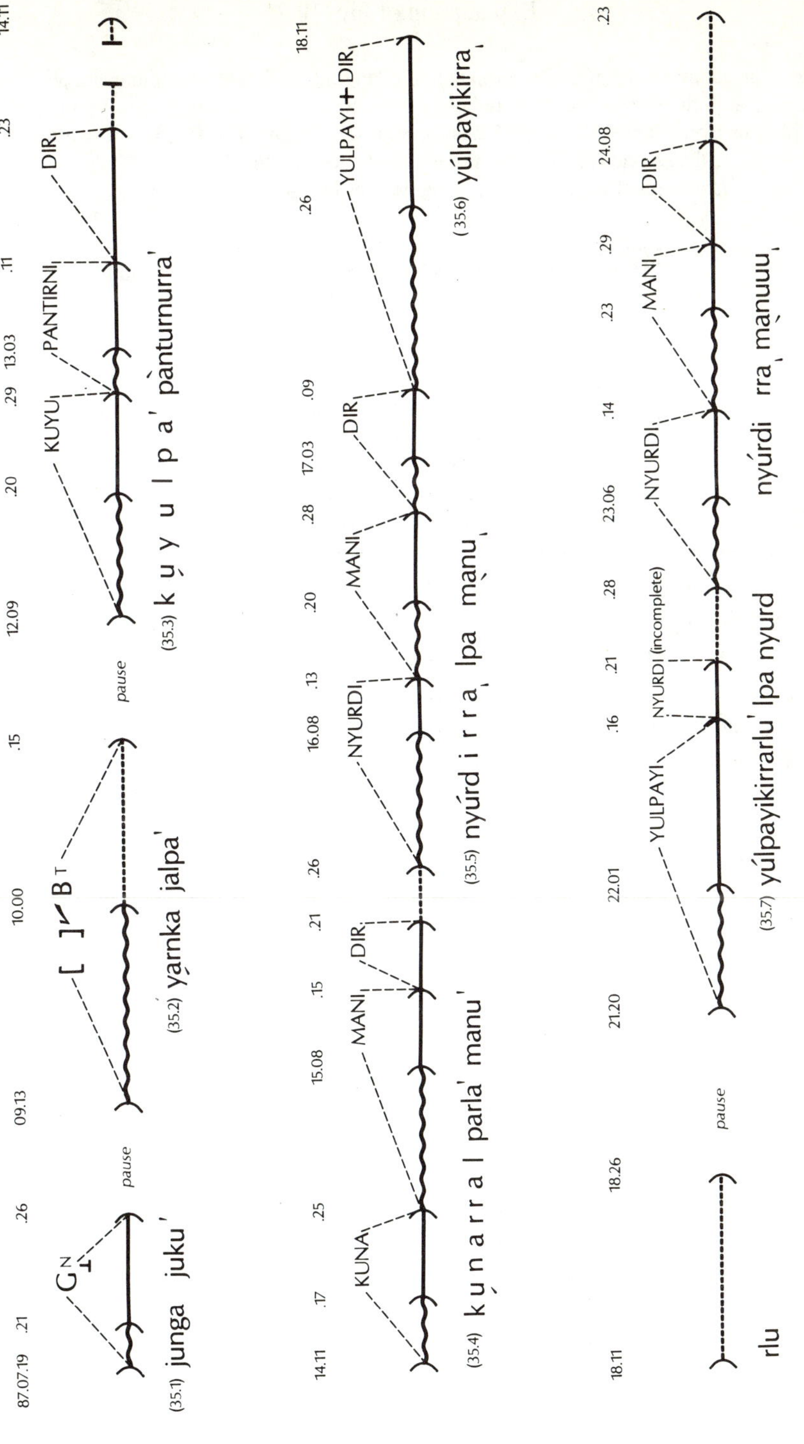
87.07.19 .21 .26 09.13 10.00 .15 12.09 .20 .29 13.03 .11 .23 14.11
G N ⊥
[ ] B T
KUYU
PANTIRNI
DIR
(35.1) junga juku'
pause
(35.2) yarnka jalpa'
pause
(35.3) k u y u l p a' pànturnurra'
14.11 .17 .25 15.08 .15 .21 .26 16.08 .13 .20 .28 17.03 .09 .26 18.11
KUNA
MANI
DIR
NYURDI
MANI
DIR
YULPAYI+DIR
(35.4) k u n a r r a l parla' manu'
(35.5) nyúrd i r r a lpa manu
(35.6) yúlpayikirra
18.11 18.26 21.20 22.01 .16 .21 .28 23.06 .14 .23 .29 24.08 .23
pause
YULPAYI
NYURDI
NYURDI (incomplete)
NYURDI
MANI
DIR
rlu
(35.7) yúlpayikirrarlu' lpa nyurd
nyúrdi rra manuuu

Explanation of Fig. 10.2

For explanation of diagram see Explanation of Fig. 10.1. Words in capitals are Warlpiri labels for signs, except that DIR indicates an index finger point in a specific direction. G-phrases over P-units 35.1 and 35.2 are gestures, not signs. The first is a forward index finger point, the second is a movement of the hand over the shoulder.

Translation of the speech in this figure is as follows:

Junga-ju-lku. Yarnka-ja-lpa. Kuyu-lpa pantu-rnu-rra.
Straight-still. Set off-PAST-IMPF. Meat-IMPF pierce-PAST-thither.
Straight away he set off. He speared meat [game] over there.

Kuna-rra-lpa-rla ma-nu
Intestines-thither-IMPF-3P DAT get-PAST
[He] gutted [his catch] for her over there.

Nyurdi-rra-lpa ma-nu yulpayi-kirra-rlu.
Carry meat on neck-thither-IMPF -PAST creek-ALL-ERG
He carried the meat on his neck thither to the creek.

---

earlier Chapters, on other grounds. It is remarkable that even when Winnie is accompanying her speech with signs, sign order is not necessarily tied to the order in which she produces the spoken units.

To conclude, we may summarize the foregoing by saying that what is left out of the signed accompaniment is what can be left out without losing the gist of what is being said. The signed accompaniment, in fact, appears to be little different from what we find when signed discourse is not accompanied by speech. That is, in signing concurrently with speaking, at least for the examples analyzed here, speakers are providing a second representation of what they are saying. When speech and sign are used together, that is, to a large degree what is spoken is paralleled by what is signed.

10.7 Unspoken meanings in co-speech signing

So far, we have been concerned to see the extent to which what is spoken is rendered in sign. However, we might imagine that in signing at the same time as one is speaking one could produce signs that might add to what is being said in words, or complement it in some way, so that an understanding of the utterance could only be complete if both the verbal channel and the manual channel were taken into account. One might suppose that this would be possible, because the vocal channel and the manual channel are apparently quite separate. Whereas, in speaking, it is impossible to say two things at once, at first sight it would seem quite reasonable that one should be able to speak one thing and sign another. Studies of gesticulation show that different aspects of the meaning of an utterance may be conveyed simultaneously by word and gesture.(Kendon 1985b, McNeill 1987). For example, McNeill (1987) reports an instance in which a narrator tells of an episode from a detective story. The speaker says: "And he seeks to protect her by hiding the glove and not telling any of the other detectives about this." Concurrently with the phrase "by hiding the glove", the speaker performs a gesture which appears to be an enactment of removing a glove from the hand and placing it in his pocket. By this action the speaker shows just how the glove was hidden, and thus adds specific detail to an utterance that, in words alone, conveyed the information about hiding the glove in a much more general way. Our question is, can signs that are produced simultaneously with speech also serve to add information to the utterance in a similar manner?

In the materials studied in this Chapter, this is found to be quite rare. There are eleven occasions when there is a discrepancy between sign and word in Yarnirnpa 2, seven in YSL IV and ten in YSL X. They may be grouped into three types. First, signs which do not match what is spoken may appear during phrases that are introductory to new segments of discourse; second, a sign for the referent of a deictic word may be made as the deictic word is uttered; third, and least commonly, the sign and the word have a different substantive reference and the two must be taken together if the full meaning of what is being said is to be grasped. Examples of each of these types follow.

1. Signs during topic introduction talk. Winnie opens her telling of the Yarnirnpa story in Yarnirnpa 2 with the following:

YARNIRNPA		WAYIL	WAYIL	YIRRARNI
Yiiiiiiiiiiiiii	puta-lpa	wayil wayil	yirra-rnu	yiiiiii
Ohhhhhhhh	incomplete action-PAST	hold in marriage-PAST		ohhh

MARDUKUJA YUNJUMU
mardukuja- jiiiiiiiiiii
woman-Phonological extension
(Oh the shy one, the incomplete marriage. Oh the woman sitting facing away)

In these phrases, Winnie announces the main theme of her story. It will be seen that she does this partly in sign and partly in speech. However, it will be seen that the signs that provide additional meaning - YARNIRNPA 'shy' and YUNJUMU 'sit facing away from others' - do not co-occur with articulate words (YARNIRNPA does not coincide with "putalpa" for example) but during the introductory "oh" or during the extension syllable of the final word - which itself conveys no lexical meaning. Thus here, though signs do complement the meanings provided in the spoken channel, they only do so by *alternating* with the articulate segments in that channel.

Throughout her narration Winnie introduces new segments of the story with the phrase:

ngula-jangka -ju
that -ELATIVE-TOP

Freely translated, this means "And then", "next". There are signs in Warlpiri sign language by which *ngula* and *-jangka* could be rendered (see Chapter 8) and in a few cases Winnie does appear to accompany this phrase with NGULA. In several other instances, however, this phrase is accompanied by a sign with quite a different meaning. Thus, Y2-14.1, the first phrase of Topic Unit 14, is as follows:

MARLU
Ngula-jangka-ju

MARLU is the sign for *marlu* 'plains kangaroo'. Here Winnie has just completed a segment of the story in which she tells of how several kangaroos were hunted and killed and brought and piled on the ground. In Topic Unit 14 she will describe how various people came to get their appointed portions of the catch. "Kangaroo", thus, is very much on her mind at this point. Although the word is not used in 14 (only names for various parts of the animal are used), 14 is all about what is done with the kangaroos that are brought. Here the sign MARLU does not add meaning to what is being said in 14.1. One might say of it that here Winnie is providing a sign of what she is thinking about.

2. Sign as the referent of a deictic word. In Yarnirnpa 2, in Topic Unit 15, Winnie explains how the hero tries to persuade his promised wife to come over and accept meat from him. She quotes his words and signs at the same time as follows:

KUYU NGARRI JARRI
Kuyu-kurra ngarra ngarri-jarri mayi
Meat-ALL FUT go-inchoative INTERROGATIVE
(Aren't you going to go to the meat?)

KUYU NGARRI JARRI
nyampu-piya-kurra ngarri-jarri-waja
this-like-ALL come-INCHOATIVE-indeed
(Come to the likes of this indeed!)

It will be seen that she specifies in 15.4 what "this" refers to by signing KUYU 'meat' at the same time as she says "nyampu-piya-kurra".

Similarly, in YSL IV (22.1, 22.2) Nelly asks who put down somewhere a bag of flour which now seems to be missing:

QUESTION YARDA
Ngana-ngku ngula-ju yarda yirra-rnu
Who-ERG this again put-PAST
(Who was it [who] put it down?)

MIYI
Nyampu-piya
This-like (The like of this)

As she says "nyampu-piya" she signs MIYI 'flour', thus indicating the referent of the deictic word.

Similarly, also in YSL IV (13.2), in the course of complaining about the behavior of a relative (he is always rushing off to town and does not stay around his wife and children as he should, it seems), she says:

SPOUSE KARIJA
Kuja-nyanu-ku karija
Thus-POSS-DAT. don't know
(His one [i.e. wife] does not know him [because of his absences])

Here we must take the signed accompaniment into consideration to know that it is his spouse that is being referred to and not some other relative (we know it is a relative because of the use of *-nyanu* as the possessive, this being a form used only with kin-terms).

In these instances, then, the manual channel is being used simultaneously with speech to provide meanings not in the spoken channel, but though we need to see the sign given in order to grasp the full meaning of what is uttered, the sign fills in a meaning that is only pointed to in the speech. As in the previous instances just given, these are not examples of *two* meanings being given simultaneously.

3. Simultaneous use of sign and word with different meanings. We now illustrate cases where a sign and a word are paired but the sign and word have different substantive meanings. Here the two channels are being used at the same time to present different referents and we observe a true complementarity between the two channels.

For example, in YSL X, in reply to someone, in the course of a discussion about how the ground must be cleaned up for ceremonial dancing to be performed at Yuendumu Sports Weekend, Nelly says:

	RAKE		JILKARLA
Yuwa	marna	manu...uu	jilkarla-ku-lku-lpa-rlipa-rla
Yes	grass	and..........	prickles-DAT-then-PAST-we-DAT

KULPA	WATIYA	CHOP
kulpa-ja...aaa	watiya-ku-lku-lpa-rlipa-rla	yawirr-pu-ngu
return-PAST	tree-DAT-then-PAST-we-DAT	chop down

(Yes, we raked the grass and prickles and went back and chopped down the bushes)

As she says *marna* 'grass' she signs RAKE - a sign in which the hand, held with the fingers spread and bent as in a claw, is flexed at the wrist and brought in towards the signer somewhat. This sign is glossed as "rake" but it also refers to the action of raking.

As another example, this time one in which the object of the verb is provided in sign and the verb itself is spoken, we may cite 17.5-17.7 in YSL IV:

CLOTHES	WURULYPA	TARNNGA
Ngurrjarli marda-rnu-jala	wuruly ka-ngu	tarnnga-juku
Steal-PAST-indeed	secretly take-PAST	long time-still

(the clothes were stolen, secretly taken away for a long time)

Here it will be seen that the object of the action of stealing is given only in the sign.

To what extent do these examples undermine the general claim made at the outset, that when signs are used concurrently with speech, because they are an alternate representation of the meaning units expressed in the words, they can only parallel word meanings and cannot, as gestures can, complement the meanings that are spoken?

In the first two types of sign-speech complementarity illustrated, it will be seen that, despite the disparity between what is signed and what is spoken, *new* meanings are being provided in only one of the channels. The phrases used at the beginnings of new segments of discourse are formulaic or, as in Yarnirnpa 2, the speaker may not actually say anything, but utter an inarticulate noise. A deictic word does not itself carry any reference and so here, too, in the second group of instances, we may say that substantive reference is being given in only one channel.

It is the third kind of instance, where two new meanings are being given at once, that would appear to be true exceptions to the general claim that has been made. Closer inspection suggests that this may not be so, however. First of all, it will be seen that the two new meanings that are given simultaneously are not unrelated. The two meanings in question are in every case components of a grammatical construction. Thus, of the eleven instances recorded of this sort (three in Yarnirnpa 2, two in YSL IV and seven in YSL X), the two referents that are produced simultaneously stand as verb to object (in five cases), verb or noun to modifier (in four cases), or as a conjunction of verbs (in two cases). Second, in all but one case, the two different but simultaneously presented meanings occur only as the initial elements in the phrase. As will be recalled from earlier discussion, in order for the stroke of a sign to occur simultaneously with the word with which it is associated, it is often necessary for the preparation of the sign to begin some time in advance of the pronunciation of the word. Thus, at the beginning of a phrase, processes for the production of a sign are put in train before processes for the production of a word. Once the sign has been selected, however, if speech is not already in progress, it may well be possible for the speaker then to prepare for the production of the next lexical item in the construction. If two channels are available, at the outset of a phrase the first item selected can be expressed in one of them, the second in the other, with the result that they both are actually executed at the same time, even though they are different. At this point, however, selection must be well advanced for the next item in the utterance and with both production channels in operation the simultaneous production of different elements in each of them is no longer possible.

10.8 Unspoken meanings: sign inflections

In the discussion of the signing of directionals we referred to a number of verb signs that can be modified in how they are performed and in this way 'incorporate' within the action of the sign a reference to the proximal and distal meanings of the directional clitics. It will be seen, however, that in making a movement towards or away from oneself it is possible to provide additional information by making the movement along lines that have different points of origin or termination. That is, for example, in using the sign KANYIRNI to render the sentence *watingki ka kuyu kanyirni* 'the man is carrying the meat hither' not only would I move my hand toward myself, but I could also begin the movement from a particular direction, so adding information about where the man carrying the meat was coming from.

In Yarnirnpa 2, Winnie appears to be fairly consistent in the way in which she directionalizes signs in this way. Indeed, on the basis of the spatial arrangements of the points of origin and termination of such directionalized signs - as well as the directions of pointings and certain other gestures to be considered below - it is possible to map out the spatial relationships of the main characters in the story and the paths that they take as they move about. Fig. 10.3 provides an overall representation of this in which it will be seen that Winnie appears to locate the creek to which the hero of the story removes, when his promised wife rejects him, as behind her right shoulder, to her northeast. His own camp, and that of his bride, are located to Winnie's left, and somewhat in front of her, to her southwest.

Winnie may provide directional information in her signs even when no directional clitic is used in the spoken channel. Two examples will be given to illustrate this, both from the Yarnirnpa story (Y-2-39.2 and Y-2-31.5):

WIRDIYI NYANYI
Wirdiyi nya-ngu-lpa-jana-rla
Road see-PAST-IMPF-3P1 DAT-3P DAT
(He looked up the road for them)

Here the sign NYANYI is performed on an upraised forearm with the hand oriented toward the southwest direction which, as we have just said, is the direction Winnie uses for the location of the home camps and the direction from which the bride and her family travel. No direction is given in speech here but by orienting the sign NYANYI in this way Winnie adds information about the spatial mapping of the story's events.

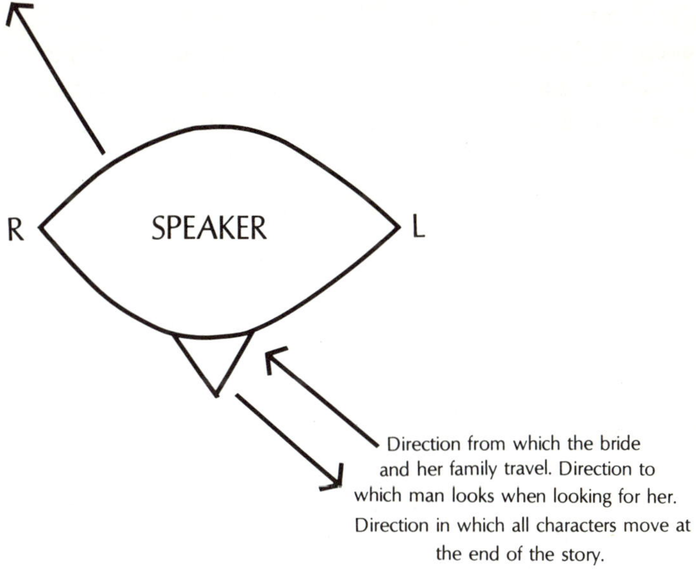
Direction used when referring
to the man's journey
R
SPEAKER
L
Direction from which the bride
and her family travel. Direction to
which man looks when looking for her.
Direction in which all characters move at
the end of the story.

Fig. 10.3 Spatial relationships of the main characters in Yarnirnpa 2, as indicated by the directions of Winnie's points, movement paths of signs gaze, and bodily orientation

Directional modification of a sign may also be used in a slightly different way, as in the following example, where Winnie is quoting the words of one of the bride's aunts, who is trying to persuade her to go with her to her prospective husband to get meat:

TARNNGA YIRNTIRRPARNI YIRRARNI
Tarnnga-juku-mayi-npa-rla kuyu-rlangu yirntirrparni yirra-rni
Long time-CONT-INTERROG-2P DAT meat-also leave-and-forget-NONPAST
(For a long time you leave and forget the meat, isn't it so?)

In this example, instead of directing the movement of the sign YIRRARNI forward in mid-signing space, as is done when this sign is not modified, Winnie directs it off to her right somewhat, rather as if it is a gesture of pushing something away from oneself and to the side. Here we do not have new information being added, but in this case we do see how a sign can be modified in its performance to add an additional graphic character to what is being said.

Another example which shows the graphic possibilities the modification of sign performance can provide is found in the signing that accompanies P-units 81.1- 81.3 and 82.1. Here Winnie refers to how the hero of the story, in the company of his new wife's uncle, went a long way round, hunting as they went. The events of spearing the kangaroo took place a long way off. Throughout these phrases, the signs are performed with arms elevated, thus adding an element that gives expression to the great distance away at which the events took place. Elevation of the arms adds this expressive element because this is a component of the signs for the demonstratives *nyampu* 'this', *yalumpu* 'that over there' and *yali* 'that yonder, far off'. These are signed simply by pointing, but the ones that refer to greater distances are signed with greater degree of arm elevation.

10.9 Unspoken meanings: pointing

Additional information may be provided in the manual channel by means of the use of gestures, rather than signs. Pointing is an example of this. It cannot be considered part of the sign language proper - although it is extensively used in signing. Pointing retains its open referential character and pointing, as used when signing, appears to be in no way different from pointing as used when speaking and not signing. There are no defined ways of pointing that have fixed meanings. Pointing remains an open ended way of directing attention to something in the environment or to indicate a direction.

In many places in Yarnirnpa 2 Winnie uses pointing to indicate directions or locations of activities within the story. She also uses pointing depictively, as in sketching out spatial arrangements of people and objects directly. These usages are just the same as the uses made of pointing by speakers who do not have available a system of lexicalized gestures.

An example of the use of directionalized pointing is to be found in Y2-13.2.

NGULA	Point (over right shoulder)
Ngula-jangka-ju	wirlinyi ka parnka-mi
And then	hunting AUX run-NONPAST

(And then [they] went hunting)

Here Winnie could have signed WIRLINYI PARNKAMI. Instead, as she says "wirlinyi ka parnkami" she points over her right shoulder as if to indicate where the people being referred to went, as they went hunting. In this way she adds information to what she is saying by pointing.

A somewhat similar example is in Y2-14.4:

Point
Yi-lpa-rla yitirli yirra-rnu
Comp.-IMPF-3pDAT apart put-PAST
(That [meat] which was put down aside for him)

Here Winnie simply points to her left, a place where she has already established that the meat she is referring to has been placed. Had she signed this, she would not have done a sign to match *yi-lpa-rla*, but she could have used NGALYA 'separate' and YIRRARNI 'put' for the rest.

Pointing may also be used depictively, as in Y2-24.2 - 24.3:

PARNTARRIMI Point Point JANKAMI
Parntarri-ja- mpa-lpa. Warlu-lpa-palangu kulkurru janka-ja
Crouch-PAST-Directional-IMPF. Fire-IMPF-33p middle burn-PAST
DAT.
([she] was crouched facing past [him]. The fire burned between them).

Here Winnie is telling how the prospective bride crouched down facing away from her husband and the fire was between them. That is, they did not spend the night sleeping together. It will be seen that she signs PARNTARRIMI, but then follows with two pointing movements. Here the index finger points downward and is drawn inwards, first to the right, then to the left. Here Winnie is drawing out the relative positions of the two people - between whom the fire was burning.

Finally, in yet another sort of usage, Winnie may use pointing as an emphasis marker, as in Y2-59.1 - Y2-59.2:

YANGKA Point down Point down Point down
Yangka-lpa nga-rnu nyanungu kalinyanu-kurlangu-rla-rlu-lku
Aforementioned-IMPF eat-PAST that spouse-belong-LOC-ERG-SEQ.
([The bride] then ate at her spouse's place)

Here, at last, the young bride has stayed at her spouse's camp and she is eating his meat. Over *ngarnu*, instead of signing NGARNI Winnie points downward vigorously, as she does twice more in the succeeding phrase, thus emphasizing the location where the eating was done, which is the important feature of what is being said here. It is of interest to note that in the phrase that follows, Y2-59.3, Winnie repeats "kalinyanu-kurlangu-rla-rlu-lku-lpa ngarnu" and with this repetition she signs KALINYANU KURLANGU NGARNI.

10.10 Expressive gesture

From time to time, in the material analyzed here, the speaker will use expressive gestures, rather than signs. This is another way in which information may be provided in the manual channel which is not given in words. This includes the use of certain movements which appear to represent aspects of a character's behavior and are thus part of what might be termed a dramatic rendering. Also included here is the use of gestures of interpersonal regulation - beckoning, for example - and certain other movements which are not signs but which appear to depict patterns of action.

An example of a use of speech-concurrent gesturing in which Winnie appears to be acting out part of a character's behavior is Y2-6.7:

WITA <u>Point forward</u>
Wita-kari yu-ngka-jala
Little-other give-IMP-EMPHATIC
(Give a little!)

This phrase comes from a passage in which Winnie is quoting the words of the young bride's aunt who tells her that she is indeed the wife of the hero and that she must stop being *yarnirnpa* and not be so proud: she must "give a little". The pointing finger is thrust forward several times, as if in emphasis, but perhaps as a finger might be "wagged" at someone who was being subjected to this sort of injunction. Evidently Winnie is here giving a dramatic rendition of an instructing aunt.

A second example is in Y2-56.1 and 56.2. Here Winnie is quoting the hero's words as he tells his prospective wife to take the meat that is offered. Here again the words are not signed. Instead Winnie points repeatedly to a space just in front of her, as if she is the hero pointing to the meat that is to be taken:

<u>Point down</u>	<u>Point down</u>	MANI
Jurru-jarra ma-nta-waja.	Manu mirdi-patu ma-nta!	
Head-dual take-IMP-EMPH.	And knee-several take-IMP.	
(Take the two heads, indeed!	And take these lower legs!)	

The use of beckoning is exemplified in the following:

KUYU Beckon PURLKA Beckon
Kuyu-ku-waja ya-nta-rni purlka-waja. Kulpa ya-ni-rni-li
Meat-DAT-EMPH Go-IMP-hither old man-EMPH Return go-NONPAST -hither-333P
(Come here old man for meat! Come back here you!)

Examples of this sort are scattered throughout Yarnirnpa 2. Although Winnie is a skillful signer and storyteller she does not embellish her telling with much dramatic rendition, at least not in this telling. These examples may illustrate, however, some of the ways in which gesture rather than sign may be employed, concurrently with words, but, in these cases, serving to give visual renditions of the kinesic activity of the characters, rather than signing what is being said.

10.11 Conclusions

The examples studied in this Chapter show that when signs are being used at the same time as speech, the meanings of the items in the two modalities *parallel* one another to a large extent. What the speaker says, she also signs. To the extent that this is so, speech concurrent signing is quite different from gesturing while speaking. In gesturing while speaking, or gesticulation, we observe the production of configurations of action which are not standardized in form and which, furthermore, relate to units of meaning that, in speech, require for their expression a syntactically organized combination of several lexical items. That is, in gesticulation, a single unit or G-phrase encodes meaning at the level of the syntagm rather than at the level of the lexical units of which the syntagm is composed. It encodes meaning *presentationally* rather than in *constructions*. In co-speech signing, in contrast, we observe a close match between signs and spoken lexical units. The signs, indeed, are the equivalent of lexical units, but rendered in manual form, and they appear to be co-selected with the spoken lexical units they match as the utterance is produced.

We saw, however, that what is rendered in sign is not a complete parallel of what is said. Several reasons were put forward to account for this. First, as we noted in earlier chapters, there are some units of spoken language that are never rendered in sign. These include endings which mark grammatical relations and endings and other forms that mark tense. We also noted that certain noun formative endings and several of the sentence particles which often receive rendition in sign when discourse is produced only in sign, often do not receive rendition in sign when signs co-occur with speech. This is probably related to the fact that signs take longer to produce than spoken elements and that, if everything said was signed, the signing could not keep pace.

In fact, as we observed, signs are allowed to lag in relation to speech, but only to a limited extent. Thus we found that the speaker does not add signs for everything that has been left out. Only the final sign of the sequence is added. Were the speaker to do otherwise, she would either have to extend the length of her inter-phrase pauses to accommodate the extra signs or she would have to permit her signs to become increasingly out of phase with her speech. Neither occurs. Signs, like words, are selected and organized together into phrases and they remain together in phrases. Although the speaker may delay her speech slightly to permit time for the completion of the preparation phase of a sign so that a word and its signed equivalent may begin simultaneously, she does not appear to prolong inter-phrase pauses so that left over signing may be completed. This we regard as a consequence of the fact that words and signs are co-selected. Any sign performed after the speech of a current phrase has been completed is a sign-equivalent of the last lexical unit selected and this is never preceded by sign-equivalents of lexical units earlier in the phrase. If more than one sign does follow speech, the additional signs are always either repetitions of the last sign or new lexical items.

There are two additional reasons why not everything spoken is signed, even though signing is so largely a parallel to what is spoken. First, for certain compound expressions, the speaker does not always sign all parts of the compound but uses a unitary sign instead, if one is available. Second, in phrases in which there is much repetition, the speaker may not sign out all of the verbal items that are repeated but will produce a succession of 'sign syllables', coordinate with the rhythmic structure of the speech, which render the sense of what is being said without rendering it in full spoken lexical detail.

We also examined the extent to which signs produced at the same time as speech may add to the total information conveyed by the utterance. We found that, when this did occur, it occurred most commonly during a vocal gesture or during the production of deictic or formulaic expressions. In such cases, we suggested, new meanings were being provided in one channel only, and these instances did not constitute exceptions to the claim that signs and words are the equivalent of one another.

A few instances were found in which a sign and a word of different meanings occurred simultaneously, and these might be thought to undermine our general conclusion. Close inspection of them suggested that they did not do so, however. In each one of them, the two lexical units were always components of the same grammatical construction and they co-occurred only at the outset of phrases, with but one exception. It was suggested that concurrent production of two different lexical meanings would be possible at the beginning of phrases, because of the need to initiate sign production in advance of word production. At the beginning of a phrase, once the first lexical item has been selected, if speech production has not yet begun, it might then be possible for the next item to be selected and produced in a different channel. It will be see that such instances can be accounted for in a way that is consistent with the general claim that signs and words are alternate expressions of equivalent units of meaning.

On the other hand, supplementary or complementary information may be provided in the manual channel from time to time if, instead of signs, expressions that are not standard forms within the sign language are being used. Thus Winnie was observed to make considerable use of pointing to add information about directions and spatial relationships. She also used expressive gestures from time to time which gave meanings additional to those provided lexically. In such cases she was using the manual channel to encode meanings presentationally, rather than as lexical constructions.

The foregoing is taken to support a general hypothesis: if a speaker is to combine different channels of expression to produce a more complex message than any one alone would provide, it seems that this is usually done only when the *mode* of encoding in the separate channels is *different*. If we were to use a lexical mode of encoding in both speech and kinesis, then we can usually only produce parallel messages. On the other hand, if we may use one of the channels (usually, but not necessarily always, the kinesic channel) for encoding meanings in single configurations of action, as presentations, then this can be combined with lexical encodings in a complementary relationship.

One final question may now be raised. If, as we have seen, in co-speech signing what is produced in the manual channel for the most part merely parallels what is said, why is signing used? At least in the instances we have examined here signing appears to be very largely redundant. It is possible that such redundancy is useful. It is possible that a parallel rendition of the narrative in sign may serve in conveying more certainly what is being said in circumstances where surrounding noise may interfere with the reception of speech. It is also possible that the coordinated manual activity of co-speech signing, like the coordinated manual activity of gesticulation, may serve in making a speaker more conspicuous and interesting to watch, and thus facilitate the attention of recipients. There is a further possibility, however. That is, it seems possible that by presenting lexically encoded units of meaning in manual form as well as in spoken form a kind of objectification of meaning is achieved. Manual signs can be visually inspected, they can be held or prolonged and they exist almost as if they are physical objects separate from the producer. In this they are somewhat like graphic forms. Thus, in giving you the sign for something it is almost as if I am giving you a token of that thing. Unlike a spoken word, which is fleeting, a sign can be held still. Thus by rendering one's discourse in signs at the same time as one is speaking, it is as if one is rendering one's meanings in the form of physical objects. The story thus comes to have a different sort of existence than if it were merely spoken. In consequence, the story will be apprehended in a different way by those that receive it from the way it would be apprehended if it were presented in speech only.

Notes

[1]This Chapter is an altered version of a paper that was published in *Multilingua*, vol. 6, no.1, pp.25-68, 1987.

[2]Meggitt (1954) also noted the use of signs in conjunction with speech, although his information concerns their use by men and does not refer to the sustained use of sign during speech that is common among women. He writes (p. 3): "..the signs are used piecemeal as a kind of embroidery on spoken Walbiri [sic] to provide required emphases". He also noted a use of sign with speech which he termed "conventional emphasis". According to him, there are some terms which are almost always accompanied by signs, whatever their context. "Notable among them are terms for circumcision, subincision, penis, vagina, semen, bullroarer, killing, and a few others. Presumably these refer to things or activities which are important to the Walbiri, and therefore this importance should be indicated as a matter of course" (Meggitt, op. cit., p.5).

[3]From author's fieldnotes, Yuendumu, 1981.

[4] From author's fieldnotes, 4 August 1984.

[5]Nelly is a pseudonym.

[6] The transcription of Yarnirnpa 2 was done by a literate Warlpiri native speaker, as mentioned in Chapter 9. The transcriptions of YSL IV and YSL X were done from the original sound recordings by Dr. Mary Laughren with the assistance of several of the speakers who had participated in the films and (for YSL X) with some assistance from Professor Kenneth Hale. Detailed English interlinear and literal translations of these transcriptions have been made with the assistance of Dr. Laughren.

[7]I am indebted to Palmer Morrell-Samuels of the Department of Psychology, Columbia University, New York, for making this video field numbered copy possible.

[8]G-units may thus be the equivalent of R-units defined in the previous Chapter. The term R-unit, however, will not be used here, since this is a unit set up in the context of discourse constructed of signs only. The term G-unit will be used as a more general term for any unit of gestural activity, whether comprising signs or not.

[9]The concept of tone unit used here is taken from Crystal and Davy (1969), which is based on British English speech. Although in Warlpiri intonation is patterned differently, intonation units comparable to tone units can readily be identified.

[10]These terms are explained in Chapter 9.

[11]It should be noted that the sign Winnie performs here is a sign that stands for all kin who are in the relation to anyone as Spouse and Spouse's siblings. The term *ngangkiri* that Winnie uses here, however, is a term that refers to the spouse of someone where the spouse is also the child of speaker's brother (woman speaking). She uses this term here because she is quoting the speech of the promised wife's Father's Sister. *Ngangkiri* is, thus, a 'triangular' kinship term (Warlpiri kin vocabulary is very rich in these) which, however, is not distinguished in sign language. For further discussion of this see Chapter 11.

[12]An exception to this is described in the next section.

11 Signs of kinship

11.0 Introduction

Kin relationships govern every aspect of social life in Australian Aboriginal society. As Elkin (1979, p. 85) puts it, "...it is the anatomy and physiology of Aboriginal society and must be understood if the behaviour of Aborigines as social beings is to be understood". Accordingly, in all Aboriginal languages, kinship terminology is highly elaborated. In the North Central Desert societies we also find well developed sets of signs for kin relations. It is appropriate, therefore, that kin signs should receive special attention. As we shall see, there are fewer kin signs than there are kin terms and, typically, several different kin relations may be signed using the same sign. The consequence of this is that the signs effectively group kin terms into equivalence classes. These turn out to be quite similar to the equivalence classes that may be inferred from a study of semantic relations among kin terms (Cf. Scheffler 1978, Laughren 1982, 1984a) and also to the equivalence classes established by the subsection system, which is in use in all these societies. The study of kin signs, thus, can throw an additional light upon our understanding of the structure of kin relations within these societies.

Signs for kin relations are also reported from many other parts of Australia, even from places where, otherwise, there is no well developed sign language (e.g. the Worora - see Love 1917, 1941). A comparative study of these signs with kin signs in the North Central Desert provides some additional insights into the nature of Aboriginal thinking on kin relations. As we have noted previously (Chapter 5), kin signs in the North Central Desert are, to a large degree, articulated by pointing to a body part. This is also true of kin signs from elsewhere, although there is considerable variation in what body parts are pointed to as a sign for a given kin relationship. The body-articulated character of kin signs appears to be a reflection of a widespread tendency to conceive of kin relations in terms of how social interaction, within a given relationship, is mediated by way of the body. The body part that is thought of as the focal point of the interaction most characteristic of the relationship becomes symbolic of that relationship. This is reflected in the spoken language, where, in many languages, kin terms can be found that are closely related to body part terms. These body parts may also become the locus of articulation for the corresponding sign. The signs, thus, are concrete manifestations of this way of thinking of kin relations.

This Chapter will begin with a brief explanation of the general principles that govern the use of kin terminology in Aboriginal societies. This will provide background for the subsequent discussion. We shall describe the kin signs used in the North Central Desert and compare the kin classes these imply with the kin classes that may be inferred from a study of the semantic relationships of the spoken terms. We shall then compare North Central Desert kin signs with kin signs from other parts of Australia. After a discussion of the significance of the body-articulated character of kin signs, we will conclude with a survey of signs for subsections.

11.1 Australian kinship terminology: some general principles[1]

Social relationships in Australian Aboriginal society are governed by general expectations about how persons should behave toward one another that depend upon the kin relationship of the persons involved. Every member of the society is reckoned to stand in a kin relationship to everyone else and the nature of this relationship provides the framework within which the social relationship between particular persons proceeds. Each type of relationship, whether of Father and Son, Uncle and Nephew, Grandmother and Grandchild, implies a set of obligations and expectations that persons standing in these relationships will bear toward one another. In effect, all members of an Aboriginal society treat each other as if they are genealogical and/or affinal relatives (although a distinction is made in practice between persons who are actual relatives and those who are classificatory).[2] This is accomplished by what amounts to an extension of terms used for family members to all members of the society. This extension is accomplished through the application of a number of general principles by which the use of kin terminology is governed. The three most general of these principles are as follows:

1. Same sex siblings are treated as equivalent. Thus Ego's Father's Brother is treated as equivalent to Ego's Father and Ego's Mother's Sister is treated as equivalent to Ego's Mother. This has the consequence that children of Ego's Father's Brothers are considered siblings of Ego, and likewise for the children of Ego's Mother's Sisters. Further, however, the children of Ego's Father's Father's brothers are considered Father's Brothers, and their children, accordingly, are siblings to Ego, and so on. In this way sibling relations may be extended laterally to an indefinite degree.

2. A distinction is drawn between the children of Father's Brothers and Mother's Sisters, on the one hand, and the children of Father's Sisters and Mother's Brothers, on the other. The children of cross-sex siblings of Ego's parents, that is to say, are called by a different set of terms and are regarded as standing in a different sort of relationship to Ego from the children of same sex siblings of Ego's parents. This is related to the fact that children of the cross-sex siblings of Ego's parents, his cross-cousins, that is, may also have an affinal relationship to Ego. This comes about because, depending upon the kinship system in operation, Ego (ideally) draws his or her spouse either from among his classificatory cross-cousins or from among some subset of the children of his parents' classificatory cross-cousins.

3. In the third place, the terminology employed does not extend indefinitely upwards to foregoing generations or indefinitely downwards to succeeding generations. Instead, the set of terms that are applied by Ego to members of his own generation are re-applied to the second generation above (the grandparental generation) and to the second generation below (the grandchild generation): these are sometimes termed 'harmonic' generations; and the set of terms applied to the first generation above (the parental generation) are re-applied to the the first generation below (the offspring generation): these generations are sometimes termed 'disharmonic'. This has the effect of establishing members of alternating generations as equivalent: grandparents and grandchildren are equivalent and one's children are equivalent to one's parents, and so on. Generations, thus, are conceived of as having a cyclic relationship to one another, rather than as extending indefinitely into the past and into the future, as with a system such as the one used in English. This last principle is of particular importance, for it is this that makes possible the indefinite extension of a limited set of terms to all members of the community.

These principles govern the application of kinship terminology in all Australian Aboriginal societies. They have the important consequence that relatives are thought of as being grouped into sets that, at some level, are equivalent, even where the terminology may draw distinctions. For example, because siblings are equated, although a terminological distinction may exist between my Mother and my Mother's Brother, there is a sense in which they are relatives of the same sort. This can become evident from how the terms are employed. As we shall see, in the application of kin signs, several of these equivalences become apparent.

Australian Aboriginal kinship systems have been classified into a number of different types, largely in terms of the rules governing which categories of kin may marry. We need not be concerned with these differences here. It is sufficient for our purposes to note that the kinship system of the

North Central Desert groups considered here is of the Arandic type. That is, four lines of descent are distinguished, terminologically, in the second ascending generation and preferred marriage, for a man, is with the daughter of one's classificatory mother's mother's brother's daughter and for a woman, with one's classificatory mother's father's sister's daughter's son. The kinship systems of the other groups to be considered later are different. Notice will be taken of this at those points in the discussion where this is needed.

11.2 Kin signs in the North Central Desert

Table 11.1 presents the signs for up to 20 kintypes for each of the seven languages investigated in the North Central Desert. It will be seen that within each language there are only nine or ten distinct signs. Thus many kintypes differentiated in the spoken language are merged in the sign language. It will also be seen that there is considerable similarity among these seven groups in how these kintypes are signed. As we shall see in 11.4, however, when we compare these signs with those for kintypes in other parts of Australia, there are many differences with kin signs outside this area.

We shall begin our discussion with a consideration of Warlpiri kin signs, since our data for this group is the most complete. We shall then compare them with the signs for the equivalent kintypes recorded from the other groups. In the discussion of Warlpiri kin expressions we shall adopt a woman's perspective, except where otherwise indicated. A diagram setting out the Warlpiri kin terminology,[3] from the point of view of each sex, is presented in Fig. 11.1.

11.2.1 Warlpiri kin signs

Siblings. In Warlpiri, there are separate words for Elder Brother, Elder-Sister, Younger Brother and Younger Sister, but only two signs are commonly used. These serve to distinguish Elder Sibling from Younger Sibling. Elder Sibling is signed by patting the ipsilateral thigh with a palm-up B hand (↖B$_{\wedge<}$$^{\vee\times}$'). Younger Sibling is signed by touching the top of the ipsilateral shoulder with the tip of the extended middle finger (⅂mϚ$^{\text{\textdegree}}$ '). Some informants suggest, however, that *kapirdi* 'elder sister' may be signed by patting the side of the left hand with a palm-up 'flat' (B) hand (.B$_{>}$$_{\perp}$\B$_{\wedge<}$$^{\vee\times}$'), thus distinguishing it from *papardi* 'elder brother'. Likewise, some informants also suggest that *kukurnu* 'younger brother' and *ngawurru* 'younger sister' can be distinguished in sign by touching the right or left shoulder, respectively.

Warlpiri Kinship Diagram (from a woman's perspective)

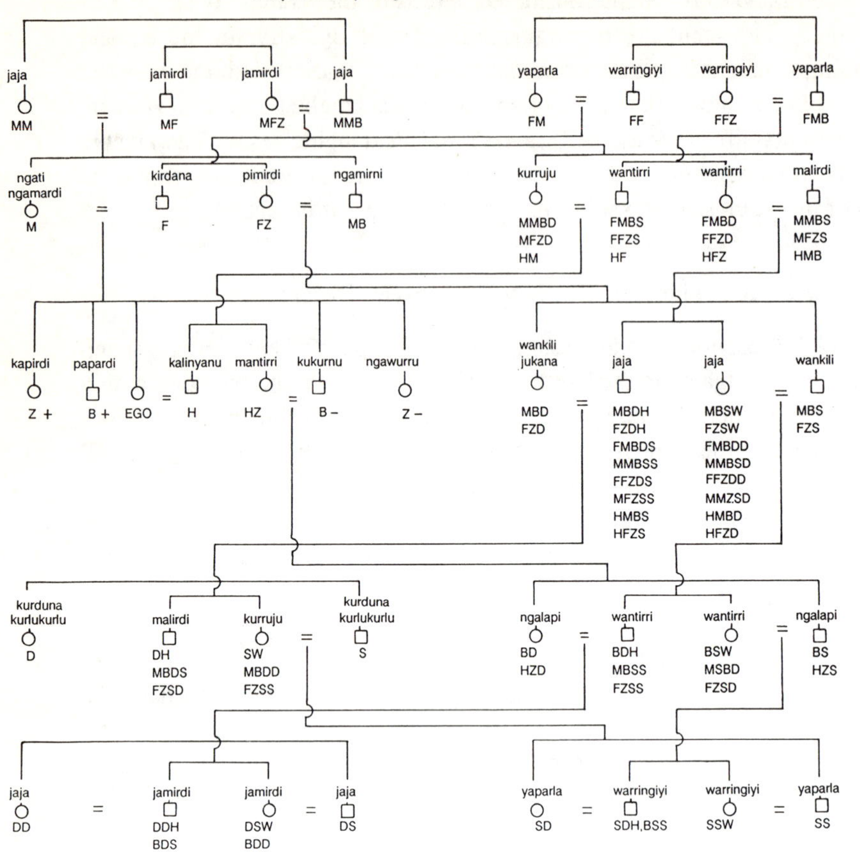

jaja MM
jamirdi MF
jamirdi MFZ
jaja MMB
yaparla FM
warringiyi FF
warringiyi FFZ
yaparla FMB
ngati ngamardi M
kirdana F
pimirdi FZ
ngamirni MB
kurruju MMBD MFZD HM
wantirri FMBS FFZS HF
wantirri FMBD FFZD HFZ
malirdi MMBS MFZS HMB
kapirdi Z +
papardi B +
EGO
kalinyanu H
mantirri HZ
kukurnu B –
ngawurru Z –
wankili jukana MBD FZD
jaja MBDH FZDH FMBDS MMBSS FFZDS MFZSS HMBS HFZS
jaja MBSW FZSW FMBDD MMBSD FFZDD MMZSD HMBD HFZD
wankili MBS FZS
kurduna kurlukurlu D
malirdi DH MBDS FZSD
kurruju SW MBDD FZSS
kurduna kurlukurlu S
ngalapi BD HZD
wantirri BDH MBSS FZSS
wantirri BSW MSBD FZSD
ngalapi BS HZS
jaja DD
jamirdi DDH BDS
jamirdi DSW BDD
jaja DS
yaparla SD
warringiyi SDH,BSS
warringiyi SSW
yaparla SS
key
M mother
F father
Z sister
S son
W wife
= marria
sibling
male
female
I descer
+ elder
– young

Warlpiri Kinship Diagram (from a man's perspective)

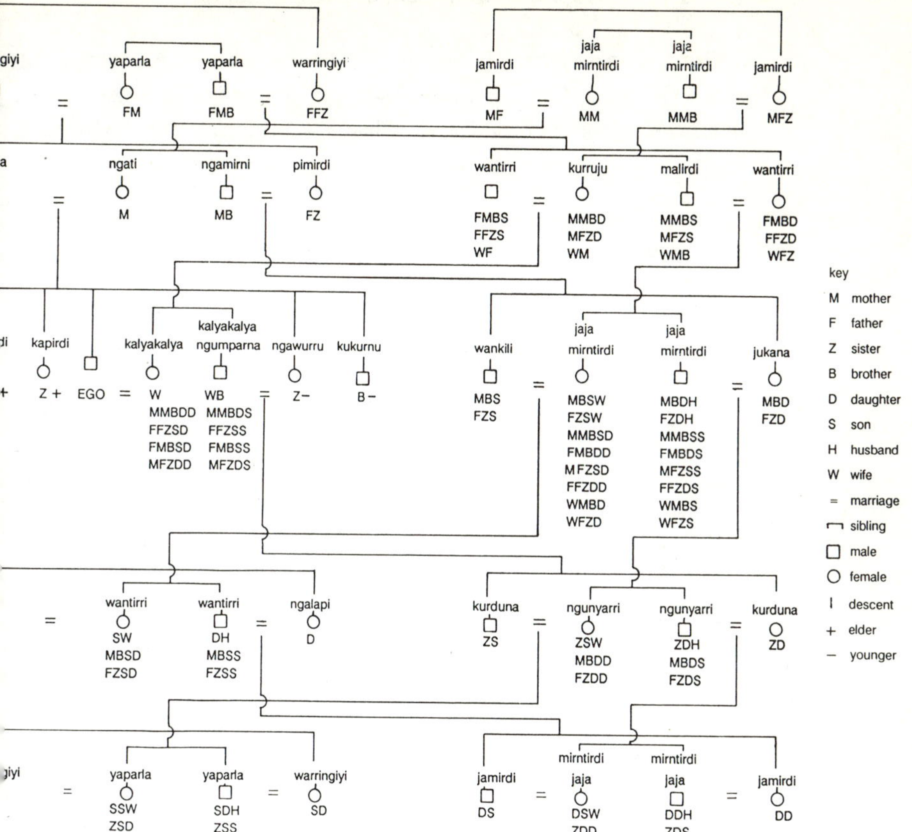

Table 11.1 Kin signs for the North Central Desert sample

Warlpiri (P), Anmatyerre (N), Kaytej (K), Warumungu (R), Warlmanpa (L), Mudbura (M), Djingili (D). F=Father, M=Mother, B=Brother, Z=Sister, + elder, - younger, Wo=Woman, Ma=Man, Ch=Child, D=Daughter, S=Son, H=Husband, W=Wife

Kintype	Groups	Sign	
B+	All	\B∧<×'	Pat thigh[4] with palm up 'flat' hand
	R, alternative	.B>⊥\B∧<×'	Pat left hand with palm-up 'flat' hand
Z+	P	.B>⊥\B∧<×'	
B-, Z-	P, N, K	˥mϚ	Touch ipsilat. shoulder with middle finger
	R, L, M, D	˥B	Touch ipsilat. shoulder with 'flat' hand
FF, SCh	P	⌒ȷ⌈tG∨<+	Forehead or front of contralat. shoulder
	K	˥B∨⊥×'	Knee
	R	˥B	Ipsilat. shoulder
FF only	R	∪B̂∨<σ'	Hand below chin
	M	∪ℓB̂∨<>'	Left hand
	D	]B⊤<~	Hand moved up and down near side of thorax
MM, DCh	P	⌒ȷ⌈B	Use of 'flat' hand in contrast with sign for FF, etc.
	N	⌈B	Front of contralat. shoulder
	K	⌈tG∨<+	
	R, L	˥B	

Table 11.1, continued

MM only	M	⌒B ᵠ	
	D	⟍ℓB‸ ˣ ˈ	Left hand contacts left thigh
DCh only	M	⅂G ᵠ	
MF, etc.	P, L	⟍B˅⊥ ˣ ˈ	Contact is made with palm of hand
	N, K, R, M	⌝B˅⊥	
	D	⟍ℷB‸ ˣ ˈ	Right hand contacts right thigh
FM, etc. FMBSS, etc.			
Spouse	All	.B˅› ⟍B˅⊥ ˣ ˈ	Right hand, palm down, pats back of left hand twice
FM, etc.	M	◡ℷB̂˅ ‹ ˈ , ⌝B˅⊥ ˣ	Move right hand under chin; pat knee with palm of B hand
	D	⌝B˅⊥ ˣ , ⋝B ˣ	Pat knee; contact shin or calf
M, MB	P, N, K	.Y‹‸ ᵃ ˈ	
	R, L, M, D	[ ]‹5 ᵠ	Contact chest
MB	P	[ ]A⊤‹ ˣ	Touch center of chest with fist, palm facing inwards
WoCh MMBD, etc. HM	P, N, R, D	⊔B ᵠ	Contact abdomen
HMB	All	3B̈⊤‸ ⁺	Contact side of face M and D use index finger
FMBS, etc. HF	P, R	[ ]A⊤‹ ˣ	Touch center of chest with fist, palm facing inwards
F, MaCh	All	◡G˅‹ ᴮ ˈ	Touch chin with back of horizontally extended index finger

Father's Father, etc.-Brother's Son's Child. These kintypes are both termed *warringiyi* in Warlpiri, and they are signed in the same way: the side of a version of the index finger hand (in which the thumb is extended and held in contact with the index finger) is brought into contact with the front of the contralateral shoulder (F tG^{+}) or, for some informants, the forehead (⌒tG^{+}).

Mother's Mother, etc.-Daughter's Daughter. These kintypes are both termed *jaja* (although Daughter's Daughter is also called *mintirdi*). They are signed in a way similar to Father's Father, etc., using either contralateral shoulder or forehead as point of contact, except that a B hand is used (all digits extended and held together) and contact is made with the palm of the hand (F $B_{\top<}^{\times}$, ⌒$B_{\top<}^{\times}$).

In terms of signs, thus, it will be seen that the distinction between male and female parallel grandkin is a sub-distinction with the framework of identical Sign Locations. To the extent that this appears to group Parallel Grandkin together, this fits with the grouping of these kintypes suggested for Warlpiri by Scheffler (1978), where he proposes that Parallel Grandkin be included as a sub-class of the SIBLING super-class.

Mother's Father-Mother's Brother's Children. Mother's Father and Mother's Father's Sister are called *jamirdi* and the male children of Mother's Father's Son (i.e. Mother's Brother) are called *wankili*, the female children *jukana.* All these kintypes are signed in the same way: pat ipsilateral thigh with palm of B hand (\\$B_{\vee\perp}^{\vee\times\prime}$).

Father's Mother-Father's Mother's Brother's Son's Children. Father's Mother and Father's Mother's Brother are termed *yaparla* and they are also the paternal grandkin of Ego's spouse and spouse's siblings. Ego's spouse is called *kalinyanu* and his female siblings are termed *mantirri*. Ego's son's children are also termed *yaparla*. All of these kintypes are signed in the same way: the back of the left hand is patted by the palm of the right hand (. $B_{\vee\perp}$ \\$B_{\vee<}^{\vee\times\prime}$). A woman speaking of her spouse's sister may use the term *kakarda*, which also means 'back of neck'. This term is signed by touching the back of the neck with the extended index finger ($\overset{b}{\pi}G^{\text{B}}$).

It will be seen that, just as with Father's Father, etc. and Mother's Mother, etc., so here, despite terminological distinctions between the second ascending generation and the second descending generation in the spoken language in each case, these distinctions are neutralized in sign. As we shall see later (11.6), the kin groupings that are implied by such sign usages correspond to the kin groupings established by the subsection system. Thus, in regard to the sign usages just discussed, the consequence is that for Ego, there is one sign for any kin found in her 'cousin' subsection and another sign for any kin found in her 'spouse' subsection.

Mother, Mother's Brother-Children, Sister's Children. Mother is *ngati* and mother's brother is *ngamirni*. A woman's children are *kurdu* or *kurduna*. In sign, Mother and Mother's Brother can both be signed as .Y$_{<}^{a}$ ' (index and fourth fingers only extended; the hand is partially supinated twice - an unusual kin sign, for it is not body-articulated), although Mother's Brother is also quite often signed by contacting the center of the chest with the fist: [ ]A$_{T<}^{\times}$. A woman's children are signed by touching the abdomen with a flat hand: ⊔B$_{T<}^{\text{?}}$ and are thus distinguished in sign as they are terminologically.

Father, Father's Sister-Brother's Children. Father is *kirda* (also *jaji* and *wapirra*), Father's Sister is *pimirdi* and Brother's Children are *ngalapi*(if male) and *yurntalpa* (if female). Despite these distinctions in the spoken language, in sign all these kintypes are represented in the same way, by tapping the point of the chin with the back of the extended index finger: ᵕG$_{\vee<}^{B}$ ' .

In sign it will be seen, thus, that whereas Ego's mother and Ego's children are kept distinct, Ego's father and her brother's children are united in a single class. This is a reflection of the fact that the children of same sex siblings are classed differently from the children of cross-sexed siblings and that the children of a woman are equivalent to her mother's mother's mother (and MMMB), rather than her mother, whereas the children of a man are equivalent to his father (and father's sister). As we shall see, in the kin categorization established by the subsection system, a man's children are in his father's subsection, whereas a woman's children are in the subsection of her mother's mother's mother.

Husband's Mother, etc.-Child's Spouse. Husband's Mother is termed *kurriji* and Husband's Mother's Brother is termed *malirdi*. Ego's son's wife is *kanajardu* and Ego's daughter's husband is *malirdi*. Ego, as a woman, must avoid her husband's Mother's Brother and her daughter's Husband. All of these kintypes, with one exception, are signed by placing a curved B hand, palm facing backwards, against the cheek: 3B̈$_{T\wedge}^{\times}$.

The exceptional kintype is *pirlipirli*, which is the term used for an actual Mother's Mother's Brother's Daughter (and also for Father's Sister's

Daughter's Son, if a woman is speaking). This is signed in the same way as the 'shoulder' version of *warringiyi* - that is, it is signed by touching the front of the contralateral shoulder with the side of a tG hand.

It is to be noted that an actual Mother's Mother's Brother's Daughter cannot be a Wife's Mother because marriage between the children of actual cross-cousins is not permitted (Meggitt 1962, p. 147) or at least it is quite rare. The person who stands in this relationship actually is thus distinguished by a special term. In view of the fact that marriage does not take place, it is interesting to note that the sign for *pirlipirli* is the same as the sign for Father's Father, etc. Such sign identity suggests that such persons who, because of closeness, cannot be connected by marriage are viewed as if they are 'honorary' members of this kinclass which, on Scheffler's (1978) analysis, is part of the SIBLING superclass. The use of the *warringiyi* sign here suggests, perhaps, that an actual MMBD is treated as a kind of 'sibling'. This in spite of the fact that MMBD and FF are members of adjacent or 'disharmonic' generations.

Husband's Father, etc.-Brother's Child's Spouse. These kintypes are all termed *wantirri* and they are all signed with a fisted hand making contact with center of the chest: []A$_{\top <}^{\times}$. That is, they are all signed in the same way as one of the signs for *ngamirni* 'mother's brother'. *Wantirri* is in fact, for Ego, like *ngamirni* a member of her opposite patrimoiety and of the generation above. At the Section level of kin classification (see below), thus, these kin are equivalent.

To summarize, it will be seen that, in Warlpiri kin signs, within each descent line, Second Ascending and Second Descending generation kin are signed in the same way, and that First Ascending and First Descending generation kin are signed in the same way within the Father's line and within the paternal line of one's Spouse. Within Mother's line, and within the Maternal line of one's spouse, the Ascending Generation kintypes are signed differently from the Descending Generation kintypes, however. Within Ego's own generation, separate signs for Elder and Younger Siblings are used and it is only here that we observe some discrimination in sign by sex.

As we will note again later, the kin classes thus implied by these sign usages are the same as the kin classes established by the subsection system except that, in sign, within Ego's own subsection, own generation and second (harmonic) generations are discriminated.

11.2.2 Comparisons with other North Central Desert groups

Siblings. In the other six groups, Siblings are signed in the same way as in Warlpiri, with only minor variation. That is, Elder Sibling is signed by patting the ipsilateral thigh with a palm-up B hand, and Younger Sibling is signed by contacting the top of the ipsilateral shoulder. In Djingili, however, for Elder Sibling, contact is made with the upper thigh, as close to the groin as possible. This ensures that the sign will be distinct from the signs for Mother's Mother, etc. and Mother's Father, etc. which are signed in the same way, but with point of contact on thigh near the knee. In regard to the Younger Sibling signs it will be noted that in Anmatyerre and Kaytej, as in Warlpiri, contact with the shoulder is made with the tip of the middle index finger. In the remaining groups contact is made with the fingertips of a B hand.

We recorded no sex differentiation in Elder Sibling signs in any group except Warlpiri. However, although, in Anmatyerre, there is but one term for Younger Sibling, Anmatyerre informants suggested that Younger Sister is indicated by touching the right shoulder, Younger Brother by touching the left (the reverse of Warlpiri). Male Mudbura informants also suggested that the sex of Younger Siblings could be distinguished in sign (in Mudbura there are separate terms for Younger Brother and Younger Sister), but for them the right shoulder should be used for Younger Brother, the left for Younger Sister. The Mudbura women I checked this with did not maintain this distinction.

Father's Father, etc.-Brother's Son's Child. We have recorded signs for both kintypes in this class for Anmatyerre, Kaytej and Warumungu, and for Father's Father only in Mudbura and Djingili. In Anmatyerre, for both kintypes, a B hand, palm down, contacts the knee. In Kaytej, a B hand touches the forehead. In Warumungu a B hand contacts the ipsilateral shoulder - the sign is thus identical to Warumungu Younger Sibling. However, in Warumungu we also recorded a separate sign for Father's Father, in which a bent B hand is held just below the chin, and moved outwards twice by forearm pronation: ᵕB̂ᵥ‹ ᵟ '. This sign was also recorded for Father's Father in Mudbura, where it was done with the left hand to distinguish it from the sign for Father's Mother which is the same, but done with the right hand. In Djingili, Father's Father is signed with a related form, by moving a B hand up and down in relation to the side of the body.

Mother's Mother, etc.-Daughter's Daughter. We have recorded signs for both of these kintypes in Kaytej, Warumungu and Mudbura. In Kaytej the front of the contralateral shoulder is touched with the side of a tG hand, in

Warumungu both kintypes are again signed in the same way as Younger Sibling, by touching the top of the ipsilateral shoulder. In Mudbura, Mother's Mother is signed by touching the forehead, Daughter's Daughter is signed by touching the shoulder with the extended index finger. In Djingili, as already mentioned, Mother's Mother is signed by patting the left ipsilateral thigh with a palm-up B hand.

Mother's Father, etc.-Mother's Brother's Children. These kintypes are not differentiated in any of the groups and they are all signed in the same way as in Warlpiri: the lower thigh (knee, in Anmatyerre, Kaytej and Mudbura) is patted with a palm-down B hand. In Djingili Mother's Father is signed in this way using the right hand and thigh.

Father's Mother, etc.-Father's Mother's Brother's Son's Children, Spouse. In all six groups both kintypes are signed in the same way and they are all signed as in Warlpiri: pat the back of the left hand twice with the palm of the right.

Mother, Mother's Brother-Children, Sister's Children. Mother and Mother's Brother are signed as in Warlpiri *ngati* 'mother' in Anmatyerre and Kaytej, although in Anmatyerre a sign in which contact is made with the ipsilateral breast was also given (ℲꟷtO ✻^ '). Woman's Child is signed in all groups, as in Warlpiri, by touching the abdomen.

Father, Father's Sister-Brother's Children. In all groups both of these kintypes are signed as in Warlpiri: the back of the extended index finger taps the point of the chin.

Daughter's Husband, etc. In all groups this kintype is signed by touching the cheek, either with a curved B hand, as in Warlpiri or, in Mudbura and Djingili, by touching the cheek with the index finger. This is also used for Husband's Mother and Son's Wife in Warlpiri, but in Warumungu, where this kintype is called *ngunyarri*, a different sign is used, in which a hand with thumb extended and abducted and index finger flexed as a hook ($X_{\square}$) is moved forward from a point of contact against the ribs.

Husband's Father, etc.-Brother's Child's Spouse. Besides Warlpiri, a sign for these kintypes has been recorded only for Warumungu and Djingili. In Warumungu two signs are used, one in which the center of the chest is tapped with an A hand - identical to the sign for Mother's Brother in

Warlpiri - and another in which the hand is supinated rapidly twice, held with index finger and thumb are extended (an L hand). This sign is used for *pirlipirli*, which is any Mother's Mother's Mother (or MMM Brother, hence classificatory husband's father). The previous sign is used for *lamparra*, which is a term used by a woman when speaking of her actual husband's father.

To summarize, with a few exceptions, it will be seen that the groupings of kintypes effected by signs in the other six groups examined are the same as those observed in Warlpiri. Thus, within each descent line, Second Ascending and Second Descending generation kin are signed in the same way, although in Warumungu a separate sign for Father's Father was recorded. In all groups Mother, etc. is signed separately from Woman's Child, but Father and man's Child are not distinguished in sign. It may be noted that this reflects the fact that Father and Father's Child constitute a symmetrical kin relationship, because they belong to the same patriline, whereas Mother and Mother's Child are not symmetric, since Mother's patriline is different from that of her Child. Spouse's mother, etc., is signed in all groups in the same way. In all groups there are separate signs for Elder Sibling and Younger Sibling.

In Warumungu, Father's Father, etc. and Mother's Mother, etc. are both signed in the same way as Younger Sibling and perhaps this offers further support to Scheffler's (1978) analysis which places these Grandkin within a SIBLING superclass. Djingili is exceptional in two ways. Except for a right-left difference, Mother's Mother and Mother's Father are signed in the same way and Father's Mother and Spouse, etc. are signed differently. This distinction is given in Mudbura sign, as well.

It will be seen that, for the most part, kin signs throughout the North Central Desert are highly similar. Almost all of them involve making contact with a part of the body and, in most cases, equivalent kintypes are signed by touching the same or very similar parts of the body. Thus we have thigh for Older Sibling, shoulder for Younger Sibling, knee or lower thigh for Cross-Cousin, hand on hand for Spouse, chest for Mother and Mother's Brother, abdomen for Child of Woman, point of chin for Father and Child of Man and cheek for the kin who are Spouse's Mother, etc.

Warlpiri, Anmatyerre and Kaytej are exceptional in that for Mother, and sometimes also for Mother's Brother, a non-body contact sign is used. We also noted special non-body contact signs for Mother's Mother's Mother etc. in Warumungu and for Father's Father in Warumungu, Mudbura and Djingili.

11.3 Signs and special features of kin terms

Besides the basic terminology referred to above, all of these languages have additional kin terms with more specialized contexts of use. Furthermore, there are special features to kin term morphology and grammar that mark it out as a special development within the lexicon of these languages (Laughren 1982). We have collected sign data for some of these expressions and this shows that within the sign language kin signs may also show some special features. Some of these have already been mentioned briefly. Thus, in Chapter 8, in the discussion of the signing of pronouns, we described how, in Kaytej, the form of plural pronouns depends upon the kin relations of the persons referred to. We saw that this was partly reflected in sign. In this section, with special reference to Warlpiri, we shall mention examples of suffixes that are special to kin terminology and show how they receive specialized representation in sign.

In Warlpiri there is a special suffix that is used with kin terms to refer to two or more individuals in terms of the kin relationship in which they stand to one another. This has already been mentioned briefly in Chapter 7. Thus *kirda* is 'father' but *kirda-rlangu* refers to a father-child pair. *Ngati* is 'mother' but *ngama-rlangu* refers to a mother-child pair. The suffix *-rlangu* in its kinship usage has been referred to as the 'gether suffix'. Suffixes with similar usage occur in Warumungu: *-nyini* and *-kurangi*. These special suffixes appear to be rendered in sign in a special way, which is similar in both Warlpiri and Warumungu.

It will be recalled from Chapter 8 that suffixes with an 'associative' meaning are all signed in the same way. However, the 'gether suffix' has a special form. It is done by sweeping the hand away from the signer while it is in contact with the other hand (or thigh, in encumbered or 'tired' signing). Thus, to sign *kirda-rlangu* the signer first touches her chin with her index finger, but as she does so, her left hand is already lifted in readiness and, immediately after touching the chin, the hand is moved forward, brushing over the raised left hand as it does so. For *ngama-rlangu* we observe something similar. To sign *ngati*, it will be recalled, the signer uses a Ψ hand in which all digits but the index finger and the fourth finger are flexed to the palm. This hand is held up and the forearm twice rapidly supinated: . Ψ º ' . To sign *ngama-rlangu*, however, the hand in Ψ form is supinated but then it is moved away from the signer and as this is done it brushes over the left hand which is raised in readiness.

In both of these examples it will be seen that the performance of a sign for the *-rlangu* suffix influences the way the sign for the kin term is performed. KIRDA is modified so that the chin is touched but once, not tapped twice. NGATI is modified so that the hand is supinated but once and immediately moved distally. In signing *jukarlangu* 'cousins together' this modification goes further and in this case there is no separate part to the sign that can be identified as the suffix sign. To sign *jukana* 'cousin' the signer pats her thigh with a palm-down B hand. To sign *jukarlangu* the palm-down B hand is swept forward and back on the thigh: ⟍B$_{\vee\perp}{}^{*\text{I}}$.

This modification to the performance of a sign, with the same semantic implication, is also found in signs for expressions which refer to a married couple, husband and wife considered together as a unit. In Warlpiri, the term *kalinja* has this meaning and this can be signed by modifying the SPOUSE sign so that the active hand sweeps back and forth over the back of the other hand, rather than patting it.[5] It appears, thus, that we may identify a 'gether inflection' in Warlpiri (and Warumungu) sign which consists in a back-and-forth sweep of the hand over either the other hand or the thigh.

A somewhat similar kind of inflection has been recorded for some of the plural kin terms in Anmatyerre. Thus in this language *matye* is 'mother' and *ampwekwe* is 'child of woman', but *mernenge-therre* is 'mother and daughter together' (*-therre* is the dual suffix). Whereas *matye* is signed as . Ɏ$^{\underline{\text{a}}}$ ', just as *ngati* is signed in Warlpiri, *mernenge-therre* is signed as . Ɏ$^{\text{a}\sigma}$⁞U$_{<\perp}{}^{>}$. Here, it will be seen that, in addition to the dual suffix sign being added, the sign for 'mother' has been modified so that the hand is now twisted back and forth, not rapidly supinated twice. In other Anmatyerre dual or plural kin signs we find the back-and-forth sweep with body contact, as in the signs for expressions meaning several siblings together. 'Sibling' may be signed by patting the thigh, but in these plural signs the hand sweeps back and forth on the thigh, as with the examples for Warlpiri.

These inflections are about the only examples we have observed in these Aboriginal sign languages where the inflection is accomplished by modifying the sign's movement pattern rather than by adding a second sign as if it were a spoken form. This kind of inflection is highly characteristic of primary sign languages, but it seems quite rare in the Aboriginal sign languages considered here. It appears to occur only in the signs for the dual and plural kin terms.

Warlpiri also has three special possessive suffixes that occur only on kin terms. These are *-na*, *-puraji* and *-nyanu*. *-na* replaces *ngaju-nyangu* 'First Person singular-Possessive' and *-puraji* replaces *nyuntu-nyangu* 'you sg.-Possessive' on kin terms, as in *Yalumpu karli ngaju-ku kirda-na-kirlangu* - 'That boomerang belongs to my father', or *Yalumpu karli nyuntu-ku ngamirni-puraji-kirlangu* - 'That boomerang belongs to your uncle.' *-nyanu* is an anaphoric possessive, as in *Kurdu ka-rla yulami ngati-nyanu-ku* - 'The child is crying for his mother.' A separate sign for *-na* has not been recorded.

However, *-puraji* and *-nyanu* are signed in a way that is similar to the associative suffix sign we have previously described, but a G handshape is used instead of a B handshape.

There are also special words that serve to indicate whether someone is of an ascending generation (any ascending generation) or of one's own generation: *palangu* and *purdangka*. These may be used to refer to one's parents, mother's brother, and the like, or to a sibling, in a more general way. The first is signed in a way that is very similar to NGATI 'mother'. The second is signed by moving to the right a B hand, held up with palm facing away from the signer - a nice representation of a laterally extending horizontal 'band'.

Finally, a note should be added here on 'triangular' kin terms. The kin terminology in all of the NCD languages is enriched by a large number of terms which indicate, at one and the same time, the relationship between the speaker and the person being referred to, and the relationship of that person to the addressee. Thus we noted in Chapter 10 (note 11) that Winnie, when quoting the words of the aunt of the promised wife as she spoke to the future husband used the term *ngangkiri*. This word means 'spouse', and in using it she makes reference to the young man's wife. However, it also indicates that the wife so referred to is, in this case, the niece (i.e. Ego's brother's daughter, where Ego is a woman) of the speaker. As we noted, in this case Winnie, as she speaks, also signs, but she uses here the same sign as she would use for any other 'spouse' term. In the case of terms for 'spouse', it would seem, at least for Winnie, the 'triangular' terms are not distinguished. This is not always so, however, for, as already noted, we have collected examples of distinct signs for 'triangular' terms in Warumungu. At present, our data are not well enough developed on this point to merit further discussion. Suffice it to say, however, that there may be greater complexity in kin signs than we have been able to indicate here and that this area of NCD signing would be well worth further study.

11.4 Kin signs from elsewhere in Australia

In this section we shall consider such data on kin signs as is available from other parts of Australia. Included here are the five kin signs described by Roth (1897) for several groups in Northwest Central Queensland, and data from the Northern Aranda of the Central Desert (Strehlow 1914), the Ngatajara of the Western Desert (Miller 1971), the Worora of the north west coast of the Kimberley (Love 1941), two groups in Arnhem Land (Warner 1937, Williams 1981), and from the Yir Yoront (Sharp 1933-1936, Sutton and Walsh 1979), the Wikmunkan (Kilham et al. 1986), the Windawinda (Hale 1960) of

Western Cape York and the Darambul centered on Rockhampton on the Queensland coast on the Tropic of Capricorn (Roth 1898). In all cases, these signs were collected incidentally to the investigator's main interest and in most cases very little information is given about how they were collected. Roth (1897, 1898) provides drawings and Love (1941) and Williams (1981) provide photographs. In other cases we must rely upon verbal descriptions only, which are not always easy to interpret. For the Wikmunkan the only information provided in the source that was available to us is simply a statement as to the body part associated with each kintype.

Table 11.2 shows the body parts used in kin signs for these groups for up to twenty kintypes. Inspection will show that many of the signs employ body parts that are not used for any signs in the North Central Desert areas and that, further, where the same body parts are used, they are often used quite differently.

Siblings. Three groups show some similarity to the North Central Desert sibling signs: the Wikmunkanin west Cape York and the Darambul on the eastern side touch the thigh to sign Older Sibling (any Sibling for the Darambul); and the northwest Queensland groups, who tap the shoulder. The Lardiil use shoulder, as in the North Central Desert, but here it is used to signify Elder Sibling, not Younger. Otherwise, the most frequently used body part to signify Sibling is the calf of the leg. The Aranda of the central desert and the Windawinda in northern Western Cape York signify Sibling by touching the back of the neck. In the published records available, no reference is made to sex distinctions in these sibling signs, or indeed for signs for any other kin types. Warren Shapiro (personal communication, 1986), however, states that the use of the left side to indicate female and right side to indicate male is widespread in Arnhem Land.

Grandkin, etc. With the possible exception of the Wikmunkan and the Darambul, none of the signs for Grandkin overlap with the North Central Desert signs for kintypes in this class. In Aranda all grandkin are signed in the same way, by touching the abdomen, with the exception of Mother's Mother which, in Strehlow's description (as translated by C.Chewings), is signed as follows: "Rest 3, 4 and 5 on the ball of the thumb, 1 under the extended index finger, and tap yourself a few times along the right eyebrow, from left to right." The handshape described here is apparently the same as the tG handshape used for Mother's Mother among the Kaytej and the Sign Location is in the forehead area, which is used for this kintype for both Mother's Mother and Father's Father by the Warlpiri, among others in the North Central

Table 11.2 Body parts touched in Non-NCD kin signs

Aranda (A), Ngatajara (NG), Worora (WR), Gupupuyngu (G), Lardiil (LD),Yir Yoront (Y), Wikmunkan (WM), Windawinda (WW), Pitta Pitta, etc. (PP),Wanamarra, etc. (WN), Darambul (DB)

Kintype	AR	NG	WR	GP	LD	YY	WM	WW	PP	WA	DB
BZ+	⫪	〉	〉	〉	┐	〉	＼	⫪	┐		＼
BZ-	⫪	〉	〉	〉	〉	〉	⫪	⫪	┐		＼
FF	⊔		〉	ʌ	]		⌒	ʌ			⌒
S Ch			〉	ʌ							
MM	⌒	Ч＼	┓	BAK	▣		⌒	ʌ			
D Ch		Ч＼	┓								
FM	⊔			◡		┐		ʌ			
MF	⊔		◡＼	◡		┐		ʌ			⌒
M	▣	▣	BUT	▣		▣		▣	▣		▣
MB	▣	[ ]	⫪					▣			
Wo Ch	▣	▣	⊔	◡		▣		▣			⊔
F	◡┐	△	┐	┐	◡	ɿ	┐	┌ ꭗ	◡		┐
Ma Ch	◡	┐	┐	┐	◡	ɿ	┐	┌ ꭗ			GEN
MBC	▣						＼				
FZC	▣			┓	]		＼				
Sp	ɿ	GRO	Ч	Ч	＼	＼	ʌ		BUT	＼	BUT
Sp B,Z		BUT									
WF	ɿ	⌒, [ ]									
WM	ɿ		┬┌ ꭗB				BUT		HAIR		⌒

Explanation: ʌ top of head, HAIR hair, ⌒ forehead, △ nose, ◡ chin, ⫪ back of neck, ┌ contralat. shoulder, ┐ ipsilat. shoulder, ɿ upper arm, ⊔ abdomen,] side, [ ] chest, ▣ ipsilat. breast, Ч hip, ＼ thigh, Ч＼ join of hip and thigh, ┓ knee, 〉 calf or shin, GRO groin, BUT buttocks, GEN genitals.

Desert. In the Windawinda all grandkin are also signed in the same way, by patting the top of the head.

In the other groups, as far as the data available go, there appears to be some differentiation between the different types of grandkin and considerable diversity in the body parts touched. Thus, for Father's Father and Son's Son, in Worora one touches the calf (thus merging these kintypes with Siblings); in Gupapuyngu and Windawinda one pats the top of the head; in Lardiil one touches the side of the thorax; in Wikmunkan the 'associated body part' is 'head'. For Mother's Mother and Daughter's Daughter in Ngatajara a point on the thigh just below the hip is touched, in Worora the knee is touched and the back in Gupapuyngu. Father's Mother and Mother's Father are signed in the same way in Gupapuyngu by touching the chin, in Yir Yoront by touching the shoulder and among the Darambul by touching the forehead with "the length of the thumb". Mother's Father is signed in Worora by touching the underside of the thigh.

Mother, Mother's Brother, Woman's Child. There is much less diversity in the body part touched for these kintypes. The breast is touched in most cases. Thus the breast is grasped or touched to sign Mother, in Aranda, Ngatajara, Gupapuyngu, Yir Yoront, Windawinda, Northwest Queensland and Darambul and the same is done for Mother's Brother in Aranda and Windawinda. For Woman's Child the breast is touched or grasped in Ngatajara, Worora (if a woman is speaking of her own children), Yir Yoront and Windawinda. Abdomen is touched for Woman's Child in Worora and Darambul, and the chin is touched in Gupapuyngu (thus, in this group, merging Woman's Child with Father's Mother and Mother's Father).

Father, Father's Sister, Man's Child. As we saw, in the North Central Desert all kintypes in this set were signed in the same way throughout, by tapping the chin with the back of the extended index finger. This sign does not occur in the non-North Central Desert sample, and although the chin is used in Aranda, Lardiil and North-West-Central Queensland, the way in which it is contacted is different. In Aranda according to Strehlow, it is stroked downward between thumb and forefinger for Father and Father's Sister but the beard is grasped for Man's Child. In Lardiil the chin is stroked downwards for all kintypes in this class in a way that is similar to the Aranda. In North-West- Central Queensland a fisted hand is held in contact with the chin and rotated back and forth. In the Ngatajara, Worora, Gupapuyngu and Wikmunkan the ipsilateral shoulder is contacted for all kintypes in this class but among the Darambul this sign is for Father only. Father's children, in this group, are signed by touching the genitals. In Yir Yoront and Windawinda, as far as we can gather from the descriptions, the contralateral shoulder or upper arm is contacted.

Mother's Brother's Children, Father's Sister's Children. For these, in Aranda, the breast is grasped (just as for Mother, etc.), in Gupapuyngu and Wikmunkan the knee or thigh is contacted (similar to the North Central Desert), in Lardiil the side of the thorax is contacted, apparently just as is done for Father's Father. Again, there is no overlap with the North Central Desert.

Spouse, etc. In the North Central Desert, as we saw, all kin grouped with Spouse are referred to by patting the back of the left hand with the right. This sign does not occur elsewhere, although there are signs from other groups that may be related to it. Thus in Aranda the upper arm is clasped, and for the Ngatajara, Miller reports a special sign for Wife only: grab beard, then grab wrist. The second part of this sign is perhaps related to the Aranda sign and can be seen as similar to the North Central Desert signs for Spouse, as will be discussed further below.

Other signs reported for Spouse or Spouse's siblings are quite different. Roth (1897, p. 82) reports that for the Pitta Pitta and related groups in northwest Queensland the buttock is slapped for Spouse, while among the Woonamurra (Wanamarra) and Goa (Koa), which are further to the east, the "middle or outer half of the thigh" is tapped. In Ngatajara the buttock is touched for Spouse's siblings and the groin is touched for Spouse, in addition to the special sign for Wife mentioned above used by these people; in Worora and Gupapuyngu the hip is touched for Spouse and Spouse's siblings; among the Lardiil and Yir Yoront the thigh is grasped; among the Wikmunkan the top of the head is patted; among the Darambul the hand is placed on the buttock.

Spouse's Father, Mother. For Wife's Father, in Aranda the upper arm is stroked with the finger tips of a spread hand, and in Ngatajara the center of the chest or forehead is touched. There may be a relationship between the first of the Ngatajara signs and the North Central Desert sign for Wife's Father, since chest is used in both cases, although in the North Central Desert a fist handshape is used, not an extended index finger. For Wife's Mother in Aranda the sign is the same as for Wife's Father (both are clearly related to the Aranda sign for Spouse). In Worora one touches under the contralateral arm, in Yir Yoront the buttock is touched and among the Windawinda the signer grabs a lock of hair. Roth reports for the northwest Queensland groups that "mother-in-law" is signed by tapping the forehead with the "closed hand and thumb". According to his drawing this would be $^{\frown}A_{\vee <}^{\times \prime}$ in our notation.

Overall, then, the kin signs within this sample show little similarity with those of the North Central Desert. This is true even for the Aranda and the Ngatajara, which are the closest, geographically and culturally. It is notable, also, that some of the body parts employed in these groups are not used at all or used very rarely in the North Central Desert area. Thus kin signs in the non-North Central Desert group include the use of the calf of the leg, the buttocks, the back of the thigh, and the back. All of these body parts are out of immediate reach and are outside the signing space of the North Central Desert signs. In the other areas, as far as we can tell (except for western Cape York), sign languages were developed to a much lesser extent and used much less than within the North Central Desert. The use of body locations that require more than minimal effort to reach within these areas is perhaps a reflection of this. As we saw in Chapter 6, if signs are used extensively, they tend to become modified in such a way that they can be performed within a fairly small spatial area, extending from the forehead to the upper thighs. We would expect locations such as the back, the buttock or the lower leg not to be used in highly developed sign languages.

There is also considerable diversity within the non-North Central Desert sample, although there are also some surprising similarities. Table 11.3 shows a matrix in which the proportion of signs using the same body part for a given kintype is entered for each group in comparison with every other group (Roth's North-West-Central Queensland data not included since he reports too few kin signs).

Table 11.3 Proportion of same body parts used in kin signs in eleven non-NCD groups

AR Aranda, NG Ngatajara, WR Worora, GP Gupupuyngu, LD Lardiil, YY Yir Yoront, WM Wikmunkan, WW Windawinda, DB Darambul

	AR	NG	WR	GP	LD	YY	WM	WW	DB	M
AR		10	0	9	25	10	22	36	13	16
NG	10		30	75	17	57	33	25	29	35
WR	0	30		40	16	25	17	0	25	19
GP	9	75	40		13	30	25	20	22	29
LD	25	17	16	13		40	0	0	0	14
YY	10	57	25	30	40		0	20	13	24
WM	22	33	17	25	0	0		16	50	20
WW	36	25	0	20	0	20	16		13	16
DB	13	29	25	22	0	13	50	13		21

The two groups showing the least similarity with the others are the Lardiil and the Aranda. The Lardiil, it may be noted, inhabit Mornington Island off the coast of the Gulf of Carpentaria and are thus geographically and culturally somewhat removed from their immediate neighbors. It is surprising, however, that the Aranda show so little similarity to the other groups. The Aranda, like the Windawinda of Western Cape York, do use back of neck for Siblings, and they also use breast for Mother, etc. (a usage one might expect separate groups would arrive at independently) and chin for Father, etc., but otherwise they show no overlap with any other group. It is surprising that they share so little with the Ngatajara and the North Central Desert groups.

Second, it will be noted that the Ngatajara, the Worora, the Gupapuyngu and the Yir Yoront show quite a high degree of similarity with one another. In particular, it is striking that these four groups all use the calf for Sibling and that three of them use ipsilateral shoulder for Father, etc., and hip or buttock for Spouse (Spouse's Siblings among the Ngatajara). As we will suggest in the next chapter, this similarity in seemingly quite arbitrary signs between such geographically diverse groups, and the dissimilarity with what is found in the North Central Desert, where there is comparative uniformity, has implications for understanding the origin and the time-depth of these sign languages.

11.5 Body parts and kinship

As we have noted, the most outstanding feature of kinship signs in all the parts of Australia where these have been reported is that almost all of them consist of pointing to some part of the body. This suggests that in Australian Aboriginal thought, kin relations are somehow identified with parts of the body. Such a notion is also indicated in other ways. The belief that telepathic knowledge of a relative may be indicated by the twitching or throbbing of a body part has been reported from several different parts of Australia, and in several languages terms for body parts are also incorporated into expressions for kin.

Elkin (1937) describes the widespread Aboriginal belief that one could know that a certain relative was thinking of one or that a certain relative was coming to pay one a visit if one felt a muscular twitch or throbbing in a specific body part. He lists the body parts that may be affected in this way and the particular relatives that are indicated by such twitching or throbbing, for two groups in the Kimberley area, one group at Hall's Creek, and one group on the Western Desert coast at La Grange. Douglas (1977) has also listed the meanings attributed to the twitching of body parts for Western Desert groups that would include the Ngatajara.

There is some degree of correlation between the body part that twitches and the body part that is touched, in sign, to symbolize a kin relation. Thus, as we saw, for the Worora, the calf is touched to indicate Sibling, the shoulder is touched to indicate Father, etc., and the abdomen is touched to indicate Woman's Child. According to Elkin, among the Ngarinyin, a Kimberley group adjacent to the Worora, a twitching in the calf indicates a Sibling is approaching or thinking of one, a twitching of the upper arm indicates Father or Son, and a twitching in the abdomen indicates Sister's Child. However, a twitching in the lower arm indicates Wife, but among the Worora, this is indicated by touching the hip. A twitching in the armpit can indicate Mother or Mother's Brother where, among the Worora, this relationship is indicated by touching the buttock. For the Western Desert groups mentioned by Elkin (the Djaru at Hall's Creek and the Karadjeri on the desert coast at La Grange) a twitch in the shoulder indicates Father or Son, a twitch in the buttock indicates Wife and a twitch in the calf indicates Sibling. All of these but the one for Wife correspond to the body parts that are touched to indicate these relations in signing among the Ngatajara.

Douglas's (1977) report also partially correlates with the Ngatajara kin signs as given by Miller. As we saw, calf is touched for Sibling, shoulder is touched for Father and Man's Child, groin is touched for Wife and the center of the chest is pointed to for Mother's Brother. Douglas shows calf as the site of twitching for elder sibling, groin or thigh for Wife, upper arm for Parent (which is perhaps close to shoulder), a throbbing heart for Mother's Brother and a whistling in the ears for Elder Brother.

Warlpiri also a believe that muscle twitches can announce the approach of a relative; however the locations of the twitches reported do not correlate with kin signs. Thus, if the left arm twitches, it means a junior relation is approaching and if a right arm twitches, a senior relation is coming. There are a number of kin terms in Warlpiri that incorporate body part terms, and for some of these there is a relationship with sign language. Thus a junior male sibling may be addressed as *jija-warnu* 'shoulder-belong' and a person may be addressed as *miyalu-warnu* 'stomach-belong' by anyone who is related to them as *ngati* 'mother' or *ngamirni* 'mother's brother'. It will be recalled that in Warlpiri sign the shoulder is touched for a junior Sibling and the abdomen is touched for a Woman's Child (i.e., child referred to by Mother or Mother's Brother). In Warlpiri, also, a maternal parent may be referred to as *lampurnu* 'breast', and while the breast is not touched to indicate Mother, Mother's Brother can be signed by tapping the center of the chest with a fisted hand, and this may well be a displacement from touching the breast. A term based on *kakarda* 'back of neck' is used by women speakers to refer to Husband's Sister and this kintype may be signed by touching the back of the neck, as mentioned above. Other kin terms in Warlpiri also make reference to body parts, but in these cases a direct connection with sign language is not so certain. The term *kirda* which is used for Father can also mean 'penis' or 'tail'.

It is also possible that the Eastern Warlpiri term *miimi* 'son-in-law (for girl), mother-in-law (for boy), is related to the term *mimi* 'forehead'. For Father, as we have seen, the chin is touched. It is possible that this location is a 'displaced' penis - displaced upwards, into signing space. The Sign Location for Mother-in-Law/Son-in-Law is the cheek, which is almost certainly a derivation by displacement from a face-covering gesture. Such a gesture could well involve placing the hand against the forehead to cover the eyes. Such location displacements certainly occur in the development of signs, as we saw in Chapter 6, and these interpretations are fully consistent with this.[6]

Heath (1982), writing of kin terminology in Dhuwal, a language of the Yuulngu group in Northeast Arnhem Land, describes how body part expressions may be employed as a supplement to certain kin expressions to make their reference more specific. Most kin categories are associated with a body part and a body part expression may be used in conjunction with a basic kin term as a way of specifying an actual relative as opposed to a more distant, classificatory relative. Thus the term *ba:pa* is used to refer to Father, etc., but when used in conjunction with the expression *mu:n-buy* 'of the shoulder', it specifies one's actual father. Likewise, to specify an actual Sibling is to combine one of the basic Sibling terms with the expression *rapari-puy* 'of the calf, of the leg'. Body part expressions may also be used to refer to relatives who must be avoided. Wife's Mother, for instance, may not be referred to directly, but may be referred to as being *bun gumu-wuy* 'of the knee'. In some contexts a speaker may not even say this, but slap his knee instead. All of the body parts referred to, we may add, are also the body parts pointed to in signing these kin relations among the Gupapuyngu, a related group. However, Heath gives many other body part expressions that are used in this way that do not always correlate with those used in kin signs.

In his discussion of the use of body parts in referring to kin, Heath points out that this usage does not arise because the human body is regarded as an analogical model of family structure. As he puts it: "It must be emphasized that Dhuwal body-part expressions do not constitute analogical mappings from one structured system (kinship) onto another (the body). Instead we have a *metonymic* system in which particular body part terms are paired on an individual basis with particular kin categories..." (Heath 1982, note 10, pp. 62-63). Heath suggests, largely on the basis of explanations offered by the Dhuwal themselves, that the basis of this pairing derives from an encoding of patterns of behavior by which interaction with a given relative is characterized. That is, "the body part expressions ... allude to stereotyped *behaviours* rather than to abstract genealogical relations as such. In particular they refer to precisely those behaviours, involving physical contact (or avoidance), which evoke the richest, most intimate affective relationships" (op. cit., p. 58, author's emphasis). Thus a Son or Father is referred to as 'of the shoulder' because of the practice of a father carrying his child on his shoulder. 'Of the belly' for Mother or Mother's Brother is a reference to the carrying of the child in the womb. 'Of the calf' for sibling appears to be associated with the practice of the elder sisters of a boy, at circumcision, gashing their shins and wailing in sympathy.

This approach to an explanation for the association of body parts with kintypes can also be applied in accounting for kin signs in other parts of Australia and several other writers have alluded to it. Roth (1897) suggested that the tapping of the shoulder for a brother or a sister "is expressive of the fact that they have both been carried on the same spot" (op. cit. p. 82) and he suggests that to slap the buttock to signify Spouse, as is done among the Pitta Pitta and related groups, is to "conjure up the idea of both mates sitting down, &c., in the same hut" (loc. cit.).

Some related observations have been made by McConnell (1934). In writing of the Wikmunkan she describes hand positions adopted by women when they dance during a certain stage of a male initiation ceremony. During the dance, different women adopt different hand positions according to their relationship with the initiate. Thus, a woman who is a Sister to the initiate will place her hand on the back of her neck, while a woman who is a Father's Sister places her hand on her shoulder. These positions are said to derive from the positions of the hands when carrying a child, and McConnell shows photographs which provide evidence for this. Small babies are supported in the back by a hand placed behind the neck. Older children are steadied on the shoulder by a hand placed on their knees. Finally, the calf is painted with a special pattern if the woman is a sister to the boy as a way of emphasizing that her legs must have strength to permit her to carry her small brother.

Strehlow (1978 [1915]) reports that the Aranda sign for Spouse is one in which the contralateral upper arm is grasped. This would appear to be derived from the action of 'grabbing the arm' referred to by Roheim (1974), in which a man grabs the upper arm or wrist of a woman he intends to take sexually (also reported for the Warlpiri). This is also a gesture by which a man may claim his promised wife. The expression of 'grabbing the arm' is used in this way in several of the Aranda texts Roheim provides in translation (e.g. *op. cit.*, p. 143). Grabbing the upper arm is employed among these groups, as among the Warlpiri, as an expression of a man's claim to his promised wife, for when a man claims her, she may express reluctance at leaving her parents to follow her husband and hence must be dragged away. It is also, according to Roheim, the gesture by which the concept of *mbanja*, or forcible intercourse, is expressed. Roheim writes (*op.cit.*, p. 228) that the term *mbanja* is used to refer to the first intercourse after marriage which, he says, is usually accompanied by force. He continues: "*Mbanja* cannot be translated easily into any European language. The Central Australians use the gesture of a man holding the left wrist of a girl with his right hand to illustrate the term."

In Warlpiri, it may be noted, stroking or patting the upper arm is a sign that refers to a man and woman going off together for sexual purposes, and among the Mudbura, patting the upper arm is a sign for *lukuwurru* 'married camp'. We may also recall, in this connection, the special compound sign for Wife that Miller reported, in which, in Part II of the sign, the right hand grasps the left wrist. We suggest that the North Central Desert sign for Spouse, etc., in which the palm of the right hand pats the back of the left hand is derived from this gesture of grabbing the upper arm or wrist. Once transformed into a mere stroking or patting of the arm or wrist, as in the North Central Desert (so we suggest), it can become generalized to serve for all kin in the Spouse category.

Where the groin or thigh is touched for Spouse (as among the Ngatajara in the Western Desert or the Wanamara and Koa of northwest Queensland) this relation perhaps is conceptualized in terms of sexual intercourse (which Roth suggests). Alternatively, this sign may be connected to a betrothal ceremony in which the man who has been chosen as promised husband sits down and the girl promised him (who may be only a few years old) is placed upon his thigh by her parents. This ceremony has been described for the Warlpiri (Meggitt 1962) and may well be practised more widely. Where the buttock is touched, as among other groups in northwest Queensland or the Darambul at Rockhampton, if Roth's suggestion is accepted, the Spouse relationship is here conceptualized in terms of sitting closely together.

Finally, the sign for Mother-in-Law and Son-in-Law in the North Central Desert, in which the side of a B hand, palm facing inwards, is placed against the cheek, is almost certainly derived from a gesture of covering the eyes so as not to look, for these relatives must avoid one another.

In Aboriginal thinking, then, part of the way in which kin relations are conceptualized is in terms of modes of bodily relationship, either derived from patterns of interaction, as in modes of carrying or avoidance, or from physiological relationships, as with the relationship of child to mother's womb or breast. These modes of bodily relationship are referred to in signing by pointing to the body part involved. In this way, the use of body parts in the signing of kin terms is to be accounted for.

11.6 Signs for kin groupings

As we have seen, in Aboriginal society kin are regarded as being grouped into sets or categories of various kinds. One category already referred to is that of generation level. Two generation levels are recognized, which alternate, as we have seen. A distinction is drawn between one's own generation, and the generation of one's parents. One's children are classed in one's parents' generation, but their children, and the parents of one's parents (the grandkin, that is) are classed in one's own generation.

A second category, or kin grouping, is the patriline. This is a grouping of persons who recognize descent through the same Father's Father or his siblings. Typically, several patrilines are associated through more remote patrilineal connections to constitute a division of the society, or *patrimoiety,* the men of which all marry women from an 'opposite' patrimoiety. This means that in one's own patrimoiety are all those who trace descent patrilineally, while in the opposite patrimoiety are all those who trace relationships through the patriline of spouse's father.

Terms used for these divisions are reciprocal. That is, Ego-1 refers to his own generation and his own patrimoiety by one set of terms, and the opposing sets by another set of terms. Ego-2, however, if a member of the opposed sets, from Ego-1's point of view, nevertheless uses the same set of terms, but in reverse. Such terms, like kin terms, are egocentric, therefore. Signs for some of these terms have been obtained in Warlpiri. As we saw in 11.3 there are signs for the generational terms *purdangka* 'of one's own generation' and *palangu* 'of an ascending generation'. We also have recorded signs for the two patrimoiety terms *kirda* 'own patrimoiety' and *kurdungurlu* 'opposite patrimoiety'.

The division of kin into alternate generations and 'opposing' patrimoieties results in a fourfold set of categories of kin. For a given Ego, within his own category are found those of his own generation and his own patrimoiety; there is another category that arises by grouping together relatives of one's own generation but of opposite patrimoiety; two additional categories are likewise produced by recognizing the same divisions in the opposite generation. In some societies adjacent to those considered in the North Central Desert (for example, the Alyawara), these four categories, known technically as sections, are recognized and named, but in the North Central Desert societies these four categories are further subdivided to produce an eightfold division into subsections. This is brought about by dividing each section into two in such a way that Cross-Cousins are found in a different subsection from the children of one's parents' Cross-Cousins of the opposite sex. This means that any person will find that the group from which his or her spouse is (ideally) to be drawn belongs to a different subsection from that of his or her Cross-Cousins. The invention and rapid adoption of the subsection system in societies where Cross-Cousin marriage is prohibited is thought to have come about in part because subsections make it easier for any person to recognize those categories of kin to which actual or potential potential marriage partners belong (Elkin 1979, p. 131). These eight divisions have received absolute, rather than reciprocal, names. They are related by marriage, matrilineal and patrilineal descent as shown in Fig. 11.2.

The subsection system provides for anyone a kind of summary of kin relations that allows a quick calculation of the sort of specific relationship anyone might have with any other. This becomes especially useful when, as at large ritual gatherings, groups from different widely separated locations come together. If there is agreement as to subsection membership it is an easy matter to reckon kinship, without having to trace out specific lineages. For instance, if I am known as Jampijinpa, then anyone I meet who is also of that subsection I can reckon as 'brother' if male or 'sister' if female. If they are much older than I, however, I may count them as Father's Father, if much younger, as Grandson. Anyone who is Jangala or Nangala is reckoned like a 'son' or 'daughter' but anyone who is Japanangka or Napanangka is reckoned like a child of my sister and is a potential spouse of my wife's mother and wife's mother's brother, and so on.

The subsection system appears to have arisen in the northwest of Australia (in the southeastern Kimberley, according to Von Brandenstein 1982 or on the Victoria River, according to McConvell 1985) and spread fairly rapidly southwards and eastwards. It is estimated to have been adopted by societies in the North Central Desert area not more than a century ago and it was still spreading to such Western Desert groups as the Pintupi as late as about 1932 (Myers 1986, p. 183). The names for subsections, though they show some variation from one group to another, can easily be shown to be cognate throughout the areas where the system is used. It is on the basis of such linguistic comparisons, in fact, that a large part of the evidence concerning the nature of the spread of the system is derived.

Signs for subsections have been reported by Strehlow (1978 [1915]) and Spencer and Gillen (1927) for the Aranda. In our own work we have recorded signs for subsections from Warlpiri and Kaytej informants. For Warumungu and Warlmanpa, signs for subsections were said not to be used, but a way of referring to individuals by subsection name was demonstrated. Signs for subsections were not known to our Anmatyerre informants, nor to our Mudbura or Djingili informants.

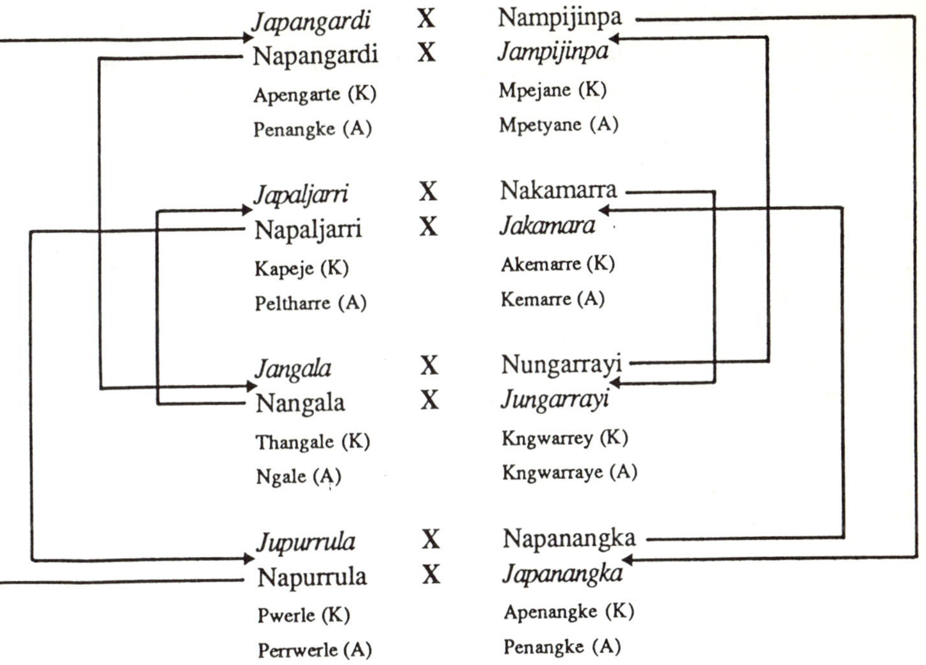

Arrows show maternal descent, X shows preferred marriage partner. Names in italics are male. Kaytej (K) and Aranda (A) equivalents given in small type.

Fig. 11.2 Subsections and their interrelations

For the Aranda, Strehlow reports four signs, one for each 'patricouple' - i.e., the subsections that are linked by Father-Son descent. The signs given are also the signs for the plants and animals that are associated as totems for each of these patricouples.[7] Thus Bangata (Pengarte)[8] and Panaka (Penangke) are signed in the same way as *eritja* 'eagle', Paltara (Peltharre) and Knuraia (Kngwarraye) are signed in the same way as *tjilpa* 'spotted wild cat', Ngala (Ngale) and Mbitjana (Mpetyane) are signed in the same way as *agia* 'Wild plum, *Canthium latifolium* ',[9] and Purula (Perrwerle) and Kamara

(Kemarre) are signed in the same way as *putaia* ' little wallaby' (probably *Bettongia lesueur*, Burrowing Bettong).

Spencer and Gillen (1927), also writing of the Aranda, report eight signs, one for each subsection. The signs they report are quite different from those given by Strehlow and we strongly suspect that they are, in fact, kin signs and not signs for subsections. In our own experience, when someone is asked to give a sign for a subsection they usually first respond in egocentric terms and give the kin sign that would be appropriate, given their own subsection and their relationship to someone in the subsection inquired about. Thus Nangala would give the sign for Father if asked for the sign for Jampijinpa, the sign for Daughter if asked for the sign for Napaljarri or the sign for Spouse if asked for the sign for Jungarrayi, and so on. This is doubtless because it is normal to think of specific individuals who thus have a specific kin relation to one, rather than to think in terms of whole categories of people. Spencer, in re-presenting this set of Aranda signs in his *Wanderings in Wild Australia,* states that the signs were shown to him "by an old Purula man amongst the Arunta ..." (i.e. Aranda) (Spencer 1928, Vol. 1, p. 437). Although the eight signs reported are not all the same as the kin signs Strehlow gives, they are similar. The sign given by Spencer and Gillen for Panunga (Penangke) "Both arms extended, the left wrist grasped by the right hand" - is clearly similar to the Spouse sign given by Strehlow and, for a Purula (Perrwerle) man, Penangke is the subsection from which he would draw his spouse. Likewise, the sign given by Spencer and Gillen for Bultara (Peltharre) - "the right arm is bent so that the hand clasps the right breast" - is almost the same as Strehlow's sign for Mother and for a Pulura (Perrwerle) man Bultara (Peltharre) would be his Mother's subsection. Spencer and Gillen do not include any kin signs in their list separate from these, so we cannot be completely certain of this interpretation, but it seems highly likely.

From our Warlpiri and Kaytej informants four subsection signs covering all eight subsections were given. The signs and the subsections they stand for in each group are shown below.

Subsection signs for Warlpiri and Kaytej

Warlpiri

.A$_{\top}$>\Y$_{<\perp}$$^{\times}$'	J/Nampijinpa and J/Nakamarra
.A$_{\top}$>\5$_{\vee\perp}$$^{\times}$'	J/Napangardi and J/Napaljarri

Each subsection within a pair belongs to the same matrimoiety. In each, the subsections are related by matrilineal descent as grandkin to one another.

$\frown 0_{\top\wedge}^{\times\perp}$	J/Nangala and J/Nungarrayi
$.\,m\varsigma x_{\mathsf{I}\top\wedge}^{\perp\blacksquare\mathsf{I}}$	Ju/Napurrula and J/Napanangka

Each subsection within a pair belongs to a different matrimoiety. In each the subsections are related as marriage reciprocals.

Kaytej

$.\,A_{\top>}\backslash B5_{\vee\perp}^{\times\mathsf{I}}$	Mpejane and Thangale
$\frown 0_{\top\wedge}^{\times\perp}$	Akemarre and Pwerle

Each subsection within a pair belongs to a different matrimoiety. In each the subsections are related as Father to Son.

$\sqsupset G_{\top<}^{\ast\wedge ?}$	Apenangke and Kngwarrey
$.\,A_{>\perp}\backslash \Psi_{\top<}^{\times\mathsf{I}}$	Kapetye and Apengarte

Each subsection within these pairs belongs to the same matrimoiety. In each they are related as grandkin.

It will be seen, in the first place, that these signs are quite unlike kin signs, for they do not consist of pointing to a body part, as is typical of kin signs (and characteristic of the signs given for subsections by Spencer and Gillen, it might be added). Second, the subsection signs given by Warlpiri informants, although similar in all but one instance to those given by Kaytej informants, 'pair up' the subsections differently in each case.

For the Warlpiri, it will be seen that two of the pairs of subsections that share signs in common are the marriage reciprocals. The two other pairs are linked as Maternal Grandkin. For the Kaytej, of the pairs created by shared signs, two pairs are 'patricouples' (subsections linked by paternal descent) and the other two are again linked as Maternal Grandkin, but different Maternal Grandkin pairs than are given in Warlpiri. These pairings of subsections are quite unexpected and puzzling. At the present time, no satisfactory explanation can be offered for them.

As to the origin of the subsection signs, as far as we can tell they appear to be arbitrary. They have nothing in common with the subsection signs described by Strehlow nor are they similar to signs for animals or plants in Warlpiri or Kaytej or associated sign languages as far as we know. They cannot be interpreted as totemic signs, that is. Two of the signs in Warlpiri are the same as signs used elsewhere. Thus the sign given for J/Napaljarri-J/Napangardi is the same as the sign used for *yirdi* 'name' and *rdangkarlpa* 'short' and the sign given for J/Napanangka-Ju/Nappurula is the same as a sign for *warlka* 'lie', but there seems little doubt that these similarities are coincidental and are not connected in any way to anything that may be associated with the subsections. Von Brandenstein (1982) has argued that the names for the subsections derive from terms for physique and temperament and he suggests that there is a tendency for subsection members to be thought of as sharing certain character traits. As far as we have been able to determine, the signs used for the subsections either by the Warlpiri or the Kaytej are not related to signs for human attributes or character traits and even where, by some stretch, they might be seen to be so, they are not applied to the subsections in a way that would suggest any relationship with von Brandenstein's observations.

In Warlmanpa and Warumungu the concept of subsection itself (*puntu* in Warlmanpa) can be referred to in sign: a downward pointing index finger touches the front of the shoulders, first left, then right (ꟳ ꓶ G $_{>\vee}^{+\quad+}$). To refer to someone by their subsection name, however, no signs for individual subsections are used. Instead, a single sign is used which appears to mean something like 'I now refer to someone in subsection name mode'. In this sign the hand is held with palm up and all fingers flexed to the palm but the index finger is flexed so that its tip is placed in contact with the tip of the thumb. The hand is then lowered by a movement of wrist extension (. ъO$_{\wedge\perp}^{\circlearrowleft}$).

If it is necessary to specify the subsection being referred to, the signer then points to any individual who is visible, using a special handshape. By doing so, the signer indicates that the person pointed to has the same subsection as the individual referred to by the subsection sign just described. In pointing in this manner, the hand is held so that all the fingers are extended at their first joints, but flexed so that their tips meet in contact with the side of the thumb (a handshape notated as ₓO). If it should happen that there is no one available who can be pointed to who has the appropriate subsection, then someone who is of the maternal subsection of the person referred to may be pointed to in this manner, but in this case the point is immediately followed by

B^6, the ASSOCIATIVE (described in 8.1.2). This means "the person I refer to is of the subsection of this person's maternal child" - i.e. child of the person pointed to, if a woman, child of person's sister, if the person pointed to is a man.

This method of referring to people by subsection may seem somewhat surprising. A proper understanding of it must turn upon an understanding of the significance of referring to someone by subsection. A very common way of referring to someone is by kin term, for personal names are generally considered too intimate a mode of reference in most situations.[10] However, such a mode of reference, being egocentric, carries with it implications for the speaker's (or signer's) mode of relationship with that person. For others, the mode of relationship may be different. For example, one person's Mother may well be another's Sister, and another's Granddaughter, and so on. subsection names are sociocentric, however. No matter what a person's kin relationship may be, he will be addressed by the same subsection name. Yet such names are not like surnames or titles. They serve to refer to someone in such a way as to imply the full range of relationships that his position in the subsection system determines for him. As Myers (1986, p. 184) has put it: "Subsection terms ... are part of a structure that does implicitly express a series of relations between social categories. Because these relations are understood by speakers, when a subsection term is applied to an individual, its use specifies this person's expected relationships to individuals of other social categories - what can be anticipated in the sense of kinship obligations." To use a subsection term, thus, is like using a kinship term that is generalized for all present, rather than one that is specific to the speaker and the person referred to. Given this special significance of using these terms, it is understandable that a way of using them in sign language should also have been developed.

11.7 Conclusion

In this Chapter we have surveyed kin signs both within the data from the North Central Desert we ourselves have gathered and from corpora provided by other investigators for other parts of Australia. We find that almost all kin signs in all parts of Australia are body-part pointing signs. This is accounted for by the fact that an important aspect of the Aboriginal conception of kin relationships is in terms of the different ways in which different kin are related to in interaction. These different patterns of behavior are symbolized by the part of the body most directly involved in the interaction. This is shown by the use of body-part terms to refer to kin relations in several Aboriginal languages and in the widespread Aboriginal belief that a twitching or throbbing in a specific part of the body can provide foreknowledge of a specific relative's movements or circumstance. The body-part indexing nature of kin signs provides further evidence for this view of kin relations.

For the Warlpiri, for which our data are most complete, we saw that there are fewer kin signs than there are basic kin terms. We examined the way in which kin terms are applied in referring to more than one kintype. We found that the groupings of kintypes that resulted are an Elder Sibling and a Younger Sibling group, four distinct Grandkin groupings, and a Father-Child of Man group. Mother, Mother's Brother and Child of Woman are all signed separately, as is Daughter's Husband-Wife's Mother. These groupings correspond closely with the kin groupings established by the subsections. All kin within each of the subsections are referred to by the same sign, except within Ego's own subsection. Here three signs are used, one for Elder Sibling, one for Younger Sibling and one for kin equivalent to Father's Father/Son's Son. Mother's Brother may also be distinguished in sign from Mother, but this is not always done.

The groupings of kin effected by signs in the other North Central Desert groups examined, insofar as our data permitted us to establish them, largely followed this pattern. However, in Warumungu a separate sign for Father's Father was recorded although, at the same time, a single sign could also be used to refer to both Parallel Grandkin classes and to Younger Sibling.

We then provided a few examples, mainly from Warlpiri, which showed that just as in the spoken language the kin lexicon shows certain special morphological characteristics, so there are certain special features to the morphology of kin signs. In particular, in looking at signs for dual and plural kin expressions, we found a mode of sign inflection not otherwise much used in these Aboriginal sign languages, although it is widely used in primary sign languages.

We then compared the kin signs found in the North Central Desert groups to those reported for groups elsewhere in Australia by other investigators. It became apparent from this that the North Central Desert kin signs show a high degree of uniformity, but are substantially different from kin signs in other places. That the same signs for Sibling, Father-Son and Spouse are used throughout the Western Desert, the Kimberley region and Arnhem Land, but that these are quite different from what is found in the North Central Desert, supports the view, to be developed in the next chapter, that the North Central Desert sign languages are all of one 'family' and probably arose much later than the sign systems in use elsewhere in Australia.

Finally, we examined signs for kinship groupings, in particular signs for subsections. We noted that these signs are quite different from kin signs: none of them are body-part pointing signs. We saw that, for the three groups for which subsection signs have been recorded (the Aranda, as reported by Strehlow, the Warlpiri and the Kaytej), there are only four signs, so that the subsections are grouped into pairs. In Strehlow's data these pairs are according to 'patricouples' and the signs are the signs for totemic animals or plants. For the Warlpiri and the Kaytej the pairings are different and do not show the sort of consistency that might have been expected. No satisfactory explanation can be offered for this. The signs used for subsections by the Warlpiri and Kaytej are very similar; however they appear to be arbitrary and cannot be associated with signs for totemic animals or plants, or with anything else. The Warumungu were found to have a method of indicating in sign that someone was being referred to by his subsection, even though no signs for the separate subsections were reported.

Kin signs in Australian Aboriginal sign languages display some unique features. A study of them throws some further light on Aboriginal concepts of kin relations. It also provides further insight into the semantic relationships that obtain between the terms within this domain.

Notes

[1]For general introductions to Australian kinship see Elkin (1979) or Berndt and Berndt (1981). For more detailed discussion see Scheffler (1978). A very clear elementary introduction is Wafer (1982). See also Appendix 2 of Bell (1983) for a more readily available exposition based on Wafer. For kinship among the Warlpiri, see Meggitt (1962). An excellent recent discussion of the operation of kinship in an Australian society quite close in culture to those considered here is to be found in Myers (1986).

[2]Thus there can be considerable variation in the ways in which people who stand in the same kin relationship behave toward one another, depending upon the closeness of the relationship. For example, a man does not avoid all of his mothers-in-law, but only those who are actually in such a relationship. With those more distant to him he may just show some degree of circumspection in his behavior. People may sometimes emphasize their kin relations with another, sometimes pay it less attention, according to how this may advantage them in interaction.

[3]The Warlpiri kin terminology is that generally in use at Yuendumu. There are some variations. Eastern Warlpiri, for instance, uses but one term for Junior Siblings, and there are other differences. These will not be noted here, however.

[4]For Djingili point of contact on thigh is near groin.

[5] In some versions of this sign the back and forth sweeping movement and contact is retained but the active hand assumes a shape in which only the middle finger is extended.

[6]Data on Warlpiri in this paragraph taken from Hale and Laughren (1983 in progress), from Nash (personal communication 1986) and from Françoise Dussart (Personal Communication 1987).

[7]Each patricouple may have several different animals or plants associated with it in this way. According to Strehlow's account, the sign selected is the sign for 'totem place' where many members of the patricouple were said once to have lived.

[8]I give Strehlow's own spellings followed by contemporary renderings in brackets. The names of the animals he lists as being signed are given in Strehlow's spellings only.

[9]This plant is also associated with this patricouple among the Warlpiri.

[10]Signs for Aboriginal and European personal names have been recorded for Warlpiri. European personal names are in general use nowadays and within many contexts they are used in the European fashion, without the reticence that attaches to the use of Aboriginal personal names.

12 Comparing Aboriginal sign languages

12.0 Introduction

In previous Chapters, although differences between the sign languages of the North Central Desert have been noticed, the main emphasis has been upon those features they all share in common. In this Chapter these differences become the focus of attention. We shall look at how the North Central Desert sign languages vary among themselves and we shall also look at differences between them and other sign languages, as described from elsewhere in Aboriginal Australia.

We shall begin by considering differences between the North Central Desert sign languages that can be attributed to differences between the spoken languages associated with them. As we have seen, to a large degree, these sign languages may be thought of as gestural representations of the meaning units that correspond to the morphemes of the spoken languages of their users. Differences between them, due to differences in the associated spoken languages, are to be expected, therefore. We shall provide examples that show that differences in signs can arise where an expression for a given meaning differs in morphological structure between languages, where there are differences in idiom or fixed collocations, or where there are differences in the semantic distinctions drawn by the vocabularies of the different languages. We shall also consider to what extent there is an overall relationship between spoken language vocabulary and sign vocabulary. Here we shall find that there is some tendency for signs to be the same between two groups when, for a given meaning, the words are the same or related, and for signs to be different where the words are different.

The main factor governing sign language differences within the North Central Desert, however, appears to be degree of geographical separation, not spoken language differences. This will be seen from a study of the extent to which sign vocabularies of the different groups overlap. Samples of signs drawn from each of the seven sign languages studied will be compared in terms of their features within each of their aspects, so that a quantitative measure of the degree to which sign vocabularies differ may be arrived at. We shall then consider how such factors as spoken vocabulary differences and geographical separation are associated with this measure. This will lead to a consideration of the principles that govern the sharing of signs between groups which, as we shall see, appear to differ somewhat from those that govern the sharing of items from spoken vocabulary.

Signs from the North Central Desert will also be compared with signs reported by other workers from elsewhere. North Central Desert signs will be compared with signs described from the Western Desert by Miller (1970), the Northern Aranda by Strehlow (1978 [1915]) and from North-West-Central Queensland by Roth (1897). Comparisons using much smaller samples are also possible with signs described from Arnhem Land (Williams 1981), Mornington Island (Woolston and Trezise 1966), the Gulf coast (Black 1975) and from several different locations in the Cape York Peninsula (Roth 1908, Hale 1960). The results of these comparisons are interpreted to suggest the presence of a number of sign language areas. It will be proposed that the highly elaborated sign languages found in the North Central Desert are a distinct and possibly relatively recent development.

12.1 Sign and spoken language differences within the North Central Desert

As we saw in Chapters 7 and 8, in many respects the North Central Desert sign languages can be described as systems in which the meaning units of the spoken languages associated with them are represented. Thus we saw how sign organization often matches spoken language morphology: signs which have a reduplicate organization are often glossed by words which are reduplicate forms, and compound signs are often glossed by compound words or by words composed of a root and a suffix. Examination of such associations makes it clear that in many cases the reduplicate or compound signs are related to unitary or simple signs in a way that closely parallels the relationship between the corresponding reduplicate or compound spoken forms with unitary or simple words.

This relationship between sign organization and word structure is the source of one overall difference between these sign languages that has already been noted. Thus, as we saw in Chapter 5 (Table 5.1), Warlpiri and Warlmanpa sign language contain a far higher proportion of reduplicate and compound signs than does the sign language of Anmatyerre or Kaytej. This is a direct reflection of the fact that reduplication and compounding are not as widespread in spoken Anmatyerre and Kaytej as they are in Warlpiri and Warlmanpa. In consequence we may expect that where, in one language, a compound expression is used for a given meaning whereas, in another, the same meaning is expressed with a unitary spoken expression, the corresponding signs for these meanings will, likewise, differ in their organization. As we shall see below, this does indeed occur.

12.1.1 Differences in sign and differences in language structure

There are at least three ways in which differences between sign languages can be attributed to lexical and morphological differences between the associated spoken languages. Differences between languages in lexical distinctions, idioms and compounds can all give rise to differences in sign, as will now be exemplified.

1. Languages can differ in the semantic distinctions established by their vocabularies and this can lead to a corresponding difference in sign. For example, in Warlpiri the verb *nga-rni* is used to refer to any sort of ingestion, whether this be eating or drinking. Correspondingly, there is but one sign for 'eat' and 'drink'. Other languages in our sample, however, distinguish 'eat' and 'drink' by different words and in these we find a sign for each also.[1] In all these languages, the sign used for 'eat' is the same: a 'claw' hand is 'trembled', usually held with palm up or towards signer, . ᶜ5$_{\wedge\perp}{}^{tr}$. In the sign for 'drink' in Anmatyerre, Kaytej Warumungu and Warlmanpa a flat hand, fingers bent at the A joints, is held just below the chin and the forearm is supinated twice: ᵕB̂$_{\vee<}{}^{\sigma\,'}$. In Mudbura 'drink' is signed by approaching the mouth with a tapered O hand: ▽ tO$_{\vee\top}{}^{><}$.

Likewise, in Warlpiri and Warumungu there are separate words for 'digging stick' and 'crowbar': *kana* and *kurupa* for both languages, respectively. In Warlmanpa and Mudbura, however, the word *kapirli* (*kapili* in Mudbura) is used for both types of implements. Correspondingly, we find that both Warlpiri and Warumungu have separate signs for 'digging stick' and 'crowbar', but Warlmanpa and Mudbura do not.

Other examples may be recalled from the discussion of pronouns in Chapter 8. Thus we saw that in Warlpiri, in which an independent third person spoken form need not be used, a fixed sign form for the third person pronoun is absent. In the other languages, on the other hand, where an independent third person spoken form is always used, sign equivalents for it are found. We also noted how, in Kaytej, different first person dual and plural pronouns are used according to the kin relationship of the persons being referred to. We found that this was partially reflected in sign. For the first person dual two signs are used, according to whether or not the two persons referred to are of the same patrimoiety and generation. Such differences in pronouns are not found in the other languages examined and, correspondingly, there are no such differences in sign.

2. For some meanings we find languages differ in the idioms used to express them. These differences may be reflected in the associated sign languages. For example, as was mentioned in Chapter 7, in Anmatyerre'lightning' may be referred to as *kwatyepwerre* which is literally 'water tail (or penis)' and it is signed, accordingly, as a compound of the signs KWATYE and PWERRE. In other languages 'lightning' is referred to by a single word (different in each case). The corresponding sign in these languages is highly similar: a rapid downward movement of a downward pointing middle or index finger.

Likewise, 'scorpion' in Warlpiri is *kana-parnta* (sometimes *karlangu-jarra-parnta*) 'digging stick-having'. It is signed as a compound sign KANA 'digging stick' followed by B^{6}, the Associative Suffix sign. In Warumungu 'scorpion' is *jalangartata* 'mouth crab' and it is signed as a compound of the signs JALA 'mouth' and NGARTATA 'crab'.

As a third example, consider expressions for 'sad'. In Warlpiri 'sad' can be referred to by *luyurrpu* and this is signed by a unitary sign. In Warumungu 'sad' is the compound *munkku wangu,*[2] literally 'stomach bad'. It is signed by first touching the abdomen, followed by the sign WANGU 'bad'. In Warlmanpa 'sad' is expressed in yet another way as *yuru-kanyanu* or 'face-other'. Correspondingly it is signed as a compound of YURU 'face' and -KANYANU 'other'.

Differences in sign that are related to idiomatic differences between spoken languages that arise in connection with expressions for modern concepts were exemplified earlier in 7.4. Some modern concepts are expressed by the use of expressions already in the language and we saw how, in such cases, signs for these concepts often reflected this with the result that where languages differ in the type of expression employed, there are corresponding differences in sign. Thus, 'policeman' in Warumungu is often termed *kili-partta* 'danger-having'. It is signed as a compound of KILI 'danger' and -PARTTA 'having'. In Anmatyerre 'policeman' is referred to as *ewrrkwetye* 'grabber',[3] It is signed by crossing the wrists one upon the other as if they were tied together. As we also noted in 7.4, whereas in Warlmanpa, Warumungu and Mudburathe word for 'rock' is extended to mean 'money' and it is signed accordingly, in Warlpiri 'money' is referred to with English derived words, either *maniyi* or *tala* (from 'dollar').[4] The sign for it in this case is to describe a circle with the index finger of the right hand, often in relation to the palm of the left hand.

3. Languages may differ in whether they use a compound or a simple expression for a given meaning. The signs for these meanings may differ in a corresponding way. We saw an instance of this in the 'lightning' example given above. The Anmatyerre expression for this is a compound, and so is the sign. In the other languages, where the expression is unitary the sign is unitary. In Kaytej, where the word for lightning is the reduplicate form *aweylewelye* , the sign also has a reduplicate form. Likewise, as we noted from the discussion of 'sad', Warlpiri uses a unitary sign and a unitary expression, where Warumungu and Warlmanpa both have compound expressions and compound signs to match.

This kind of difference may be further illustrated by comparing verb forms between languages where, in one case, the verb has a preverb-verb structure and in the other case the verb is a root form only. Thus in Warumungu we have *pakurr ja-nta* 'descend, get off (e.g., get off a horse)' where, in Warlpiri, for the same meaning we have the root verb *jiti-mi*. Correspondingly, in Warumungu the sign is a compound. In Part I, the hand, with only index and fourth fingers extended, is moved downwards. Part II is the sign for *ja-nta* 'stand': . Ч$_{\vee\perp}^{\vee}$ʔ⁾ ⁞ tG$_{\top\wedge}^{\perp\blacksquare}$. In Warlpiri *jiti-mi* is signed with a unitary form in which a closed hand is lowered rapidly and, at the same time, the first and second fingers are opened to form a V hand: . 0$_{\top\vee}^{\vee}$[U]. Again, in Warlmanpa *ngapi nya-* 'to smell (tr.)' is a compound of a preverb and the root verb *nya-* 'see, perceive'. This is signed as a compound in which a V hand, digits curved, is directed toward the nose, followed by the sign for *nya-* 'see': △Ü$_{\top\wedge}^{\top}$ ⁞ U$_{\vee\perp}$. The Warlpiri expression for this is *parnti nya-nyi* and it is signed in the same way. In the other languages considered, besides these two, 'smell, tr.' is expressed by a root verb and the sign is also unitary. A third example: 'look after, e.g. look after a child' is a compound in Warlpiri, *jina marda-rni* , and it is signed as a compound in which Part I is a special form and Part II is the sign for the root verb *marda-rni* 'have, keep, possess'. In Anmatyerre and Katej this meaning is expressed with a root verb, and in each case the sign is unitary in organization.

4. In comparing meanings in which, in each case, a compound expression is used, we sometimes find that, although the preverb is the same, the root verb is different. In such cases we again find a corresponding difference in how the meaning is signed. Thus in Warumungu we have *pina ja-* 'to hear', which is a compound of a word for 'ear' and the root verb 'to stand'. This is signed as a compound in which in Part I the ear is pointed to, while Part II is the sign JANTA 'stand'. In Warlpiri the same meaning is also expressed as a compound, *purda nya-nyi*. This is composed of a word for 'ear' and the verb *nya-nyi* 'see, perceive'. Again we have a compound sign in which, in Part I, the ear is pointed to, but in Part II we have the sign NYANYI 'see'.

As another example, consider the activity of tracking an animal. In Anmatyerre we have *impatye are-me* 'to track, follow footprints' which is literally 'foot see', and this is how it is signed. In Warlpiri there are two expressions: *wirli nya-nyi* and *yitaki ma-ni*. The first of these is parallel to the Anmatyerre expression, for 'foot' in Warlpiri is *wirliya* so this compound could be glossed as 'foot see'. It is signed as a compound, in which Part II is the sign NYANYI 'see', but the sign that corresponds to the preverb here is a special kind of downward pointing movement (. Ⴤ$_{<\perp}$$^{\sigma\vee\}}$). The second of these expressions involves a special preverb, followed by the root verb *ma-ni* 'get, cause'. The sign is also a compound in which Part I is a special form and Part II is the sign for the root verb *ma-ni*.

12.1.2 Sign differences and word differences

In the foregoing section we have seen how differences between languages, in respect to the morphological structure of expressions for the same meaning, can result in differences in how that meaning is rendered in sign. Here we shall ask if differences in spoken language vocabulary make a difference in their own right. Between languages, where words are the same or closely similar, do we tend to find the same or similar signs, and do we tend to find different signs where the words are different?

Examples can readily be found which illustrate both possibilities. Thus the sign for 'initiated man' is the same in all the languages considered, but the word for this meaning is different in each language. On the other hand, 'water' is *ngapa* in both Warlpiri and Warumungu,[5] but the signs are not the same. However, if there is a relationship between the spoken language vocabulary and the sign vocabulary, we would expect to find that the number of instances in which the same meaning is expressed by the same word, in any two languages, will include more instances where the signs are shared, than where they are different. Similarly, we may expect that where signs differ for a given meaning, words will differ more often than where signs are the same. This can be the case, regardless of the actual proportion of signs or words shared. To examine this, an analysis is required in which the relationship between sign and word for each meaning taken separately can be compared between each of the groups investigated.

To undertake this a selection was made of meanings for which we have signed expressions and corresponding spoken expressions in each of the seven groups studied. For each meaning the signs and the words recorded from the seven groups were compared. Signs were recorded as the same only when they were identical in all three Aspects of Sign Actor, Sign Location and Sign Action. Words recorded as the same included all those that are obviously similar, including words that are the same, once allowances are made for systematic sound differences between the Arandic languages in the sample (Anmatyerre and Kaytej) and the others.[6] We also counted as the same all instances where the same English word occurred, regardless of how it had been transformed when assimilated to the phonology of a given language. From these comparisons, a table was constructed from which it was possible to count the number of meanings for which any two groups were found to share the same sign but differed in word, differed in both word and sign, shared both word and sign, or differed in word but shared in sign. The results of these counts are presented in Table 12.1.

Table 12.1

[P Warlpiri, N Anmatyerre, K Kaytej, R Warumungu, L Warlmanpa, M Mudbura, J Djingili]

Comparison	DIFFERENT SIGN AND		SAME SIGN AND		
	Different word	Same word	Different word	Same word	Total
P/N	53	6	106	21	186
P/K	81	6	91	18	196
P/R	80	15	79	27	201
P/L	60	23	48	44	175
P/M	111	9	38	16	174
P/J	114	9	27	0	150
N/K	59	15	64	45	183
N/R	80	8	90	8	186
N/L	67	8	66	6	147
N/M	102	11	48	1	162
N/J	101	6	34	1	142
K/R	88	7	90	11	196
K/L	72	12	82	10	176
K/M	110	9	51	2	172
K/J	105	7	35	0	147
R/L	36	10	87	44	177
R/M	86	13	61	14	174
R/J	88	8	31	8	135
M/J	36	12	63	29	140
Total	1701	217	1264	343	
Mean	81	10.33	60.19	16.33	

It will be seen from this that although one is always more likely to find that a given meaning is expressed by a different word in any two languages, the number of instances in which different words are associated with different signs tends to be higher than the number of instances in which different words are associated with the same signs; likewise, the number of instances in which the same words are associated with the same signs is higher than the number of instances in which the same word is associated with different signs.

Thus for 13 out of the 21 comparisons, signs are different when words are different more often than they are the same when words are different; and in 11 out of the 21 comparisons, signs are the same when words are the same more often than signs are the same when words differ. The mean number of instances per comparison where signs differ and words differ is 81, but the mean number of instances per comparison where signs are the same and words differ is 60. The mean number of instances per comparison where the signs are the same and the words are the same is 16, whereas the mean number of instances per comparison where the signs differ but the words are the same is 10.33. Because the comparisons made here are not made between independent observations, these differences cannot be evaluated by tests of probability. Nonetheless, it will be seen that these figures are in the direction we would expect if there is some degree of relationship between sign and word.

In 12.2.1 we offered examples which show how differences in sign language between two groups may be attributed to differences in the morphological structure of spoken expressions or to differences in the idioms employed to express the same meanings. In this section, however, we have offered evidence that suggests that there may also be some tendency for signs in two languages to be similar when words are similar, different when they are different. How might this be accounted for?

In previous discussion we have suggested that signs in these sign languages represent the meaning units of the associated spoken language, and not the surface forms, that is, not the actual words. As we showed in Chapter 6, many signs (perhaps almost all) can be understood as originating as gestural representations of images (bases) selected to represent concepts. They come to represent the meaning units of the spoken language as a result of their continued use. There is thus no obvious reason why a gestural representation of a meaning unit should be the same in two different groups just because the words happen to be the same. The relationships between words and signs suggested in Table 12.1 calls for some explanation, therefore.

As a working hypothesis we propose the following. Where signs and words are shared between groups, direct borrowing has occurred. That is, both word and sign have been borrowed from one language into another as a unit. Where the signs are different and the words are different, we may suppose that the signs arose independently. This must also be the case where the signs are different but the words are the same (the least common case). Where the signs are shared but the words are different, however, it may be the case that the signs have been in use longer than their corresponding words. As will be explained later, there is in Australia a widespread practice whereby words that sound similar to the names of deceased persons may not be spoken for an extended period after their death. Such tabooed words must be replaced, either by borrowing from a neighboring language, by an extension in the use of existing words or by the creation of altogether new forms. The result is that there is a relatively rapid turnover in vocabulary and considerable sharing of vocabulary between adjacent languages. In addition, many languages are found to have a large number of synonyms. Such taboos do not apply to signs, as far as is known. Thus, even if there was originally a close link between sign and word, this link may often be undone, because the word may be replaced because of taboo, leaving the sign unchanged.

12.2 Sign vocabulary comparisons

In this section we shall undertake quantitative comparisons between the North Central Desert sign vocabularies by estimating the degree to which the seven groups studied share the same signs for the same meanings. These estimates are examined in relation to the degree of similarity in vocabulary of the respective languages and the degree of geographical separation of the groups considered. The data are set out in Table 12.3. The geographical positions of the groups are given in Fig. 4.1, p. 70.

For the purposes of estimating the extent to which signs are shared between these groups, 250 meanings were selected, covering all semantic domains, for which signed expressions had been recorded in most of the groups studied. The actual number of items compared ranged between 256 for the Warlpiri/Warumungu comparison to 164 for the Warlmanpa/Djingili comparison. The mean number of items per comparison is 213. In making these comparisons signs were judged Same if they were found to be the same in respect to all three aspects of the sign, they were judged Similar if they differed in respect to only one aspect and they were judged Different otherwise.

Some examples will help to clarify how these judgements were made and also serve to illustrate something of how signs can vary. In Warlpiri 'dog' is signed by moving a vertically extended index finger back and forth, palm facing outwards: $.G_{\perp\wedge}^{\wr}$. In Warumungu, in contrast, the hand is held so that all the fingers, held straight, are bunched together, the hand then being lowered by an arm movement, at the same time as the wrist is flexed: . ьB⊥^ˇ ʔ }. Again, in Warlpiri and Anmatyerre, 'water' is signed by holding the hand up in the form of a fist. The hand is then thrust forward slightly, the forward movement terminating in a rapid and repeated supinatory movement of the forearm: . J A<^ ⊥• a •• }. In Warumungu 'water' is signed by holding the hand up in front of the signer, the fingers all extended but held together (a 'flat' or B hand) and with the palm facing the signer. The fingers are then partially flexed rapidly two or three times: . B⊤^ Ω ". In Warlpiri, 'big' is signed by holding the hand as a V in front of the face, but with the two extended fingers slightly bent. The hand is then lowered and flexed at the wrist, and, while being moved toward the face, it is shaken back and forth slightly: ⌒V̈⊤^ ʔ I }. In Mudbura 'big' is signed by holding the hand like a claw, palm down, lowering it and closing it to a fist at the same time: . ˂5∨⊥ ˇ[A]. All these signs would be considered Different.

Signs may differ in respect to only one feature, however, in which case they are considered Similar. For example, in Warlpiri 'old man, elder' is signed by holding a claw-like hand toward the face and moving it forward and back slightly: ⌒˂5⊤^ I (see Fig. 5.9). In the Warumungu version the same handshape is used, but the hand is now twice twisted away from the signer by forearm pronation: . ˂5<⊥ б '. In Warlpiri 'camp' is signed by touching the cheek with an O hand: 3O<^ ×. In the Warumungu version the cheek is touched with the tip of the extended index finger: 3G ˀ . In Warlpiri 'mother's brother' is signed by tapping the center of the upper chest with the hand held as a fist: ⌐A⊤< × '. In Warumungu it is signed by holding the hand with fingers straight and spread, but bent at the first joints, and tapping the center of the chest with the tips of the fingers: ⌐˂5⊤< ˀ '. All these signs would be considered Similar because they differ in respect to one feature only: by Sign Action in the first example, and by Handshape (Sign Actor) in the second two.

In some cases, it should be noted, signs which are considered Different by these criteria nevertheless do retain some similarities at a more general level of analysis. For example, although we distinguish three signs for 'woman', two of these share a supinating motion of the forearm and thus appear to have a 'scooping' movement in common. Thus, in Warlpiri, 'woman' can be signed as . ˂B<⊥ a̲, a 'cupped' hand is partially supinated. In Warumungu a similar motion is involved but the action is otherwise different: the hand begins as a spread hand with palm facing downwards. Then, as the forearm is supinated, the fingers of the hand close to the palm, the terminal handshape being the G shape: . 5∨⊥ a[G]. Again, although two different signs for 'boy' are distinguished, both share the feature of a single extended finger. In Warlpiri, 'boy' is signed by holding out the middle finger only and twice pronating the forearm: $.\mathrm{m}\varsigma_{<\perp}^{\sigma}{}'$ (cf. Fig. 6.7). In Mudbura 'boy' is signed by holding out the index finger and twice flexing at the first joint: $.\mathrm{G}_{\vee\perp}^{\Omega}{}'$.

A number of signs recorded as Different, thus, can nevertheless be interpreted as variants on a theme. This suggests that, even where signs have been created independently of one another, what is selected as base for a concept is the same and similar strategies of representation have been followed. As we shall see later, the occurrence of similar signs in widely separated parts of Australia may, in some cases, be better understood in these terms. In many other cases, however, it seems highly likely that the sign forms themselves have undergone diffusion.

The extent to which signs within the North Central Desert area differ from one group to another varies somewhat according to semantic domain. Table 12.2 shows the proportion of signs that are the Same in five or more of the seven North Central Desert groups in each of several semantic domains. It will be seen that kin signs, as we saw in Chapter 11, with a few exceptions, are the same for all groups in this area. Perhaps this is related to the importance, in Aboriginal society, of ensuring that, in any encounter, kin relations are understood. On the other hand, about three quarters of the signs for articles of manufacture, just under two thirds of human classification and animal signs, and half of all verb signs, are different from one group to another. From this it is clear that there is a large measure of local development in signing.

For the purposes of comparing spoken vocabularies, between 176 and 166 items were used. The mean number of items per comparison is 172. The vocabulary items are all included in the set of meanings used in the sign languages comparison. The number of items compared is somewhat less than the number of signs compared because we excluded all words based on English and all words of which we were uncertain. All obviously identical words were counted as shared, including words that are the same once allowances are made for systematic sound differences between the Arandic languages in the sample, and the others (see note 6). In comparing verbs we have made comparisons only in respect to the root. Where verbs are compounds of a preverb and root, if, for the same meaning, the languages differ in the root verb employed but not in the preverb, a score of difference has nevertheless been recorded.

Table 12.2

Domain	Percentage of items with same sign in 5 or more groups	Items per domain
Kin	73	15
Plants*	50	18
Verbs	50	48
Time	40	10
Animals	38	18
Human Classification	35	20
Adjectives	27	33
Artefacts†	26	43
All	40	205

*Includes Topography. † Includes Camp and Consumables

It will be seen that the percentages for shared vocabulary given in Table 12.3 are in reasonable agreement with those to be expected on the basis of the language groupings presented in Wurm (1972). Such deviations from Wurm's figures as there are probably arise from the fact that the word lists we have used were not designed for systematic lexicostatistical comparisons. In particular, our list contains very few body part terms, in contrast to the lists employed in the comparisons discussed by Wurm. In any case, our interest here is not so much to compare our lexicostatistics with Wurm's, but to see whether there is a relationship between sign and word similarities or differences within the particular population of meanings here selected.

For the purposes of comparing the groups studied in terms of geographical distance, locations for each group were selected that have been recorded on a map and therefore convenient to make measurements from, but which, also, either are close to the center of the traditional area of the group in question, or close to the area where our informants grew up. The locations selected (see Fig. 4.1, p. 70) are Willowra for Warlpiri, Ti Tree township for Anmatyerre, Neutral Junction station for Kaytej, the town of Tennant Creek for Warumungu, Banka Banka station for Warlmanpa, Newcastle Waters station for Mudbura and Beetaloo for Djingili. Willowra was chosen for Warlpiri, even though the material used here was gathered at Yuendumu, because our two main informants for Warlpiri grew up in the Lander River area and have spent much time at Willowra. Ti Tree township is very close to the area where Anmatyerre informants grew up, Neutral Junction is the birthplace of all of the Kaytej informants and is a location that is central in the traditional area of the Kaytej. Tennant Creek is located at about the center of the area traditionally used by the Warumungu. Banka Banka has been a center for Warlmanpa people for several generations (their traditional area was somewhat to the west of this). Newcastle Waters was for many years a center for Mudbura people and all of my Mudbura informants grew up there. Beetaloo has been a center for Djingili people and my principal Djingili informant was for a long time associated with it.

Table 12.3 shows the proportion of signs that have been judged the Same, Similar and Different between all of the seven groups from which we have gathered data. Proportions of words shared between each of these seven languages are also given. The groups in the Table are arranged from left to right in order of increasing distance from Warlpiri. Since the geographical locations selected for each group, with one exception (Ti Tree), extend from the location selected for Warlpiri in a northerly direction, this arrangement ensures that groups that are closest to one another geographically are next to one another in the Table. Inspection of Table 12.3 reveals the following:

1. In every case but one, the proportion of signs shared is higher than the proportion of words shared, in most cases substantially higher. Sign language vocabularies, in other words, are more similar between groups than spoken language vocabularies. Evidently signs diffuse more widely than words.

2. The proportion of signs shared is highest between groups that are on the diagonal of the matrix. That is to say, groups that are geographically closest share the highest proportion of signs. Indeed, it will be seen that the proportion of signs shared declines as one moves from left to right in the Table in every row. This suggests that the further apart two groups are, the less likely they are to share signs.

3. The proportion of words shared does not follow the same pattern as the proportion of shared signs. In fact it will be clear that geographically adjacent groups share a high proportion of signs, regardless of whether or not their spoken languages have much in common. Thus, Warlpiri and Anmatyerre share many more signs than Warlpiri and Warlmanpa, despite the fact that Warlpiri and Warlmanpa are very closely related spoken languages, whereas Warlpiri and Anmatyerre are not closely related. Similarly, Mudbura and Djingili, close geographically, share more signs than Mudbura shares with either Warlmanpa or Warlpiri. This is notwithstanding the fact that Mudbura and Djingili, linguistically, are quite unrelated, while Mudbura, Warlmanpa and Warlpiri all belong to the same language group.

Table 12.3

This Table presents the proportion of signs that are the Same, Similar or Different between each of seven NCD sign vocabularies. Based on sign vocabulary samples ranging from 256 to 164 and spoken vocabulary samples ranging from 176 to 166. Numbers labelled (Distance) are distances measured in kilometers between locations for each group compared. See text for definition of locations. Numbers in square brackets are % range of words shared between groups from Wurm (1972).

	N	K	R	L	M	J	
P	61(125)	48(150)	47(238)	43(313)	27(438)	19(463)	% signs same (Distance)
	17	18	14	17	16	10	% signs similar
	22	34	39	38	57	71	% signs different
	16	12	20	47	17	5	% words shared
	[16-25]	[16-25]	[16-25]	[50-70]	[26-50]	[≤15]	% range words shared [Wurm]
N		57(88)	41(275)	41(375)	26(519)	23(538)	
		13	17	19	15	13	
		29	42	40	59	64	
		35	6	7	4	3	
		[26-50]	[16-25]	[16-25]	[16-25]	[≤15]	
K			46(200)	45(300)	28(450	26(475)	
			13	17	15	11	
			41	37	57	62	
			7	5	2	2	
			[16-25]	[16-25]	[16-25]	[≤15]	
R				65(100)	37(250)	27(275)	
				15	15	12	
				20	48	61	
				31	13	5	
				[16-25]	[16-25]	[≤15]	
L					42(163)	30(175)	
					20	13	
					38	57	
					38	26	
					[26-50]	[≤15]	
M						58(50)	
						12	
						30	
						26	
						[≤15]	

We must conclude, then, that the strongest factor governing the degree of similarity between sign language vocabularies is geographical distance separating the communities using them. Despite some evidence that there is a weak relationship between sign and spoken language differences, it seems that the geographical factor governing sign language distribution appears to operate regardless of whether the spoken languages are related or not. This finding, taken together with the observation that the proportions of shared signs are generally much higher than the proportions of shared words, suggests that signs are much more readily borrowed from one community to the next than are words. Possible reasons for this will be discussed below (12.4).

12.3 Comparison with other findings

From the analyses discussed in the preceding section we have seen (1) the degree of similarity of sign language between any two groups varies inversely with the geographical distance between them, (2) the proportion of signs shared between any two groups tends to be higher than the proportion of words shared and, for the most part, it is much higher, and (3) geographically adjacent groups share a high proportion of signs, regardless of whether or not their spoken languages have much in common - as witness the findings in respect to Warlpiri and Anmatyerre or Mudbura and Djingili.

These results may now be compared with those reported by Meggitt (1954), who undertook an analysis of the data presented by Roth (1897) for a number of groups in North-West-Central Queensland. The area for which Roth provides sign language data is roughly centered on Boulia (see the location marked PP in Fig 12.2, p. 395) and extends from Cluny near the Georgina River in the south, to Canobie on the Cloncurry River in the north; and from just east of Lake Nash in the west, eastwards, as far as Cambridge Downs near the Flinders River. Roth's area is thus comparable in size and latitude to our own, but it is geographically and culturally well separated from the North Central Desert.

Roth provides a description of 213 signs which he attributes to ten different groups in this region. He also provides a comparative table of vocabulary with 90 words from nine of the groups for which sign data is also available. Meggitt undertook analyses of these data in which, as we did, he compared each of the ten groups in terms of the proportion of signs and words Roth reports to be the same. Meggitt's comparative matrices are reproduced in Fig. 12.1.

Meggitt's findings are threefold, each directly comparable to our own: he finds that in every comparison the proportion of signs shared is substantially higher than the proportion of words shared; that groups that are geographically adjacent share significantly more signs than groups that are

Proportions of signs in common between ten groups in North-West Central Queensland

Tribes	Woo	Goa	Wal	Wan	Pit	Ula	Und	Boi	Mit	Kal
Woonamuna		100	50	50	60	55	54	57	64	57
Goa	100	(I)	50	50	60	55	54	57	64	57
Walookera	50	50		100	94	89	91	81	53	57
Wankajera	50	50	100		94	89	91	81	53	57
Pitta Pitta	60	60	94	94	(II)	94	91	89	57	61
Ulaolinya	55	55	89	89	94		90	88	58	55
Undekerebina	54	54	91	91	91	90		80	48	65
Boinji	57	57	81	81	89	88	80		56	57
Mitakoodi	64	64	53	53	57	58	48	56		75
Kalkadoon	57	57	57	57	61	55	65	57	75	(III)

Comparisons as presented in Table 2 in Meggitt (1954, p.12) from data provided by Roth (1897). Sections of table labelled I, II and III indicate the three groupings of tribes that have high proportions of signs in common. These tribes are closest to one another geographically.

Proportions of words in common between nine groups in North-West Central Queensland

Tribes	Woo	Goa	Wal	Wan	Pit	Ula	Und	Mit	Kal
Woonamuna									
Goa	32								
Walookera	4	3							
Wankajera	14	16	9						
Pitta Pitta	14	18	7	62					
Ulaolinya	13	13	5	74	56				
Undekerebina	3	3	5	11	5	12			
Mitakoodi	51	20	3	10	11	7	2		
Kalkadoon	21	13	2	9	12	7	2	19	

Comparisons as presented in Table 4 in Meggitt (1954, p. 15) from data provided by Roth.

Fig. 12.1 Matrices comparing signs and words among North-West Central Queensland groups. After Meggitt (1954)

geographically separate; and that this is the case, regardless of whether or not geographically adjacent groups speak closely related languages.

Thus Meggitt reports that the proportion of signs shared ranges from over 94% (in five cases) to as low as 48%, with a mean of 60%. The proportion of words shared, on the other hand, averaged only 16%, although there are three comparisons where the proportions were between 56% and 74%. For our own results we report a mean of shared signs of 40% (with a range from 65% to 19%) and mean for shared words of 16% (with a range of 47% to 2%).

Meggitt shows that the variation in proportion of signs shared is closely related to geographical adjacency. Thus the Woonamurra and the Goa,[7] who share 100% of their signs, are adjacent groups in the east of the region studied, while the Mitakoodi and the Kalkadoon, who share 75% of their signs, are neighbors to the north. The five groups which live in the area referred to by Roth as the Boulia district, all quite close to one another and considered by him to be "messmates" (these are the Wankajera, the Pitta Pitta, the Ulaolinya, the Undekerebina and the Boinji) all share between 89% and 94% of their signs. In contrast, these five groups, when compared to the more remote Woonamurra and Goa, or the Mitakoodi and Kalkadoon, all share 65% of their signs or less.

Variation in proportion of words shared between these groups does not follow the principle of geographical adjacency to nearly the same extent. Meggitt shows that while the Pitta-Pitta, Ulaolinya and Wankajera share over 55% of words with one another, other groups who are geographical neighbors do not. This point is especially well illustrated in the case of the Walookera, as compared to the Wankajera. According to Roth (1897, p.42) the Wankajera were to be found in the neighborhood of Glenormiston and Herbert Downs, while the Walookera are described as being found between Roxburgh and Carandotta, "with their headquarters at the latter locality" (Roth, loc. cit.). This makes them the immediate northern neighbors of the Wankajera. Nevertheless, these two groups share only 9% of their vocabulary. Indeed, of the Walookera Roth says they are "a small tribe using words absolutely distinct, showing no traces of contact with neighbouring peoples". The Walookera are today referred to as the Warluwara, their language is perhaps related to Wakaya, and in any case it is considered quite distinct from the Pitta Pitta dialects of the groups immediately to the south (see Wurm 1972, pp.129-130). All the more striking, then, that the Walookera should share 100% of their signs with the Wankajera, and 80-90% of their signs with the other Pitta-Pitta dialect using groups. Evidently, although linguistically quite distinct from all other groups, in terms of sign language they must be considered part of the Boulia district group.

Meggitt's analysis of the data Roth provides, thus, produces results that are just the same as our own and lend support to the general hypothesis that Meggitt put forward in his 1954 paper, that signs vary on a strictly geographical basis, ignoring spoken language differences, even when these are very marked, as between the Pitta Pitta dialect speakers and the Walookera, as in Roth's material, or between the Mudbura and the Djingili, in our own. As we shall suggest in 12.7, this strictly geographical hypothesis must be modified to take into consideration two factors: differences in the extent to which adjacent groups interact with one another and variations in the functions of sign language within the community. However, the fact remains that, within a given area such as the North Central Desert or Northwest Central Queensland, adjacent groups share more signs than separated groups, regardless of their linguistic affiliations.

12.4 Sign and word diffusion compared

Signs cross linguistic boundaries more readily than words, so the results just discussed suggest. Why should this be? Why should it be possible for such groups as the Warlpiri and the Anmatyerre, the Mudbura and Djingili or the Pitta Pitta and the Walookera, while maintaining such close interaction between themselves, at the same time to maintain extensive linguistic differences but not maintain sign language differences, at least not nearly to the same degree? Evidently the processes that lead to convergence or differentiation between spoken languages operate differently when it comes to signs. Here six reasons for this difference are suggested, all of which could play a part in these processes.

1. Native ideologies. A number of writers have reported that Aborigines maintain that members of different social groups 'possess' different ways of speaking and that group membership is partly manifested by speaking a given 'language'. Such a view does not appear to apply to sign languages. If this is so, whereas the native view of language would appear to encourage the maintenance of difference, the native view of sign language would offer no impediment to sign language blending.

The view that the language one speaks is an important part of what one can claim to possess in consequence of one's group membership has been described for parts of Arnhem Land and Cape York, in particular, though it applies in other parts of Australia as well. Thus Schebeck (1968), writing of the language situation in Northeast Arnhem Land (the region of the 'Murngin' of Lloyd Warner or the 'Yolngu' of more recent writers), states that a widely held native theory of language is that each *mala* (i.e. land holding patriline) has its own *matha*, or mode of speech. He shows that this theory does not actually work out in practice - several different *mala* may actually speak in the same way. Nevertheless, it is clear from his discussion that the idea that each *mala* owns a given way of speaking contributes to the maintenance of different dialects between groups who are otherwise in close interaction with one another. Similarly, Rigsby and Sutton (1980-1981) write: "In the Cape Keerweer region of western Cape York Peninsula, as elsewhere in Aboriginal Australia, language is *owned* and not merely spoken. According to the Aboriginal model, one inherits language from one's father, along with many other important forms of property such as land and major totems" (p. 18, emphasis in original). While this is probably somewhat too general statement - Heath (1979) finds no comparable native model in Southeastern Arnhem Land - it seems clear that this linguistic ideology is an important factor in the process by which language differences between interacting groups are maintained. As Rigsby and Sutton point out, it is because members of such interacting groups routinely learn each other's languages that language differences are maintained. One does not give up the language one learns from one's patriline, for to speak it is part of being a member of that group, a membership which, of course, is never relinquished. Such an 'ownership' view of language, together with the practice of multilingualism (Brandl and Walsh 1982), ensures the maintenance of different languages or dialects and constitutes a counterforce to processes of language blending.

As we have seen, it appears that blending in regard to sign languages is much more likely to occur. Perhaps this is because there appears to be no comparable ideology attached to sign language. Virtually every Aboriginal person I have spoken to about this in the North Central Desert region maintains that the sign languages of all the other groups they know about are "the same" as their own. This view I found to be held by sophisticated and knowledgeable sign users as well as by those who knew little about it. Sophisticated signers, within the context of my elicitation sessions, would sometimes recognize differing signs to belong to, say "the Warumungu side" or they might insist that a given sign was "properly Warlmanpa" but despite this they would still maintain that the sign languages are all the same. Evidently the native theory of sign language is just the opposite of the native theory of spoken language. Just as an ideology of difference surely contributes to the maintenance of language differentiation, so an ideology of sameness would at least make signers in adjacent communities much less resistant to new forms. This could mean that signers in a given community are much more ready to absorb new forms from their neighbors than are speakers. In other words, whereas the ideology of language encourages differentiation and the maintenance of distinctness, the ideology of sign does not discourage sameness.

2. Taboo words and language change. It is a widespread custom that, when someone dies, their name may not be spoken, nor may any word that bears some phonological resemblance to the name (Nash and Simpson 1981) It has been argued by some (e.g. Dixon 1970, 1972) that this has contributed in an important way to one of the most striking features of Australian languages: that so many of them are lexically very different from one another, yet grammatically very similar. The taboo on words homophonous with names of the deceased does not apply to the *signs* associated with them, as far as is known. This being the case, we might expect that languages might replace their spoken vocabulary faster than their sign vocabulary. Assuming that the sign vocabularies of adjacent groups already show some degree of overlap, if the two languages were then to replace words at a faster rate than they replace signs, as would be expected from the practice of word taboo just mentioned, we would expect a much higher proportion of shared signs than shared words.

3. Structural impediments to language spread. Heath (1979) showed that the diffusion of forms from one language to another may sometimes be subject to impediments that stem from structural differences between the languages. Such structural differences probably have little effect on sign language diffusion.

Heath studied linguistic diffusion between adjacent languages in Arnhem Land. He found that some linguistic forms diffused much more readily than others. For instance, between Nunggubuyu and Warndarang lexical diffusion in the case of verbs was found to be virtually absent because, Heath suggests, the verbs in these languages have a totally different structure. In Nunggubuyu verb roots are inflected with pronominal prefixes and tense-aspect suffixes, whereas Warndarang has a system of verbal auxiliaries. Between Ngandi and Ritharngu, however, two adjacent languages that are found to the north, verb diffusion has occurred. Verbs which, in Ritharngu, can occur in the form of an uninflected 'naked root', have been borrowed into Ngandi, while those that cannot occur in the language in this way have not. Structural differences may also serve as impediments to linguistic diffusion elsewhere in Australia. For instance, in Warlpiri, verbs are always accompanied by an auxiliary to which are suffixed tense and person clitics. Such auxiliaries are absent in the neighboring language of Anmatyerre in which, also, there are no conjugations but only one set of inflections attached directly to the verb root to mark tense and aspect. Such differences may well be a barrier to verb borrowing between the two languages.

Such structural differences between spoken languages are unlikely to give rise to impediments to diffusion between associated sign languages, however. As we have seen (Chapter 8), signs are not found which represent grammatical case markers, markers of tense, or the verbal auxiliary, where it occurs. Thus, although, as we have seen, differences between sign languages can arise where the languages they are associated with differ in whether the same concept is expressed by a compound in one language but in a simple form in the other, differences do not arise, say, in verbal signs between Warlpiri and Anmatyerre or between Mudbura and Djingili, even though the forms of the verbs in these languages differ considerably.

4. As we saw in Chapter 6, for many signs it is possible to show a motivated or 'iconic' connection between form and meaning. There is some evidence that signs with such a relationship between form and meaning are easier to learn than those which have an arbitrary relationship (Brown 1978). This could have the result that signs which are iconic are less likely to change their form, when borrowed into another system, than signs that are arbitrary. This might also lead to a higher proportion of signs in adjacent sign languages remaining the same or similar.

5. In Chapter 5 we suggested that although there is a considerable degree of systematization at the formational level, there is evidence that the North Central Desert sign languages are quite open ended in this regard, at least in comparison to the phonology (formational system) of a spoken language. As a result, a borrowed form may be less likely to be transformed, because there is less pressure to make it conform to the formational system of the existing sign language.

6. Themes in sign formation. As suggested above, signs for a given meaning that differ from one another from one place to another may nevertheless show thematic similarities. This may be due to the fact that there is a tendency for the same base to be selected for a given concept - for instance, horns to represent 'cattle' or the crescent shape of the moon to represent 'moon'. Since strategies for representation are fairly limited, it is quite possible that signs created separately from the same base could turn out to be highly similar, if not identical. This could be another reason why signs appear more widely shared than words.

In the light of such considerations, it seems reasonable that we should find, as we do, both from our own analyses, as well as the results of Meggitt's analyses of Roth's data, than sign language expressions are more widely diffused that words.

12.5 North Central Desert signs and signs from elsewhere: Aranda, Western Desert and Queensland

In Chapter 5 we saw that, in formational terms, the North Central Desert sign languages have much in common. We have also seen, in Chapter 11, that signs for kinship in this region are the same throughout, but that kin signs from elsewhere are, for the most part, quite different. In addition, as we saw in 12.2, in regard to other semantic domains, although there are many very different signs in the North Central Desert, there are also many that are the same or highly similar. It would appear that the sign languages of the Warlpiri, Anmatyerre, Kaytej, Warumungu and Warlmanpa, at least, do have much in common and can be regarded as all being closely related. This view is reinforced when we compare signs from the North Central Desert with signs from other areas, as we shall now see.

Three authors have recorded extensive sign lists from elsewhere in Australia which contain a considerable number of signs that can be compared with items in the sign vocabularies we have collected. These lists are those of Roth (1897) who, as stated above, described 213 signs from several different groups in North-West-Central Queensland, Strehlow (1978 [1915]), who described 290 signs covering 454 meanings from the Northern Aranda at Hermansburg, and Wick Miller (1971), who described 297 signs collected from two elderly male Ngatajara speakers at the Warburton Ranges Mission in the Western Desert. These lists contain between 80 and 160 signs that can be compared with our own sign vocabularies.

There are a number of difficulties involved in making these comparisons. The descriptions of the signs in these lists vary in quality and consistency and it is often difficult to be certain of the form of a given sign. Of the three lists, Roth's is the best, because he accompanied his descriptions with excellent line drawings (see Fig.2.1), but even here one often cannot be certain about a sign's form, especially in regard to the pattern of movement involved. Second, in going through the lists, it is often difficult to be sure what signs can be compared. This is especially true in regard to signs for animals and plants where, unless scientific names are provided (which is not always done), one cannot be sure that the same species are being referred to, except where the animal is very well known, such as the echidna, emu or turkey bustard. Finally, we can make no judgement about the reliability of the descriptions provided by Roth and Strehlow. Neither author provides information about how they obtained the signs they describe so we do not know whether the informants these authors used were particularly well versed in sign language or not. Miller gives more information on this point and he also indicates when he suspected that a sign was not a traditional form, but improvised for his benefit. Signs thought by Miller to be improvised have been excluded from our comparisons.

As we saw in Chapter 2, it is probable that the sign languages described by these authors differ from the North Central Desert sign languages in who uses them and for what purposes. Roth indicates that signs were widely used for distance communication and also in connection with certain phases of male initiation. He makes no reference to their use by women and does not make any references to speech taboos as part of mourning. Miller lists a variety of circumstances of sign use among the Ngatajara, but does not refer to speech taboos in mourning. He indicates that, in his observation, men were more proficient at it than women. Other writers on the Western Desert have indicated that, in addition to the use of signing in hunting, periods of silence are imposed on young male initiates and that they may learn to use some sign language at this time. Among the Aranda, silence appears to have been observed by widows, but it is clear, both from Strehlow and from Spencer and Gillen (1927), that sign language was also used by men. It is unfortunate that Strehlow does not tell us whether the signs he described were obtained from men or women. In any case, the signs described by Roth, Strehlow and Miller appear to belong to systems that have a somewhat different status from the North Central Desert systems, but we remain uncertain as to what that status is.

Table 12.4 gives the number of signs examined in each comparison and the proportion of signs in each case that were judged Same, Similar or Different. The comparisons given are for each of the seven North Central Desert lists with the lists of Roth, Strehlow and Miller, and also for the comparison of Strehlow's and Miller's lists with each other and with Roth's list.

It will be seen that, in all but three comparisons, the proportion of signs recorded as Same is much lower than any reported from the North Central Desert comparisons given in Table 12.2. For the seven North Central Desert groups, it will be recalled, the average proportion of signs recorded as Same was 40%, with a range of 19% to 61%. Here, for the twenty-one North Central desert comparisons, the average proportion of Same signs is 11.5%, with a range of 5% to 22%. From this it is clear that the North Central Desert signs constitute a relatively homogeneous set, clearly different from the sets of signs from Queensland, Western Desert and Northern Aranda.

Nevertheless, there is some variation in the proportion of Same signs that is consistent with the geographic and cultural relationships of these groups. Thus, for the Warlpiri, who are neighbors to the north of the Northern Aranda studied by Strehlow, and the Anmatyerre and Kaytej, the two Arandic speaking groups in our sample, just over 20% of the signs compared with

Strehlow's list are the Same. For the more northerly groups in our sample (Warumungu, Warlmanpa, Mudbura and Djingili), the average proportion of Same signs is 15%. On the other hand, for the four northerly groups, 11.75% of their signs, when compared to Queensland signs, are the Same, whereas for the three southerly groups, the average proportion of Same signs in this comparison is 9.6%. The lowest proportion of overlap is with the Ngatajara sample, but even here the figures pattern in a way geography might lead one to expect: the southerly groups show, on average, 7% Same signs, while for the northerly groups the proportion is only 5%.

The comparisons between the Aranda, Ngatajara and Queensland lists also show low rates of similarity. However, these do not show a pattern that accords with geographic or cultural relations. Ngatajara does show a higher proportion of Same signs when compared to Aranda than does Aranda when compared to Queensland, but it shows a surprising 17% of Same signs for its Queensland comparison. These comparisons involve much smaller samples of signs and are thus less reliable. Nevertheless, they all indicate that there is considerable difference between the sign vocabularies drawn from these areas.

Taken together, these figures provide an overall picture which suggests that the sign languages of the North Central Desert are quite similar to one another, but markedly different from sign languages in other areas, although the more northerly part of the North Central Desert has faint affinities with the Queensland area to the East, and the more southerly part of it has somewhat stronger (but still weak) affinities with the Northern Aranda to the south and west. The Western Desert sign vocabulary appears to be very different, both from Aranda, which it adjoins, and from the North Central Desert and the Queensland areas.

12.5.1 Identical and similar signs

We turn now to discuss particular signs that are found to be identical or closely similar between the groups considered. There are a few signs that are found to be identical or similar throughout. In other cases we find that signs found to be the same in one comparison are different from those found the same in another. For example, several of the signs that are shared between the southerly groups of the North Central Desert and the Aranda are different from those that are shared between the northerly groups of the North Central Desert and Queensland.

Table 12.4

	Queensland	**Aranda**	**Ngatajara**
Warlpiri			
Same	12%	21%	8%
Similar	15%	18%	18%
Different	72%	60%	78%
Total	110	137	160
Anmatyerre			
Same	8%	22%	7%
Similar	11%	15%	18%
Different	80%	62%	76%
Total	93	107	124
Kaytej			
Same	9%	21%	6%
Similar	13%	18%	19%
Different	78%	60%	76%
Total	95	102	127
Warumungu			
Same	11%	15%	5%
Similar	16%	20%	18%
Different	72%	64%	77%
Total	99	104	132
Warlmanpa			
Same	12%	14%	5%
Similar	15%	16%	19%
Different	73%	69%	76%
Total	94	117	116
Mudbura			
Same	11%	17%	5%
Similar	16%	19%	22%
Different	73%	64%	73%
Total	102	95	126
Djingili			
Same	13%	15%	5%
Similar	17%	18%	15%
Different	70%	66%	80%
Total	84	94	114
Aranda			
Same	9%		12%
Similar	17%		24%
Different	73%		64%
Total	53		83
Ngatajara			
Same	17%		
Similar	12%		
Different	71%		
Total	59		

Eleven signs in the samples studied are found to be the same or highly similar throughout the entire region. They are as follows. 'Boomerang' is represented by a curved index finger in the Western Desert, Aranda, all of the North Central Desert groups except Mudbura and Djingili, and among the Pitta-Pitta and associated groups in Queensland. 'Horse' is represented in Aranda, throughout the North Central Desert and in Queensland by a sign in which the hand, with all fingers fully flexed at the second and third joints, is held forward and then moved back and forth, in a pattern reminiscent of pulling on reins. 'Boy' is represented among the Ngatajara, Aranda, and the North Central Desert by an extended finger, either the middle finger or the index finger. 'Echidna' is represented in all areas by a sign in which either the index finger or the fourth finger is extended. This sign is evidently based upon a representation of its foot, which has one very extended toe. Number signs throughout the region are similar in that they employ the display of one, two, three or all extended digits to indicate 'one', 'two', 'few', or 'many', although the manner in which the fingers are displayed and how they are moved varies. 'Axe' is signed throughout with a flat hand making chopping movements. 'Forget', and related meanings, in all regions is signed with a gesture that points to the ear, reflecting the widespread concept of the ear as the channel of cognitive functioning. 'Far' is indicated throughout the region by extending the arm rapidly in the direction referred to and terminating the extension by snapping the fingers. 'Wait, hold on, etc.' is signed throughout by shaking a fisted hand up and down: $.\lrcorner A_{<\perp}^{\sim}$. Except in the Western Desert, 'father' is signed by touching the chin, although how the chin is touched varies.

Several of these signs may well be similar in all parts of the region because of similar processes of sign creation, rather than because of diffusion. Some of the signs that are found in common only between the Aranda and the North Central Desert, or between the North Central Desert and Queensland, on the other hand, appear to be better interpreted as true shared forms. Examples illustrating this from these comparisons are as follows.

First, consider signs shared between the Aranda and the southerly North Central Desert group, the Warlpiri, Anmatyerre and Kaytej, that is. In all these groups, 'water' is signed by 'trembling' an upraised fist: $.\lrcorner A_{<\perp}^{\underline{\mathrm{a}}\,\mathrm{tr}}$. 'eternal, always' is signed by 'shaking' the hand back and forth with only the index and fourth fingers extended: $.\Psi_{<\wedge}^{\mathrm{I}}$. 'see' is signed by holding the hand in a V shape: $\cup_{\vee\perp}^{\perp\blacksquare}$. 'red kangaroo' is signed by first placing all the tips of the fingers onto the tip of the extended thumb - forming an O hand - and then opening the hand rapidly, twice: $.0_{\vee\perp}[5]'$. These signs seem to be highly evolved and therefore unlikely to have developed separately through parallel invention. For some of them, to be sure, we may be able to propose ways in which they can be seen as derived from base representational gestures. The sign for 'see', for instance, perhaps may be derived from an action that depicts two eyes looking; the reduplicated expansionary movement of the sign for 'red kangaroo' may be somehow analogous to the characteristic mode of progression of this animal. However, they appear to have developed away from base representation in a highly specialized manner and it seems more plausible to suppose that it is these forms that have spread, rather than that these forms should have been invented separately more than once.

Some of these forms also extend to the Ngatajara. Thus the southern North Central Desert Group, the Aranda and the Ngatajara all sign 'honey ant' in the same way.[8] The hand is held palm up, with only the index finger extended. The index finger is then repeatedly flexed: $.\,G_{\wedge\perp}^{\Omega}\,'$. The sign for 'see', as described above, is also the same among the Ngatajara as it is among the Aranda and the North Central Desert groups.

In addition, there are a number of signs which, though different, appear to be related in form. Thus, for Ngatajara there is a sign for 'water' in which both shoulders are tapped. This may be related to a sign for 'water' recorded among the Warlpiri and Warumungu in which the signer taps center of the chest with a flat hand: $[\,]B_{T<}^{\times\,'}$. Throughout the North Central Desert 'creek' is signed by moving a hand upwards with the finger tips in contact with the center of the thorax, or very close to it: $[\,]\hat{B}_{T<T}^{\ast\wedge}$. A similar sign for 'creek' occurs among the Ngatajara.[9]

Comparing the North Central Desert lists with the Queensland lists, most of the overlapping signs are those already mentioned above that are the same or similar throughout the entire central region here being dealt with. However, there are a few signs that are shared between Queensland and the North Central Desert groups, especially the more northerly of these (Warumungu, Warlmanpa, Mudbura, Djingili), that are of the sort that suggest that sign diffusion may have occurred. They are not found in Aranda or Ngatajara. Thus, as we saw in Chapter 11, 'Younger Sibling' is signed by touching the ipsilateral shoulder throughout the North Central Desert and 'Sibling' is signed in this way also in Northwest Central Queensland. 'Water' is signed among the northern North Central Desert groups by holding up a flat hand, palm inwards, and flexing the fingers several times ($.\,B_{T\wedge}^{\Omega}\,'$). The same sign is also reported from Queensland. The sign for 'woman', among the Mudbura and Djingili, appears to be the same as that reported by Roth for the Pitta Pitta. In this sign a fisted hand, held up in front of the chest, is moved back and forth: $.\,J\,A_{T\wedge}^{\int}$. There are also similarities between Queensland and North Central Desert in regard to one sign for 'rock, hill' and, with the northern group, in regard to signs for 'turkey bustard' and 'dog'.

If we now consider the Queensland data in relation to Ngatajara and Aranda we again find, as will be clear from Table 12.4 , a number of signs that are apparently the same. However, most of these, unlike those just discussed, appear likely to be the same because of parallel invention, rather than as true shared forms. Thus, comparing Roth's Queensland lists with the Ngatajara list we find 'bullock' is signed in both areas by extending index fingers from either side of the head, clearly derived from a depiction of the bullock's horns. 'Eagle' is signed in both areas by forming the hand into a claw shape. 'Man' is signed by a gesture of grasping the beard. 'Mother' is signed by grasping the nipple. 'Sleep' is signed by laying the palm of the hand along the side of the face.

In the Aranda list, in addition to those signs common to the entire region already described, we find only 'mother', 'native bee' and 'bad, as in bad person' signed similarly to signs reported from Queensland. The signs for 'native bee' and 'bad' may be examples of shared forms. They also seem to be related to forms found in the North Central Desert. In both the Aranda and in Queensland 'native bee' can be signed by a rapid repeated outward flicking of the index finger from a closed position (probably .X$_{\vee\perp}$[Gt]').[10] In Warlpiri a similar sign for this is also is found. Among the Warumungu and Warlmanpa this meaning can be signed by extending all fingers from an initially closed position (.O$_{\vee\perp}$[‹5]'), perhaps a related form. 'Bad', according to Strehlow's description,[11] appears to employ the Ⴤ hand (index finger and fourth finger only extended) with a motion pattern that appears to make it quite similar to the Warlpiri sign for *wingki* 'bad behavior'. In Roth the same handshape is reported for a sign glossed as "Bad: person, or thing" (No. 211).

12.6 Comparisons with northern Australia and Cape York

In addition to the sign lists of Roth, Strehlow and Miller, sign lists of varying lengths have also been provided by several other authors for other parts of Australia. These include kin signs for the Worora in the coastal northwest (Love 1941), the Gupupuyngu of Arnhem Land (Williams 1981), the Lardiil of Mornington Island (Woolston and Trezise1966) and the Kukutja at Normanton on the Gulf coast (Black 1975). Roth (1908) has described signs for groups near the Pennefather (now Archer) River in Western Cape York, at Princess Charlotte Bay and Cape Bedford in Eastern Cape York, the Palmer River in southern Cape York, and a few signs for a group at Rockhampton. Some of these lists are quite short, and in the case of the longer ones of Woolston and Roth, many of the signs listed are for various aquatic animals

Fig. 12.2 Geographical locations of the sign languages compared and tentative sign language dialect areas. Heavy broken line encloses North Central Desert. Sign languages of the Warlpiri (P), Anmatyerre (N), Kaytej (K) are closest to Warumungu (R) and Warlmanpa (L); however P, N and K show some slight sign vocabulary overlap with Northern Aranda (AR); R and L, together with Mudbura (M) and Djingili (J) show some slight overlap with groups in N. W. Central Queensland: Undekerebina (UND), Kalkadunga (KAL), Waluwara (WAL), Pitta Pitta (PP), Wongkadjera (WON), Julaolinja (ULA), Koa (GAO), Wanamara (WAN), Maithakari (MIT). Other groups shown are Ngatatjara (NG), Worora (WR), Gupupuyngu (GP), Lardiil (LD), Kukutja (KJ), Yir Yiront (YY), Wikmunkan (WM), Windawinda (WW), Darambul (DB). PCB Princess Charlotte Bay, CB Cape Bedford, PR Palmer River

Meaning	NG	AR	PNK	RL	MJ	PP	MWG	DB	WR	GP	KJ	LDL	WW	PR	PCB	CB
Man	∪A⊤<×	ɹG^ ∂	⊓B⊤ ›Ω	⊓B⊤ ›Ω	⊓B⊤ ›Ω	∪A⊤<×	∪A⊤<×	∪A⊤<×		∪A⊤<×	∪A⊤<×		∪A⊤<×	∪A⊤<×		∪A⊤<×
Woman	Ï	×B∨⊥ tr	‹B‹⊥ Ω	×B‹⊥ Ω	ɹA⊤^ ʃ	ɹA⊤^ ʃ	∃	∃			∃		∃			
Infant	‹B^⊥ ∪'	0σ'	0σ'	0σ'	‹B∨⊥ ˇ	G‹⊥ ∂	⊸H⊤^ φ							⊔B^'B^~		
Siblings	⟩	╪	⟍,˥	⟍,˥	⟍,˥	˥		⟍	⟩	⟩	ɿ	˥,⟩	⟩	╪,⟍		
Mother	∃	∃	Ψ∞	[]‹5φ'	[]‹5φ'	∃	∃	∃	BUT	∃		∃				
Father, etc.	˥	∪A×	∪G∨<×	∪G∨<×	∪G∨<×	∪A×		˥	˥	˥			Γ			
Spouse, etc.	GR	ɿB⊤ ✱~	B∨›\B∨×'	B∨›\B∨×	B∨›\B∨×'	BUT	⟍	BUT	⟩	⟩		⟍	^			
Dog	ℓ˥A bn	G⊥^ ʃ	G⊥^ ʃ	to⊥ ʔ	to⊥ ʔ	to⊥ ʔ	to⊥ ʔ			to⊥'to⊥~	⊽G φ		G⊥^ ʃ	˥B φ	˥B φ	
Horse	B∨'B∨~~	E∨⊥ ɪ	E∨⊥ ɪ	E∨⊥ ɪ	E∨⊥ ɪ	E∨⊥ ɪ	E∨⊥ ɪ				A'A⊤'		ɹA'ɹA		A'Aˇ'	[]ʃɹA'ɹA
Emu	Ψ‹⊥ tr	A^⊥ ∪'	ɹX⊤^ ∪'	ɹO⊤^ ∪'	ɹO⊤^ ∪'	U‹⊥ tr, ɹB̂⊥ ⊥'	3∨⊥ ˇ'			ɹB̂⊥ ⊥'	ɹB̂⊥ ⊥'				ɹB̂⊥ ⊥'	
Bustard	G̈∨⊥ ⊥[G]	G̈∨ ∪a	mϚ⊤ Ω	mϚ⊤ Ω	ɹB aσ	ɹB aσ	ɹB aσ					ɹ to ʔ			ɹ to aσ	ɹB̂ ɪ
Digging stick	A\Aˇ'	Aˇ'	B∨⊥ ɪ	×B⊤< ɪ	B∨⊥ ɪ	G‹⊥ ˇ'	Aˇ'				Aˇ'					
Boomerang	G̈∨⊥ ⊥ʔ	G̈‹⊥ a	G̈‹⊥ a	G̈‹⊥ a	‹5⊥ ∞	Ψa	G̈					ɹB⊥	ɹB⊥			
Spear	U⊥[G]	Xa	Xa‹⊥ tr	R∨⊥ ⊥[U]	≥G›^'ɹG^	G⊤‹ σ›					≥G›^'ɹG^	≥G›^'ɹG^				
Water	Γ˥B ××	ɹA atr	ɹA atr	⊓B×'	B⊤^ Ω'	B⊤^ Ω'	B⊤^ Ω'			p3B×			p3B×	p3B×	p3B×	B⊤^ Ω'
Water				B⊤^ Ω'												
Fire	toBL	0σ	0σ	0σ	0σ	toBL	toBL				toBL	toBL	toBL			
Eat	‹5σ	⊔‹5⊤ ʃ	‹5^ ɪ	‹5^ ɪ	‹5^ ɪ	▿to σ[5]				▿to ›‹	▿to ›‹		▿to ›‹			▿to ›‹
Sleep	⊦3B×	A‹ σ	A σ	⌓Gˇ Ωˇ Ω	33ɹG'ɹG⊥	⊦3B×	⊦3B×				⊦3B×				⊦3B×	
Sleep			⌓Gˇ Ω ˇ Ω													
No	Üt σ	5σ	5σ	5σ	5σ	5σ	5σ			B̂∨⊥ a			ɹ5∞		ɹ5∞	
Question	ɹB⊤ ⊥[G^]	L a	L a	L a	L a	A› a	A› a				B∨⊥ a		ɹB∨ˇ[A]			

Table 12.5 Signs for twenty meanings compared between twenty four groups. Signs are given in abbreviated notations. Where only a body part is given, assume this is touched by the hand, usually a 'flat' hand or index finger. For explanation of symbols see Appendix I. For descriptions see text. NG Ngatatjara (Miller 1970); AR Northern Aranda (Strehlow 1914); PNK Warlpiri, Anmatyerre, Kaytej; RL Warumungu, Warlmanpa; MJ Mudbura, Djingili; PP Pitta Pitta and associated groups (Roth 1897); MWG Maithakari, Wanamara, Koa (Roth 1897); WR Worora (Love 1941); GP Gupupuyngu (Williams 1980); KJ Kukutja (Black 1975); LDL Lardiil (Woolston 1966); WW Windawinda, Yir Yiront, Wikmunkan (Roth 1908, Hale 1960); PR Palmer River (Roth 1908); PCB Princess Charlotte Bay; CB Cape Bedford (Roth 1908).

---

and other species that do not occur in the deserts. For this reason, we have found only twenty meanings that can be reliably compared in most of these places, as well as in the locations discussed hitherto. Although this is a rather small number, the comparisons seem worth discussing here, for they contribute to the rather interesting conclusions suggested in the next section. The distribution of signs for these twenty meanings is given in Table 12.5. The geographical locations of the groups compared are given in Fig. 12.2.

The twenty meanings listed include some of those that we have already discussed. As we saw in 12.5, above, the signs for several of them are the same, or similar, in the North Central Desert, as they are in either Aranda, Northwest Central Queensland, or both areas. As we suggested, this may indicate that there are some connections between the sign languages of these areas. The signs for these meanings, as reported from the northern regions, Cape York and the east coast, however, in most cases are quite different from the signs in the center. Furthermore, many of the signs in these more peripheral regions are themselves very widespread. Thus, in the Western Desert, on the Northwest Coast, in Arnhem Land and in Cape York, the calf is touched to sign Sibling, the shoulder is touched to sign Father, the buttock, hip or thigh is touched to sign Spouse and the nipple is grasped to sign Mother, but these signs are all quite different from the North Central Desert versions. There is also a very wide distribution of similar signs for 'water', 'fire', 'digging stick', 'eat' and 'sleep'. Thus 'water' is signed by tapping a puffed out cheek, not only in Arnhem Land, but throughout Cape York Peninsula as well. 'Fire' is signed everywhere except in the North Central Desert and among the Aranda, by holding the hand up as if grasping something and blowing on it. 'Digging stick' is signed everywhere except in the North Central Desert by moving one or two fisted hands up and down, in imitation of digging movements. 'Eat' is signed by moving a bunched hand toward the mouth in Arnhem Land and in Cape York, and a variant of this is also found in Queensland. Again, with the exception of the North Central

Desert, 'sleep' is signed everywhere by placing a flat hand against the side of the face.

12.7 Conclusions

In the light of the comparisons just discussed, together with the findings presented earlier, we suggest the following conclusions.

(a) The North Central Desert area is quite distinct as far as sign language goes. Though there is variation within it, this variation is less than the variation found between it and other areas.

(b) Nevertheless, there are certain connections between the North Central Desert and adjacent areas. The northern part of the North Central Desert seems to share some signs with the area in Queensland to the east, studied by Roth. The southern part of the North Central Desert area shares some signs with the northern Aranda immediately to the south, and to a more limited extent, with the Ngatajara in the Western Desert.

(c) These connections notwithstanding, the sign languages of the Aranda, Ngatajara and Northwest Central Queensland are all very different from one another, and just about as different from one another as they each are from the North Central Desert.

(d) Signs reported from the extreme northwest, Arnhem Land and Cape York, on the whole, are different from those reported from the more central regions. With some exceptions, however, several of these signs reported from widely separated areas are strikingly similar to one another, if not identical.

The picture these conclusions suggest is not incompatible with the view that sign language in the North Central Desert is a separate development from sign languages elsewhere in Australia. In view of the extraordinarily widespread distribution of some of the non-North Central Desert signs, especially some of the kin signs, we suggest that it is a more recent development, as well.

We have seen, from Chapter 3, that the functions of sign language in the North Central Desert are different from their functions elsewhere. In the North Central Desert, at least among the Warumungu, the Arandic groups and the Warlpiri, sign language is primarily, if not exclusively, the province of women. Under certain conditions, such as when speech is avoided because of mourning, they must use it extensively and for long periods, in all communicative circumstances. These conditions of use appear not to obtain elsewhere. This probably accounts for the distinctiveness of North Central Desert Sign Language. The very wide distribution of certain signs that are quite different from those in the North Central Desert suggests the antiquity of those forms and hence, perhaps, the relative recency of the forms found in the North Central Desert.

It will be seen that these conclusions lead to a modification of the strict geographical hypothesis that Meggitt's consideration of Roth's data and our own analysis of the North Central Desert data separately support. We suggest that the geographical hypothesis will apply only within areas where sign language has the same function throughout. When we compare areas where there are differences in the circumstances of its use and differences in which segments of the population use it, as is the case when we compare the North Central Desert with other regions, then we may find much greater differences in sign language than geography alone would lead us to expect.

12.8 Summary

This Chapter began with examples to illustrate the way in which, within the North Central Desert, differences between sign languages can arise, due to differences in the spoken languages associated with them. We showed that differences could arise in association with differences in spoken vocabulary, in the use of idioms and in the morphological structure of spoken expressions for the same meanings. A statistical analysis showed that there is some overall tendency, albeit not a strong one, for it to be more likely that signs will be the same between any two groups if the words they are associated with are the same and that signs will be different if the associated words are different. Some suggestions were offered by which this association might be accounted for.

Notwithstanding these relationships between spoken language and sign language, a comparison of the proportions of signs shared between the seven North Central Desert groups showed that the strongest factor affecting sign language difference is geographical distance. Despite major differences in spoken language, the sign vocabulary of such neighboring groups as Warlpiri and Anmatyerre or Mudbura and Djingili is shared to a greater extent than is the sign vocabulary of more distant groups, even if their spoken languages are more similar.

Overall, we found that the proportion of signs in common between any two groups was higher than the proportion of words in common. Signs appear to be more widely diffused than words, that is to say. Such a conclusion is very similar to the conclusion reached by Meggitt in an analysis of data gathered by Walter Roth from groups in Northwest Central Queensland in 1897.

To account for the greater diffusion of signs as compared to words, six factors were suggested as being at work. It was noted that there appears to be no native ideology of sign language difference, where there is an ideology of spoken language difference, and thus no particular effort to keep sign languages distinct would be expected; processes of name-taboo which induce relatively rapid vocabulary change do not apply to signs; structural differences between spoken languages which impede lexical diffusion would not affect the diffusion of signs; the iconicity of signs makes them easier to learn, and they are thus less likely to be distorted in memory; the formational system of these sign languages is relatively open and new signs are less likely to be transformed to conform to a local formational system than would be the case with spoken words; finally, processes by which concrete images receive gestural representation and cultural similarities giving rise to the selection of the same bases for the same things could also encourage similarity of signs as compared to words.

Comparisons with signs reported from other areas, including the Western Desert, Aranda, Queensland, Arnhem Land and the Cape York Peninsula showed the high degree of distinctiveness of sign language in the North Central Desert area. It was suggested that this distinctiveness is due to the fact that sign languages in this area have a somewhat different range of functions from those it serves elsewhere. In particular, it is only in the North Central Desert that prolonged speech taboos are observed by women in association with mourning. It was suggested that this has meant that sign language in this area is a separate development. Because certain apparently arbitrary signs are found to be the same in widely separate locations, but different from signs for equivalent meanings in the North Central Desert, it was suggested that North Central Desert sign languages may be a relatively more recent development, as well.

Notes

[1]Thus in Warumungu we have *jajja-* 'eat' and *jalupu-* 'drink', in Warlmanpa the corresponding words are *nga-nyja-* and *nguka-*, in Mudbura *nga-* and *pi-*, in Kaytej *aye-nke* and *kwathe-nke* and in Anmatyerre *arlkwe-me* and *antye-me*.

[2]In Warlpiri 'sad' can also be expressed in this way, as in *miyalu wangu* 'stomach bad'.

[3]Cf. *yurrkunyu* in Warlpiri which is a cognate of the Anmatyerre expression.

[4]In Warlpiri coins may be referred to as *pirli*, 'rock', and may be signed accordingly (Mary Laughren, personal communication, 1986).

[5]The form in Warumungu is written as *ngappa* because there is a phonemic distinction between 'long' and 'short' stop consonants. This does not occur in Warlpiri, nor in the other languages of the area.

[6]Arandic languages, when compared to languages in the Southwest (Nyungic) group - which includes Warlpiri, Warlmanpa and Mudbura - show extensive initial dropping of consonants and often of the following vowel, also. Thus *warlalja* (Warlpiri) and *araltye* (Anmatyerre) 'one's own, especially one's own kin' or *purlka* (Warlpiri) and *erlkwe* (Kaytej) 'old man'. In the present analysis, words showing this kind of relationship are considered the same.

[7]Roth's spellings for these groups are used throughout this discussion.

[8]There is no sign for 'honey ant' in the northern part of the North Central Desert, because this species does not occur there.

[9]Among the Pitjantjatjara and Aranda 'creek' is used as a metaphor for female genitalia and the male subincision wound (Roheim 1945, pp. 163-169). This could well account for the form of the sign for this.

[10]Strehlow's sign No. 151, Roth's sign No. 82, attributed to the Woonamurra and Goa. Roth suggests that the form of this sign is an imitation of the action of tapping a tree to see if it is hollow, and thus a possible location for a bee's nest. If this was a common practice throughout the North Central Desert and among the Aranda as well, then the wide distribution of this sign could be as well attributed to parallel invention, after all.

[11]No. 325, *kunna*, in Strehlow's list.

13 Australian Aboriginal sign languages and other semiotic systems

13.0 Introduction

In this Chapter we shall compare the Aboriginal sign languages we have studied with a number of other semiotic systems. This will permit us to see what some of the factors are that contribute to their structure. In addition, by showing what they have in common with other systems, and also how they differ, their particular semiotic status may be clarified.

In previous chapters we have examined the relationship between the NCD sign languages and the spoken languages of their users and we have seen that there are several ways in which spoken language influences them. Thus, as we saw in Chapter 7, for many signs there is a correlation between sign organization and morphology. In Chapter 8 we saw that there is extensive representation in sign of semantic cases, pronouns and directional enclitics. In Chapter 9 we saw that if signed discourse is compared to spoken discourse, discourse units can be established that are equivalent in the two media, and that the organization of constituents within such units is closely similar. We concluded that, at least for the examples considered, it appeared that the signed discourse units were transpositions into sign of spoken discourse units. To an extent, therefore, the sign languages investigated here may be characterized as systems which *represent* their associated spoken languages. This invites a comparison with other systems of language representation, for example writing. First, however, we shall compare them with other sign languages.

We shall begin (13.2) with a look at the NCD sign languages in relation to primary sign languages and versions of signing used among the deaf which are heavily influenced by spoken language, such as sign English.[1] Here we shall see the important part played by a previously established language model in guiding the structure of a system that is secondarily acquired. We shall also see that, although the medium of linguistic expression is very important as a factor affecting language structure, it is not overriding. We shall then compare the NCD sign languages with two other alternate sign languages: a version of the sign language used by the Plains Indians of North America (13.4) and one variety of monastic sign language (13.5). These comparisons will show that the extent and the nature of the relationship between a spoken language and an alternate sign language can vary with several factors. These may include the size of the sign language vocabulary, the functions of the alternate sign language, the presence or absence of writing systems and the nature of the spoken languages used by the signers. The Chapter will conclude (13.7) with a discussion of the NCD sign languages as language codes (systems of spoken language representation) and they will be compared with other language codes, such as whistle and drum 'languages' and writing.

13.1 Primary sign languages and spoken language influenced sign systems

Recent work has shown that in primary sign languages various morphological and syntactic processes are employed that are radically different from those employed in spoken languages. These differences arise because the kinesic medium makes available modes of expression that have no counterpart in spoken language. As discussed in Chapter 1, the kinesic medium makes possible the employment of space as well as time. This allows for a number of modes of expression that are not found in spoken languages. For example, relations between verbal arguments can be displayed spatially and spatial relations can be given directly, without separate prepositional signs. In addition, because signs can be accomplished by several different parts of the body simultaneously, it is possible for signs to overlap in time with one another. Syntactic relations may be marked by 'bracketing', which, most especially, has been shown to be done by actions of the face.

Our analyses of the alternate sign languages considered in this book suggest a number of ways in which they are different from primary sign languages. In the alternate sign languages of the NCD, signing is confined almost exclusively to the hands, typically to one hand only. The face and head are used neither in the production of lexical signs (with but one or two exceptions), nor for grammatical purposes. It appears that, for the most part, the lexical units of these sign languages are directly dependent upon the lexical units of the spoken languages, albeit at various levels, and that the morphological and syntactic devices that appear to be so distinctive of primary sign languages are employed to a much lesser extent. Inflection of movement, as a morphological device, is used only to a limited degree, spatial location for pronominal reference is not well developed and we have not observed anything comparable to the 'predicate classifiers' (McDonald 1983, Supalla 1986) that have been described for primary sign languages.

On the other hand, several of the features we have described for Australian Aboriginal sign languages are quite reminiscent of those forms of signing used in deaf communities that are influenced by the spoken language of the larger community within which they live. In both the United States and Britain, for instance, a form of signing referred to variously as 'manually coded English', 'pidgin sign English', 'sign English' or 'signed English'.[2] has developed which is used mainly in contexts where there is a need for hearing and deaf persons to interact, or where something that is originally in English is to be conveyed to deaf persons - as in the presentation of sermons in churches, news broadcasts, or lectures.

Some description of the properties of this form of signing has been given by Woodward (1973) for American pidgin sign English. In this form of signing there are sets of signs that stand for English nouns, verbs and adjectives. These signs include many that are derived from the local sign language, many initialized forms[3] and also forms derived from fingerspelling, which may also be used extensively. These signs are deployed in English word order and the system may include signs for prepositions, auxiliary particles and one or more signs for the copula and for some verbal inflections as well. Limited use may be made of sign language forms - such as reduplication of nouns for pluralization and reduplication of verbs to express the progressive aspect and the use of a completive sign for the perfect tense. The extent to which the system used follows English patterns or sign language patterns varies according to circumstances, what is being signed and the relative competence in sign or English of the hearing and deaf participants.

Students of these spoken language based forms of signing (e.g. Deuchar 1977 for British signed English and Reilly and McIntire 1980 for American signed English) have remarked on the lack of the use of the face and the much reduced use of various forms of simultaneous expression. In these respects, then, Australian Aboriginal sign languages would appear to resemble such systems. In the circumstances of their development and use they are otherwise quite different, of course.

The characteristics that have been noted for signed English in its various forms are said to be present both because the availability, in this form of signing, of English-like grammatical devices obviates the need to use sign-language-like devices, and also because hearing users lack familiarity with sign language devices. In the case of deaf users, who would otherwise use a form of primary sign language, there is evidence that, in interaction with hearing persons, even where sign is being used, there is a strong tendency to 'tone down' primary sign language expressive devices and to conform much more closely to spoken language influenced forms of signing.

It is widely supposed that such signed English forms are, thus, a compromise. With continual use of such signing and a progressively increasing degree of familiarity with sign language by hearing users, it is expected that there will be a change away from spoken language forms in the direction of sign language forms. There is some evidence for this. Thus, when the American Asylum for the Deaf was established in the United States by Thomas Gallaudet at Hartford, Connecticut, in 1817, the medium of instruction was a form of manually coded English, adapted from the *signe methodique*, a version of manually coded French originally developed by Abbé L'Epée and brought to the United States by Laurent Clerc, a pupil of L'Epée and Sicard, the founders of the use of sign in deaf education in France (Lane 1980). However, by 1830 the manually coded English established at Hartford, and also in use at the New York Institution for the Deaf, was found to be too cumbersome to use and a form of sign language quite rapidly replaced it. Lane (1980, p. 128) states that "At the turn of the century, the head of the American Asylum [for the Deaf] could affirm that the useless and cumbersome parts [of manually coded English] had been removed once and for all in the 1830s and that every teacher of the deaf must master ASL." More recently, studies of the linguistic skills of deaf children who have been taught some form of manually coded English have been reported (Suty and Friel-Patti 1982, Livingston 1983) which show that while such children are quite slow in acquiring manually coded English, they show considerable sophistication in the use of morphological and syntactic devices of primary sign language. Livingston (1983, pp.281-282) concludes that this indicates that children create their own modes of expression and that, for them, the external model of manually coded English is something they only come to acquire at a much later stage. Gee and Goodhart (1985) likewise suggest that in acquiring a sign system such as Signed English children will 'nativize' it - that is, they will modify it in the direction of the structure of the language they learned first - in this case that of sign language. Gee and Goodhart suggest (p. 308) "there are reasons to believe that the gestural modality may impel nativization towards a synthetic norm [i.e. toward having a fusional morphology]".

It is proposed, in short, that where the kinesic medium is the only available medium for linguistic expression, linguistic forms will emerge that have a complex 'layered' morphology (movement morphemes modifying sign performance), that make extensive use of spatial reference and use a variety of devices which amount to the 'incorporation' of verbal arguments into verb signs (e.g. sign 'predicate classifiers'). These features are clearly those that are possible because of the kinesic medium. They appear to be found in all primary sign languages. A comparison of recent work on several different sign languages (including British, Norwegian, Danish , French and Russian sign languages) shows them to be common to all of them. Evidently, though divergent lexically, modes of grammatical expression are fundamentally the same.[4]

On this basis, one might expect that a system of signing such as that developed by the Aborigines of central Australia would show a tendency to diverge from spoken language and become more 'sign-language-like'. Yet, as we have reported, the opposite seems to be the case. It is among those who are most practised in the use of these sign languages that we find the most detailed representations of spoken language in sign. Instead of diverging from a spoken language and developing sign-language-like structures, they appear to converge toward spoken language structure. To be sure, as we noted in the conclusions to Chapter 8, there are several ways in which these sign languages do employ strategies of expression that are characteristic of primary sign languages, but there seems to be much less divergence from spoken language structures than might have been expected, given what is known about the fate of spoken-language based signing systems in deaf communities.

Why should this be? In attempting to answer this question, it should be emphasized that not only are Aboriginal sign languages elaborated by speaker-hearers, but they are used within communities of speaker-hearers. This means that all users have the same access to a very well elaborated spoken language model, which is always available to guide their linguistic output. Spoken language manual coding systems, on the other hand, are used between the hearing and the deaf. They are used, that is to say, in situations where the interactants do not all have access to the same linguistic model. Since the deaf must use the kinesic medium all the time as a means of linguistic communication, modes of expression characteristic of this medium are, for them, likely to be highly developed, but this will not be so for the hearing. Hence, *deaf* who are taught a manual code for a spoken language are highly likely to alter it in the direction of kinesic or primary sign language modes of expression, just as hearing users are likely to do the opposite.

In this connection, it is relevant to note that deaf Aborigines do not, apparently, become highly fluent in the prevailing Aboriginal sign language. Like isolated deaf elsewhere,[5] they rely upon a sign system improvised within their immediate family circle. This may include some elements of the prevailing Aboriginal sign language but, as far as is known, this system is not the main means of communication used with them. Green (1975), in an unpublished survey of deaf Aborigines in the Western Desert, reports examples of deaf Aborigines who may have used some Aboriginal signs, but relied mainly upon a locally developed family sign system. It is of interest to add the observation by La Mont West (1960) on this point. In his study of the sign languages of the Plains Indians of North America, he writes (1960, II p. 64): "Indian deaf mutes often develop a home made sign language within the family or neighborhood circle, rather than learning the fuller Plains Indian sign language." Very little is known about this topic, it should be added, and I have myself come across no accounts of the position of deaf Aborigines in traditional Aboriginal society. From the few observations available, however, it looks as if deaf persons, in a community where an alternate sign language is in use, do not themselves use this sign language, but develop one of their own.[6]

It would seem, then, that the statement of Gee and Goodhart, quoted above, is too strong. The kinesic medium does not 'impel' language structure, at least not to the degree that they seem to suppose. It does provide possibilities for special modes of expression, and these will be adopted if the kinesic medium is the only one available for the development of a linguistic system, as is the case with the deaf. As the studies of Sutyand Friel-Patti and Livingston show, for people who do not have access to spoken language but can use only the kinesic medium, any sign system they may be taught from outside they are likely to reorganize for their own purposes, according to their own strategies of expression. In doing so they will fully exploit the possibilities of the kinesic medium, with the result that the system that is developed will have much in common with an established primary sign language. Users of Australian Aboriginal sign languages, on the other hand, already have a language model available. Like the deaf children who are taught a manual code for a spoken language, they adapt what they acquire of this sign language to their own existing strategies of expression. For them, however, these are based on spoken language. In consequence, as they learn the sign language, they model it on spoken language structure. They do not develop new linguistic structures. The situation of these Aborigines is, in a sense, the reverse of the situation of the deaf subjects in the studies just referred to, and the process by which sign language is adapted to spoken language is, accordingly, the reverse of the process observed in them.

13.2 Comparisons with other alternate sign languages

The development of systems of conventionalized gestures among speaker-hearers as a replacement for speech has arisen many times. Most of these systems are specialized, however, in that they have been developed for use only within specific contexts or domains of activity. They are not used to replace speech in all circumstances of interaction. In the present work we shall compare NCD sign languages with other generalized alternate sign languages. However, a few remarks on specialized systems will be offered first.

We include as instances of specialized alternate sign languages the more or less simple gesture signalling systems that have been developed to meet the communication requirements of specific tasks. For example, among the !Kung San (Bushmen) of the Kalahari Desert in southern Africa, a set of signs has been developed so that, in hunting, hunters may let each other know what animal they have sighted without making any sound (Marshall 1976, p. 136). Some of the sign usages among Aborigines reviewed in Chapter 3 are also of this type (e.g. Berndt 1940). In industrialized societies many highly specialized systems have been described that serve the communication necessary in a wide range of tasks such as crane operation, aircraft marshalling, stock exchange transactions, auction transactions, broadcast studios, communication among skin divers and communication between workers in factories with high noise levels.

Most such systems, or *occupational sign languages*, as they may be called, are quite simple (Brun 1969 describes many of these; an analysis of one such system may be found in Crystal and Craig 1978). Occasionally, they have become elaborated into something more complex, however. The best documented examples of elaborated systems of this sort are those developed in the sawmills of Oregon (Johnson 1978) and British Columbia (Meissner and Philpott 1975). In these cases, what began as a system of gesture signals, established to permit task coordination between workers in circumstances where spoken signals would have been difficult or impossible to use, became a system which made possible the exchange of joking comments on fellow workers, brief exchanges of news, such as sporting results, and small pieces of gossip. This system, like the others mentioned, however, is quite restricted in the circumstances in which it is used. None of these systems completely replace speech as NCD sign languages do and all of them are thus more or less restricted in vocabulary and are quite simple in their modes of expression.

Another specialized context in which gesture systems or sign languages have developed is that of the theatrical performance. These systems may be termed *performance sign languages*. They may become quite complex and, in the case of the system used in Hindu dance drama, it may rival a well developed primary sign language in the degree of its elaboration, although in use its scope is restricted to the narration of traditional Hindu stories within the context of danced drama. West (1960, II, pp. 10-16) provides a preliminary sketch for a systematic analysis of one of these systems, based on the account given in the Bharata-Muni text, which dates from about 600 A.D. or earlier (he relies upon the 1951 edition of Manomohan Ghosh's translation). He shows that this system is amenable to a systematic linguistic analysis comparable to that applicable to primary or to generalized alternate sign languages. He shows that it makes use of a repertoire of phoneme-like elements of movement, position and handshape which combine according to rules of formation into units comparable to morphemes. These in turn are assembled within the performance to create units that are analogous to units of discourse. For accounts of these systems see Coomaraswamy and Duggiralla (1936), La Meri

(1941) and Ghosh (1967). For a modern analysis within a linguistic framework, besides West, see Ikegami (1971).

We may now take up the consideration of NCD sign languages in relation to other generalized alternate sign languages. Besides the Australian systems, three others have been described. These are: an alternate sign language used by married women in certain remote regions of Armenia whenever they were in the presence of their affinal relatives; the sign languages used by the Plains Indians of North America; and the various sign languages used in several European monastic orders which follow a rule of silence.

The system described from Armenia appears to be the closest in function to the Australian Aboriginal systems we have dealt with. As described by Karbelashvili (1936), in the Baraninsky region of Armenia (in the Soviet Socialist Republic of Armenia) women, once married, were not permitted to speak whenever they were in the presence of a wide range of their affinal relatives. A complex sign language for use in these circumstances was developed. The sign languages used by the Plains Indians of North America included a widely shared system that was used in part as a means of communication between groups that did not speak the same language. The sign languages developed in monasteries are, in comparison, relatively restricted. In monastic orders that follow the rule of silence, all forms of communication are discouraged and, originally, only a limited number of signs were permitted to meet essential communication requirements. Despite these restrictions, however, more complex systems have developed. One of these has been quite well described by Barakat (1975).

In the sections to follow we first provide some account of the signing used by the Plains Indians, with special reference to West's (1960) analysis of the widely shared version he termed Plains Standard.We then discuss the monastic sign language described by Barakat. Throughout, we draw comparisons with NCD sign languages. As we shall see, Plains Standard and the monastic sign language to be described differ from one another, and also from the NCD sign languages, in several ways. In particular, they differ in how they relate to spoken language. Plains Standard sign language appears to show no specific relationships with any spoken language and it shows many of the characteristics of primary sign languages. This may be because it was used between people whose spoken languages were mutually unintelligible. The monastic sign language we shall examine shows a closer relationship with spoken language than Plains Standard sign language, but it is still not as closely related to it as NCD sign language is. Furthermore, its relationship is somewhat different because it is, in part, mediated by writing.

13.3 Sign language among the Plains Indians of North America

Besides the Australian Aborigines, the people who made the most widespread use of alternate sign language were the Plains Indians of North America.[7] The signing they employed received considerable attention in the nineteenth century (Mallery 1978 [1880], 1972 [1881]; Clark 1982 [1885]; Hadley 1893; Scott 1978 [1893]) but little was added to our knowledge of it in the present century, until the study by La Mont West (1960). Apart from West's work, the most important contributions to this topic since 1900 include Tomkins' (1969 [1929]) presentation of a large number of signs for use by Boy Scouts, the efforts of Scott to record it cinematographically in 1934, a series of papers by Harrington (1978 [1938]), and a critical discussion by Kroeber (1978 [1958]). Since West's work, which remains only as a Ph. D. dissertation, no original work has been done.[8] A survey and evaluation of the most important literature has been published by Taylor (1978).

13.3.1 Origin and distribution

Sign language appears to have been widely used by the Plains Indians as a means of communication between groups speaking unrelated languages, and its development may have been brought about by a need for intertribal communication in circumstances in which groups speaking quite different languages came into brief but repeated contact with one another. It is by no means certain that this was so, however. As West has pointed out (1960, II, p. 63), there is evidence that spoken lingua francas were widespread in the Plains area, even before European contact. Furthermore, traditionally, sign language use was by no means confined to inter-lingual interactions. It was used within a tribe in oratory, ceremonial performance, storytelling, and as a convenient form of communication in circumstances where speech is difficult to use. However, its use as a lingua franca appears to have been very important, and may be the reason why its use became so widespread throughout the Plains culture area.

The best available evidence indicates that the use of signs by North American Indians was well developed in the area of the Gulf Coast of Louisiana, South Texas and Tamaulipas in Mexico (see Fig.13.1) long before they were used further to the north. Coronado reported the use of signs in this area in 1541 (Winship 1896, cited by Taylor 1978), and there are subsequent accounts in the eighteenth century (e.g. Santa Ana 1740 as quoted by Goddard

Fig. 13.1 North American Indian tribes reported to have used sign language. Tribes that used sign language underlined. The Plains culture area outlined by heavy black line. Note that some tribes contiguous to Plains area also used signs. The map does not show tribes not native to the Plains who were crowded onto the Plains from the East and the Southeast during the late 18th and 19th centuries. Many of these Indians (e.g. Delaware, Shawnee, Wyandot, Kickapoo, Cherokee) also learned and used sign language. Note: Santee, Yankton and Teton equal Sioux; Bungi equals Ojibway; Blackfoot, Blood and Piegan equal Blackfoot; Jicarilla and Mescalero equal Apache; Wind River equals Shoshoni. Map drawn by A.R. Taylor, from p. 221 in Clark Wissler, *The American Indian,* Oxford University Press, 1922. Tribal entries based on West 1960, Vol. 2, pp. 61a-61b. Reproduced with adapted legend from Taylor (1978, p. 227) with permission of author and Plenum Publishing Company, New York

1979). This area is (or was) an area of extreme linguistic diversity. Goddard (1979), in a survey of the languages there, concludes that languages of at least seven unrelated families were in use and he, like Taylor (1978), suggests that the sign language of the Plains in all probability originated in this area as a response to this linguistic situation. Sign language spread northwards until, by 1880, it was in use all over the Plains area. This spread is part of the process by which the Plains culture complex came to be established. This was greatly facilitated by the introduction of the horse by the Spanish in the seventeenth century. With the horse, tribes who already engaged in buffalo hunting were able to extend their hunting territories considerably. Tribes who previously were agriculturalists, such as the Cheyenne, upon acquiring the horse, also became highly mobile buffalo hunters, even abandoning their settled agricultural life in the process. The result was that many groups, speaking several quite different languages, came into contact with one another for the first time (Lowie 1954). It is widely supposed that this facilitated the spread of sign language, even if sign language was not devised, in the first instance, for inter-lingual communication.

The details of how sign language came to be established as a lingua franca in the Plains are not known. It is possible that sign languages were already in use by tribes to the north and that existing sign languages were thus adapted for inter-tribal communication. Taylor (1978) shows, however, that there is evidence that signs were not in use in the northern Plains as late as the eighteenth century and that their use spread over the whole area only within the last 250 years. It is more likely, thus, that the use of signs spread northwards, as groups from the north and the east moved into the southern Plains, after they had acquired the use of the horse. If this is so, then the Plains sign language of the nineteenth century could be a development from the sign language previously in use in southern Texas and northern Mexico.

13.3.2 Plains Standard and NCD sign languages

West (1960), at the instigation of Kroeber (1978 [1958]) and working under the guidance of Voegelin (1958), attempted a structural linguistic analysis of a version of Plains Indian sign language that he termed Plains Standard, as expounded by an Arapaho, Mr. William Shakespeare. He proposed an analysis of signs into what he termed their component *kinemes* (a term he borrowed from Birdwhistell 1955) and *morphemes*. A *kineme* he defines as "the largest structural unit of motion, shape, direction or tempo not consistently assigned a conventionalized meaning, but which behaves as a unit when entering combinations that are consistently assigned a meaning or meanings..." (1960, II, pp. 11-12). These are comparable to the handshapes, loci of articulation and movements that have been used in the analysis presented in Chapter 5. West's treatment is somewhat different, however, for he distinguishes direction and movement pattern as separate kineme classes, his treatment of location includes several external (non-body) locations, and he also establishes a class of dynamic kinemes, which includes manner of movement and a specification of how the hands participate in enacting the sign. He thus distinguished five kineme classes, where we have distinguished only three.

The *morpheme* in West's analysis is the smallest unit of motion, shape, direction or tempo, or any combination of such, that is consistently assigned a conventionalized meaning or which serves to indicate a relationship between two or more morphemes. A morpheme may comprise a single sign, but, more usually, a sign can be analyzed as containing several morphemes. One of West's major claims is that the grammar of Plains Standard is to be understood almost wholly in terms of the internal morphological organization of signs and their spatial relationships with one another, rather than in terms of how signs are sequentially arranged in time within an utterance. Thus he says that Plains Standard is "strikingly inflectional in regard to internal sign morphology… [it] largely ignores the fourth dimension, time, but intensively employs the three spatial dimensions to express relationships and to structure formal components. Both the 'syntax' and the semantic logic of sign language are spatially oriented, and it is this spatial orientation that accounts most strikingly for the high degree of integration and rigidity of sign languages at the morphemic level" (1960, I, p.1b).

We may now consider various aspects of Plains Standard, mainly as described by West, and compare them to features of the NCD sign languages. So far as body part involvement is concerned, from West's account it would seem that Plains Standard, like NCD sign languages, is predominantly manual in character. West does recognize that facial expression may play some role, but he appears to regard this as paralinguistic and he accords it no place in his linguistic description. Thus he says that (1960, II, p. 77) "…a good sign user avails himself of face and tongue to lend dramatic impact and emotional force to his sign productions, though a graceful sign talker's facial expression and speech are not permitted to be obtrusive". In other forms of Plains Indian sign language, however, the face may have a more important role to play. West states: "Sign talkers unfamiliar with the standard tend toward larger, freer movements, exuberant use of facial expression and posture, and frequently voluble running commentary in some spoken language. This tendency is especially developed in the far northern dialect area, where sign language is used almost exclusively for story telling". (1960, II, p. 75). Whether, in fact, the face plays the kind of grammatical role it has recently been shown to do in primary sign languages remains somewhat of an open question, it would seem.

There are two accounts of handshapes used in Plains Indian signing, one by West, the other by Mallery. All of the handshapes described by West and all but one of those described by Mallery are also employed in the NCD sign languages. However, seven of West's handshapes do not appear to match handshapes in Mallery, while eight of Mallery's handshapes do not match those described by West. Both authors distinguish several versions of A, B and G handshapes on the basis of hand orientation. If we ignore these distinctions we find that, to use our symbols, both West and Mallery list A (fist), to (fingers 'tapered' together, tips on extended thumb), G (index finger only extended), L (index finger and thumb extended and abducted), U (index and second finger extended, abducted: 'V' hand), c5 (all fingers extended, spread, curved: 'basket' hand) and B ('flat' hand). West also lists the following handshapes which are not given by Mallery: L̈ (as L but digits bent), Â I ('fist' with thumb and little finger extended) 5t (all fingers spread, but thumb opposed) G̈ (as G but index finger bent) Ü ('bent V) C (all digits extended, adducted, bent, with thumb opposed and bent), bO (tip of index finger rests on tip of thumb, other digits flexed to palm), bO2 (tips of index and second fingers rest on tip of thumb, fingers spread). The handshapes which Mallery lists but which are not given by West are: Â (fist with thumb extended), X (index finger flexed so nail lies against tip of extended thumb, other digits flexed), E (digits extended and adducted, but fully flexed at B and C joints), a handshape described as "hooked, thumb against side of forefinger", which does not occur in the NCD set, xO (all fingers curled so that their tips rest on the side of the the thumb), 5 (all digits extended and spread), cB (all digits extended, adducted, somewhat bent: the hand forms a 'cup'), a version of cB in which the thumb is crossed on to the palm, and U (the hand held in a relaxed fashion). These differences doubtless arise from the very different samples these investigators had studied. West's set of handshapes is drawn from his analysis of sign language as expounded by a single Arapaho informant. Mallery does not attribute his handshapes to any sign language group, but he had gathered material from many different groups. These differences suggest that there may be kinological differences between sign languages in use by the Plains Indians as well as lexical differences and differences in style of sign performance. It is of interest, however, that both investigators report a closely similar number of handshapes - 14 by West and 18 by Mallery (ignoring orientation distinctions) - and that all but three of these handshapes are also found to be used by all seven of the NCD groups we have investigated.

As in NCD, so in Plains Standard, the way in which the hand or hands are disposed in space in relation to the signer's body is an integral feature of the sign. West terms this spatial component of the sign its *referent.* He lists thirty three Body Referents and seven External Referents. The Body Referents include twenty main body locations (head, face, trunk and legs) and thirteen locations that refer to the left hand. The External Referents specify the compass directions of the signs and three are also established to specify the location of a current sign in relation to the spatial location of a previously performed sign. Of the main body referents, there are 15 that are also found in NCD sign languages, but we also find Foot, Ankle, Spine and Coccyx, which do not occur in NCD sign languages. Locations not mentioned by West, but found in NCD sign languages, include Forehead, Cheek, Face, Below Eyes, Below Nose, Chin, Side of Torso, Breast, and Under Arm. So far as main body referents are concerned, thus, Plains Standard makes fewer distinctions than NCD, but it also uses several body locations that are out of the range found in NCD.

Movement is less easy to compare directly, since in his analysis West treats movement patterns separately from direction, whereas in our system this is not done. West distinguishes only Curved, Straight, Oscillation or Vibration and Circular movements. To these, for NCD sign languages, we should add Forearm Pronation and Supination, Wrist Flexion and Wrist Extension and Tremble.

In general, then, in Plains Standard, signs are made manually and the face has no linguistic role. Signs may be made by one hand only or by both hands acting in unison or alternately, and there are also many signs in which one hand (usually the left hand) serves as a location for action by the right hand. In Plains Standard there are fewer handshapes than in NCD, although almost all those used in it are the same as the most widely used handshapes in NCD. There appear to be fewer locations of articulation in relation to the body than in NCD, although Plains Standard employs both the dorsal surface of the the body and the ankle and foot as locations, which NCD does not. Movement patterns are harder to compare. It does seem that certain movements, which are common in NCD, are not employed in Plains Standard. A great many signs in Plains Standard are made by whole arm actions. From West's description, it would seem that Plains Standard is less fine grained in its movements than NCD.

West maintains, as do most other authors, that there is a very high degree of iconicity in Plains Indian signing. Harrington (1938) attempts a systematic analysis of the forms of signs from this point of view (this analysis has provided some of the inspiration for the system we followed in Chapter 6 of this book). West does not himself attempt any analysis of the signs in his corpus of this sort, although his analysis of signs into their component morphemes, to be outlined below, depends in part upon a recognition of the meaningful elements of signs, interpreted iconically. In Chapter 6 we suggested that an explanation of the current form of a sign often requires an understanding of the processes of *image representation*, by which some concrete object or pattern of action taken as symbolic for a given concept (the 'base') is given gestural representation, and the processes of *sign formation*, by which such a gestural representation becomes altered in various ways, under the influence of a number of general processes, as it becomes incorporated into the system of signs in the sign language vocabulary. It is clear that these processes are also in operation in Plains Indian signing, and indeed they are explicitly referred to by several authors (including Mallery and Kroeber). A consideration of a selection from the sign descriptions provided by Mallery (1972 [1881]) or by Clark (1982 [1885]) strongly suggests, nevertheless, that a high proportion of Plains Indian signs retain much of the character of image representations. Whereas in the NCD languages there are many signs for which it is hard to perceive any connection between form and meaning (few are 'translucent', that is, to use Klima and Bellugi's term), this appears to be less the case for Plains Indian signs. This suggests that at least some Plains Indian signing may not have been established for very long. If we accept the suggestion that sign language spread throughout the Plains only within the last 250 years, some versions of it would have been much younger than this at the time Mallery collected his material and, in consequence, almost certainly much younger than the NCD sign languages.

According to West, signs in Plains Standard are well separated from one another in discourse and signs that occur in sequence do not tend to fuse together in any way. As West puts it (1960, I, p. 52) "external sandhi is almost unknown in American Indian sign language". Although we have not examined external sandhi in NCD sign languages systematically, it certainly occurs and a few examples have been provided. In NCD signs in discourse are often minimally separated from one another (see Ch. 9). In general, American Indian signing, as reported by West, is fairly slow (between two and one and a half signs per second). Most of West's material may have been somewhat formally presented stories and statements. However, it should be noted that Plains Indian signing was, and perhaps still is, mainly used as an oratorical form, for story telling and formal addresses to large meetings. Such a use might encourage a rather slow and deliberate mode of delivery. NCD sign languages, of course, like primary sign languages, are used in rapid everyday face-to-face interchanges and this would encourage a much greater degree of running together of signs in discourse, or external sandhi, to use West's term, which we certainly find.

West describes three levels of juncture. These are the 'paragraph final' juncture, in which both hands are folded or crossed over the lower abdomen or in the lap (if the signer is sitting); the 'phrase final' juncture, in which the hands relax and move toward the lower abdomen or lap, but rebound before reaching it; and the 'sign final' juncture, in which the hand, upon the completion of a sign, either remains still before proceeding to the next sign or, more commonly, moves toward the shoulder or toward the chest, and then pauses, before proceeding. Such sign final junctures are absent between signs within a sign compound, but occur almost everywhere else. The first two of these junctures correspond quite closely to the R junctures and C junctures described in Chapter 9, and they appear to have a very similar pattern of occurrence. However, from West's description, it would seem that 'paragraph final' junctures are performed in a much more formal and consistent way than are the R junctures we have described. It also appears that there is much greater marking of the boundary of signs in the signing of West's informant than there is in our material. This is no doubt a reflection of the slower and more deliberate manner in which signing appears to be done, as compared to either NCD or everyday primary signing.

It appears to be a feature of Plains Standard, and apparently of Plains Indian signing, generally, that many referents require a string of two or more signs for their designation. Where this is so, it is usually the case that the first sign in such a string designates the general class to which the referent belongs, while subsequent signs qualify it and make it specific. For example, a widely used sign for Negro was the string WHITEMAN + BLACK; a sign for Infantry was WHITEMAN + SOLDIER + WALK. West refers to such strings as 'open compounds', for the same referent may be designated by several different sign groupings. He writes (II, p. 55) "It is common for an American Indian to specify an animal by as many as 5 or 6 separate signs, each portraying pantomimically some attribute or habit of the animal and each sufficient alone for identification of the animal." As an example (I, p. 121), West shows how 'skunk' may be represented by an open compound of as many as seven signs: 1. SMALL ANIMAL + 2. PLUMED TAIL + 3. STRIPED BACK + 4. ODOR + 5. BAD + 6. EGG + 7. SMASH, although various shorter combinations of signs from this set may, at times, be used. With regard to NCD sign languages, it will be noted that although such open compounding is occasionally resorted to by a signer when she does does not know a sign for something, it is not a widespread practice and is not a feature of the sign language, as it appears to be for Plains Indian signing.

It is possible that open compounding is a feature of Plains Indian signing because it has so often been used as a means of inter-lingual communication. In a discussion of the ability of people from different tribes to talk with one another using sign, West refers to the redundancy introduced by the use of open compounds as a feature which greatly facilitates this. Thus West writes, "such elaboration [open compounding] can be introduced at will in order to compensate for any misunderstanding on the part of the observer and is readily resorted to whenever the observer is one unfamiliar with the local sign dialect" (II, p. 55).

Within an utterance the ordering of signs (including sign compounds) is fairly free. West found that his informant gave the same sentence with numerous different sign orderings, although some of these orderings, when re-submitted to him, were rejected, showing that there were some preferences. In general it appears that, within an utterance, topics precede qualifiers, so that noun signs occur early in the sequence, while verb signs tend to be placed toward the end. An interrogative sentence is always begun by a question sign and a negation sign always follows that which is negated. If the temporal frame of an utterance is to be specified, temporal adverbial signs will be placed initially. As will be recalled from Chapter 9, these statements could equally well apply to NCD sign language. There, however, we pointed out that the ordering of signs in discourse appeared to be highly similar to word order in spoken discourse and we suggested that sign order in fact follows the preferential word order of the sign talker, since we supposed that she was simply providing signed versions of words she otherwise would have spoken. In the case of Plains Standard sign talkers, however, this would not necessarily apply. As we shall see below, there is little evidence that Plains Standard is parasitic on any particular spoken language in the way that NCD sign languages are.

In West's view the sequential ordering of signs within an utterance is not the main means by which grammatical relations are expressed. Rather, he says, "obligatory grammatical relationships are established ... by spatial relationships, both within the execution of single signs and between positions of execution of succeeding signs. ...[T]he ...grammatical structure of American Indian Sign Language ...is almost entirely a matter of internal sign morphology and that syntactic order is in most cases a redundant, non-obligatory stylistic matter" (1960, I, p. 90). He notes (pp. 68-69) that "one of the most distinctive and important features of sign language involves its technique of assigning a previously executed sign to some point in space and using that point as a *referent* for subsequent signs, when it is desired to refer to the previous sign". By adding, in the transcription of a sign, a symbol to indicate the spatial position of its execution, relative to the spatial location used for the execution of the preceding sign, West can incorporate the spatial relationship of a given sign to another into its morphological description. This use of spatial location for pronominal reference is well known for ASL and other primary sign languages, and indeed it has been cited as a prime example of how a kinesic language may differ from a spoken language because it can use space as an expressive resource (e.g. Stokoe 1980, p. 384).

West's analysis of signs into their component morphemes further shows how grammatical relationships in Plains Standard are conveyed through sign inflection, not through sequencing. He notes that this can be shown most clearly in the case of verb signs. For example, in Plains Standard the sign for 'attack' is to thrust a fisted hand forward, opening it to a spread hand in the course of doing so. West gives the example of how 'he attacks him' is signed. Here, both hands are employed. The fisted hands are first placed in the position previously designated for the first third person (the first 'he') and the movement of the sign is now in a direction toward the position previously designated for the second third person (the second 'he'). This is a simple example of the 'incorporation' of subject and object into the verb, a phenomenon well known for ASL (Fischer and Gough 1978) which can also occur for some verbs in NCD sign languages. In West's analysis, this sign is composed of two morphemes: the fist expansion combined with the thrusting movement ('attack'), and the direction of movement from the first to the second third person positions ('He-to-him').

West notes that most instances of Verb signs provide not only information about the action performed but, in addition, they may incorporate information in respect to several additional categories. For many Verb signs much of this additional information is unavoidably or obligatorily provided. Thus it is obligatory for many Verb signs to provide information about the relationship between actor and object, spatial location of action, person, spatial relationship to sign talker, transitivity, speed or force of action, scope or extent of action, multiplicity of action, repetition, and seriality-distributivity. Noun signs may also incorporate information about spatial location of any attribute, spatial relationship to sign talker, juxtaposition, and whether visible or non-visible.

It will not escape notice that, in many respects, West's account of the morphology and grammar of Plains Standard anticipates the insights reported more recently concerning the morphology and grammar of ASL and other primary sign languages. Workers such as Bellugi (1980), Supalla and Newport (1978) and McDonald (1983) have emphasized the highly inflectional character of ASL and have proposed that signs should themselves be analyzed into morpheme components. For example, after reviewing much of this most recent work, McDonald (1983) recommends that we "change our assumptions about ASL". She says that " ...the sign is not the smallest unit of meaning. ...[A] single sign is made up of many morphemes which combine in an incredibly tight fashion" (p. 35). She then goes on to provide examples which show that particular handshapes may recur in many different verbs in ASL, reflecting a semantic theme that is common to them. Thus a fisted hand occurs in verbs in which a small compact object is being handled, a cupped spread hand occurs in verbs in which a round object is being handled, or a handshape in which one or two fingers are extended and curved occurs in verbs in which the motion or location of narrow curved objects is being expressed. Her analysis is very close to that proposed by West, but neither she, nor any of the other leading workers in sign language today, make any reference to his work.

The NCD Aboriginal sign languages discussed in this book, as we have previously observed, do not appear to display the degree of internal morphological complexity that West described for Plains Standard or that has been described recently for ASL. To a limited extent, in the NCD sign languages, some verb signs can be modified both directionally and iteratively to convey information about Subject-Object relations and about repetition, prolongation or distribution of action, but since signed utterances in these sign languages so often match the morphemic organization of the spoken language so closely, the development of a spatially organized grammar of the kind found in ASL or PSL appears to be much less advanced.

13.3.3 Plains Indian sign language and spoken language

Several writers on Plains Indian signing who preceded West have suggested that there is a relationship between it and spoken language, although none provide much in the way of exemplification. Thus, Clark (1982[1885]) provides examples which suggest that signs for new things introduced by Europeans also followed the structure of the spoken language expressions of them. Harrington (1978 [1938]) provides as typical an example which shows that sign order in descriptive phrases may be determined by the spoken language of the signer. He illustrates this with examples of how the concept of God is signed in Kiowa and Ojibway. According to Harrington, both groups signed this as a compound of signs for 'big' and 'spirit' or 'medicine'. In Kiowa the sign for God was MEDICINE+BIG, whereas in Ojibway it was BIG+SPIRIT. In the corresponding spoken languages Harrington gives *daa'k'ia-'eidl* 'medicine-big', whereas in Ojibway he gives *kihtci-manitoo* 'big spirit'. The signs, in each case, as they are illustrated, are the same, but the order within the compound is different, according to the order of noun and its modifier that is followed in the spoken language. He maintains that "[t]he signs are everywhere based on spoken language and reflect it at every turn.

The word order, the syntax, the vocabulary (the peculiar bundles of concepts tied together under the label of each word) of the American Indian sign language all prove it to be based, originally and constantly, on the spoken language of the user, whatever Indian idiom he happens to use as his daily speech."

Kroeber (1978 [1958]) also maintained that American Indian sign language, "like writing, is a substitute for speech ...The concepts which sign language communicates are basically concepts already developed in speech but translated into a non-spoken medium." His evidence for this is similar to Harrington's, but with more examples. He reports the results of an examination of the signs described by Tomkins in his *Universal Indian Sign Language*. This book was written mainly for the benefit of Boy Scouts; however the signs described in the book, according to Kroeber, appear to be based mainly on the sign language of the Western Dakota Indians. Kroeber gives many examples of compounded signs in which one sign denotes a concrete object, the other serves as a specifier or qualifier. He shows that in most instances the order is that of 'noun' followed by 'qualifier'. He states (p. 193) that "Siouan, Kiowa, Athabaskan and Muskogian compound nouns by having the qualifying or determining noun precede, the verb or adjective follow the noun element; which is also the apparent sign language order." Several other languages spoken in the Plains region had a different order, but over half of the Indians inhabiting the Plains in the nineteenth century spoke either Siouan or one of the other languages (such as Kiowan or Athabascan) that had the same order in compounds as is found in the sign language. Kroeber concludes (ibid) "The suggestion is that the Siouan compositional order of elements was adopted for sign language compounds." However, Kroeber goes on to suggest that, because of the "slow and incomplete development with which gestures proceed" greater clarity of exposition would be achieved if concrete objects were mentioned first and their qualities later. He concludes (p. 194): "It remains to be discovered, accordingly, whether it is general considerations of this nature which have chiefly established sign order, or the influence of translation from speech. Both may have been at work."

It is, of course, possible that, locally, sign language did show some degree of influence from the local spoken language. This is apparently what Harrington (1978 [1938]) believed. At the same time, the version employed widely at inter-tribal gatherings which West designates as Plains Standard, could well have developed as a system independent of any spoken language. West undertook a very thorough comparative study of the various Plains Indian sign vocabularies that were available to him, and he also himself collected sign language samples from many different places in the northern Plains and showed that there was considerable dialectal variation. However, it remains for future research, if indeed such can still be undertaken, to determine how far there may have been local influence from spoken language on Plains Indian sign language structure.

So far as the widely used Plains Standard is concerned, there appear to be strong reasons for accepting the view that this does not relate structurally to any spoken language. First of all, the grammatical character of the sign language, as described by West, in itself makes it highly unlikely that it could be considered as a representation of any particular spoken language. Thus, as West writes (1960, II, p. 29):

> In view of the strong individualistic bent of internal grammatical structure observed by the writer for American Indian sign language...it seems highly unlikely that any American Indian sign language dialect has a syntax that could be consistently correlated with a spoken language syntax of the tribes concerned, for sign syntax is characterized most prominently by flexibility, the obligatory grammatical mechanisms being largely confined to the internal morphology of signs. This internal morphology, in turn, represents the point at which sign language differs most fundamentally from spoken language and neither morpheme classes nor combinatorial possibilities find much common ground between sign language and spoken.

Second, as West also points out, as have others, in the area where Plains Standard was used there are several different spoken languages. Indeed, in the Plains area the languages spoken belonged to eight different language families (Sherzer 1976) and most, thus, had little or nothing in common with one another lexically, morphologically or grammatically. In the light of this, it seems highly unlikely that a sign language used throughout this area, as Plains Standard appears to have been, would be modelled upon one, rather than another, of the spoken languages that were in use. Kroeber, as quoted above, did suggest that the noun-qualifier order common in many sign expressions could reflect the influence of Siouan languages which, he said, were spoken by about half of the groups in the Plains area. West, on the other hand (1960, I, 91-92), states that Siouan speaking Plains Indians were actually quite marginal to the main sign language area and suggests that a better choice for a linguistic influence would have been Kiowan. The Kiowa, who also have a noun-qualifier order in their speech, have often been credited with being the originators of Plains Indian signing. West goes on to point out, however, that the Comanche, Arapaho, Cheyenne and Blackfoot were also very important in disseminating sign language and all of these groups spoke languages in which syntax would dictate a qualifier-noun order, rather than a noun-qualifier order. He adds, as a further point, and perhaps a more telling one, that the compounds that Kroeber is referring to in the spoken languages in question cannot be compared to the compounds that occur in Plains Indian sign language. As he put it (p. 92)"...the 'compound noun' situation referred to by Kroeber comprises compounding in a formal, structural sense for the spoken languages cited; but in sign language there are no formal, structural criteria of the sort intended. There is compounding in the sign language, but the analogue to the spoken language compounds cited by Kroeber are [sic] not compounds in sign language, but simple sequences of signs related only by juxtaposition and some conceptual common-denominators, but by no formal features." Elsewhere, West also points out that he found only some degree of preference for particular syntactic ordering in signed utterances and that there was no evidence that the syntactic ordering of the signer's spoken language exerted influence of any strength on sign order. As we have seen, given the spatial nature of Plains Standard syntax, as West describes it, sign order in utterances would not, in any case, be very important - as indeed it proved not to be.

We see, then, that there are quite strong grounds for accepting the view that Plains Standard was not structured by any spoken language. It is for this reason, we suggest, that it has developed characteristics that are very similar to those found in a primary sign language, and in this it is clearly different from the Australian Aboriginal NCD sign languages we have considered here.

It should be added here that, according to West, speech is quite often used simultaneously with signing. He reports that of the 116 informants he recorded sign language from, 47 spoke continuously as they signed. He undertook no detailed analysis of how this continuous speech is related to the signing; however he remarks (1960, II, p.76): "The spoken harangue in some cases paralleled the sign language, in some cases involved comments *about* what was being simultaneously signed, and in some cases was an independent lecture or conversation intended for the writer or some by-stander." West further adds that fluent signers were just as likely to speak as to remain silent; however Plains Standard signers were more likely to remain silent while signing.

13.4 Monastic sign languages

Several monastic Orders, founded as long ago as the fourth century, A.D., follow a rule of silence. Ideally, the members of these Orders are to devote all their time to contemplation, and communication with others, especially by speech, is regarded as a distraction from this. At the present time the Cistercians, the Cluniacs and the Trappists follow a version of a rule of silence that was first laid down by St. Benedict in the sixth century. In the monasteries of these Orders, silence is enjoined from seven in the evening until seven the next morning, and it is also required during mealtimes, and at all times in certain parts of the monastery. When speech is permitted, it should be kept to a minimum and confined to decorous subjects.

However, the necessity for a minimal degree of communication was always recognized and, from the first, a number of signs were permitted. The first lists of permitted gestures were drawn up in the tenth century, and it is from these lists of official signs, revised from time to time, that the present day monastic sign languages partly derive. 'Unofficial' signs also evolved. These are used to add to and to make possible richer communication during periods of silence than the official signs permit. The use of these unofficial signs is frowned upon and their use may sometimes incur punishment. However, though the development of unofficial sign vocabularies was restricted it could not be entirely prevented and each monastery evolved its own version of sign language. Differences between the sign languages used in different monasteries could be considerable, so that visiting Brothers often found that they could not use sign language to communicate easily, beyond the minimum permitted by the official signs of the Order. West (1960, II, pp. 39-44) undertook a comparative study of monastic signs, as these have been compiled by van Rijnberk (1953), from several different Orders and a number of different monasteries. He showed that there was remarkably little overlap. He writes (II, p. 39): "Rather than a monastic species of sign language with dialects, there appears to be a group of independent sign languages which share only the characteristic of being used by Roman Catholics in monastic seclusion and under silence ban. Each order, and in some cases each monastery, seems to have its own, strongly individualized sign language."

Although there are a number of published lists of monastic signs from various monasteries in Europe (Umiker-Sebeok and Sebeok 1987 comprise a recent compilation) only one detailed linguistic study of a monastic sign language has been undertaken. This is the study by Barakat (1975) of the sign language in use at St. Joseph's Abbey, in Spencer, Massachusetts. In this study, Barakat provides some analysis of the manner in which the signs relate to their referents, he examines sign language syntax and provides descriptions of over 1200 signs.

The sign descriptions provided by Barakat are organized into three sections. In the first section he gives the official list of 324 basic signs. This is followed by descriptions of 208 derived signs that are formed from the basic signs by compounding. These lists have official recognition in the Cistercian Order and these signs are thus likely to be found in use in other Cistercian monasteries. In the second section, Barakat describes the officially sanctioned vocabulary for St. Joseph's Abbey. This shows some overlap with the list sanctioned by the Cistercian Order. However, not only are some of the signs variants of those in the official list of the Order, there are also some additional items that permit reference to aspects of contemporary life that are not included in this other list. Some of these items reflect features peculiar to St. Joseph's Abbey. This second section includes 180 basic signs and 112 derived signs. The third section of Barakat's dictionary comprises the unofficial vocabulary of 'original' or 'useless' signs elaborated at St. Joseph's Abbey. This is an open set, including many short-lived inventions. These signs permit reference to things beyond the rather strict limits imposed by the use of the official signs and they make possible a certain amount of joking and humor, as well. Barakat says that these signs "are constantly being invented for immediate purposes and rarely gain recognition beyond the exchange in which they are used" (p. 88). Barakat describes 627 of these signs. He also describes an unofficial set of signs for conveying the twenty-six letters of the alphabet, and a set of numeral signs.

Barakat classifies the signs in these lists into five partially overlapping classes, according to how they relate to their referents. These are pantomimic signs (i.e., obviously iconic signs); pure signs, that is, signs that appear to be purely arbitrary; qualitative signs, or signs which refer to their referent by assigning one or more qualities to it; signs that are partly related to a spoken expression for the referent; and signs that are attempts at a phonetic representation of a word. A comparison of the different sign lists shows that they differ in the frequency with which signs from these different classes occur in them. Thus, as Barakat points out, most of the basic signs in the two official lists have a pantomimic character: that is, they comprise schematized enactments of action patterns or schematized characterizations of objects that are taken as symbolic of their referents (i.e bases; see Chapter 6). All of the phonetic signs, on the other hand, are found in the unofficial list of signs.

It is of interest to note that some 47 of the basic signs in the list sanctioned by the Cistercian Order are compounds in which one sign serves to stand for a general class of object and another serves to specify it.[9] For example, to sign 'cat' one moves the hands laterally from either side of the mouth, as if depicting whiskers, and follows with the sign for ANIMAL. Likewise for 'pig' the sign ANIMAL is combined with a sign in which one points to the side of the nose. Again, to sign 'cabbage' one first clasps one's head with two hands, and then makes the sign VEGETABLE. To sign 'onion' one makes the sign VEGETABLE and then draws the outer edge of the extended thumb along the lower edge of the right eye. It will be recalled (p.417) that a similar kind of compounding has been frequently reported in Plains Indian signing and it is notable that it also occurs in the Baraninsky sign language from Armenia as described by Karbelashvili (1936). Karbelashvili describes signs for twelve different animals. All of them are compounds of two signs, one of them the same in all cases, the other specific to each sign.

Similarly, he describes five water-related signs - 'river', 'sea', 'well', 'fish' and 'bank'. All of these are compounds, all using as the first element the same sign as the sign glossed simply as 'water'.[10] This suggests that the formation of such 'classifier compound' signs may be a general strategy for sign formation and it would seem to deserve further investigation. If this is so, it is all the more striking that this kind of compound sign formation is not encountered at all in the NCD sign languages.

The derived signs in both the Order's list and in that of St. Joseph's Abbey are all compounds of signs from the basic list. In most cases these are compounds of only two signs, but occasionally three or more may be used. These compounds differ from the 'classifier compounds' just mentioned for they comprise a combination of two or more basic signs which serve as a kind of translation of the referent into component concepts. Thus, in St. Joseph's Abbey's list 'snow' is signed as WHITE+RAIN, 'storeroom' is signed as HIDE+HOUSE and 'refectory' is signed as EAT+HOUSE. According to Barakat, the derived signs in the Order's list are based on translations from French so that where a compound consists of a sign for something and a modifying sign, the modifier typically is placed after the topic sign, as in French.

In the list of 'original' signs the large majority are compounds and many of them are compounds of three or more signs. These compounds are made up on the spur of the moment and they may or may not gain currency among the monks. Even if they do, however, they are not officially sanctioned. Many of the compounds found in this list are similar to the open compound signs that West described for Plains Standard sign language. For example, 'Easter' is signed as GOD+UP+DAY, 'grounds keeper' is signed as RELIGIOUS (i.e. monk) + CHARGE + FLOWER, 'literature' is signed as READ + ALL + BEAUTIFUL + WRITING and 'Noah' is reported to be signed as OLD + SAINT + ARRANGE + BIG + BOAT + TIME + BIG + WATER + FILL + COME.

Many other compounds in the 'original' list, however, arise as a result of attempts to create a sequence of gestures that will be understood as a representation of the spoken sound of a word that refers to what is meant. Where an English word can be analyzed into component words, or into parts that sound somewhat like English words, if signs already exist for these parts, then a compound will be formed from them. Thus, 'hurricane' may be signed as HURRY + CANE, 'hardship' may be signed as HARD + SHIP, 'Philip' may be signed as FILL+ UP, and 'Czech' may be signed with a sign in which a check mark or tick is sketched. Where this cannot be done, then letter signs will be used. However, letter signs are not used as a way of spelling the word intended. They are used, rather, as representations of speech sounds, generally as sounds that stand for syllables that cannot otherwise be equated with words for which a sign can be found. For example, 'pumpernickel' may be signed as PUMP + R + FIVE + CENTS, 'Ohio' may be signed as O + HIGH + O, 'Iowa' may be signed as EYE + O + A and 'Hawaii' may be signed as HIGH + Y + E.

In some cases letter signs may be used as a kind of identifying initial, as in 'Jerusalem', which is signed as NUMBER + ONE + JEW + SECULAR + COURTYARD + J or as in 'John the Baptist', which may be signed as BLESS + WATER + OUR + SAINT + J. However, in most cases letter signs are signed as representations of speech sounds in the manner just described. It will be seen that insofar as the 'original' signs of the the Cistercian monks studied by Barakat do tend to represent English words, they do so as if they are syllabic signs, rather than signs for morphemes. It is also worth noting that in regard to the strictly 'phonetic' signs many are signs for names of places. As we have mentioned in Chapter 7, in the NCD sign languages the few signs that we have found which have a 'phonetic' character include a high proportion of signs for names. We shall return to this point below, when we discuss the relationship between type of medium and units of representation in language codes.

In the NCD sign languages, as we noted in our discussion of Plains Indian sign language above, we do not find the kind of open compounds that are so freely invented by the Cistercian monks that Barakat studied. In this case, it seems likely that the open compounds are developed not so much because of a need to build in redundancy as a way to avoid misunderstanding - although this certainly may be an important factor - but because the monks have so few signs at their disposal. In consequence they are forced to improvise. In doing so, they follow two main strategies. They use such signs as they have available to indicate combinations of concepts that can match the intended referent. They also develop ways of representing the sounds of words. The first strategy is clearly similar to Plains Indian practice of open compounding. The second strategy, however, is not used by Plains Indians (as far as has been reported) and it is used to only a limited degree in the NCD sign languages. The extent to which it is used by the Cistercians perhaps reflects the fact that they are literate. It is the availability of alphabetic writing that makes it possible for these signers to call upon letters as symbols to represent speech sounds. We may see, thus, how the existence of another means of spoken language representation may influence the way in which signs in an alternate sign language may relate to their referents.

Barakat includes an examination of various syntactic features of the sign language. Apparently his method was to present English sentences to the monks which they then translated into sign. Although English syntax clearly played an important part in influencing how the monks structured their translations, since there are no signs in their system to match English grammatical words, no copulative, no pronominals, and no system of sign affixes by which, say, tense markers for verbs might be conveyed (as is found, for instance, in various forms of signed English), various strategies of expression were employed which, as Barakat puts it, often led the monks to restructure the sentence when translating it into sign. The examples he gives show much variation. It appears that, once the need for expressions beyond those commonly used in the sign language arises, as it did in Barakat's examples, it seems, individual ingenuity was employed to produce the translations. Examining Barakat's examples, one has the strong impression that the sign language has not developed a productive system of syntax that can be learned by its users, beyond the simplest kinds of sequencing which matches English word order, wherever possible. The extensive use of open compounds often leads to signed sentences that are quite different from English. It would seem that the sign language has not developed a sufficient lexical resource for it to develop, as NCD sign languages have, into a true sign representation of the morphemes of the spoken language.

13.5 Sign language comparisons: conclusions

Four main conclusions may be drawn from the foregoing:

1. As we saw in 13.2, where deaf persons are taught a sign system that is based upon a spoken language, there is a strong tendency for it to be modified and incorporated into a system of expression that uses modes of expression that are characteristic of primary sign languages. In contrast, where, as in the case of the NCD sign languages, sign language is secondary to spoken language, it is adapted to spoken language structures and there is but little elaboration of a spatial morphology and grammar. Hence, although the medium of language expression can have profound consequences for language structure, it will only do so if a spoken language is not already in place to provide a matrix for its development.

2. As in the NCD sign languages, so also in Plains Indian signing and Cistercian sign language, most signs have an iconic origin. Where they represent spoken language elements they do so at the semantic level. However, in the sign language of St. Joseph's Abbey there are many signs that represent spoken words or syllables, rather than meanings. For example, letter signs are used to symbolize the sounds of monosyllables of English words. To some degree, the spontaneously elaborated aspects of St. Joseph's

Abbey sign language is like a kinesic syllabary. We suggest, in consequence, that an alternate sign language is likely to represent phonetic features of associated spoken language elements only if a visual means of such representation already exists. Otherwise it will be the semantic value of spoken language elements that is represented, much less often their phonetic form.

3. Plains Indian signing (at least the Plains Standard described by West) differs from the NCD sign languages because it appears to have developed as an autonomous system and has not been structured by any one specific language, probably because the signing community, in this case, included speakers of very different, unrelated, languages. In consequence, we may conclude that, where an alternate sign language develops within a community where one language only is in use, then the spoken language will exert a strong influence on the sign language. Where no such commonly shared spoken language exists, the alternate sign language may go its own way, and make far more use of the expressive potentialities of the kinesic medium.

4. Since the members of St. Joseph's Abbey share one spoken language, one would expect that their sign language would show more evidence of spoken language influence than Plains Standard. This proves to be the case. However, St. Joseph's Abbey sign language does not map English as closely as, say, Warlpiri sign language maps Warlpiri. This is in part because, like Plains Indian sign language, but unlike the NCD sign languages, Cistercian sign language makes much use of open compounding. It probably does so because it has a limited vocabulary, and this is doubtless a consequence of the limitations placed on its use. This supports our view that for an alternate sign language to reflect spoken language structures extensively, more than some minimum level of development is required. If its development is restricted, or if it is at an early stage, an alternate sign language will show less influence from spoken language than later on, provided, of course, that the other factors that favor the influence of spoken language are also operating.

13.6 North Central Desert sign languages as language codes

If, as we have suggested, the Aboriginal sign languages considered here may be referred to as 'signed Warlpiri' or 'signed Warumungu', etc., we may think of them as systems that *represent* these spoken languages, at least to a degree. They may be thought of, thus, as species of *language codes*. A *language code* is any system in which a set of signals have been established which stand for elements in a spoken language. These signals may be oral, as in the 'whistle language' of the Mazatecos of Mexico (Cowan 1964 [1948]); acoustic, as in the 'drum languages' of many West African tribes (e.g. Herzog 1964 [1945]); or graphic, as in writing systems of various kinds. From this point of view, the sign languages considered here may be looked upon as kinesic language codes. It is also possible to speak of linguistic language codes, where the signals in the code are items that are themselves part of a spoken language. Thus the 'special language' systems, such as Damin, employed by the Lardiil, that were discussed in 3.15, could be regarded in this way.

The language codes just mentioned are all *first order* codes, it should be noted, for the signals comprising them stand for spoken language elements directly. There are also *second order* language codes, in which the signals refer to signals in an already existing language code, rather than to linguistic elements directly. In most such cases, the signals referred to are alphabetic. Second order language codes include morse code, which is acoustic, semaphore and fingerspelling, which are kinesic, Braille, which depends on touch (haptic), and systems such as the cypher used by Samuel Pepys to write his diary, which is graphic. For the present discussion, only first order language codes need be considered.

Language codes, as we have indicated, may be classified in terms of the medium employed as signal. They may also be compared in terms of the linguistic elements represented in them. That is to say, language codes may represent phonetic, morphological or semantic units of the spoken language they are related to. Further, they will also vary in 'completeness'; that is, the extent to which all of their elements are to be accounted for as representations of spoken language forms. Probably there is no first order language code that is complete, in this sense, but some are much more complete than others are. As we have seen, in the sign languages considered in this book, not all signs can be shown to have a spoken language form as their correlate. Indeed, we have several times indicated that we believe that in the first development of these alternate sign languages rather few of the properties of a language code will be observed. These properties become increasingly marked as the system becomes elaborated. Thus we must recognize that the concept of a language code is not sharply bounded. Systems may vary in the extent to which they show language code properties.[11]

13.6.1 Oral and acoustic language codes

Oral and acoustic language codes have been reviewed by Stern (1957). Systems in which oral whistling is employed include the system used by the Mazatecos of Mexico described by Cowan (1964 [1948]), the system in use by the youth of the Sizang of Northern Burma, as mentioned by Stern, and the system used in the Canary Islands and still in use recently on the island of La Gomera (Classe 1957). The system in use on La Gomera is well adapted to long distance communication in the rugged and well wooded terrain of that island. The system described by Cowan in use by the Mazatecos is used for distance communication but it may also be used in close conversations, as well.

The languages of the Mazatecos and of the Sizang are tone languages, and in whistling utterances the whistler varies pitch to represent the succession of phonemic tones that would be used were the utterance spoken. Inevitably, since vowel and consonant contrasts are not conveyed by this method, considerable ambiguity can arise which, nevertheless, can usually be resolved by context. On the island of La Gomera, on the other hand, the language represented in the whistle system is Spanish, which is not a tone language. According to the analysis outlined by Classe, a whistler moves the tongue as if articulating a spoken utterance. This produces a series of pitch changes which can be recognized as resulting from the tongue movements and so the words intended may be understood. Classe gives the impression that virtually anything can be conveyed in this way and that there is little ambiguity.

Stern cites numerous examples of acoustic language codes from many different parts of the world in which membrane drums, slit gongs, bell like instruments and xylophones, horns and flutes are employed. The most well known examples have been described from West Africa. In all the cases where these systems are well attested as language codes, the languages in question are tone languages, and the instruments employed are capable of producing two, three or even four different pitches. Spoken utterances are played out by varying the tones to correspond to tone variation in the spoken utterance, rhythmic patterns of notes or beats match the syllabic structure of the speech forms.

From Stern's review, it appears that of those oral and acoustic systems that do encode features of spoken language, it is phonological features that they encode, predominantly. These may be syllabic units, tone differences or, as in the case of the Canary Island whistle system, segmental phonemes transformed into pitch variations. In these respects, they differ markedly from the sign languages we have considered. As we have seen, in these systems, representation of phonological features is extremely limited. In contrast, in the oral and acoustic systems considered, although there are elements that represent words and even phrases directly, as well as elements that are not language code elements, these are not prominent features of these systems, which must be considered to be mainly phonological representation systems.

13.6.2 Graphic language codes

Graphic communication systems take a wide variety of forms, and previous writers have proposed comparisons between some of these and sign language. Thus, both Mallery (1972 [1881] and Kroeber (1978 [1958]) have discussed Plains Indian sign language in relation to North American Indian pictography. In this section we discuss NCD sign language only in relation to graphic language codes, that is, writing systems. However, before coming to this I will comment briefly on the relationship between NCD sign language and the graphic system that has been described by Munn (1973) for the Warlpiri. As she shows, this comprises a set of graphic elements which can be combined in various ways to create designs which convey definite meanings. The system may be used as part of the process of story telling and it thus might be thought to function rather like sign language. However, the graphic elements in the system do not relate to elements in the spoken language and, when used in story telling, they are not combined into units of discourse but into figures that represent what is referred to in the discourse. They are not analogous to words, that is, but are the building blocks of pictures.

The graphic system Munn describes is used in ceremonial designs of various sorts, both in body paintings, and as carvings or paintings on ceremonial objects. When used in this way, the designs are considered to have considerable power and to be derived from the ancestors of the *jukurrpa* ('the dreaming'). Similar designs may also be drawn in the sand, as part of the process of informal story telling. When used in this way, they provide a kind of running illustration of the human actors, the animals, the camps and the waterholes that are told about in the story, which is typically a recitation of the ordinary daily events of the traditional life of hunting and gathering, making camp and holding ceremonies. These stories are told by women in the informal context of the camp and may be a source of entertainment for anyone around, especially children.

In the construction of these sand drawings a limited set of graphic elements are employed. These elements are arranged together in certain standard configurations which Munn terms 'figures'. The graphic elements include u-shaped forms, straight lines, wavy lines, circles, curved lines and ovals. A 'figure' might comprise, say, a long curved line, with two straight lines, one longer than the other, extending vertically from the concave side of the curved line. This would stand for a man and his wife lying next to one another in a bough-shade. Each of the elements that recur in such 'figures' is used to stand for a range of meanings. Thus a straight line may serve to indicate a human being lying down, as in the example, but it may also be used to indicate any elongate stationary object, such as a spear, a fighting stick, or an animal lying down stretched out. A circle may indicate closed roundish objects such as a hole, a nest, a tree, a hill, an egg or a billy can. These graphic elements only gain specific meaning when organized into 'figures' and when embedded within the context of running narrative, which is typically a combination of speaking and signing. The 'figures' are like highly schematized illustrations, providing a display of the spatial relationships of the people, events and locations that are expounded in the story. As Munn (p. 87) puts it "...the graphs are arranged as 'pictures'; that is, they are organized not simply in a linear way following speech sequence, as is characteristic of a script, but also as images in pictorial arrangements". The drawings serve as the scenes that the spoken and signed utterances refer to, and are, thus, extra-linguistic. They therefore have a quite different semiotic status from either speech or sign.

We turn now to consider NCD sign languages in relation to graphic language codes, or writing systems. In the world today, these divide into two main types. There is the logographic system of Chinese, in which the graphic signals employed ('characters') stand for individual morphemes in the spoken language, and there are various phonographic systems in which aspects of the phonology of the language are represented. Some of these are syllabic, such as the system used by the Vai of Liberia (Scribner and Cole 1981) or the system of *kana* used in Japan; Han'gul, used for writing Korean, is what Sampson (1985) terms a featural script; and then there are various alphabetic systems, such as the Semitic system which represents only consonants, and the Graeco-Roman system which represents vowels as well.[12] In comparing the North Central Desert sign languages with contemporary writing systems it will be clear that the only possible similarity could be with Chinese writing. However, any comparison with contemporary Chinese would not take us very far. More to the point, perhaps, is a comparison with early systems of writing and their subsequent development. There are some suggestive parallels.

As far as can be told, writing did not emerge in the first instance as a language code. It began as what Sampson (1985) has termed a semasiography. That is, it began as a system of graphic signals which expressed concepts independently of how these were expressed in spoken language. These graphic signals were, for the most part, recognizable as pictures of things that represented the concepts to be communicated. Only as these pictures became standardized and used repeatedly did they come to represent elements in the spoken language. This development appears to have taken place in the evolution of Egyptian writing (Gelb 1963), Chinese writing (Gelb 1963, Sampson 1985) and Sumerian writing (Driver 1976).

To illustrate this we may consider the writing system of the Sumerians in a little more detail. Sumerian writing is the earliest known writing system and recent interpretations of early archaeological finds in the area have suggested a way in which this writing system may have come about from a previous system, that definitely is not to be considered writing. A useful summary of the development of the earliest form of writing from its Sumerian beginnings is given by Sampson (1985), whom we follow below.

The Sumerian civilization flourished between perhaps 6500 and 3750 years ago in lower Mesopotamia - what is now southern Iraq. The first Sumerian inscriptions that are known were written with a stylus on clay tablets. The inscriptions were brief and appear to have served administrative purposes, recording such matters as tax payments and the distribution of goods. The graphs employed in this early system were quite restricted in number compared to the elements of spoken Sumerian (one authority counts about 1200 graphs in archaic Sumerian script). These graphs referred to various kinds of goods, animals, units of measurement, graphs indicating number, and personal names. Most of the graphs for material objects of various kinds are recognizable as pictures of them.

In its earliest stage, then, Sumerian writing appears to have been a system of pictorial signs, augmented by a few other apparently arbitrary marks, which could be used to record brief statements about people in association with goods, animals, pieces of land, and so on. Sampson suggests that in its first form it should be considered as closer to a semasiographic system, than as a glottographic system (i.e. a graphic language code), although, as he points out, at a relatively early stage conventions of linear order appeared in the script and this appears to have reflected the linear arrangement of spoken elements in an utterance. Furthermore, when numbers of objects were referred to, numeral signs were combined with a sign for the object to be numerated. This also suggests that the the system is encoding spoken language elements, rather than representing concepts directly. The spoken language elements archaic Sumerian script appears to have encoded, however, are words or morphemes: units of meaning, that is, not units of sound. Only later did some degree of phonography enter the system. Phonography was introduced by using graphs for things that had names that shared similar sounds. This was a way of overcoming ambiguities in the system. To give the examples provided by Sampson, the graph used for /a/ 'water' was used for the word /a/ 'in' and the graph used for /ti/ 'arrow' was used for the word /til/ 'life'. Somewhat later, this principle was extended so that grammatical suffixes in the spoken language could be represented. Thus, the graph for the word /me/ 'oracle' was extended to stand for /-me-/, the plural suffix.

With further development of this script the use of the phonographic principle became more widespread, so that later versions of Sumerian script began to show some of the properties of a syllabary. Sampson states, however, that logographic forms continued to be used and that most of the extension of the written vocabulary followed logographic, not phonographic principles. As he puts it (p. 55) "The Sumerians tended to use signs phonographically only when the limitations of their logographic system forced them to."

So far as our comparison with NCD sign languages is concerned, there are two points to note at this stage. First, graphic marks, like movements of the hand, share no properties in common with the sounds of speech. Whereas, as we have seen, systems of signalling that employ sounds encode features of *speech* when they develop into language codes, this does not seem to be the case when we are dealing with systems that use a completely different medium for its codes. As we argued in Chapter 6, signs are created in the first instance as representations of concrete images that are symbolic of their meanings. That is, signs are first of all developed to represent meanings in their own right and not as representations of already existing symbolic expressions such as words or other spoken language forms. Likewise, it appears that when graphic forms are first used as a means of communication, the same principle is followed: images are created that serve as representations of concrete objects that are symbolic of their meanings.

Secondly, one may perhaps be struck by the apparent fact that, in early Sumerian script the logographic principle appears to have been very persistent. In Chapter 7 we noted some examples of phonological representation in sign (which are very similar in principle to the device of phonographic extension adopted in early Sumerian script) but we noted, too, what a very limited role it appears to play. It would seem that when a language code is established in a non-acoustic medium the logographic principle is not only the first principle to be adopted, it is also not easily abandoned. However, Gelb (1963, p. 66) among others supposes that the impetus for a graphic system first to develop graphs that refer to units of speech, the impetus for the system to move towards phonography, that is, comes from the need to represent names. There are serious limitations to any attempt to represent individual persons semasiographically. The second impetus may have come from the need to represent foreign expressions. It is interesting to note that in Warlpiri sign language although, as we saw, the phonographic principle is applied but little, rather a high proportion of phonographic signs are name signs, and there are also a number of examples of phonographic signs serving to represent concepts that derive from English.

According to Sampson, it was not until the Akkadians (Babylonians) adopted Sumerian cuneiform for their own purposes that the script developed more fully as a phonographic system. He suggests that this may have been because of differences in the morphological character of the Akkadian language, as compared to Sumerian. Spoken Sumerian was an agglutinative language and such a morphology is quite easy to represent by a system of signals in which each element stands for a morpheme. Akkadian, on the other hand, was an inflecting or fusional language and this creates much greater difficulties for a language code if it is to remain mainly as a code for morphemes.[13]

This point may be clarified by a simple example. In English, a partially inflecting language, the first person pronoun inflects for case. Thus 'I' refers to 'self' as subject or agent, whereas the possessive form, 'my', combines or 'fuses' both the concept of 'self' and the concept of 'possession'. In contrast, in Warlpiri, which is a highly agglutinative language, the same two concepts are expressed by two separate morphemes: *ngaju* 'First Person' and *-nyangu* 'Possessive'. It will be seen that with a language with a fusional morphology it would be much more difficult to set up signals, whether graphic or kinesic, that can serve as morphemic equivalents.

As we suggested at the end of Chapter 8, it is possible that the agglutinative character of Warlpiri and the other North Central Desert languages makes it easier for the corresponding sign languages to develop as systems in which signs match morphemes, for in these languages there is, on the whole, a direct correspondence between the minimum units of meaning in the language and morphemes as they appear in linear order within an utterance. If an alternate sign language in a community in which a fusional language was in use could be studied, it would be of great interest to see the manner in which it corresponded to spoken language organization. We suggest that it might show a relationship very different from that shown in the case of the sign languages studied here.

13.7 North Central Desert sign languages and language codes: conclusions

The main conclusion to emerge from 13.7 is that the medium in which a language code is developed governs the aspects of the spoken language which it comes to represent. Thus, language codes developed in the acoustic medium, such as drum or whistle 'languages', have developed as speech code systems or speech surrogates. The elements in these codes encode phonetic features of the spoken language. Language codes developed in the graphic medium did not, in the first instance, develop in this way. They began as semasiographic systems and, at least in the case of Egyptian, Sumerian and Chinese writing, evolved first in the direction of morpheme representation systems. To this extent there is some parallel with the development of the NCD sign languages.

All writing systems further developed to include at least some representation of the phonetic features of spoken language. The initial impetus for this, so several scholars believe, was the need to represent personal names. It is of interest to note in this connection, therefore, that where phonetic representation has developed in the NCD sign languages, this has tended to be in connection with the development of signs for personal names, or for signs for non-traditional things with names in English. Likewise, in the sign language of St. Joseph's Abbey, a rather high proportion of phonetic signs are signs for place names and people.

In short, where a language code develops in the same medium as speech, it is likely to develop in the first place as a system representing sounds of speech. Where a language code develops in an alien medium - graphic or kinesic - it first shows a relationship with spoken language by developing units that match semantic units in the spoken language. The representation of phonetic units in writing systems is a much later development which emerged over a very long period of time. It perhaps would never develop to any degree at all in kinesic systems except, as we have seen, if the kinesic system evolves in a community that is already literate.

13.8 General conclusion

At the outset of this study we proposed that the sign languages to be considered here should be distinguished as *alternate* sign languages, because they have been developed in communities of speakers, for use by them at times when, for various reasons, speech could not be used. An important question to investigate is that of the possible relationship between such a sign language and the spoken language of its users. Accordingly, this has been a major theme of this book. As we have seen, although there are several important qualifications, there is justification for the view that the NCD sign languages can be characterized as spoken language representation systems. As such, they show several differences from primary sign languages. Space is little exploited for the expression of grammatical relations, the 'layered' inflectional system is little developed and the use of so-called 'classifier' forms is not found. Head and face action is scarcely used for the production of lexical signs, and not at all as a means of bracketing segments of discourse to display their grammatical status.

These features, so widely found in primary sign languages, show how the special properties of the kinesic medium may be exploited in shaping a language. However, as our study of the NCD sign languages clearly shows, a sign language is not compelled by the the medium it uses to develop in this way. It will only do so if there is no prevailing spoken language, shared by all users as a first language. As we have seen in the present Chapter, where no single spoken language model prevails, as in the case of the Plains Indians of North America, then the alternate sign language that develops emerges as an autonomous system with many of the characteristics of a primary sign language.

Viewing the NCD sign languages as kinesic language codes, we noted that the spoken languages are encoded in terms of semantic units, as these are defined at the morphemic level. Representation of spoken language phonetic features, whether segmental or syllabic, is present only to a very limited extent indeed. Comparison with other language codes, both acoustic and graphic, suggested that this may result from the character of the medium. Where acoustic signals are employed in a language code there is extensive representation of the phonetic features of the spoken language but not of semantic units directly. Where graphic elements are employed, if these map a spoken language then, at least to begin with, spoken language meaning units are represented. Phonetic units gain representation only as a much later development. A language code that develops in a visual medium, whether kinesic or graphic, will develop in the first instance as an encoding of the semantic units of the spoken language, not of its phonetic units.

An exception to this general principle, however, was suggested by an examination of the sign language in use in the Cistercian monastery, St. Joseph's Abbey. This sign language appears to have developed partly as a kinesic syllabary. The main factor contributing to this development, we suggested, was that the users of this alternate sign language are literate. The idea of representing speech sounds by visual means is already well ingrained for them. This shows that how an alternate sign language may represent elements of its associated spoken language may be partly dependent upon what other systems of language representation may also be in use.

Another factor may also be playing a part here, however. The highly agglutinative character of the spoken languages of the North Central Desert may facilitate the development of a system in which individual morphemes can be represented in sign. English, in contrast, has many characteristics of a 'fusional' or inflecting language and this makes it more difficult to establish a straightforward sign-morpheme match. Consequently, an English alternate sign language may very well develop other strategies for language representation and the sign language of St. Joseph's Abbey may provide an example of this.

In sum, we see that how an alternate sign language may develop in relation to spoken language depends upon several factors. These include the extent to which a single spoken language is shared within the alternate sign using community, whether other methods of spoken language representation are already in use and perhaps also on the morphological character of the spoken language involved. We have seen, too, that the medium employed for the development of a secondary communication system has an important influence on the way in which a primary system may be represented in it. For a given semiotic system, thus, medium of expression, function, and relationship to other semiotic systems interact in a complex way in shaping its character.

Notes

[1]Educationists of the deaf, from L'Epée onwards (see Lane 1980), have devised systems which represent spoken language in manual form; however we shall not discuss any of these here, since our interest is in what may evolve within a communication community, rather than in what may be invented by specific individuals. Thus we shall not consider fingerspelling in its various forms nor the many systems in which manual gestures are established as the equivalents of words and morphemes in the spoken language. For English these systems include the Paget-Gorman system (Paget and Gorman 1968), Seeing Essential English (Anthony 1971), Linguistics of Visual English (Wampler 1972) and Signed English (Bornstein et al. 1975). Some of these systems adapt signs from an existing primary sign language, but some use newly invented signs. All of them are deliberately constructed systems designed as a means of conveying spoken language to the deaf. They show a heavy reliance upon written forms of the language, which is generally taken as the norm. A review of the English systems may be found in Wilbur (1979).

[2]'signed English' as distinct from 'Signed English'. Signed English is Bornstein's name for a particular system he invented. We use the expression 'manually coded' as a generic term for invented systems which attempt to represent a spoken language as a system of manual gestures.

[3]That is, signs that take the form of a letter from the manual alphabet which is used to stand for the initial letter of a word in spoken language that is commonly used to gloss the sign in question (see Battison 1978).

[4]As Grigley (1983, p. 368) remarks in his review of Kyle and Woll (1983), the proceedings of a symposium in which primary sign languages from several different countries are discussed, "...Sign may indeed be more 'universal' than we have yet conceded --- universal not in terms of lexical structure (as early researchers believed) but in terms of grammatical structure. This is not to say we are dealing with one Sign Language and numerous national dialects; ...Instead, evidence is beginning to suggest that we are slowly recognizing a set of sign universals based on constraints of the visual gestural medium."

[5]That is, deaf who live separately from other deaf and who have no contact with a community of deaf persons, such is provided in the United States or Britain by deaf educational institutions and social clubs for deaf people.

[6]A deaf Warlmanpa man I met briefly in Elliott used a 'home sign' system and the few signs for common items such as 'dog', 'cat', 'truck' and 'water' that he showed me were quite different from any of the local Aboriginal sign language forms. It is also worth noting that he used his face a great deal as he signed in a way that was quite different from the virtual non-use of facial action that is characteristic of NCD signing.

[7]Throughout, I shall write as if sign language is no longer used by the Plains Indians. As far as I know, it is not widely practised today, although West was able to record a good deal as late as 1959. In various places there has been some effort to revive it, mainly in connection with programs of cultural re-education.

[8]Brenda Farnell, of Indiana University, initiated dissertation research on Plains Indian sign language in 1986.

[9]In the basic signs that are sanctioned by St. Joseph's Abbey only, however, only two are compounds of this sort. Several of the signs which overlap with those in the Order's official list are simplified, in that the classifier sign is not used.

[10]I am indebted to Margaret Kendon for translations from the Russian.

[11]The term 'language code', in the sense we intend it here, has not been used before, as far as I know. Stern (1957) employed the term 'speech surrogate' to refer to whistle and drum 'languages' and Hymes (1964, p. 325) suggests that this term should be extended to include writing and other systems, such as Plains Indian sign language. He thus sets it up as a term equivalent to what we intend by 'language code'. However, 'language code' seems preferable as a general term for these systems since they vary quite a bit in the extent to which they encode elements of speech, as such, or elements of language that are more abstract. For example, Chinese writing is a system that encodes the morphemes of Chinese, but it does not really encode how they are pronounced, the presence in compound characters of elements which have a phonetic function notwithstanding. It is unquestionably a system for encoding the Chinese language, therefore, but it does not encode Chinese speech. On the other hand, Han'gul, the writing system invented by the Korean ruler Sejong in the Fifteenth Century as a means for writing Korean, is a system designed to encode in graphic form how units of Korean speech are pronounced. Both are graphic language codes, but Han'gul is a system that encodes the segmental phonology of Korean, whereas Chinese writing encodes at the level of the word or morpheme (Sampson 1985).

[12]Almost none of these systems are pure representatives of their type, it should be noted. Compound characters in Chinese are often composed of a 'phonetic', which indicates (it does not represent) the pronunciation, while most phonographic scripts, so called, include logographic features. Han'gul comes perhaps the closest of any phonographic system to representing the segmental phonemes of Korean, but the others all contain logographic features in varying degrees. English, for instance, although it uses an alphabetic script, is notorious for the unphonetic character of its orthography. However, as several authors have pointed out (Sampson 1985, Halliday 1985b), English writing is in part a logographic system. For example, it makes visibly apparent the differences between words that, in speech, sound the same, as in the different spellings of /rait/: wright, rite, right, write.

[13]Driver (1976, p. 59) writes: "...the Sumerians had little need for signs representing syllables, not only because those which they were using had been designed to represent

their own names of common objects in daily use, but also because their own words were largely monosyllabic and underwent no internal alteration through inflexion, which was indicated mostly by simple prefixed and suffixed syllables, and comparatively few syllabic signs sufficed for this purpose... On the other hand the Babylonians, except when they used the old signs as ideograms, which were foreign to their language, as a kind of short hand, were compelled to spell out every single word by syllables. Hence the development of the syllabic use of these signs was their work."

14 Aboriginal interaction and Aboriginal sign language

14.0 Introduction

In Chapter 3 we suggested that the distribution of complex sign languages in Aboriginal Australia is correlated with the practice of speech taboos, either those observed by the bereaved, or as imposed upon male novices in initiation. Such speech taboos, especially the former, since they are so prolonged, and shared by so many individuals at the same time, would appear to account for the development of truly complex sign languages. However, as we saw from the survey presented in Chapter 3, as well as from Chapters 11 and 12, some use of signing has been recorded from many parts of Australia, including areas where extended speech taboos have not been reported. Furthermore, in those areas where speech taboos are followed, the use of sign language is not confined to periods of speech taboo, nor is it necessarily confined to those who normally observe such taboos. It would seem, thus, that signing is a widely favored mode of communication in Aboriginal society and that its elaboration in association with speech taboos is, perhaps, but a particular development within the context of a more general predisposition towards its use. What is the reason for this widespread tendency to use signs among Aborigines?

In this Chapter we suggest that signing, as a mode of communication, has properties that suit it well for certain communication requirements that are a recurrent feature of Aboriginal interaction. These requirements arise as part of the special character of Aboriginal face-to-face interaction, which, itself, is a consequence of the kind of sociality that is found in Aboriginal society.

In what follows, we shall first (14.1) present an account of Aboriginal sociality. We shall describe the nature of the groupings in which Aborigines live, and the character of interpersonal relations within them. This has received especially detailed attention in the work of Sutton (1978), Sansom (1980) and Myers (1986). These authors write of Aboriginal society in Western Cape York, in the urban fringe camps of Darwin and in the Western Desert, respectively, but their accounts have much in common, and it would appear that, in many respects, the kind of sociality they describe is characteristic of

Aboriginal society generally, including the societies of the North Central Desert. As a part of this discussion, we shall refer to recent interpretations of the Dreaming in which its role in the maintenance of Aboriginal sociality has been proposed. We shall suggest a relationship between this and the prevalence of speech taboos associated with the dead (14.2). Here, also, a few suggestions will be made as to why, in the North Central Desert, these speech taboos apply to women, in particular, and why it is in this region, accordingly, that we find that signing has become elaborated into complex sign languages.

The peculiar characteristics of Aboriginal interaction will then be summarized (14.3), as these have been noted by a number of authors, including Harris (1977, 1980), Von Sturmer (1981), Malcolm (1982), Eades (1982, in press), and Liberman (1982a, 1985), as well as by Sutton, Sansom and Myers. These characteristics appear to fit well with the special communication requirements that Aboriginal sociality seems to impose and provide a context in which the proliferation of a variety of communicative styles can take place. Some of the properties of signing, considered as a mode of communication, will then be discussed (14.3). It will be suggested that because signing is silent, less intimate, and perhaps less complex in information than speech, it is particularly well suited for the indirect, semi-explicit, communication that is so often required in Aboriginal interaction. In short, the hypothesis presented in this Chapter is that signing is widely used in Aboriginal society because its special properties as a mode of communication suit it to the communicative tasks Aborigines face daily among each other.

It should be added that this hypothesis is not meant to imply a causal relationship. Face-to-face interaction in other hunter-gatherer societies, such as the !Kung San, is reported to have many features that are quite similar to those described for Aborigines (cf. Liberman, 1985, p. 103). However, the !Kung do not make extensive use of signs, as do the Aborigines. What is being suggested is that if people, for whatever reason, resort to signs as a means of communication, if the society they live in conducts interaction in the way to be described here for Aborigines, the practice of using signs will be favored, and may spread. This does not mean.that the development of signing in a society is an inevitable consequence of particular modes of interaction.

This Chapter is necessarily somewhat speculative and may be regarded as a prolegomenon to further research. There are few detailed studies of Aboriginal interaction, and no studies have been carried out on the use of signing in daily life which would show what the circumstances are in which it is chosen instead of speech and what communicative functions it appears to serve. Aborigines have an especially well elaborated range of communicative styles. A detailed study of how these are employed, which would include detailed attention to the modality of signing, could be highly illuminating for an understanding of how communicative purpose, communicative modality and code structure all interact.

14.1 Aboriginal sociality

As we stated in Chapter 4, in the North Central Desert, as elsewhere in Australia, Aborigines lived in small groups of variable size and composition, usually of two or three families, each with a man and his wife or wives and children, but often including other relatives as well. In the history of the anthropology of Australian Aborigines, there has been much controversy about the nature of these small groups. When regarded as descent groups with territorial rights they have been termed 'hordes'. 'Band' has also been used, usually as a more neutral term,to refer to an actual group of individuals living together day to day. Following Radcliffe-Brown's (1930) formulation, it was widely supposed that the basic unit of Aboriginal society was the territorially bounded patrilineal and patrilocal horde. However, as fieldwork progressed, this model came under increasing criticism (Hiatt 1962, Meggitt 1962, Peterson 1986) and the most recent treatments make it clear that, as originally formulated, it never had any reality. There were, to be sure, patrilineal groupings related to specific tracts of country (throughout all but the Western Desert); however these groupings were not residential and they did not correspond to the actual bands within which individual Aborigines lived from day to day. For Myers (1986), writing of the Pintupi in the Western Desert, as for Sansom (1980), writing of the Darwin fringe dwellers and Sutton (1978), writing of Western Cape York, the basic grouping of daily life was not and, today, is not like a clan, it does not exist as a separate entity to which individual members can be attached. Rather, the groups in which Aborigines are found to live are aggregates of individuals who are associated with one another because of ties of kinship and affection, as well as ties to country. Sansom refers to these groupings as 'mobs', following the usage of English speaking Aborigines in the Northern Territory. Myers refers to them as 'bands'.

For Sansom, mobs are aggregates of individuals who sustain co-association with one another for a period of time. Mobs, as Sansom writes, "are not entities as are corporations. Rather a mob brought into being [as an aggregation] is, at any moment of its existence, a realization." Members of mobs "live in lively appreciation of social continuity. They know that any lasting mob in which a degree of continuity of membership is achieved must be sustained in a realization day by day" (p.16).[1] That is to say, people in mobs associate with one another out of their own choice. They can, and do, leave to join other groups at any time and the maintenance of a group over time is the outcome of a continual process of interaction. It should be regarded as an achievement and not taken for granted as a background feature for the rest of what takes place.

Among the Pintupi of the Western Desert the system is similar. Thus Myers says (p. 43)[2] that the "Pintupi communities are not anything like a clan or series of clans. They are much more an aggregation of individuals based on complex, bilateral ties." Myers stresses that bands were highly variable in composition. A given individual did not always live with the same group, or within the same area or territory. He states (p. 71) that "the mobility of individuals is a primary feature of social structure". He speaks of bands as having an egocentric structure; they arise through dyadic ties between members and endure just as long as particular individuals prefer to remain associated with one another: "bands are largely the outcome of individual decisions, and their actual composition can be explained only through the history and processes of individual affiliation" (p. 97). Membership in a band is thus negotiable, "the formation of a group should be seen as a social accomplishment, and not simply taken for granted" (p. 72). That is to say, in order for a collection of individuals to stay together as a band, to 'run together', in the terminology of Sansom's fringe dwellers, the interpersonal ties that make this possible have to be continuously negotiated.

In the light of this, it will be seen that, in their interactions with one another, people cannot take each other for granted. A fundamental assumption that guides people in their interactions with one another is that each person is autonomous. That is, people behave toward each other in such a way as to make it clear that they are respecting each other's rights to be a free agent. In most circumstances people do not attempt to constrain others to do their bidding in a direct, overt manner, and nobody is prepared to take orders from others as to what should be done. Thus Myers writes (p. 159) that relationships "among people are not totally 'given' in the defining rules of landownership, residence or kinship. Instead, relationships must be worked out in a variety of social processes." In the practice of daily interaction, thus, people must continually compromise with one another, if they are to sustain relationships. Yet, inevitably, no one is willing to compromise all the time. People have strong needs, opinions and desires and further, although autonomous in the sense that people regard themselves and others as free agents, they are nevertheless bound to one another by obligations of all kinds. People are therefore limited in several ways in the degree to which they can accommodate to one another. As a result, negotiation can fail and when it does the parties may resort to violence. The possibility of violence in everyday life is ever present, in fact. It is the other side of the coin of the congenial relatedness which is continually aimed at in interaction and which is valued so highly, precisely because interpersonal violence appears as the inevitable alternative.

This is clear from the work of both Myers and Sutton. Myers writes (p. 179), "the ever present possibility of conflict lends enormous value to sustaining shared identity as a precondition for social action". Sutton (1978) writes of the people of Cape Keerweer in Western Cape York that "...people live under fairly constant tension, suspicion and even threat of physical violence... At my field base vigorous arguments erupted frequently, many of them between brothers and sisters, husbands and wives, or between different families." He adds, however, that nevertheless people continually seek to avoid violence. Indeed, great value is placed upon congenial, shared relatedness. But because of the ever-present possibility that this sort of relationship may break down, social life is a matter of continual diplomacy. As Sutton puts it (p. xiv) "...people try to avoid violent confrontation in most cases, and personal diplomacy publicly recognizes the rights of others to be the equivalent of one's own".

A further feature of everyday Aboriginal sociality that it is important to mention is its highly public character. People must live out their lives in continual co-presence. Individuals are almost never alone and there is almost no privacy. This means not only that everything that one does may be open to observation by others, it also means that others have a right to observe what one is doing, so that to attempt to conceal one's activities may give rise to resentment and suspicion. Thus Sansom writes (p. 82):

> In-camp activity is always wholly public unless special measures are taken. And acting in front of one another, viewing and in view, the people of a mob are 'known' to one another. ...It is very difficult, for as long as one is in camp, to hide facts about oneself and one's doings. The general precondition that makes camp life public and open is not merely that 'everybody watchin', but that everybody has, implicitly, by being there, the right to be a watcher 'watchin for witness'.

Elsewhere in the same book, Sansom describes how people who wish to have private conversations, using a language not shared by everyone present in the camp, apologize for doing so and may seek permission to do so. Anyone who 'goes into language' without doing so is likely to be called to account. Hamilton (1979) likewise emphasizes the disapproval of privacy among the Pitjantjatjara. Commenting on the use of shelters in camp she writes (p. 17) "Normally the interior [of the shelter] is used for sleeping only, as privacy is frowned upon during the day, and most activities take place in full sight and sound of everyone else." Myers, similarly, writes of the resentment of secrecy

(p. 100). To travel unannounced, or to approach a camp at night without making a noise to indicate one's presence, is to invite attack. Anyone who is regarded as acting in a manner to hide the nature of what he is doing is immediately suspected of being up to no good. This condition of social life means that everyone is highly aware of the informational consequences of their activities. Sutton describes how careful one must be, even in how one walks. He says that to walk briskly may indicate a state of emergency or aggression: "...it is wise to saunter about camp if one wishes to be 'read' as having no argument with anyone" (p. 214).

14.2 The Dreaming, sociality and speech taboos

The social order of group life in Aboriginal society is thus highly fragile. It depends upon continual negotiation and is constantly threatened with breakdown. However, the maintenance of social order is made less problematic than perhaps has been indicated because, although it is a matter of continual negotiation, this negotiation is carried out within the context of a view of the enduring nature of relationships which is enshrined in what is referred to as the Dreaming.[3] This is the 'time out of time' when the totemic heroes travelled through the landscape and established the natural and the social order and prescribed the rituals through which this is to be maintained. Recent interpretations of the Dreaming have stressed its function as an extra-human domain which can be appealed to as an authority for which one is, oneself, not accountable. It serves as a means of denying creative significance to individual human action and thus permits people to propose courses of action without themselves being accused of attempting to assert their own individual wills over others. As Myers puts it (p. 52), "it represents all that exists as deriving from a single, unchanging, timeless source". All things have always been the same, forever deriving from the basic pattern. The Dreaming cannot be altered by human action. Hence it may serve as the source for what should be done and as an explanation for what is done for which no particular individual or group can be held responsible.

In fact the content of the Dreaming does change. It evolves over time as circumstances alter. New events and historical changes are continually incorporated into it. However, these changes in content are regarded as new discoveries about the nature of the Dreaming, not as changes to the Dreaming itself. New items that are incorporated into the Dreaming are treated as if they are pieces of new knowledge about it. Thus Myers writes (p. 53), "the Dreaming organizes experience so that it *appears* to be continuous and permanent. For the Pintupi, the dynamic, processual aspect of history seems to exist as one of discovering, uncovering, or even re-enacting elements of the Dreaming."

Myers gives as an example to illustrate this an instance where a change in Pintupi geographical distribution was interpreted as a disovery of a hitherto unkown aspect of the Dreaming. The Dreaming track from which present day Pintupi originate was supposed to extend northwards only as far as a place called Pinari, near Lake Mackay. However, some Pintupi from Papunya had travelled to visit distant relatives who were living at Balgo, a mission station very far to the north (near the northern edge of the Western Desert). When they returned they told Myers that they now knew that the Dreaming track did not stop at Pinari, but went under the ground all the way to Balgo. They learned this from a revelation a Balgo man had received in a dream. Thus the new distribution of Pintupi established a new piece of knowledge about this Dreaming. The alteration in the story, thus, was not regarded as an alteration but as a discovery about an aspect of it that had been there all along.

In Myers' interpretation, the Dreaming appears as a part of the solution to the problem of maintaining continuity and stability to social life in the light of the continual tension that is experienced between the need to maintain relatedness, and the need to maintain personal autonomy; and the need to maintain equality in the face of the hierarchic inequalities that arise between generations. Myers suggests that the Dreaming serves to place outside of individual human responsibility events which are, nevertheless, human creations. Current action, thus, may be seen not as a consequence of human alliances, preferences and choices, but as imposed by a wider social order. By establishing a domain 'outside' human responsibility, a way is provided by which the two basic problems of Aboriginal society may be overcome: that of the web of mutual obligations within which each individual is embedded, and the value that is placed upon personal autonomy, which means that, generally speaking, people are not under much obligation to obey orders from others about what to do.

It should be added that people certainly may attempt to order others about and in certain relationships this may be acceptable. For example, elder brothers have considerable authority over younger brothers and men often assert authority over their wives. Young men, when going through initiation, also, are often subjected to severe discipline. This, however, is sanctioned by 'the Law' and is not interpreted as attempts to gain and maintain power by specific individuals. Except for this, giving orders to others and an expectation that these orders will be obeyed is not characteristically part of how Aborigines conduct their affairs. Armies, gangs, and other such organizations which depend upon the issuing of orders by a central authority and obedience to them by subordinates, are not a feature of Aboriginal society.

Sansom, in his work with Darwin fringe dwellers, describes how events or happenings become characterized in summary statements that he refers to as the 'given word'. These statements are established as the possession of a particular group or mob, they become a sort of objectification of mob experience. Those who are members of the mob 'know' the word, and may have a right to speak it. Those who are not members do not. Although Sansom does not deal with whether or not these summary accounts of past events are incorporated into the Dreaming, he nevertheless likens their establishment to the process of the objectification of experience that Munn (1970) has described for the Pitjantjatjara. The 'given word' acquires an objective, external status and can be appealed to, much as the Dreaming can be, as a source of extra-human authority.

Aboriginal social order is dependent upon a kind of running agreement which is highly fragile and easily threatened. The objectification of group experience as Dreaming myth or as 'given word' provides a means whereby this running agreement can be preserved from individual challenge. As Sansom shows, events are witnessed and become labelled in a certain agreed manner, and these 'words', these objectified summary descriptions, constitute the foundation of the social order. To re-open discussion of the now defined past is to threaten this order. Sansom writes (p. 159): "When that order [i.e. Aboriginal social order] is based on syntheses of words and happenings, the raising of problems from the past is an act of deaggregation in which the constituted reality of a mob is exploded."

It is in the light of this that we may understand why the mentioning of the names of the dead creates such anxiety and is, accordingly, so scrupulously avoided. To refer to the deceased by name is to resurrect them and this is, in some measure, to resurrect the problems that were attendant upon the disruption caused by their death. It is, too, to re-evoke the past and the memory of the changes that continually occur. It undermines in a particularly vivid way the denial of time that seems to serve as a bulwark against the social disintegration that is so ever present. Thus to speak of the dead, like attempts to 're-open' or to 'revise' the 'given word', is like challenging the reality of the Dreaming. Thus the strong resistance to referring to the dead may be understood, and this it is that accounts for the taboo placed upon the pronunciation of the names of the dead and, by extension, of words that sound like these names.

The speech taboo observed by bereaved women in the North Central Desert may be understood as a further extension of this taboo on references to the dead. Why this should have come about in this part of Australia to the degree that it has, we shall probably never know, for relevant historical data are unobtainable. As suggested in Chapter 12, however, in the particular form in which it occurs in the North Central Desert, this custom may be of relatively recent origin and has probably spread southwards and westwards, possibly beginning with the Warumungu.

Although no definite account of this is possible, there are two points to be noted that may have contributed to the spread of this custom in this part of Australia. First, as Myers notes - among the Pintupi, but his observation probably applies elsewhere - women identify most strongly with immediate kin, whereas men identify with the broader relationships of descent groupings (p. 253). Thus women are, in some sense, more closely connected to the deceased and may, perhaps, be more in danger of reminding others of the deceased than are men. As Rose (1984) has written of the Ngaingman and Ngaliwurru people in the area of Victoria River Downs, a widow is regarded as especially dangerous for she has become a woman married to a dead man.[4] Women must, therefore, defend themselves more strenuously against reminding others of the deceased than men. Social withdrawal is an obvious solution. As suggested in Chapter 3, sign language permits one to remain in communication with others, even as one is, at the same time, something less than a fully social person. Using sign language, thus, when, as a widow, one is in a dangerously close association with a dead person, is a way of making oneself relatively safe for others.

Second, the extension of the speech taboo to classificatory female relatives of the deceased, which is such a marked feature of the Warumungu, the Warlpiri and other NCD groups, may perhaps be accounted for by the corporate nature of women's society in these areas. In these parts of Australia, as in the other arid areas, as we noted in Chapter 4, women lead highly autonomous, almost separate lives from men, to the extent that, in Hamilton's (1980) view, desert Aboriginal society must be regarded as being organized as a dual system. White (1974), as we noted, observed that the segregation of men and women, both economically and ceremonially, is more pronounced in the arid regions of Australia than it is in the lusher regions of the North, and that it is in the central desert regions that rituals that parallel those of the men are found. It is here, also, that women are found to camp together in 'single women's quarters'. Perhaps it is this very autonomy that has encouraged the observance of extended speech taboos by women relatives of the deceased, especially the extension of this observance to classificatory female kin, and not just to actual wives or mothers. Where women constitute more of a separate society among themselves, as they do in the North Central Desert, speech taboos may become more extended in this way because women may have more solidarity with one another than they do, say, in Arnhem Land where they lead much less segregated lives (Hamilton 1981).

Spencer and Gillen's observations, quoted in Chapter 2, may be relevant here.They noted that, in the Warumungu camps, they encountered large numbers of women observing the speech taboo. They added "they[i.e. the women] did not seem to mind in the least". Perhaps this was correct. It may be, that where women constitute something of a separate society from men, the use of sign language, which men do not use, can serve as a means of reinforcing this separateness. In these societies, as we have seen, sign language is a mode of communication that is used more or less exclusively by women. Its may become, thus, a feature of 'women's way' and to use it is a mark of being fully involved in the culture of women's society. As we noted in Chapter 4, signing among women at communities like Yuendumu appears to be a way in which a woman may show that she is knowledgeable in 'women's business' and is fully a part of the community of women at the settlement.[5]

14.3 Some characteristics of Aboriginal interaction

The aggregate character of Aboriginal sociality, the negotiable nature of interpersonal relations, the continual need to maintain personal autonomy and equality in the face of generational hierarchy, the need to sustain relatedness and identity, and the highly public character of daily life, impart a special character to Aboriginal interaction. As has been noted by a number of observers, Aborigines interact with one another in what appears to be a very polite, indirect fashion, they avoid putting themselves forward and attempt not to impose upon others with direct orders or requests. There is a continual endeavor to establish and maintain congeniality. This appears to be because, if congeniality is not maintained, resort may be had to interpersonal quarrelling, often of a violent nature. Furthermore, people may readily become jealous of one another, and there is a continual underlying suspicion of each other's intentions. In interaction, thus, individuals must be highly diplomatic, continually negotiating with one another, attempting to achieve satisfaction of their own needs and desires, at the same time as they try to ensure good relations and continued cooperation with others.

The first study in which aspects of Aboriginal interaction were characterized was carried out by Harris (1977, 1980). He worked among Yolngu people at Milingimbi, in Arnhem Land, analyzing the situations in which learning took place traditionally. As part of this work he undertook an ethnography of speaking in this community. Many of his observations are cast in terms of the way in which Yolngu etiquette of speaking appears to differ from European Australian etiquette.

He notes that Yolngu avoid what they refer to as 'strong talk'. That is, Yolngu do not engage in direct debate with one another, as European Australians do. They prefer to let each person present his point of view without offering any criticism of the points of view of others. This is one obvious strategy by which interpersonal conflicts may be avoided. Other strategies he mentions are the manner in which people introduce what they have to say at public meetings. Typically, remarks are prefaced by self-deprecatory comments, by saying things like "This is just a little story I have to tell" or by speaking in an impersonal way, as if what is being said is what 'anyone' might say. Putting forward one's views as a personal contribution is avoided at all costs.

Other strategies which Harris mentions, observed in conversations, include not indicating what the main business of a conversation may be for a very long time. If someone is to ask a favor of another, for instance, the actual request, if made at all, will be made in a most indirect fashion, and only after long preparatory talk. If the request is to be refused, the person asked will often not express refusal directly, but will most likely indicate that he has other things to do first, or find some other way to put off action. Where differing points of view are to be discussed, allegories or stories will be used, rather than talk which directly addresses the issues.

Harris notes that among Yolngu there is no requirement that a question, if asked, deserves an answer. If someone asks a question, silence, inactivity, or talk on irrelevant topics may be quite common and apparently acceptable. This, it will be seen, reflects the ethic of personal autonomy, for to insist on an obligation to reply is to impose oneself upon the other. In Aboriginal society a question may be answered, but the answer is given the questioner not as a right, but as a privilege (Harris 1977, p. 442). Eades (1982), in her analysis of information seeking in conversation among people of Aboriginal descent in south east Queensland, has made a similar observation. She shows that in interactions in which information is transferred from one person to another, this does not come about through a sequence of answers being given to direct questions. Rather, the participants question each other indirectly, often by seeming to offer information they already possess, so that the other's response serves as a confirmation, an extension or a correction of this information.[6]

Eades, in another publication (Eades, 1988) suggests, further, that the indirectness by which questions are both asked and answered among Aborigines provides a means whereby people can preserve some measure of privacy. She suggests that the lack of obligation to answer questions, or the acceptability of delaying an answer, the indirect manner in which questions are asked and the circumspect way in which people put forward their own opinions or inquire about those of others, are all strategies that permit people to preserve a measure of privacy about themselves and their motives in the context of the highly unprivate nature of the circumstances of interaction.

This manner of handling questions is also related to the Aboriginal attitude to knowledge. Whereas, in European society, knowledge tends to be thought of as something that is freely available, in Aboriginal society knowledge may be owned by individuals or groups and, as such, may be made available to others on a highly selective basis (Michaels 1985). This applies, in particular, to knowledge having to do with the Dreaming and details of designs, songs and other matters connected with ceremony. As Sansom (1980) has shown, however, it can also be true of other kinds of knowledge as well. Only those who have shared fully in a mob's experience have the right to speak the 'given word'. Knowledge in Aboriginal society may only be transmitted by selected individuals at appropriate times to selected others, who stand in the right sort of kin relationship. Others may also possess the knowledge in question, but this does not mean that they thereby have a right to divulge it. Thus in making inquiries, one has to be very circumspect, lest the information being sought may not be given or lest one is oneself someone who does not have a right to it.

Another feature of Aboriginal interaction remarked on by both Harris and others concerns the way in which requests for goods or services are commonly handled. Very often, people do not make such requests directly. Rather, they let their needs be generally known, but within the earshot of others who are in an appropriate kin relationship. For example, if someone is in need of firewood, they do not always just ask someone to get firewood for them directly. Rather, they may indicate that they have no firewood within the hearing of relevant kin who may be obligated to them. Such an indication will be taken up and firewood will be fetched, but this is not always done directly in response to a request for it. Harris indicates that too direct a request and too direct a response to the request is demeaning. It is incompatible with the ethic of personal autonomy.

Harris also notes that Yolngu, in their dealings with one another on a day to day basis, do not enter into commitments to do something with others at some future time.[7] European Australians readily agree to make appointments and expect them to be kept. The unwillingness of Aborigines to do this can be a source of considerable difficulty and frustration in interactions between European Australians and Aborigines. An Aboriginal may readily agree to do something with a European the next day, go fishing, for instance, but yet fail completely to keep the appointment and show no remorse about this when a subsequent meeting occurs. Harris suggests that this comes about because Yolngu are highly opportunistic, are disinclined to make plans. An agreement to meet on the following day only indicates a willingness to do so, it implies no intention.

This feature of Aboriginal interaction, however, can also be interpreted as reflecting the value placed on personal autonomy. To make an appointment with someone and to be bound by this is to compromise one's own autonomy, as well as that of the other person. Traditionally, on a day to day basis, advance appointments were not usually made.[8] The way in which people organized to do things together followed a quite different course. People might indicate their intention to do something by moving in a certain direction, sitting in a certain place, or just by beginning to engage in the activity on their own. Others, observing this, might join in as they chose. In this way a cluster of individuals engaging in some activity jointly could become established. Von Sturmer (1981) describes this process in giving an account of how ceremonies are organized. The principal person responsible for the ceremony will simply be available at an appropriate spot, for example by sitting in the shade of a tree removed from the main camp, or in a bough shade that has been made on the ceremonial ground. Others may then gather there and work may begin on preparing the paraphernalia. Those who gather in this fashion may sing together, and also exchange comments on how the ceremony should be performed. Whether it actually is performed, eventually, will depend upon the extent to which the persons relevant for its performance join in the gathering. Particular individuals who fail to come but who are expected to be there are not criticized individually. Remarks may be made critical of the group as a whole, instead. This will make the delinquents feel shame, and motivate them to join in. If an insufficient number of people gather in this manner, the main person responsible may simply withdraw, perhaps choosing another time later to be available again.

Liberman (1982a, 1985) has made very similar observations regarding interactions among Pitjantjatjara speaking peoples in the Western Desert. He emphasizes that a strikingly salient value for these people is that interaction should be congenial, argument should be avoided and a state of friendly togetherness should be the overwhelming aim of any interaction. He points out that, relative to European interactions, among the Aborigines there is a great de-emphasis on personal identity. As far as possible, speakers at meetings seek to present what they have to say as 'mere remarks', what 'anyone' might say, or, at times, as a view that derives from 'Aboriginal Law' or the Dreaming. Aboriginals in interaction with one another aspire to act in ways that do not appear to be egoistic.[9] As Liberman says (1985, p. 69): "imposing one's self upon another is a cardinal error in Aboriginal relations". Participants in meetings show tremendous respect for the primacy of the groups in which they find themselves and also for the other persons who compose such groups. This respect is displayed by showing a proper degree of embarrassment or shame in doing anything, and at the same time always trying to act in such a way as to avoid embarrassing others. They avoid forcing their own individual ideas upon a group and work to harmonize with others.

Through an anonymous style of discourse Aboriginals de-emphasize personal interests. Though such interests may continue beneath the surface of the talk, the talk itself has the character of being oriented to the group as a whole, and so there are fewer opportunities for argumentation. Liberman notes that if arguments occur, they are likely to escalate very rapidly and do serious damage to social relations. For this reason, every effort is made to avoid them and when argument is likely there is frequent invocation of the rule that talk must be kept harmonious. Thus he explains (1985, p. 14) how he was himself advised by his Aboriginal companions: "Don't *arkamin* [from English 'argument']" and how Aboriginals would often advise each other: "Let's keep it nice, we don't like too much *arkamin*.... Speak softly always".

We see, then, that everyday interaction among Aborigines has a highly complex and delicate character. Accordingly, it perhaps may not seem so surprising that there is much interest in the techniques of interpersonal communication and that many different modes of communication have been elaborated. This has been widely noted. The 'special' languages, such as the so-called 'mother-in-law' languages and the 'mystic' languages taught to male initiates referred to in Chapter 3, are but the most well known and obvious examples. Observers have also been struck by the widespread phenomenon of multilingualism (Brandl and Walsh 1982). As has been shown by several different writers, in Australia the language one speaks is part of what one 'owns'. People may speak several different languages, not so much because they need to do so to make themselves understood in different places, but because these languages serve as a means of expressing the multiple social identities that they can lay claim to through their network of kin relationships. Having a range of different languages available can serve as a means of having available a range of communicative codes that facilitate the maintenance of a complex and delicate range of social relationships. This is a central thesis of Sutton's (1978) work. The Wik people of Cape Keerweer speak several different languages, but the different languages a given individual might command is related to the network of social relationships he is involved in. Each time a person speaks he must choose among several different communicative codes. Sutton states that people are multilingual not because they are frequently having to change their language to make themselves understood. Rather, the code one speaks in is a matter of choice and by means of this choice one can give expression to one's view of the kind of social relationship one is engaging in. As Sutton (1982) puts it: "...language is not primarily a means of conveying information [about one's own status, kin relationships, etc.], although it may contain it. ...what is really being indexed are *states of intention*"[emphasis in the original]. In other words, the choice of which language or dialect to speak in, which register of that language, or which other communicative mode, is to a considerable degree governed by an individual's attempt to *manipulate* the social context of the interaction, it does not just index the social context in a passive way. The elaboration of many different modes of communication, thus, is a reflection of the complexity and multiplicity of social relationships that must be sustained and negotiated.

14.4 The fitness of sign

Sign language, as we pointed out at the outset (Chapter 1), being a kinesic system, has a number of structural properties that set it apart from spoken language. However, as we also pointed out, it not only differs from spoken language in how it encodes information, it also differs in how it may be employed in interaction. As a silent, visual mode of communication, produced by actions of the hands and arms, it has a number of properties that seem to make it more useful than speech for certain kinds of communication. These will now be discussed and it will be suggested how well fitted it may be for many of the communicative situations that are common in Aboriginal interaction.

First of all, we may note that in order for signs to be successfully transmitted, they must be seen. This means that, in respect to the signer, the recipient must be oriented in an appropriate way. This does not mean, necessarily, that the recipient must gaze directly at the signer, but it does mean that some kind of definite orientation is required. Receipt of speech, on the other hand, does not require any definite orientation. That is, whereas p may overhear q without giving any particular overt evidence of doing so, it is much harder for p not to give overt evidence of receiving visual information. Because of this it is easier for the transmitter of visual information to know who its recipients are. A signer, thus, may more readily see to whom she is signing than to whom she is speaking. This means that she can exercise greater control over who her signed messages are received by than she can over her spoken messages.

This ability to control who one's recipients are is further enhanced by the fact that signs may be varied in where they are made. Although, as we have seen, signs are typically performed within a fairly restricted space in front of the signer, more or less at shoulder level, this is not an absolute requirement. Signs that do not require any articulation in relation to a specific body part may, in fact, be produced in a variety of locations. Thus many signs may be done above the head, over the shoulder, down low, to one side of the body or the other, and even behind the signer's back. This means that a signer can sign in a particular location, using her body as a screen, so that her signs can be observed by others selectively. These considerations suggest that it is possible for a signer and a recipient to collaborate in the establishment of an exclusive communication channel much more easily than can be done with speech. Given the highly public nature of everyday interaction that we have noted, it may well be that signing proves a useful alternate mode of communicating when some degree of concealment of one's communications is desired.

Signing makes it possible for articulated messages to be transmitted over longer distances with less effort than if speech is used. Although the human voice can be heard over quite long distances, due to medium turbulence and echo its articulate character is quite quickly lost. This is not so with sign, hence it may serve as a convenient and relatively effortless means of communication over distances that would be much more difficult to cope with, using the voice. Furthermore, since signing is silent, it can be used where a raised voice or shouting would otherwise be necessary. Raising the voice is generally frowned upon, especially if relatives are about for whom respect must be shown, hence the use of signs for communicating at a distance may be favored for reasons of etiquette as well as economy. The dispersed and open arrangement of Aboriginal camps, in which people tend to place themselves so that they can both be seen and be able to see others (Tonkinson and Tonkinson 1979, White 1977) and the general assumption of camp life that any one who is around is a likely witness to anything anyone is doing ('everybody watchin', as Sansom says), also would appear to favor the use of signs as a means of articulate communication between people who are visible to one another but separated by some distance. Its use for brief exchanges over distances of many yards may indeed be observed, both among seated people in camp and also among people who are moving about. At Yuendumu, for instance, it is not uncommon for women who can see each other, often at distances much too great for casual spoken interchange (say, up to a hundred paces, or so), to use signs to exchange information about where they are going and what they have been doing. For instance, sign is quite often used between people as they pass to and fro in the settlement, to indicate the purchases they have made at the store or what they have caught when on a hunting expedition. Earlier observers of Aborigines have often noted this. The passage by

W.E.Roth, quoted in Chapter 3, in which he describes how he first became aware of sign language in North West Central Queensland, provides a good example.

Another feature to be considered is that signs may be varied in the degree of explicitness with which they are performed.[10] When performed in a minimal fashion, many signs may be hard to distinguish from casual physical acts. It is possible, thus to disguise them as actions that have no particular explicit communicative character. Speech cannot be performed as an ambiguous activity in the same way. It is not possible to speak in such a way that a hearer might not be certain whether an utterance had been engaged in or not. This 'graded' character of signing makes it a useful modality for handling interaction situations in which communication must be indirect. It makes it possible to communicate in a tentative fashion, so that messages can easily be denied, if necessary. This makes signing highly suitable in many circumstances of Aboriginal interaction. It will be recalled, for instance, that people rarely ask each other direct questions, and may often not make requests for goods or services directly. Sign may sometimes be used instead of speech as a way of making known one's needs, for it can be used as a way of doing this in a casual, indirect, semi-explicit fashion. Further, when people who have not met before make contact with one another for the first time or when people who have been absent for a long time meet again, a variety of background information is needed before explicit interaction can easily proceed. People meeting for the first time must establish each other's position in the kinship system. This may be done using sign, which is regarded as a kind of 'off the record' mode of communication. Likewise, sign may be used when people who have been absent for some time meet again as a means of establishing whose relatives have died in the meantime, something that it is very important to know because of the extremely delicate way in which deceased persons must be referred to.

We saw above that the indirect, highly diplomatic character of much Aboriginal interaction also derives from the great importance that is attached to self-effacement in many situations. As we saw, Aboriginal people have great respect for each other's personal autonomy and individuals try to avoid any suggestion that they are putting themselves forward. At meetings where matters must be decided, for instance, as Liberman among others has described, when people express their views, they tend to do so in an impersonal manner, with as little indication of their own involvement in the position being expressed as possible. Signs may be used in such circumstances for in this way people are able to express their views without being directly noticed as doing so. Thus, as an observer of meetings at a community in the Western Desert has reported to me,[11] many cross-conversations in sign may be carried on, often with the result that the chairman is able to announce the consensus of the meeting on a matter that has never been explicitly discussed in words. It seems that there is considerable reluctance to wrangle over things verbally. It is much more acceptable for people to put their varying viewpoints in sign.

Signing may be used in such situations at times, not only because it may be employed in a highly indirect fashion, and provide a means of communicating without drawing attention to the communicator. It may also be used because it is a less intimate, less personal mode of communication, with a more object-like character than speech. Signs that do not require a bodily location, for instance, may be held away from the body, and may thus, to some extent, be distanced from the self. This cannot be done with speech. The voice, issuing as it does from inside the person, has a more intimate connection with the person, as if it is a manifestation of his invisible essence or soul. Signs formed by the hands, however, can be treated almost like physical objects. They have an objective, de-personalized character. It is probably for this reason that, as noted in Chapter 4, signs are often used when reference is made to sacred matters which must be spoken of with respect. We may add here that Sutton (1978) noted that signs were used when making reference to persons who deserve the greatest respect. Their use seemed to be the least personal way of referring to someone.

Finally, signing probably has a more neutral character because the information it conveys is less complex than the information conveyed by a spoken utterance. A spoken utterance conveys meaning at many different levels at once. In speech almost anything can be said in many different ways. Even within a given dialect, the words chosen, the voice quality employed, the pattern of stress, the rapidity of speech, and the like, all of these may vary. The particular choices that a speaker makes in respect to all these different aspects convey information at many different levels, both in regard to the content of the utterance and also in regard to his attitude to his recipient, to himself, to the interaction in which the utterance takes place, to the relationship that obtains between the interactants, and to many other things. Signed utterances almost certainly do not have the same degree of complexity. Sign vocabulary is more restricted, so there are fewer different ways in which a thing may be said. In addition, because sign language is something that is acquired late in life it seems likely that signers do not exercise the same level of subtle control over it as they can over speech. Signers thus have fewer choices and they thus cannot convey nuances of meaning to the same degree as is possible with speech. The more neutral character of sign that follows from this means, again, that sign is a suitable medium for impersonal, neutral utterances that are so often demanded in Aboriginal interaction.[12]

For these various reasons, signing appears to be a medium of communication well fitted to many of the interactional circumstances of Aboriginal life. It can be used with a great deal of discretion, making private exchanges possible even in quite public circumstances; it can serve usefully as a mode of communication for people who are much of the time visually co-present but often at considerable distances from one another, nevertheless; it can be varied in the explicitness of its performance, and so is useful as a vehicle for tentative communications; it has a less personal, more objective and neutral character, and may thus be suitable for conveying messages in a more anonymous, objective style. In all these various ways, it would seem, signing is a valuable communicative modality within the context of Aboriginal interaction. In this way, perhaps, we may understand why it is that sign use and sign languages have developed so widely among Australian Aborigines.

[1]Page references to Sansom are to Sansom (1980), unless otherwise specified.

[2]Page references to Myers are to Myers (1986), unless otherwise specified.

[3]Classic discussions of this concept may be found in Spencer and Gillen (1899), Roheim (1945) and Stanner (1979).

[4]Compare the bereavement terms in Warlpiri which use the suffix *-puka*, as in *ngati-puka* 'bereaved mother' or *ngangkiri-puka* 'bereaved spouse', etc. As we noted in Chapter 8, *-puka* may be related to *puka* 'stinking, rotten', and the bereavement terms are thus to be understood literally to mean 'mother of stinking one', etc.

[5]Isobel White has suggested to me that some women may prolong their observance of the speech taboo as a way of avoiding re-marriage. Until a widow is released from the taboo she may not be re-married. Among the older women, especially, the cosy communal life of the 'single women's quarters' may well be preferred to the obligations of marriage.

[6]Eades' work was carried out among English speaking descendants of Aborigines living in south east Queensland. It is especially interesting that many of the characteristics of interaction that she describes among these people, who are in many ways integrated into European Australian ways of life, are highly similar to those described for the much more traditional Aborigines of Cape York, Darwin, or the Western Desert.

[7]Yolngu, like other Aborigines, certainly enter into long term commitments, such as marriage agreements. Such commitments, however, do not require the coordination of behavior at a particular 'slot' in time, and it is this kind of coordination that Harris is concerned with in his observations.

[8]Arrangements to meet at a specified time were, traditionally, sometimes made in advance, especially when such a meeting involved people from distant groups, for example, when holding large gatherings connected with male initiation ceremonies. As described in Chapter 4, shortly after the young man has been removed from his immediate family at the start of the initiation process he is (or was) taken on a long journey, during which he learns the topography of the region, but in which he visits many neighboring groups who are invited to attend the ceremonies that are to be held later. Some of the people

visited may thereupon accompany the party escorting the youth back to his home camp, but others may agree to come later. Peterson (personal communication, 1988) says that it may be agreed to hold the ceremonies when a certain constellation of stars has appeared in the sky and this provides a way in which those invited may know when to arrive. Piddington (1932-1933), writing of the Karadjeri of the Western Desert, describes how the days of the journey are counted on the novice's hands. This enables the visitors to explain to those they invite how many days journey away they are and in this way those invited can arrange to set off so that they will arrive at the home camp of the novice in time for the ceremonies.

[9]This characteristic is one that Aborigines are explicitly trained to have. Young men who appear restive, demanding, boastful, may find themselves subjected to much more severe treatment at initiation than those who are meek. The general view is that the disciplines of initiation ceremonial have the effect of 'making men', reshaping behavior, that is to say, in a self-effacing, quiet, respectful direction. I am indebted to Ian Keen for drawing my attention to this point.

[10]This point receives further discussion in Kendon (1986b).

[11]Letter from Joan Kweck, January 31 1986.

[12] I am indebted to Michael Jackson for drawing my attention to the point made in this paragraph.

Appendix I: Sign Notation Symbols

The principles governing the use of these symbols are outlined in Chapter 5. The symbols are modified from Stokoe, Casterline and Croneberg (1965) and have been adapted for the Apple Macintosh ™ computer by a modification of 12 pt. Monaco using Font Editor I.

Sign Location Symbols

1.	·	Neutral space.
2.	∩	Upper space.
2a.	∪	Lower space.
2b.	BB	Any convenient body part.
3.	^	Top of head.
4.	⌒	Forehead.
5.	○	Face.
6.	⌓	Eyes.
7.	⌓̲	Immediately below eyes.
8.	3	Side of face, cheek, temples.
9.	?	Ear.
10.	△	Nose.
11.	△̲	Upper lip, just below nose.
12.	▽	Mouth.
12a.	▼	Mouth, with tongue protruding.

12b.	ʊ	Mouth with lips drawn back, exposing teeth.
12c.	-◇-	Mouth with lips parted and protruded.
12d.	ᴗ	Chin.
13.	π	Front of neck or throat.
14.	π̊	Back of neck.
15.	Γ	Contralateral shoulder, top.
16.	˥	Ipsilateral shoulder, top.
17.	Ϝ	Contralateral shoulder, front.
18.	ꟼ	Ipsilateral shoulder, front.
19.	⊓	Upper chest.
19a.	]	Ipsilateral side of thorax.
20.	[]	Thorax.
21.	⊔	Abdomen, stomach region.
22.	[▪, ▪]	Contralateral, ipsilateral breast (both together indicates both breasts).
23.	1	Armpit.
24.	ʅ	Upper arm.
25.	ɺ	Forearm.
26.	⊻	Elbow.
27.	ʮ	Hip.
28.	╲	Thigh.
29.	˥	Knee.

30. ᐳ Lower leg.

Sign Actor Symbols

Arm Position

1. ʅ Abducted upper arm (upper arm is lifted away from the shoulder).

2. J Forearm held in a vertical position.

3. ⩦ Arm fully extended forward.

4. ⊁ Arm fully extended laterally.

5. ʅJ Arm upraised above head.

6. › Upper arm rotated forward, elbow flexed so that elbow protrudes laterally. The 'arms akimbo' position.

Handshapes

In the descriptions to follow, the fingers are numbered from the index finger to fourth finger as 1 to 4. The thumb is abbreviated as tb. Digit joints are referred to as A (proximal), B(medial), C (distal). Drawings of most of these handshapes may be found in Figure 5.2, pp. 121-125.

Unspecified

1. U Unspecified. Used when hand shape is not critical (e.g. in Warlpiri RDANGKARLPA 'short' where the subordinate hand may vary from a fist to a loosely open hand, or in POLIJIMANI 'policeman' where the wrists cross on one another, but hand shape is variable).

Closed Hands

2. A Fist: all digits fully flexed at all joints.

3. Ȧ Fist but with thumb extended.

4. Ả A 'fist' in which the fourth digit protrudes as a 'hoop':1, 2 and 3 and tb fully flexed, 4 flexed at B and C joints, but extended at the A joint.

5. Ảt As Ả but with thumb extended.

5a. B̂t4 As B̂ but with thumb and digit 4 extended.

6. T The 'fig' hand: 1, 2, 3, 4 fully flexed, tb opposed, with tip placed between digits 1 and 2.

7. X Digits 2, 3 and 4 fully flexed, tb extended and opposed, digit 1 extended at A joint, fully flexed at B and C joints. Tip of digit 1 pressed on to tip of thumb, contacting the thumb with the nail.

8. XẢ As X, but with digit 4 extended at A joint so it forms a 'hoop'.

9. ЬO Digits 2, 3 and 4 fully flexed. Thumb extended and opposed, digit 1 extended at A joint, partly flexed at B and C, tip of digit 1 in contact with tip of thumb.

10. ЬO2 Digits 3 and 4 flexed to palm. Tips of digits 1 and 2 rest in contact with tip of thumb.

11. tO Digits 1 to 4 extended at A joints, partly flexed at B and C joints, all converging so that their tips are in contact with extended and fully opposed thumb.

12. ťO As 11, but finger tips not quite in contact.

13. O Digits extended at A joints and adducted, bent at B and C joints. Thumb opposed, bent at B joint so its tip is in contact with tip of digit 1.

13a. ×O Digits 1 to 4 extended at A joints but flexed at B and C joints, thumb fully opposed. Tips of fingers rest along side of thumb.

13b. O+ Symbol for handshapes 13 and 13a.

14. ỏ As in 13, but digit 4 is fully extended at A joint so it protrudes in a 'hoop'.

Open Hand - Digits in Adduction (drawn together)

15. B — All digits extended and adducted. The 'flat' hand.

15a. B̂ — As B, but the thumb fully abducted.

15b. B̈ — As B, but digits 1-4 slightly flexed at B and C joints.

15c. Bt — As B, but thumb is opposed. If digits 1-4 are curved, as in 16, but thumb is opposed, the handshape may be notated as B̈t.

15d. B̂ — All digits adducted and extended at B and C joints, flexed at right angles at A joints.

15e. B5 — All digits extended but partly or slightly abducted. 'Half way' between B and a 5 hand.

15f. B+ — Symbol for handshapes 15-15e.

16. Bt432 — A 'B' hand with thumb opposed. Digits 4, 3, and 2 somewhat flexed at A joints, 4 the most, 3 the next most and 2 the least.

17. cB — All digits extended and abducted, but flexed slightly at all joints to produce a slightly 'cupped' shape.

17a. t cB — cB but with thumb opposed and in contact with palm of hand.

18. bB — All digits extended, but 1 and 3 make contact at their tips; 2 rests on top of 1 and 3; tip of thumb in contact with tip of 4.

19. ×B — Digits 2, 3 and 4 fully extended and adducted; 1 extended at A joint, flexed at B joint; thumb fully extended and abducted. In some occurrences digits 2, 3 and 4 are spread apart (abducted). If this is to be noted one may write X5 or XB5.

20. ×B+t — As ×B but with thumb extended but pressed against side of hand.

21. C — Digits 1-4 extended, adducted, partially flexed at B and C joints. Thumb extended, opposed, partially flexed. Hand makes a 'C' shape when viewed laterally.

22. E — Digits 1-4 extended at A joints, fully flexed at B and C joints.

22a. Ê — As E, but thumb conspicuously abducted.

22b. E5 — As E, but the digits somewhat abducted or spread.

22c. E+ — Symbol for handshapes 22-22b.

Open Hand - Digits in Abduction

23. 5 — All digits fully extended and abducted.

24. 5t — A 5 hand, but with the thumb opposed and abducted.

25. c5 — All digits abducted, but partially flexed at all joints. Thumb slightly opposed. A 'basket' hand.

25a. 5̈ — All digits abducted, but slightly flexed at B and C joints. A 'curved' 5 hand.

26. c5mʕ — As c5, except that 2 is only slightly flexed or fully extended.

27. F — Thumb and digit 1 in contact at tips. Other digits fully extended and abducted.

Hands with one or two digits extended

28. G — Digit 1 fully extended, all other digits fully flexed. The 'pointing' hand.

28a. tG — As G, but thumb extended and opposed and in full contact with digit 1.

28b. G+ — Symbol for handshapes 28 and 28a.

29. Gt As G, with thumb extended and opposed but partially abducted, so it is not in contact with digit 1.

30. L As G, but thumb fully extended and abducted. In some cases the digits are slightly or partially flexed. If this is to be noted it may be written L̈.

31. G̈ Digit 1 fully extended at A joint, partially flexed at B and C joints. All other digits fully flexed. A 'hooked' index finger.

32. X□ Digit 1 extended at A joint but partially or almost fully flexed at B and C joints. Thumb fully extended and abducted.

33. H Digits 1 and 2 extended and adducted. All other digits flexed to palm.

33a. tH H but with thumb extended and opposed and in contact with palm of hand.

34. mH Digits 3 and 4 extended.

35. R Digits 1 and 2 extended, with digit 2 flexed in an ulnar direction so it rests in top of digit 1. 'Crossed' fingers.

36. U Digits 1 and 2 extended and abducted. Other digits flexed to palm.

36a. Ut V with thumb extended and opposed, but not in contact.

37. Ü As in 36, but digits 1 and 2 slightly flexed at B and C joints.

38. U_2 Digit 1 fully extended. Digit 2 extended at B and C joints, partially flexed at A joint.

39. Ч Digits 1 and 4 fully extended. Thumb and 2 and 3 fully flexed. The 'horns' hand.

39a. Ӵ As 39 but digits 1 and 4 slightly flexed at B and C joints.

39b. Ч+ Symbol for handshapes 39 and 39a.

40. mϚ Digit 2 extended. All other digits fully flexed.

40a. MG̈ Digit 2 extended and partially flexed at B and C joints ('curved') All other digits flexed.

40b. mϚx_1 Digit 1 extended at A joint, partially flexed at B and C joints, adducted to digit 2. Digit 2 extended. 3 and 4 flexed to palm.

40c. ьOϚm As 40, but thumb opposed, with tip in contact with base of second digit.

40d. mϚ+ Combined symbol for 40-40c.

41. I Fully closed hand but with digit 4 fully extended.

41a. Ï As I but with extended 4 slightly or partially flexed at B and C joints.

42. W Digits 1, 2 and 3 extended. 4 and thumb flexed to palm.

Digits

1. t Thumb

2. 1, 2, 3, 4 For index finger, second, third and fourth fingers, respectively.

Right and Left

1. ʎ Right side of body, arm, hand.

2. ℓ Left side of body, arm, hand.

Hand Orientation Symbols

1. ⊤ Toward signer.

2. ⊥ Away from signer.

3. ^ Facing or pointing upwards.

4. ˅ Facing or pointing downwards.

5. ‹ Facing or pointing left.

6. › Facing or pointing right.

7. ∠ Facing left and partly down.

8. ⦣ Facing right and partly down.

9. ⩲ Facing away and partly down.

SIGN ACTION SYMBOLS

Path of Movement of Hand

1. ^ Upwards.

2. ˅ Downwards.

3. › To the right.

4. ‹ To the left.

5. ⊥ Forward, to front of signer.

6. ⊤ Backward, toward signer.

7. ~ Up and down.

8. ʃ Left and right.

9. I Forward and back.

10. ᘓ Circular motion.

11.)(Approach.

12. ÷ Separate.

13. ǂ Cross over.

Rotational Movements of the Forearm

1. ɑ Forearm supination (clockwise rotation in right arm).

2. ɑ̱ Partial forearm supination.

3. ɒ Forearm pronation (anti-clockwise rotation in right arm).

4. ɒ̱ Partial forearm pronation.

5. ɒɑ Combination of pronation-supination into one action.

6. tr Tremble. A very rapid, small amplitude movement.

Movements of the Wrist

1. ɔ Wrist flexes.

2. ɔ Wrist extends.

3. ɷ Wrist flexion-extension: wrist 'flap'.

4. wɑ Wrist deviation (radial).

4a. wɑ ^ Wrist deviation (ulnar).

5. wɑ ⦧ Rotational movement executed from the wrist .

Movements of the Fingers

1. [HS] Handshape symbol in square brackets indicates terminal hand shape as a result of finger movement.

Contact

1. × Simple contact.

2. ⋇ Contact that occurs during movement, such as rubbing or brushing.

3. ! Audible contact, as when one hand slaps the other or slaps the thigh.

Contact Points

1. ᵖ Digit tip. If digit is to be specified this symbol is to be followed by a digit symbol.

2. ▮ Digit joint.

3. + Side of hand or digit, where this symbol is immediately followed by a digit specifier.

4. h 'Heel' of hand.

5. p Palm of hand.

6. bn B joints.

Movement Modifiers

1. ' Action is repeated.

2. " Action is repeated more than once.

3. ▪ Action is of restricted amplitude.

4. d Spatial movement has specific direction.

5. ↔ Hand is moved back and forth as Sign Action is performed.

6. ← Hand is moved to the left as Sign Action is performed.

7. → Hand is moved to the right as Sign Action is performed.

Movement Symbol Operators

1. ⟩ Interpret preceding symbols as combined.

2. ~ Action alternates.

Conventions for Two Handed Signs

1. ' Both hands are held in parallel. Action in each is the same.
2. ‡ Hands are held crossed over.
3. ↑ Right hand held directly ahead of left hand.
4. \ Right hand is above (or in front of) left hand and functions as the active hand. This symbol indicates an asymmetric relationship between the two hands.
5. / Right hand is below (or just behind) left hand yet functions as the active hand. This symbol also indicates an asymmetric relationship between the two hands.

Sign Juncture Symbols

1. ¦¦ Placed between two sign notations to indicate that two signs are parts of a compound expression.
2. ; Indicates that there are two phases to a sign.
3. , Symbols or complete sign notations separated by this symbol are alternate forms.

Signed Discourse Juncture Symbols

1. | Juncture bracket.
2. |R| Rest juncture. Hands are lowered to a position of complete relaxation.
3. |pR| Partial rest juncture. Hands are returned part-way toward their position of relaxation.
4. |R,| Hands move to Rest position but do not cease motion, moving immediately onwards to next signing position.
5. |,| Hands slow up, or pause briefly, but do not move towards Rest position.
6. |+| Signs succeed one another directly with no intervening recovery or repositioning. Indicates suffixing of one sign on to another.

Appendix II

Two Versions of a Warlpiri Story

Introduction

In this Appendix transcriptions of a Warlpiri story are presented, first in sign and then in speech. Both versions were told by Winnie Nangala and recorded at Yuendumu, Northern Territory in 1981. The sign version was recorded on video-tape in July 1981. The spoken version was recorded on audio tape only, several weeks later, at the end of August 1981.The sign version was transcribed by the author with the assistance of Winnie Nangala. The spoken version was transcribed by June Napanangka and revised by Mary Laughren in consultation with Winnie Nangala. The English translation and interlinear was undertaken by the author, with revisions and corrections provided by Mary Laughren.

The story belongs to the Dreaming and is part of a complex of stories that are concerned with the star constellation the Pleiades or Seven Sisters (Western Desert stories about the Pleiades have been recounted by Tindale 1959, but these appear to be rather different from the Warlpiri complex). These stars are thought of by the Warlpiri as a group of women associated with the Napaljarri subsection. The constellation is called *Napaljarri-warnu* . The story, here titled *Parraja-kurlu* , concerns an old man who is fed by his daughters. They repeatedly bring him edible seed, ground up and made into a batter, which they carry on a variety of dishes. The old man not only eats the food but he swallows the dishes as well. Eventually his daughters wonder where all their dishes are disappearing to and they ask him to give them back. He replies that he has lost them, and in any case he refuses to return them. The women then find dishes belongng to other people on which to bring him food, but he swallows these as well. He gets fatter and fatter. Eventually the women have no more dishes to carry food with and they resolve to do something to the old man. They get together as a group and chase him with their fire sticks. They catch him and shove their fire sticks into him. This makes him vomit up all the dishes he had swallowed. The women then go off to dig for yams and gather seed. While they are away, the old man gathers together their grinding stones and casts a spell upon them, so that when the women return they will be killed. However, when they come back they throw their digging sticks at him and, after a chase, they take off and go up into the sky to become the *Napaljarri-warnu* constellation. The old man also goes up into the sky and sits there with them.

The sign version is incomplete. A recording was being made both on video-tape and on super-8mm film. Unfortunately, the film cassette ran out just before the end of the story and Winnie, on hearing the film camera stop, assumed that the recording was finished and stopped signing.

In the translations to follow note that since there are no separate terms in English for the different kinds of dishes mentioned in the story (in English they would all be referred to as 'coolamons'), I have retained the Warlpiri terms. A *parraja* is a flat dish, a general purpose carrier, but commonly used for carrying and preparing edible seed; a *kurlinjirri* is also a flat dish of a similar type; a *pangurnu* is a small dish, used for digging out sand in soaks to obtain water; a *mardu* is a small bowl-like dish used for carrying water; a *yanurrpu* is a large bowl for carrying water.

Explanation of transcription conventions

Sign Version. For the sign version, the signs are labelled with Warlpiri words written in upper case. In a few cases, where no Warlpiri label could be given, a sign has been transcribed in sign notation. Occasionally, an action may also be described in words, as when a path of movement must be indicated, as in R-sequence 16, or where there is non-sign action.

Sign junctures, where marked, are enclosed in vertical lines.They are as follows: I+I 'affix' juncture; I , I recovery after stroke or a slight pause before next sign; IR,I the hands are lowered to a neutral or resting position but do not stay; IRI the hands are lowered to a neutral or resting position and remain there; IpRI, as for IRI, but the hands do not relax; ITRI a rest position is reached, but it is not a neutral posture; I I I an "irrelevant" action, as in rubbing the eye, etc. A more detailed explanation of sign junctures is given in Chapter 9.

Features of sign action are enclosed in slashes. Thus: /h/ indicates a hesitation or pause within a segment of sign movement; /ss/ indicates that the action is sustained or "overslow"; /i/ indicates that the sign segment is interrupted; /H/ indicates that the position reached at the end of the sign is held or sustained. Inc. means "incomplete" sign. Prepr. indicates "preparation" (the phase of movement by which the limb executing the sign is got ready).

An English gloss for each sign is written on the line immediately below. On the third line a free English translation is given. The numbers on the line immediately below indicate in minutes, seconds and thirtieths of seconds the video frame at which each R-sequence begins. These numbers are visible on a video-tape copy of this recording which it is hoped we shall be able to publish. At present, this recording may be viewed at the Australian Institute of Aboriginal Studies in Canberra or at the Archives of Traditional Music, Indiana University, Bloomington, Indiana.

On the line above the sign labels, the facial address (orientation) of the storyteller is indicated. A symbol indicating the address is followed by a dotted line to indicate the period during which the address indicated was sustained. 0 indicates that the signer is oriented frontally, toward the camera (and so toward the author, who was sitting beside the camera as the story was being told); † indicates that the signer is looking downwards, into her lap; > indicates the signer has turned her face to her right; < indicates that the signer has turned her face to her left. When combined with † this shows that the storyteller is looking downwards and to her left or right, at the same time. These different orientations are figured in Figs. 9.3 -9.7, pp. 292-294.

Spoken Version. The Warlpiri, given on the first line, is written with all morpheme breaks indicated by hyphens. Interlinear conventions are as follows:

ABL, Ablative; ALL, Allative; AUX, Auxiliary; CAUS, Causative; COMP, Complementizer; DAT, Dative; DET, Determiner; DIMIN, Diminuitive; EMPH, Emphatic; ERG, Ergative; IMP, Imperative; IMPF, Imperfect; INC, Inceptive; INCH, Inchoative ('become'); INF, Infinitve; LOC, Locative; NPAST Nonpast; OBJ, Object; PAST, Past; PERL, Perlative ('alongside of'); POSS, Possessive; PROG, Progressive; PROP, Proprietive ('having'); REFLX, Reflexive; SBJ, Subject; SEQ, Sequential ("then"); TOP, Topicalizer. Notation for pronouns follows Hale (1974). 1, 1st person singular ('I'); 2, 2nd person singular ('you, thou'); 3, 3rd person singular 'he, she, it'); 12, 1st person dual inclusive ('you and I'); 11, 1st person dual exclusive ('he/she and I'); 22, 2nd person dual ('you two'); 33, 3rd person dual ('they two'); 122, 1st person plural inclusive ('they and I'); 222, 2nd person plural ('you all'); 333, 3rd person plural ('they all').Pronouns occur as independent forms and also as clitics, suffixed to the auxiliary base.

***Parraja-kurlu:* About the coolamons. Sign language version**

o...........   †................................>.................†...............o.......

[1] NGURLU YURRPARNI PARRAJA KANYI{L} | , | MURUPINYI | pR |

Edible seed grind *parraja* carry Shove inside

Edible seed was ground, [placed in] a *parraja*, carried [to him], [he] shoved it inside himself.

69.10.29

†...o...

[2] MURUPINYI PARRAJA JINTANGKU NGURLU JINTANGKU MUKU NGARNI | R,| inc.| R |

Shove inside *parraja* together with seed together with everything eat

[He] shoved inside himself the *parraja* together with the seed together all was eaten.

69.22.28

†...>..................o....

[3] NGULA JANGKA PANGURNU YURRPARNI KANYI /ss/ | R,|

DET. CAUS. *pangurnu* grind carry

(And then) [they took] a *pangurnu*, ground seed on to it, carried it to [him].

69.31.00

>.........†............o...
[4] KANYI MURUPINYI | pR, | KIRDA NYANU | , | MURUPINYI | R |
Carry shove inside father of them shove inside
[They] carried it to him, he shoved it inside himself, that father of theirs, he shoved it inside himself.
69.49.02

>.......................................<†...†...
[5] NYAPARRA PARRAJA | , | Point WAJAWAJA MANI Point NGAYI | R |
Where *parraja* Over there lost there indeed
[The women said to him] "Where are our *parrajas*" "Over there I lost them indeed" [said the old man].
69.57.18

<†............................
[6] KULKUL KARRI | R |
Wait stand (i.e. wait awhile)
"[You'll have to] wait [for them]."
70.05.07

†..................................>..................................o...
[7i] YANURRPU YURRPARNI NGULA JANGKA KANYI | R,|
Yanurrpu grind and then carry [to him]
[The women took a] *yanurrpu*, ground [seed] and then carried it [to him].
70.09.01

o............................>........ †....................................o..
[7ii] KIRDA NYANU | , | YINYI YANURRPU MURUPINYI | R |
Father of them give (to him) *yanurrpu* shove inside
[To that] father of theirs they gave to him the *yanurrpu* [with the food], he shoved it all down.
70.17.01

o........... †....................o...........
[8] MIYALU PIRDA MARDARNI | pR |
Stomach full have
His stomach was full up.
70.25.08

†.............o...>†...............†...........................o..........
[9] PARRAJA | R | YANURRPU PANGURNU MURUPINYI | R |
Parraja *Yanurrpu* *Pangurnu* shove inside
The *parraja*. The *Yanurrpu*, the *pangurnu*, he had shoved inside himself.
70.28.23

†..>....
[10] NGULA JANGKA PANGURNU / i / PARRAJA KARI YURRPARNU NGURLU | R,|
And then *pangurnu* *parraja* other grind edible seed
And then they got a *pangurnu* and another *parraja*, they ground seed,
70.36.18

.................†.......................................>............o....
KANYI / i / JIRRIMA PARRAJA JIRRIMA | , | KANYI | R |
carry to him two *parraja* two carry to him
they carried it to him, two *parrajas*, two they carried to him.
70.44.04

>.......................†....
[11] YINYI | + | Point | pR |
Give to him
[They] gave them to him.
70.49.21

o.......................†...o.....................
[12]MURUPINYI | pR, | NGURLU JINTANGKA MURUPINYI PARRAJA JINTANGKA MURUPINYI | R |
Shove inside seed together with shove inside *parraja* together shove inside
He shoved inside himself the food together with the *parraja*, all together he shoved them inside.
70.54.11

†..o.........>..........

[13] NGULA JANGKA Prepr. / h / MARDU WITA YURRPARNI | , | KANYI | I | (Rubs eye).

And then mardu small grind carry (to him)

And then they ground seed and carried it to him on a small *mardu*.

71.03.03

†.............................o..............>.....................o..

[13a] PANGURNU MARDU WITA | , | JIRRIMA KANYI | R |

Pangurnu *mardu* small two carry (to him)

On a *pangurnu* and a small *mardu*, on two dishes they carried food to him.

71.13.18

†.........................o...........

[14] NGANJINI MURUPINYI | pR |

On arrival shove inside.

As soon as they arrived with the food, he shoved it inside himself.

71.20.08

o...

[15] MIYALU MARDARNI RDANJARR MARDARNI | R |

Stomach possess load possess

His stomach had a very full load.

71.23.00

†..o.......................................

[16] PARRAJA YANURRPU | R,| MIYALU (Downward moving point) RDANJARR MARDARNI | pR |

Parraja *yanurrpu* stomach (down into) load possess

Parrajas, yanurrpus were down in his stomach it was fully loaded.

71.27.03

o.....................................†........o..

[17] RDANJARR MARDARNI | R | | I | | R |

Load possess

It was fully loaded.

71.33.06

>.............................†..

[18] NGULA JANGKA | , | WAPALWAPAL WANGKAMI PATU Prep / h / MARDUKUJA PATU . G> ⊥ 'G< ⊥ ˇ | R |

And then in expectation talk several woman several Dative

And then several of the women wondered about [the whereabouts of the dishes].

71.41.20

†...>.......................................

[19] WAPALWAPAL WANGKAMI | , | JAPUKUKARI PAYIRNI | R |

In expectation talk next time ask

[They] wondered about [the dishes], next time they would ask [about them].

71.49.09

>..

[20] PAYIRNI PARRAJA YINYIRNI |R |

Ask *parraja* give hither

[They] ask: give back the *parrajas*!

71.54.25

>.....................................o.......................>................

[21] LAWA | R | [22] LAWA . G ˇ ˇ | , | Prepr. / i / [23] (Interchange with Ruby)

No No 3rd P

No! No! [said] he.

71.59.20 72.01.13

†....................................

[24] PARRAJA | + | WAJA | R |

Parraja indeed

Parrajas, indeed!

72.13.23

†..>....................................o....

[25] NGANA KANYIRNI . G⌄⊥ ˇ (nyampu-kurra) | , | NGURLU YUNGU YINYIRRA | pR, | NYUNTU | pR |
Who carry hither to this food causal give thither you
Who can carry here food in order to give it to you?
72.16.28

†.. †..

[26] . B^⊥\B⌄< ⊥* LAWA / h / | TR | [27] WURRA MANI (?) . G⊤^ | pTR |
Everything nothing — hold back
All our dishes are gone. — [We] hold back [giving you food].
72.24.00

†........>...........................

[28] KIRDA NYANU . G⌄⊥ ˇ | TR |
Father of them ?Dative
For their father.
72.28.26

†......................... †...>...........................o..

[29] NGULA JANGKA | R | [30] PARRAJA PALKA MANI | , | . G⌄> 'G⌄< ϭ▪ . G⊥^ 'G⊥^ ⊥▪ | , | YURRPARNI KANYI | R |
And then *Parraja* find throw there grind carry
And then [they] found a *parraja* that had been thrown away, [they] ground food and carried it to him.
72.34.13

>.........†..   >...........................†....................

[31] KANYI | R | [32] YINYI KULPAMI | + | . G⌄⊥ ˇ | pR |

Carry (to him)   give   return

[They] carried [food] to him. [They] gave it to him, returned.

72.47.25

†...o...........>†...........>......................................o.....

[32] YARDA YURRPARNI YURRPARNI YURRPARNI YURRPARNI PANGURNU KURRA | R,| NGULA YARDA YINYI | + | . G⊥› ʔ | pR |

Again grind grind grind grind *pangurnu* ALLATIVE thus again give to him.

Again they ground and ground and ground and ground food, put it in a *pangurnu*, thus again they gave food to him.

72.56.12

o.....†...o............   †..........o...........

[34] MURUPINYI | pR | [35] MURUPINYI | pR |

Shove inside   Shove inside

He shoved it down.   He shoved it down.

73.04.08

†.................................o.........

[36] MIYALU PIRDA MARDARNI | R |

Stomach full   possess.

His stomach was full up.

73.09.25

o....................†......................   †.....................o.......†...........................

[37] MUKU NGARNI | I Extended pause. | [38] MUKU NGARNI | pTR, | MUKU NGARNI | R |

All eat   all eat   all eat

He ate everything.   He ate everything.   He ate everything.

73.15.10   73.39.26

>..†..   †...

[39] NYAPARRA PARRAJA YINYI /H/ YARUJU YINYI | R | [40] YARUJU YARUJU YINYI YARUJU YARUJU YINYI | R |

Where *parraja* give hurry give   hurry hurry give hurry hurry give

"Where are the *parrajas* we have given you. Hurry, give them back. Hurry, give them back."

73.46.19

†..............>...o...

[41] YANURRPU ?YINYI | , | PANGURNU KURRA | , | YURRPARNI YURRPARNI YURRPARNI YURRPARNI YURRPARNI | R |

Yanurrpu ?give *pangurnu* ALLLATIVE grind grind grind grind grind

[They] ground and ground, etc. [food] on a *yanurrpu*, on a *parraja*.

73.58.20

†...>.........o...

[42] YURRPARNI YURRPARNI YURRPARNI YURRPARNI YURRPARNI KANYI | R |

Grind, etc.   carry

[They] ground and ground and ground, etc. [food] and carried it to him.

74.08.26

†....................................>....................................o.......... †.................o....
[43] YURRPARNI YURRPARNI KANYI | R,| YINYI | + | KULPAMI | R | [44] MURUPINYI | pR |
Grind grind carry give return shove inside
[They] ground and ground and carried [food] to him, [they] gave it to him and returned. [He] shoved it all inside himself.
74.17.01

†..o..........
[45] WIRI WIRI NYAMPU | , | Prep. / h / YANURRPU WIRI WIRI NYAMPU MURUPINYI | R |
Big big this *yanurrpu* big big this shove inside.
This was a big dish, the *yanurrpu* was very big, this one that he swallowed.
74.23.29

o..
[46] MIYALU JINTA RDANJARR MARDARNI | R |
Stomach one load possess
His stomach had a full load.
74.30.00

†........................... <.....................>....†..>..................................
[47] NGULA JANGKA | R | [48] MARLAJARRA | , | MUKU NGARI RDAKA JIRRIMA NYINA PATU MARDUKUJA | + | . G‹⊥~ | R |
And then empty handed all just hand two sit several woman
And then the women were empty handed. They had just their own two hands.
74.37.06

>......<...........†...   †..........<...........†...<.....>...†..

[49] WARNTAMARRI | R | [50] Prep /h/ PURAMI WARLU NGIJI   PATU MUURLPA WARLU NGIJI   PARNTA PURAMI | R |

Large women's quarters   follow   fire   firestick several together   fire   firestick having   follow

From the large women's camp they followed [the old man] with burning firesticks.

74.48.23

†.............>..........   †..<...........†..>

[51] PURLKA . G‘ | R | [52] Prep./ i / NYANUNGU PATU MARDUKUJA PATU PURAMI | R |

Old man ran   He   several woman   several follow

The old man ran away. Several women followed him.

75.09.20

o..........<.......†...>...............

[53] WARLU MURUPINYI YURLKULYU YIRRARNI NGAKA WARLU JANGKA | R |

Fire   shove inside vomit   put   soon   fire   causative

[The women] shoved the fire sticks inside [the old man] and the he vomited soon because of the fire.

75.18.17

†...>...............   o.......................

[54] WARLU JANGKA NGAKA YURLKULYU YIRRARNI YURLKULYU YIRRARNI | R | [55] WINKIRRPA | R |

Fire   causative soon   vomit   put   vomit   put.   Wrong one.

The fire soon caused him to vomit and vomit. Naughty old man.

75.25.17

>........................<....................†...................

[56] [Arms extended forward alternately] NGUNAMI | R |
Gesture indicating things spread out on the ground.
The things he had swallowed lay everywhere.
75.33.15

†...>.......................................

[57] NGULA JANGKA | , | WARLU JANGKA MARA MARA | + | G YANIRRA NYANUNGU PURLKA | R |
And then fire causative half baked that one go hither he old man.
And then, half baked from the fire, the hold man went off.
75.38.15

>.....................................†...

[58] |Posture shift, Wave | , | PAMARRPA | , | WIRLINYI JUUL KARLAMI | , | KULPAMI NYANUNGU PURLKA WARLU WARNU | TR |
Stone hunting stop dig return he old man fire elative
The grinding stones, [left behind by the women who] went hunting and stopped to dig for yams, the old man returned for, because of the fire (i.e. because he had been burned).
75.49.18

>..†.......................<........†...............................>..............................<...

[59] PAMARRPA | + | ?Come back ?WIRIYI (tracks) MANI PUNPUN WANGKAMI PAMARRPA NYAMPU | R |
Stone come back tracks get advise speak stone this
The grinding stones the old man told them to look for the tracks of the women (i.e. he cast a spell on the stones so they would either follow the women, or find their tracks and await their return).
75.58.09

<............†.........................o..

[60] NYANYI NGAMA RLANGU | R |

See mother-daughter pair. [Here this refers to the pair of stones, one large, on small, used for grinding seed]

[He] saw the mother and daughter stones.

76.05.22

>..o....

[61] NGAMA RLANGU KARI NGAMA RLANGU KARI KANARDI YIRRARNI PAMARRPA | + | NYAMPU | R |

Mother-daughter pair other mother-daughter pair other in a row put stone this

He placed the mother-daughter stones in a row, one after the other.

76.13.03

Parraja-kurlu: About the coolamons. Spoken version

(1) Pangurnu-rla-lpa yurrpa-rnu, yarda-lpa yurrpa-rnu,

Pangurnu-LOC-IMPF grind-PAST, again-IMPF grind-PAST

ngula-lpa-rla jirrima-rla yi-nja-ya-nu-rra mardu-ngka, pangurnu-rla.

that-IMPF-3DAT two-on give-INF-PROG-PAST-thither *mardu*-LOC,

pangurnu-LOC.

On to a *pangurnu* was ground [seed], again was ground, it was for him, two for him went and gave thither, on a *mardu*, on a *pangurnu*.

(2) Pangurnu-rla, yi-nja-ya-nu-rra-lpa-rla

Pangurnu-LOC, give-INF-PROG-PAST-thither-IMPF-3DAT

On the *pangurnu*, went and gave thither to him

yi-lpa-rla yinya kuju-rnu-lpa-lu-rla.

COMP-IMPF-3DAT that-beyond throw-PAST-IMPF-333SBJ-333DAT.

over there they threw to him [food].

(3) Ngula-warnu-ju, yanurrpu-rla-lku-lpa-lu yurrpa-rnu ngurlu-ju.

Then, *yanurrpu*-LOC-SEQ-IMPF-333SBJ grind-PAST seed-TOP

And then, on the *yanurrpu* now they ground seed.

Yurrpa-rnu-lpa-lu.

Grind-PAST-IMPF-333SBJ.

They ground seed.

(4) Ngayi-lpa pulapi nungu-ju ka-ngu-rnu.

Indeed-IMPF full up batter-TOP carry-PAST-hither.

Indeed the [containers] carried hither [to him]were full up with batter.

(5) Ka-ngu-lpa-rla,

Carry-PAST-IMPF-3DAT,

yi-nja-ya-nu-rra-lpa-rla yu-ngu.

give-INF-PROG-PAST-thither-IMPF-3DAT give-PAST.

Carried to him, went and gave to him thither, gave.

(6) Ngayi-lpa muru-pu-ngu.

Indeed-IMPFswallow-PAST.

Indeed he swallowed it.

(7) Ngula-lpa muru-pu-ngu yawalati ---- parraja-rlangu, pangurnu-rlangu.

That one-IMPF swallow-PAST whole lot --- *parraja*-also, *pangurnu*-also.

That one (old man) swallowed the whole lot, the *parraja* and the *pangurnu* as well.

(8) Ngula-warnu-ju, yarda-rni-lpa ka-ngu.

And then, again-hither-IMPF carry-PAST.

And then, again (they) carried (food) hither (to the old man).

(9) Yarda yurrpa-rnu-lpa-rla parraja-rla-lku wiri-ngka,

Again grind-PAST-IMPF-3DAT *parraja*-LOC-SEQ big-LOC,

Again (they) ground seed for him and put it on a big *parraja*,

parraja-rla-lpa-lu-rla yurrpa-rnu

parraja-LOC-IMPF-333SBJ-3DAT grind-PAST.

on the *parraja* they (put the seed they) ground.

(10) Pulapi-lpa-lu-rla ka-ngu.

Full up-IMPF-333SBJ-3DAT carry-PAST.

They carried full dishes to him.

(11) Yu-ngu-lpa-lu-rla.

Give-PAST-IMPF-333SBJ-3DAT.

They gave (the food) to him.

(12) Ngayi-lpa parraja muru pu-ngu manu ngurlu muru pu-ngu ---

Indeed-IMPF *parraja* swallow-PAST and seed swallow-PAST

purlka-ngku-ju.

old man-ERG-TOP.

Indeed the *parraja* and the seed were by the old man.

(i.e. he ate both the food and the dishes).

(13) Nga-rnu-lpa panu-juku.

Eat-PAST-IMPF everything.

Everything was eaten.

(14) Muru-pu-ngu-lpa.

Swallow-PAST-IMPF.

(It was all) swallowed.

(15) Ngula-warnu-ju, mardu-ngka-lku-lpa-lu-rla yurrpa-rnu.

And then, *mardu*-LOC-SEQ-IMPF-333SBJ-3DAT grind-PAST.

And then they ground seed (and put it) on a *mardu.*

(16) Pangurnu-rla-lpa-lu-rla yurrpa-rnu.

Pangurnu-LOC-IMPF-333SBJ-3DAT grind-PAST.

They ground [seed] for him [and put it] on a *pangurnu.*

(17) Ngula-warnu-ju, jirrima-rla-lpa-lu-rla yi-nja-ya-nu-rra.

And then, two-LOC-IMPF-333SBJ-3DAT give-INF-PROG-PAST-thither.

And then, on two [containers] they went and gave [food] to him.

(18) Panu-juku-lpa-jana muru-pu-ngu.

Many-still-IMPF-333DAT swallow-PAST.

He swallowed all of them.

(19) Miyalu-ju-lpa yali-lki nyina-nja-rra ya-nu.

Stomach-TOP-IMPF that-SEQ sit-INF-thither go-past.

His stomach was sticking right out

(20) Ngula-warnu-ju, yanurrpu-rla-lku, palkarni-rla-ju,

And then, *yanurrpu*-LOC-SEQ, last one-LOC-TOP,

yurrpa-rnu-lpa-lu-rla, panu-kari ngari.

grind-PAST-IMPF-333SBJ-3DAT, much other ones just.

And then they ground more seed on to the last *yanurrpu* they had..

(21) Yi-nja-ya-nu-rra-lpa-lu-rla.

Give-INF-PROG-PAST-thither-IMPF-333SBJ-3DAT.

They went and gave it to him.

(22) Ngayi-lpa muru-pu-ngu yanurrpu wungu.

Indeed-IMPF swallow-PAST *yanurrpu* together

Indeed the *yanurrpu* together with [the food] he swallowed.

(23) Yanurrpu wungu-lpa muru-pu-ngu.

Yanurrpu together-IMPF swallow-PAST.

The *yanurrpu* together with [the food] he swallowed.

(24) Ngula-warnu-ju, parraja-rlangu-rla-lku, pangurnu-rlangu-rla-lku,

And then-TOP, *parraja*-also-LOC-SEQ, *pangurnu*--etc.

mardu-ngka-lku-lpa-rla yurrpa-rnu,

mardu-LOC-SEQ-IMPF-3DAT grind-PAST,

yurrpa-rnu-lpa-lu-rla, yurrpa-rnu.

grind-PAST-IMPF-333SBJ-3DAT, grind-PAST

And then on a *parraja* and a *pangurnu* and a *mardu*, [they] ground and ground and ground [seed] for him.

(25) Ka-ngu-lpa-lu-rla, ka-ngu-lpa-lu-rla.

Carry-PAST-IMPF-333SBJ-3DAT, Carry-etc.

They carried to him, they carried to him

(26) Yi-nja-ya-nu-rra.-lpa-lu-rla.

Give-INF-PROG-PAST-thither-IMPF-333SBJ-3DAT.

They kept on giving [the food] to him over there.

(27) Ngayi-lpa wanapi ngurlkurr kuju-rnu, muru pu-ngu-lpa.

Indeed-IMPF one piece gulp down-PAST, shove inside-PAST-IMPF.

Indeed he gulped it down, whole he swallowed it.

(28) Ngula-warnu-ju, yanurrpu-rla-yijala-lpa-lu-rla yurrpa-rnu.

And then-TOP, *yanurrpu*-LOC-also-IMPF-333SBJ-3DAT grind-PAST.

And then on a *yanurrpu* -also they ground [food] for him.

(29) Mardu-ngka wita-ngka-lku-lpa-lu-rla yurrpa-rnu.

Mardu-LOC little-LOC-SEQ-IMPF-333SBJ-3DAT grind-PAST.

Then on a little *mardu* they ground [food] for him.

(30) Yurrpa-rnu, yurrpa-rnu ....

Grind-PAST, etc.

[They] ground and ground.

(31) Pulapi-lpa-lu-rla yi-nja-ya-nu-rra ngami-ngka, parraja-rla.

Full up-IMPF-333SBJ-3DAT give-INF-PROG-PAST-thither *ngami*-LOC, *parraja*-LOC.

They kept giving it all to him [food] on a *ngami*, on a *parraja.*

(32) Ngayi-lpa ngurlkurr kuju-rnu.

Just-IMPF gulp down-PAST.

[He] just gulped it down.

(33) Kurlinjirri-rla, kurlinjirri-rla wungu-ngka-lku-lpa-lu-rla yurrpa-rnu.

Kurlinjirri-LOC, *kurlinjirri*-LOC, together-LOC-SEQ-IMPF-LOC grind-PAST.

They ground [food] for him on to a *kurlinjirri*, a *kurlinjirri.*

(34) Yurrpa-rnu, yurrpa-rnu ...ka-ngu-lpa-lu-rla.

Grind-PAST, grind-PAST ... carry-PAST-IMPF-333SBJ-3DAT.

They ground, they ground, they carried [the food] to him.

(35) Ngayi-lpa ngurlkurr-kuju-rnu. (36) Ngurlkurr-kuju-rnu-lpa ngari.

Indeed-IMPF gulp down-PAST. Gulp down-PAST-IMPF just

Indeed [he] gulped it down. [He] just gulped it down.

(37) Ngintirrki-ngintirrki-kirra-lpa pardi-ja-rra.

Swell up-ALL-IMPF grow-PAST-thither.

[He] was swelling out, getting bigger and bigger.

(38) Ngintirrki nyina-ja-lpa ngari yalarni-lki miyalu-ju

Swell up be-PAST-IMPF just there-SEQ stomach-TOP

marilpi-piya-lku.

moon-like-SEQ

[His] stomach was then swollen up like the full moon.

(39) Yurrpa-rninja-rla-lpa-lu-rla yu-ngu.

Grind-INF-SEQ-IMPF-333SBJ-3DAT give-PAST.

And then they went and ground [more food] and gave it to him.

(40) Yurrpa-rninja-rla-lpa-lu-rla yu-ngu.

Grind-INF-SEQ-IMPF-333SBJ-3DAT give-PAST.

And then they went and ground [more food] and gave it to him.

(41) Panu-juku muru-pu-ngu ---- parraja-nganja-nganja.

Many-still swallow-PAST ---- *parraja*-etc.-etc.

Everything was shoved down --- the *parraja* and all.

(42) Parraja, kurlinjirri. (43) Wanapi-lpa muru-pu-ngu-lku.

Parraja, kurlinjirri Whole-IMPF swallow-PAST-SEQ.

The *parraja*, the *kurlinjirri*. He swallowed it whole.

(44) Parraja-rla, kurlinjirri-rla-lku, mardu-ngka-lku-lpa-lu-rla

Parraja-LOC, *kurlinjirri*-LOC-SEQ, *mardu*-LOC-SEQ-IMPF-3DAT

yurrpa-rnu, yurrpa-rnu,

grind-PAST, grind-PAST

Then on a *parraja*, a *kurlinjirri*, a *mardu* they ground food for him.

(45) Yiii ... ngurlkurr-kuju-rnu-lpa.

Oh ....gulp down-PAST-IMPF

Oh it was all gulped down.

(46) Yi-nja-ya-nu-rra-lpa-lu-rla,

Give-INF-PROG-PAST-thither-IMPF-333SBJ-3DAT

ngurlkurr kuju-rnu-lpa.

gulp down-PAST-IMPF.

They kept giving him food and he gulped it all down.

(47) Wanapi-lpa muru-pu-ngu --- parraja-kurlu.

Whole-IMPF swallow-PAST --- *parraja*-PROP

He swallowed it in one go - with the *parraja*..

(48) Ngula-warnu-ju, yapa-kari-kirlangu-lku-lpa ma-nu.

And then, person-other-POSS-SEQ-IMPF get-PAST

And they got someone else's [dishes].

(49) Yapa-kari-kirlangu-lku-lpa ma-nu.

Person-other-POSS-SEQ-IMPF get-PAST

They picked up someone else's [dishes].

(50) Yurrpa-rnu-lpa-lu-rla, yurrpa-rnu-lpa-lu-rla ...

Grind-PAST-IMPF-333SBJ-3P, grind-PAST-IMPF-333SBJ-3DAT

They ground for him, they ground for him.

(51) Yurrpa-rninja-rla, yi-nja-ya-nu-rra-lpa-lu-rla.

Grind-INF-SEQ, give-INF-PROG-PAST-thither-IMPF-333SBJ-3DAT

They ground [food] and then they went on giving it thither to him.

(52) Ngula-lpa-lu-rla kurlinjirri-kirra-lku jinta-kurra-lku

That-IMPF-333SBJ-3DAT *kurlinjirri*-ALL-SEQ one-ALL-SEQ

yurrpa-rnu yurrpa-rnu.

grind-PAST grind-PAST

Then they ground [food] for him into one *kurlinjirri*.

(53) Yi-nja-ya-nu-rra-lpa-lu-rla.

Give-INF-PROG-PAST-thither-IMPF-333SBJ-3DAT.

They went on giving [it] to him.

(54) Ngula-warnu-ju, parraja-rla-lku-lpa-lu-rla yurrpa-rnu.

And then-TOP, *parraja*-LOC-SEQ-IMPF-333SBJ-3DAT grind-PAST

And then they ground [food] for him on a *parraja*.

(55) Ngula-warnu-ju, pangurnu-rla-lku-lpa-lu-rla yurrpa-rnu.

And then-TOP, *pangurnu*-LOC-SEQ-333SBJ-3DAT grind-PAST

And then they ground [food] for him on a *pangurnu*

(56) Jirrima-rla-lku-lpa-lu yi-nja-ya-nu-rra.

Two-LOC-SEQ-IMPF-333SBJ give-INF-PROG-PAST- thither.

On two[dishes] they then went and gave him food.

(57) Yii .... Wanapi ngari-lpa ngurlkurr-kuju-rnu,

Ohh ... one piece just-IMPF gulp down-PAST

yi-lpa-rla jirrnganja -- ngurlu-ku-ju.

COMP-IMPF-3DAT with -- edible seed-DAT-TOP.

Oh he gulped it down in one go with the edible seed.

(58) Ngula-warnu-ju, rdapardapa-rla-lku-lpa-lu-rla wangka-ja.

And then-TOP, nothing-LOC-SEQ-IMPF-333SBJ-3DAT speak-PAST.

And then when there was nothing left they asked him.

(59) Wangka-ja-rra-lku-lpa.

Say-PAST-THITHER-SEQ-IMPF

They said

(60) "Parraja-nganpa yu-ngka!"

"*Parraja*-133OBJ give-IMP

"Give us the *parrajas*!"(61) "Lawa-waja!"

"No-EMPH"

"There's none I tell you!"

(62) "Parraja-nganpa yu-ngka! Yangka panu-ja yu-ngka-wurru ngurlu-ku."

"*Parraja*-us give-IMP! DET many-EMPH give-IMP-just food-DAT.

"Give us the *parrajas!* Just give us those many [things] used for the food"

(63) "Lawa-waja! Lawa-waja!"

"No I won't! No I won't!"

(64) "Ngayi? Kala nyiya-rla-rlipa yurrpa-rninja-rla nga-rni-waja?"

"Indeed? But what-LOC-122SBJ grind-INF-SEQ eat-NPAST-EMPH?"

"Indeed? But then what are we to grind food into?"

(65) Palka-ma-nu-lpa yangka yapa-kurlangu.

Find-PAST-IMPF DET someone-POSS.

[They] found one that belonged to someone.

(66) Parraja-puka, mardu-puka-lpa-lu palka ma-nu.

Parraja-only, *mardu*-only-IMPF-333SBJ find-PAST.

They only found a *parraja* and a *mardu.*

(67) Ngula-ngku-lpa-lu ma-nu-lpa-lu, ma-nu-lpa-lu, ma-nu-lpa-lu.

That one-ERG-IMPF-333SBJ get-PAST-IMPF-333SBJ, etc.

With that they gathered, gathered, gathered (seed)

(68) Ka-ngu-rnu-lpa-lu, ka-ngu-rnu-lpa-lu.

Carry-PAST-hither-IMPF-333SBJ, etc.

They carried them hither, they carried them hither.

(69) Yurrpa-rnu-lpa-lu, yurrpa-rnu-lpa-lu ..

Grind-PAST-IMPF-333SBJ, etc.

They ground [seed], they ground [seed].

(70) Mardu-ngka-lpa-lu-rla yi-nja-ya-nu-rra

Mardu-LOC-IMPF-333SBJ-3DAT give-INF-PROG-PAST-thither.

They [put the food] on the *mardu* and went and gave it thither [to him].

(71) Mardu-lpa-rla jirrnganja ngurlkurr-kuju-rnu.

Mardu-IMPF-3DAT with gulp down-PAST

He gulped down *mardu* with [the seed batter].

(72) Ngayi-lpa miyalu yalarni-lki nyina-ja pulapi-lki.

Indeed-IMPF stomach there-SEQ be-PAST full up-SEQ

Indeed his stomach then became full up.

(73) Ngula-warnu-ju, parraja-rla-lku-lpa-lu

And then, *parraja*-LOC-SEQ-IMPF-333SBJ

yurrpa-rnu, yurrpa-rnu, yurrpa-rnu.

grind-PAST, etc.

And then on to the *parraja* they ground and ground and ground [food].

(74) Yi-nja-ya-nu-rra-lpa-lu palkarni-rla-lku

Give-INF-PROG-PAST- thither-IMPF-333SBJ scarce-LOC-SEQ

jinta-ngka-lku kurlinjarri-rla.

one-LOC-SEQ *kurlinjirri*-LOC.

They went and gave him [food] on the one last *kiurlinjirri* [they had]

(75) Kurlinjirri-rla-lku-lpa karri-ja.

Kurlinjirri-LOC-SEQ-IMPF stand-PAST.

It was on the *kurlinjirri*.

(76) Ka-ngu-rra-lpa-lu-rla.

Carry-PAST- thither-IMPF-333SBJ-3DAT

The carried it thither for him.

(77) Yiii...wanapi ngari-lpa punta-rninja-rla-lku

Oh ...one piece just-IMPF take away-INF-SEQ-SEQ

muru-pu-ngu.

swallow-PAST

Oh! he took it from them and swallowed it all down.in one go.

(78) Ngula-warnu-ju, kurlinjirri-rla-lpa-lu jinta-ngka yurrpa-rnu...

And then, kurlinjirri-LOC-IMPF-333SBJ one-LOC grind-PAST

And then they ground food onto one *kurlinjirri*.

(79) Ka-ngu-lpa-lu-rla.

Carry-PAST-IMPF-333SBJ-3DAT

They carried it to him.

(80) Yi-nja-ya-nu-rra-lpa-lu-rla.

Give-INF-PROG-PAST-thither-IMPF-333SBJ-3DAT.

They went on giving food thither to him.

(81) Wanapi ngari-lpa-rla jirrnganja muru-pu-ngu.

One piece just-IMPF-3DAT with shove inside-PAST.

He swallowed it whole [with the seed batter on it]..

(82) Rdapardapa-rla-lku-lpa wangka-ja.

Nothing-LOC-SEQ-IMPF speak-PAST

Then when there was nothing left he spoke.

(83) Parnka-ja-rni-lpa-lu.

Run-PAST-hither-IMPF-333SBJ

They ran hither to him.

(84) Wayi! parraja, wayi! yanurrpu. Kala pangurnu. Kari lawa.

Where *parraja*, where *yanurrpu*. but *pangurnu*. well no.

Where are the *parrjaas*, where are the *yanurrpus*, what about the *pangurnus*? They seem to be all gone.

(85) "Kala nyarrpara-npa yirra-rnu yangka-ju panu?"

"But where-2SBJ put-PAST DET-TOP many?"

"But where did you put them all?"

(86) "Wajawaja-rna ma-nunju-nu.

"Forget-1SBJ get-INC-PAST

Wirlinyi-rla waja-rna wajawaja ma-nunju-rnu."

Hunting-LOC EMPH-1SBJ forget-INC-PAST

"I lost them when I went hunting"

(87) "Ngayi? Nyiya-rlipa-rla yi-nyi-waja.

"Indeed? What-122SBJ-3DAT give-NPAST-EMPH.

"Indeed! what can we give it to him on then?

Nyarrpa-ma-ni-rlipa-waja?"

How get-NPAST-123SBJ-EMPH"

"What will we do to him?"

(87.1) Wurntali-jarri-ja-mpa

Distant-become-PAST-accross

[He] moved away in front of them.

(88) Nyanungu-lu-rla kalyi pu-ngu.

DET-333SBJ-3DAT intercept-PAST

They intercepted him.

(89) Rdululu nga-rnu-lu.

Take off one by one-PAST-333SBJ

They each took off

(90) Miyalu nyampu-juku pulapi ka nyina.

Stomach this-still full up NPAST be.

This stomach is still full up

(91) Yijardu-rlu warlu ngiji-kangukangu-kurlu-rlu,

True-ERG fire burning stick-several-PROP-ERG

ngiji-panji-kirli-rli papapa.

firestick-PL-PROP-ERG papapa (Onomatapoeic)

Truly each with a burning stick papapapa

(92) Kirdirr-karri-ja-lu-rla.

Attack-PAST-333SBJ-3DAT

They attacked him

(93) Ngula-lpa-lu-rla puta muru-muru pu-ngu-lpa-lu-rla kulkurru-wiyi.

DET-IMPF-333SBJ-3DAT try shove inside-IMPF-333SBJ middle-first

They tried to shove their firesticks down inside him.

(94) Ngula warnu-ju, yarda-rra yarnka-ja.

And then, again-THITHER set out-PAST

Then they again set out.

(95) Parnka-jaaaaa, parnka-jaaaa.

Run-PAST, run-past

[He] ran, ran

(96) Wajirli pu-ngu-lpa-luuuuu, wajirli pu-ngu-lpa-luuuu

Chase-PAST-IMPF-333SBJ, etc.

kirdir-karri-ja-lu-rla.

attack-PAST-333SBJ-3DAT

They chased and chased.him.

(97) Kirdirr-karri-ja-lu-rla.

Attack-PAST-333SBJ-3DAT

They attacked him.

(98) Nyanungu-ju-lpa palpal karri-ja-lku.

DET-TOP-IMPF stop-PAST-SEQ

Then he tired and stopped

(99) Nganayi purlka-pardu.

That old man-DIMIN

That little old man.

(100) Warlu-ju-lpa-lu-rla muru-muru pu-ngu muru-muru-pu-ngu.

Fire-TOP-IMPF-333SBJ-3DAT shove inside-PAST, etc.

They shoved the fire sticks inside him.

(101) Wuu! Wurruluku yirra-rnu-lpa, wurruluku yirra-rnu-lpa,

Wow! Vomit-PAST-IMPF, etc.

wurruluku yirra-rnu-lpa warlu-jangka-rlu-lku.

etc. fire-CAUS-ERG-SEQ.

Wow! he vomited, vomited, vomited, because of the fire-sticks.

(102) Muru-muru-pu-ngu, muru-muru-pungu ngiji-lpa-lu-rla.

Shove inside-PAST, fire-stick-IMPF-333SBJ-3DAT

They shoved and shoved the fire sticks into him.

(103) Ngiji-ji, warlu-ju, ngiji-lpa-lu-rla muru-muru pu-ngu.

Fire-stick-TOP, fire-TOP, fire-stick-IMPF-333SBJ-3DAT shove inside.

Burning fire sticks they shoved into him.

(104) Ngiji-ji muru-muru-pu-ngu, muru-muru pu-ngu

Fire-stick shove inside-PAST, etc.

muru-muru pu-ngu-lpa-lu-rla.

etc.-IMPF-333SBJ-3DAT.

They shoved and shoved the fire sticks into him.

(105) Wurruluku yirra-rnu-lpa. Wurruluku yirra-rnu-lpa.

Vomit-PAST-IMPF. Etc.

He vomited and vomited.

(106) Wurruluku yirra-rnu-lpa, yangka kuja kuju-rnu

Vomit-PAST-IMPF, DET thus throw-PAST

He vomited, the things [he had swallowed] were thrown out

yangka-ju ngurlu jinta-kumarrarni.

DET-TOP food one-all.

that food and everything.

(107) Wurruluku yirra-rnu-lpa, wurruluku yirra-rnu-lpa: parraja, yanurrpu, pangurnu, kurlinjirri.

Vomit-PAST-IMPF, vomit-etc.: *parraja, etc.*

He vomited, vomited the *parrajas*, *yanurrpus*, *pangurnus*, *kurlinjirris*

(108) Wurruluku yirra-rnu-lpa, wurruluku yirra-rnu-lpa.

Vomit-PAST-IMPF, etc.

He vomited and vomited.

(109) Paka-rnu-lku-lu, paka-rnu-lku-lu ....

Hit-PAST-SEQ-333SBJ, etc.

Then they hit [him], then they hit [him]

(110) Karrka-ja-lu. Yarnka-ja-lu. Yarnka-ja-rra-lu.

Walk-PAST-333SBJ, set off-PAST-333SBJ, set off-etc.

He set off walking, set off walking

(111) Kala-nyanu turnu-turnu-ma-nu --- parraja manu ngami --- kurlinjirri

PAST-REFLX gather together-PAST --- *parraja* and *ngami* --- *kurlinjirri*

jintangka.

together.

He gathered up to himself all the *parraja* and *ngami*, the *kurlinjirri* - all together.

(112) Warru-rra-lku kankaly-kankaly yarnka-ja.

Around-thither-SEQ swaying set out-PAST

He then set off swaying from side to side as he moved around.

(113) Juulpa-lpa-lu karla-ja. Wunju ngurlu-lpa-lu ma-nu.

Stop-IMPF-333SBJ dig-PAST yams. Edible seed-IMPF-333SBJ get-PAST

[The women] stopped and dug for yams. They got edible seed.

(114) Wunju, wunju, ngulu. Ma-nu-lpa-lu.

Yam, Yam, edible seed. Get-PAST-IMPF-33SBJ.

Karla-ja-lpa-lu. Ma-nu-lpa-lu.

Dig-PAST-IMPF-333SBJ. Get-PAST-IMPF-33SBJ.

Karla-ja-lpa-lu, Karla-ja-lpa-lu.

Dig-PAST-IMPF-333SBJ., etc.

They dug and they gathered. They dug and dug.

(115) Yangka kulpa-ja yinya.

DET return-PAST yonder

He returned yonder.

(116) Ngurrju ma-nu-jana jangkardu pirli-kangukangu.

Make-PAST-333DAT against stone-several

He did something to all the stones so they would harm the women.

(117) Kanardi yirra-rnu. Kanardi yirra-rnu-rraaaa.

In a row put-PAST. Etc.

He put [the stones] in a row

(118) Yirra-rnu-rra, yirra-rnu-rra, yirra-rnu pirli-ji.

Put-PAST-thither, etc., etc., stone-TOP

He put the stones in a row.

(119) Punpun-wangka-ja-lku-lpa-rla --- pirli-ki-ji, pirli-patu-ku-ju.

Advise-PAST-SEQ-IMPF-3DAT stone-DAT, stone-several-DAT-TOP

He advised [i.e. 'sang'] the stones, the several stones.

(120) "Nya-ngka-jana wirdiyi nyangka-jana.

"See-IMP-333DAT tracks see-IMP-333DAT

"Look for their tracks, look for their tracks"

(120a) "Nya-ngka-jana wirdiyi, nya-ngka-jana.

"See-IMP-333DAT tracks, see-IMP-333DAT

"Look for their tracks, look for their tracks"

(121) Jalangu ka-npa-jana purrju-ngkuju yilya-nja ngurlu ma-nu-waja

Now AUX-2SUBJ-333OBJ hurriedly-ERG-TOP send away-PAST-EMPH

Today you will chase them away.

(122) "Kaji-li kulpa-mi-rni, kaji-li rdipi-mi-rni ----

If-333SBJ return-NPAST-hither, if-333SBJ meet-NPAST-hither ---

wirlinyi-jangka."

hunting-CAUS

When they come back, when they return from hunting.

(123) Murlurru-rlu-jana jirriny-pu-ngu kirda-nyanu-rlu-juku.

Completely-ERG-333DAT send a curse father-REFLX-ERG-yet.

Their father put a curse on all of them to kill them.

(124) Jirriny-pu-ngu-jana, rdipirdipi-ja-rni-li.

Send a curse-PAST-333DAT, meet-PAST-hither-333SBJ

He put a curse on them. They returned.

Rdipi-ja-rni-li kanardi-rla rdipirdipi-ja-rni-li.

Meet-PAST-hither-333SBJ row-DAT meet-PAST-333SBJ

They returned to the row of stones, they returned.

(125) Ngari-lpa-lu nguna-njina-nu.

Just-IMPF-333SBJ lie-INC-PAST

They just went and lay down.

(126) Ngari-lpa-lu nguna-njina-nu wunju-kurlu-ju, ngurlu-kurlu-ju.

Just-IMPF-333SBJ lie-INC-PAST yam-with-TOP seed-with-TOP.

They just went and lay down with the yams and with the seeds.

(127) Yurnujumpurru-yurnujumpurru kulpa-ja-rnu-lpa-lu.

Laden-laden return-PAST-hither-IMPF-333SBJ.

They returned heavily laden.

(128) Jarntantarru-jarri-ja-lku yangka pirli-kangukangu

Bent over-PAST-SEQ that stone-several

He then bent over all these stones

nyampu ngama-rlangu-jarra.

this mother-pair-DUAL.

these mothers and daughters.

(129) "Muurlpa-rlu-jana yilya-nja-ngurlu ma-nta."

"Together-ERG-333OBJ send away-INF-ABL CAUS-IMP"

"Chase them all away together."

(130) Ngula-warnu-ju yirra-rnu-lu yuka-piya-juku.

And then put-PAST-333SBJ [?]-like-still.

?And then they put them

(131) Yilya-nja-ngurlu ma-nu parrparrparrparr ....

Send-INF-ABL CAUS-PAST parrparrparr... (onomatapoea)

warru-kirdi-kirdi-kirdi-kirdi yintirdi-wana-rlu

around-around stump-PERL-ERG

warru-kirdikirdi-kirdikirdi wajirli-pu-ngu.

around-around chase-PAST

Round and round the tree stump they chased

(132) Karlangu-lu yurrujurujuru-rra kuju-rnu.

Digging stick-333SBJ-thither throw-PAST

They threw lengthwise their digging sticks away from them.

(133) Yapa-lku-lu warrka-rnu-rra, wira-nga-rnu-rra.

Person-SEQ-333SBJ climb-PAST-thither, take off-PAST-thither.

They climbed up, they took off [up into the sky].

(134) Nyanungu-lku, nyanungu-lku wira-rra nga-rnu-jana pirdangirli wungu-panji-jiki.

DET-SEQ, DET-SEQ took off-PAST-333DAT behind company-several-still.

The old man then took off after them staying with them forever.

(135) Jinta-ku-marrarni-lki-li muku ya-nu

One-DAT-all-SEQ-333SBJ all go-PAST

All of them went

kankarlarra yalkiri-kirra-jarri-ja-lpa.

up sky-ALL-INCH-PAST-IMPF.

up into the sky.

(136) Jinta-ku-marrarni-li ya-nu

One-DAT-all-333SBJ go-PAST

They all went.

(137) Wanjilypiri-jarri-ja-lku-lu-jana jirrnganja kirda-nyanu-ju nyanungu ----

Star-INCH-PAST-SEQ-333SBJ-333DAT with father-POSS TOP

Napalajarri-warnu-jala.

Napaljarri-ASSOC-EMPH

They all became stars along with their father.The Napaljarris.

(138) Nyanungu ka-lu Napaljarri-warnu yarnka-mi-rni,

DET AUX-333SBJ Napaljarri-ASSOC set out-NPAST-hither,

Those Napaljarris come out,

nyanungu ka yarnka-mi-rni.

DET AUX set out-NONPAST-hither.

He comes out.

(139) Napaljarri-warnu-lpa-lu yalkiri-rla-lku lirri nyina-ja.

Napaljarri-ASSOC-IMPF-333SBJ sky-LOC-SEQ sit in a group-PAST

The Napaljarris then sat in a group in the sky.

References

Anthony, D. *Seeing Essential English, Vols. 1 and 2.* Anaheim, California: Educational Services Division, Anaheim Union School District, 1971.

Argyle, M. A. and Cook, M. *Gaze and Mutual Gaze.* Cambridge: Cambridge University Press, 1976.

Baker, C. and Cokely, D. *American Sign Language: A Teacher's Resource Text on Grammar and Culture.* Silver Spring, Maryland: T.J. Publishers, 1980.

Barakat, R.A. *Cistercian Sign Language.* Kalamazoo, Michigan: Cistercian Publications, 1975.

Basedow, H. Anthropological notes made on the South Australian Government north-west prospecting expedition, 1903. Royal Society of South Australia. *Transactions,* 1904, 28: 12-51.

Basedow, H. *The Australian Aboriginal.* Adelaide: F.W.Preece and Sons, 1925.

Bates, D. Native Vocabularies. Manuscript 365, Section XII , c. 1904. In Australian National Library, Canberra.

Bates, D. Smoke signals [and Sign Language].Manuscript 365, Section XI, 5 c.1904. In Australian National Library, Canberra.

Bates, D. *The Native Tribes of Western Australia.* Isobel White, ed., Canberra: National Library of Australia, 1985.

Battison, R. *Lexical Borrowing in American Sign Language.* Silver Spring, MD: Linstok Press, 1978.

Bell, D. *Daughters of the Dreaming.* London: Allen and Unwin, 1983.

Bellugi, U. Clues from the similarities between signed and spoken languages. In U. Bellugi and M. Studdert-Kennedy, eds., *Signed and Spoken Language: Biological Constraints on Linguistic Form.* Deerfield Beach, Florida: Verlag Chemie, 1980, 115-140.

Bellugi, U. and Studdert-Kennedy, M. eds. *Signed and Spoken Language: Biological Constraints on Linguistic Form. Report of the Dahlem Workshop on Sign Language and Spoken Language: Biological Constraints on Linguistic Form, Berlin 1980, March 24-28.* Weinheim, Deerfield Beach, Florida and Basel: Verlag Chemie, 1980.

Berndt, R.M. Notes on the sign language of the Jaralde tribe of the lower River Murray, South Australia. *Transactions of the Royal Society of South Australia,* 1940, 64: 267-272.

Berndt, R.M. and Berndt, C. *The World of the First Australians.* Sydney: Landsdowne Press, 1981.

Berndt, R.M., and Johnston, T.H. Death, burial and associated ritual at Ooldea, South Australia. *Oceania,* 1942, 12: 189-208.

Birdwhistell, R.L. *Introduction to Kinesics: An Annotation System for the Analysis of Body Motion and Gesture.* Washington, D.C.: Foreign Service Institute, 1955.

Birman, W. *Gregory of Rainsworth: A Man of His Time.* Perth: University of Western Australia Press, 1979.

Black, P. Sign Language Film with Rolly Gilbert, Normanton, Queensland, 1975. Library, Australian Instititute of Aboriginal Studies, Canberra.

Blake, B.J. *Australian Aboriginal Languages.* London and Sydney: Angus and Robertson, 1981.

Blake, B.J. *Australian Aboriginal Grammar*. London and Sydney: Croom Helm, 1987.

Bloomfield, L. *Language*. New York: Holt, Rinehart and Winston, 1933.

Bonython, E. *Where the Seasons Come and Go*. Melbourne: Hawthorne, 1971.

Bornstein, H., Hamilton, L., Kannapell, B., Roy, H. and Saulnier, K. *The Signed English Dictionary for Pre-School and Elementary Levels*. Washington, D.C.: Gallaudet College, 1975.

Bradshaw, J. Journal, 31st January 1891 to 6th June 1891. Manuscript, NPL: M-B967, Mitchell Library, Sydney.

Brandl, M.M. and Walsh, M. Speakers of many tongues: toward understanding multilingualism among Aboriginal Australians. *International Journal of the Sociology of Language*, 1982, 36: 71-81.

Brennan, M. Marking time in British Sign Language. In J.Kyle and B. Woll, eds., *Language in Sign*, London and Canberra: Croom Helm, 1983.

Brown, R. Why are sign languages easier to learn than spoken languages? Part One: Keynote Address to the National Association of the Deaf, 1977. Part Two: *Bulletin of the American Academy of Arts and Sciences*, 1978, 32: 25-44.

Brun, T. *The International Dictionary of Sign Language*. London: Wolfe, 1969.

Cameron, A. L.P. [Letter to A.W.Howitt], Balranald, Nov. 13th 1881. In Howitt Papers, Box 2, Folder 5. Library, Australian Institute of Aboriginal Studies, Canberra, 1881.

Capell, A. Language and social distinction in Aboriginal Australia. *Mankind*, 1962, 5: 514-528.

Chadwick, N. *A Descriptive Study of the Djingili Language*. Canberra: Australian Institute of Aboriginal Studies, 1975.

Chakravarti, P. A Report on WaRumungu. Document No. 69/839, 1967. Library, Australian Institute of Aboriginal Studies, Canberra.

Chewings, C. *Back in the Stone Age*. The Natives of Central Australia. Sydney: Angus and Robertson, Ltd., 1936.

Clark, W.P. *The Indian Sign Language*. Lincoln, Nebraska: University of Nebraska Press, 1982 [= reprint of original publication in Philadelphia, L.R. Hamersly, 1885], 1982 [1885].

Classe, A. The whistled language of La Gomera. *Scientific American*, 1957, 196: 111-120.

Cohen, E., Namir, L. and Schlesinger, I.M. *A New Dictionary of Sign Language*. The Hague: Mouton and Co., 1977.

Coomaraswamy, A. and Duggiralla, G.K. *Nandikesvara The Mirror of Gestures*. New York: Wehye, 1936.

Cowan, G.M. Mazateco whistle speech. In Dell Hymes, ed., *Language in Culture and Society: a Reader in Linguistics and Anthropology*. New York: Harper and Row [Reprinted from Language, 24: 280-286], 1964 [1948].

Crauford, L. Victoria River Downs Station, Northern Territory, South Australia. In Notes on the Aborigines of Australia [Responses to questions prepared by J.G. Frazer and circulated by E.C.Stirling]. *Journal of the Anthropological Institute of Great Britain and Ireland*, 1895, 24: 180-182.

Crystal, D. and Craig, E. Contrived sign language. In I.M. Schlesinger and L. Namir, eds., *Sign Language of the Deaf: Psychological, Linguistic and Sociological Perspectives*. New York: Academic Press, 1978, 141-168.

Crystal, D. and Davy, D. *Investigating English Style*. Bloomington, Indiana: Indiana University Press, 1969.

Curr, E.M. *Recollections of Squatting in Victoria*. Melbourne: Robertson, 1883.

Curr, E.M. *The Australian Race: Its Origins, Languages, Customs, Place of Landing and the Routes by which it Spread Itself over that Continent*.Melbourne: John Ferres, Government Printer, 1886.

Dail-Jones, M. A Culture in Motion:A Study of the Interrelationship of Dancing, Sorrowing, Hunting and Fighting as Performed by the Warlpiri Women of Central Australia. M.A. Thesis, University of Hawaii, Honolulu, 1984.

Dawson, J. Australian Aborigines. *The Languages and Customs of Several Tribes of Aborigines in the Western District of Victoria, Australia.* Facsimile of the original edition published by George Robertson, Melbourne, 1881. Canberra: Australian Institute of Aboriginal Studies, 1981[1881].

de Graaf, M. The Ngadadara at the Warburton Ranges. Typescript, 1968. Australian Institute of Aboriginal Studies Library, Canberra.

de Zwaan, J.D. Material on Gogo-Yimidjir Sign Language. In material for a Ph. D. thesis submitted to University of Queensland, 1969. Library, Australian Insitute of Aboriginal Studies, Canberra.

Dell, C. *A Primer for Movement Description Using Effort-Shape and Supplementary Concepts.* New York: Dance Notation Bureau, Inc., 1970.

DeMatteo, A. Visual imagery and visual analogues in American Sign Language. In L.A. Friedman, ed., *On the Other Hand: New Perspectives on American Sign Language.* New York: Academic Press, 1977, 109-136.

Deuchar, M. Sign language diglossia in a British deaf community. *Sign Language Studies,* 1977, 17: 347-356.

Divale, W. T. and Zipin, C. Hunting and the development of sign language: a cross cultural test. *Journal of Anthropological Research,* 1977, 33:185-201.

Dixon, R.M.W. Languages of the Cairns rainforest region. In S.A.Wurm and D.C.Laycock, eds., *Pacific Linguistic Studies: Essays in Honour of A. Capell* (= Pacific Linguistics, Series C, No. 13). Canberra: Department of Linguistics, Research School of Pacific Studies, Australian National University, 1970.

Dixon, R.M.W. A method of semantic description. In D.D. Steinberg and L.A.Jakobovits, eds., *Semantics: An Interdisciplinary Reader in Philosophy, Linguistics and Psychology.* Cambridge: Cambridge University Press, 1971, 436-471.

Dixon, R.M.W. *The Dyirbal Language of North Queensland.* Cambridge: Cambridge University Press, 1972.

Dixon, R.M.W. *The Languages of Australia.* Cambridge: Cambridge University Press, 1980.

Douglas, W.H. *Topical Dictionary of the Western Desert Language. Warburton Ranges Dialect, Western Australia.* Canberra: Australian Institute of Aboriginal Studies, 1977.

Driver, G.R. *Semitic Writing: From Pictograph to Alphabet.* Third Edition. Oxford: Oxford University Press, 1976.

Duncan-Kemp, A. M. *Our Sandhill Country: Nature and Man in Southwestern Queensland.* Sydney: Angus and Robertson, Ltd., 1933.

Eades, D. "You gotta know how to talk...": Information seeking in South East Queensland Aboriginal society. *Australian Journal of Linguistics,* 1982, 2: 61-82.

Eades, D. They don't speak an Aboriginal language, or do they? In I. Keen, ed., *A Way of Life: Aboriginal Cultural Continuity in 'Settled' Australia.* Canberra: Aboriginal Studies Press, 1988.

Eco, U. *Theory of Semiotics.* Bloomington: Indiana University Press, 1977.

Elkin, A.P. Notes on the psychic life of the Australian Aborigines. *Mankind: The Journal of the Anthropological Society of New South Wales,* 1937, 2: 49-56.

Elkin, A.P. The development of scientific knowledge of the Aborigines. In W.E.H.Stanner and H. Shiels, eds., *Australian Aboriginal Studies.* Melbourne: Oxford University Press, 1963, 3-29.

Elkin, A.P. *The Australian Aborigines: How to Understand Them.* North Ryde, N.S.W.: Angus and Robertson, 1979.

Elwell, Vanessa M.R. Some social factors affecting multilingualism among Aboriginal Australians: a case study at Manningreda. *International Journal of the Sociology of Language*, 1982, 36: 83-103.

Evans, N. *A Learner's Guide to Warumungu*. Alice Springs: Institute of Aboriginal Development, 1982.

Fischer, S. and Gough, B. Verbs in American Sign Language. *Sign Language Studies*, 1978, 18: 17-48.

Fison, L, and Howitt, A.W. *Kamilaroi and Kurnai*. Melbourne: Robertson, 1880.

Fraser, J.F. The Aborigines of New South Wales. *Journal and Proceedings of the Royal Society of New South Wales*, 1882a, 16: 193-233.

Fraser, J.F. *An Australian Language, etc.*, by L.E.Threlkeld. Sydney: Charles Potter, Government Printer, 1882b.

Fraser, J.F. *The Aborigines of New South Wales*. Sydney: Government Printer, 1892.

Freedman, N. Hands, words and mind: On the structuralization of body movements during discourse and the capacity for verbal representation. In N. Freedman and S. Grand, Eds., *Communicative Structures and Psychic Structures: A Psychoanalytic Approach*. New York and London: Plenum Press, 1977.

Freedman, N., Van Meel, J.M., Barroso, F. and Bucci, W. On the development of communicative competence. *Semiotica*, 1986, 62: 77-105.

Friedman, L.A. Space, time and person reference in American Sign Language. *Language*, 1975, 51: 940-961.

Friedman, L. A. Formational properties of American Sign Language. In L. A. Friedman, ed., *On the Other Hand: New Perspectives on American Sign Language*. New York: Academic Press, 1977, 13-56.

Frishberg, N. Arbitrariness and iconicity: Historical change in American Sign Language. *Language*, 1975, 51:696-719.

Gason, S. *The Dieyerie Tribe of Australian Aborigines*. Adelaide: W.C.Cox, Government Printer, 1874.

Gason, S. Of the Tribes, Dieyerie, Anminie, Yandrawontha, Yarawuarka, Pilladapa. In Notes on the Aborigines of Australia [Responses to questions prepared by J.G. Frazer and circulated by E.C.Stirling]. *Journal of the Anthropological Institute of Great Britain and Ireland*, 1895, 24: 167-176.

Gee, J.P. and Goodhart, W. Nativization, linguistic theory and deaf language acquisition. *Sign Language Studies*, 1985, 49: 291-342.

Gee, J.P. and Kegl, J.A. Narrative/story structure, pausing and ASL. *Discourse Processes*, 1983, 6: 243-258.

Gelb, I.J. *A Study of Writing*. Revised (Second) Edition. Chicago: University of Chicago Press, 1963.

Ghosh, M. *The Natyasastra (A Treatise on Ancient Indian Dramaturgy and Histrionics) ascribed to Bharata-Muni. Vol. I (Chs. I-XXVII)*. Completely transcribed for the first time from the original Sanskrit with an Introduction, Various Notes and an Index by Manomohan Ghosh. Revised 2nd Edition Calcutta: Manisha Granthalaya Private Ltd., 1967.

Glowczewski, B. Death, women and value production: the circulation of hair strings among the Warlpiri of the central Australian desert. *Ethnology*, 1983, 22: 225-239.

Goddard, C. *A Grammar of Yakunytjatjara*. Alice Springs: Insititute of Aboriginal Development [= A Semantically Based Grammar of the Yakunytjatjara Dialect of the Western Desert Language. Ph. D. thesis, Australian National Univeristy, Canberra], 1983.

Goddard, I. The languages of South Texas and lower Rio Grande. In Lyle Cambell and Marianne Mithun, eds., *The Languages of Native North America: Historical and Comparative Assessment*. Austin, Texas: University of Texas Press, 1979, 355-389.

Goody, J. *The Domestication of the Savage Mind*. Cambridge: Cambridge University Press, 1977.

Gould, R.A. *Yiwara: Foragers of the Australian Desert*. New York: Charles Scribners and Sons, 1969.

Green, J. *Learner's Guide to Arrernte*. Alice Springs: Institute of Aboriginal Development, 1984.

Green, N. J. Survey of Former and Current Aboriginal Students at W.A. [Western Australia] School for Deaf. An Innovation Project funded by the Australian Schools Commission. Mount Lawley College of Advanced Education, Mount Lawley, Western Australia, mimeographed, 1975.

Greenway, J. *Bibliography of the Australian Aborigines and the Native Peoples of Torres Strait until 1959*. Sydney: Angus and Robertson, 1963.

Gregory, A.C. and Gregory, F.T. *Journals of Australian Explorations*. Brisbane: James C. Beale, Government Printer, 1884.

Grigley, J. Perspectives on perspectives (Review of *Language in Sign*, J. Kyle and B. Woll, eds.). *Sign Language Studies*, 1983, 41: 365-374.

Hadfield, B. Wangkatja Sign Language, Videocassette. Perth: Mount Lawley Teachers College, Learning Resources Centre, 1977.

Hadley, I.F. *Indian Sign Talk, Being a Book of Proofs of the Matter Printed on Equivalent Cards Designed for Teaching Sign Language by In-go-nom-ishi (pseud.)*. Chicago: Baker and Co.,1893.

Hale, K. Notes on the signing of Sam Kerundun. Manuscript,1960.

Hale, K. Introduction to Wailbry Domains and Selection. Typescript, 1959. Library of Australian Institute of Aboriginal Studies, Canberra.

Hale, K. A note on the Walbiri tradition of antonymy. In D.D. Steinberg and L.A.Jakobovits, eds., *Semantics: An Interdisciplinary Reader in Philosophy, Linguistics and Psychology*. Cambridge: Cambridge University Press, 1971.

Hale, K. *Grammatical Outline and Vocabulary for Warlpiri*. Alice Springs: Institute of Aboriginal Development, 1974.

Hale, K. The logic of Damin kinship terminology. In J. Heath, F. Merlan and A. Rumsey, eds., *Languages of Kinship in Aboriginal Australia*. Sydney: Sydney University [= *Oceania Linguistics Monographs No. 24*], 1982.

Hale, K.L. Warlpiri and the grammar of non-configurational languages. *Natural Language and Linguistic Theory*, 1983, 1: 5-47.

Hale, K. and Nash, D.G. Lardil and Damin Phonotactics Draft. Unpublished draft, March 29th, 1987. Presented by David Nash to the Australian Linguistics Scoiety, Canberra, August, 1987.

Hale, K.L. and Laughren, M. Warlpiri-English Dictionary [in progress]. Cambridge, Mass.: Lexicon Project, Center for Cognitive Science, Massachusetts Institute of Technology, 1983.

Hall, T. *A Short History of the Downs Blacks known as the Blucher Tribe*. Warwick, New South Wales: Thomas Hall (privately printed), c.1925.

Hall, T. *The Early History of Warwick District and Pioneers of the Darling District*. Warwick, New South Wales: Thomas Hall (privately printed), c.1935.

Halliday, M.A.K. *Introduction to Functional Grammar*. London: Edward Arnold, 1985a.

Halliday, M.A.K. *Spoken and Written Language*. Victoria: Deakin University, 1985b.

Hamilton, A. Timeless Transformation: Women, Men and History in the Australian Western Desert. Ph. D. Thesis, Sydney University, Sydney, 1979.

Hamilton, A. Dual social systems: Technology, labour and women's secret rites in the eastern Western Desert of Australia. *Oceania,* 1980, 51: 4-19.

Hamilton, A. A complex strategical situation: gender and power in Aboriginal Australia. In N. Grieve and P. Grimshaw, eds., *Australian Women: Feminist Perspectives.* Melbourne: Oxford University Press, 1981, 69-85.

Hannah, W. *Darkness Visible: A Revelation and Interpretation of Freemasonry.* 5th Edition. London: Augustine Press, 1953.

Hardman, W., ed. *The Journals of John McDouall Stuart, etc.* Second Edition. London: Saunders, Otley and Co., 1865. Facsimile Edition, Adelaide: Libraries Board of South Australia, 1975.

Harney, W.E. Peck-marked carvings and sign talk. *Mankind,* 1952, 4: 345-346.

Harrington, J.P. American Indian sign language. In and D.J. Umiker-Sebeok and T.A.Sebeok eds., *Aboriginal Sign Languages of the Americas and Australia, Vol. II: The Americas and Australia,* pp. 109-142. New York: Plenum Press 1978 [Reprinted from Indians at Work, 1938, March, pp. 8-15, July, pp. 28-32, August, pp. 25-30], 1978 [1938].

Harris, S.G. Milingimbi Aboriginal Learning Contexts. Ph. D. Thesis, University of New Mexico, Albuquerque, New Mexico, 1977.

Harris, S.G. *Culture and Learning: Tradition and Education in North East Arnhem Land* [An abridgement by J. Kinslow-Harris of a Ph. D. thesis by S.G. Harris]. Darwin: Northern Territory Department of Education, published for the Professional Services Branch, 1980.

Haviland, J.B. Guugu Yimidhirr brother-in-law language. *Language and Society,* 1979a, 8: 365-393.

Haviland, J.B. How to talk to your brother-in-law in Guugu Yimidhirr. In T. Shopen, ed., *Languages and their Speakers.* Cambridge, Mass.: Winthrop, 1979b, 160-239.

Heath, J. *Diffusional linguistics in Australia: Problems and prospects.* In S. A. Wurm, ed., Australian Linguistic Studies. Canberra: Department of Linguistics, Research School of Pacific Studies, Australian National University. [= Pacific Linguistics, Series C, No. 54], 1979, 395-418.

Heath, J. Where is that (knee)?: Basic and supplementary kin terms in Dhuwal (Yuulngu/Murngin). In J. Heath, F. Merlan and A. Rumsey, eds., *Languages of Kinship in Australia.* [= *Oceania Linguistic Monographs No. 24*]. Sydney: University of Sydney, 1982, 40-63.

Herzog, G. Drum-signalling in a West African tribe. In Dell Hymes, ed., *Language in Culture and Society: a Reader in Linguistics and Anthropology.* New York: Harper and Row. [Reprinted from Word, 1: 217-238], 1964 [1945].

Hewes, G. W. Gesture language in culture contact. *Sign Language Studies,* 1974, 4: 1-34.

Hiatt, L.R. Local organization among the Australian Aborigines. *Oceania,* 1962, 32: 267-286.

Hill, E. *The Territory.* Sydney: Angus and Robertson, 1951.

Howitt, A.W. Notes on the use of gesture language in Australian tribes. *Australian Association for the Advancement of Science,* 1890, 2: 637-646.

Howitt, A.W. The Dieri and other kindred tribes of Central Australia. *Journal of the Anthropological Institute of Great Britain and Ireland,* 1891, 20: 30-104.

Howitt, A.W. *The Native Tribes of South East Australia.* London and New York: Macmillan, Co.,1904.

Hughes, A.N. Notes by A.N. Hughes sent to A.W.Howitt. In Howitt Papers, Box 1, Folder 8, Paper 2. 16pp, c. 1880. [Copy in Library of Australian Institute of Aboriginal Studies, Canberra].

Hymes, D., ed. *Language in Culture and Society: A Reader in Linguistics and Anthropology*. New York: Harper and Row, 1964.

Hymes, D. *Foundations of Sociolinguistics*. Philadelphia: University of Pennsylvania Press, 1974.

Ikegami, Y. A stratificational analysis of hand gestures in Indian classical dancing. *Semiotica*, 1971, 4: 365-391.

Johnson, R.E. A comparison of the phonological structures of two northwest sawmill sign languages. *Communication and Cognition*, 1978, 11: 105-132.

Kaberry, P. M. Death and deferred mourning ceremonies in the Forrest River tribes, Northwest Australia. *Oceania*, 1935, 6: 33-47.

Karbelashvili, D. *Ruchnaija Rech' Na Kavkaze [Manual Speech in the Caucasus]*. Nauchno-Issledocatel'skii Institut Kavkazovedenija Imeni Akademii Nauk CCCP, Tiflis [Research Institute of Caucasian Studies, Academy of Sciences of the USSR, Tiflis], 1936.

Keen, Sandra N. [Transcript of Tape A1793, field tape 42] Normanton, Queensland, 1969. Library, Australian Institute of Aboriginal Studies, Canberra. Library, Australian Institute of Aboriginal Studies, Canberra.

Kelly, G.T. Tribes of the Cherbourg Settlement, Queensland. *Oceania*, 1935, 5: 461-473.

Kendon, A. Some relationships between body motion and speech: an analysis of an example. In A. Seigman and B. Pope, Eds., *Studies in Dyadic Communication* Elmsford, N.Y.: Pergamon Press, 1972, 177-210.

Kendon, A. Appendix. In A. Kendon, *Studies in the Behavior of Social Interaction*. Lisse: Peter De Ridder Press, 1977, 225-240.

Kendon, A. Sign language of the women of Yuendumu: a preliminary report on the structure of Warlpiri sign language. *Sign Language Studies*, 1980a, 27: 101-112.

Kendon, A. Gesticulation and Speech: two aspects of the process of utterance. In M.R.Key, ed., *Nonverbal Communication and Language*. The Hague: Mouton and Co., 1980b, 207-227.

Kendon, A. A description of a deaf-mute sign langauge from the Enga Province of Papua New Guinea with some comparative discussion. Part III: Aspects of utterance construction. *Semiotica*, 1980c, 32: 245-313.

Kendon, A. The study of gesture: some observations on its history. *Recherches Semiotique/Semiotic Inquiry*, 1982, 2: 45-62.

Kendon, A. Gesture and speech: how they interact. In J. Wiemann and R. Harrison, eds., *Nonverbal Interaction* [= Sage Annual Reviews of Communication, Vol. 11]. Beverly Hills, California: Sage Publications 1983, pp. 13-46.

Kendon, A. Knowledge of sign language in an Australian Aboriginal community *Journal of Anthropological Research*, 1984, 40: 556-576.

Kendon, A. Variation in central Australian sign languages: a preliminary report. *Language in Central Australia*, 1985a, 1 (4): 1-11.

Kendon, A. Some uses of gesture. In D. Tannen and M. Saville-Troike, Eds., *Perspectives on Silence*. Norwood, N.J.: Ablex Corporation, 1985b, 215-234.

Kendon, A. Iconicity in Warlpiri sign language. In P. Bouissac, M. Herzfeld and R. Posner, eds., *Iconicity: Essays on the Nature of Culture. Festschrift for Thomas A. Sebeok on his 65th Birthday*. Tübingen: Stauffenburg Verlag, 1986a, 437-446.

Kendon, A. Current issues in the study of gesture. In J-L. Nespoulous, P. Perron and A.R. Lecours, eds., *The Biological Foundations of Gestures: Motor and Semiotic Aspects*. Hillsdale, New Jersey: Lawrence Erlbaum Associates, 1986b, 23-47.

Kendon, A. Speaking and signing in Warlpiri sign language users. *Multilingua*, 1987, 6: 25-68.

Kendon, A. and Silverstein, M. 16mm film of Worora signs demonstrated by Sam Woolagoodja, Derby, Western Australia, 1975. Copy on deposit, Library, Australian Institute of Aboriginal Studies, Canberra.

Kilham, C., Pamulkan, M., Pootchemunka, J. and Wolmby, T. *Dictionary and Sourcebook of the Wik Mungkan Language*. Darwin: Summer Institute of Linguistics Australian Aboriginal Branch, 1986.

Klima, E. Sound and its absence in the linguistic symbol.In J.F. Kavanagh and J.E. Cutting, eds., *The Role of Speech in Language*. Cambridge, MA: MIT Press, 1975, 249-270.

Klima, E. and Bellugi, U. *The Signs of Language*. Cambridge, Mass.: Harvard University Press, 1979.

Koch, H. *A Simple Sketch of the Kaitiji Language*. Alice Springs: Institute of Aboriginal Development, n.d.

Koch, H. Kinship categories in Kaytej pronouns. In J. Heath, F. Merlan and A. Rumsey, eds., *Languages of Kinship in Australia.* [= *Oceania Linguistic Monographs No. 24*]. Sydney: University of Sydney, 1982, 64-71.

Kolig, E. *The Silent Revolution*. Philadelphia: Institute for the Study of Human Issues, 1981.

Kroeber, A.L. Sign language inquiry. In D.J.Umiker Sebeok and T.A. Sebeok, eds., *Aboriginal Languages of the Americas and Australia. Volume II: The Americas and Australia*. New York: Plenum Press, 1978, pp. 185-201 [Reprinted from *International Journal of American Linguistics,* 24: 1-19], 1978 [1958].

Kyle, J. Looking for meaning in sign language sentences. In J. Kyle and B. Woll, eds., *Language in Sign*. London and Canberra: Croom Helm, 1983, 184-194.

Kyle, J.G. and Woll, B. *Sign Language: The Study of Deaf People and their Language*. Cambridge: Cambridge University Press, 1985

La Meri. *Gesture Language of the Hindu Dance*. New York: Columbia University Press, 1941.

Laban, R. and Lawrence, F.C. *Effort*. London: Macdonald Evans, 1947.

Lamond, G.H. *Tales of the Overland. Queensland to Kimberley in 1885*.Carlisle, W.A.: Hesperian Press, 1986.

Lane, H. A chronology of the oppression of sign language in France and the United States. In H. Lane and F. Grosjean, eds., *Recent Perspectives on American Sign Language*. Hillsdale, New Jersey: Lawrence Erlbaum Associates, 1980, 119-161.

Laughren, M. Warlpiri kinship structure. In J.Heath, F. Merlan and A. Rumsey, eds., *Languages of Kinship in Aboriginal Australia.*[= *Oceania Linguistics Monographs No. 24*]. Sydney: Sydney University, 1982, 72-85.

Laughren, M. Warlpiri baby talk. *Australian Journal of Linguistics,* 1984a, 4: 73-88.

Laughren, M. Some focus strategies in Warlpiri. Paper presented to Australian Linguistics Society, Alice Springs, 1984b.

Levy, C. Lurugu. Archival Footage, 16mm. film, 1974. Library, Australian Insititute of Aboriginal Studies, Canberra.

Liberman, K. Some linguistic features of congenial fellowship among the Pitjantjatjara. *International Journal for the Sociology of Language,* 1982a, 36:35-51.

Liberman, K. The economy of central Australian Aboriginal expression: an inspection from the vantage of Merleau-Ponty and Derrida. *Semiotica,* 1982b, 40: 267-346.

Liberman, K. *Understanding Interaction in Central Australia: An Ethnomethodological Study of Australian Aboriginal People*. Boston: Routledge, Kegan Paul, 1985.

Liddell, S. *American Sign Language Syntax*. The Hague: Mouton and Co., 1980.

Liddell, S. THINK and BELIEVE: Sequentiality in American Sign Language. *Language,* 1984, 60: 372-399.

Linklater, W. Notes, Sydney. Manuscript PMS 3926, 1940. Library, Australian Institute of Aboriginal Studies, Canberra.

Livingston, S. Levels of development in the language of deaf children. *Sign Language Studies,* 1983, 40: 193-286.

Lockwood, D.W. *I, the Aboriginal.* Adelaide: Rigby, 1962.

Love, J.R.B. Notes on the Worora tribe of North-Western Australia. *Transactions of the Royal Society of South Australia,* 1917, 41: 21-38.

Love, J.R.B Worora kinship gestures. *Transactions of the Royal Society of South Australia,* 1941, 65: 108-109.

Love, J.R.B. Notes on the Natives at Ernabella 1941-1945. Manuscript PRG214/24, South Australian Archives, Adelaide, South Australia.

Lowie, R.H. *Indians of the Plains.* New York: McGraw Hill Book Co., Inc. [= Anthropological Handbook Number One, American Museum of Natural History, New York], 1954.

MacPherson, J. Ngarrabul and other aboriginal tribes. *Journal and Proceedings of the Linnean Society of New South Wales,* 1902, 27: 637-647.

MacPherson, J. Ngarrabul and other aboriginal tribes: distribution of tribes. *Journal and Proceedings of the Linnean Society of New South Wales,* 1904, 29: 677-684.

Malcolm, I.G. Speech use in Aboriginal communities: a preliminary survey. *Anthropological Forum,* 1982, 5: 54-104.

Mallery, G. *Sign Language Among the North American Indians Compared with that of Other Peoples and Deaf Mutes.* The Hague: Mouton [= pp. 263-552 in Bureau of American Ethnology First Annual Report, Vol I, 1879-1880. Washington D.C.: Government Printing Office, 1881], 1972 [1881].

Mallery, G. A Collection of Gesture-Signs and Signals of the North American Indians with some Comparisons. In D.J.Umiker-Sebeok and T.A. Sebeok, eds., *Aboriginal Sign Languages of the Americas and Australia. Volume I: North America: Classic Comparative Perspectives.* New York: Plenum Press [Originally published in 1880 by United States Bureau of American Ethnology, Smithsonian Institution, Washington, D.C.], 1978[1880].

Mandel, M. Iconic devices in American sign language. In L. A. Friedman, ed., *On the Other Hand: New Perspectives on American Sign Language.* New York: Academic Press, 1977, 57-108.

Marshall, L. *The !Kung of Nyae Nyae.* Cambridge, Mass.: Harvard University Press, 1976.

Mathews, R.H. Initiation ceremonies of Australian tribes. *Proceedings of the American Philosophical Society,* 1898, 37: 54-73.

Mathews, R.H. Wombya organization of the Australian Aborigines. *American Anthropologist,* 1900, 2: 494-501.

Mathews, R.H. Notes on the Aborigines of the Northern Territory, Western Australia and Queensland. *Proceedings of the Royal Geographical Society of Australia, Queensland,* 1907, 22: 1-13.

McBride, G. Sign Language Films, 8mm, Edward River Mission, Queensland, c. 1970. Library, Australian Institute of Aboriginal Studies, Canberra holds one roll. Other material at University of Queensland.

McConnell, U. The Wik-Munkan and allied tribes of Cape York. *Oceania,* 1934, 4: 310-367.

McConnell, U. Mourning ritual among the tribes of Cape York Peninsula. *Oceania,* 1937, 7: 346-371.

McConvell, P. Mudbura Sign Language. Film, 1976. Library, Australian Institute of Aboriginal Studies, Canberra.

McConvell, P. The origin of subsections in northern Australia. *Oceania,* 1985, 56: 1-33.

McDonald, B. Levels of analysis in signed languages. In J. Kyle and B. Woll, eds., *Language in Sign*. London and Canberra: Croom Helm, 1983, 32-40.

McKay, G.R. Rembarnga Field Notes, Maningrida, etc., from 1972. Library, Australian Instititute of Aboriginal Studies, Canberra.

McKay, G.R. Rembarnga: A Language of Central Arnhem Land. Ph. D. Thesis, Australian National University, 1975.

McLaren, J. *My Crowded Solitude: The Author's Life among the Aborigines of Farthest North Australia.* 7th Edition. [Original date of publication: 1926]. London: Quality Press, 1946 [1926].

McNeill, D. So you think gestures are nonverbal? *Psychological Review,* 1985, 92: 350-371.

McNeill, D. *Psycholinguistics: A New Approach.* New York: Harper and Row, 1987.

Meggitt, M. Sign language among the Walbiri of central Australia. *Oceania,* 1954, 25: 2-16.

Meggitt, M. *Desert People*. Sydney: Angus and Robertson, 1962.

Meissner, M. and Philpott, S.B. The sign language of sawmill workers in British Columbia. *Sign Language Studies,* 1975, 9: 291-308.

Michaels, E. Constraints on knowledge in an economy of oral information. *Current Anthropology,* 1985, 26: 505-510.

Miller, W. R. Western Desert Sign Language. Mimeograph, 1971. Library of the Australian Institute of Aboriginal Studies, Canberra.

Miller, W.R. A report on the sign language of the Western Desert (Australia). In D.J.Umiker-Sebeok and T.A. Sebeok, eds., *Aboriginal Sign Languages of the Americas and Australia. Volume II: The Americas and Australia.* New York: Plenum Press, 1978, 435-440.

Mountford, C.P. [The Anjamatana Tribe]. Manuscript plan for proposed book. In the Mountford-Sheard collection, South Australian Museum, Adelaide. n.d.

Mountford, C.P. Gesture language of the Ngada tribe of the Warburton Ranges, Western Australia. *Oceania,* 1938, 9: 152-155.

Mountford, C.P. Gesture language of the Walpari tribe, central Australia. *Transactions of the Royal Society of South Australia,* 1949, 73: 100-101.

Mountford, C.P. *Nomads of the Australian Desert.* Adelaide: Rigby, 1976.

Mulvaney, D.J. The ascent of Aboriginal man: Howitt as anthropologist. In Walker, M. H. *Come Wind Come Weather: A Biography of Alfred Howitt.* Melbourne: Melbourne University Press, 1971.

Mulvaney, D.J. and Calaby, J. H. *'So Much that is New'. Baldwin Spencer 1860-1929, a Biography*. Melbourne: Melbourne University Press, 1985.

Munn, N.D. The transformation of subjects into objects in Walbiri and Pitjantjatjara myth. In R. M. Berndt, ed., *Australian Aboriginal Anthropology: Modern Studies in the Social Anthropology of the Australian Aborigines*. Nedlands, Western Australia: University of Western Australia Press, for the Australian Institute of Aboriginal Studies, 1970, 141-163.

Munn, N. *Walbiri Iconography*. Ithaca, New York: Cornell University Press, 1973.

Myers, F.R. *Pintupi Country, Pintupi Self: Sentiment, Place and Politics among Western Desert Aborigines*. Washington, D.C.: Smithsonian Institution Press, 1986.

Nash, D.G. Preliminary Vocabulary of the Warlmanpa Language with Grammatical Preface. Unpublished Manuscript. Department of Linguistics, Massachusetts Institute of Technology, Cambridge, Massachusetts, 1979.

Nash, D.G. Warlpiri roots and preverbs. In S. Swartz, ed., *Papers in Warlpiri Grammar: In Memory of Lothar Jagst*. Darwin: Summer Institute of Linguistics, Australian Aborigines Branch [=Work Papers of SIL-AAB], 1982, 165-216.

Nash, D.G. The Warumungu's reserves 1892-1962: a case study in dispossession. *Australian Aboriginal Studies*, 1984, 2:1-15.

Nash, D. G. *Topics in Warlpiri Grammar*. Outstanding Dissertations in Linguistics, Series 3. New York: Garland Publishing Co., 1985.

Nash, D.G. and Simpson, J. 'No-name' in Central Australia. In Carrie S. Masek et al., eds., *Papers from the Parasession on Language and Behavior. Chicago Linguistic Society*, 1981, 165-177.

O'Grady, G. N. A secret language of Western Australia - a note. *Oceania*, 1956, 27: 158-159.

O'Grady, G. New concepts in Nyanumarda: some data on linguistic acculturation. *Anthropological Linguistics*, 1960, 2: 1-6.

Paget, R. and Gorman, P. *A Systematic Sign Language*. London: National Institute for the Deaf, 1968.

Parkhouse, T.A. Native tribes of Port Darwin and its neighbourhood. *Australian Association for the Advancement of Science*, Report, 1895, 6: 638-647.

Peterson, N. The natural and cultural areas of Aboriginal Australia: A preliminary analysis of population groupings with adaptive significance. In N. Peterson, ed., *Tribes and Boundaries in Australia*. Canberra: Australian Institute of Aboriginal Studies, 1976, 50-71.

Peterson, N. with Long, J. (coll.). *Australian Territorial Organization. Oceania Monograph 30*. Sydney: Sydney University, 1986.

Piddington, R. Karadjeri initiation. *Oceania*, 1932-1933, 3: 46-87.

Plomley, N.J.B., ed. *Friendly Mission: The Tasmanian Journals and Papers of G.A. Robinson*. Hobart: Tasmanian Historical Research Association, 1966.

Pope, K. and Moore, D.R. The story of the Roth ethnographic collection. *Australian Natural History*, 1967, 15: 273-277.

Priest, C. A. V. *Northern Territory Recollections*. Benalla, Victoria: Charles A.V. Priest, 1986.

Purle, C., Green, J. and Heffernan, M. *Anmatyerre Word List*. Alice Springs: Institute of Aboriginal Development, n.d.

Radcliffe-Brown, A.R. The social organization of Australian tribes. *Oceania*, 1930, 1: 34-63, 322-341, 426-456.

Ray, S.H. The Languages of Cape York Peninsula, North Queensland. In A.C.Haddon, ed., *Cambridge Anthropological Expedition to the Torres Straits, Volume 3, Linguistics*. Cambridge: Cambridge University Press, 1907: 264-283

Reilly, J. and McIntire, M.L. American sign language and pidgin sign English: What's the difference? *Sign Language Studies*, 1980, 27: 151-192.

Reynolds, H. *The Other Side of the Frontier: Aboriginal Resistance to the European Invasion of Australia*. Ringwood, Victoria: Penguin Books, 1982.

Rigsby, B. and Sutton, P. Speech communities in Aboriginal Australia. *Anthropological Forum*, 1980-1981, 5: 8-23.

Robinson, E.O. [Notes on Port Essington]. In Howitt Papers, Box 3, Folder 8, Paper 4, c.1880. Library, Australian Institute of Aboriginal Studies, Canberra.

Roheim, G. *The Eternal Ones of the Dream*. New York: International Universities Press, 1945.

Roheim, G. *Children of the Desert*. New York: Harper and Row, 1974.

Rose, D.B. Dingo Makes Us Human: Being and Purpose in Australian Aboriginal Culture. Ph. D. thesis, Bryn Mawr College, Bryn Mawr, Pennsylvania, 1984.

Roth, H.L. *The Aborigines of Tasmania*. Halifax: F. King and Sons [add modern edition], 1899.

Roth, W.E. *Ethnological Studies Among the North-West-Central Queensland Aborigines.* London: Queensland Agent-General's Office, 1897.

Roth, W.E. The Aborigines of the Rockhampton and Surrounding Coast Districts. Report to the Commissioner of Police. Manuscript, 1898. Original in Queensland State Archives. Photocopy in Library, Australian Institute of Aboriginal Studies, Canberra.

Roth, W.E. [Report to the Commissioner of Police, Brisbane]. An account of the Koko-Mini Aboriginals occupying the country drained by the Middle Palmer River, Cooktown, May 12, 1899. Photocopy of original, Library, Australian Institute of Aboriginal Studies, Canberra.

Roth, W.E. Report [to the Undersecretary, Home Department, Brisbane], on the Aboriginals of the Pennefather (Coen) River district and other coastal tribes occupying the country between Batavia and Embley Rivers. Cooktown, January 8th 1900a.

Roth, W.E. On the natives of the (lower) Tully River; and Appendix. Scientific Report to the Undersecretary, Queensland Home Secretary's Department, Office of the Northern Protector of Aboriginals. Manuscript, 1900b.. Original in Queensland State Archives. Photocopy in Library, Australian Institute of Aboriginal Studies, Canberra.

Roth, W.E. Notes of savage life in the early days of West Australian settlement. *Proceedings of the Royal Society of Queensland,* 1902, 17: 45-69.

Roth, W.E. Burial ceremonies and disposal of the dead. *North Queensland Ethnography Bulletin Number 9. Records of the Australian Museum,* Sydney, 1907, 6: 365-403.

Roth, W.E. Signals on the Road; Gesture Language. *North Queensland Ethnography Bulletin, No. 11. Records of the Australian Museum,* Sydney, 1908, 7: 74-107.

Roth, W.E. On certain initiation ceremonies. *North Queensland Ethnography Bulletin No. 12. Records of the Australian Museum,* Sydney, 1909, 7: 166-185.

Roughsey, D. *Moon and Rainbow: The Autobiography of an Aboriginal.* Sydney: Reed, 1971.

Rowley, C.D. *The Destruction of Aboriginal Society.* Canberra: Australian National University Press, 1970.

Rowley, C.D. *The Remote Aborigines.* Harmondsworth: Penguin Books, 1976.

Salter, E. Daisy Bates: *The Great White Queen of the Never-Never.* Sydney: Angus and Robertson, 1971.

Sampson, G. *Writing Systems.* London: Hutchinson, 1985.

Sansom, B. *The Camp at Wallaby Cross: Aboriginal Fringe Dwellers in Darwin.* Canberra: Australian Institute of Aboriginal Studies, 1980.

Schebeck, B. Dialect and Social Groupings in North-East Arnhem Land. Manuscript, 1968. Library of Australian Institute of Aboriginal Studies, Canberra.

Scheffler, H. W. *Australian Kin Classification.* Cambridge: Cambridge University Press, 1978.

Schegloff, E.A. On some gestures' relation to talk. In M. Atkinson and J. Heritage, eds., *Structures of Social Action.* Cambridge: Cambridge University Press, 1984, 266-298.

Schenkein, J., ed. *Studies in the Organization of Conversational Interaction.* New York: Academic Press, 1978.

Scott, H.L. The sign language of the Plains Indian. In D.J.Umiker-Sebeok and T.A. Sebeok, eds., *Aboriginal Languages of the Americas and Australia. Volume II: The Americas and Australia.* New York: Plenum Press [Re-printed from Archives of the International Folk-Lore Association, 1893, Vol. I, 206-220], 1978.

Scribner, S. and Cole M. *The Psychology of Literacy.* Cambridge, Mass.: Harvard University Press, 1981.

Sharp, R.L. North Queensland Expeditions: Field Data 1933-1935, 1957. [Mitchell River, Queensland, 1933-1936, 1957, 1973]. 11 Parts. Manuscript, Library, Australian Institute of Aboriginal Studies, Canberra.

Sharp, R.L. Ritual life and economics of the Yir-Yoront of Cape York Peninsula. *Oceania,* 1934, 5: 19-42.

Sherzer, J. *An Areal-Typological Study of American Indian Languages North of Mexico.* New York: Elsevier Publishing Co., Inc., 1976.

Simpson, J. How Warumungu people express new concepts. *Language in Central Australia,* 1985, 1: 12-24.

Simpson, J., and Heath, J. A Warumungu Sketch Grammar. Unpublished Manuscript, 1984.

Siple, P. Visual constraints for sign language communication. *Sign Language Studies,* 1978, 19: 95-110.

Smyth, R.Brough. *The Aborigines of Victoria.* Melbourne: John Ferres, Government Printer, 1878.

Sommerlad, J. [Transcriptions of AIAS tape A. 21437: Interview [with] Mr. G. Purvis-Smith, Boorook, Sandy Hills]. 1966. Library, Australian Institute of Aboriginal Studies, Canberra.

Spencer, B., ed. *Report of the Work of the Horn Scientific Expedition to Central Australia.* London: Dulan and Co., Melbourne: Melville, Mullen and Slade, 1896.

Spencer, B. *The Native Tribes of the Northern Territory.* London: MacMillan and Co., 1914.

Spencer, B. *Wanderings in Wild Australia.* London: MacMillan and Co., 1928.

Spencer, B. and Gillen, F.J. *The Native Tribes of Central Australia.* London: Macmillan and Co., 1899.

Spencer, B. and Gillen, F.J. *The Northern Tribes of Central Australia.* London: Macmillan and Co., 1904.

Spencer, B. and Gillen, F.J. *Accross Australia.* London: Macmillan and Co., 1912.

Spencer, B. and Gillen, F.J. *The Arunta: A Study of a Stone Age People.* 2 Volumes. London: Macmillan, Co., 1927.

Stam, J.H. *Inquiries into the Origin of Language: The Fate of a Question.* New York: Harper and Row, 1976.

Stanner, W.E.H. The Dreaming (1953). In W.E.H. *Stanner, White Man Got No Dreaming: Essays 1938-1973.* Canberra: Australian National University Press, 1979, 23-40.

Stationmaster. On the habits, etc., of the Aborigines in district of Powell's Creek, Northern Territory of South Australia. In Notes on the Aborigines of Australia [Responses to questions prepared by J.G. Frazer and circulated by E.C.Stirling]. *Journal of the Anthropological Institute of Great Britain and Ireland,* 1895, 24: 176-180.

Stern, T. Drum and whistle 'languages': an analysis of speech surrogates. *American Anthropologist,* 1957, 59: 487-506.

Stirling, E.C. Anthropology. In W.B.Spencer, ed. *Report of the Work of the Horn Scientific Expedition to Central Australia,* 1896, 4: 1-157.

Stokoe, W.C. *Sign Language Structure.* Buffalo, N.Y.: Studies in Linguistics Occasional Papers No. 8., University of Buffalo, 1960.

Stokoe, W.C. *Semiotics and Human Sign Languages.* The Hague: Mouton and Co., 1972.

Stokoe, W.C. *Sign Language Structure.* Revised Edition. Silver Spring, Maryland: Linstok Press, 1978.

Stokoe, W.C. Sign language and sign languages. *Annual Review of Anthropology,* 1980, 9: 365-390.

Stokoe, W.C., Casterline, D. and Croneberg, C. *A Dictionary of American Sign Language.* Washington, D.C.:Gallaudet College Press, 1965.

Stone, W.W., ed. *Charles Pearcy Mountford: An Annotated Bibliography, Chronology and Checklist of Books, Papers, Manuscripts and Sundries from the Library of Harold L. Sheard.* Cremorne, New South Wales: The Stone Copying Company, 1958.

Strehlow, C. *Die Aranda-und-Loritja-Stamme in Zentral-Australien.* Frankfurt: Baer, 1907-1922.

Strehlow, C. The Sign Language of the Aranda [An extract from *Die Aranda-und-Loritja-Stamme in Zentral-Australien*. Frankfurt: Baer, translated by C. Chewings]. In D. J. Umiker-Sebeok and T.A.Sebeok, eds., *Aboriginal Sign Languages of the Americas and Australia. Volume II: The Americas and Australia,* 1978[1915], 349-370.

Stuart, J. McDouall. *Fourth Expedition Journal 1860*. J.B., ed. Sullivan's Cove: Adelaide [Re-issue of J. McDouall Stuart's Journal of Fourth Expedition 1860, corrected against the original. Limited edition of 220 copies of which the first 10 are special], 1983.

Stubbs, M. *Discourse Analysis: The Sociolinguistic Analysis of Natural Language*. Oxford: Basil Blackwell, 1983.

Studdert-Kennedy, M. and Lane, H. Clues from the differences between signed and spoken language. In U. Bellugi and M. Studdert-Kennedy, eds., *Signed and Spoken Language: Biological Constraints on Linguistic Form*. Deerfield Beach, Florida and Basel: Verlag Chemie, 1980, 29-39.

Supalla, T. The classifier system in American Sign Language. In C. Craig, ed., *Noun Classes and Categorization: Proceedings of a Symposium on Categorization and Noun Classification, Eugene, Oregon, October 1983*. Philadelphia: John Benjamins Publishing Company, 1986, 181-214.

Supalla, T. and Newport, E. How many seats in a chair? The derivation of nouns and verbs in American Sign Language. In P. Siple, ed., *Understanding Language through Sign Language Research,* New York: Academic Press, 1978.

Sutton, P.J. Wik: Aboriginal Society, Territory and Language at Cape Keerweer, Cape York Peninsula, Australia. Ph. D. thesis, University of Queensland, Brisbane, 1978.

Sutton, P.J. Personal power, kin classification and speech etiquette in Aboriginal Australia. In J. Heath, F. Merlan and A. Rumsey, eds., *Languages of Kinship in Australia*. [= *Oceania Linguistic Monographs No. 24*]. Sydney: University of Sydney, 1982, 182-200.

Sutton, P.J. and Walsh, M. *Revised Linguistic Fieldwork Manual for Australia*. Canberra: Australian Institute of Aboriginal Studies, 1979.

Suty, K. and Friel-Patti, S. Looking beyond signed English to describe the language of two deaf children. *Sign Language Studies,* 1982, 35: 153-166.

Swartz, S.M., ed. *Papers in Warlpiri Grammar: In Memory of Lothar Jagst*. Darwin: Summer Institute of Linguistics, Australian Aborigines Branch [= Work Papers of SIL-AAB], 1982.

Swartz, S.M. Warlpiri topicalized clauses. Unpublished manuscript, 1984.

Taylor, A.R. Nonverbal communication in aboriginal North America: The Plains Indian sign language. In D.J.Umiker-Sebeok and T.A. Sebeok, eds., *Aboriginal Sign Languages of the Americas and Australia. Volume II: The Americas and Australia*. New York: Plenum Press, 1978, 223-244.

Teichelmann, C.G. and Schürmann, C.W. *Outlines of a Grammar, Vocabulary and Phraseology of the Aboriginal Language of South Australia, Spoken by the Natives in and for Some Distance around Adelaide*. Adelaide, 1840.

Terry, M. *The War of the Warramullas*. Adelaide: Rigby, 1974.

Tervoort, B.T. Esoteric symbolism in the communication behavior of young deaf children. *American Annals of the Deaf,* 1961, 106: 436-480.

Thomas, N.W. *Natives of Australia*. London: Archibald Constable and Co., 1906.

Thompson, J.M. The Aborigines. *Science of Man,* 1902, 5: 15.

Tindale, N.B. Totemic beliefs in the Western Desert of Australia. Part I. Women who became the Pleiades. *Records of the South Australian Museum,* 1959,

Tindale, N.B. *Aboriginal Tribes of Australia*. Berkeley: University of California Press, 1974.

Tindale, N.B. and Birdsell, J.B. Tasmanoid tribes in North Queensland. *Records of the South Australian Museum,* 1940, 7: 1-9.

Tindale, N.B. and Fry, H.K. Ernabella Expedition, 16 mm. Film, 1933. Library, Australian Institute of Aboriginal Studies, Canberra.

Tomkins, W. *Universal Indian Sign Language of the Plains Indians of North America.* New York: Dover Publications 1969 [= reprint of original publication, San Diego: William Tomkins 1929], 1969 [1929].

Tonkinson, M. and Tonkinson, R. Modern housing for sedentarised nomads. In M. Heppell, ed., *A Black Reality: Aboriginal Camps and Housing in Remote Australia.* Canberra: Australian Institute of Aboriginal Studies, 1979, 196-206

Tonkinson, R. *The Mardudjura Aborigines.* New York: Holt, Rinehart and Winston, 1978.

Trager, G. and Smith, H.L. *An Outline of English Structure.* Studies in Linguistics, Occasional Papers No. 3. Norman, Oklahoma: Battenburg, 1951.

Tsunoda, T. *The Djaru Language of the Kimberley, Western Australia.* Pacific Linguistics, Series B, No. 78. Canberra: Department of Linguistics, Research School of Pacific Studies, 1981.

Turner, M. M., and Breen, G. Akarre Rabbit talk. *Language in Central Australia,* 1984, 1(1): 10-15.

Tylor, E. *Researches into the Early History of Mankind and the Development of Civilization.* Boston: Estes and Lauriat, 1878.

Umiker-Sebeok, D.J. and Sebeok, T.A., eds. *Aboriginal Sign Languages of the Americas and Australia.* In Two Volumes. New York: Plenum Press, 1978.

Umiker-Sebeok, D. J. and Sebeok, T.A., eds. *Monastic Sign Languages.* Berlin: Mouton De Gruyter, 1987.

Van Rijnberk, G. *Le Langage par Signes Chez les Moines.* Koninklijke Nederlandse Akademie van Wetenschappen. Amsterdam: North Holland Publishing Co., 1953.

Voegelin, C.F. Sign language analysis, one level or two? International Journal of American Linguistics [Reprinted in D.J.Umiker Sebeok and T.A. Sebeok, eds., *Aboriginal Languages of the Americas and Australia. Volume II: The Americas and Australia.* New York: Plenum Press, 1978], 1958, 24: 71-77.

Vogt-Svendsen, M. Lip movements in Norwegian sign language. In J.G. Kyle and B.Woll, eds., *Language in Sign: an International Perspective on Sign Language.* London: Croom Helm, 1983, 85-96.

Von Brandenstein, C.G. *Names and Substance of the Australian Subsection System.* Chicago: Chicago University Press, 1982.

Von Sturmer, J. Talking with Aborigines. *Australian Institute of Aboriginal Studies Newsletter,* 1981, 15: 13-20.

Wafer, J. *A Simple Introduction to Central Australian Kinship Systems.* Alice Springs: Institute for Aboriginal Development, 1982.

Walsh, G.L. Mutilated hands or signal stencils? A consideration of irregular hand stencils from Central Queensland. *Australian Archaeology,* 1979, 9: 33-41.

Wampler, D. *Linguistics of Visual English.* Santa Rosa, California: Early Childhood Education Department, Aurally Handicapped Program Santa Rosa City Schools, 1972.

Warner, W.L. *A Black Civilization.* New York: Harper and Row, 1937.

Webbink, P. *The Power of the Eyes.* New York: Springer, 1986.

West, La Mont. The Sign Language: An Analysis. Vol. 1: The Sign Language: An Analysis, Vol. 2: Dialects. Ph. D. thesis, Indiana University, Bloomington, Indiana [Ann Arbor, Michigan: University Microfilms], 1960.

West, La Mont. Sign Language Films, A20-7-1 to A20-7-6, 1961-1965. Library, Australian Institute of Aboriginal Studies, Canberra.

West, La Mont. Aboriginal sign language: a statement. In W.E.H. Stanner and H. Shiels, ed., *Australian Aboriginal Studies*. Melbourne: Oxford University Press, 1963, 159-165.

White, I.D. Aboriginal women's status: a paradox resolved. In F. Gale, ed., *Women's Role in Aboriginal Society*. Second Edition. Canberra: Australian Institute of Aboriginal Studies, 1974, 36-49.

White, I.D. From camp to village: some problems of adaptation. In R. M. Berndt, ed., *Aborigines and Change: Australia in the '70s*. Canberra: Australian Institute of Aboriginal Studies, 1977, 100-105.

Wilbur, R.B. *American Sign language and Sign Systems*. Baltimore: University Park Press, 1979.

Williams, D. *Learning an Aboriginal Language [Gupapuyngu]*. Canberra: Curriculum Development Center, 1981.

Winship, G.P. The Coronado Expedition 1540-1542. *Annual Report of the Bureau of Ethnology, No. 14*. Washington, D.C.: United States Government Printing Office, 1896, 329-637.

Wong, J. The sound of one hand talking. *National Times*, Sydney, April 1st, 1974.

Woods, J.D., and others. *The Native Tribes of South Australia*. Adelaide: E.S. Wigg, 1879.

Woodward, J.C. Some characteristics of pidgin sign English. *Sign Language Studies*, 1973, 3: 39-46.

Woolston, F. P. and Trezise, P. Reel 2 and 3, 16mm film footage, with transcribed list of signs depicted in Reel 2 and 3, 16mm film footage, Mornington Island. Library, Australian Institute of Aboriginal Studies, Canberra, 1966.

Wright, C. *Walpiri Hand Talk*. Darwin: Northern Territory Government Department of Education, 1980.

Wundt, W. *The Language of Gestures*. With an introduction by Arthur L. Blumenthal and additional essays by George Herbert Mead and Karl Bühler. The Hague: Mouton & Co. [= Translation by J.S.Thayer, C.M. Greenleaf and M.D. Silberman of Ch. 2, Vol. 1, Part 1 of *Völkerpsychologie: Eine Untersuchung der Entwicklungsgesetze von Sprache, Mythus und Sitte*, Fourth Edition. Stuttgart: Alfred Kröner Verlag, 1921], 1973 [1921].

Wurm, S. *Languages of Australia and Tasmania*. The Hague: Mouton & Co., 1972.

Wurm, S.A. and Hattori, S., eds. *Language Atlas of the Pacific Area*. Canberra: Australian Academy of the Humanities in collaboration with the Japan Academy, 1981.

Yallop, C. *Australian Aboriginal Languages*. London: André Deutsch, 1982.

Young, E. *Tribal Communities in Rural Areas*. Canberra: Australian National University, Development Studies Centre [= The Aboriginal Component in the Australian Economy, Vol. 1], 1981.

Index of signs

Signs listed are those described. Bold numbers refer to illustrations.

General index